SteubenGlass

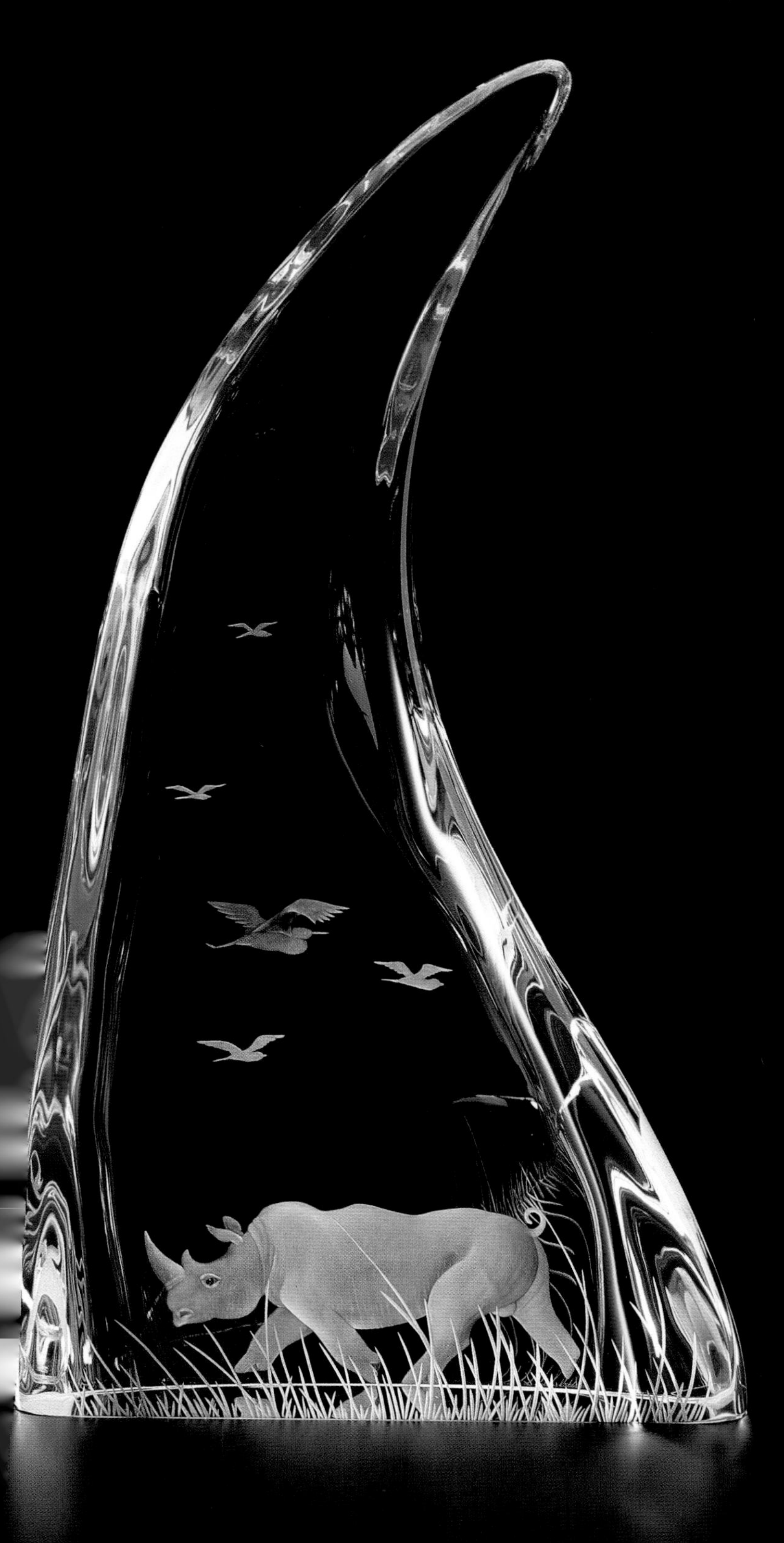

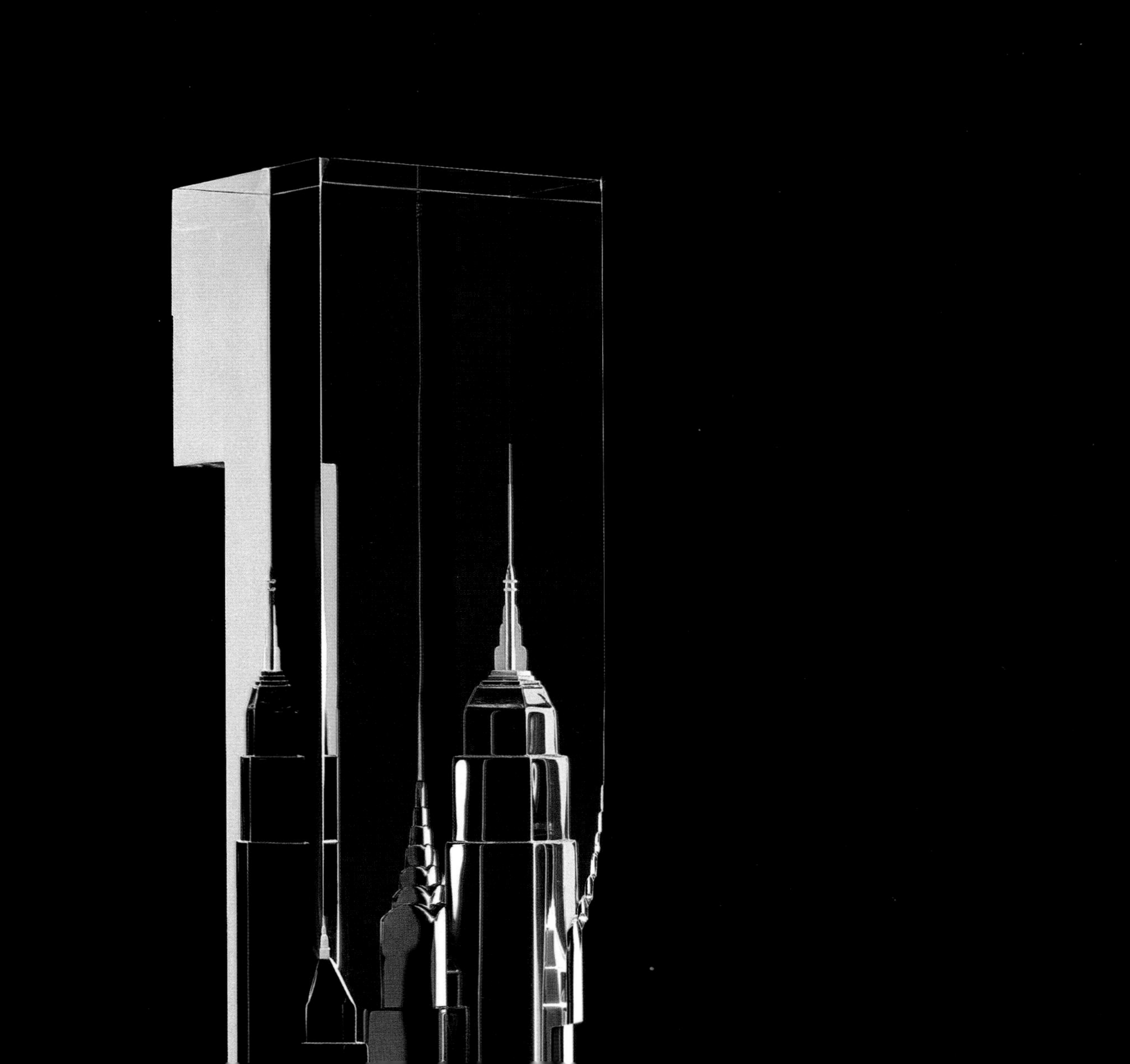

SteubenGlass

REVISED AND EXPANDED

AN AMERICAN TRADITION IN CRYSTAL

Mary Jean Madigan

HARRY N. ABRAMS, INC., PUBLISHERS

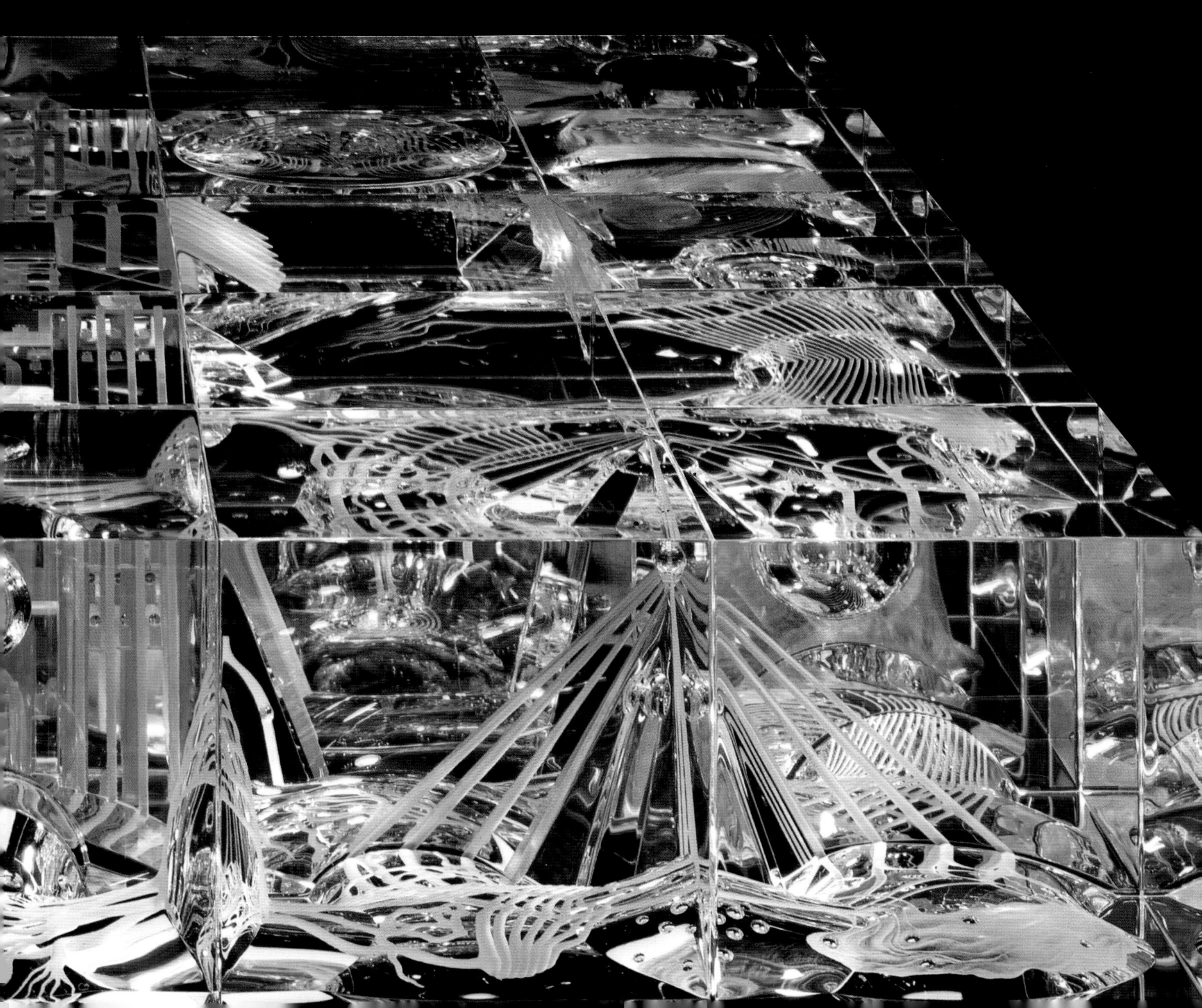

David Dowler. Grotto. 1997. Height 22½".

Donald Pollard, Alexander Seidel. The Four Seasons. 1969. Height 7⅜".

Julie Shearer. Iris Vase. 1986. Height 13½".

Bernard X. Wolff. Hercules: The Third Labor. 1983. Height 7¾".

Donald Pollard, Beni Montresor. Crown of Oberon. 1982. Height 9½".

David Dowler, Zevi Blum. Odyssey. 1984. Height 10¾".

Stephen Dale Edwards. Swimmers. 1986. Width 17½".

Eric Hilton. Dreams of Alice. 1987. Height 16¼".

Peter Yenawine, David Johnston. Butterfly Girl. 1973. Height 11".

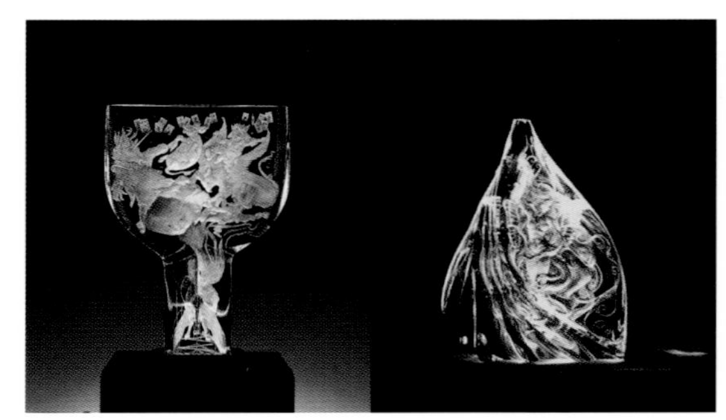

Eric Hilton. Ruby-Throated Hummingbird. 2000. Height 8½".

Taf Lebel Schaefer. Herons. 2000. Height 14½".

James Houston. Elephants of Kilimanjaro. 1987. Height 8½".

James Houston. Rhino Horn. 1984. Height 10¼".

Peter Drobny. Mobius Prism. 1993. Height 11⅝".

Paul Schulze. New York, New York. 1984. Height 17".

Robert Cassetti. Exploration and Discovery. 1993. Height 8½".

Joel Smith. Sundial. 1997. Diameter 9¼".

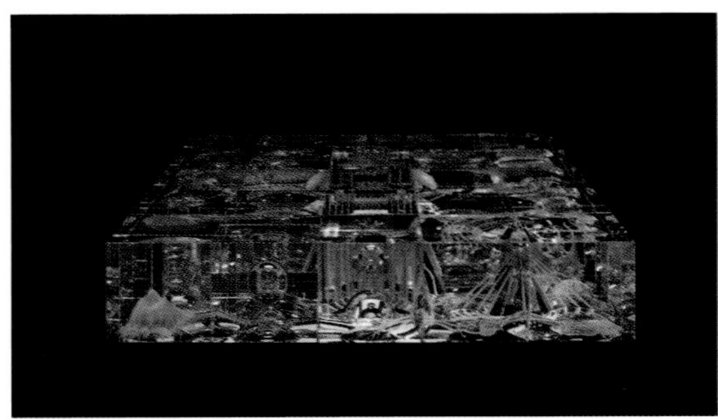

Eric Hilton, Ladislav Havlik, Lubomir Richter, Peter Schelling, Roger Selander. Innerland. 1980. Length 19⅜".

To my grandchildren,

Sarah Myles Madigan and Andrew Richard Kyle Madigan

EDITOR: Andrea Danese
DESIGNER: Darilyn Lowe Carnes
PRODUCTION MANAGER: Maria Pia Gramaglia

Library of Congress Cataloging-in-Publication Data

Madigan, Mary Jean Smith.
Steuben glass : an American tradition in crystal / Mary Jean Madigan.— Rev. and expanded.
p. cm.
Includes bibliographical references and index.
ISBN 0-8109-3492-2
1. Steuben Glass, Inc.—History. 2. Glassware—United States—History—20th century—Catalogs. 3. Cut glass—United States—Catalogs. I. Title.

NK5198.S7 M3 2003
748.29147'83—dc21 2002015972

Published in 2003 by Harry N. Abrams, Incorporated, New York.

Printed and bound in Japan
10 9 8 7 6 5 4 3 2 1

Abrams is a subsidiary of

Paul Schulze, Steuben's former director of design, wrote eighteen commentaries on the changes in Steuben's design philosophy for the 1982 edition. These appear again in this revised edition, and are found, illustrated and within boxes, on pages 67, 68, 73, 79, 88, 98, 111, 125, 126, 128, 137, 145, 154, 155, 157, 163, 168, 173.

CONTENTS

FOREWORD

On two occasions twenty years apart (the first in 1959, the second in 1979) I had the revealing and gratifying experience of serving as a juror for international exhibitions of newly designed glass. They were organized by the Corning Museum of Glass. The shows were international not just in the sense that the glass came from many nations, but, once assembled, that they travelled widely here and abroad. In all, about 7,500 pieces were submitted to the judgment of the jurors of these two exhibitions, glass objects of almost every conceivable sort. There was glass for everyday use, for decoration and ornament. There was glass sculpture, ceremonial glass, glass to touch, to look at, to play with; stained and painted glass, blown, molded, cut, and etched glass, figurative and abstract glass, glass like froth (the spume of waves), like gossamer, like lead, like distilled water. There was glass of rich and subtle colors and brilliantly clear glass. But whatever sorts of glass it was my pleasure to choose among (for each exhibition I was to select a hundred pieces), the human eye and hand and imagination and at least some of the human heart were in all of them, just as they are in every Steuben piece illustrated, or only spoken of, in this book.

I hark back to the international glass exhibitions for two reasons: the first is to suggest the range of kinds and uses of glass (I have mentioned only a few and no industrial ones), its flexibility and adaptability and brilliance; and, second, to suggest that objects of glass are artifacts that can tell us a great deal about the aspirations and tastes of the society that makes them. Glass reflects a great deal more than light and images. If the decorative arts, in which glass has played a lively role for five millennia, are, as I believe, the artifacts of social history, then what appears in this book is a clue to understanding much of the character of American taste during the last century.

When Steuben was founded at the turn of the twentieth century, its direction was determined and its path guided by Frederick Carder, an English glassmaker filled with experience of his exacting craft and with an artist's eye. The America to which he came was not, where taste was concerned, in the least sure of itself, and what was considered acceptable by the genteel classes (gentility was more than a pose, it was a principle of behavior) came inevitably from Europe. The taste of what the historian Mark Sullivan in *Our Times* called "the average man" was in genteel terms "vulgar" as far as the arts were concerned. It was a time when American painters and sculptors, architects and writers went to Paris and London, Berlin and Rome as a matter of course to drink at the aesthetic springs where the arts were purer and the patrons more sophisticated and sensitive. Culture, which they hoped to bring back to America, was a European monopoly as surely as jazz was regarded as an American aberration better not mentioned in artistic circles, much less in genteel society. It was the age of Edith Wharton and Henry James (who thought America so crass that he gave up his citizenship), when "suitability," as preached by Mrs. Wharton and Elsie de Wolfe, who called herself America's first woman decorator, was the *sine qua non* of "good taste"; in their view this meant a leap backward to the quiet refinement of pre-Victorian days, an escape from flowered Brussels carpets, fringed draperies, wax flowers in bell jars, and conspicuously ornate furniture. It was also a time when American audiences gave their hearts to operettas from Vienna, Paris, and London, when Edward MacDowell's *To a Water Lily* was regarded as a modern classic, and aspiring citizens led suburban lives in little chateaux, English manors, and Spanish villas.

The art glass that was being made widely

Peter Aldridge and Jane Osborn-Smith. Swan Bowl. 1985. Diameter 9".

in Europe and by a few Americans, most notably Louis Comfort Tiffany, at the turn of the century did not quite suit the doctrine of "suitability" or the Wharton-de Wolfe concept of "good taste." It was called Art Nouveau, and it became a fashion that spread over Europe in the 1890s and the first years of this century. To conservative taste here and in Europe, it was considered raffish, even decadent. In glass and ceramics, and even in wood and metal, sensuously flowing patterns of stems, leaves, and flowers (most particularly irises and lilies) seem to wave languidly. To respectable Victorian eyes, Art Nouveau suggested the kind of uncorseted abandon that they witnessed in the dances of Loïe Fuller with her yards of billowing and flaming silk. To the younger generation, turning away from their parents' taste for Victorian clutter and what seemed to them pomposity, Art Nouveau and the products of its contemporary, the Arts and Crafts Movement with its four-square furniture and homespun "honesty," were more attractive than Miss de Wolfe's "suitability." Art Nouveau and the Crafts Movement arrived in America almost simultaneously, the former from the continent and the latter from England, where it had been inspired by William Morris, a philosopher of design, an artist, and a greatly respected seer.

In 1903, the same year that Steuben was established in Corning, still another revolt in the world of design was taking place. The architect and designer of decorative arts, Josef Hoffmann, led the Secession in Vienna and established the Wiener Werkstätte as a rebellion against the Academy. Like Art Nouveau, the Secession had its roots in the doctrines and designs of Morris, but unlike Art Nouveau, which Morris despised and which led to nothing but more of itself, the Secession was a direct forerunner of the Bauhaus, which the architect Walter Gropius established in Weimar in 1919. "Functionalism" was to Gropius what "suitability" had been to Miss de Wolfe. In other words, when Carder arrived in America to direct the destiny of Steuben, the design world was in a state of vigorous ferment.

Carder brought with him from England the design vocabulary of Art Nouveau and applied it with great skill to the products of the Steuben factory. As a result, Steuben in its earliest days was very much *à la mode* and to some degree avant-garde, or, perhaps more accurately, it was avant-garde in the *à la mode* Art Nouveau manner of its time with some of William Morris' Crafts Movement flavor as well. When the impact of Bauhaus functionalism began to make itself felt in the 1920s in architecture and furniture, in textiles, ceramics, and glass, when, it might be said, purity of design in some influential quarters was considered to be more important than flavor, Steuben went its own decorative ways. There was no perceptible response in Steuben's products to this new avant-garde. To the designers of the new "modern," ornament for ornament's sake was looked upon as "dishonest." (Moral epithets like "honest" and "sincere" are common in the vocabulary of design, though their meanings differ from generation to generation.) To them, any plain surface was preferable to an ornamental one, however discreet. The most honest, and by their standards the most beautiful, glass was laboratory glass, glass insulators, any glass, in other words, whose aesthetic was based solely on the practical, nondecorative functions it was made to perform. A tumbler with straight vertical sides was considered honest; one with curved sides was not. Geometry, it seemed, was not just a tool of design; it had become an end in itself . . . and Plato was quoted to prove it.

When the team of Arthur A. Houghton, Jr., John M. Gates, and Sidney Waugh (with Houghton as captain, Gates as tastemaker, and Waugh as designer) changed Steuben's direction in 1933, it was not the modern movement as typified by the Bauhaus that it espoused. It leaned toward (but did not swallow whole) Art Deco as it had declared itself at the Exposition des Arts

Décoratifs et Industriels in Paris in 1925. There were elements of "machine art" and streamlining in Art Deco's geometrical shapes, and traces of Art Nouveau in its free spirit and its use of flowing figures and floral ornament. As a style, it was disdainfully called "modernistic" by the functionalists; they thought it impure, adulterated. But the public liked it because it was up-to-date but not aseptic. They were entranced, for example, by the Chrysler Building in New York City with the silvery waves of its tower topped by a gigantic, gleaming spike, its gargoyles shaped like Chrysler radiator caps, and its lobby a rich tangle of inlaid woods and ornate pierced metal screens. If the public thought that it and other buildings and ornaments of the same nature were fun, the functionalists were "not amused."

Like most styles, Art Deco in the hands of astute designers and excellent craftsmen retained its essential virtues and at the same time yielded to experiment and the imprint of its designers' personalities. This is what happened at Steuben. In the 1930s and 1940s, the firm produced glass of superb quality which was at the same time both classic in many of its basic shapes and up-to-date but not doctrinaire in the Art Deco spirit either in the forms imposed on it or its engraved and often figurative ornament. "Good taste" as it was characterized by the products of Steuben at that particular time was at loggerheads with what the Museum of Modern Art and its satellites, which had set themselves up as arbiters of what was "good design," were exhibiting. "Good design" in their terms was based on the Bauhaus concepts of honest design. You would be no more likely to find a Steuben wine glass, cocktail shaker, or engraved bowl in the Modern's exhibitions than a design approved by the Museum for its machinelike functionalism in a Steuben showroom. Obviously, two quite different theories of design and definitions of what is meant by "good" were at work, both valid and both productive of excellence.

Styles grow tired, wear out, and collapse into clichés. Bauhaus functionalism is now passé, Art Deco has become a collector's item, and the new trend is toward an eclecticism in which old styles thought dead a few decades ago are being revived, adapted to new functions and new materials in what appears to be a romantic concern with man's spirit as well as with his basic functional needs. In the world of glass, this new freedom from doctrine is epitomized by the Studio Glass Movement in which glassmakers by the thousands are developing new forms and finding new vitality in this most ancient of man-made materials.

The Studio Glass Movement is nothing new to Steuben. Since its inception in 1903, Steuben has been a studio. It has always gone its own way, sure and uncompromising in its quality, jealous of its undisputed position as a leader in the world of glassmaking, and confident that it is cherished by an audience to whom its name is synonymous with style and elegance.

Steuben's evolution is traced both verbally and visually in the illuminating pages of this book in ways that reflect the dignified good taste of the eras in which it has been made. It is no wonder that Steuben glass has been the official gift of our government on many occasions to other governments and their dignitaries, of friends to their most cherished friends, and of institutions to their most valued patrons and leaders. It has cachet, suitability, and richness. But more than that, it has the honesty of the most exacting craftsmanship, the purity of the most beautiful crystal, and the refinement of sensibility and imagination in the quality and character of its design.

Russell Lynes
1981

INTRODUCTION

Joel Smith and Meredith Hamilton.
Evening in the Park. 2000. Height 9½".

The story of Steuben, nearly a century in the telling, is a story of people. It is the story of glass chemists, factory technicians, toolmakers, gaffers, servitors, apprentices; of polishers, inspectors, finishers, washers, and packagers; of engravers, inventory clerks, and the countless other men and women of Corning, New York, who spend each working day performing many of the same careful tasks that earlier generations of their families did before them. It is also the story of designers and librarians, of secretaries, and sales people and behind-the-scenes support staff who work at the Steuben shop on Madison Avenue in New York City. It is the story of executives, who shuttle between these places, cementing the bonds of aesthetics and commerce. Not least, Steuben's story is the story of a succession of presidents—people of taste and vision, ranging from founder Frederick Carder to incumbent president Marie McKee—whose leadership styles have dictated Steuben's evolution over the course of a century.

The character of Steuben Glass changed most abruptly in the five years after 1933, when Arthur A. Houghton, Jr., became president. Enlisting the support of architect John M. Gates and sculptor Sidney Waugh, Houghton phased out the colored glass that had been the mainstay of the Carder era, resolving to create "the most perfect crystal the world has ever known." As Houghton put it, "Crystal is the ultimate, the real perfection of the material of glass, with its great transparency and fire and light."

Steuben's history prior to that watershed was first charted by Paul V. Gardner, Frederick Carder's longtime personal assistant, in his exhaustive study, *The Glass of Frederick Carder* (New York: Crown, 1971), which catalogued the virtuoso range of exuberantly eclectic glass made by Carder. Thomas P. Dimitroff's comprehensive biography and collector's guide, *Frederick Carder and Steuben Glass*, published by Schiffer Publishing Ltd. in 1998, opened still another window on the Carder era, offering additional scholarly insights into Carder's life and throwing new light on his post-1933 contributions to Steuben and Corning Glass Works.

While the early colored pieces of Steuben were thus well documented by Gardner (and later by Dimitroff), there existed no comparable collector's guide for the *colorless* post-1933 Steuben until the original edition of this book, *Steuben Glass: An American Tradition in Crystal*, was first published by Harry N. Abrams in 1982. In addition to relating—for the first time—the complete story of Steuben and the people who made it, a primary purpose of the original version was to provide collectors with an unprecedented and much-needed tool for identifying and dating individual pieces of colorless Steuben crystal produced in the Houghton era and beyond. The original book was reprinted in 1983, and again in 1987 with some corrections and additions to the catalogue section. This new edition carries Steuben's history forward from 1981 to the present, and updates the catalogue to identify all pieces of Steuben crystal made through 2001. Like the original version, it is envisioned as a resource for collectors and connoisseurs.

In the twenty years since the first edition of this book was published, the ranks of sophisticated collectors focusing exclusively on brilliant, colorless post-1933 Steuben crystal have grown significantly. Some collectors are seduced by the stunning technical expertise inherent in Steuben's meticulously engraved exhibition pieces from the 50s, 60s, and beyond; they understand that today's economy can no longer sustain the traditional expressions of virtuoso craftsmanship found in such early pieces. They know that these stunning, elaborately engraved examples of exhibition crystal will become ever more rare, expensive, and difficult to acquire. Still other people collect Steuben—both classic pieces and new designs purchased directly online or from the shop—because it is simply the best of its class: the purest crystal, embodying the highest standards of design and the finest examples of American craftsmanship that money can buy.

It is hoped that everyone who values and collects Steuben will find in this updated volume a clearer understanding of the company and its people, and a definitive guide to every piece of utilitarian, ornamental, and exhibition glass produced at the Steuben factory from 1933 through 2001. Ironically, while the many pieces of glass catalogued in this book can be identified individually by number (if not always by name), limitations of time and space have prevented us from identifying the individual craftspeople, scientists, and engineers whose cumulative efforts over the years have lifted Steuben to its present position of eminence. Their contributions have been largely anonymous, and so they remain. As Steuben approaches its one-hundredth anniversary, however, we honor each member of this nameless legion. Their work has fulfilled Arthur Houghton's vision for a truly American crystal, unsurpassed in its beauty and purity by any in the world.

Mary Jean Madigan
February 2002

I.

HOW STEUBEN GLASS IS MADE: FORMING, FINISHING, DECORATING, DESIGNING

In ancient Egypt, during the eighteenth dynasty, people first had the desire to create perfect crystal glass, unclouded by any foreign substance, as pure as water and as light-refractive as the finest of diamonds. It was to be an elusive search, continued through many centuries, in particular by the Venetians with their misty *cristallo,* and by George Ravenscroft in England, who discovered that by adding lead to the glass compound he could greatly increase its clarity and brilliance. Today's Steuben glass is the culmination of that search—the most perfect crystal yet achieved. Fittingly, it is made a stone's throw from The Corning Museum of Glass, where the finest efforts of historic glassmakers such as Ravenscroft and Verzelini are displayed. Seven days a week, year round, visitors to the museum may finish their tour at the Hot Glass Show at the entrance to the attached Steuben factory, which was built in 1951 as part of the Corning Glass Center. Seated on stadiumlike benches in front of an open platform equipped with a "glory hole" or glass reheating furnace, visitors can observe a "gaffer," or glass artisan, demonstrate all the procedures involved in blowing and forming a handmade glass object. Just beyond the open demonstration platform, the airy, open floor of an actual Steuben blowing room may be glimpsed. Renovated in July of 2000, the Steuben blowing room is dominated by four silvery, tentlike structures that house three barrel-sized glory holes apiece. It is quieter than in former years, when the roar of big central gas burners in each of six four-door glory holes drowned out conversation. Steuben's great melting tank, once open to view, has been partitioned off to lower factory temperatures and minimize airborne particles that can compromise the quality of the glass. Rising heat

Servitor and gaffer transfer a partially formed Steuben Trout from blowing iron to pontil rod. Designer's sketch is clipped to the wall of the "glory hole" or reheating unit.

Opposite: John Dreves. Olive Dish. 1939. Width 5⅝".

Overview of the blowing room at the Steuben factory shortly after its completion in 1951.

from the glass furnaces is still dissipated by Robinson ventilators in the roof, abetted by a new air conditioning system that ensures worker comfort and further reduces particulate matter.

On the factory floor, casually dressed groups of men and women work around the evenly spaced reheating units. Their deliberate, unhurried movements convey the sense of a slow-motion ballet. Each team of workers, or "shop," has its own glory hole and is led by a senior gaffer.[1] Traditionally, a glassmaking shop was a five- to seven-person team: the gaffer, the gatherer, and the servitor, who gather and form the gob of molten glass, and the bit gatherer, the stick-up boy, and the carry-in boy. Today, however, a single apprentice may be responsible for many of these functions: fetching small gathers of glass from the tank for application to the object being blown, transferring the half-formed glass object from the blowing iron to the pontil rod or "punty," and carrying the completed piece to the annealing ovens.

Melting the Glass

Until the process was computerized and automated in 1988, workers constantly shoveled precisely measured quantities of dry "batch"—sand, potash, lead, and other additives—mixed with "cullet," or broken shards of pure Steuben crystal, into the batch-loading door of the great melting tank to assure a constant level of molten "metal" within. The Steuben tank, one of the first of its type to be used in the production of fine crystal, is partially lined with platinum, which resists corrosion by molten glass. (Still, the tank must be shut down every few years for the replacement of its interior components, a three-week process that is scheduled during the factory's summer break.) A platinum stirring rod constantly agitates the glass to assure uniform melting temperatures of about 2,500 degrees Fahrenheit. A narrow central chamber, or dividing wall, collects glass that has

Lloyd Atkins. Hand Coolers. 1974. Length or height 2¼" and 2½".

melted to the right degree and directs its steady flow at two pounds per minute through an opening into the "cave" or cellar below.

"Let It Down Easy"

There, unfazed by the tons of molten fire overhead, an operator monitors the narrow, free-flowing stream. When a gather of glass is wanted for a specific piece of Steuben, the monitor is alerted by a signal from the blowing floor to position a mold (or cup) under the flow, catching a precisely timed portion of molten glass. (Since glass at the same temperature flows at the same speed, the timed gather ensures that stock pieces are virtually uniform in size. It takes a fifty-three-second gather, for example, to form the classic Olive Dish.) As the glass is poured, its weight gently depresses a flexible floor in the mold. For this reason, the method of pouring became known to the trade as "let it down easy." When no mold is in position, the flowing column falls into a continuously circulating stream of pure water. It cools, hardens, and cracks into pieces that are eventually re-fed into the tank above as cullet. Pioneered by Steuben, this process of drawing molten glass from the tank by gravity is now used by crystal manufacturers the world over. It ensures that the body of the gather will be of uniform temperature and consistency throughout, with no cords or specks due to uneven melting. Test samples or "patties" shaped like large flat lozenges are drawn from the tank every hour for visual analysis. Three times a week, the samples are also analyzed by spectograph to assure the crystal's uniformity and purity.

Molding and Pressing Facilities

Adjacent to the cave, on a subterranean level of the blowing room, is the mold shop, where plaster models of certain new designs are converted

Gatherer shapes a large gather of molten glass in a cherrywood form to give it consistency of shape.

Craftsman blows a small puff of air into the gather, creating the basic glass bubble or "parison."

into metal molds for pressing. Although most Steuben is mouth-blown, about six or seven of the thirty new designs presented each year—including the popular hand coolers and some small animals such as the eagle, cat, and sea horse—are pressed. Pressing takes place on the factory's third shift or press shift, from ten o'clock at night until six in the morning. During these hours, the entire output of the melting tank is fed into two adjacent presses—one a century-old hand model. No off-hand blowing takes place during the press shift.

Still other pieces are formed by "sagging," an exacting procedure used with increasing frequency through the late 1980s and 1990s for major sculptural pieces. In this process, the designer first creates a three-dimensional model out of clay, wood, or plaster. Molten rubber is poured over the model to form a negative image of it—the "master" mold. From the master rubber mold a second plaster mold is formed, and a roughly shaped piece of cold glass is slowly heated in a low-temperature sag kiln until it melts enough to "sag" into the mold. After the glass is slowly cooled and rehardened, the plaster mold—which can be used only one time—is chipped away from it, revealing the glass form, ready for finishing. The sag molds are made in a mold shop next to the sag kiln room.

Off-Hand Blowing

By far the largest number of Steuben objects is formed by the off-hand method of blowing. The process begins in the cave below the melting tank. When a precisely timed gather of glass has been caught by the operator who monitors the molten stream, it is hoisted by elevator to the blowing room floor where a craftsman—usually the servitor—waits to receive it. He removes the gather from its metal mold, and carries it on the end of a blowpipe to his shop's glory hole for

Servitor rolls a small gather of glass on the flat marver to cool the surface prior to blowing and to make it uniform.

Guilding the gatherer's iron with a pair of bit shears, the gaffer directs the application of a "bit" to a larger glass form.

forming. By this time, the gather has cooled to a solid but still viscous and malleable consistency; it is the color of amber and about 1,500 degrees Fahrenheit. To maintain proper working temperature, it will be reheated in the glory hole several times. The first step in forming may involve thrusting the gather into a metal or graphite box for uniformity of shape, then rolling it on a flat metal "marver" to smooth its surface. Then, with a quick expert puff the servitor or the gaffer blows a small amount of air into the gather of glass at the end of the blowpipe. The temperature of the glass causes the air bubble to expand to the desired size. The gaffer controls the shape of this "parison" or viscous glass bubble by swinging or spinning the blowpipe on the projecting arms of the bench on which he is seated. This prevents the glass from sagging due to its own weight. While manipulating the parison, the gaffer may shape it with a small paddle of dampened cherrywood[2] or a pair of wooden pincers known as a "wood jack."

Early in the forming process, after the parison of glass has achieved the desired shape, it is transferred from the blowing rod to the pontil rod, or "punty." This solid piece of metal is dipped in molten glass to make it adhere to the parison, then manipulated by the servitor or other shop helpers. The developing object is cut away from the blowing rod with a pair of shears. While attached to the pontil rod, the object is continually rotated and reheated. The bit-gatherer may bring additional elements of glass from the furnace to add to it, forming stems, bases, or whatever is required. Known as "gaffered forms," these elements are added while the glass is still hot and malleable. From time to time, the gaffer measures the dimensions of the glass object with a pair of calipers, checking its size and shape against the specifications of a designer's drawn-to-size blueprint spread out on a bench or tacked to the wall of the glory hole.

The mouth of the object may be opened

up with the wood jack, or it may be further shaped with the help of other traditional tools of the glassmaker's trade—the "steel jack" or pucellas, the calipers, the forming tool, the bit shears, and the wooden or graphite pallet. "So ancient and changeless is this craft that certain tools used by the modern glassblower still retain their Latin names," noted Steuben's foremost designer, Sidney Waugh.[3] Today's gaffers are aided by still other advances in technology. For example, the gas-powered, fuel-efficient glory holes have an improved ceramic lining that lasts four years (new ones, installed in the 2000 factory renovation, can be individually taken out of service for repairs while others within the same four-furnace unit continue to operate). Attached within the gaffer's reach are nozzles for air (to freeze the outer shell of the piece, giving it stability), for vacuum (to draw out specific elements of a gather, such as the tails of tiny crystal mice), and for a gas torch (to heat a small section of the glass or give it more polish). Despite these technical improvements, all of Steuben's more traditional tools are handmade in the company tool shop.

When a specific Steuben object has been fully formed "at the fire," it is solid but still too hot to touch. The gaffer's apprentice grasps it with a pair of insulated pincers, and with a sharp, accurately directed blow, the gaffer "cracks off" the object from the pontil rod. At 350–400 degrees Fahrenheit, the completed piece can light a cigarette. The apprentice removes it—again using insulated pincers—to the annealing ovens, where a moving belt transports it through a controlled atmosphere of slowly decreasing temperatures. This process of annealing, or slow cooling, eliminates interior stresses that might otherwise cause the glass to crack. There are two kinds of annealing ovens in the Steuben factory: the slow "kiln" in which heavy pieces take as much as two and one-half days to cool, and the fast "lehr," which can cool small objects in as little as eight hours.

Finishing Procedures

Drawn through the annealing ovens on conveyor belts, the cooled-down objects emerge in the adjacent finishing area, where they are inspected and marked with orange crayon for the appropriate procedures. Some pieces, such as certain animals and traditionally shaped bowls, are completely formed in the blowing room and need only touch-up finishing—grinding out rough spots and polishing. Other pieces require cutting to assume their final form. These go to the diamond-saw operator, or cutter, for further shaping or "cold cutting."

The glass cutter works at a "frame"—a rotating wheel of sandstone or carborundum, or one edged with industrial diamonds, above which he positions the piece of glass. Holding the crystal object over the wheel, observing the progress of his work through it, the cutter sometimes makes only a few delicate surface cuts for decorative purposes, but sometimes it is necessary for him to grind away large masses of glass to obtain the desired shape. A stream of water pours down steadily on his wheel, carrying away silica dust and cooling the friction-heated surfaces. Cutting wheels may vary from three to eighteen inches in diameter. Rough-cutting, with a sandstone or carborundum wheel, may leave the surface of the glass matte and dull, without sparkle. The cutter can restore brightness by polishing the piece on wooden and felt wheels, sometimes fed with putty powder. Today, some cutting operations are automated, using new computerized equipment that can deliver perfectly faceted surfaces.

For pieces that do not require further "cold cutting," pontil marks and rough edges are smoothed with diamond-dust emery wheels fed with successively finer grit powders—carborundum and aluminum oxide—to grind down unwanted roughness. Luster, which may have been lost in the forming process, is restored to the glass, and minor scratches are removed on

Final drawing for water pitcher #7837, clipped to a board, will be hung on the "glory hole" wall for the gaffer's guidance.

Gaffer shears off unwanted glass to form the lip of a pitcher.

Using a cherrywood paddle, gaffer smooths the side of a Steuben Snail.

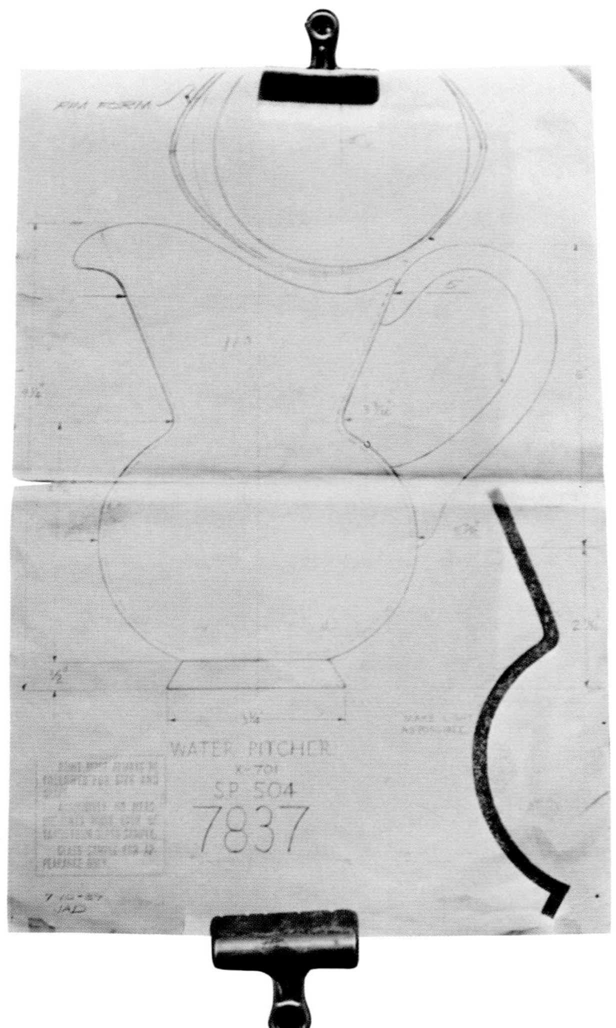

polishing wheels using pumice and a putty of cerium oxide.

In the last few years, the process of finishing the hand-blown, pressed, or sagged glass has been speeded by the use of automated and semiautomated devices such as the Blanchard grinders and polishers, the Rociprolap (which smooths the bottoms of vessels), and the Bridgeport and Maho cutting machines.[4] Some of this equipment is computer-programmable to exquisitely fine tolerances. By introducing a degree of automation to certain of the finishing processes, Steuben has raised its operational efficiency while reducing the risk of repetitive motion injuries and workers' exposure to particulate matter containing lead. However, the important work in terms of engraving, design cutting, and repair work is still done by hand. There is no piece of glass that

Paul Schulze. Nimbus Bowl, Nimbus Vase, Nimbus Dish. 1980. Diameter 7" each.

Finisher is smoothing the bottoms of glasses on a carborundum wheel.

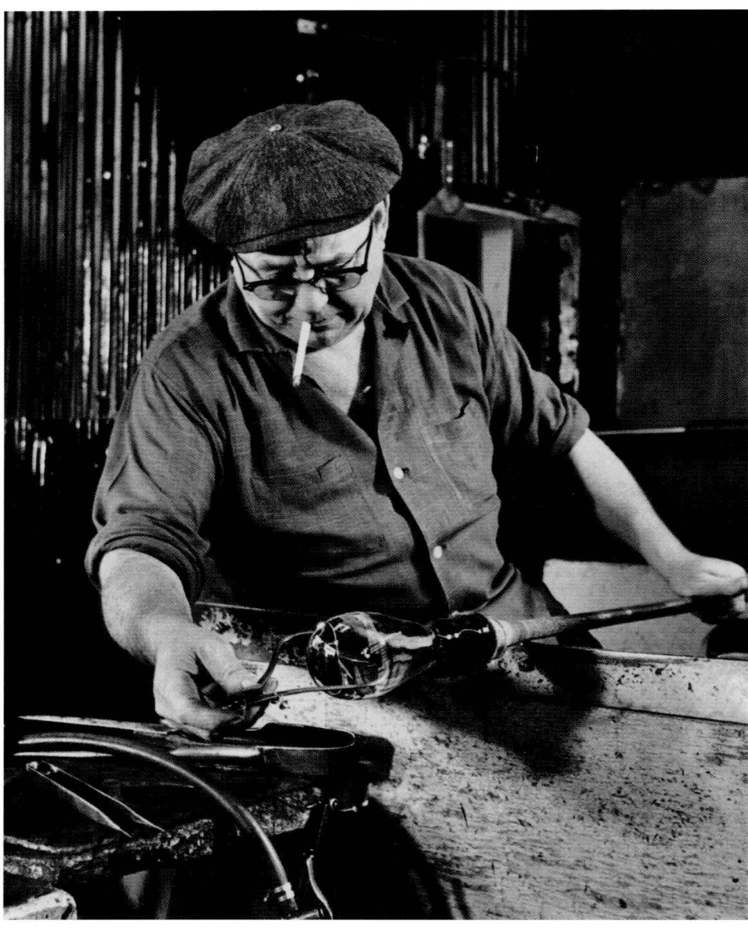

Gaffer uses calipers to check the size of the parison.

Carry-in boy deposits a goblet, grasped in asbestos-tipped pincers, into the mouth of the annealing oven.

is untouched by the hand of man. Steuben is unique among contemporary glass houses in its avoidance of acid-polishing to restore shine to the surface of a piece.

Smoothed and polished pieces are carefully washed, dried, and inspected before qualifying for the Steuben signature, which is affixed to the underside of each perfect piece with a diamond-tipped stylus. If a piece has even one scratch or imperfection at this point, it is destroyed; Steuben sells no seconds. Since 1933, every piece of glass to leave the Steuben factory has been marked with the characteristic script signature, except for some tablewares made prior to 1947, which were signed with the initial "S."

Engraving and Decorating

Steuben enjoys a well-deserved reputation for the splendid artisanship of its glass engravers. In the twentieth century, most American glass engravers came from Austria, where they learned the old craft traditions through long years of apprenticeship. Before the 1974 slump in the demand for engraved crystal, Steuben had eleven full-time engravers on staff; today there are six, who work most of the time from home shops, coming into the plant for six weeks each year on a rotating basis. It takes at least a half-dozen years for a glass engraver to learn this exacting trade, and Steuben ensures there will be continuity by directing an apprenticeship program in conjunction with Corning Community College.

Working from the designer's drawing, the engraver first coats the glass with protective shellac, then transfers the image onto its surface with India ink. To cut the design, the glass is pressed upward against the edge of a fine copper wheel attached to a rapidly rotating lathe under a constant feed of linseed oil and emery powder. In the process of engraving a single object, as many as fifty different handmade wheels—ranging from an eighth of an inch to four inches in diameter—may be used. To obtain a stippled effect, a diamond-tipped stylus is used, conveying the impression of light and shadow.

Although engraved portions of a piece of Steuben glass appear to be in low relief, that is an optical illusion. The engraved cuts are actually concave—a shallow intaglio carved into the surface of the glass. Some intricate designs may require as many as three hundred hours or more to engrave. In addition to the copper wheel and diamond stylus, the engraver may use other methods to achieve particular effects. For example, a stream of sand, driven by compressed air and applied with an air brush, may be used to tunnel deeply into the glass. The sides of such a tunnel have a matte finish, which appears semiopaque when viewed through the glass object. Eric Hilton's Innerland makes excellent use of the sandblasting technique to achieve its decorative effect.

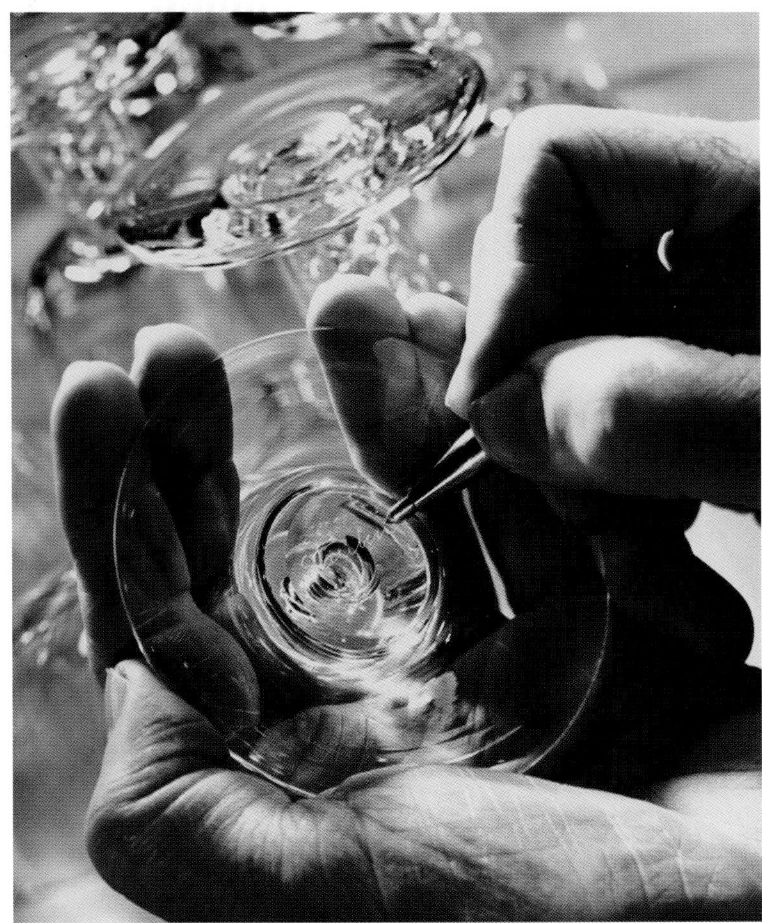

Only after a piece has met Steuben's exacting standards of quality is the script signature affixed to the base with a diamond-tipped stylus.

The Monair Process

Some pieces of Steuben, particularly those decorated with lettering, calligraphy, or other designs (such as monograms) that are linear and two-dimensional rather than sculptural, may be engraved by the exacting "Monair" process. Unlike copper-wheel engraving, which gives a rounded cut and subtle variations in depth to achieve an intaglio effect, Monair provides a sharp, precise edge, ideal for lettering. The method was developed in 1949 by Corning and Eastman Kodak to ensure exact duplication of the designer's two-dimensional drawing on the glass.

The process begins in the Corning-based design department, where a scaled drawing of the desired monogram or inscription is enlarged or reduced to size, then converted to a photographic negative. The film is sent to the factory, where pieces of glass to be decorated are painted with a protective shellaclike covering that is sensitive to light. The negative is affixed to the glass and exposed to an intense light, transferring the image. The protective covering is removed in the area of the image, and the exposed section is carefully engraved with fine sand driven through an air brush.

The resulting design is an absolutely accurate, hard-edged reproduction of the original sketch. The bud vases lettered with inscriptions from Shakespeare or Elizabeth Barrett Browning are good examples of the Monair technique applied to ornamental Steuben.

Designing Steuben Glass

For centuries, it was traditional for the owner or chief official of a glasshouse to design the shape and decoration of the glass produced. This was

Bases of bowls and vases are made flat by grinding on horizontal wheels.

In the finishing room, a "stopperer" grinds stoppers to fit precisely the mouths of Ships' Decanters.

Polisher uses a buffing wheel to remove tiny scratches from the interior of the engraved Colorado Bowl.

Jack Hultzman inspects a finished piece of Steuben. If there are flaws, it will be smashed in the "cullet" barrel.

Opposite:
Eric Hilton. Innerland (detail).

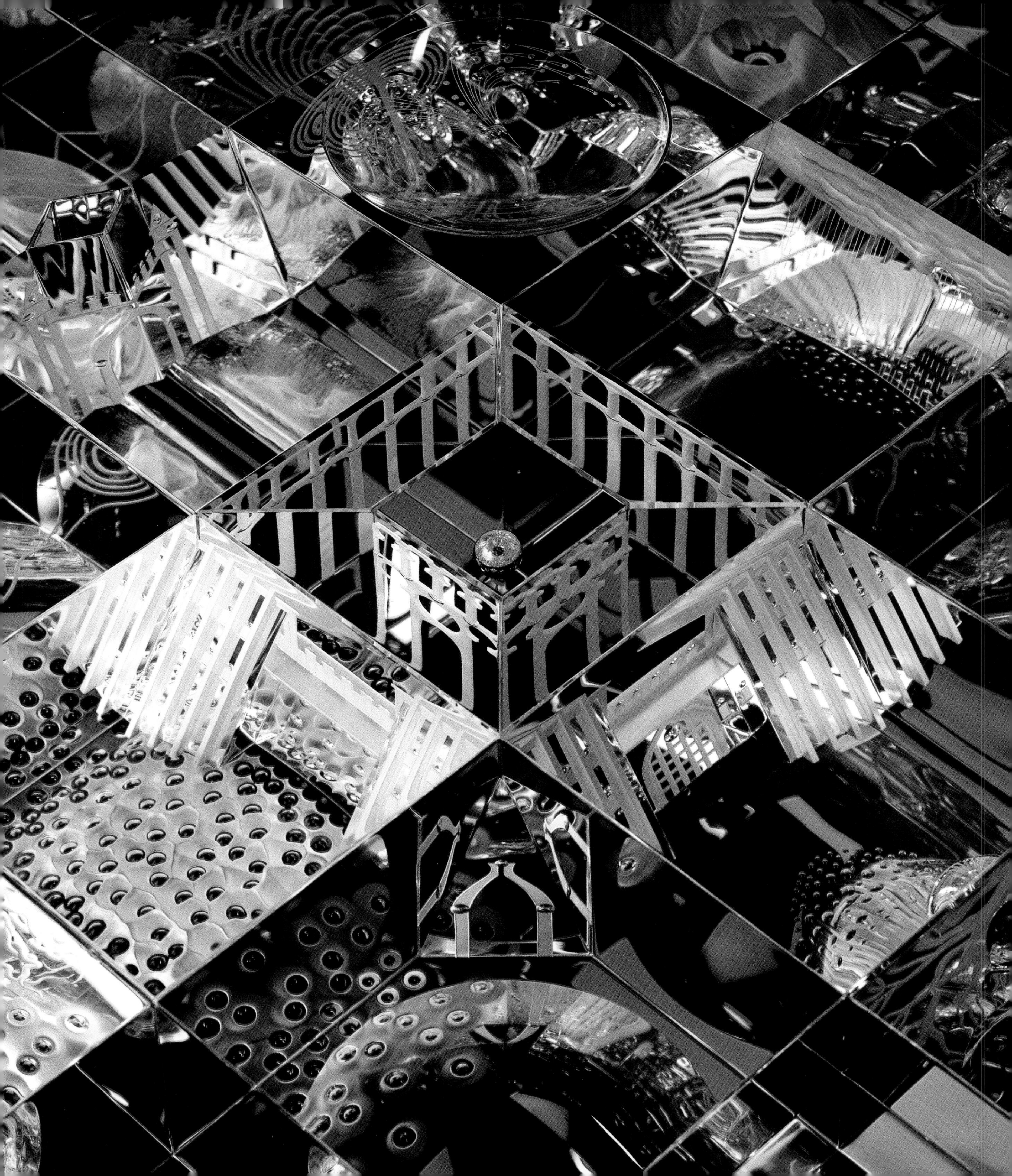

certainly true during Frederick Carder's years at Steuben, when he functioned not only as the company's administrative head, but also as its chief designer. When Arthur Houghton reorganized Steuben in 1933, he broke with tradition by handing total responsibility for design over to John Monteith Gates, and separating the design department physically from the factory. Under Gates's direction, Steuben designers were headquartered in their own atelier in New York City, away from Corning, where they would not interact with the blowers and would therefore remain unconstrained by the fetters of glassmaking tradition. In New York, too, were the museums, galleries and other sources of design inspiration that Houghton deemed essential to the design process. Houghton himself enjoyed taking Steuben designers to the great museums of Europe, where they could absorb masterpieces of art. Steuben's design department remained in New York City for nearly sixty years, until it was moved to Corning during a corporate reorganization in 1989.

Design Procedure

Each year, hundreds of proposals for new designs are drawn up by Steuben's design staff. Most new stock designs are in response to requests from the sales department. At a monthly staff meeting, proposals are evaluated and those selected for further development are given a design number. The designer then develops the concept through drawings, models, or further experimentation in glass, culminating in a final scaled drawing that the gaffer may use to set measuring calipers. Steuben's designers invariably accompany their trial sketches to the factory to watch while an experimental sample of the new object is made.

Even before the design department moved to Corning in 1989, Steuben maintained at least one staff designer-in-residence there to work with the glassblowers in developing new pieces. Samuel Ayres and John Dreves were two of the earliest. Peter Yenawine and Katherine De Sousa were placed in Corning in 1969 during a time of philosophical transition in the design department: it was reasoned they could develop their own concepts most fully by being near the glassmaking process. David Dowler and Peter Aldridge were the second generation of designers to work in Corning, primarily on their own creations, joined soon after by Eric Hilton. Today, staff designers work from studio offices adjacent to the factory, and some also maintain home studios. (Steuben's consulting and guest designers, including those who contribute drawings for engraving, may be based anywhere in the world.)

Once a trial sample is under way, the designer and glassblower work closely together to iron out the wrinkles in order to assure successful production of the experimental design, and to get an estimate of its cost to produce. The completed trial sample is further evaluated by the director of design and other members of top management. If the piece is accepted for production, the designer will make a revised drawing, based on the trial sample, for use in the factory. These final drawings have been filed and recorded by Steuben, and they provide a good record of past production. Steuben's design procedures are the same for blown, sagged, cut, or molded pieces. Often two or more designers may collaborate on a single piece, particularly if it is to be engraved or otherwise embellished. Outside designers and artists frequently are invited to submit sketches for the engraving—or less often, for the shape—of a particular piece.

Steuben takes as much time and care as may be required to produce the best glass. It imposes no production quotas on its designers and craftspeople, and imperfect pieces—perhaps 20 to 30 percent of the production—are destroyed immediately. For this reason, Steuben remains a luxury product—the finest glass that can be made. It is priced to reflect the exacting conditions of its design and production.

Engraver Edward Palme draws the outline of a bird design on an Audubon Plate in India ink.

Then the lines are cut into the glass, using many interchangeable copper wheels powered by a rotating lathe.

II.
FOUNDATIONS: 1903–1929

Steuben Glass, now a century old, has always been a company of dedicated visionaries and craftsmen. Two men have dominated the course of its history: Frederick Carder, a brilliant English glass designer and chemist, who founded Steuben in 1903 with Thomas Hawkes to supply crystal blanks for Hawkes' glass cutting shop in Corning, New York; and Arthur Amory Houghton, Jr., fourth-generation member of a great American glassmaking family, who reorganized the company in 1933 with the goal of making "the most perfect crystal the world has ever known." To understand Steuben's evolution under the direction of Arthur Houghton and his successors Thomas Buechner, Davis Chiodo, Kirtland Gardner, Susan King, Don Rorke, and Marie McKee, it is necessary to explore its early development in the years from 1903 to 1932, when the firm was guided by Frederick Carder.

Frederick Carder in England

Born in 1863 in Brockmoor, Staffordshire, England, to a family of potters who owned a salt-glazed stoneware manufactory in nearby Brierley Hill, Frederick Carder spent the first forty years of his life in these industrial environs. After learning all he could about ceramic glazes and chemistry as an assistant in the family business, studying nights at both the Stourbridge School of Art and the Dudley Mechanics Institute, Carder came under the tutelage of John Northwood, famed for his exquisite cameo glass designs. Northwood taught him to carve glass and marble, and soon recommended him for the position of designer at Stevens and Williams, a Brierley Hill glassmaking firm. The year was 1880, and Carder was seventeen when he began his career in glass.

Frederick Carder. Vase. 1917. Tyrian with trailed decorations in gold Aurene, height 10½". Collection Corning Museum of Glass.

Henning Overstrom, the first glassblower Frederick Carder hired for Steuben, 1903.

At the time, Stevens and Williams was engaged primarily in making colorless cut crystal tablewares, which Carder considered "the quintessence of vulgarity."[1] He persuaded the factory supervisor to produce some of his own designs in colored glass, which sold well. The following year, Carder's mentor, John Northwood, came to work for Stevens and Williams. The two men turned out various types of colored art glass, including the cased and cut cameo glass for which Northwood was best known. They collaborated on various technical problems, but the relationship began to sour in the years just prior to Northwood's death in 1902.

During the two decades he spent at Stevens and Williams, Carder honed his skills as a designer of colored and cameo glass and of delicate Art Nouveau patterns destined to be cut into "rock crystal"-style tablewares. He took many prizes in various British competitions for his designs. Throughout his years at Stevens and Williams, Carder maintained his connections with the Stourbridge School of Art, where he had part-time teaching duties. During summer vacations, he used a national scholarship award to travel around England and the continent, studying the great museum collections of historic glass.

In 1891, at the invitation of local authorities, Carder started the Wordsley School of Art to train talented glassworkers in the rudiments of drawing and in advanced glass production techniques. As the skills of his students became more and more evident in the glasshouses of the Stourbridge area, Carder's reputation as a designer and teacher grew. In 1902, the local government sent him on a fact-finding tour to the glassmaking centers of Germany and Austria. His report of the trip was well received and in 1903 he was again sent on a fact-finding mission—this time to the United States. It was a trip that would profoundly affect the course of his career.

After touring New York, Washington, and various glasshouses in the Pittsburgh area, Carder traveled to Corning, New York, to meet with Alanson Houghton and other officials of the Corning Glass Works, a diversified manufacturing concern that had begun business in 1868 in the small upstate New York glassmaking community. During his stay in Corning, Carder also met with Thomas G. Hawkes, president of T.G. Hawkes and Company, a glass engraving firm that had for many years purchased blanks from Stevens and Williams.

Details of the Carder-Hawkes meeting, which took place on a day in early March 1903, are sketchy. But Paul Gardner, Carder's assistant and biographer, has surmised that the two men were previously acquainted, having met during the course of Hawkes' various trips to Brierley Hill, and that prior to Carder's arrival in Corning, they had already laid out the basic terms of agreement to start a new company in Corning—the Steuben Glass Works, named for Steuben County in which the town was located.[2] According to an account in the *Corning Leader* of March 11, 1903, articles of incorporation for the new firm were filed with the New York secretary of state on March 9 of that year. As might be expected, the Stourbridge city fathers were less than delighted with the defection of their foremost glass designer and chemist on a tour they themselves had underwritten.[3] There is evidence to support the contention that Carder's career at Stevens and Williams had reached an impasse when John Northwood's son was appointed chief designer in 1902. Carder looked to America for a new beginning.

Steuben Glass Works: The First Years

There are no records to indicate the precise terms of the agreement between Carder and Hawkes to found the Steuben Glass Company. Throughout his long life, Carder was close-mouthed on that particular issue, if little else. It has been generally assumed by scholars that Hawkes provided the firm's financial backing, while Carder's broad experiences as an English glassmaker were brought to bear as planner, administrator, production manager, and artistic head of Steuben Glass. Hawkes' motivation in luring Carder away from Brierley Hill is not entirely clear. In all likelihood, he wished to free his glass-engraving firm from dependence on other manufacturers—Corning Glass Works, Dorflinger of White Mills, Pennsylvania, and Stevens and Williams, all of which had supplied glass blanks for decoration by Hawkes' Corning firm.[4]

Once in America, Carder began immediately to arrange for a ten-pot, coal-fired furnace to be installed in a converted foundry building Hawkes had purchased on Erie Avenue. When union difficulties, precipitated perhaps by the disgruntled glassmen he had left behind in England, prevented him from bringing fifteen English glassblowers over to work for him in Corning, Carder hired Swedish workers away from Dorflinger and other American manufactories.[5] By late October 1903, Steuben Glass Works was turning out the blanks Hawkes required for his engraving business.

Frederick Carder's talent and imagination were hardly taxed by such routine manufacture. By the following spring, he was experimenting with colored glass, including a new iridescent gold-toned glass similar to Louis Comfort Tiffany's vaunted Favrile. Carder patented his discovery in September 1904, naming it Aurene. Steuben was soon a commercial success. Paul Gardner recalls him boasting that he "bought the materials, built the furnace, and retired 40 percent of the $50,000 indebtedness in the first year of operation."[6]

Over the next decade, Steuben grew steadily; by World War I, there were twenty-seven employees. From the original Paynes Foundry Building, the company annexed several structures along Erie Avenue until its various cutting, blowing, warehousing, etching, and decorating operations filled an entire city block.[7] A second sixteen-pot furnace was added to the blowing room in 1908, enabling Carder to keep up with the demand for glass blanks, as well as for fixtures, tableware, colored art glass, and cut crystal that Steuben gradually added to its line. In the words of Tom Buechner, who was Steuben's president from 1973 to 1981 and who knew Carder well in his later years, the man from Brierley Hill was "a one-man band." He experimented on and perfected the formula for Steuben's various melts, designed both the shape and decoration of the glass, hired the workers, administered the factory, and planned the sales and

Overleaf, left: Frederick Carder. Cologne Bottle. c. 1928. Blue and pink Cintra center cased in heavy crystal with controlled bubbles and cut decoration, height 11½". Collection Smithsonian Institution.

Overleaf, right: Frederick Carder. Vase. Late 1920s. Blue Aurene cased over jade yellow with etched decoration, height 8½". Collection Corning Museum of Glass.

marketing for the glass through a network of travelling Steuben salesmen.[8]

Introduced in 1915, frosty white Calcite glass used for lighting fixtures comprised much of Steuben's business, together with the crystal blanks manufactured for Hawkes' engraving firm. Carder's strong creative drive inspired a variety of ornamental colored glasswares, signed with Steuben's distinctive fleur-de-lis trademark, among other signatures. His greatest innovation, Aurene, brought on the threat of litigation from Louis Comfort Tiffany, who resented its similarity to Favrile. Alone and in combination with other kinds of colored glass, Aurene was the most popular and best-known type of art glass made by Steuben during its first decades. Other kinds of prewar Steuben art glass included Verre de Soie, Alabaster, and Tyrian glass.

Corning Glass Works Buys Steuben

With the outbreak of World War I, certain kinds of raw materials including lead—a basic compound of crystal glass—and all fuels were in short supply. The government curtailed sale of these scarce items to firms manufacturing nonessential goods. Carder was no longer able to obtain enough coal to keep his pot furnaces at full production. An article in the *Corning Leader* noted that Steuben was forced to go on short time "because of fuel shortages and curtailment of orders."[9] At the same time, however, Corning Glass Works was working at full productive capacity, spurred by wartime demand for insulating, laboratory, and optical glass products. The outcome was inevitable. According to the *Corning Leader* of January 7, 1918, "The Corning Glass Works today acquired by purchase the plant of the Steuben Glass Works, a noncompeting concern which has hitherto confined its manufacturing operation to the manufacture of art and ornamental glassware. All present employees will be retained."[10]

The Houghtons of Corning Glass Works

The Houghton family ran Corning Glass Works. Its members had been prominently involved with American glass manufacture for nearly a century. In 1851, Amory Houghton, Sr., established the Union Glass Company in Somerville, Massachusetts. Soon he was known as the ablest authority in America on glass mixing and chemistry. It was natural for his son, Amory, Jr., to come into the family business at Somerville. There, early in his career, he established a laboratory and devoted most of his time to experimenting with new mixes and glassmaking techniques. Father and son sold the Union Glass Company in 1864, acquiring an interest in the Brooklyn Flint Glass Works, which was founded in 1827.[11] They soon discovered that New York in the troubled Civil War years was an expensive place to do business, lacking a well-priced supply of coal to fuel the glass furnaces and rife with labor unrest.

In 1868, hoping to find a situation where labor, fuel, and glassmaking materials could be obtained more cheaply, the Houghtons moved their operation to Corning, New York, and called it the Corning Flint Glass Company. The town was an attractive site for glassmaking. Its relatively rural populace had not yet become infected with the labor malaise that plagued New York and other large cities. Local fortunes, secured by "lumbering off" the nearby forested hills, were available for investment in other manufacturing concerns. There was good transportation: Corning was situated on the Chemung River, from which a feeder canal provided a link to the Erie Canal system, the vital commercial waterway joining the Hudson River and Port of New York to the Great Lakes and Mississippi. Furthermore, Corning was a railroading hub. Several small lines extended to Pennsylvania's coal fields in the south, providing cheap fuel, while legs of the Erie railroad connected with markets in New York City, Rochester, and the West.[12]

Sixteen-pot furnace used from 1908 until the 1930s. Erie Avenue, Corning.

Old warehouse, Erie Avenue, c. 1917, shows variety of Steuben designs in stock.

North facade of the old Erie Avenue plant as it appeared about 1908.

Steuben showroom, Erie Avenue, c. 1915, with much of the product line on display.

Opposite: Frederick Carder. Gold Aurene Glass. Left to right: Disk. 1920s. Diameter 10½"; Vase. c. 1905–10. Height 10⅞"; Vase. c. 1904. Height 5". First Vase, Collection Smithsonian Institution; others, private collection.

By October 1868, the Houghtons' glassmaking venture was in full swing, taking full advantage of all the resources Corning had to offer. The upper floor of their brick building was leased out to another firm, the Hoare and Daily cutting shop, where glass blanks made by Corning Flint Glass and other manufacturers were cut into decorative designs under the supervision of one Thomas Hawkes. John Hoare, a proprietor of the firm, had previously worked with the Houghtons in Brooklyn, it being customary in those days for cutting firms to set up operation near their source of supply for undecorated glass blanks.

Despite the advantages of its location in the southern tier of New York State, just above the Pennsylvania border, Houghton's fledgling company had some rocky years. Demand for decorative art glass was slow, and the country's economy was in a period of general decline. In 1872, after shutdown followed by bankruptcy, the company was reorganized and named the Corning Glass Works. Amory Houghton, Jr., was president; his brother, Charles, was vice president. Carrying on in the tradition established by the senior Amory Houghton in Massachusetts, they pursued a corporate policy that put a high premium on scientific research leading to the development of special products and to new fields of applied glass technology.

In the Houghton firm, discovery followed discovery. Corning was the first to develop ruby-colored glass made with copper for railroad danger signals. Previously, railroad signals, given their characteristic color by the addition of gold salts, changed to pale yellow in foggy weather—an obvious hazard to public safety.

In 1878, working from Thomas A. Edison's sketches, Corning blew the first electric light bulbs. The subsequent manufacture of this revolutionary invention constituted a large part of the company's business. In 1890, Charles Houghton patented a new type of railroad lens

Interior of the old Erie Avenue plant showing calcite light shades in foreground.

having corrugations inside rather than outside, to prevent their dimming from road dust. A few years later, Arthur A. Houghton pioneered a method of drawing thermometer tubing vertically rather than horizontally, as had been the practice for centuries in European glasshouses.

The Houghton inventiveness peaked in 1915 with the discovery of heat-resistant glass—a borosilica compound suitable for diverse uses. A full line of borosilicate glass products was marketed under several trademarks, including Pyrex. Ovenware, electric insulators, and components for industrial use were made of the revolutionary new glass, which was extremely resistant to the destructive forces of heat, chemicals, and electricity. When the supply of laboratory glass in the United States was cut off by World War I, Corning developed beakers, test tubes, and other technical wares made of the Pyrex formula. The Navy used Pyrex insulators, and Admiral Byrd carried them to Antarctica.

All during the time it was pioneering new applications in scientific and industrial wares, Corning Glass Works continued to make decorative lead crystal glass blanks for sale to the many cutting shops that sprang up in Corning by the turn of the century. The Philadelphia Centennial Exposition of 1876 displayed many examples of glass cut in the British style, spurring the American demand for such wares and boosting production of blanks in Corning. By the 1890s, many European craftsmen, trained primarily in the Bohemian countries, were working in various Corning cutting shops. When Corning Glass Works took out its papers of incorporation in 1872, four to six shops of the firm's glassblowers were busy turning out blanks for engraving and cutting. That same year, Hoare and Daily—the firm that rented part of the Corning Glass premises—had two hundred people on its payroll. In 1880, Thomas Hawkes, superintendent of Hoare and Daily, left that company to start his own

Finishing department, Erie Avenue, c. 1910.

firm. By 1903, he was sufficiently prosperous to lure Frederick Carder away from Stourbridge to start the Steuben Glass Works.

In the meantime, a third generation of Houghtons entered glassmaking at Corning. In 1887, Amory Houghton, Jr.'s sons, Arthur and Alanson B. Houghton, joined the family firm. Arthur Houghton gave his name to a son who would become Steuben's innovative head in the decades following 1933; Alanson was later the United States ambassador to England (1925–28) and to Germany. His son, Amory, would later become president of Corning Glass Works and a staunch friend and supporter of his cousin Arthur during Steuben's period of reorganization. This enterprising third generation carried on the family's long-established commitment to research and development of new products, and under its direction Corning Glass Works continued to flourish.

The Steuben Division

Carder and the Houghton family were brought together in 1918 by the advent of war, and by the nature of a wartime economy that necessarily gave a higher priority to the production of industrial glasswares than to the production of art glass. Though Carder was kept on as managing director of the new "Steuben Division" of Corning Glass, few of his beloved artwares were manufactured for the duration of the war. Instead, bulbs, tubing, and optical glass for use in aviators' goggles were produced on a large scale in the Steuben plant. Corning Glass appointed John Hostetter assistant manager of the Division, diminishing Carder's authority to a certain extent. With the advent of Hostetter, Carder was named art director of the firm, though he also retained the title of "manager."

When normal times returned after the war, Corning's management somewhat relaxed its hold on Steuben manufacture, although "the boys from Smokestack University," as Carder liked to call them, made unstinting efforts to bring the Steuben Division's accounting procedures into line with those used by the parent company. In 1921, Carder's responsibility for the production of Steuben art glass, illuminating wares, and crystal blanks for engraving—if not for the optical products still made by the Division—was confirmed.[13] He turned his attention once more to ornamental glasswares. Since the original Steuben ten-pot furnace was no longer in use, colored melts were now made entirely in the newer sixteen-pot furnace of 1908. Steuben introduced a variety of new art glass types in the postwar years: Cintra and Cluthra; etched opaque or semi-opaque wares were top-of-the-line items together with the ever popular Aurene.[14]

During the 1920s, Carder introduced his most prized innovation—Intarsia glass, extremely difficult to produce, incorporating a delicate trellis or floral pattern of colored glass between two clear crystal layers. The upsurge of interest in American antiques during the 1920s was reflected to a certain extent in the art glass of the Steuben Division. Carder's Pomona Green and Amethyst wares, for example, often resembled the threaded and lily-pad glass of the eighteenth century. In the late 1920s, architectural glass panels with Art Deco designs were brought into the line. Many kinds of decoratively cased, etched, and engraved wares were also made at Steuben during these years (Thomas Dimitroff's *Frederick Carder and Steuben Glass* provides a definitive listing).

Like other Corning firms making engraved glass, Steuben relied on the services of skilled outside engravers, many of them trained in the glass and hardstone cutting centers of Bohemia. These engravers worked from shops in their homes in Corning, and according to Jane Spillman and Estelle Farrar in their definitive book, *The Complete Cut and Engraved Glass of Corning,* they were a common sight on Corning streets during the first three decades of this century, as they trudged home from the glassblowing factories each day with baskets of blanks tucked under their arms. Without question, the concentration of so many skilled engravers in Corning helped Steuben to change successfully its artistic direction after 1933, away from colored art glass and toward the manufacture of crystal, clear as water.

The Resources for Reorganization

By the early 1920s, several men were already in Steuben's employ who would continue to play an important role in the company during the next several decades. Robert J. Leavy, Carder's office manager, began his career as an accountant with Corning Glass Works in 1916 and came to Steuben as factory accountant when the firm was purchased by Corning in 1918.[15] By 1926, he was sales manager. Bolislav Manikowski, foreman of the etching shop during the 1920s, had been hired by Carder in 1917 as an etching worker. According to Paul Gardner, Manikowski's primary job during the years between 1920 and 1933 was to etch Carder's designs on the metal plates used to make wax transfer prints to be applied to objects.[16] Manikowski sometimes "improved" Carder's designs, changing the plates to suit his own taste. For a time after the 1933 reorganization, Manikowski was listed on company records as Steuben's resident designer, and it is often difficult to be certain whether specific designs were Carder's or Manikowski's.

Frederick Schroeder, whose detailed memoirs helped to trace the early history of the firm, was in charge of Steuben's blowing room during much of the 1920s and continued in Steuben's employ after 1933.[17] Perhaps the most skilled Steuben glassblower during these years was Johnnie Jansen, a Swede who joined Carder in 1905 or 1906 and continued to work at Steuben until the late 1930s, imparting his incredible range of glassblowing knowledge to his young apprentices.

Frederick Carder stands in front of a pillar in the Steuben office, about 1915.

III.

THE TROUBLED YEARS: 1929–1932

By the mid-1920s, it became increasingly clear that all was not well. Although Corning Glass Works gave Frederick Carder his head in administering the business as well as the artistic affairs of Steuben, sales were dropping. Sophisticated buyers were beginning to turn from the shimmering colors and sinuous organic design of Art Nouveau–inspired glasswares. They preferred the more "modern," clean-lined, geometric, and colorless crystal glass made popular by Swedish designers in the years following the war. Carder, of course, grew up in an era when colorless glass was also popular, albeit cut in overly ornate, detailed patterns that he considered vulgar. As a result of this early conditioning, he retained little affection for "colorless" crystal and during the 1920s, counter to world design trends, Steuben produced as little of it as possible. A vast array of unsold iridescent and colored glass shimmered on the shelves of Steuben's storerooms.

The problem was compounded by Carder's style of sales management. Instead of using agents, Steuben employed its own traveling salesmen who visited various retailing outlets across the country. They would often return to Corning with orders for special variations on stock pieces and for new designs suggested by their clients. These were obligingly turned out by workers in the blowing and finishing rooms, resulting in a growing overstock of unsalable, few-of-a-kind pieces. Corning management tried to regain control by making Robert J. Leavy liaison between sales and manufacture, heading off the special orders. But Carder disregarded this dictum, the problem continued, and the unsold stock grew.

The situation reached a head around the time of the 1929 stock market crash. In a report to Dr. E.C. Sullivan, then president of the parent company, a Steuben employee (probably the sales manager, M.J. Lacey) noted that Steuben had run a deficit in every year since Corning acquired it "except for briefly in 1926."[1] The report blamed not only an "inactive market," but manufacturing and sales methods. Carder was pictured as a despot, "unwilling to delegate authority even to packing and shipping; most details are carried on in his own head." The company had nearly three thousand accounts in all sections of the country, and it attempted to cater to individual tastes. In addition, Steuben's prices were not competitive with those of other suppliers of art crystal components to chandeliermakers such as Pairpoint. The company's crystal glass blanks for engraving were also priced too high for the market.

Morale was said to be low throughout the firm, in part due to Carder's autocratic management style which was not open to suggestions for improvement. The Lacey report concluded by recommending that the Steuben Division be "officially" turned over to Carder on the condition that he hire an understudy and report monthly to the Corning management. Under such a plan, Carder would run the Division as a separate unit, with books kept apart from those of Corning Glass Works, for an eighteen-month period in which he would either "make it or break it" with his methods. At the end of the trial period, it was expected that if Carder and his understudy had failed to make the Division profitable, he would quietly step aside and permit "the boys from Smokestack University" to take over.

Finally, the report suggested that a small retail outlet be set up in Corning's Baron Steuben Hotel, where overstocked items could be sold to

Strawberry Mansion Urn and tableware, designed by Frederick Carder, 1931. An engraved goblet of the Federalist period, c. 1790, was found in Painted Post, New York, in the summer of 1931. Steuben copied the design for presentation to Strawberry Mansion, a historic Philadelphia house restored in 1932. The pattern was subsequently produced for sale.

local customers and tourists. The recommendations in the report were apparently not followed, but the handwriting was clearly on the wall: Carder's days at Steuben were numbered.

On September 23, 1929, a fourth-generation member of the Houghton glassmaking family, fresh from Harvard, came to Corning Glass Works as an assistant timekeeper in "A" factory. He was Arthur Amory Houghton, Jr., a scholarly twenty-three-year-old who loved old books and would soon become responsible for the future of Steuben.

In the meantime, however, the situation continued to deteriorate. The Steuben factory, still in its original series of old buildings, was beginning to show its age; in the words of one employee, working conditions were "slightly less than deplorable."[2] Carder persisted on his own independent path, ignoring the requests of Corning management to institute better production and sales controls. Even the most mundane and predictable category of Steuben's production—the lighting fixture and globe manufacturing department—failed to keep competitive prices with other firms.[3]

Steuben's dilemma was summarized in a memorandum written in 1931 by Corning executive R.C. Vaughn to Amory Houghton, the young president of Corning Glass Works.[4] "Certain deficiencies are apparent in plant organization, cost planning, cost efficiency, morale, working conditions, sales assistance and general cooperation, and they are present in such degree as to make it clear that a change must be effected within a comparatively brief time if continued and increasing losses are to be avoided" within the Steuben Division, he noted. Vaughn reiterated the shortcomings of Carder's administration. He pointed out that it was impossible for the same salespersons to promote effectively all of the drastically different types of merchandise then being produced by Steuben—everything from lighting fixtures and architectural glass panels to "art glass," tablewares, vases, and bowls. Vaughn suggested that there was a large potential market for the high-quality art glass then being made by Steuben, but that it had to be defined and cultivated by careful advertising. The Vaughn report concluded with a recommendation that the Steuben Division either be closed or moved to the Corning Glass Works' main plant where production—and Frederick Carder—would presumably be subject to greater scrutiny and control.

The Move to "B" Factory

Possibly as a result of the report, in February 1932, the Steuben Division offices were moved several blocks from their Erie Avenue location to "B" factory in building 21 of Corning Glass Works' main plant: "They sat between two pot furnaces that held 32 big pots—a ton of glass."[5] Following the move, the old Steuben plant on Erie Avenue was largely used for the storage of old machinery and records.[6]

At the same time, Frederick Carder's title was changed to that of art director of Corning Glass Works. His office-studio was moved to the top floor of building 21, near the Corning Glass Works' administrative offices and away from the blowing room floor. John Mackay, a Corning Glass Works employee formerly situated in the company's New York offices, was brought in to be manager of the Steuben Division with responsibility for both production and sales.[7]

Having founded Steuben and managed it with a relatively free hand for nearly thirty years, Carder was understandably embittered by his loss of control.[8] Although he continued in a *pro forma* sense to advise on the design of Steuben's new products, his involvement with their cut and engraved designs was virtually over. He spent most of his time working on his own projects—primarily sculpture created by the lost-wax method—and on architectural glass, which was sold for a time under the Steuben trademark. He was assisted during these years by Paul Gardner,

Gaffer Theodore Swenson, servitor Junius Heydolf, and gatherer Sam Gullo, c. 1932, at "B" factory in Corning Glass Works. Because of deteriorating conditions in the Erie Avenue plant, Steuben was moved to the "B" factory of the main plant, Corning Glass Works, in 1932.

Carder, c. 1930, designing engraved decoration for a goblet amid various kinds of decorative Steuben being made at that time.

who tells the complete story in his definitive biography of Carder.

At the close of World War II, Carder moved back to his old offices in the Erie Avenue building, where he continued to pursue his various projects until his official retirement in 1959, at the age of ninety-six. He remained an outspoken, well-respected public figure in the Corning community, where he was often seen attending service club meetings, puttering in his petunia beds, or strolling along the shaded streets near his home on the hill. Although many townsfolk gave Carder's peppery tongue a wide berth, he nevertheless maintained warm relationships with many old glassworks associates until he died, still indomitable of spirit and quick of mind, at the venerable age of one hundred.[9]

Following a few months of correspondence in late 1931, Amory Houghton appointed the well-known industrial designer Walter Dorwin Teague as design consultant to Corning and Steuben under a one-year contract commencing in

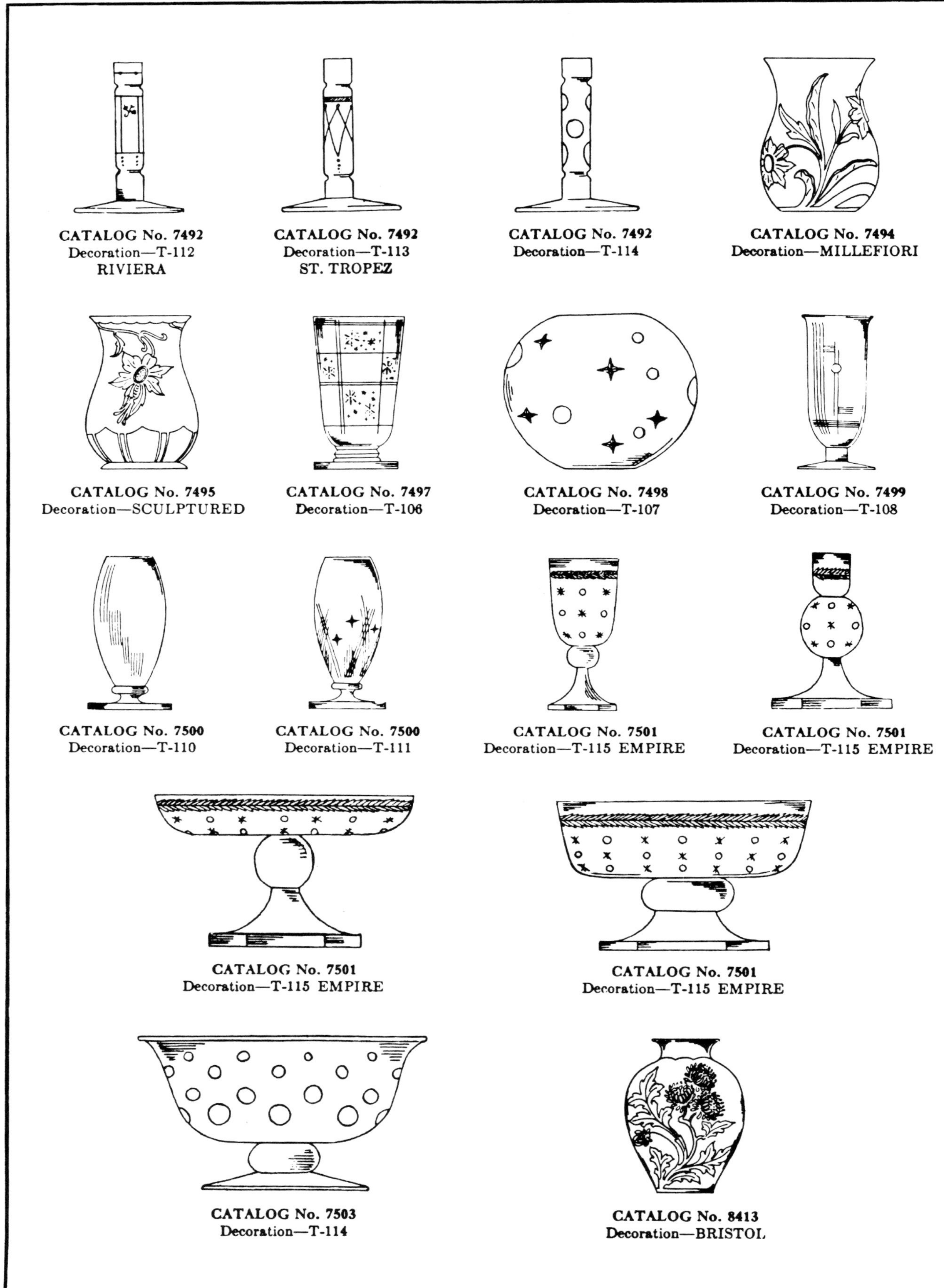

CATALOG No. 7492
Decoration—T-112
RIVIERA

CATALOG No. 7492
Decoration—T-113
ST. TROPEZ

CATALOG No. 7492
Decoration—T-114

CATALOG No. 7494
Decoration—MILLEFIORI

CATALOG No. 7495
Decoration—SCULPTURED

CATALOG No. 7497
Decoration—T-106

CATALOG No. 7498
Decoration—T-107

CATALOG No. 7499
Decoration—T-108

CATALOG No. 7500
Decoration—T-110

CATALOG No. 7500
Decoration—T-111

CATALOG No. 7501
Decoration—T-115 EMPIRE

CATALOG No. 7501
Decoration—T-115 EMPIRE

CATALOG No. 7501
Decoration—T-115 EMPIRE

CATALOG No. 7501
Decoration—T-115 EMPIRE

CATALOG No. 7503
Decoration—T-114

CATALOG No. 8413
Decoration—BRISTOL

February 1932. From his Madison Avenue offices in New York City, Teague was to work out a series of new "modern" designs for Steuben tableware, visiting the Corning plant monthly to supervise production. Teague made it clear that he did "not expect to have any modifications made in my designs except with my approval" and that he could not "share responsibility for my own work with anyone else."[10]

As Steuben Division plant manager during 1932, John Mackay did his best to turn the unprofitable business around. "Steuben Must Make Money!" he exhorted the sales and production staff in emphatic capitals in an early memorandum.[11] His reorganization plan involved cutting the active production line to a few best-selling numbers, closing out the rest at bargain prices, cutting costs of manufacture, and presenting a trendy new line of Walter Dorwin Teague's designs "which will be a Knockout . . . We are going to be Creators," Mackay averred. "We will establish a leadership in the Quality glassware field that will make the name Steuben stand for the highest in quality, workmanship, and creative effects." He also recognized the importance of a well-labeled product, and ordered that "every piece of glass leaving Corning be marked with the word 'Steuben.'"[12]

Enthusiastic Mackay was not above a trick or two. He urged stem and artware salesmen to get their customers to order extra "replacement" pieces at the time of the original order to avoid the costs of special replacement production later on. If the customer refused, the salesman was to have extra pieces made up anyway and held in stock against the time when the customer might indeed enter a replacement order. Then the customer was to be charged a much higher fee for "special production" of these replacements. "This arrangement is under no circumstances to be divulged to the customer," Mackay emphasized.[13] Rather than save the costs of special production, in all likelihood Mackay's scheme contributed to the glut of overstocked pieces cluttering the storerooms.

Teague, meanwhile, embarked on the design of a line of "extremely simple" crystal cut with geometric motifs. About thirty-two of his patterns were incorporated into the last Steuben Division catalogue, published in 1932.[14] However, he did not confine his involvement with the Steuben Division to matters concerning design. In a series of letters during 1932 to Amory Houghton, he analyzed production and sales problems, suggesting possible solutions: "It will be necessary to decide on a volume of business which will make Steuben a paying plant, plan a definite program which will bring us to this volume within a specific length of time, and begin at once to figure costs based on this volume."[15] Teague suggested still other ideas to Houghton: "Plans should be made for as much advertising as the business will stand . . . in class publications such as *Vogue, House and Garden, Harper's Bazaar*." And he thought it possible to "arrange an exhibition of Steuben glass which will be routed among the art museums of the inland cities such as Rochester, Buffalo, Cleveland, Toledo, et cetera" in the same manner that a successful exhibition of Swedish glass had been circulated some years before.

Image was paramount to Teague. "We must work to establish Steuben as the finest glassware in America, worth all we ask for it. I believe we can make the ownership of Steuben glass one of those evidences of solvency—like the ownership of a Cadillac sixteen or a house in the right neighborhood." Teague's outspoken consultancy culminated in a memorandum on Steuben policy circulated to Amory Houghton and other Steuben officials in October 1932.[16] This document is the first written expression of the so-called Steuben Trilogy—the corporate philosophy that guided Steuben's course after 1933. "This is what we have to sell: *that delicate excellence possible only when the finest crystal is worked with the ultimate in craftsmanship into designs that come alive with style*." Wisely, Teague

A group of Walter Dorwin Teague's designs as they appeared in the last catalogue to be published by the Steuben Division of Corning Glass Works, December 1932. The Teague designs are distinguished by a "T" before the stock number.

realized that Steuben could not compete with mass-produced wares in a general market. The appeal was to status: "Steuben can achieve universal recognition as the ultimate in glass. It can become a demonstration or an advertisement of its owner's good taste and savoir faire. To have Steuben glass in your home and on your table will register you among those who know the right things."

Despite his astute reading of the potential market for Steuben glass, Teague was apparently not retained as a design consultant beyond the expiration of his first year's contract. Although some of his designs continued to be made and shown in exhibitions of Steuben glass through the 1930s (though most were discontinued in the fall of 1933), Walter Dorwin Teague is not mentioned in company records after 1932, nor is Steuben listed among Teague's industrial design clients in his biography in *Who Was Who in America*.[17]

A New Glass Formula Is Discovered

Neither the forward-looking Teague nor the confident John Mackay brought an answer to Steuben's troubles in 1932. However, a striking technological breakthrough that year was to have a decisive impact on the company's future. For some time Corning Glass Works' chemists had been trying to achieve an optical glass that would transmit, instead of absorb, ultraviolet light. Experiments begun in the fall of 1929 yielded, by the following spring, an exceptional glass of extremely high refractive quality (approximately 1.584) that permitted the whole spectrum of a light wave, including the ultraviolet range, to pass through. This was accomplished by removing from the glass batch most of the iron impurities responsible for trapping ultraviolet light. Since minute traces of iron give glass a greenish cast, all Steuben made up to 1932 had been decolorized by the addition of manganese dioxide, which neutralized the greenish tint of the iron by imparting a slight pink color of its own. This new and pure glass required no decolorizing agent.

Since only small amounts of the newly discovered glass—dubbed "10-M" by Corning Glass chemists—were needed for commercial optical applications, other large-volume uses were sought to increase the economy of the purifying procedures. It seemed logical to use the brilliantly refractive new metal in the production of decorative Steuben objects. Experimentally, in early 1932, two line items were made from the new crystal—the Warwick pattern stemware set, and a cut Warwick console set consisting of a center bowl in two sizes and a candlestick.[18]

Before Steuben could put the new glass into production for its entire line, two problems had to be solved. The new glass had a coefficient of expansion different from that of the glass Carder had used since 1904; any cased object combining the new and the old glass would crack from the disparate stresses as it cooled. The 10-M glass also had a relatively short pot life—it apparently reacted with the porcelain pots in which it was melted, causing them to wear down or break in a shorter-than-normal time. (The first experimental pot of 10-M glass, containing 600 pounds, broke the second day it was placed in the furnace.) Because it takes many months to temper and prepare a porcelain-lined pot for melting glass, no one at Steuben in mid-1932 felt confident that enough pots could be made to melt sufficient quantities of the new glass for high-volume production. Later that year, after ten 2,500-pound pots were tested and delivered to the Steuben plant, it became feasible to produce the new crystal in large quantities. The problem of different coefficients of expansion for the old, often colored glass and the new crystal was solved by avoidance: old Steuben glass continued to be used for cased colored wares. After the company's reorganization in 1933, all colored glass was gradually phased out, paving the way for exclusive use of the brilliant 10-M metal.

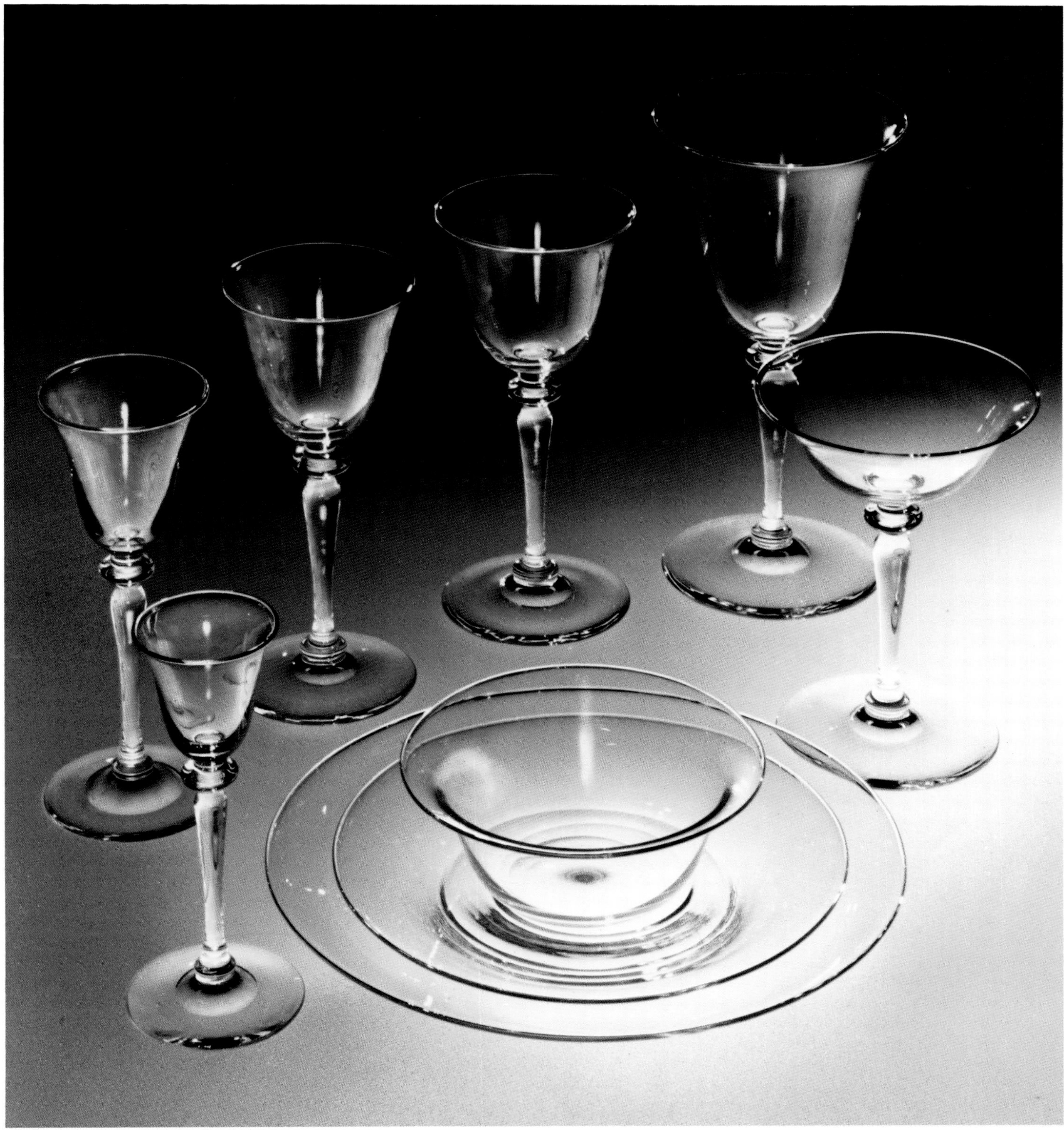

Almost all of the objects produced at Steuben in the first years after 1933 were stemware, bowls, drinking glasses, candlesticks, and urns. Although many new styles were introduced, some forms were carried over from Frederick Carder's designs. The pieces shown here were designed by Carder and had been available both in colored and clear glass of the old variety; from 1933 they were made only in the fine, new glass formula.

The new shapes brought forward under the design influence of John M. Gates and Sidney Waugh took on a different character, reflecting not only the characteristics of the new glass but the sculptural and architectural backgrounds of the two men. This massive vase (1935), designed by Waugh, consists of two thick-walled blown forms (the large vase body and the sturdy base), which were fused together, cut in bold facets, and then polished.

IV.
A NEW BEGINNING: 1933–1937

The various panaceas proposed to revitalize the ailing Steuben Division in the years between 1929 and 1932 were to no avail: without a workable, cohesive business philosophy, it was a money-losing proposition for the Corning Glass Works. By the middle of 1933, Corning's directors were ready to throw in the towel.

One of Corning Glass Works' youngest directors at the time was Arthur Amory Houghton, Jr. Educated at St. Paul's and Harvard, young Houghton had started work in 1929 as assistant timekeeper in "A" factory. He was later appointed a director of the family firm, at the age of twenty-four. Between 1930 and 1932, he served as assistant to his cousin, Corning Glass president Amory Houghton. In this position, young Houghton observed at first hand the trial-and-error efforts of Steuben's new manager, John Mackay, to turn the firm around; and he was aware of the arrangements with Walter Dorwin Teague.[1] The pivotal year for Steuben's history was 1933. As Arthur Amory Houghton, Jr., later recalled:

> *Around 1932 or 1933 the question came up in a directors' meeting at Corning as to whether or not the division should be discontinued. I was a director at that time and I asked if I could take a crack at it, because although not really knowledgeable about glassmaking or the arts, I was fascinated by the prospect.*[2]

Young Houghton was apparently given *carte blanche,* and in October 1933 the Steuben Division was reorganized as Steuben Glass, Incorporated.[3] The New York State papers of incorporation noted that 100 percent of the stock of the new corporation was held by the Corning Glass Works. In the months preceding incorporation, Houghton wasted no time familiarizing himself with Steuben's production team. "Manufacturing had been discontinued at the old Erie Avenue plant, moved over to pot melting in a factory, and finishing was up in 'B' factory with Bob Leavy as plant supervisor," he recalled. "I went over and introduced myself to Bob and we started along on this thing."[4]

With a young man's idealism and the patrician tastes of a bibliophile and scholar, Houghton was confident he could rejuvenate Steuben by creating an aesthetically superior glass and marketing it as "the finest in the world." In some ways, his analysis of the situation did not differ radically from Teague's assessment. "Knowing we had skilled craftsmen . . . and a really beautiful composition for crystal," Houghton recognized that "the needed elements were design and also how to sell the product."[5]

For assistance in redirecting Steuben's approach to design, he enlisted John Monteith Gates, "who was then in New York working as a young architect—I'd known him since my childhood." The Gates and Houghton families had summered near each other at the Massachusetts seashore for years. Gates was a year older than Houghton. In 1933, he agreed to become Steuben's managing director, at the age of twenty-eight. Like Arthur Houghton, "Jack" Gates had attended Harvard. He was already well launched on a successful career as an architect with the New York firm of Charles A. Platt. In 1932, Gates helped his firm win the coveted Phelps-Stokes Competition with a plan for low-cost housing on New York's Lower East Side; in 1933, shortly before joining Houghton's venture, he entered an international competition to replan central Stockholm. A month or so after he joined Steuben the telephone rang and Gates learned he would receive the 15,000-kronor first prize. "Gates had never visited Stockholm—that was a considerable intellectual triumph," Arthur Houghton later remarked.

It is a tribute to Houghton's innate persuasiveness that he convinced Gates to set aside his promising architectural career to assist in the regeneration of a failing company. Gates, in turn, was responsible for recruiting the third man in the young triumvirate. As Houghton later recalled: "Jack felt it necessary to have a skilled professional artist associated with us. He told me about a young sculptor . . . Sidney Waugh . . . by nature a poet." One balmy afternoon early in the autumn of 1933, Houghton and Gates talked Waugh into associating himself with them over a spaghetti lunch at an Italian restaurant under the el, not far from Waugh's Bleecker Street studio. It must have been a formal meeting, for Houghton recalled, "we called each other Mr. Waugh and Mr. Houghton."[6]

Sidney Waugh was a man of many talents. One of six children of a mathematics professor, he studied at Amherst College before taking up architecture at the Massachusetts Institute of Technology. Glass was an early enthusiasm: in 1930, he visited the Orrefors glasshouse in Sweden and was much impressed. From 1929 through 1932, he worked in Italy as a Fellow in Sculpture at the American Academy in Rome. His sensibilities found additional expression in the poetry he composed. Sidney Waugh's business arrangement with Houghton and Gates was evidently conceived to safeguard his professional independence. "He said he would not be willing to give up his world of sculpture, but he would be willing to work for us one-third of the time," Houghton remembered. "Waugh was serious about his work: he disdained affectation. He thought a good sculptor was a first-class craftsman. Even in the depression, Waugh was able to make a good living off his sculpture."[7]

Manufacture at Corning

In reorganizing Steuben, Houghton, Gates, and Waugh could place their confidence in a superior production team of glassworkers. In late 1933, almost one hundred people were on the plant payroll in Corning: thirty-nine craftsmen in the blowing room; thirty-two involved in finishing procedures such as smoothing, grinding, polishing, and washing; seven involved in acid-decorating; seven in packing and shipping; twelve in administration.[8]

Each of the half-dozen six-man shops on Steuben's blowing floor had its specialty. Olaf Johanson, for example, was gaffer of a shop excelling in stemware, while Tommy Swanson's shop turned out two-handled vases. At this time all of Steuben's shops were headed by Swedish gaffers, many of whom Frederick Carder had recruited decades earlier from competing glass factories in White Mills, Pennsylvania.

The year Steuben was reorganized under Arthur Houghton, the only decorating procedure carried on in-house was acid etching; all cutting and engraving was performed off the premises by independent contractors who worked from their homes in Corning. Many of Corning's engravers and cutters acquired their expertise in the Bohemian gem-and-glass-cutting centers. Joseph Libisch, the virtuoso of Corning's engravers, had such a background. Others who worked for Steuben at the time of Houghton's reorganization were Henry and Anthony Keller, Clem Nitsche, Ed Palme, Tom Miller, Gus Cummings, Roger Kingle, Joe Orencoy, Fred Haselbauer, and Tony Kroll.[9] Robert J. Leavy was plant manager at the time; his unqualified support of the new regime, marked by his strong personal loyalty to Arthur Houghton, was instrumental to its success.[10] Frederick Schroeder, who came to Corning from White Mills where he learned to blow glass at the age of twelve, was foreman of the blowing room; Bolislav Manikowski was resident designer. All were anxious to see Steuben remain a viable business and to help it grow.

New Directions in Design and Marketing

Confident of a loyal and capable production staff in Corning, and eager to exploit the "beautiful new crystal" found in 10-M glass, Arthur Houghton turned his attention to building an innovative marketing organization, backed by a superior design staff. Sidney Waugh was charged with developing a series of designs that would bring out the beauty of Steuben's new crystal contemporary designs, free of color, that could compete in a sophisticated world marketplace with the best glass sold by Orrefors, Lobmeyr, and other well-established European firms.

It seemed obvious that Steuben could no longer rely on three thousand indiscriminate retail outlets for what was to be "the best crystal the world had ever known." As Houghton recalled the circumstances: "We decided we must . . . have a first-class outlet in New York, one run and controlled by us so we could set the highest standards in merchandising, and Jack located for us at 748 Fifth Avenue . . . a handsome shop that had been a restaurant of Sherry's."[11] The former restaurant was completely redesigned by John Gates in architectural consultation with his former employers, the Charles A. Platt firm. McMillen, Incorporated—New York's leading decorating company—was brought in to execute Gates' vision of serene elegance. Quiet tones of white and grey were chosen to complement the "brilliant color and lustre of the glass" to be displayed in the shop.[12] When it opened on February 19, 1934, 748 Fifth Avenue evoked the atmosphere of a fine art gallery rather than a shop. The staff of seven, including three saleswomen, were selected for their knowledge of the fine arts.

Sidney Waugh's illuminated crystal fountain sculpture, a slender column of concentric glass cylinders topped by an alert gazelle, dominated the decor. "This is Mr. Waugh's first use of glass as a sculptural medium," the *Corning Leader* noted. To stock the new shop, however, Arthur Houghton had to rely on many of the line items carried over from previous years. "Three men are responsible for the beautiful examples of glass you'll see," observed Fern Fenton, a *New York*

Times columnist, in an article covering the shop's opening. "Walter Dorwin Teague contributes praiseworthy designs—versatile man, he jumps about from designing Kodaks to oil stoves . . . to these exquisitely frail things. Frederick Carder, another of the triumvirate, has been at this glass business for many a day. Sidney Waugh contributed an amazingly beautiful glass sculpture, framed against a gun metal mirror."[13] A section of the new Steuben store was also given over to the display of architectural glass panels, in production at Steuben since the late 1920s. Sales in the first year were less than $74,000 gross, but Arthur Houghton was not discouraged: "With youthful idealism we set ourselves the highest possible and the most vigorous standards, determined that we were going to attempt to make the finest glass that had ever been made in the history of the world."[14]

While plans for the shop were progressing under Gates' direction, Houghton was busy at Corning clearing the decks for the production of Waugh's new lines of colorless crystal. The Steuben stockroom was cluttered with the accumulation of many years' unsold glass, and decisive action was taken. In Houghton's words:

> *We broke up a substantial amount of obsolete, unsalable inventory in autumn of 1933. Our shelves were overcrowded . . . we had no space for a new inventory. I participated in and approved the decision to break it up. The decision was made after exhaustive and unsuccessful attempts to sell it, even at a giveaway price. Nobody wanted it. We had endless sets that did not match; colors that were not uniform . . . it was the accumulation of years of obsolescence and errors—in one word, dregs. We were quite aware of historical value, and first removed and put away in an upstairs room . . . those few items that might be of historical interest and examples of all variant techniques and colors.*[15]

Despite the care Houghton took to preserve worthwhile examples of earlier Steuben glass made during the Carder years, the "smashup" incident assumed mythic proportions in Corning, and Frederick Carder was clearly embittered by what he regarded as the symbolic destruction of his own contributions to Steuben.[16]

Within a year after the New York shop opened, John Gates had succeeded in launching a New York–based design department staffed by six recent graduates of well-known architectural schools. "At the time," Gates later recalled, "there was no such thing as a trained glass designer. There were, however, young and talented men coming from the architectural schools, and since I was an architect by profession, I believed that this training was a fine discipline for expanding the design of crystal within the laws of balance, proportion, profile, and scale."[17] Of the six original designers recruited by Gates, James McNaughton came from Carnegie Tech, and George Thompson was trained at M.I.T. Thompson and William Pollock remained with Steuben for years.

From the start, Houghton and Gates decided that design in a new Steuben organization should be physically separated from production, based on their belief that throughout the history of glassmaking it had been customary for the owner or the craftsman—the glassblower—to be the designer of the articles he made. Many such craftsmen-designers were "prone to engage in extravagances of technical virtuosity, to the detriment of good design."[18] To avoid this, Steuben's new design team would work in New York City, unhampered by pressure from the glassblowers. New York's cosmopolitan environment, with its variety of cultural activities, was deemed a more stimulating atmosphere for the encouragement of contemporary design than that of a small industrial town in New York state. Nevertheless, each designer engaged by Steuben was indoctrinated in the techniques of glassmaking at the Corning factory, and visits to the factory were mandated, for two or three days out of every month, to work with the glassblowers and finishers. "The designers spent a great deal of time with the

Among the key influences on the 1930s Steuben style were Swedish simplicity and the massive geometry of Art Deco. Pieces were cut, engraved, sometimes adorned with smaller elements (called "bits") of hot glass, but always with a fine sense of proportion, a feeling of fullness, and a restrained manner. The engraving designs of Waugh, such as shown here in his classic Gazelle Bowl (1935), were bold in character and composed of large shapes easily reproduced by the round cutting wheels of the engraver; they are similar to the architectural sculpture of the period. For years to come, the hallmark of Steuben would be weighty pieces, volumetric in character, with elements added to embellish or decorate the basic forms.

Sidney Waugh. Mariner's Bowl. 1935. Diameter 15¾".

Sidney Waugh. Zodiac Bowl. 1935. Diameter 16".

craftsmen, and struck up strong affinities," according to Houghton.[19]

Publicizing the New Steuben

Having worked out an efficient organizational and marketing structure, with the reorganized design program well under way, Houghton turned his attention to publicizing the "new" Steuben in the right circles. By 1935, he had something to work with: new Sidney Waugh designs were in production, and more were on the drawing board. He decided to give the new Steuben the cachet of a European launch. "I met a delightful Englishman, twenty years or so older than me, by the name of C. David Stelling, a professional journalist and a very cultured man. . . . He was a public relations advisor for the Conservative Party and a speechwriter for Winston Churchill," said Houghton. It was Stelling who selected the Fine Arts Society Gallery on elegant Bond Street in London for Steuben's first exhibition abroad.[20]

To get things rolling, on February 27 and 28, 1935, Knoedler and Company, the New York art gallery, showcased fifteen pieces of Sidney Waugh's new glass prior to its shipment to London. A warm English reception for the artist's work was assured by Arthur Houghton's good timing: "On March 12, 1935," *The New York Times* reported, "Arthur Amory Houghton, Jr., nephew of Ambassador to England Alanson Houghton, presented (Waugh's) Zodiac Bowl to the Victoria and Albert Museum. It was accepted by Eric Maclagan, the Director."[21] Subsequent stories in the American press changed the word "accepted" to "bought." On March 19, *Ceramic Industry,* a trade paper, duly noted the embarkation for England of Arthur Houghton and John Gates aboard the S.S. *Majestic,* adding: "After the exhibition, Steuben will be sold by the firm of Edward Trower Company, LTD."[22] Houghton convinced the officers of the *Majestic* that the Steuben crystal had to be carried in the secure "gold room," usually reserved for the transport of bullion.[23]

In London, meanwhile, David Stelling had done his work well. A great deal of genteel hoopla accompanied the March 19 vernissage at the Fine Arts Society. Since it was the first time American art of any kind had been shown in Bond Street, the event attracted a horde of curious well-wishers. Stelling persuaded Lord Lee of Fareham, a noted British collector, to preside over the occasion. "Society women, beautifully gowned and richly jewelled, were jammed together in the narrow space," observed London's *News Chronicle*. "When Lord Lee of Fareham arrived to open the exhibition, he had to stand on a chair to make himself heard. 'I know less about this kind of art than a Hindu does about skates,' he said."[24] Nevertheless, as Houghton recalled, the event was a "*succès fou*."

More than two hundred pieces of Steuben—at least twenty of them new designs by Sidney Waugh in colorless crystal—were seen by visitors to the Fine Arts Society between March 20 and April 18, 1935. In the exhibition catalogue, the whole range of glass then being produced by Steuben was represented. Sidney Waugh's Gazelle Bowl, Zodiac Bowl, and Narcissus Vase; Carder's classic Strawberry Mansion Urn and Intarsia goblets; and Walter Dorwin Teague's pressed lens bowls and tableware in the star-engraved Empire pattern were among the items illustrated. The show received an excellent press in England. The Sunday *Times* wrote: "The work of Mr. Sidney Waugh attains a classic beauty and perfection quite unrivalled . . . in contemporary glass engraving. His taste is unfailing as his line is exquisite, delicate, and expressive."[25] Waugh's work was, in fact, distinctively different from anything turned out by Steuben in the past. His Gazelle Bowl—its base cut into a clean Art Deco geometry and its rounded shape defined by attenuated, engraved gazelles—expressed a new Steuben aesthetic of simple forms accented by shallow relief engraving.

Steuben's exhibition at the Fine Arts Society was not without its touch of Barnum. The London *Catholic Herald* wrote that "slippers worn by Miss Gloria Swanson in *Cinderella* are an object of veneration for the many American ladies paying tribute to the first exhibition of American Art in Bond Street."[26] Papers in the United States relayed United Press coverage of the show, emphasizing Sidney Waugh's new designs, which as Houghton intended attracted the greatest attention. Ironically, in many of the American write-ups, the name "Steuben" was not mentioned; an apocryphal "American Glass Laboratory at Corning, New York" received credit for sponsoring the show.

Immediately after the exhibition closed on Bond Street, selections of Steuben were circulated to other parts of England. Clearly, the London exhibition succeeded in establishing the "new" Steuben as a well-designed luxury and a desirable symbol of status. Houghton's ambition to have Steuben achieve international acclaim was no mere public relations ploy, however. It was a

Sidney Waugh. Europa Bowl. 1935. Diameter 8".

From February 11 to March 24, 1938, this selection of Steuben appeared at the Art Institute of Chicago. Sidney Waugh's Trident Bowl on the pedestal at center, classic in its rounded simplicity, contrasts with the thick-walled, massively cut bowls to either side.

Opposite: Several of Walter Dorwin Teague's designs for Steuben were shown at the Contemporary American Industrial Art Exhibition at the Metropolitan Museum, November 6, 1934, to January 16, 1935. His Lens Bowl appears on its edge in the left foreground, while examples of his tableware are on the top shelf, left.

The Corning-Steuben building at 718 Fifth Avenue, home of Steuben's New York shop from 1937 to 1959, as it appeared in the late 1930s.

deeply felt ambition that remained with him throughout his life. "Perhaps a bit of it was jingoism," he later reminisced. "The Europeans thought they were the greatest glassmakers in the world. I always thought, 'Let's see what we can do, and let them judge.'"[27]

To capitalize on the momentum generated by the London show, Houghton and Gates arranged a subsequent series of Steuben exhibitions in American museums. From November 1 through 29, 1935, the Fogg Museum of Art at Cambridge, Massachusetts, displayed Steuben in "Modern American Glass," concurrently with an exhibition of early American glass from the Metropolitan Museum of Art, the Boston Museum of Fine Arts, and Yale University.[28] Four of Sidney Waugh's works were already in the permanent collection of the Metropolitan Museum—Zodiac Bowl, Gazelle Bowl, Agnus Dei, and another piece. This was a signal event for Houghton, Gates, and Waugh. As Houghton later put it: "Our ideal was to see if we could possibly make glass that a museum would buy; that would be the apotheosis of our existence."[29] To have achieved this goal a mere two years after launching the "new" Steuben must have been extremely satisfying to the triumvirate. Compounding their gratification, in November 1936 the Metropolitan included Waugh's works in its comprehensive "History of Glass" show. When Blake-More Godwin, director of the Toledo Museum, visited Corning in September 1935, he saw Waugh's designs and other Steuben pieces in production, and he arranged to exhibit them the following spring.

New Shops Are Opened

From 1934 through 1937 Arthur Houghton launched a nationwide advertising campaign for his new crystal. "We were a little bit arrogant when we took full-page advertising in *The New Yorker*," he remembered. "*Always* the most expensive packaging."[30] But the strategy worked. Steuben's marketing organization grew along with its reputation as the country's finest glassware. By mid-1935, Shreve, Crump and Low, the jewelry store of Boston, was selling Steuben in its only major outlet outside of New York. Late that same year, Steuben opened its own store on North Michigan Avenue in Chicago. Like its predecessors, and like all the Steuben retail shops that would follow, the Chicago store had a distinctive interior, designed by John Gates in a signature combination of grey and white. J. Parker Cushman, formerly of the New York store, was made Chicago manager. To attract the right sort of clientele, Cushman hired socially prominent young women to staff the shop, reaping a free publicity bonus in Chicago's rotogravures. A third Steuben store made its debut on Palm Beach's deluxe Worth Avenue in June 1937.

Less than a month later, the New York shop moved half a block down Fifth Avenue to

John M. Gates designed the interior of Steuben's 718 Fifth Avenue shop in subdued tones of white and grey, with iridescent capiz shells covering the walls of the foyer and stairwell to the mezzanine.

Steuben's staff designers at work in their atelier in the Corning-Steuben building at 718 Fifth Avenue, c. 1937.

Corning Glass Works' new six-story building at the corner of 56th Street. This so-called House of Glass had exterior walls of Pyrex building block, designed by Geoffrey Platt and William Platt, architects, in association with John Gates. Sidney Waugh provided a distinctive frieze for the facade. The Steuben shop, all subdued elegance, occupied the ground floor and mezzanine of the building. Its walls were papered with a thin layer of capiz shells, and a circular staircase with posts of air-twist cane glass rose to the mezzanine.

Like the shop itself, Houghton's and Gates' merchandising tactics were without precedent. "One of my fights until the day I left Steuben," Houghton later recalled, "was to try to keep our sales department from trying to *sell* glass. I said, 'Don't you do it; your job is to be of assistance to the customer who comes to buy it.' We always ranked our salespeople on how gracious they were to people who came in the front door."[31] Steuben always provided its customers with small comforts and amenities—fresh flowers among the displays "because glass is sort of a cold material," courtesy telephones, and free delivery.

More conservative Corning Glass executives were skeptical about the Steuben merchandising efforts. "Older associates at Corning, top officials there, were a little concerned after we'd been running things for a while," Houghton remembered. "They got the Amos Parrish firm, experts on retailing, unbeknownst to us. They sent their people around to act as customers, and that kind of stuff. Then they sent a report back to Corning saying, 'these young crazy men are violating every rule of merchandising, but it seems to work, so let it alone, for God's sake.'"[32]

Arthur Houghton had a strong ally in the person of his cousin, Amory Houghton, then an executive of Corning Glass Works. "Like our fathers before us, we were the only two males in our generation and we were as close as brothers. . . . From the very beginning, Amory grasped what I wanted to do with Steuben. Had it not been for

In the opening decades of the "new" Steuben, two basic design attitudes emerged. The first indicated a bold set of forms with sensitive proportions and a full exploration of the new transparent material. The second led to a refinement of the eighteenth-century English glass traditions, of which spindle and baluster forms (similar to those seen in the turned and carved furniture of the period) proved well suited to Steuben's glassmaking style. Adding part to part and capturing air traps, skilled glassworkers built columns for candlesticks, finials, and goblet stems, as demonstrated in these Teardrop Candlesticks designed by F. B. Sellew (1937). The abilities thus developed evolved into a design characteristic during the 1940s and 1950s. The "applied bit" embellished most forms.

him, Steuben would have been stopped by Corning Glass. It was so incompatible with what they were trying to do up there, and it was not successful financially. Though it made some money some years, we lost considerably other years. But Amory was always interested, always encouraging."[33]

Clear Crystal Predominant

No better setting than the new Fifth Avenue shop could be imagined for Sidney Waugh's designs and the whole range of new glassware Steuben was beginning to turn out. "By 1936 or 1937," Gates recalled, "we carried no more colored pieces except for cased table crystal—made until we had to discontinue making all table glass in the early years of the war because of the unavailability of lead. Other than cased table crystal, Carder's 'Ivrene' was the last colored glass to be made by Steuben."[34] Instead, Waugh's designs and those of Gates' recently hired atelier of young architects were setting a new aesthetic standard. Because the basic "metal" of which Steuben was blown was more than one-third lead, it lent itself to massive, thick, and heavy forms that could be cut to good advantage, and to simple "bit" ornament, gathered from the pot of molten glass and applied to the primary form to create sparkling handles, finials, and bases. Waugh's designs tended toward rounded shapes dictated by gravity, simplicity of form, and ornamentation by simple cutting and by spot engraving in bas-relief that appeared to "float" on the surface of the glass. Gates' own designs, predictably, were more architectural in nature, with elements inspired by the classic forms of the eighteenth century: scrolled handles, flaring rims, baluster stems, and finials. Other individual designers in the atelier contributed thick-walled, massive vases and bowls with an Art Deco flavor. "We tried not to force this fluid medium of crystal into shapes that would make it unhappy or that it didn't want to take," explains Arthur Houghton. "When we first started coming out with our designs, we were very much complimented on their simplicity. Well, there was a damn good reason for it, and that was we didn't know how to make a complicated piece."[35]

Back in Corning, craftsmen at the Steuben factory were at first skeptical about the success of glass with no color. Jack Hultzman, for many years Steuben's assistant factory manager, whose career began in 1934, remembers: "Everytime I walked into 'B' Factory, Steuben gaffers yelled, 'You better look for a job someplace else,' or 'Goodbye Steuben!'"[36] Frederick Schroeder, who supervised the blowing room during the years colored glass was being phased out, later recalled that the gaffers had a problem with off-premises design:

We had a fling with one of the industrial designers (Teague) doing work for us prior to 1933 and the experience was a flat failure. I was not so sure we really knew what we were doing. Workmen at first had difficulty . . . there was still a tendency to inject their expression into these new forms . . . it became a handicap for the designer for it was easy for us to tell what could or could not be made in glass by hand. Gradually and by close association, this feeling dissipated and as the years passed we found a much closer interest on the part of the workmen, striving to do their best, probably because the designers' expressions and fancies were a challenge to the workmen's glassmaking talents.[37]

By 1937, another long-standing tradition was broken. Instead of sending completed pieces of glass out of the factory to be engraved in various home shops around Corning, Robert Leavy, Steuben's plant manager, convinced the engravers—many of them his friends and neighbors—to work for Steuben inside the factory. One by one they came, and the transition was complete in 1938, when the master engraver Joe Libisch himself entered Steuben's employ.

In the early years of the "new" Steuben, many designs, such as Samuel Ayres' massive, thick-walled bowl, were cut into faceted panel shapes that reflected the Art Deco aesthetic then prevalent.

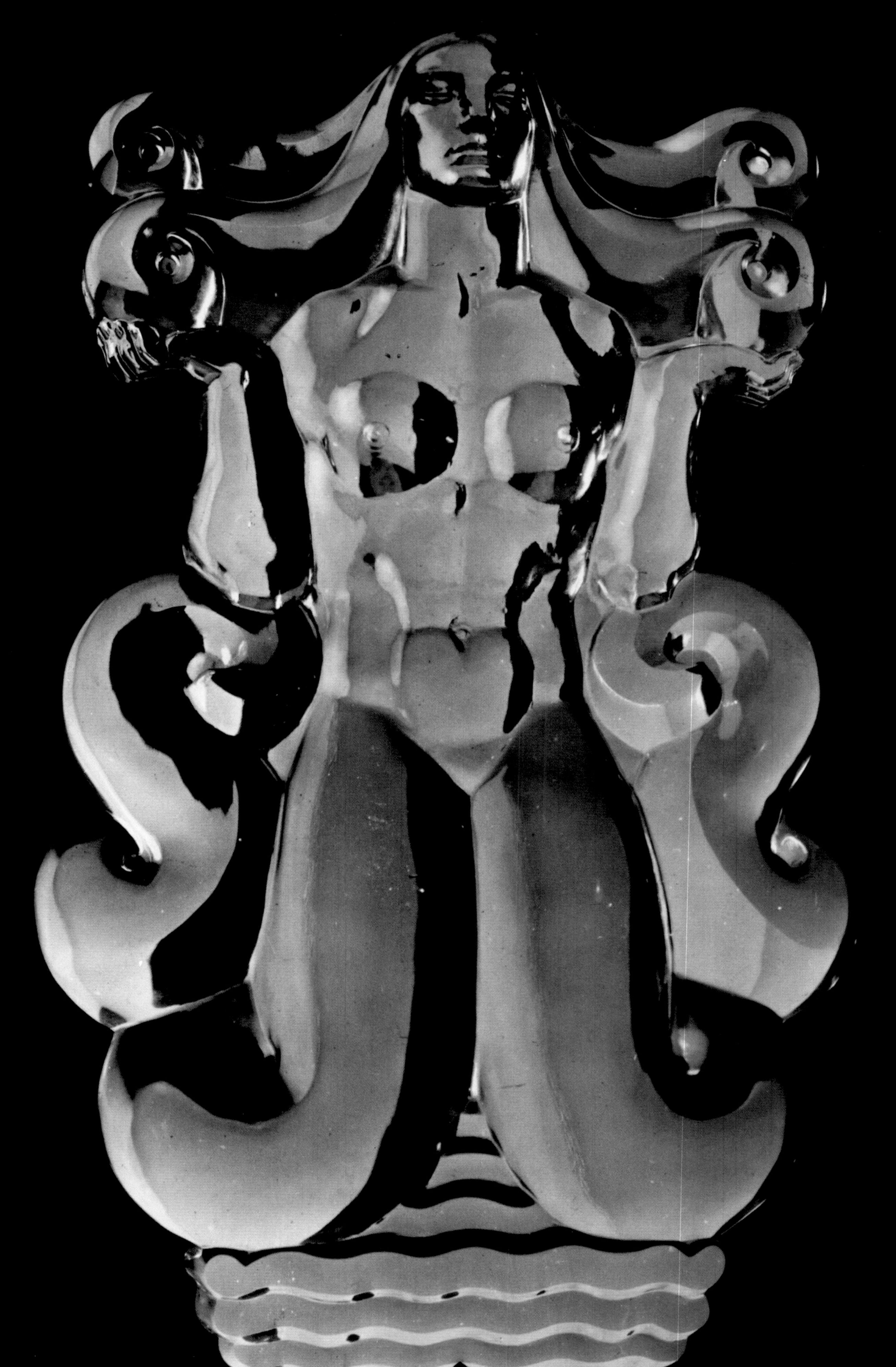

V.
WORLD'S FAIR AND WORLD WAR: 1938–1946

Fewer than five years after Steuben's reorganization, its success seemed assured. There were three Steuben shops in operation in New York, Chicago, and Palm Beach, in addition to a retail outlet in one of Boston's best jewelry stores. In production was a much-praised line of distinctive new crystal, capturing the fiery brilliance of pure lead glass with a remarkably high index of refraction. Some of the country's best young designers joined the skilled glassblowers and old-world engravers who were already at work in Steuben's Corning plant. But Arthur Houghton, who had become president of Steuben Glass in 1936 at the age of twenty-nine, was not content to rest on his laurels: "The World's Finest Glass" deserved an international reputation at least equal to the one it enjoyed throughout the United States.

In early 1937 Steuben was featured in a major architectural exhibition at the Art Gallery of Toronto, Canada. "Even the advance heralding of the exhibition of Steuben glass afforded no adequate anticipation of the glory which now shines from the Octagonal Gallery," effused a Toronto newspaper. From Canada, the glassware went to France. There, as part of Corning Glass Works' display in the American Pavilion at the Paris Exposition that summer, it stole the spotlight from other Corning wares. Designs by John Gates, Sidney Waugh, and George Thompson were featured in the show. Steuben received a Gold Medal for general excellence at the Paris Exposition, and for some years thereafter used the distinctive gilt award insignia on its announcements and official stationery.[1]

Late in 1937 Steuben officials began to plan for the company's representation in "The World of Tomorrow"—the 1939 World's Fair,

A worker smoothing and polishing Sidney Waugh's Atlantica prior to its installation in the World's Fair exhibition. Months of skilled craftsmanship went into the casting and finishing of this unparalleled piece.

Opposite: Sidney Waugh's Atlantica.

Steuben's World's Fair display highlighted exhibition glass designed specifically for the fair. Sidney Waugh's Atlantica, symbolizing the seventeenth-century arrival in America of the ancient art of glassmaking—and one of the largest pieces of cast crystal ever made—is mounted on the wall in the foreground.

to be held in Flushing Meadow, New York. Each Thursday afternoon, a five-man committee, including Arthur Houghton and John Gates, met to discuss the arrangements.[2] Steuben's booth was to be part of the Corning Glass Works' presentation in the modernistic Glass Industries Building, where other American companies such as Owens-Illinois and Pittsburgh Plate would also be represented. Among these industrial giants, Steuben's delicately engraved crystal would stand out as the very pinnacle of the American glassmaker's art.

The committee planned a semicircular booth, with seven pedestals arranged in front of a curving, back-lighted screen to display special exhibition pieces designed just for the fair. Four cases at the center of the booth, illuminated from underneath, would hold stock pieces of the Steuben line—bowls, stemware, ashtrays, table accessories, animal figures, and other pieces that showed the entire range of Steuben's production. A literature counter was to sell photographs of individual glass pieces, postcards, and two books written by Sidney Waugh: *Modern Glass* and *The Art of Glassmaking*.

When Steuben's World's Fair booth finally opened on April 30, 1939, its effect was one of subdued silvery light. Against a backdrop of black and white, John Gates' World's Fair Cup, with its trylon and perisphere and an engraved figure of the Goddess Mithrana, taken from a relief on the Administration Building, sparkled on its pedestal. Inset into the semicircular front wall was "a mermaid of rich baroque curves, glistening in polished crystal" and lighted from behind. This 300-pound piece of cast glass was Atlantica, designed by Sidney Waugh to symbolize the coming of glassmaking to the New

At the 1939 World's Fair, Steuben shared part of Corning Glass Works' exhibition space in this million-dollar Glass Center, where products of Owens-Illinois and Pittsburgh Plate Glass were also on display. Steuben was the only crystal shown.

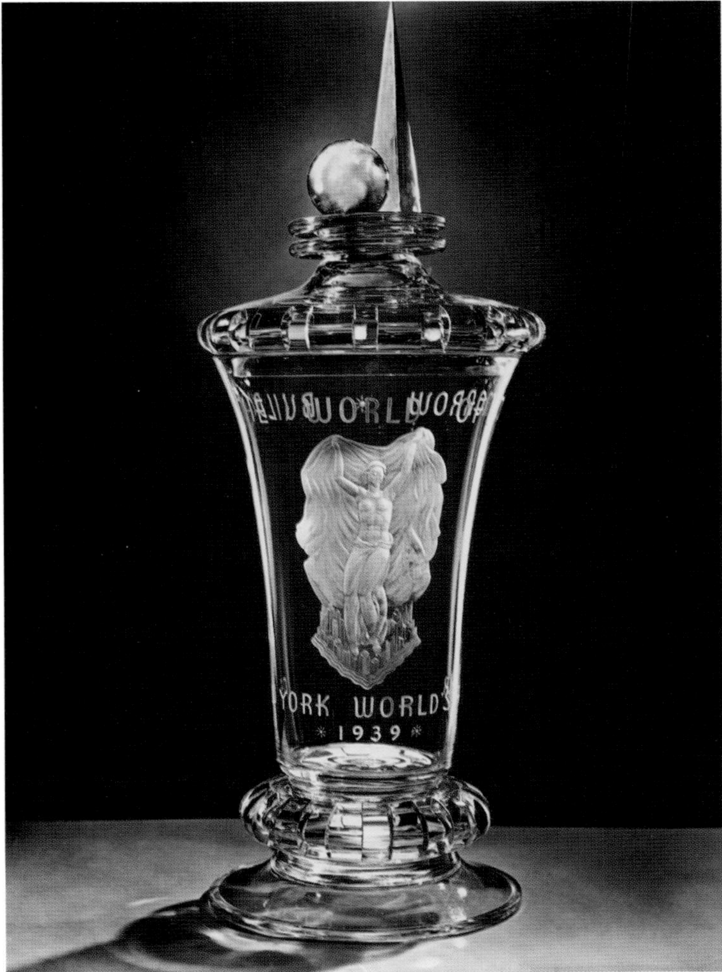

Exhibition pieces designed especially for the 1939 World's Fair included the World's Fair Cup, designed by John M. Gates to incorporate the symbols of the fair—the trylon, perisphere, and Goddess Mithrana.

World. Three feet high, it was one of the largest pieces of clear crystal sculpture ever cast, requiring five men to pour it and three to polish it.

Five young men staffed the booth and kept the crystal sparkling: the pieces on the pedestals had to be cleaned every hour, while the glass enclosed in cases was polished three times each day. The case lights made the booth stifling in those pre-air conditioned days; although fans were kept running, at least four pieces of glass cracked from heat stress and had to be replaced.

From ten each morning until ten at night, April through October of 1939, 2,860,000 people filed through the Steuben display. A poll revealed that the public's favorite pieces were Sidney Waugh's Wine, Women and Song Bowl, Samuel Ayres' Whirlpool Vase, and the Dolphin and Galapagos Bowls. Of the stock glass, visitors liked Waugh's cast pigeons best. During the final months of the fair, as Hitler launched his war machine, booth attendants recorded some harsh criticism from people who thought Steuben was a German company. Though millions saw and admired Steuben crystal during the 1939 season, the firm elected not to participate in the 1940 session of the fair: it was "too costly." Besides, Steuben was well launched on an exciting new project of international scope.

"Twenty-seven Artists in Crystal"

In 1937, John Gates became acquainted with Henri Matisse in Paris. The famous painter was intrigued with the idea of using glass as an artistic medium, and he offered to provide Gates with a sketch to be engraved on a piece of Steuben. Gates quickly agreed. Excited by the possibility of an entire series of such pieces, he sought out twenty-six other internationally renowned painters, sculptors, and printmakers to commission designs for engraving on Steuben. The project took three years. When all the vases, bowls, and urns in the series were engraved, Gates

At the opening preview of "Twenty-seven Artists in Crystal," John M. Gates chats with contributing artist Georgia O'Keeffe.

Salvador Dalí contemplates the bowl he designed for the "Twenty-seven Artists in Crystal" series.

George Thompson. The Galapagos Bowl.

James McNaughton. The Lotus Vase.

brought them together in a stunning exhibition, "Twenty-seven Artists in Crystal," that opened at the New York shop on January 10, 1940.

Such diverse artists as Paul Manship, Georgia O'Keeffe, Aristide Maillol, Isamu Noguchi, and Salvador Dalí were represented in the show. Noguchi's simple cat was one of the most successful designs, rendered in a few fluid strokes on the gently concave surface of a wide plate. Before the exhibition closed on Valentine's Day, attendance grew so large that the doors of the Steuben Building had to be locked several times a day while lines of people waited on Fifth Avenue.[3] Although some designs translated more successfully than others into the medium of crystal, the exhibition was generally well received by New York's art critics. Royal Cortissoz told *Herald Tribune* readers:

> *Each piece is confined to an edition of six, five of which are for sale. It will be surprising if they are not all soon sold off. They deserve to be. It is surprising, meanwhile, that these designs should be as successful as they are. To translate pictorial conceptions into intaglios—which yield an effect as of sculpture in relief—would seem to have been impossible, and the drastically divergent styles of the artists involved would appear to have introduced another obstacle. But the legerdemain of the glassmen works. It reduces the whole company to a common denominator of whitish grey effectiveness against a crystalline background and leaves the designs charming.*[4]

Installation of "Twenty-seven Artists in Crystal" at Steuben's Fifth Avenue shop, 1940. Ranged around the gallery (left to right) are works by Giorgio de Chirico, Thomas Hart Benton, José Maria Sert, Aristide Maillol, Muirhead Bone, John Gregory, and André Derain.

The Valor Cup (1941), designed by John M. Gates, exemplifies a fully designed piece—entirely premeditated and intentional—carried out faithfully by expert craftsmen, unlike earlier creations and interpretations made by the artisans themselves. Though functional in form, objects like the Valor Cup were intended more for decoration than use.

Efforts for England

Soon after "Twenty-seven Artists" closed, the world situation became a pressing concern at Steuben. England's involvement in the war seemed certain to be followed by that of the United States. Early in 1941, to express support for the British, John Gates was charged with designing a special piece of glass, the Valor Cup. This scroll-handled, covered urn, engraved with the arms of Britain, was displayed at the Steuben shop for two weeks in May, then presented to the British War Relief Society in commemoration of the Battle of Britain. Houghton hoped that the Society could sell the urn for two thousand dollars, a healthy sum at that time.[5] Striking a patriotic note on the home front, Sidney Waugh designed the Cincinnati Urn in 1941. It was given to the Society of the Cincinnati by Steuben Glass that October, accompanied by a manuscript letter on the 1783 founding of the Society by General Friedrich von Steuben—after whom Steuben County, and Steuben Glass, were later named.

Since 1938, John Gates had been in touch with Cecil Davis, a noted London glass dealer, concerning a proposal to exhibit Davis' collection of antique glass, including some superb pieces by England's first glassmaker, Giacomo Verzelini, and the man who invented lead glass, George Ravenscroft. On at least two occasions, dates were set for the exhibition at Steuben, then cancelled as Davis grew more apprehensive over the war conditions.[6] In 1941, however, he agreed to act as Steuben's agent in London, buying antique glass from the hard-pressed English gentry for resale in Steuben's New York shop, where the mezzanine floor was refurbished as the "Antique Room." Arthur Houghton persuaded Douglas Carson, who then worked for Stair and Company—noted antique dealers—to join Steuben and run the antique glass department.[7] Houghton thought the department would not only aid British exports, it would also educate Americans in the appreciation of early English and Irish glasswares, which were not at that time well represented in United States museums. By late 1941, Steuben was advertising antique glass in several magazines.

The Valor Cup, designed by John M. Gates to commemorate the Battle of Britain, is examined by (left to right) Arthur A. Houghton, Jr., F. Cecil Baker, and Mrs. Rex Benson.

When the firm's first annual catalogue was published later that year, in addition to illustrations of various pieces of Steuben stock, it pictured the Antique Room with its "many rare and unusual pieces of interest to the collector."[8] About 1943, Steuben Glass published a separate catalogue of its antique offerings.[9] The earliest piece pictured, a footed salver of 1674 by George Ravenscroft, was not for sale. (It later became part of the collection of The Corning Museum of Glass.) The collection ranged from the mid-sixteenth through the early nineteenth centuries. The latest piece, a Regency candlestick, dated from about 1820. Provenances for most items were prominently listed.

While the Antique Room may have had an altruistic inspiration, it also fulfilled an

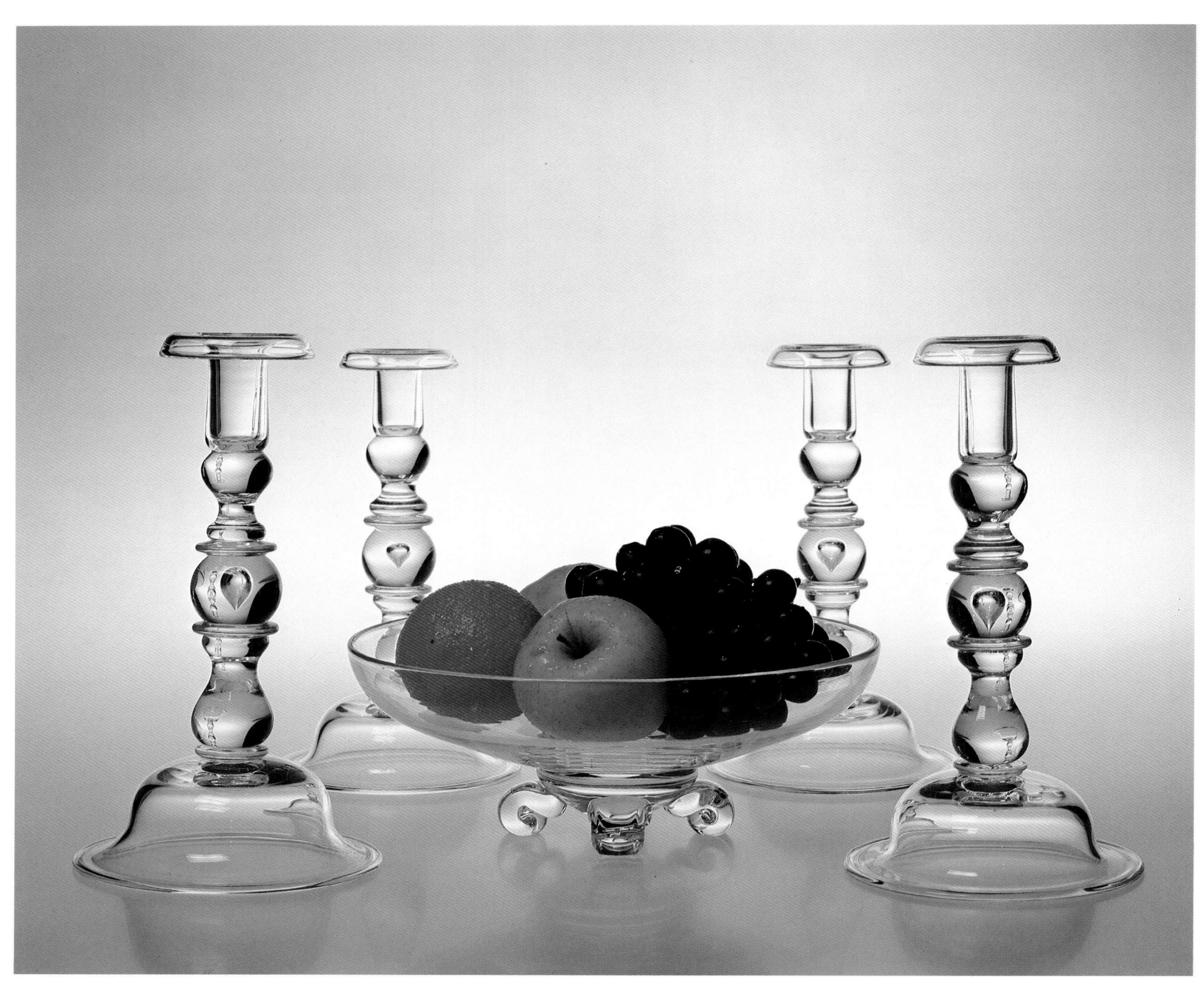

John Dreves. Low-footed Bowl. 1942. Diameter 10⅝". Baluster Candlesticks. Height 10½".

Ship's Decanter. 1942. Height 9¾". Donald Pollard. Old Fashioned Glasses. 1953. Height 3¾".

Installation of Steuben's "Spring Flower Show," 1942. Shortly after the exhibition opened, Steuben's top management departed for duty in the armed forces.

eminently practical need. Houghton recalled that "Steuben could not be considered a necessity in time of war," therefore it was difficult to obtain the necessary lead to manufacture the standard glass formula. "They were able to make a substitute formula—a little like making bricks out of straw—that carried us through." But it was the Antique Room that "gave us a certain volume of sales and kept the store operating."[10] Though most of the experienced glassworkers at Corning were too old to enlist in the war effort, the younger men joined, and production was cut back to six "shops" for the duration of the conflict.

Since the factory was no longer able to supply adequate quantities of glass to the Chicago and Palm Beach shops, where demand for luxury items was dropping anyway, these expensive-to-maintain facilities were closed. By late 1941, Steuben was being retailed outside of New York through franchises in the top department and specialty stores of Boston, Dallas, Cleveland, Providence, St. Louis, Detroit, and Chicago.[11] Perhaps to boost the demand for small line items that could still be produced during the wartime conditions, Steuben rented a showcase in the Savoy Plaza Hotel in New York, where drinking accessories were displayed.

Steuben's 1943 Christmas catalogue pictured only nineteen pieces of glass, including Sidney Waugh's patriotic American Ballad series, designed the previous year, before Waugh enlisted in the Army.[12] Each member of Steuben's young triumvirate joined the war effort. Before going off to service, they organized a lighthearted exhibition that seemed to celebrate the endurance of beauty in the world, despite the overshadowing clouds of war. In April 1942, the Steuben showroom became a bower of cut blossoms in a

Beginning in 1941, Steuben's Antique Glass Collection was housed in this special room on the mezzanine of the New York shop. Fine-cut, blown, and pressed pieces purchased from British collections were offered for sale to augment Steuben's own war-depleted line.

colorful event remembered as the first "Spring Flower Show." Flowers in various glass containers were replaced every other day for the duration of the two-week event. A Hammond organ played every afternoon; pigeons in white cages cooed among the blossoms and sparkling crystal; and each male visitor received a red carnation—red, perhaps, for valor.

Like many other American businesses, the Steuben shop during wartime was a feminine domain. Robina Haynes became temporary manager of design in John Gates' absence. There was "a spirit of camaraderie, of idealism" in the shop at that time, according to Betsy Pollard, who arrived at Steuben to do the window displays in early 1944 and eventually became manager of design. "The friendships fostered in those years endured for life. There was great loyalty to the company."[13] Sally Walker, later named executive vice president, joined the firm during the war years. And a young saleswoman, Isobel Lee (who became Steuben's director of public relations), served the war effort as a Red Cross worker in the South Pacific. There, she met government officials who would later play an important role in Steuben's history.

When Arthur Houghton left to serve in the armed forces, he recalls: "I put Bob Leavy in as president of Steuben to hold things together until I got back. He'd take the train down (from Corning) every week or so, the night train, and spend a few days."[14] The most notable event in Steuben's wartime history occurred during 1942, while Leavy was in charge. In that year, the American Flint Glass Worker's Union became the official bargaining agent for Steuben's heretofore nonunion laboring men and women in the Corning plant.[15]

VI.
GEARING FOR EXPANSION: 1946–1950

Production and sales were at a low ebb during World War II, but Steuben, like many other American industries, anticipated expansion at the war's end. By 1947, Arthur Houghton was back at the helm as president; Robert Leavy stepped over into the permanent position of vice president and general manager. America was eager to get on with the business of living, and Steuben was ready to provide the accoutrements of a gracious lifestyle.

As production soared, so did prices in the inflationary postwar economy. A pair of Steuben teardrop candlesticks that sold in 1941 for $25.00, for example, were listed in the 1947 catalogue for $50.00.[1] This did not deter the steady demand for fine crystal. Steuben was now in a position of unique advantage. The depredations of warfare had seriously affected glass production in the traditional European manufacturing centers. This fact was confirmed for Arthur Houghton in the summer of 1947, when he sent James Plaut, then director of Boston's Museum of Contemporary Art, "over to Europe to find out what was going on."[2] Plaut was to visit the major glasshouses of Europe and to assess the state of the art in glass design and postwar manufacture.

On his travels through Belgium, France, Holland, Sweden, and Czechoslovakia, Plaut found the industry shattered and backward, clinging to conservative tradition. Many craftsmen had been lost in the war and its aftermath of suffering. Only neutral Sweden, relatively unaffected by the events of the previous decade, was near normal. But Sweden's major glasshouse, Orrefors, maintained the design stance it had pursued with such success in the years before the war. Orrefors' plant was still under the direction of Edvard

David Hills. Bud Vase with Rose. 1949. Height 8".

Hald, turning out a great deal of glass in the Graal and Ariel patterns.

On his return to the United States, Plaut reported to Houghton that "the general debilitation of Europe has compromised greatly any opportunity which the glass industries of the liberated countries—and of Sweden—might have of evolving a successful and promising post-war pattern of recovery." He added: "The implications of this situation for American industry and for Steuben-Corning in particular, are arresting."[3]

Plaut's assessment was right on target: the physical plant at Corning was not at all affected by the war; most of Steuben's craftsmen were too old to join the services, and were anxious to stoke up the furnaces and turn out more, newer, and better designed pieces of crystal. In the New York design rooms, Sidney Waugh was back at the drawing board; and John Gates once more took up the title of director of design.

Design: A Postwar Priority

Tasteful design, in all its manifestations, was very much a priority at Steuben in the early postwar years—not just for the crystal itself, but for every aspect of its packaging and promotion. "We were not satisfied with the quality of our printed material," Houghton recalls. At the suggestion of Phillip Hofer, a Harvard curator, he sought out Joseph Blumenthal of the Spiral Press to redesign Steuben's printed matter.[4] It took three years to establish a consistent, distinctive graphic style for the firm's many catalogues, monographs, company stationery, and other printed materials. Blumenthal asked designer Philip Grushkin to work out a design for a snow crystal to be used as the Steuben trademark.[5] Houghton regarded the snowflake as the most appropriate symbol: "The snow as nature's most perfect form of crystal; Steuben as man's."[6] The snowflake, after Grushkin's design, was ultimately patented in 1950 as Steuben's trademark.

The Corning-Steuben Design Project

While its graphic image was in the process of transformation at the hands of Blumenthal and Grushkin, Steuben pressed forward to maintain its own unique position in the world of glass design. Early in 1948, Corning Glass Works and Steuben established a "working relationship" with the Institute of Contemporary Art in Boston to "improve design in all consumer products bearing the Corning or Steuben name." Under the direction of James Plaut, who had gone fact-finding the previous year on Steuben's behalf, ICA was eager to enter into the project to fulfill its responsibility as an educational institution "midway between art and industry as counselor, intermediary, and critic." Institute officials agreed to co-sponsor a program wherein trained artists and designers would spend a summer at Corning studying the problems of glass manufacture in order to gain a thorough working knowledge of glass as a material for design. At the time, there were no glass designers in America educated specifically to that trade.

From hundreds of talented young design school graduates, twelve trainees were selected to participate in the pilot program at Corning. Adjacent to the blowing room at Steuben's Corning factory, a special training area was set up. In addition to the usual offices and design studio, the project area had a demonstration amphitheater complete with a "glory hole," or glass reheating furnace, where the students could observe gaffers working with glass.

During the eight-week course, jointly supervised by J.B. Ward, Corning Glass Works' director of design, and John Gates of Steuben, the students became familiar with the working qualities of glass and the techniques used in its forming and finishing. Student designs were executed by skillful Steuben glassblowers in the amphitheater, and the "resultant product evaluated by the group from the standpoint of the best use of

Designers for Steuben and for the Corning Glass Works busy in their atelier at 730 Fifth Avenue, c. 1949. Left, far to near: Helen Nichols, Lee Goldman, Bob Simmons, Jeanne Leach. Right, far to near: Walter Budd, Zosia Jezowski, David Hills, Lloyd Atkins.

By the end of the 1940s, Steuben designers were becoming more familiar with the unique properties of glass and the possible techniques for forming it, and they began to produce designs suited expressly to glass, not translatable to any other medium. This Air-Trap Vase (1948), designed by John Dreves, relates specifically to the fluid and transparent nature of glass itself; unlike a cut vase, which could be crafted in stone, clay, or even wood, this piece could be achieved only in hot glass.

material and techniques without any reference to the validity of the design for (Corning's commercial) use."[7] At the end of the program, four of the trainees were offered jobs as Steuben staff designers, and three were retained for further instruction in machine production methods before going to work for the Corning Glass Works' design department.[8] Three participants contributed free-lance designs to Steuben over the next few years, after Plaut urged Steuben to accept work from outside designers not accorded "staff" or "associate" status.

The program, however, was hardly an unqualified success. Two participants failed to complete the course; and, as Plaut later pointed out, because the glassblowers conducting the live demonstrations were Steuben's best, the students were inclined to think their designs were rendered only through the gaffers' "miraculous" handling of the metal, leading to "a distortion of normal design expectancy." Plaut also criticized the students' competing to enhance their chances for hire by working mainly to please their Corning supervisors, which "resulted in the suppression of genuine creative effort and often led to the execution of forced designs like those already in the line."[9]

Ironically, Ward found quite another kind of fault with the program. He felt that all architectural and design students—including those in the trainee program—received inadequate training in design history, and that "decoration of any sort is completely against their concept of good design." Their work therefore "had no relation to our past, present, or forecasted production and distribution economy . . . these designs will not gain consumer respect today."[10]

Despite Ward's gloomy assessment, which more than anything else pointed up the differences in design philosophy that existed between Corning Glass Works and Steuben during the postwar years, several of the young men hired by Steuben produced glass of enduring commercial appeal. David Hills' 1949 Bud Vase, for example, is still a popular line item at Steuben. Don Pollard and Lloyd Atkins also joined Steuben in 1948; each designer gave many years of service to the company and each had many best-selling designs to his credit.

The Corning-Steuben-ICA Design Program is worth remembering not just for its tangible results, but because it was a pioneering effort to use the technological resources of a major manufacturing firm for the hands-on training of design students—an instance of unprecedented cooperation between education and industry. It certainly highlighted the intense concern Steuben felt for design excellence in the immediate post-war years. Arthur Houghton later emphasized this concern in a paper presented to the International Congress of Industrial Design at the Royal College of Art in London. Houghton stressed that the integrated design program successfully adopted by Corning Glass Works was first initiated at Steuben. "At Steuben we began with the realization that good design must be integrated and extended throughout the company's every activity. If we were to convince the public that Steuben represents the very highest level of design in glass, then our advertisements, display rooms, catalogues, booklets, stationery, and packages, all of these auxiliaries must be designed as carefully as the product and must present to the public the same high standard of design as does the glass itself. And in addition, their design must be harmoniously integrated."[11]

Technological Innovations: Tank Melting and Monair

Important as it seemed in the postwar years, design was not Steuben's only concern. Technological innovation was to be just as crucial to the firm's expansion. Perhaps the most important event of the late forties and early fifties was the production change from traditional pot furnaces to tank melting. Previously, Steuben glass was melted in ceramic pots set into the arches of the large melting furnaces. This method had certain disadvantages: impurities were apt to fall into the pots; and uneven distribution of the basic elements in the "melt" led to cords (wavering lines) or seeds (minute particles of unmelted matter) in the glass. Further, the ceramic pots themselves had a relatively short life span, and "setting a pot"—replacing a newly filled one in the arches of the furnace—was perhaps the most arduous and dangerous chore in the glass-making industry.

Since 1940, Corning Glass Works had been experimenting with melting techniques that would achieve greater clarity and purity in the final product. Optical glass of a composition similar to Steuben's had been tank-melted at Corning as a quality control measure beginning in 1942. By 1951, at the urging of Corning managers George Macbeth and Walter Oakley, tank melting for Steuben Glass was under development in Pilot Plant Number One, a Corning Glass Works facility on Chestnut Street. Charles De Voe directed the work. Gathers of molten glass from these tank-melted batches were superior in their uniformity and perfection to gathers made from pot-glass in the Steuben plant. Shops of glass-blowers were dispatched to Pilot Plant Number One to experiment with the new method. The results were so promising that it was decided to install a melting tank, from which all Steuben metal would be drawn, in the new Steuben factory then in the planning stages.[12]

Another postwar innovation was the Monair technique of glass engraving using an air-powered abrasive. In 1948, Hugh Smith, whose position as research associate in glass at the Metropolitan Museum of Art was funded by Steuben, was sent abroad to attend the Fiftieth Anniversary Celebration of Orrefors Glassworks in Sweden. There, Smith observed and reported on a new technique of photoengraving, introduced by John Selbing. Steuben wasted little time developing its own counterpart to the Orrefors process, with assistance from Eastman Kodak. Monair was brought into production in 1949 as a means of speeding the monogramming of stock pieces. At first, Steuben's design staff expressed misgivings about the mechanized process. Gates wrote to Houghton: "My feeling is that we are lousing up the crystal."[13] However, most opposition melted away when it became apparent that the Monair technique could provide incredibly exact and swift duplication of certain hard-edged designs. Monair was applied only to precise patterns such as monograms and inscriptions where the design is not pictorially free. Decorative engraving that required shading to give the illusion of depth remained for the most part the province of the hand-engraver. However, Arthur Houghton was one of those at Steuben who remained somewhat ambivalent about the process, even in retirement. "I don't feel too highly about it because it has been used as a way of doing copper wheel engraving cheaply," he said. "People should look upon it as a new tool, to see what it can do, not to replace copper-wheel engraving."[14]

Fit for a Princess

In 1947, Arthur Houghton engaged in a bit of personal salesmanship that laid the groundwork for Steuben's later acceptance as the official diplomatic gift of United States presidents. He learned that the United States Embassy in London was seeking an appropriate gift for presentation to Princess Elizabeth upon the occasion of her forthcoming marriage. A new Sidney Waugh design, the Merry-Go-Round Bowl, with its gay carrousel figures and regal, crownlike finial, seemed the ideal choice. Houghton packed it up together with a set of Audubon Plates and sailed to London. The ambassador selected several plates from the Audubon series as his personal gift to the princess, and he convinced President Truman to purchase

Steuben's Merry-Go-Round Bowl and Audubon Plates, presented to Princess Elizabeth on the occasion of her wedding in 1947, are displayed at St. James Palace, London, together with other royal wedding gifts. The Steuben articles are on the middle shelf of the vitrine.

the Merry-Go-Round Bowl as the official American gift of state for Elizabeth's wedding.

The royal marriage captured America's imagination, and Steuben made the most of its contribution to the event. A duplicate of the Merry-Go-Round Bowl, together with the selected Audubon Plates, were placed on exhibition in the Fifth Avenue shop and elsewhere. In a few short weeks, Steuben's image as a luxury product was immeasurably reinforced—crystal "fit for the tables of royalty."

The Americana Series: "United States in Crystal"

During the early years of the war, Sidney Waugh designed a patriotic series of bowls that were well received by Steuben's American market. Now at peace again, the country was in a mood to celebrate its early heritage—and Steuben was ready to oblige. Late in 1948, Arthur Houghton wrote to his old friend, the distinguished historian and librarian of Princeton University, Julian

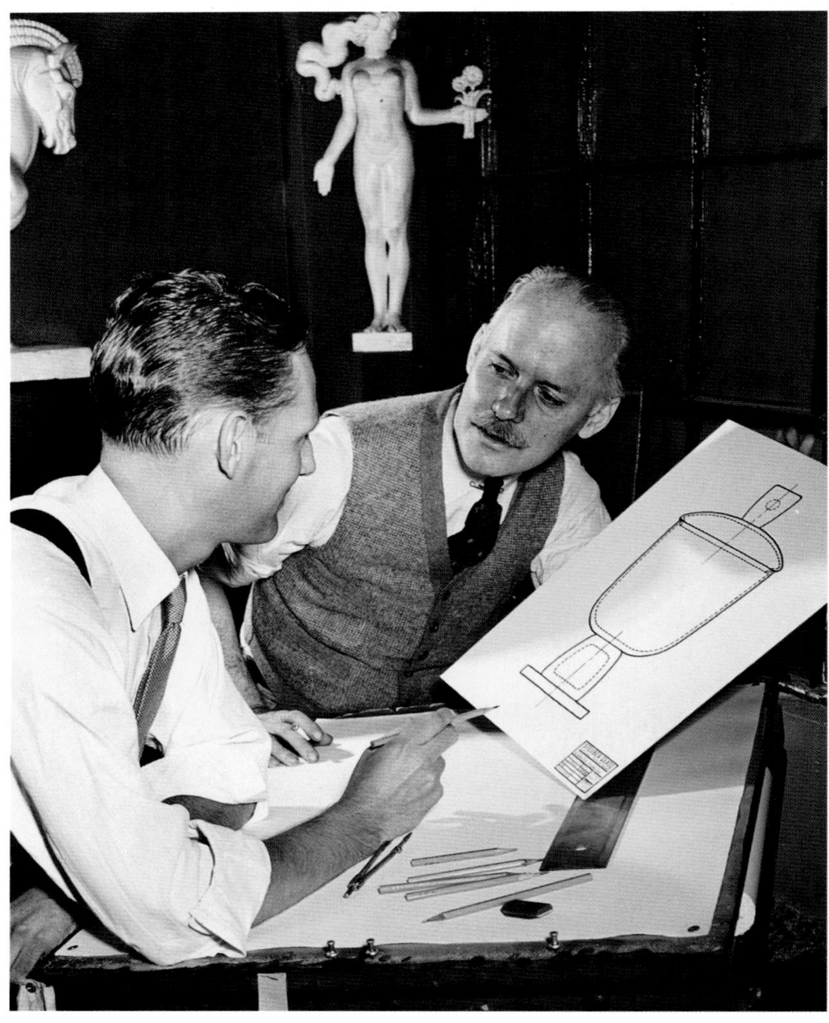

Sidney Waugh, at right, consulting with Steuben designer George Thompson on the working drawing for his United States in Crystal Bowl, c. 1950.

Boyd, that he wished to "produce a glass of such quality that a new chapter will be written in the history of glassmaking" to help America "demonstrate its ability to make great accomplishments in the arts."[15] Houghton suggested that a series of forty-eight engraved bowls, one for each of the states then in the Union, depicting scenes from their histories might be the most appropriate vehicle for these ambitions. Boyd liked the idea of the state bowls and agreed to bring it before the Institute of Early American History and Culture, a scholarly organization, to enlist their help in selecting the themes and researching the topics to be engraved on Steuben crystal. "We didn't want the responsibility for picking the themes . . . that was a hot potato," Arthur Houghton remembers.[16]

Historian Carl Bridenbaugh was then director of the Institute. He had some misgivings about finding historical vignettes sufficiently important to commemorate each of the states in engravings and tried to persuade Arthur Houghton to consider another kind of series.[17] They compromised. Themes of general importance to American history would be chosen, and a bowl for each state would carry an engraved picture relating that state's image to one of the general themes. "America in Crystal" was to be one of Steuben Glass' most ambitious and extensive series. The project was not completed until 1959, some eleven years later.

Sidney Waugh was vital to the success of the plan. Based on recommendations of subject matter presented by the member historians of the Institute of Early American History and Culture, Waugh created a drawing for each bowl's engraved design. He also wrote a short text explaining his selection of a specific visual theme based on the suggested topics. His completed drawings, with explanatory text, were circulated to the Steuben staff and to Carl Bridenbaugh for final approval. As each sketch passed muster, it was sent to Corning for engraving.[18]

There were many problems connected with the project. Waugh's schedule—he was head of the Rinehart School of Sculpture in Baltimore as well as an associate designer for Steuben—prevented him from completing all the sketches as quickly as Houghton would have liked. There were several personnel changes at the Institute of Early American History and Culture, which tended to delay the transmission of research data to Steuben. Two more states entered the Union between the time the project was conceived and the time it was finished. Finally, John Gates chafed at the idea of fifty identical bowls, differing only in their engraved decoration and objected to organizing a comprehensive exhibition of all the bowls. When all the difficulties were finally overcome, "America in Crystal," born in patriotic zeal in 1948, was

Twenty-one new designs in Steuben crystal were introduced at the special exhibition, "A Spring Festival in Crystal and Flowers," 1950.

finally completed and shown as "United States in Crystal" in 1959 at Steuben's new New York gallery, in the first summer of its operation.

The Flower Show: 1950

While "United States in Crystal" was under way, Steuben celebrated the return to postwar normalcy with a second flower show in the spring of 1950—a lighthearted repetition of the 1942 exhibition. Nearly 36,000 people thronged the Fifth Avenue shop to view cascades of flowers arranged in Steuben containers in settings designed by Charles Lin Tissot, a noted fabric designer. In the large front show window, crystal elephants cavorted around a floral maypole. Singing canaries upheld the lighthearted mood inside the shop, but after a few days "the bird cages were removed since it was felt we could not cope with both the SPCA and the care and feeding of canaries," Tissot reported.[19] The cages were replaced with espaliered trees supplied, like the rest of the flowers, by Judith's Garden, an exclusive New York flower shop. Music, however, was not lacking in the absence of the feathered singers. Zither player Karl Schmidt appeared each afternoon, to the great delight of the Steuben sales staff.

The crystal in the second flower show was broader in its aesthetic range than had been the prewar pieces, dominated by Georgian taste. Asymmetrical shearing, and oval and triangular shapes were prominent among the containers in the 1950 show, giving the Steuben a "new look" not unlike the pinch-waisted asymmetry of the "modern" ladies' fashions of those years.

B O M B U S

VII.
FROM AMERICA TO THE WORLD: 1951–1961

The 1950s were pivotal years in the history of Steuben Glass. With a distinctive new graphic image, an administrative staff full of energy and imagination, ready to build on the foundations laid during the first few postwar years, and a state-of-the-art new manufacturing facility, capable of turning out greater quantities of perfect crystal than ever before, Steuben began to assume a unique position in the world marketplace.

The decade began with a burst of energy. Corning Glass Works' centennial year, 1951, most appropriately coincided with the one hundredth anniversary of London's Crystal Palace, the architecturally memorable iron-and-glass structure that housed the 1851 World's Fair. To commemorate this banner year for the glass industry, John Gates and Steuben's staff designer Don Wier collaborated on a magnificent Centenary Cup. An engraving of the historic Crystal Palace structure embellished one side of the cup, while the new Corning Glass Center building appeared on the other. Corning Glass Works presented this unique piece of Steuben to the British Royal Society of Arts during the 1951 Festival of Britain. Princess Elizabeth accepted the cup during the ceremonial opening of the festival's "Exhibit of Exhibits" in May 1951.[1]

Steuben's New Factory

The same month, on the other side of the Atlantic, the Corning Glass Center opened its doors to the first of thousands of visitors who flocked to a new attraction during its initial summer of operation. One of the most interesting parts of the Glass Center, the new Steuben factory was designed to permit access to visitors.

Bruce Moore. Bombus. 1953. Height 10".

Walking along a special route, or standing in the observation gallery, visitors could watch the intricate processes of blowing, finishing, and decorating. Steuben's gaffers and finishers, used to working in the close confines of "B" factory, soon adjusted to performing under the scrutiny of hundreds of curious eyes. The new blowing room was more than just a visitor attraction; it was also a vast improvement over the old production facility. Steuben's new melting tank, which dominated one end of the blowing room, yielded the most flawless crystal the firm had yet produced. Constant agitation of the molten glass mixture by a nonreactive platinum rod, together with a new procedure wherein the melted glass was poured in a steady stream to a gathering point in the "cave," or cellar, beneath the huge furnace, eliminated virtually all the tiny impurities and striations that had previously marred even the finest crystal. To keep the molten glass at the required level, the tank was fed batch continually. It had to be fired day and night.[2]

Two shifts of skilled workers normally drew glass during the course of an average working day for "off-hand" blowing by gaffers in several shops on the factory floor. But the question of how to utilize the steady stream of molten glass pouring from the tank during the third, or night, shift, when the skilled gaffers were not required to be on duty, became a matter of some concern. Many suggestions were made; many were rejected as impractical. It was proposed to use the night shift to produce a line of molded, rather than free-blown, crystal tablewares for inexpensive sale to a middle-class market under the brand name of "Crystex."[3] The idea was scuttled. For some time the third shift produced repress cane, a technical product used by optical manufacturers, since the Steuben formula was practically identical with that of the best optical glass.[4] The third-shift problem was finally resolved in the 1970s to everyone's satisfaction, when Steuben introduced its line of hand coolers—small rounded animal forms of pressed glass, polished to a high brilliance. These are now made one by one during the third shift on innovative presses fed constantly from the steady stream of molten crystal flowing from the tank during the night hours. Still other new designs are formed on a technologically advanced press that can produce as many as twenty pieces an hour.

Steuben's innovative melting tank with its unique "let it down easy" process of shearing off the molten stream in seconds' worth of pouring time was an industry first—and for some years, a closely guarded secret. Eventually, other crystal manufacturers learned about and adopted this method for making virtually flawless glass, but Steuben must be remembered as the pioneer.

The Antique Glass Collection Goes to Corning

Another integral part of the new Corning Glass Center, The Corning Museum of Glass, explained the history and art of glassmaking, primarily with well-labeled examples of historic glass. Steuben provided the nucleus of this collection by transfer from its Antique Room in the New York shop.

Beginning in 1941, Steuben purchased every important piece of English glass to come on the market, not only for resale to augment its flagging production of crystal, but also to form a teaching collection of exemplary pieces. Steuben's Antique Glass Room served its purpose well during the war years, when the firm was short of stock, but by 1950 manufacture had surpassed the prewar volume. Because more space was needed to show new pieces of ornamental engraved crystal, Houghton decided in 1952 to renovate the mezzanine level of the shop, disposing of the Antique Glass Collection and replacing it with a display area for engraved glass. The best pieces were consigned to The Corning Museum of Glass at cost. Somewhat less important pieces were

Arthur A. Houghton, Jr., examines the Centenary Cup as John M. Gates (center) and Don Wier (left) observe, 1951.

The Steuben factory, adjacent to the Corning Glass Center in Corning, New York, shortly after its opening in 1951. Note the large Robinson ventilator used to diffuse heat from the factory floor. The great window wall lets light into the blowing room.

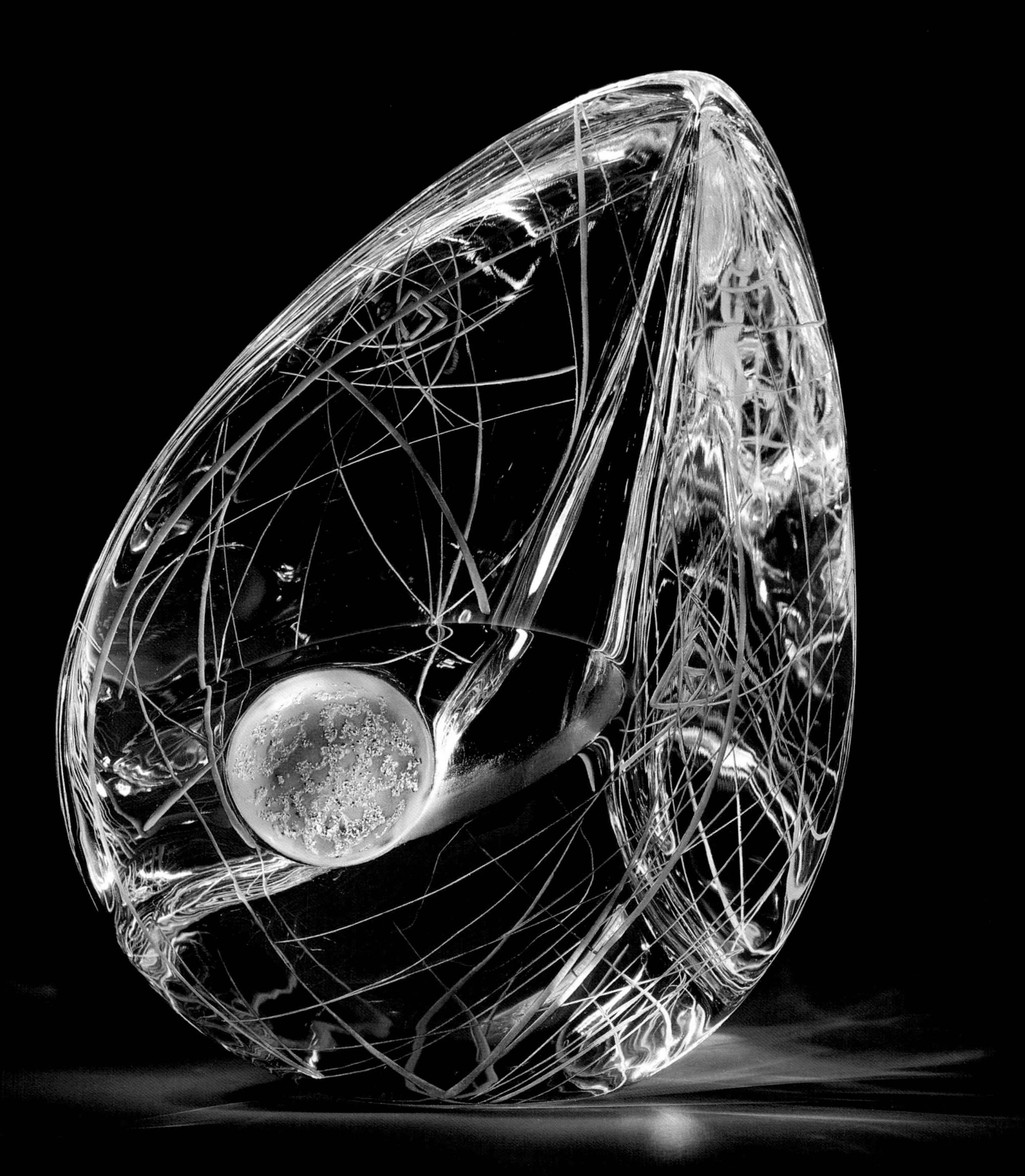

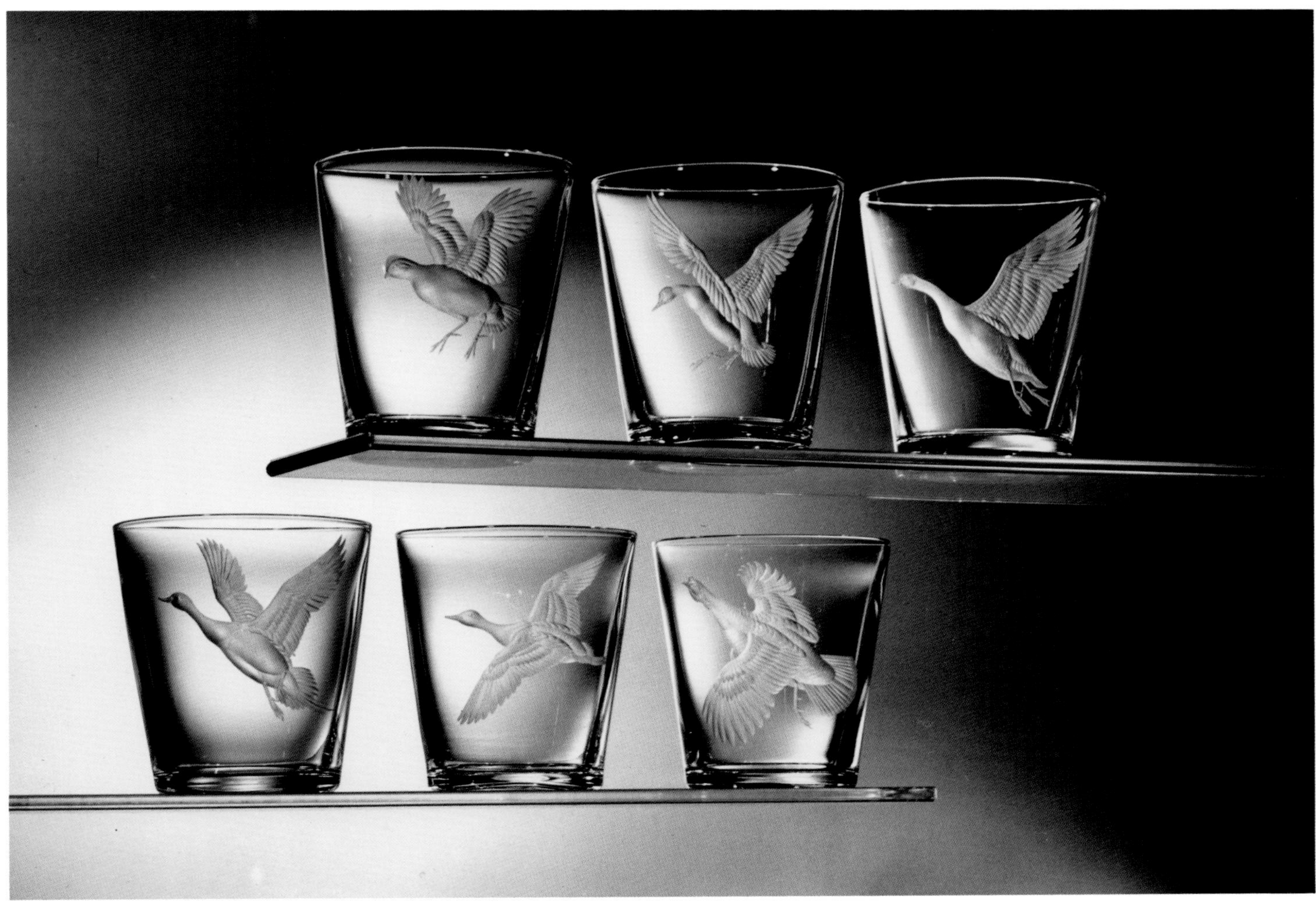

sold through Stair and Company of New York, while relatively common examples were sold to still other antique dealers. The remainder of the Steuben Antique Glass Collection was liquidated early in February 1953, when the last pieces were consigned to auction at Parke-Bernet.[5]

New Directions in Design

The mezzanine floor in Steuben's New York shop, newly cleared of English glass, was redecorated to provide a striking backdrop for the new engraved "line" items, including sets of drinking glasses embellished with printers' devices and with game birds, after designs by Charles Liedl. These were relatively conservative additions to Steuben's repertory, which during the 1950s took on a much broader aesthetic dimension.

Most free-blown Steuben objects of the late thirties and early forties adhered to Sidney Waugh's philosophy that "the objects produced must be round or the modification of round forms: with all curves firm and robust."[6] Such glass tended to be massive and weighty, either cut into the angular planes so favored by the waning Art Deco movement, or reminiscent of classic eighteenth-century design, with traditional knops, baluster stems, and other details. Ornaments during this period were usually gaffered bits—handles and finials—and the engraved decoration, most of it designed by Waugh himself, tended to emphasize the natural roundness of the glass. In the late forties and fifties, however, several innovative young designers joined the New York staff, and well-known artists such as Gwen Lux, the sculptor, were invited to submit their creations.

A new set of drinking glasses sported these designs of game birds by Charles Liedl.

Opposite: Donald Pollard (designer), Terry Haass (engraving designer). Genesis. 1959. Height 9".

View of seven of the twelve initial pieces of the "Studies in Crystal" series, on display at the New York salesroom, 1955.

Before the 1950s the design repertoire depended mainly on proportional aesthetics. New directions taken by Steuben's glass designers in the 1950s were experiments intended to expand design possibilities and to broaden glassmaking techniques. The various objects that resulted from this innovative attitude were presented simply as "Studies." The designers became more identified with their own work as it took on their individual creative notions. Here is a piece by George Thompson, Sea Breeze (1955).

Section of the Steuben display at "L'Art du Verre," Paris, 1951.

Opposite: John M. Gates designed this installation for "British Artists in Crystal" at the New York shop, 1954.

New kinds of decorative techniques, including asymmetrical shearing and air trapping, were used with greater frequency on the line items, while special exhibition pieces made daring excursions into experimental design.

Among these, twelve pieces of glass displayed in the New York shop during the spring of 1955 were the first examples of an ongoing series entitled "Studies in Crystal" that eventually grew to a collection of over two hundred works. Free from functional purpose, these innovative pieces included both engravings on prismatic forms—shapes defined by cutting after the blown glass had hardened—and free sculptural abstractions calling to mind wind-blown waves or birds in flight.

"Studies in Crystal" signified a true change of direction for Steuben. While the firm continued to produce a large and varied line of tablewares, vases, bowls, and other utilitarian objects, the new, purely decorative pieces exploited glass's potential as a medium for sculpture. It is a direction that Steuben continued to follow for many years thereafter.

Exhibitions Abroad: "L'Art du Verre"

As James Plaut observed during his 1947 fact-finding tour of the European glasshouses, the war had taken a serious toll on production facilities throughout the continent.[7] By 1950, however, most of the old European manufactories were back in business. The French glassmakers, in particular, were eager to resume their traditional preeminence in the international marketplace. With that object firmly in mind, the French government set about organizing an ambitious exhibition, "L'Art du Verre," under the auspices of the Musée des Arts Décoratifs at the Palais du Louvre.

The show was to have three parts: a historic display of masterpieces of French glass from Franco-Roman times to 1940, including the work of such greats as Maurice Marinot and Emile Gallé; a section highlighting contemporary French verriers such as René Lalique, Daum, Henri-Edouard Navarre, Aristide-Michel Colotte, and others; and an international section, representing major glasshouses from around the world. Steuben was invited to participate in the international display—the only American glasshouse so honored.[8]

Though Arthur Houghton was no doubt eager to have Steuben exhibited in such prestigious surroundings, he withdrew from participation during the planning stages, when it seemed apparent that Steuben was being asked to foot far more than its rightful share of the exhibition costs. Houghton was persuaded to reconsider by French friends, who pointed out the Louvre's delicate political dilemma: every French glasshouse had to be included in the exhibition, but rampant postwar inflation kept most of them from being able to contribute substantially to the overhead. (The British, who were also invited to send glass to the international section, declined to participate, claiming that during the ten distracting years of wartime they had been unable to create anything new. Scandinavia, Italy, Belgium, Holland, and Argentina did accept the invitation of the French government to send samples of their glass for display.)

WHISTLER
GOODEN
SMITH

President René Coty of France with the Marquis de Lafayette Medallion, presented by President Dwight D. Eisenhower in commemoration of the bicentennial of Lafayette's birth, 1957.

When all problems had been overcome, "L'Art du Verre" opened on the first day of June 1951. One-fifth of the entire display was reserved for Steuben. John Gates designed the Steuben area with typical subdued elegance: an entrance colonnade of white columns fronted two large wings decorated with dark blue felt and gun-metal tinted mirrors. One hundred and fifty pieces of Steuben crystal, including twenty-two important engraved works, glittered and sparkled against this setting—which *Le Matin,* the irreverent Paris newspaper, deemed "reminiscent of a funeral wake."[9] *Midi Libre* expressed a less cynical reaction: "The Americans, sons of a mechanized and industrialized race, have sent engraved pieces and pieces blown in the tradition of an age-old art, which do not cease to astonish us."[10]

This, of course, was precisely the image Steuben's management wished to project. When the president of the French Republic, Vincent Auriol, visited "L'Art due Verre," John Gates presented him with an engraved Steuben bowl designed by the French artist Marie Laurencin. Attendance at the exhibition continued high throughout the summer and was said to be the largest on record for the Musée des Arts Décoratifs.

Back in New York, Steuben publicized its participation in "L'Art du Verre" by installing five specially designed exhibition pieces (together with invitations to the Paris vernissage upon which the words "Palais du Louvre" were prominently lettered) in the large window of the Fifth Avenue shop. On both sides of the Atlantic, the message came through clearly: Steuben Glass was installed at the Louvre; it had entered the sacred precincts of high art.

Arthur Houghton was pleased to receive a letter from a young Frenchwoman, who wrote: "We are inundated by your mechanics and your treatises on the art of selling, efficiency, etc. (But) I am happy to find . . . America . . . can and does preserve a little time and a few men to create pure art."[11]

The Frenchwoman's words seemed to corroborate Houghton's own thoughts that Steuben had a positive and natural role to play in postwar diplomacy. By representing the sensitive, artistic, and beauty-loving aspects of American society, Steuben could soften this country's international image as a crass industrial giant. During the next decade, Houghton missed few opportunities to implement Steuben's role as an international agent of good will. He sent the Frenchwoman's letter to business associates and eminent people around the world, inviting their comments. Dwight David Eisenhower, who earlier that year bought his first Steuben—a pair of saltshakers for Mamie Eisenhower's birthday—was one of those who responded. Eisenhower himself eventually acquired a number of important pieces of Steuben, and, during his tenure as president, he often gave Steuben crystal as an official gift of state.[12]

"British Artists in Crystal"

Spurred by the success of the earlier "Twenty-seven Artists in Crystal," Steuben's leadership was eager to repeat the experiment of commissioning well-established painters and sculptors to design engravings for Steuben Glass. Shortly after "L'Art du Verre" closed, Arthur Houghton traveled to London to read a paper at the International Congress of Industrial Design. There, he conceived the plan for a second artists' exhibition to be entitled "British Artists in Crystal." David Stelling, Steuben's British representative, was called in to confer with Houghton and John Gates, and by late fall he commissioned Robin Darwin, the noted English painter, to design the first work for the projected series. Over the next twenty-seven months, Stelling circulated throughout the British art world, interviewing artists for possible inclusion in the show. After Gates approved the participation of specific candidates, it was Stelling's job to extract from them the promised sketches. It was decided that Steuben's staff designers, principally George Thompson, would design a selection of blanks appropriate for artistic engraving, and that the participating British artists would tailor their works to fit one or another of the blank crystal forms. Some artists, like John Nash, were unhappy about this restriction, but most succeeded in adapting their individual styles to the parameters of the unaccustomed medium of glass. Oliver Messel, the last person to submit a drawing for the series, late in the spring of 1954, was the only artist in the final group of twenty to design his own glass blank.[13]

According to the reception given it by the press, the series was an aesthetic victory. Gates observed that "the most astonishing feature of the collection is the success with which the distinctive individuality of the artist has been impressed upon the crystal. There is no color and no high relief. Yet a serious observation of the pieces loosens the memory, and the artists, so well known in paint or bronze, suddenly come to life in all vigor again on the glass. No one who is familiar with the works of such masters as Jacob Epstein, Frank Dobson, Matthew Smith, or Graham Sutherland could fail to recognize their characteristics transfixed in crystal. That is the exciting element, to see the individual arising in a new medium."[14]

"British Artists in Crystal" opened at Steuben's New York shop in late April 1954, with a gala preview to benefit the English-Speaking Union. Gates' exhibition design suggested a formal garden court on a summer evening, highlighted by the engraved pieces of glass and by George Thompson's Crystal Fountain that shimmered at the end of the gallery. The glass remained on display for two weeks, then traveled to Chicago where another benefit was held.

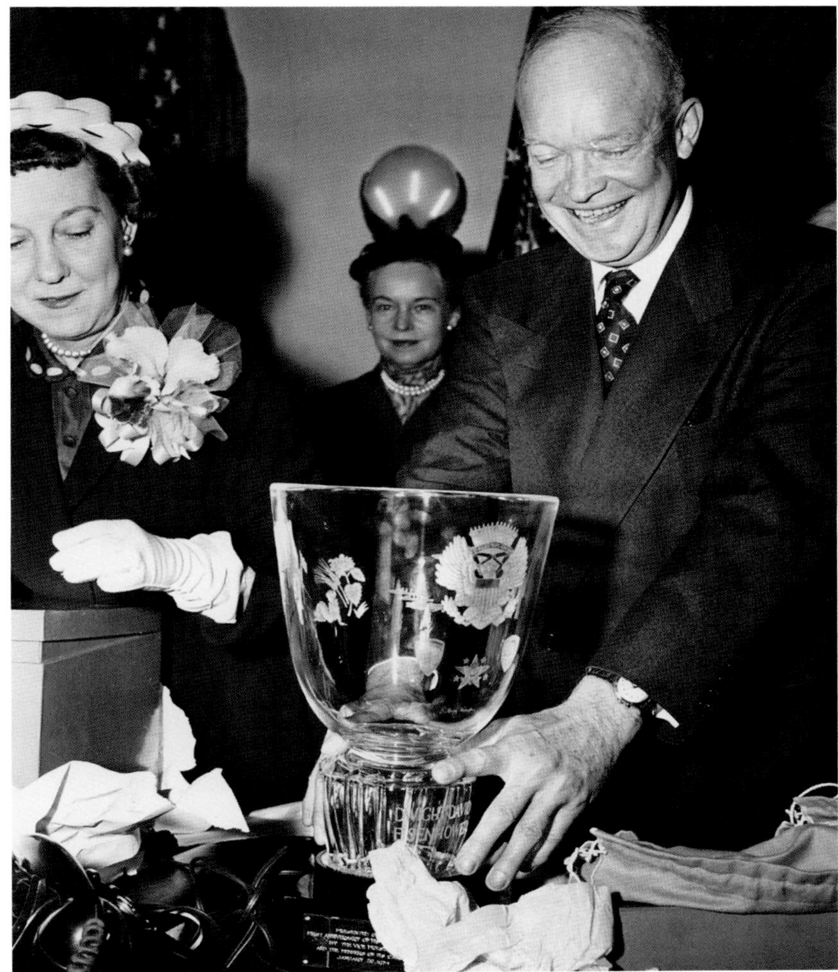

Dwight and Mamie Eisenhower admire the Steuben glass cup given to the president by his cabinet, 1954. Oveta Culp Hobby is in the background.

Queen Elizabeth II examines Enigma in the Park Lane House Exhibition, London, 1955. Arthur A. Houghton, Jr., is behind the Queen and the American ambassador to Britain is on the right.

Park Lane House

Perhaps recalling the nationalistic enthusiasm for Marie Laurencin's pieces expressed by French visitors to the show "L'Art du Verre," Steuben officials planned to take "British Artists in Crystal" to England for exhibition. They decided to enlarge the presentation to include not only the British artists' series but also engraved works by American designers, and utilitarian objects from the regular Steuben line. It was first planned to have the exhibition at London's Victoria and Albert Museum.[15] After initial expressions of interest, however, the museum staff became uneasy over the prospect of including "commercial" glass in the exhibition, but Steuben was not willing to relinquish the right of selection. David Stelling scouted about for an alternative location, settling on the Curzon Suite at Park Lane House. But the difficulties were not ended. English customs routinely excluded luxury products of foreign manufacture and they balked at permitting the American-made crystal into the country. Only after the United States Information Service intervened on Steuben's behalf, and after Steuben posted a bond to assure that no glass would be sold in England, did the exhibition clear customs.

To draw attention to the exhibition, President Eisenhower lent a unique cup, which had been presented to him by his staff, and both Queen Elizabeth and the Queen Mother permitted their Steuben to appear at Park Lane House. During the three-week exhibition, from mid-October to mid-November 1955, curious Britons filed past the Steuben vitrines, paying a small admission fee to benefit the English-Speaking Union. The Queen herself made a visit to the show, stopping to be photographed with Arthur Houghton as she puzzled, appropriately, over Enigma. Attendants noted that the crowd pleasers on display were Don Wier's Flower Plates and George Thompson's Cathedral.

"Asian Artists in Crystal"

At Park Lane House, the United States Information Service did well to intervene on Steuben's behalf, for elsewhere in the world Steuben was engaged in a joint project with the United States government, one that would confirm Steuben's growing reputation as an agent of international goodwill. Seeds of this undertaking had been sown during the war, when Isobel Lee, a Steuben employee on leave to serve the Red Cross in the South Pacific, became acquainted with many high-ranking military and government officials, who stayed in touch at war's end.[16] One of Lee's friends, Harold Stassen, became director of the Foreign Operations Administration in the early 1950s. At that time, Communism was perceived as a threat to many underdeveloped Asian nations, and Stassen had a mandate to strengthen ties between those countries and the United States. Isobel Lee kept Stassen abreast of the success of the "British Artists in Crystal" exhibition, and it seemed to him a logical extension of principle to undertake a similar series with Asian artists. After discussing his idea with Lee, Stassen wrote to Houghton: "It would be possible for Steuben glass to be of very significant service to our country."[17]

"There is a marked tendency for people (of non-Communist areas of Asia) to think wrongly of our country as being interested only in the materialistic and militaristic aspects," he continued. "We are thinking of methods by which the people of the United States might demonstrate an interest in the cultural attainments and artistic interests of the people of Asia. Noting the exceptional success of 'British Artists in Crystal,' it seemed to me if something similar could be done in relationship to Asian artists it might have a very marked result in contributing toward our objective."[18]

Houghton was no doubt delighted to comply. Stassen's request confirmed his own view of Steuben as emissary of international goodwill—a sparkling exemplar of the finest traditions of American art and American craftsmanship. A plan was quickly drawn. Karl Kup, curator of prints at the New York Public Library and newly returned from an extensive Asian trip that gave him a thorough overview of contemporary Asian art, was selected to represent Steuben in sixteen participating countries.[19] Before leaving to select the works of art to be engraved on Steuben crystal, Kup was thoroughly briefed on the basics of glass design and production. At every stop on Kup's itinerary, he met with prominent local artists, viewed their works at exhibitions arranged by the USIA, and, whenever possible, visited their studios. He had instructions to accept only those linear works and drawings that would best lend themselves to interpretation in crystal. No paintings could be considered. Selected subjects were to "please the man in the East as well as the man in the West," in keeping with guidelines set forth by the Foreign Affairs Office. Steuben also stipulated that the selections were to be "Asian" in feeling.[20]

Kup acquired a total of 130 drawings, which were all purchased by Steuben and later donated to the New York Public Library. Of the group, thirty-six works were chosen for translation into crystal. Steuben's design staff and engravers collaborated closely on the project, making two examples of each piece in the series. By late 1955, the two-year whirlwind project was nearly complete. All the glass had been blown, finished, and engraved. "Asian Artists in Crystal" was ready for unveiling. Never before had an individual American industrial firm been accorded such national attention: Secretary of State John Foster Dulles presided over the opening of "Asian Artists in Crystal" at the National Gallery of Art in Washington on January 17, 1956. Appearing concurrently at the National Gallery was the exhibition "Contemporary American Glass," comprising fifty or sixty pieces

George Thompson. Cathedral. 1955. Height 15¾".

Opposite: An example of the OX line: Steuben crystal vase presented to the prime minister of Togo on the occasion of that nation's independence, April 27, 1960.

made by nineteen different American artists and manufacturers. Without question, the National Gallery exhibition was the crowning achievement of Steuben's postwar history.

During the four weeks that the exhibition remained on display in the nation's capital, many prominent figures in government and international diplomacy, including President Eisenhower, visited the show. From Washington, "Asian Artists in Crystal" traveled to New York's Metropolitan Museum of Art, where Dag Hammerskjold, secretary general of the United Nations, accompanied by the ambassadors of the sixteen countries represented in the exhibition, officiated at the opening.

After a month's residence at the Metropolitan Museum, "Asian Artists" embarked on a tour of the sixteen participating nations, financed by the Corning Glass Works Foundation and arranged by the American Federation of Arts and the USIA. First stop on the itinerary was the National Museum at Seoul, Korea; last stop, in June 1957, was the Museum of Modern Art in Cairo. By the close of the exhibition, Steuben glass was well-known beyond the traditional art-collecting circles of Europe and the Western hemisphere. To perpetuate the good feelings generated by the project, the government presented each participating country's major museum or state collection with the pieces of glass representative of that nation's art.[21]

The duplicate set of "Asian Artists in Crystal" appeared at the Corning Glass Center in the summer of 1956 as the featured exhibition of the Glass Museum's fifth anniversary year. Thereafter, selections from this set were circulated to Steuben's regional shops in various parts of the country. (By 1956, Steuben had nineteen exclusive dealers throughout the country, mostly in prestigious department and specialty stores, in addition to its New York and Corning shops.)

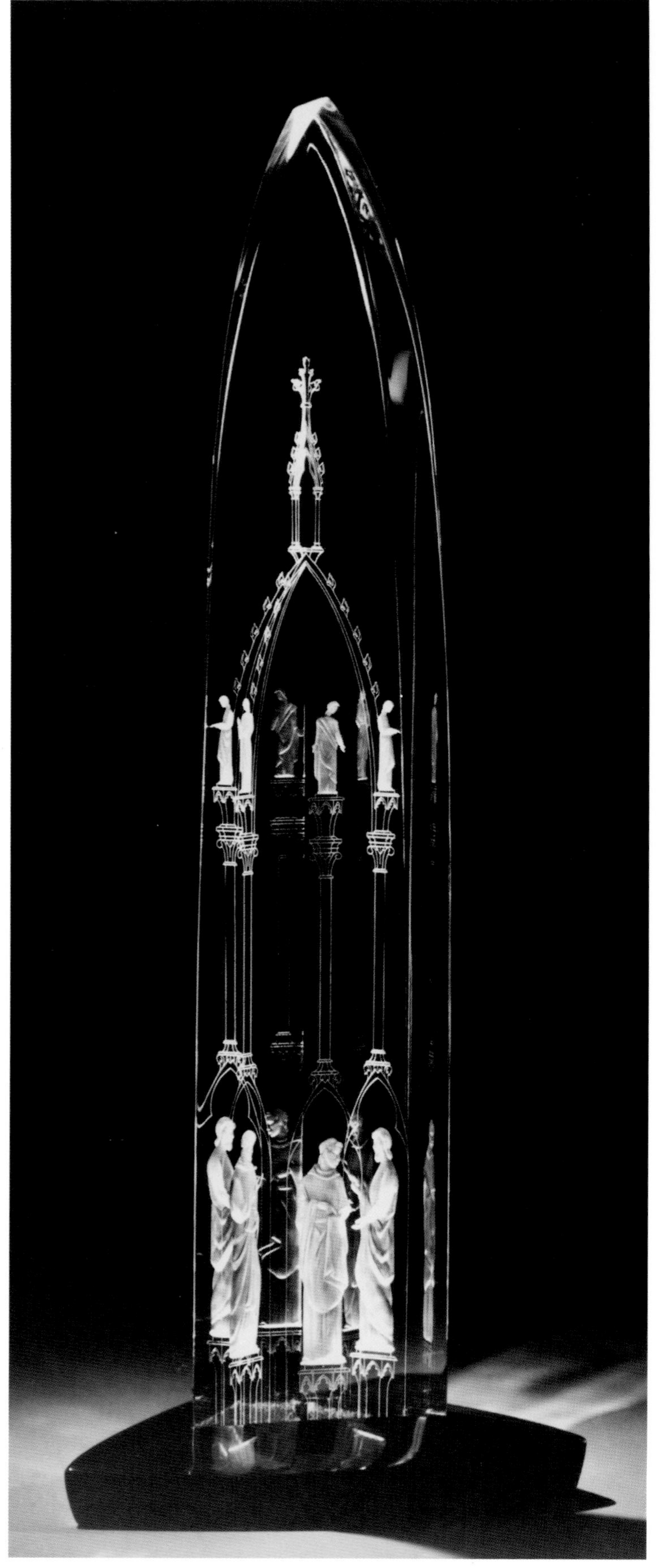

E PLURIBUS
UNUM

The OX Collection

By the mid-1950s, as a result of extensive and well-timed exposure at home and abroad, Steuben achieved the kind of reputation most traditional luxury products acquire only after a half-century or more of acceptance among the upper classes. In just a few short years, Arthur Houghton had brilliantly succeeded in presenting his crystal as the pinnacle of American craftsmanship. Furthermore, as the result of skillfully publicized gifts to important persons, Steuben was widely accepted as "the" usual gift of state. Beginning with President Truman's gift of Sidney Waugh's Merry-Go-Round Bowl to Princess Elizabeth on the occasion of her marriage, and followed in short order by other official presentations to Queen Wilhelmina, the Pope, and the Shah of Iran, Steuben could be found in state collections all over the world. Although very few of these early state gifts were designed with that particular purpose in mind, there were exceptions. The Papal Cup, for example, was especially created for presentation to Pope John in 1956.

In order to better accommodate and encourage Steuben's use as a state gift, the so-called OX Collection (O for "official" and X the usual designation for formative designs) was developed in 1955. "A special group of pieces set aside for official government gifts," announced Sally Walker to the Steuben staff in early 1955, "will eventually consist of twenty pieces, ten cut and blown, ten engraved."[22] The initial OX group consisted mainly of new designs, but it did include some existing pieces that were transferred out of the regular stock to be used henceforward only as state gifts. Certain pieces, such as the popular ashtrays and some Audubon Plates, were considered both OX and stock items.

Three sets of books picturing the OX Collection were made up. One copy remained in the Steuben shop; one was sent to the White House; and one went to the Department of State. It became a relatively simple matter for a high-level official to thumb through this "catalogue" and decide upon an appropriate gift for a visiting dignitary of any level. During the Eisenhower, Johnson, and Nixon administrations, Steuben became perhaps the most preferred state gift; it was easily portable, distinctive, American-made, and defied easy assessment of monetary value. The OX Collection no longer exists, though Steuben remains a frequent gift of state.

Steuben sales associates Ann Mount, Sally Walker, and Janet Wallace toast the opening of the newly redecorated mezzanine area for engraved glass, 1952.

Opposite: Another OX example: Vase with engraved seal of the United States of America, presented to the head of the government of Thailand by John Foster Dulles, secretary of state, when he visited Thailand in 1955.

"Steuben Crystal in Private Collections"

To celebrate and publicize the number of pieces of Steuben represented in state collections throughout the world, an exhibition of thirty-one works, entitled "Steuben Crystal in Private Collections," was held at the Steuben shop in 1961. Following a benefit preview for the Institute of International Education on May 15, the exhibition was opened for public viewing. Among the twenty-two heads of state and other notables whose pieces of Steuben comprised this display were Charles de Gaulle, Konrad Adenauer, Jawaharlal Nehru, Chiang Kai-shek, Queen Elizabeth, and the Emperor of Ethiopia. Many of the pieces were on public view for the first time. The exhibition was well received. It had originally been scheduled to remain on display for a month, but 45,000 persons visited the show during the first twenty days of its exhibition, so it was extended through midsummer.

VIII.
EXPERIMENT AND CHANGE: 1958–1972

The decade of the sixties, a time of social upheaval and change in the United States, was a time of experimentation and new directions for Steuben as well. Laying the groundwork for future stability through a basic change in accounting procedures, Steuben, which had been a wholly owned but administratively and fiscally independent subsidiary of Corning Glass Works, was "brought into the company" in 1958. Arthur Houghton's Steuben Glass, Incorporated, officially became Steuben Glass, a division of Corning Glass Works, in July of that year. The merger had been discussed for years by officials of Steuben and its parent company; it was a move designed to save taxes by joining the two firms as one financial entity.

Houghton insisted that Corning Glass Works uphold the objectives he had worked so diligently to establish for Steuben: only the highest standards of design were to be maintained; hand methods alone would be used in the manufacturing process; and the merchandising program would continue to promote crystal as a medium for artistic expression through sponsorship of exhibits and the general encouragement of artists in glass.[1] The change, therefore, was basically on paper: no substantive alterations of the administrative, design, or production functions occurred under the merger.

The Corning-Steuben Building: A New Space for New Design Trends

In March 1959, Steuben's New York shop moved across Fifth Avenue to new quarters in what was at that time the city's highest glass skyscraper, the just completed Corning-Steuben building at the corner of 56th Street. Like all previous

The Steuben showroom in New York City.

Poet Marianne Moore and Arthur A. Houghton, Jr., at the benefit preview of "Poetry in Crystal," April 17, 1963.

Steuben shops, the new facility was designed by John Gates to provide an elegant but unostentatious background for the crystal—a selling space with the ambience of a fine art gallery. The new, larger location permitted Steuben to expand both its sales staff and its production line. Veteran employees recall the move as the end of an era: "Business increased. We gained a lot, but we lost the closeness."[2]

A collection of thirty-one "Collector's Pieces," new ornamental designs, many of them elaborately engraved and primarily the work of Steuben's in-house design staff, opened on March 18, 1959, as the new shop's inaugural display. This grouping of glassware was the culmination of a tendency at Steuben during the fifties to produce major designs of a purely ornamental nature. One of the works, Moby Dick, designed by Donald Pollard and Sidney Waugh, marked a watershed in Steuben's use of engraving: no longer was the engraved decoration merely "an illustration on glass," but an integral component of the form, giving it depth, shape, and definition.

During the first few weeks it was open to the public, Steuben's new shop received thousands of visitors and well-wishers. In the summer, "United States in Crystal" was displayed for the first time. It had special appeal for many out-of-town visitors, who enjoyed finding "their" state bowl among the fifty on display.

On two floors above the salesrooms, fine new quarters were furnished for Steuben's administrative and design staff. In addition to Sidney Waugh, who retained the status of associate designer, the design department consisted of permanent full-time staff designers Donald Pollard, George Thompson, Don Wier, and Lloyd Atkins. (From time to time, Steuben invited outsiders to join the group briefly or to contribute sketches on a freelance basis.) Steuben's in-house staff exhibited a remarkable aesthetic range and versatility, which did full credit to Steuben's renewed emphasis on experimentation. The "Studies in Crystal" series, initiated in 1955, grew larger year by year as new designs involving geometric and free-form approaches were added.

"Poetry in Crystal"

By 1961, Steuben's various production, design, and sales components were well established in their various new facilities and functioning smoothly. Arthur Houghton turned his attention to yet another series, this one intended to cross-fertilize the arts. "Poetry in Crystal" would challenge Steuben's designers to interpret visually and convey the mood of specific poems commissioned from major poets under the auspices of the Poetry Society of America. "It was one of the most fascinating shows we ever did," Houghton recalls. "I established contact with the Poetry Society and explained that Steuben wished to employ poets to write poetry . . . nothing like this had happened before. We set the ground rules."[3] Through the Society, letters were sent to forty members offering the sum of $250 for each poem submitted for Steuben's consideration.[4] The poems had to be new, unpublished works between eight and forty lines long; and they were not to focus on the topics of crystal or glass.

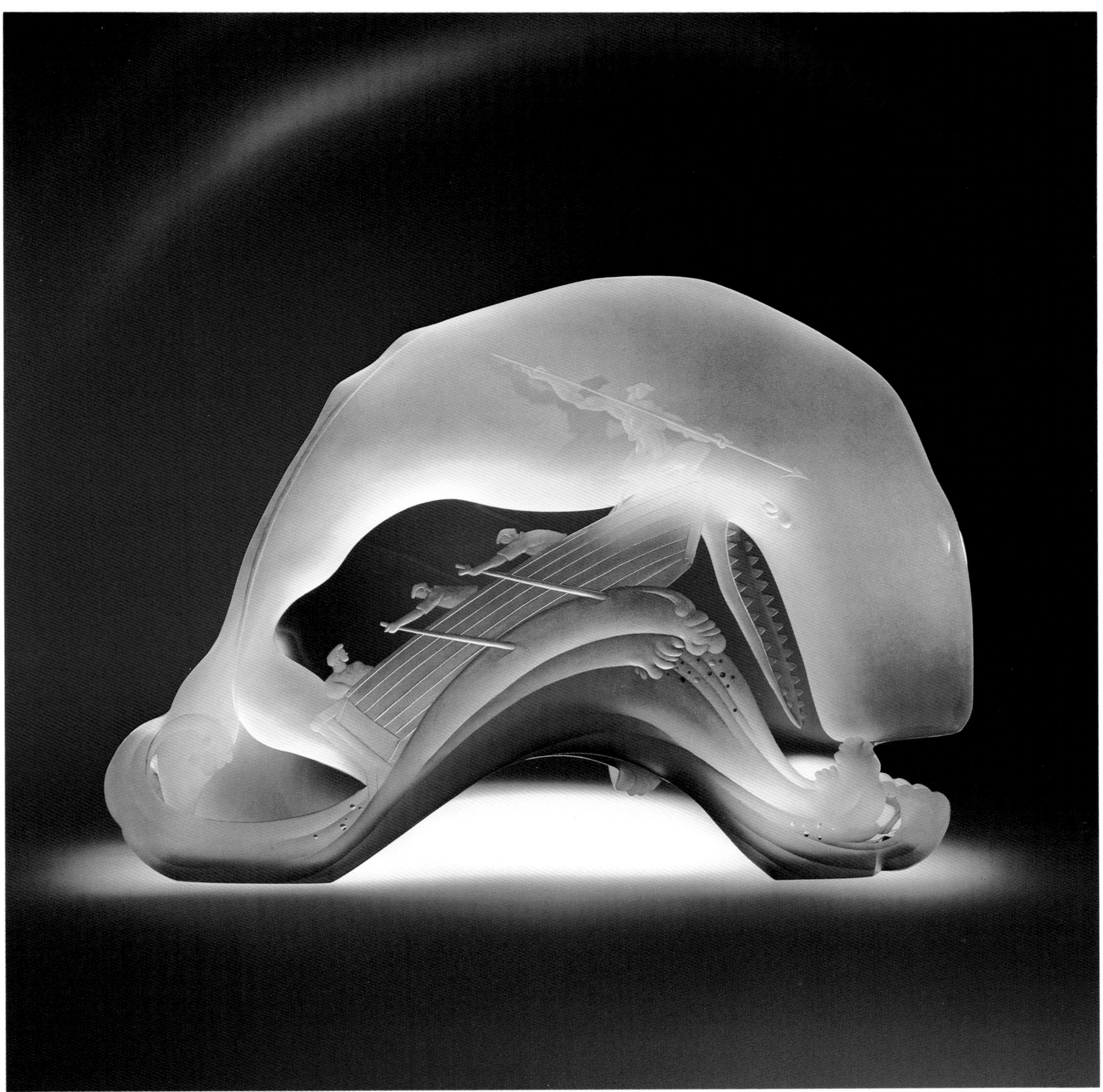

As Steuben's first generation of designers matured, and as new individuals joined the group in the 1950s, several key changes took place. In essence, asymmetry for the first time challenged symmetry, and the traditional dominance of utilitarian and functional objects was ended. Simultaneously, the previous relationship between engraving and form was revolutionized: where before, an engraving design submitted itself to the shape of the object (which in turn had been dictated by its use), now a new, organic relationship emerged—the engraved image became integral with the crystal shape. Nowhere is this better seen, perhaps, than in Moby Dick (1959), where Donald Pollard's glass design and Sidney Waugh's engraving combine for an unusually unified effect.

The experimental energy generated in the 1950s continued into the next decade, though many design variations failed to find a permanent place in Steuben's offerings. And as the trend away from functional objects continued, the demands of a new, affluent society—with a strong bent toward collecting—seemed to call for decorative objects of a representational nature. Among the examples created for this audience was Trout and Fly (1966), designed by James Houston, which also capitalized on a new perception of preciousness that combined crystal and metal.

Thirty-one works were submitted by such well-known figures as Marianne Moore, Conrad Aiken, Robinson Jeffers, and W.H. Auden, and were translated into glass. For the next two years, Steuben's designers, gaffers, and engravers were busy with the project. On April 18, 1963, "Poetry in Crystal" opened at the New York shop, under the direction of Lelia Tomes, with a gala preview party to benefit the Poetry Society.

As John Gates recalled: "This enterprise was of absorbing interest to our designers. Never before had a project so captured their imagination. As the poems were received, they were retyped without the name of the poet. When several poems had been assembled, copies of each were given to the artist-designers for their study and selection. Only after a poem had been chosen by an artist or glass designer was the poet's name disclosed."[5] Occasionally, an outside artist, such as Leon Kroll or Robert Vickrey, was called in to help interpret a mood or a theme. There were some innovations in "Poetry in Crystal," chief among them Don Pollard's incorporation of precious metal in his interpretation of A.M. Sullivan's "Who Hath Seen the Wind."

While "Poetry in Crystal" was in progress, two gifted people, whose work helped to shape Steuben's artistic evolution, joined the design team. They were James Houston, fresh from twelve years in the Arctic where, as civilian administrator, he had worked with and taught Eskimos, and Paul Schulze, a young graduate of the Parsons School of Design. In such distinctive pieces as Trout and Fly or Excalibur, Houston combined precious metals with Steuben's pure crystal. Schulze, who later became director of design at Steuben, exhibited a virtuoso fluency with all aspects of design.

The Masterworks Series

Carrying to its ultimate the idea of combining crystal with precious metals and jewels in objects of decorative art was a series of Steuben Masterworks—one-of-a-kind objects, in the tradition of Cellini or Fabergé—begun in 1966. "From time to time the combined talents at Steuben's command are focused upon the creation of a single masterwork—the imaginative concept of a senior staff artist," Houghton observed. "He is free to call upon associate artists, designers, artisans, engravers, and goldsmiths to bring into being, under his direction, a unique object of the finest design and craftsmanship."[6] Each masterwork required, on average, two to three years for planning and execution. This series came about as a result of Houghton's deeply felt conviction that "many, perhaps most, of the greatest objects that have ever been made combined more than one material. The French cabinetmakers, for instance, went beyond the English because they used far more in the way of metals and inlays, ceramics and other things."[7]

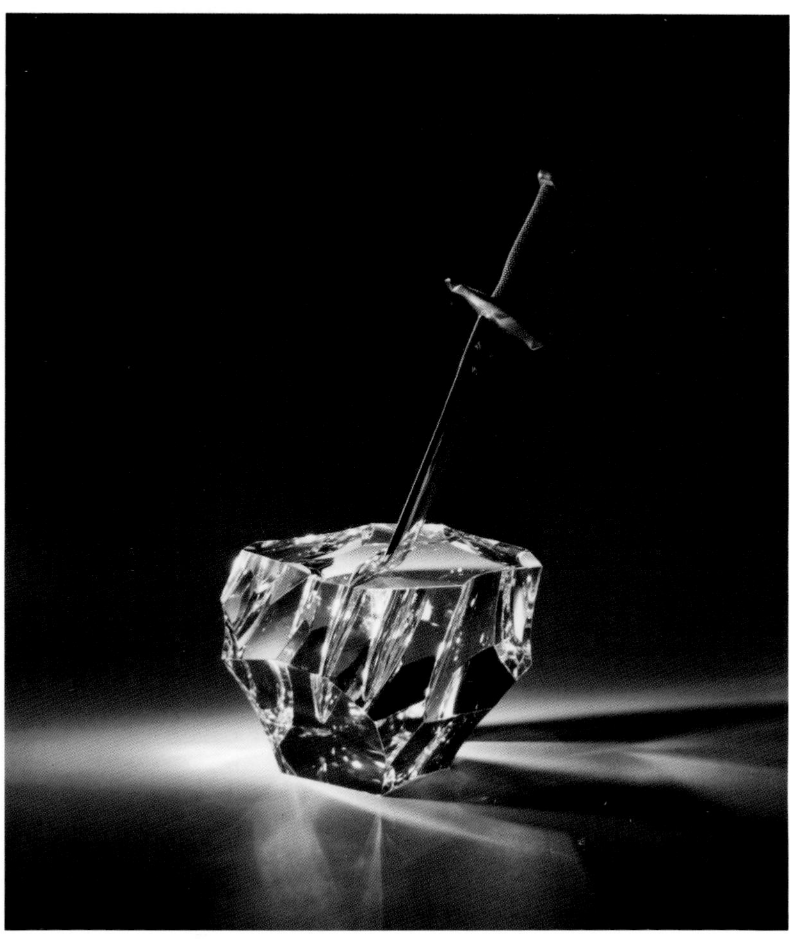

James Houston. Excalibur. 1963. Crystal, width 4½"; silver sword, height 8".

Overleaf, right: George Thompson (designer), Alexander Seidel (engraving designer). The Carrousel of the Sea. 1970. 18-karat gold, malachite, height 9¾".

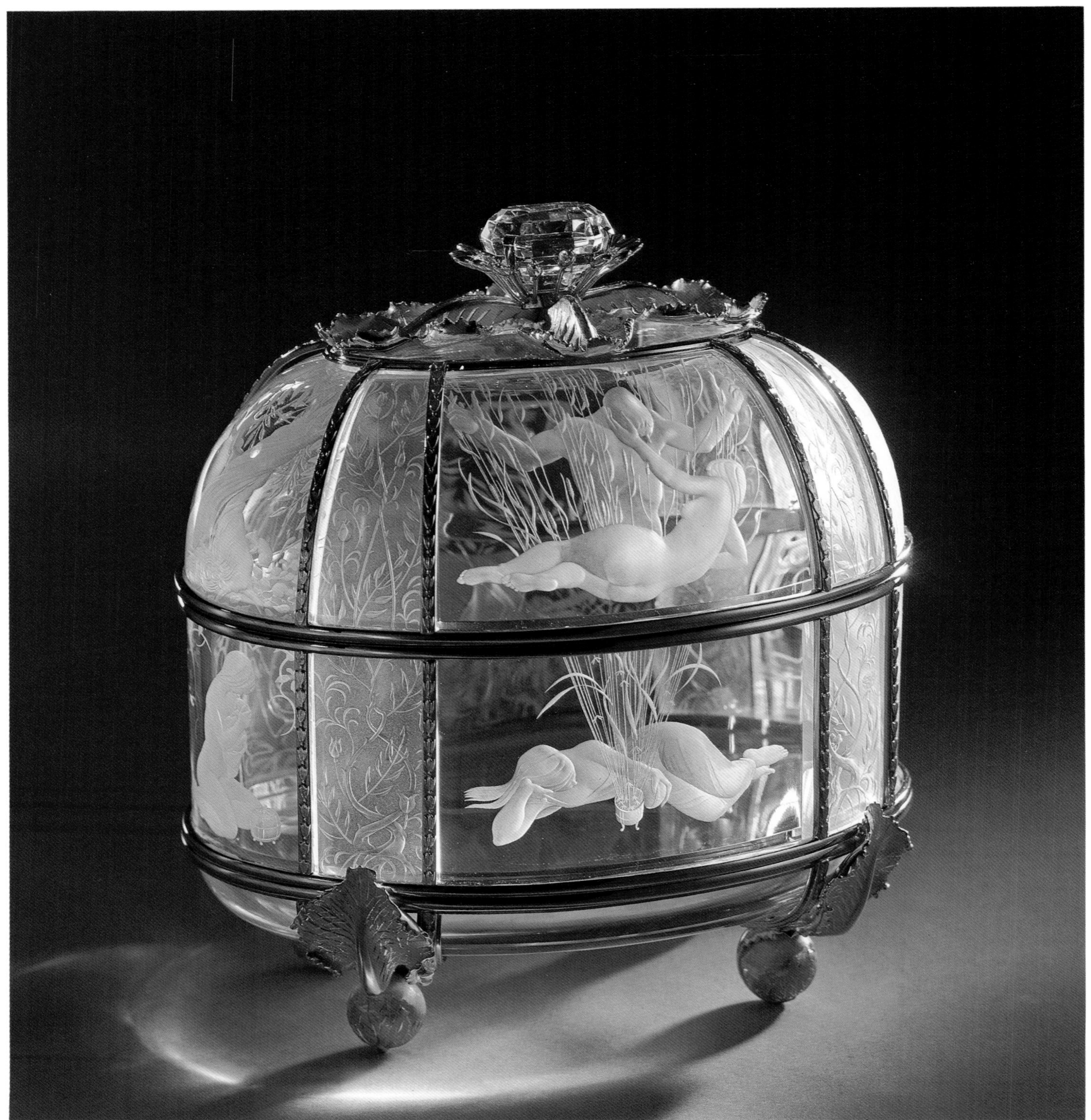

The combination of glass cutting and engraving with embellishments of gold and precious stones was achieved in The Myth of Adonis, created as a unique piece in 1966. The glass design is by Donald Pollard; the engraving was designed by Jerry Pfohl and executed by Roland Erlacher. The engraving style has a greater realism than in earlier pieces, with emphasis away from a bold outline and toward a flowing line and subtle shading of form.

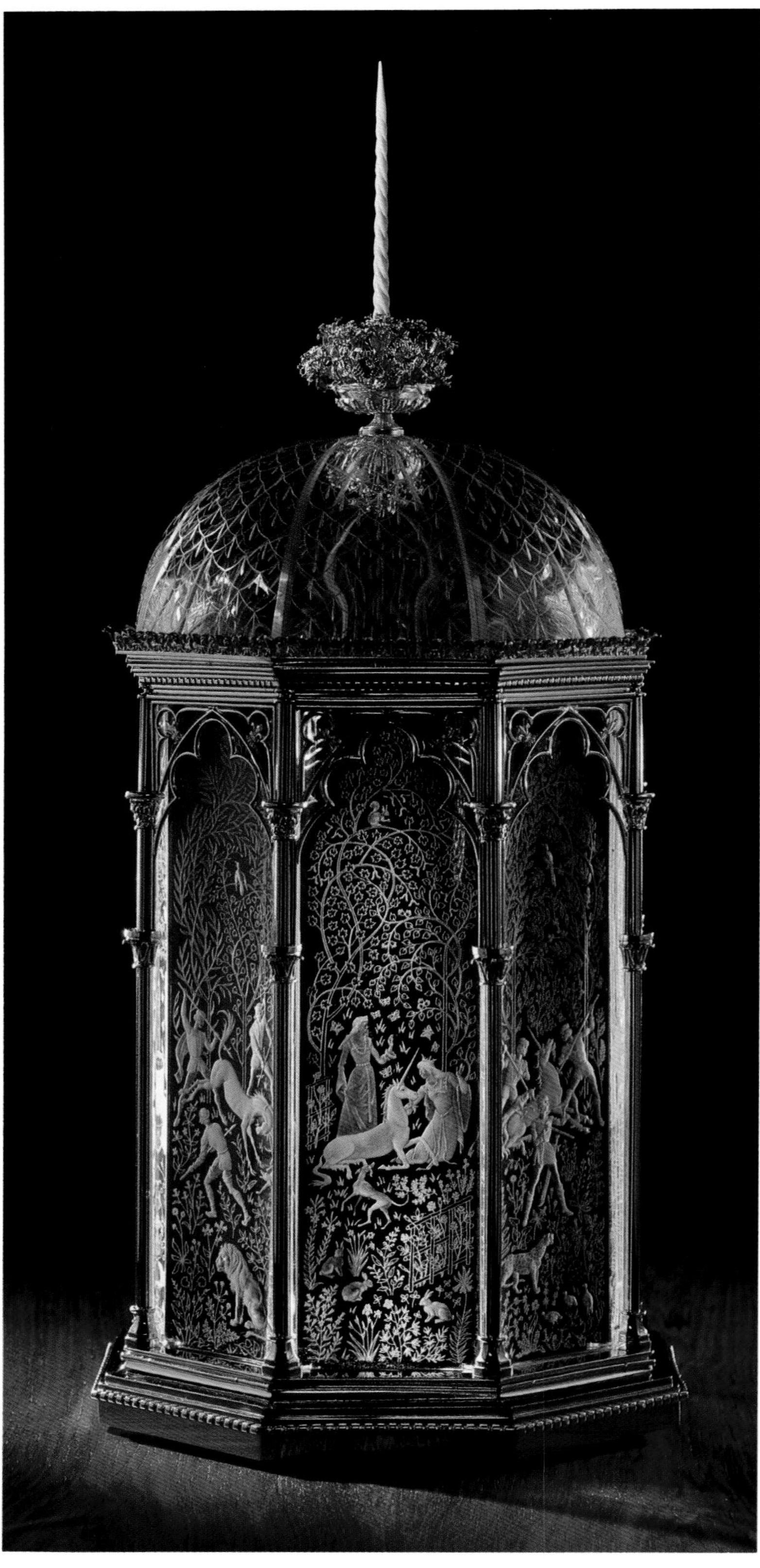

Donald Pollard (designer), Alexander Seidel (engraving designer). The Unicorn and the Maiden. 1971. 18-karat gold, ivory, diamonds, sapphires, height 14½".

Opposite: Donald Pollard (designer), Alexander Seidel (engraving designer), Roland Erlacher (engraver), Louis Feron (goldworker). Chinese Pavilion. 1975. 18-karat gold, jade, seed pearls, emeralds, diamonds, height 11¼".

The first object of this unique series was Enchanted Birds, a collaboration between George Thompson (glass design) and Alexander Seidel, whose drawing of four delicate birds was skillfully captured in crystal by Steuben's master engraver Roland Erlacher. The Myth of Adonis, a gold-framed casket by Donald Pollard and Jerry Pfohl, followed later that year. Other masterworks, most of which have been purchased by collectors at "a price equivalent to that of a major work of art" include Four Seasons (1969), Carrousel of the Sea (1970), Unicorn and the Maiden (1971), Chinese Pavilion (1974), Sphere of the Zodiac (1976), Romance of the Rose (1977), and Innerland (1980).[8]

Islands, Explorers, and Presentation Pieces

Throughout the sixties, Arthur Houghton continued to be the primary driving force behind Steuben's artistic pursuits. A bibliophile and scholar, Houghton's close ties to the academic world had fostered such collaborative efforts as the "United States in Crystal" and "Poetry in Crystal" series. His ideas did not always bear fruit: in 1962, for example, envisioning a series of twenty new pieces on the general topic of "Angels," he invited philosopher Mortimer Adler to address the New York staff on the cosmology of that heavenly hierarchy. The lecture came off, but the series did not.[9] In retrospect, Houghton felt that this was because "God doesn't want us to do angels. You just can't do angels in glass; it did not find favor with the Almighty."[10]

More successful was Steuben's collaboration with Alexander D. Vietor, curator of maps at the Yale University Library, in planning the "Islands in Crystal" series.[11] Maps and symbols of a dozen real and mythical islands, which throughout history have fired the imagination or forged important links in the progress of civilization, were engraved on free-form pieces of Steuben designed mainly by the in-house staff. At Vietor's

Previous pages, left: Donald Pollard (designer), Alexander Seidel (engraving designer; adapted from the Uranographia of Johann Elert Bode), Roland Erlacher (engraver). Sphere of the Zodiac. 1976. Stainless steel, height 19¼".

Previous pages, right: Donald Pollard (designer), Howard Rogers (engraving designer), Roland Erlacher (engraver), Louis Feron (goldworker). The Romance of the Rose. 1977. 18-karat gold, rubies, diamonds, width 9½".

Above: James Houston. Arctic Fisherman. 1970. Rhodium-plated sterling silver, height 6½".

Opposite: James Houston. Diving Seals. 1972. Height 8¾".

Overleaf: James Houston. Robert Falcon Scott. 1972. Length 14½".

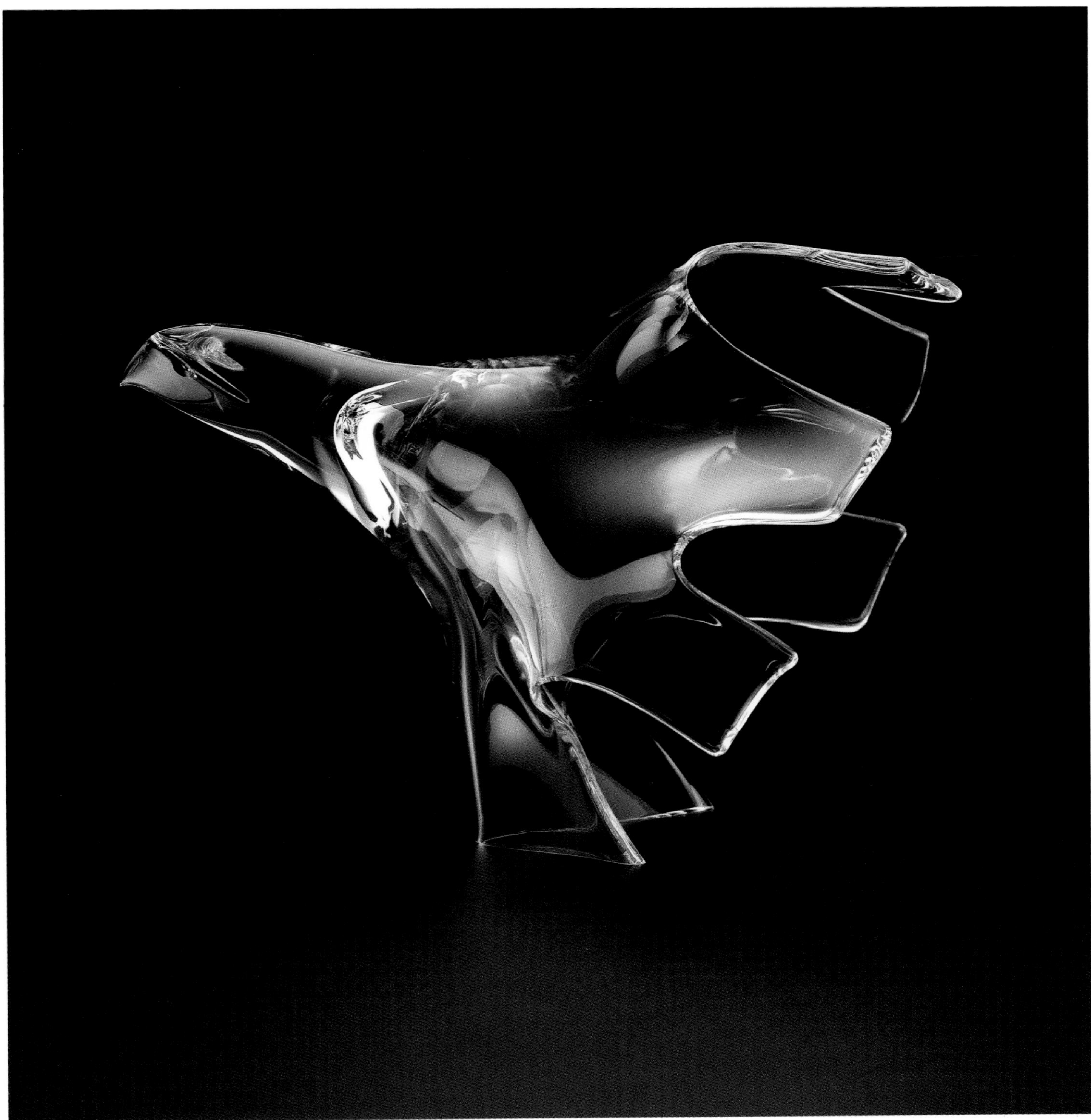

A new feeling toward decorative objects and animal forms also swept in during the 1970s. The attempt was made to simplify these forms to their essentials rather than achieve realistic detail or narrative form alone. The Flying Eagle (Paul Schulze, 1975) demonstrates this; the idea is to portray the flow of the body, tail, and wings, the fluidity of the bird's powerful, forward motion, instead of recording details such as the precise number of feathers.

MARI USQUE AD MARE
A MARI USQUE
NEWFOUNDLAND
PRINCE EDWARD ISLAND
NOVA SCOTIA
NEW BRUNSWICK
OF THE UNITED STATES OF AMERICA

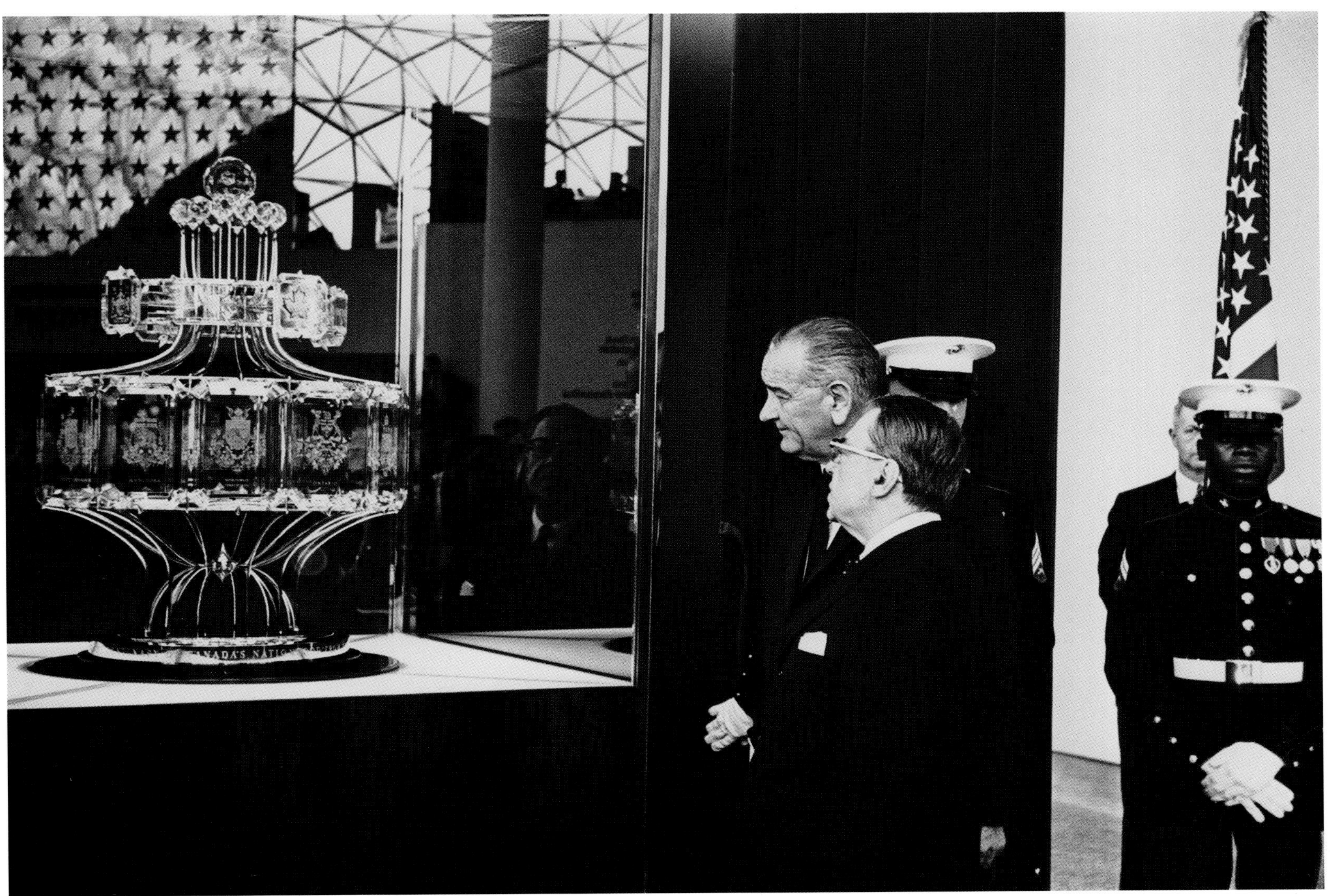

suggestion, some sketches were made directly from ancient cartographical sources, including maps from the Yale Collection. "Islands in Crystal" was well received by the press when it opened at the New York gallery in May 1965.

A similar series of ornamental Steuben designs, taking as their subject the world's great explorers, was begun during the early 1970s.

Throughout this period, during the administrations of John F. Kennedy, Lyndon Johnson, and Richard Nixon, Steuben continued to be a favorite state gift of American presidents and diplomats. In 1967, President Johnson commissioned what is perhaps the best-known Steuben gift of state, The Great Ring of Canada, for presentation to Prime Minister Lester Pearson "For the People of Canada on the Centenary of Canada's Nationhood from the People of the United States of America." Designed by Donald Pollard and Alexander Seidel, and engraved by Steuben's master craftsmen Roland Erlacher and Ladislav Havlik, The Great Ring stands forty inches high. In a setting of rhodium-plated steel, it holds twelve engraved plaques and a dozen faceted spheres of Steuben crystal, symbolizing the ten provinces and two territories of Canada. Visitors from throughout the world viewed this massive crystal artwork at Expo '67, the Montreal World's Fair, where it was displayed throughout the centennial year.

President Lyndon Baines Johnson and Paul Martin, Canada's minister for external affairs, examine The Great Ring of Canada at Montreal's Expo '67.

Opposite: Donald Pollard (designer), Alexander Seidel (engraving designer). The Great Ring of Canada. 1967. Height 40".

Changes in Staff

In 1963, the Steuben triumvirate—John Gates, Sidney Waugh, and Arthur Houghton—was shattered by the untimely death of Waugh, whose masterful command of design and sculptor's sensibilities had helped to define Steuben's aesthetic character from 1935 onward. Waugh's contributions to the early success of the "new" Steuben were inestimable; the legacy of his talent, indelible. Waugh's loss was sorely felt by his peers at Steuben, for it signaled the end of an era.

Another member of the pioneering generation of crystalmakers, Robert J. Leavy, reluctantly retired in 1963 from his post as executive vice president for staff operations. A veteran of the Carder years, Leavy had a bond with Arthur Houghton of unquestioning loyalty. As the "new" Steuben's first production manager, as its stand-in president during Houghton's wartime absence, and throughout the many years he diligently supervised the Corning operation as senior resident executive, Leavy was largely responsible for the perfection of the crystal itself. As Houghton remarked: "The many public tributes to the perfection of Steuben's craftsmanship are a recognition of the contribution that Bob Leavy has made to the history of fine glass."[12]

Over his long career, Leavy was always concerned with the perpetuation of Steuben's tradition of fine craftsmanship. "In my experience," he wrote to Houghton in 1968, "I saw four different generations of glassworkers—but weeks, months, and years in advance, I planned each single replacement. The transition worked out perfectly."[13] Now facing his own retirement, he worried that no new artisans were being trained to take the places of the aging master-craftsmen. Partly as a result of Leavy's unremitting reminders, Houghton dispatched Myron Hamer—who eventually replaced Leavy as director of production—and Leavy himself to Europe, in 1961, with the express purpose of finding "new blood" trained in

John D. Rockefeller III, chairman of the board of Lincoln Center, accepts Steuben sculpture The Performing Arts from David M. Keiser, president of the New York Philharmonic, September 10, 1962.

Opposite: Paul Schulze (designer), Donald Crowley (engraving designer). Dandelions. 1973. Width 7¾".

Dr. Martin Luther King, Jr., receiving an engraved Steuben bowl from the citizens of Atlanta, January 27, 1965.

Opposite: American Ambassador William R. Tyler presents President and Mrs. Johnson's wedding gift to Princess Beatrix of the Netherlands, while her fiancé, Claus Von Amsberg, observes.

Europe's exacting craft traditions to infuse fresh energy into Steuben's blowing, cutting, and engraving operations.

Leavy was not alone in his concern for the potential decline of Steuben craftsmanship. John Gates, in a taped interview shortly before his own retirement, expressed similar feelings about the less arduous training of Steuben's younger workers. "I confess, they cannot make perhaps some of the things made by Johnny Jansen in 1935," he admitted, recalling the great Swedish gaffer of Steuben's early days. The fact was that Steuben's craftsmen and facilities were hard put to meet the demand for handmade crystal. Because of imminent production shortfalls, on April 1, 1969, Steuben closed out its nineteen American dealerships, retaining only the company-owned shops on Fifth Avenue and at the Corning Glass Center. The great French company Baccarat took over the "Steuben Rooms" at Gump's store in San Francisco and at other locations.[14]

The Changing of the Guard: Design

After nearly thirty-six years as director of design at Steuben, and since 1957 design director for all of Corning Glass Works, John Monteith Gates retired on the first day of July 1969. As a remembrance, he received a replica of his own 1940 Valor Cup—a most appropriate gift, considering Gates' considerable bravery in abandoning a promising architectural career in 1933 for an uncertain future with a foundering, money-losing glass company. With unflagging energy and dedication, Gates had helped to shape Steuben's image of elegance. "You have guided Steuben Glass from its unformed infancy to its magnificent maturity," Arthur Houghton told his old friend and co-worker at the retirement dinner. "You have written a noble chapter in the history of glassmaking."[15] For a brief while following Gates' retirement, Paul Perrot, director of The Corning Museum of Glass, temporarily took on the responsibility for design leadership at Steuben. Perrot brought in some interesting new artists, including Katherine De Sousa, who lived for a time at Corning as designer-in-residence. Due to his other pressing responsibilities, Perrot's brief tenure ended early in 1970, and Paul Schulze, who had been assistant director of design for a little more than a year, took the vacant position.[16]

Schulze first came to Steuben as a staff designer in 1961. A native New Yorker, he was committed to innovation in glass. His own contributions to the "Studies in Crystal" series, frequently distinguished by their bold angularity, embodied his personal fascination with "cold-working" the glass—cutting it into shape after the gather has been blown into a compatible form. Schulze, however, did not impose his own vision on Steuben's other designers; he encouraged diversity and recognized that many different approaches to crystal design could coexist.

During this fast-paced decade, Steuben's line of metal-embellished crystal was conceived and developed, despite the misgivings of some Steuben staffers who felt the crystal required no further ornament. "I was the one who suggested and advocated the use of precious metals in glass," Arthur Houghton has said. "I take the responsibility for it. I wanted to see something that in price was between your simple pieces of glass and your very expensive engraved pieces; I felt this would fill a gap." Furthermore, Houghton felt that such pieces should not be utilitarian in any way, because "it is only by shaking off the utilitarian . . . that you can really accomplish something that exists for no other reason than the conveyance of beauty." Houghton was especially pleased with some of the metal-embellished major ornamental pieces. "I think the 'Mouse and Cheese' is intensely amusing. And Jim Houston's 'Arctic Fisherman' is a lovely piece."[17]

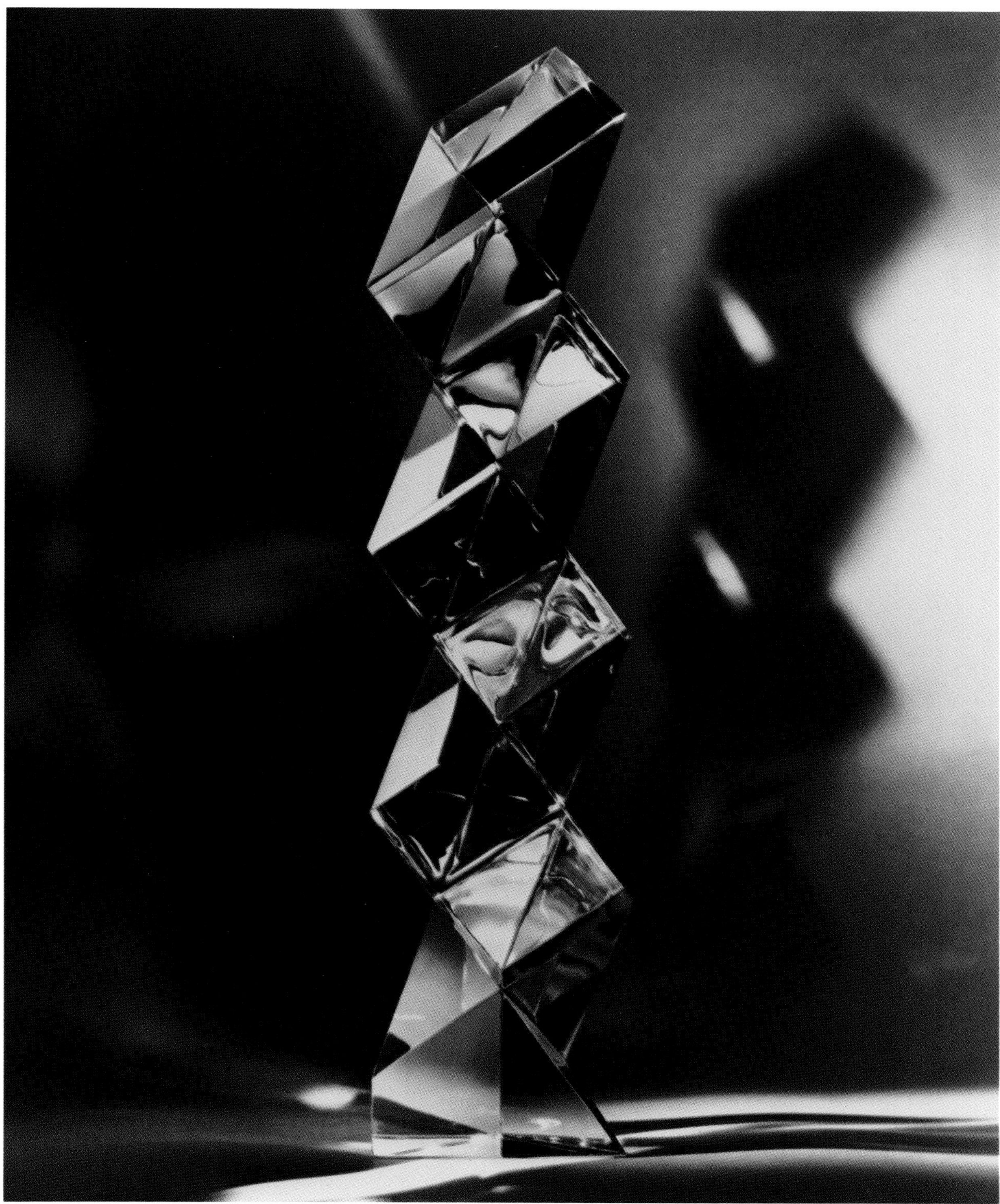

Geometric sculpture in glass found a place among Steuben pieces in the 1960s, paralleling a similar trend in the abstract painting of the period. Now, too, the techniques of handling glass permitted the casting of flawless solid blocks and the cutting of geometric forms. Transparency was juxtaposed with reflectivity to enhance these prismatic phenomena, as in Prismatic, designed by Paul Schulze in 1965.

COME TO THE ANIMAL FAIR
STEUBEN GLASS
ENTRANCE TO
717 5TH AVE.
AT 10 EAST 56
COME TO THE ANIMAL FAIR

IX.
CELEBRATING THE ARTIST: 1973–1982

When Robert Leavy was finding it difficult to come to terms with the inevitability of retirement in 1962, Arthur Houghton sent him an encouraging message. "I wonder," he wrote, "whether the great contribution we can now both of us make to Steuben, which we love, is not to provide for an orderly transition into younger hands. It is a thing we must do, despite natural reluctance. Anything else would be to destroy what we have built."[1] Yet it was a decade before Houghton himself was ready to put the presidency of Steuben into "younger hands."

In the meantime, change was in the air. Making art less elitist and more accessible was a theme of the activist 1960s, and Steuben's designs reflected this trend. By 1970, among the most popular stock items were the moderately priced, whimsical animal figures. More than sixty of these appealing little creatures were gathered into an "Animal Fair" exhibition at the New York shop. Crystal birds and beasts of many sorts—eagles, cats, owls, even a vermeil-embellished turtle with emerald eyes—arranged in what was described as a "fanciful spring landscape," attracted some fifty thousand visitors in a four-week period.[2] The exhibition, which later spent the summer at the Corning Glass Center, had opened on April 15, 1971.

That same month, Houghton announced the appointment of Thomas Scharman Buechner as vice president of Steuben Glass and president of The Corning Museum of Glass and the Corning Glass Works Foundation. Houghton was well acquainted with Buechner's talents, having recruited him in 1950 to be first director of The Corning Museum of Glass. As Buechner recalled it, "In December 1950, I was twenty-four years

A bright banner and an eye-catching sidewalk sculpture welcome visitors to the "Animal Fair" at Steuben's shop, April 1971.

Lloyd Atkins. Hippopotamus.
1980. Length 6¼".

Paul Schulze. Walrus. 1977.
Sterling silver, length 7".

James Houston. Night Owl.
1975. Width 7¾".

old and an assistant in the display department of the Metropolitan Museum of Art. On the director's recommendation, Arthur Houghton gave me responsibility for The Corning Museum of Glass, which was scheduled to come into existence only six months later. In other words we had six months to finish the building itself and to put together the collection, catalogue it, design the display, and get it installed. I remember coming into his office on my first day at work—an awesome experience in itself—and asking 'What would you like me to do?' He replied, 'That's what we are paying you to tell us.' And that is the way it has always been—great freedom, great opportunity, great responsibility."[3]

Educated at Princeton, the Art Student's League, and L'Ecole des Beaux Arts in Paris, Tom Buechner was not just an outstanding museum executive, but an established portrait painter, designer, and author. During his decade at the Museum of Glass, he had earned Arthur Houghton's friendship and trust, and that of Frederick Carder as well. Steeped in the history of glass, he founded the prestigious *Journal of Glass Studies* before leaving Corning for an eleven-year stint as director of the Brooklyn Museum.

With a background so well suited to carry on Houghton's legacy at Steuben, as well as a persuasive demeanor and scholarly bent not unlike Houghton's own, Buechner was officially named president on January 1, 1973. Houghton took on the title of chairman and moved from New York City to Wye Plantation, an historic estate near Queenstown on Maryland's Eastern Shore. It was a retirement in name only for the energetic chairman, who kept a hand on Steuben's reins, coaching and offering prodigious advice to his successors, until his death in 1990. But Buechner gave notice, ever so tactfully, of his intention to be his own man. "Arthur Houghton has continuously developed the Steuben enterprise in pursuit of a single objective—excellence—in material, in workmanship, and in design," Buechner stated in his inaugural remarks as president. "Steuben reflects his taste and his imagination. Changes will occur which will reflect his successor's, but the objective will remain the same. Having spent twenty-two years working in museums, preserving the achievements of others, I am looking forward to the unequaled opportunity to help make the most beautiful glass the world has ever known."[4] This set the tone for the coming decade at Steuben, one marked by change but always within the context of the company's traditional goals of perfection in material, design, and craftsmanship.

One of Buechner's first efforts was to lend support to the exhibition, "Steuben: Seventy Years of American Glassmaking," organized by the Toledo Museum of Art in 1974. It encompassed the entire span of Steuben's history with thirty-eight examples of Frederick Carder's colorful glass and more than sixty pieces of Steuben crystal tracing the stylistic evolution of Steuben design during the Houghton years. A catalogue written by Paul Gardner, Paul Perrot, and James Plaut documented the exhibition, reaffirming Steuben's image as the foremost American crystal of the twentieth century. After opening in Toledo, the show toured eight American museums, including the Smithsonian Institution, for two years. Many people who saw it became interested in acquiring Steuben glass and called the New York office asking to buy such out-of-production classics as George Thompson's elegant 1938 Rope Twist Candlesticks.

The Heritage Series

Responding to this unprecedented demand for classic pieces of crystal, Buechner initiated the Steuben Heritage Series in 1978—Steuben's 75th Anniversary year. The first Heritage piece was a faithful reissue of the popular Thompson candlesticks, offered in a limited edition to established Steuben customers. Additional Heritage designs,

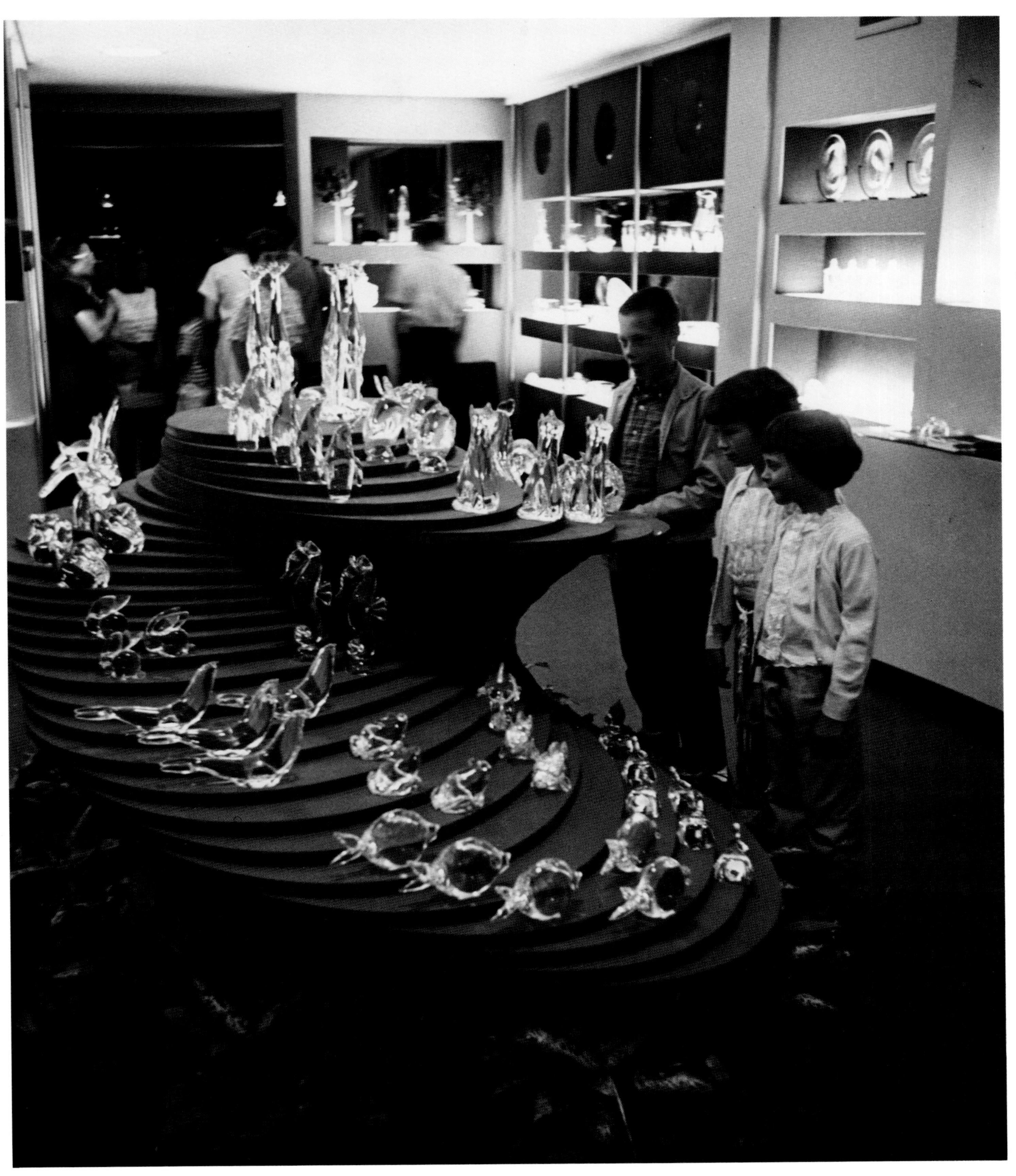

Schoolchildren admire a family of Steuben cats, part of the "Animal Fair" exhibition, 1971.

each "an example of past excellence consistent with contemporary living," were reintroduced periodically during Buechner's tenure. Heritage pieces continue to be produced. They carry a special insignia, in addition to the usual Steuben diamond-pen signature, to set them apart from their prototypes.

Another tradition-focused series, "The Classics" by Donald Pollard—ten bowls and vases inspired by the traditional shapes of ancient Chinese vessels—was presented in a September 1977 exhibition at the New York shop. These striking, unadorned pieces emphasizing the harmonious relationship between the outer form and the inner shell were displayed with traditional arrangements of flowers created by Mutsuo Tomita, a master of ikebana, the Japanese art of flower arranging.

Exhibitions of Historic Glass

Steuben's tradition of educating the public in the history and techniques of glassmaking continued under Buechner with a series of exhibitions at the New York shop. The first of these focused on Harvard University's Ware Collection of Blaschka Glass Models of Plants, made between 1884 and 1936 by German artisans Leopold and Rudolf Blaschka. Admission fees to this event, which opened in March 1976, were used to benefit a fund for the preservation of the Blaschka Collection at Harvard.[5] In April 1977, another benefit exhibition—this one to aid the restoration of Canterbury Cathedral—opened. Cosponsored by the American Committee to save Canterbury Cathedral, it featured fragments of the cathedral's historic twelfth- and thirteenth-century stained-glass windows.[6] Chinese glass snuff bottles from a private collection were displayed at Steuben in September 1980 to benefit the World Wildlife Fund.[7] In January 1980, "Small Wonders," an exhibition of 151 scent bottles dating from 1450 B.C. to 1940, was organized with the cosponsorship

Paul Schulze (designer), Frank Eliscu (engraving designer). The Carrousel of the Seasons. 1966. Height 12".

Thomas S. Buechner (left) greets the Right Honorable Lord Astor of Hever, president of the International Appeal to Save Canterbury Cathedral, at the benefit preview of the Canterbury Cathedral Windows Exhibition at Steuben, 1977.

With the retirement of Arthur Houghton and John M. Gates at the beginning of the 1970s, it seemed appropriate to use the period of transition to reaffirm the idealism of design, material, and craft with a view toward preserving the best of the past while clearly moving into the future. One of the first steps was a major effort to resume the design and production of functional glass objects. Rather than repeat older designs, a new generation of forms devoid of added exterior decoration was produced to accentuate a contemporary aesthetic. The Lunar Vase was designed by David Dowler in 1977.

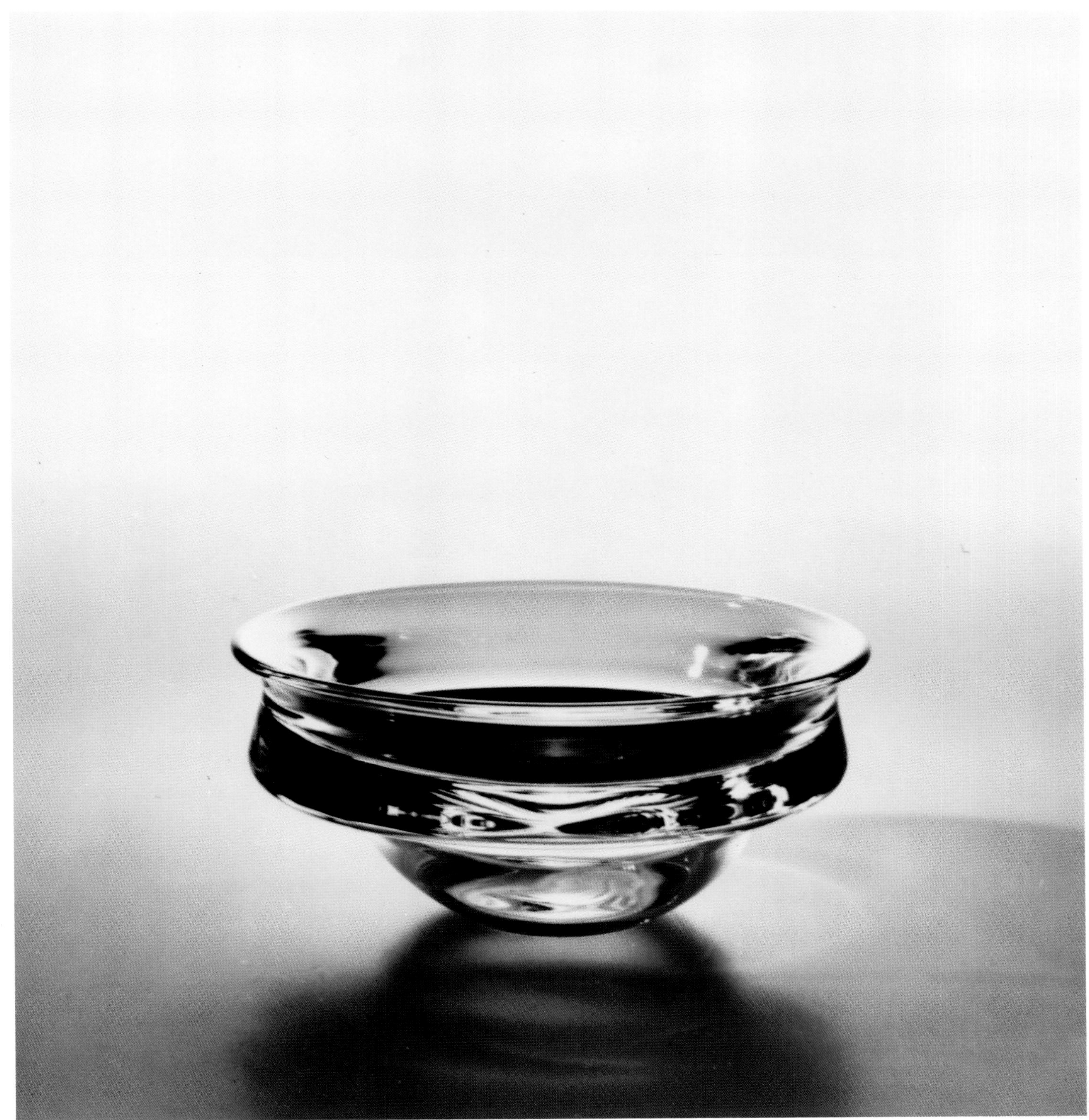

Among the new functional objects there emerged a strong feeling for shape, internal and external surface relationships, entrapments (the enclosure, for example, of a bubble inside a volume of crystal), and the prismatic effect created by concentrating weights of crystal in selected areas. James Carpenter designed this bowl in which the heavy-walled section is lifted up to the center of the design, thus intensifying the refraction and reflection of light.

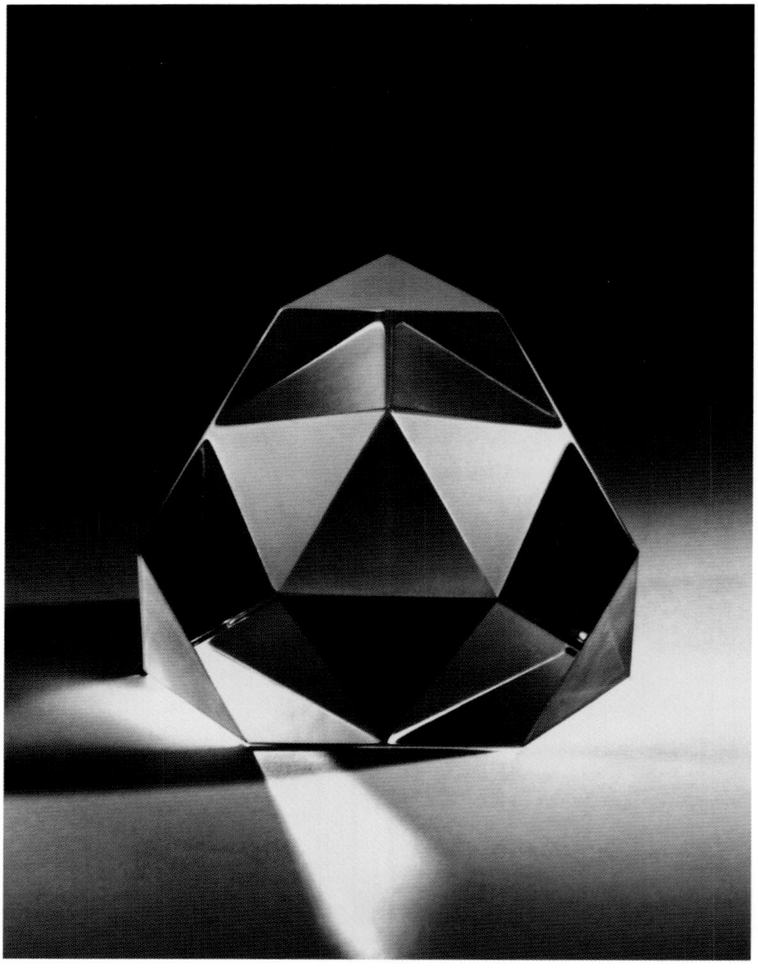

Lloyd Atkins. Octron. 1974. Width 3".

Eric Hilton. Heart. 1974. Length 2¼".

of The Fragrance Foundation, with an opening benefit for the Brooklyn Botanic Garden's Fragrance Garden for the Blind. And in 1981, "Masterpieces of Cameo Glass," selected items from a scholarly exhibition organized by The Corning Museum of Glass, went on exhibit at the New York shop. All these exhibitions emphasized Steuben's link with the centuries-old art of glassmaking by placing it in an historical context. This, Buechner believed, would enhance its appreciation as "the ultimate material in man's 3500-year search for transparency."

Autonomy for the Glass Designers

A major philosophical shift during the Buechner years was the new freedom given individual artist-designers. While Houghton had always given credit to the designers of major engraved pieces, he considered design to be essentially a group effort, resulting in a nearly anonymous corporate look for many of the stock pieces as well as the small ornamentals. Frederick Carder, by contrast, had either personally designed—or was closely involved in the design of—most Steuben pieces. Ever trend-conscious, Carder took great pains to keep up with prevailing tastes and styles. Buechner's inclination was to seek out the best talent he could find, then permit the artists to develop their own directions—not surprising, considering his museum background. He encouraged major artists working in glass to come to Steuben to continue their creative efforts within the company, and in concert with director of design Paul Schulze, he gave Steuben's staff designers the autonomy to conceive and carry out their own ideas. "My job is to make sure we have the best artists and designers and to do everything

Also in the early 1970s a greater emphasis was placed on prismatic geometric objects to capitalize once again on the remarkable essential quality of transparency and brilliance of the Steuben glass material. Innovation and refinement of articles that demonstrated this singular advantage caused narrative objects to be moved aside. Peter Aldridge's Centroid (1977) is such a geometric sculpture.

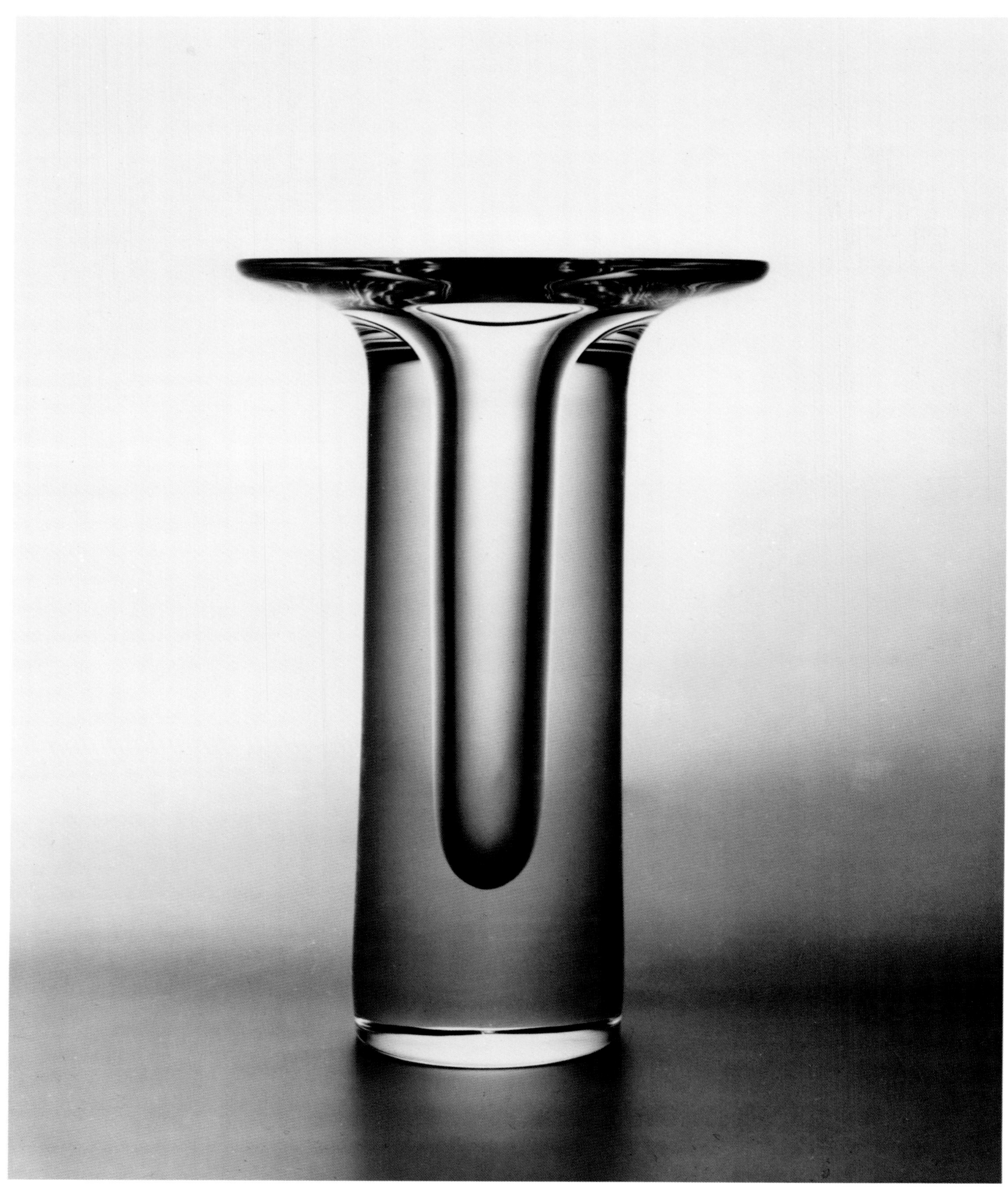

David Dowler. Pedicel Vase. 1975. Height 7¾".

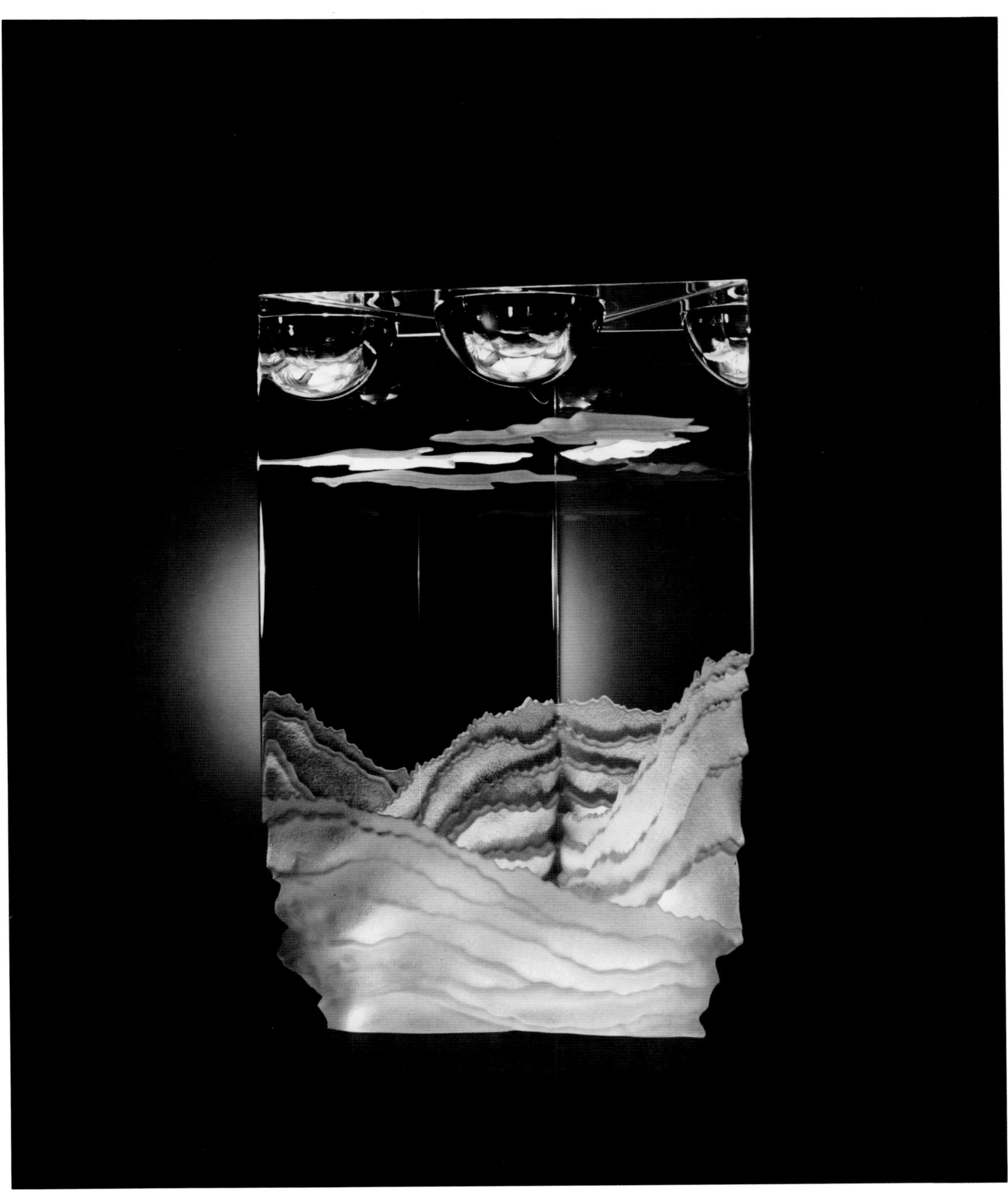

Paul Schulze. Earth Zone. 1979. Height 8".

1776
1976
E PLURIBUS UNUM
The Bicentennial of the United States of America

Peter Yenawine. Desk Set. 1975. Stainless steel. Letter Opener, length 8"; Magnifier, diameter 4"; Crystal Ball, height 4¾"; Pencil Holder, height 4¾".

Previous pages, left: Donald Pollard (designer), Patricia Weisberg and Pollard (engraving designers). The Bicentennial Goblet. 1975. Height 7¾".

Previous pages, right: Zevi Blum (designer), Roland Erlacher (engraver). The Crusaders Bowl. 1975. Diameter 13".

With a view toward exploring the pristine quality of crystal, David Dowler produced this piece, Oracle (1980), in which the viewer's eye moves from surface to surface, from smooth textures to coarse, and from reality to reflection.

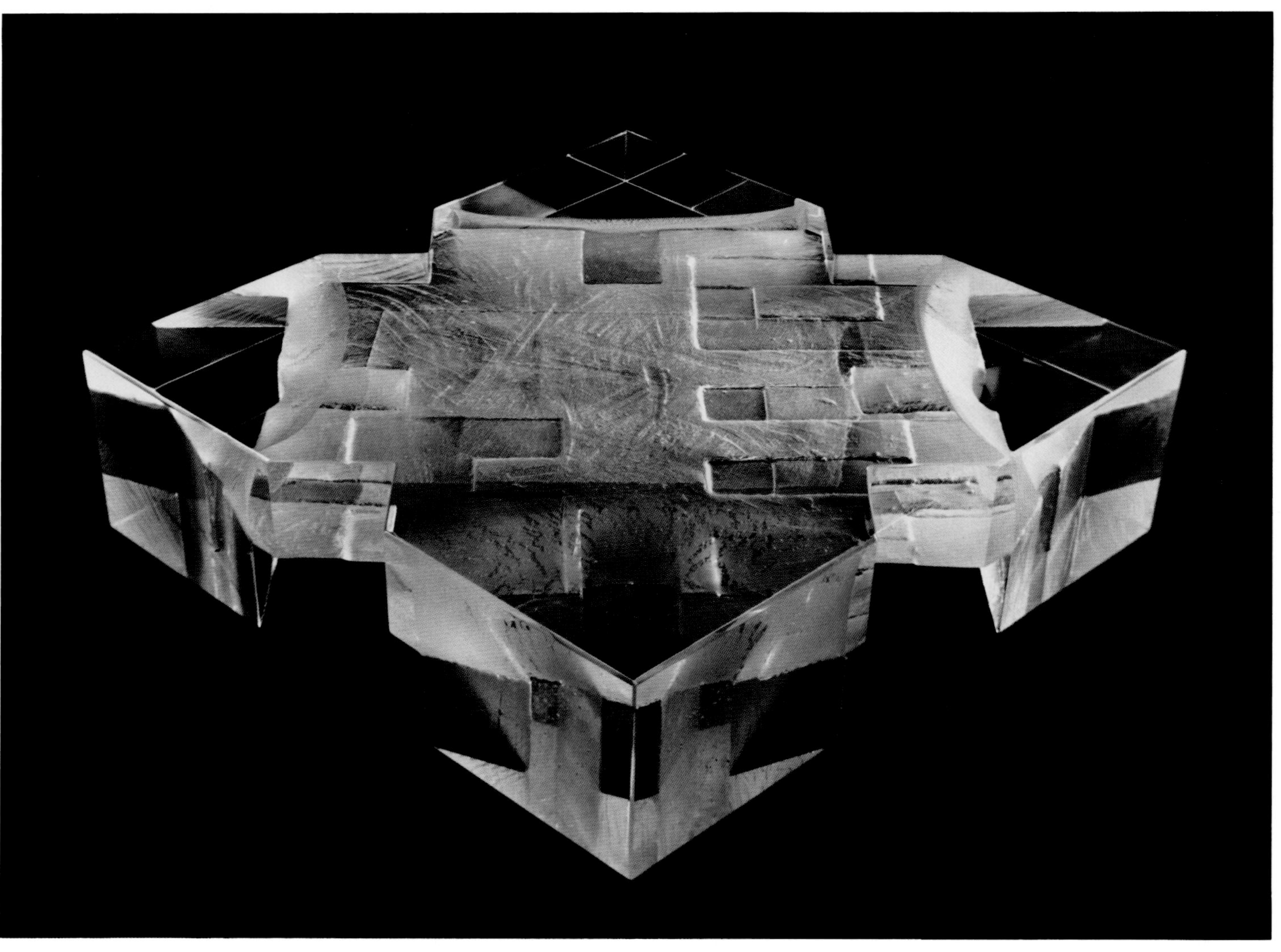

David Dowler. Four Bright Corners. 1980. Height 10".

we can to stimulate them to do their best work—in a medium appropriate to Steuben," Buechner stated in a 1981 interview.

Jewelry was one such medium. Steuben's first piece was a two-part pendant by Scottish designer Eric Hilton, introduced in March 1975; and the fall line of new pieces that year emphasized nothing so much as creative diversity. Hilton's designs inaugurated a special jewelry gallery that opened at the New York store in May 1977. His necklaces, bracelets, rings, and brooches were delicately engraved with "enigmatic motifs inspired by the mystic atmosphere of the artist's native lochs and moors."[8] In April 1977, for the first time in Steuben's history, early examples of newly introduced pieces were numbered and signed with the designer's mark in addition to the traditional Steuben signature. Among the works in this precedent-setting group of objects were five conceived by British designers Peter Aldridge and Eric Hilton, and some unique pieces both designed and executed by Laurence Whistler, England's leading glass engraver.[9] Whistler worked in diamond-point engraving, a technique not shown to advantage in the conditions of lighting and display available in the average household; the inclusion of his work underlined Buechner's stewardship of the craft tradition.

Single-artist Exhibitions

A series of important single-artist exhibitions was mounted during Buechner's tenure, beginning

David Dowler: Interception. 1980. Length 11¼".

Overleaf, left: Eric Hilton. Pendant of the Four Winds. 1979. 18-karat gold, width 2½".

Overleaf, right: Peter Aldridge. Passage: An Interval of Time. 1980. Height 10¾".

with the retrospective that marked George Thompson's February 1975 retirement after nearly forty years as an immensely prolific Steuben designer. Subsequent one-artist shows highlighted the works of Steuben designers James Carpenter, Eric Hilton, David Dowler, Peter Aldridge (who would later become director of design), and Donald Pollard.

Carpenter's works went on view in the New York gallery in March 1979. "An artist who uses glass as a medium," Carpenter was charged with creating new forms suitable to Steuben crystal. From this exhibition of contemporary vases and bowls, two of his most striking designs were chosen for the international "New Glass" exhibition, which toured major museums in the United States and abroad.[10]

David Dowler, who joined Steuben's design staff in 1972, broke tradition in October 1980 with an exhibition of eighteen abstract crystal sculptures and boxlike ceremonial vessels that for the first time combined both brilliant-polished and rough, unpolished areas for innovative textural contrast. One of Dowler's favorite techniques combined lenslike and flat cutting to create fascinating spatial and visual relationships in his objects, which change with the angle of view.[11] (Among Dowler's more traditional Steuben designs, the Eagle-Base Bowl in various versions has often been used as a gift of state.)

"When you treat a designer as an artist, he does what he *wants* to," Buechner observed. This supportive attitude helped foster such one-of-a-kind abstract works as Eric Hilton's

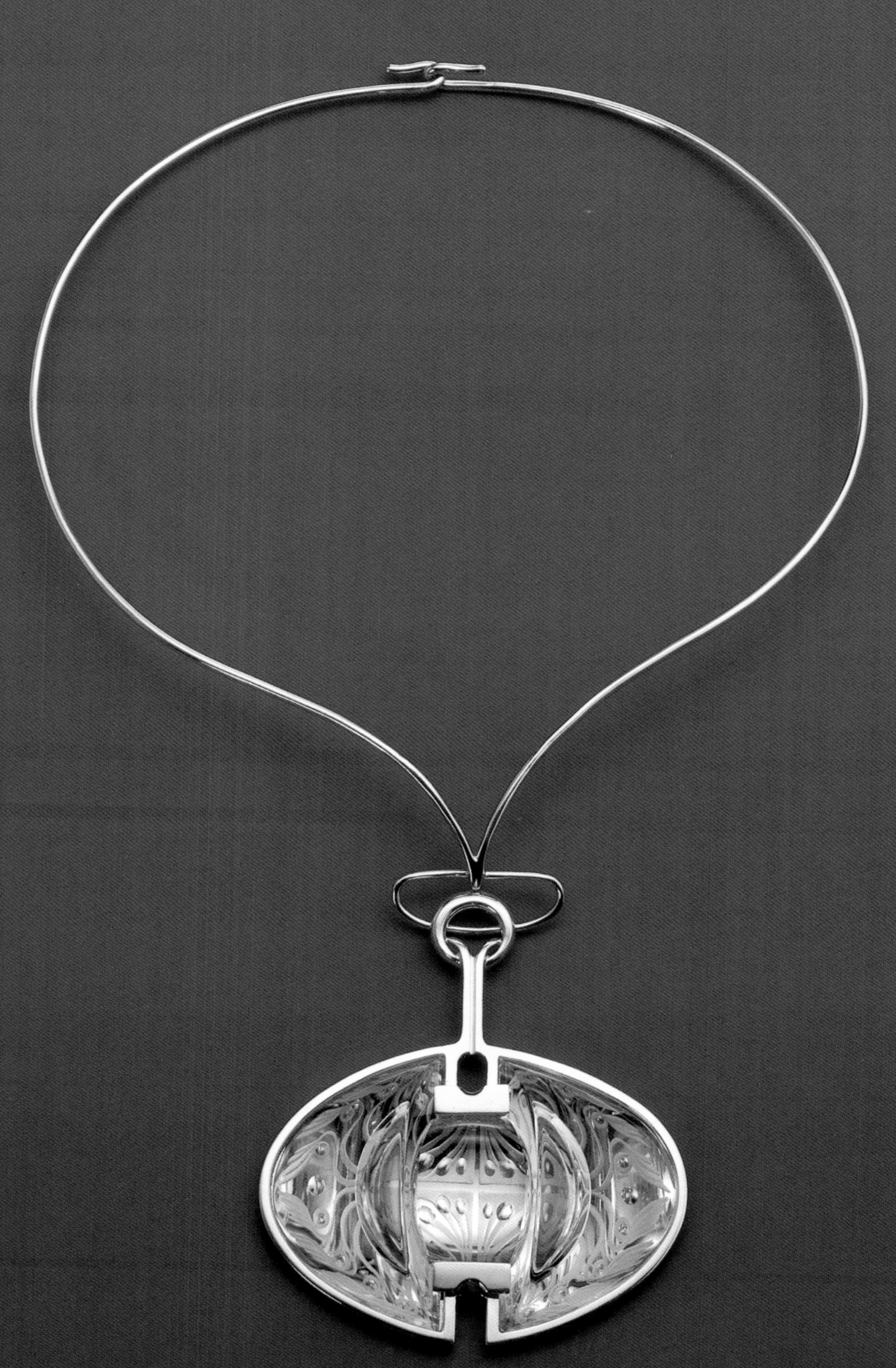

Finally, in the 1970s, a few of the glass designers and artists, who had been maturing in the previous decade, were brought closer to Steuben and encouraged to contribute directly from their personal experience and aesthetics. Eric Hilton's fascination with the sea and its endless reflective patterns, coupled with his own glass-casting and cutting background, finds tangible form in this seascape. The Wave (1975).

monumental Innerland and the crisply planed sculptures shown by Peter Aldridge in his single-artist exhibition at Steuben in April 1981. Innerland, which took four years to make, is perhaps the defining piece of the Buechner years. It is a modular crystal landscape comprised of many small, painstakingly engraved and sandblasted cubes expressing Hilton's concept of the unity of life and the inner being. Initially priced at a quarter of a million dollars because of the thousands of manhours required to plan, execute, and engrave it, Innerland was displayed at Steuben's new shop in November and December of 1980, before being shown at the Metropolitan Museum of Art as part of the "New Glass" exhibition. For the next several years, it was exhibited at regional Steuben shops around the United States. In 1986, Steuben presented it to The Corning Museum of Glass, where it remains on display as a popular addition to the permanent collection.

Innerland broke new ground for Steuben, both aesthetically and technically. It was followed by Peter Aldridge's 1981 "Passages" show of thirteen precisely cut prismatic pieces—far different from anything seen at Steuben's New York gallery. "Crystal is the ideal medium in which to express options and illusions in space," Aldridge said, noting that the works convey an idea of passage in time and space, combining concepts of modern physics with ancient mystical perceptions about the nature of reality.[12] These pristine works demonstrated the growing sophistication of Steuben's technology; many of the prismatic planes were invisibly joined with a special epoxy having the same index of refraction as the glass itself.

In a kind of aesthetic counterbalance to the forward-looking glass of Hilton and Aldridge, Donald Pollard was honored with a retrospective exhibition of fifty pieces, "Masterworks in Crystal," that opened in October 1981 to mark his retirement after thirty-five years as a Steuben designer. Fittingly, Pollard's final masterwork, the Crown of Oberon, four years in the making,

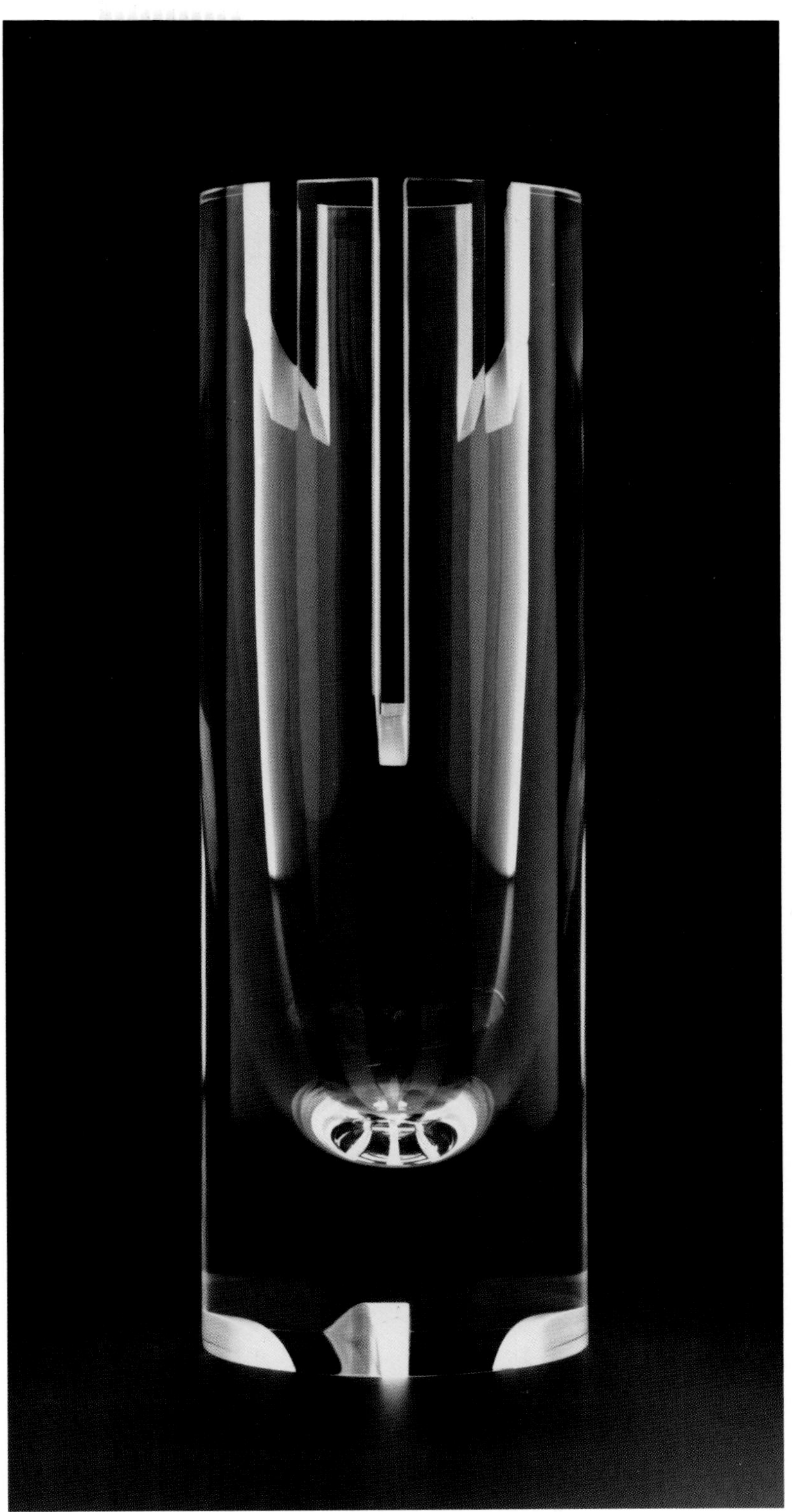

Peter Aldridge. Channeled Vessel. 1981. Height 14½".

Eric Hilton. Innerland (detail).

Opposite:
Eric Hilton. Innerland.

Overleaf:
Luciana G. Roselli. Tulip Bowl. 1981.
Diameter 12½".

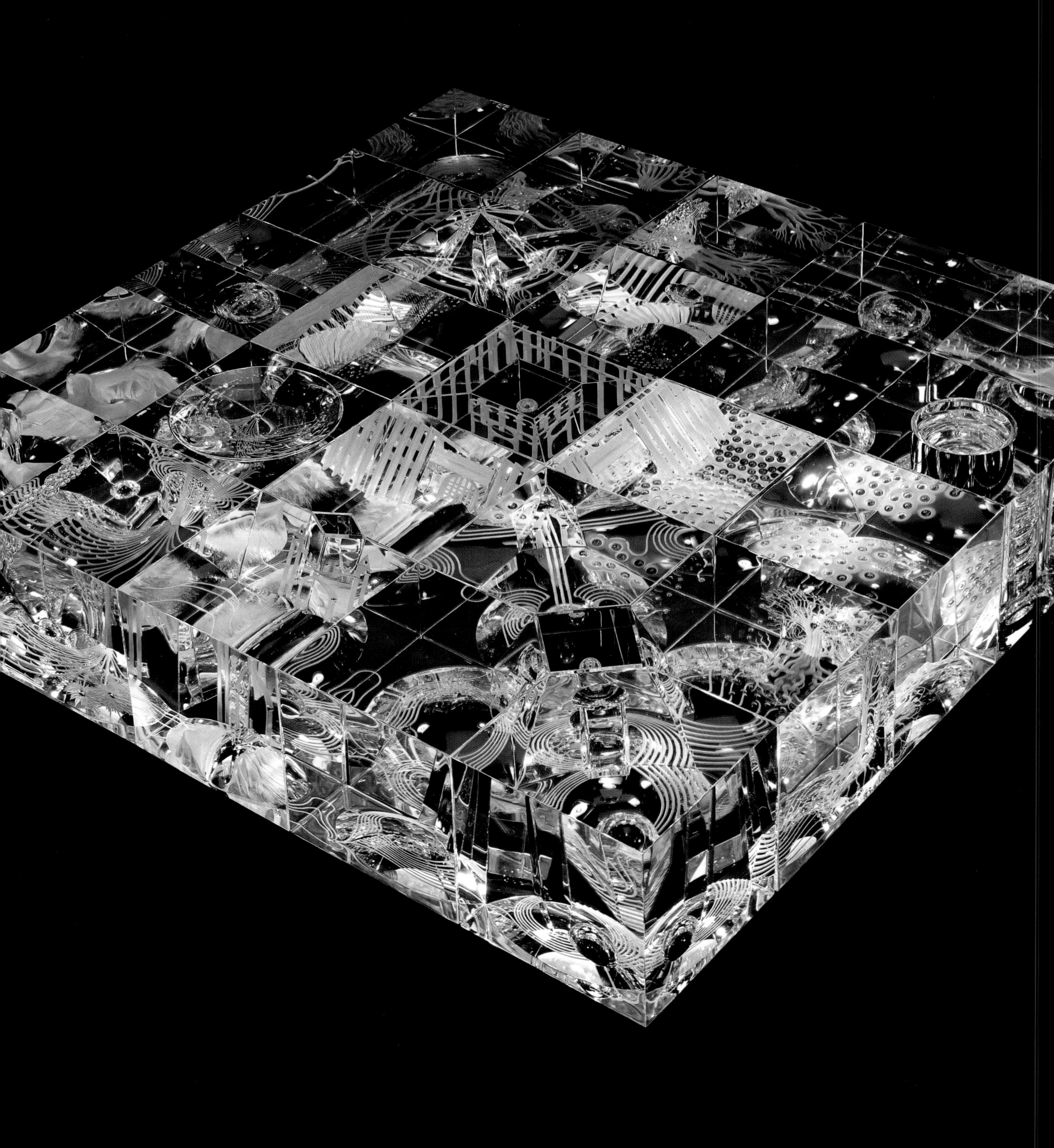

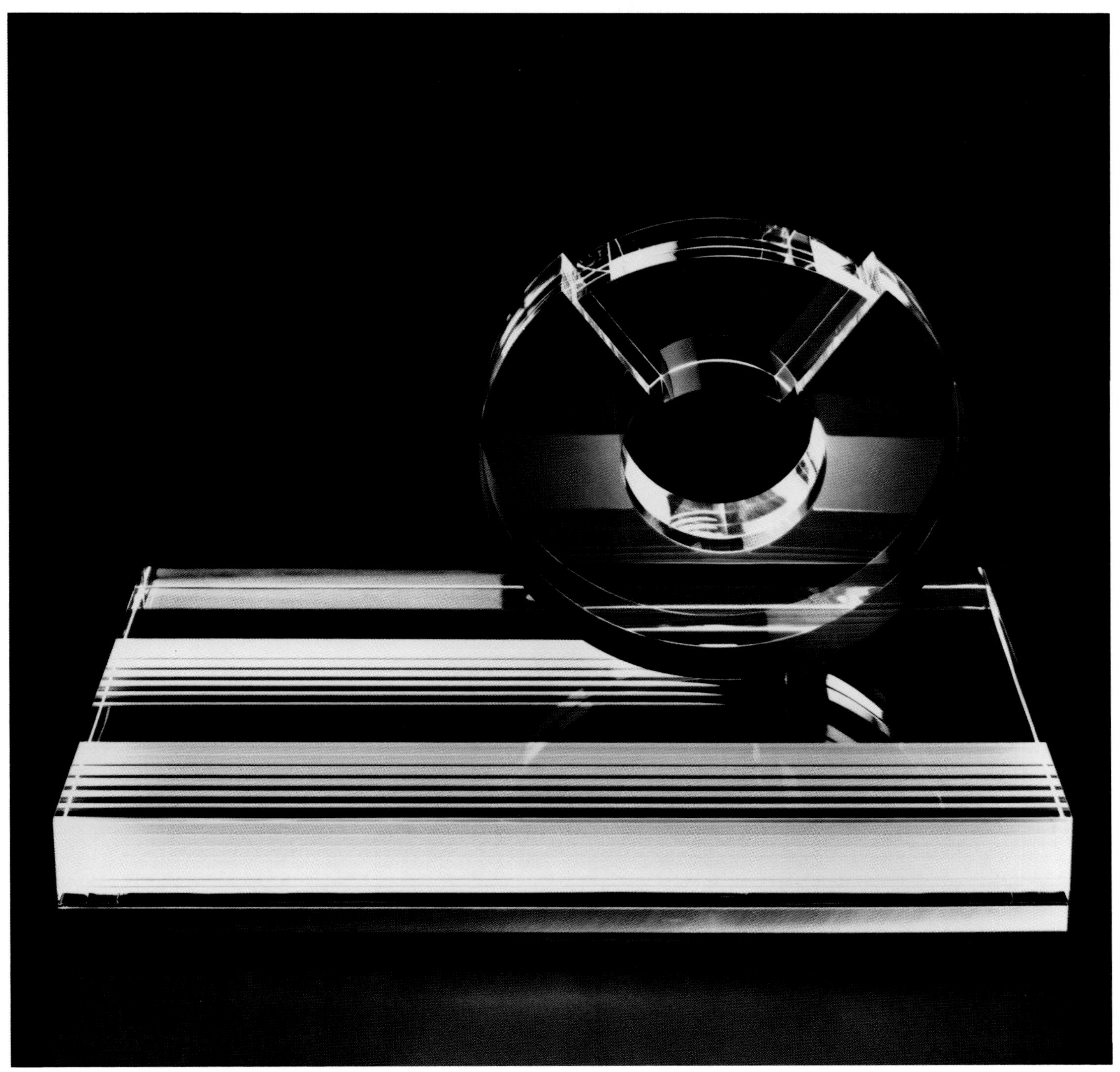

Artist-craftsmen like Peter Aldridge possess the unequaled ability to fulfill accurately their intentions. In Encounter (1981), his precisionist attitude is expressed both in shape and production process.

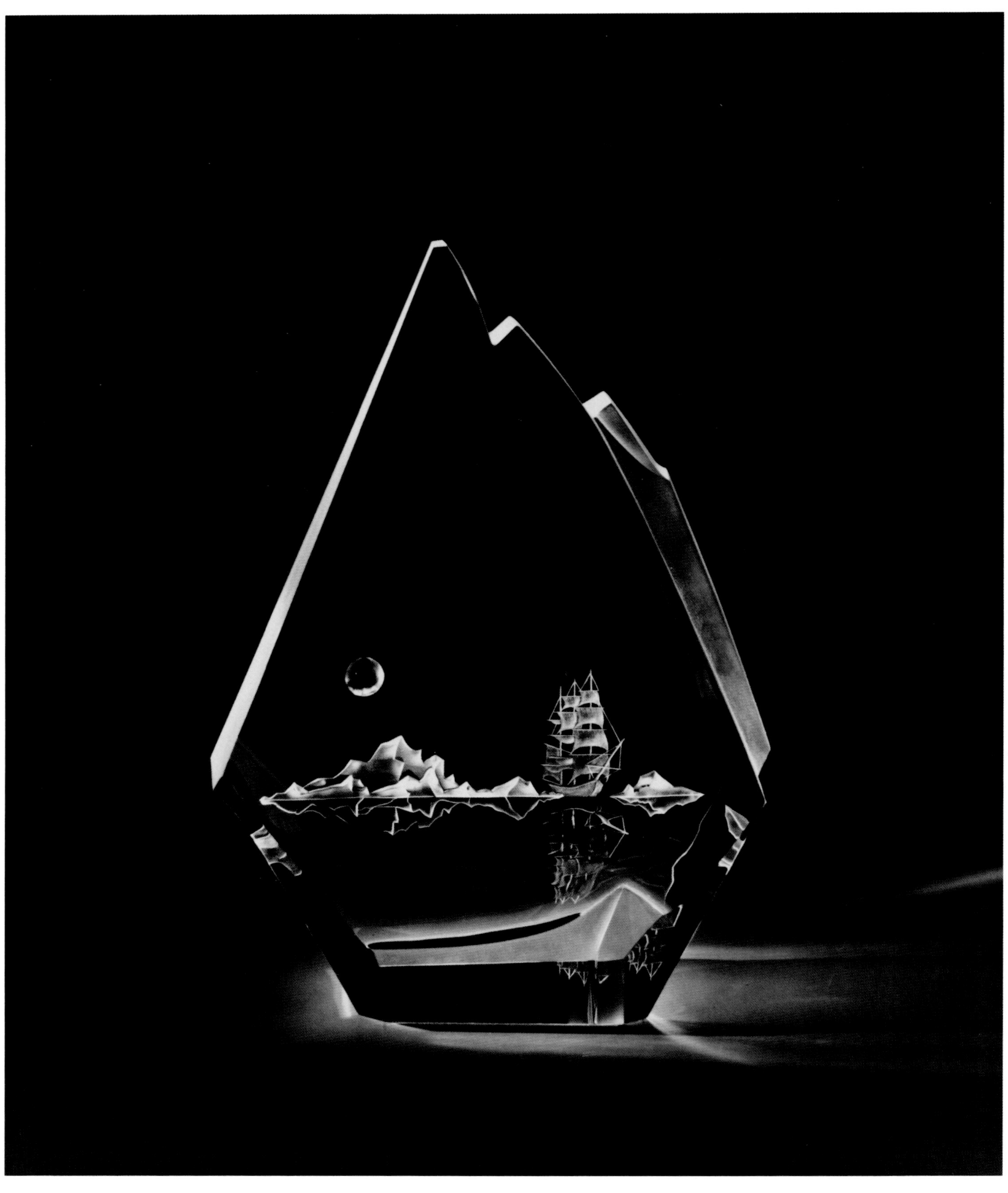

was introduced at the same time. Inspired by scenes from "A Midsummer Night's Dream," this lavish addition to the one-of-a-kind Steuben Masterwork series was a blown crystal dome surmounted by a jeweled crystal-and-gold butterfly. Pollard designed the glass, while illustrator Beni Montresor created the images for engraving by master copper wheel artisan Ladislav Havlik. The delicate gold work, fashioned by Louis Feron, was set with diamonds, emeralds, pearls, and a magnificent tourmaline.

New Technology, Old Craftsmanship

During Buechner's watch, Steuben's new stock designs began to reflect technological progress at the factory. Susan Smyly's sinuous Roman Cat, for example, was made on a new glass press that could produce twenty pieces in an hour. Well aware that pressing was regarded as "typically imitative and cheap," Buechner liked to describe these objects as "molded" to avoid negative connotations. "But we realized pressing gave us another medium, a way to form glass differently than you could by cutting or blowing. For example, in a mold you have absolute control and can handle curves precisely," he explained.

In addition to the pressing operation, other new technologies allowed Steuben to experiment with designing and forming glass in new ways. For example, mechanically perfect faceting of some prismatic pieces was made possible by a finely calibrated machine, while flexible shaft engraving—using an instrument like a dentist's drill—resulted in tonal shifts that could not be achieved with the essentially sculptural copper wheel process. Buechner saw these advances as a means of fostering new glassmaking skills unrelated to the traditional gaffering ones where a gather of glass is blown and shaped with tools by hand. He did not view the use of technology as compromising, "as long as it is not done with deceptive intent."

While embracing new techniques, Steuben continued to emphasize the importance of craftsmanship. Buechner invited several American and European glass masters to Corning to assist in the training of apprentice glassmakers. Willie Anderson, a Swede, visited three times to take part in six-month-long factory training programs, while Laurence Whistler from England and Gianni Toso from Murano, Italy, also participated.

Lighter Moments

Though the Buechner years were a time of serious artistic exploration for Steuben, there were lighter moments as well as concessions to popular taste. In the spring of 1982, continuing the Steuben tradition of spring flower shows, nine prominent New York City florists were invited to design floral centerpieces contained in crystal vessels of their choosing. Under the direction of New York interior decorator (and frequent Steuben advisor) Mario Buatta, dubbed "The Prince of Chintz," the show attracted 42,000 visitors during its two-week run from April 27 to May 8.[13]

Steuben was often in the news as a gift of state during these years, despite the company's policy of keeping a discreet silence on its sales to the government. For the wedding of Britain's Prince Charles and Lady Diana Spencer in 1981, Mrs. Ronald Reagan selected as the official gift of state the Crusader's Bowl, an elliptical piece designed by Zevi Blum and engraved by Ronald Erlacher in high relief ("hochschnitt") around the rim. The one-of-a-kind bowl took 670 hours to engrave; it was made in 1975 for a client who did not complete the purchase. When the bowl was displayed along with the other royal wedding gifts, a reporter tracked down its $75,000 retail price, setting off a controversy that obliged Mrs. Reagan to state she had obtained it for just $800—well under the $1,000 government ceiling for state gifts. Though Steuben declined

Opposite: James Houston. Arctic Exploration. 1981. Height 7¾".

Overleaf, left: Susan Smyly. Roman Cat. 1979. Length 5¼".

Overleaf, right: Lloyd Atkins. Tetrasphere. 1974. Height 7½".

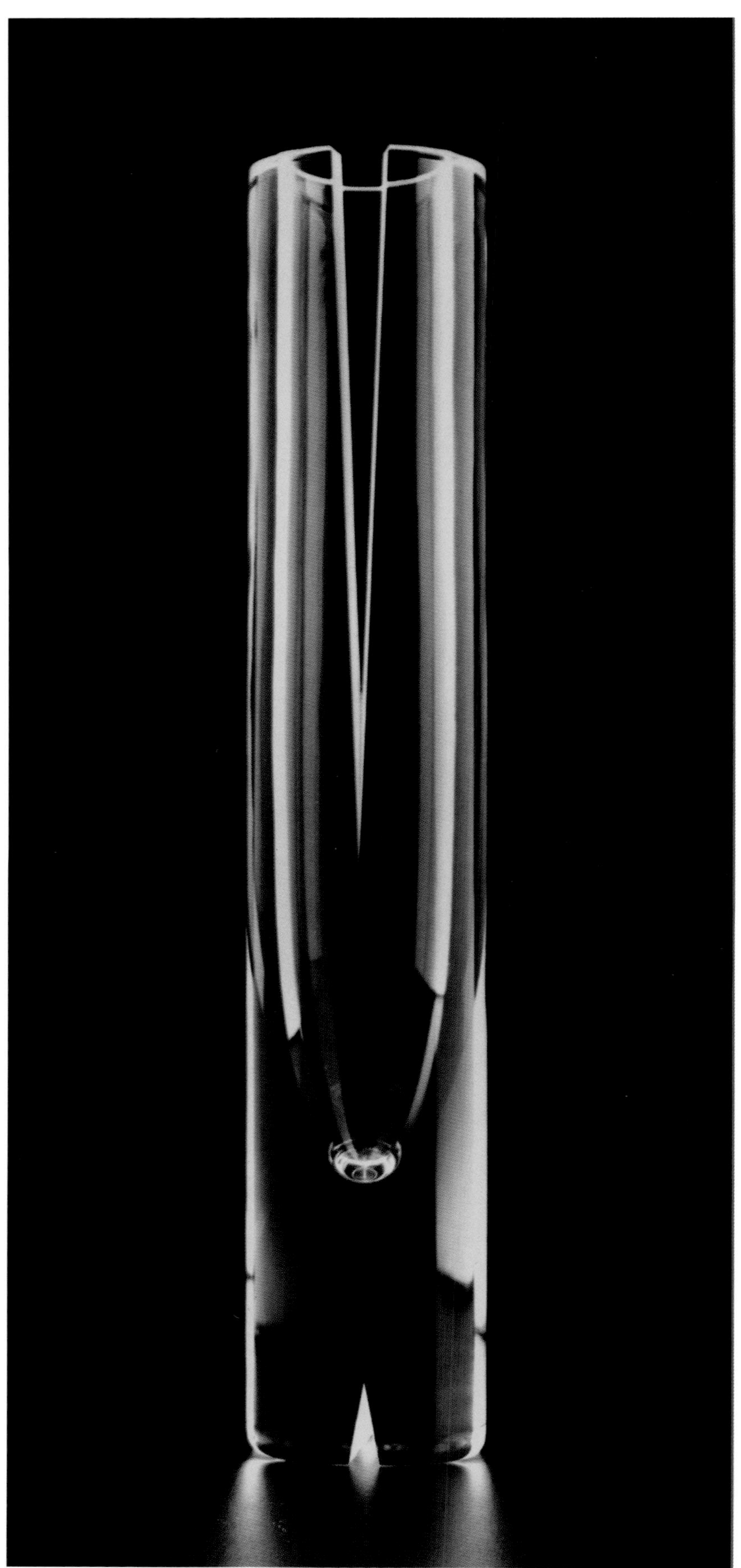

Peter Aldridge. Cleft Vase. 1981. Height 19".

comment, as always, a thick book of press clippings attests to media interest in both the costly bowl and the First Lady's "remarkable bargaining skills."[14]

Function versus Ornament

Summing up his years as president in an epilogue to the first edition of this book (which went to press in 1982), Tom Buechner touched upon an issue that continues to resound at Steuben. "The question of functional versus ornamental pieces is constantly before us," he wrote. "The only way to make functional objects to sell at prices comparable to those charged by other companies is to make them in comparable quantities. The more you make, the more efficient you can be. And the fastest way to make glass by hand is on the assembly line . . . Arthur Houghton chose not to do this, so the cost of our stemware rose above our competition"—and was discontinued for lack of sales.[15] Buechner investigated ways to offset Steuben's artistic investments in contemporary sculptural pieces with a new line of stemware that would be less costly to produce than earlier handmade versions. He proposed establishing "an additional manufacturing procedure, especially for stemware, using whatever system seems best in terms of both quality and efficiency. If we couple this with our glass and design, we should be able to resume our place in the 3,500-year-old competition to make the best drinking glasses and functional vessels measured both by quality and acceptability."[16] But Arthur Houghton was unswerving in his opposition to any kind of volume-oriented production, and Buechner's proposal to invest in new stemware facilities was not carried out.[17]

The Changing of the Guard

While president of Steuben, Buechner was deeply involved with other commitments in

Corning, most notably in his role as president of The Corning Museum of Glass. Corning had been hit with a disastrous flood during Hurricane Agnes in June 1972. The entire downtown area, the Corning Glass Works factories and corporate headquarters, the Steuben factory, and the Museum of Glass were devastated (though remarkably little of the glass collection was damaged). The company immediately turned its resources to community recovery, and plans were initiated for a new Museum of Glass, which opened in 1981. Buechner was instrumental in shaping plans for the new museum, and tireless in his involvement with other aspects of Corning's civic renovation.

With a growing slate of civic and corporate responsibilities as well as his personal goals as an artist to consider, Buechner relinquished the day-to-day operation of Steuben in July 1982 to his successor, Davis A. Chiodo. He was appointed chairman of Steuben Glass, a title Arthur Houghton had held until then. Both Buechner and Chiodo reported to James R. (Jamie) Houghton, Corning Glass Works' chief strategic officer, who was soon to succeed his brother Amory as company president. Buechner was also named chair of the Market Street Restoration Agency, while retaining his titles as chair of the Corning Glass Works Foundation and the Steuben Advisory Group, and as president of both The Corning Museum of Glass and the Rockwell Museum, which now occupies Corning's restored City Hall.[18]

As a highly visible representative of Corning Glass Works in these community endeavors, Buechner nonetheless maintained an ongoing interest in Steuben. His legacy as a champion of the history and art of glassmaking was carried forward by a notable group of exhibitions at Steuben's New York shop during Davis Chiodo's tenure.

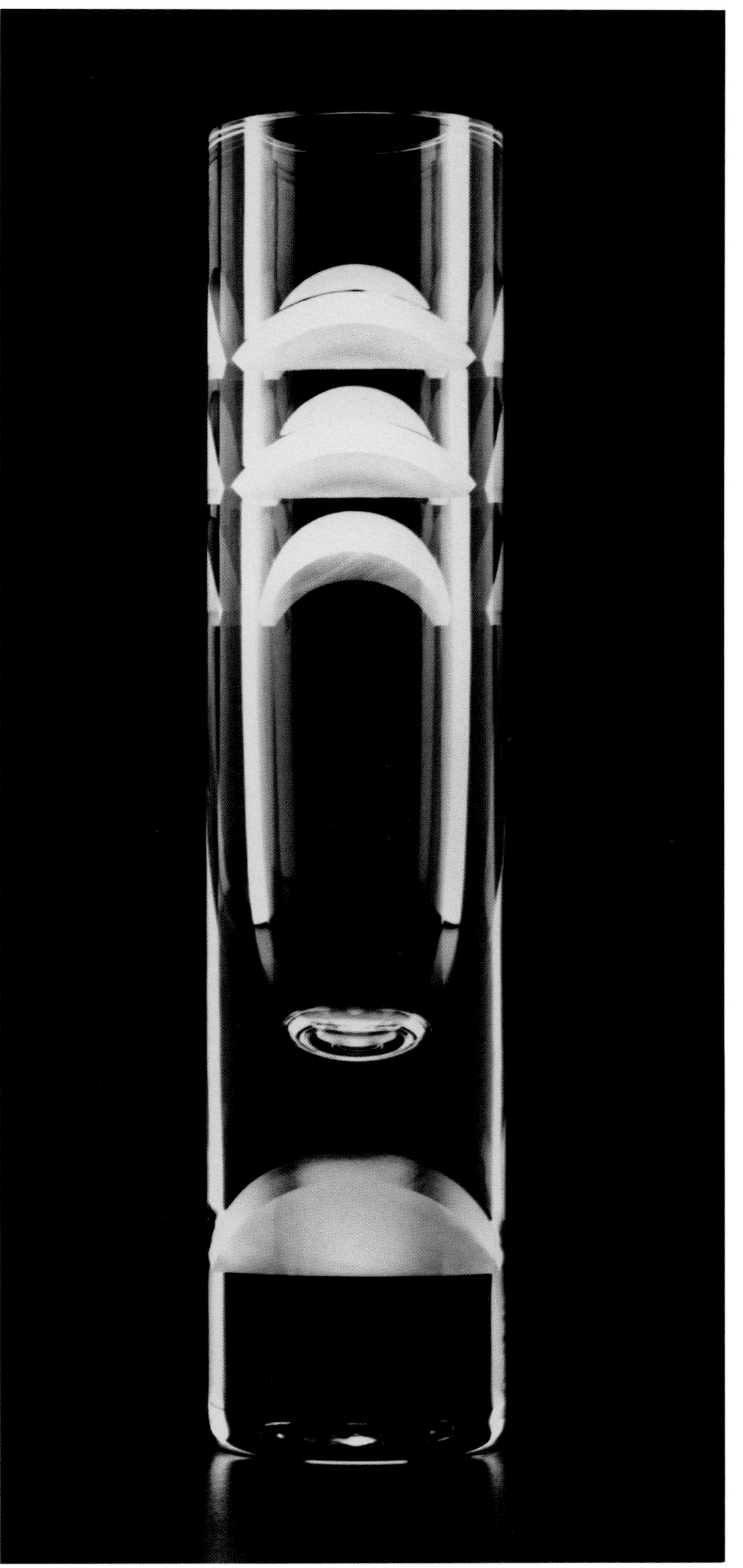

Peter Aldridge. Pierced Vessel. 1981. Height 15½".

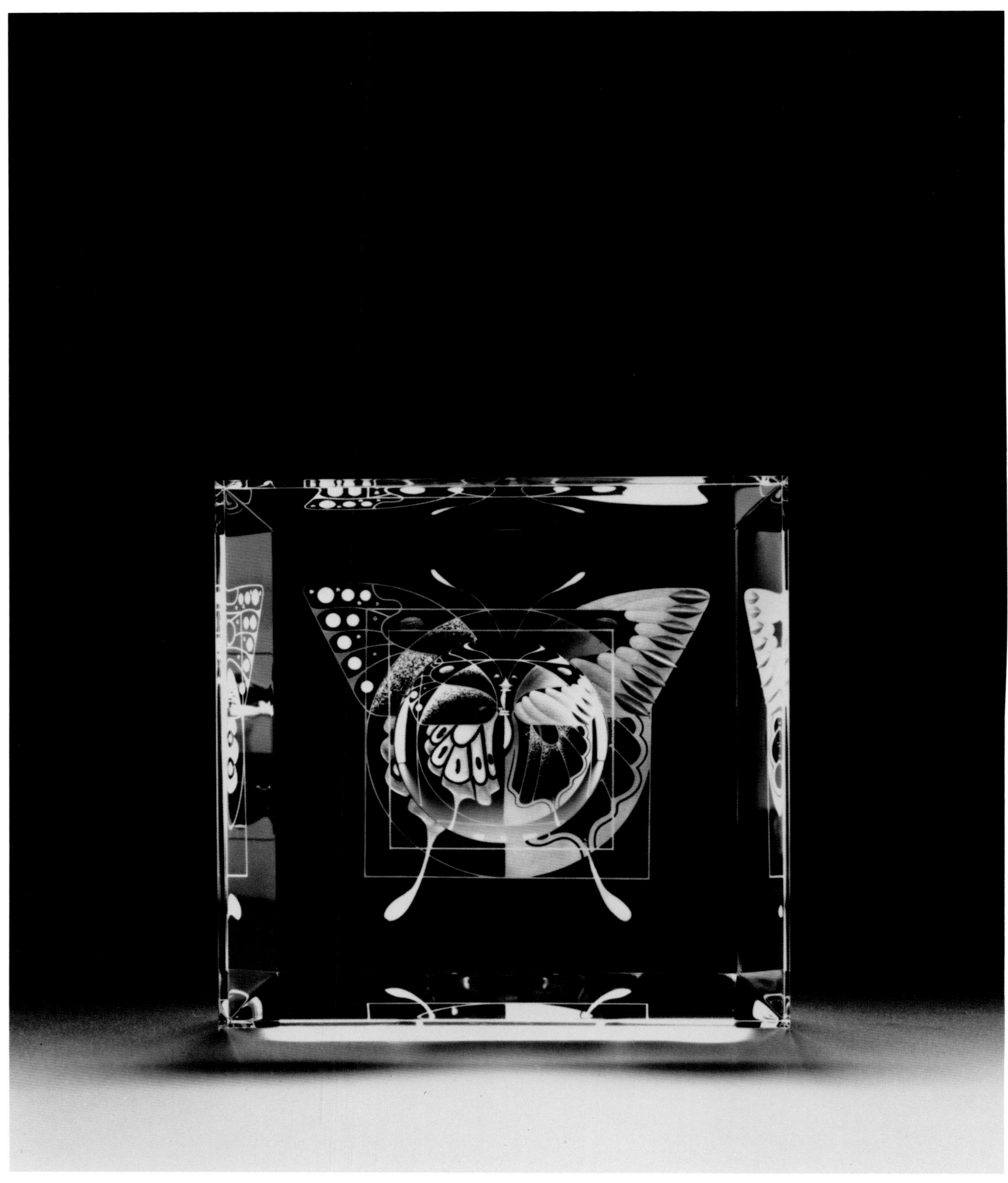

Bernard X. Wolff. Dreaming Butterfly. 1981. Height 6".

Peter Aldridge. The George Meany Human Rights Award. 1981. Height 15".

Peter Aldridge. Passage II. 1981. Height 3".

Donald Pollard. Fire Ball. 1981. Height 5½".

X.
STEUBEN IN TRANSITION: 1982–1992

Arthur Houghton had been Steuben's president for nearly forty years; Tom Buechner for ten. In the next decade, however, Steuben would welcome a succession of three new leaders, each recruited from the executive ranks of Corning Glass Works. Presidents Davis Chiodo, Kirtland Gardner, and Susan King would all confront the same basic challenge: how to make Steuben more businesslike and profitable, while meeting changing customer and corporate expectations.

The promise of operational independence Arthur Houghton extracted from Corning's directors had been honored at Steuben for fifty years, but corporate priorities were shifting as Corning Glass Works transformed itself into a high-tech conglomerate. In April 1983, Jamie Houghton succeeded his brother Amory as Chairman of Corning Glass Works, soon after completing a major strategy study that underlined the need for better financial results in every company division.[1] Self-sustaining if not always greatly profitable, Steuben had been largely exempt from corporate scrutiny, valued more for its image than its revenues. But much as Jamie Houghton appreciated Steuben's role in setting the benchmark for corporate design, it was clear that he also expected a better bottom-line performance from Corning's "crown jewel."[2]

Davis Chiodo: A Bridge to Change

Against this backdrop of corporate evolution, Davis Chiodo—an architect by training—arrived at Steuben in July 1982 after spending twenty years in design-related jobs at Corning Glass Works, the last as director of facilities engineering.[3] New president Chiodo was soon

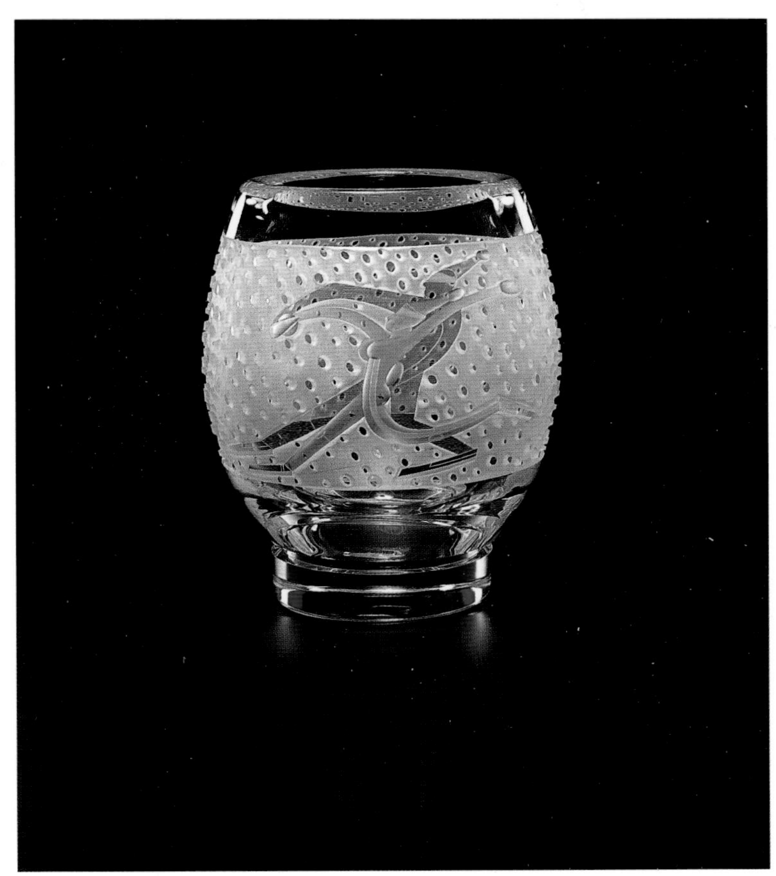

Dan Dailey. Ice Dancers. 1983. Height 9½".

Opposite: Bernard X. Wolff. Hilltown. 1982. Height 8¾".

invited to Wye Plantation for a strategy session with Arthur Houghton, who proposed a regular schedule of meetings "if you wish."[4] Chiodo dutifully went, and like his successors, was thereafter careful to include Houghton in the informational loop. Though nominally retired, Houghton kept close tabs on the New York office through frequent conversations with trusted associate Sally Walker, who succeeded Robert Leavy as executive vice president for operations in 1962.

Updating Gifts of State

Within months, Houghton proposed a plan of "corrective action" on the Gifts of State program, which he deemed the wellspring of Steuben's prestige. "Steuben is in a precarious position today," he wrote to Chiodo. "It does not have a close association with the White House or the Chief of Protocol (or) a reserve collection of items that can be used as Gifts of State. Unless Steuben takes action without delay, it risks other American products being used as the primary Gifts of State. If this takes place, the process will be irreversible. Steuben will lose its preeminent position. Its prestige will disappear and its future will be a disaster."[5] He proposed putting Sally Walker in charge of a new department to strengthen the Gifts of State program. While retaining her title as Steuben's executive vice president, Walker—as well as the other department heads she supervised—would then report directly to Chiodo, giving him more latitude to manage.

Chiodo adopted the suggestion gratefully, and the arrangement worked well. Walker established solid relationships within the State Department and Office of Protocol, visiting Washington frequently until her official retirement in 1987. Her efforts ensured that Steuben was often in the news as an important gift of state through the Ronald Reagan and George Bush administrations.

Guarding Tradition

Despite such positive contributions, Arthur Houghton often criticized his successors' efforts to make Steuben more businesslike, putting a damper on ideas he feared might turn it from the high-minded course he had set.[6] "The priority mission of Steuben is to enhance the reputation of Corning Glass Works, not to add to its sales and profitability. Although Steuben should carry itself, it should be judged not on volume and profits but on how successful it is in performing its mission," he advised Chiodo, who wanted to open more shops and expand sales through a direct mail program.[7] When young Amory Houghton, III (who joined Steuben as vice president for sales in 1983) groused that Steuben's prices were much higher than those of its competitors, Houghton wrote Chiodo, "Please impress upon (Mory) that Steuben does not make glass merchandise. It makes objects of art in crystal."[8] And when Chiodo suggested renovating the New York shop, Houghton cautioned, "we should go very slow, perhaps redoing one area each year . . . a complete change would shock our conservative clientele."[9] Ironically, Houghton himself had earlier proposed an entirely new shop in a townhouse "on the East Side of Madison Avenue" with room for design and executive offices, a cafeteria, dining rooms, and rentable floors for outside tenants.[10]

Design, Production, and Exhibitions under Chiodo

Designwise, Chiodo supported the modernization of the line that began under Buechner—and like Buechner, he gave design director Paul Schulze and his team great artistic latitude.[11] During Chiodo's tenure, Steuben designers David Dowler, Peter Aldridge, and Eric Hilton maintained an office in a small house across from the factory in Corning, while Schulze and his

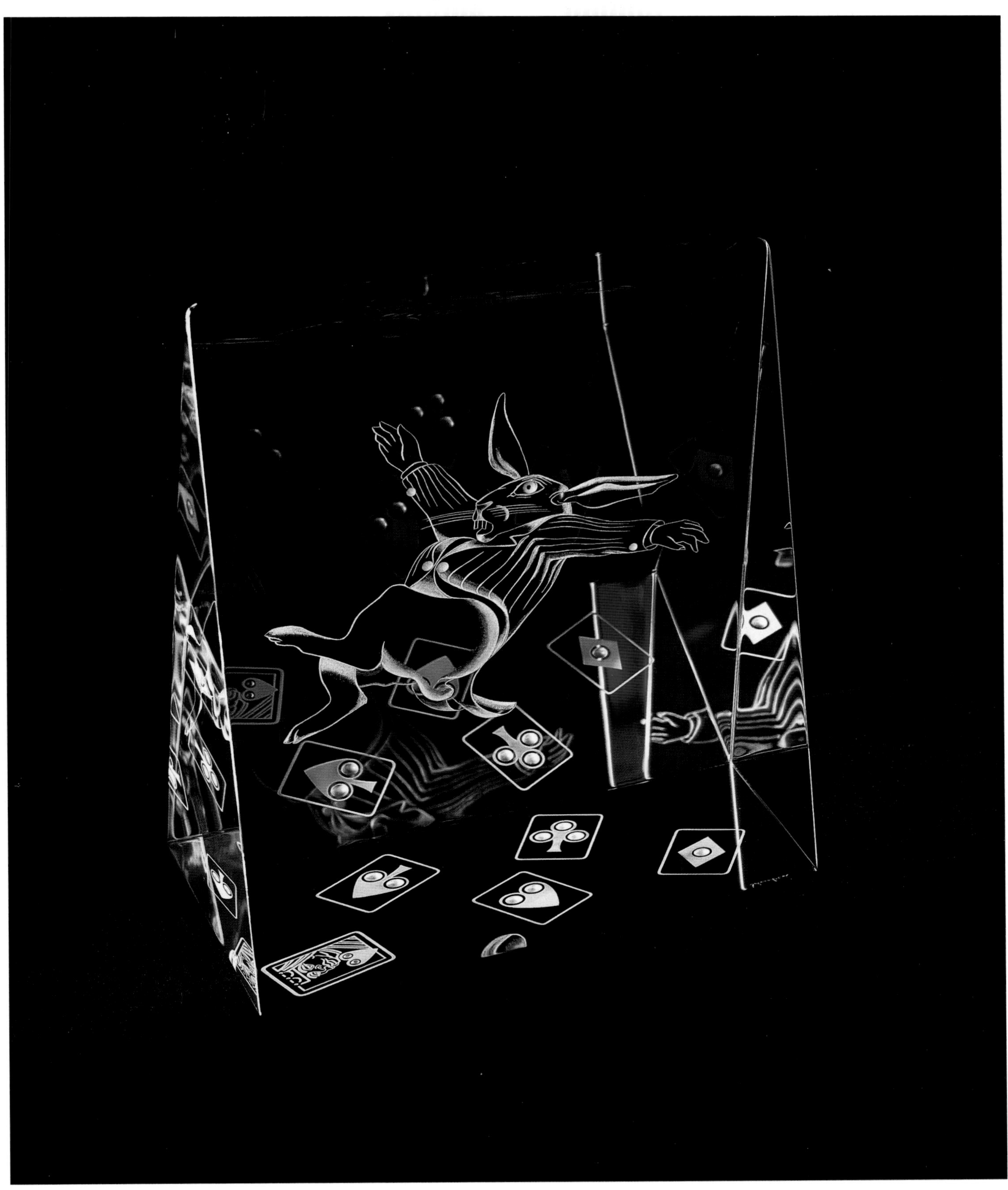

Eric Hilton. Alice in Wonderland. 1983. Height 6¾".

Eric Hilton. Deco Vase. 1986. Height 14".

assistant Bernard X. Wolff, along with designer Neil Cohen, who arrived in 1984, worked from the New York City headquarters.[12] Chiodo's goal was to increase sales by bringing together Steuben's designers and its marketing and sales team into a cohesive unit in support of "a higher aesthetic that would work in the marketplace." But sales slipped, partly because scheduling and manpower problems at the factory hampered the timely shipment of orders.[13] A rebuild of the main Steuben tank in early 1984 also contributed to production delays, affecting financial projections for the year.[14] Among other strategies, Chiodo considered making a line of bowls, decanters, and stemware without lead, but did not follow through with the commercial production of the unleaded pieces.[15]

In the New York shop, meanwhile, a series of special exhibitions intended to attract new customers bore the imprint of Buechner's ongoing influence. "One Dot at a Time: Masterpieces of 18th Century Stipple Engraving," included thirty-nine masterpieces of English glass decorated by Dutch engravers with a painstaking technique in which a diamond-point tool is used to stipple images "one dot at a time." The show opened in April 1983 with a benefit preview for the English-speaking Union, and drew 24,000 visitors to Steuben in three weeks.[16] "One of a Kind," a collection of thirty unique Steuben masterworks, was on view later that summer. Anchored by Eric Hilton's Innerland (priced at $275,000), the show also introduced six new Steuben designs, including sculptural pieces by Peter Aldridge, Eric Hilton, David Dowler, and Jane Osborn-Smith, and by guest British designer Simon Whistler. Works by Donald Pollard and Lloyd Atkins were also included in the show, while replicas of important gifts of state underlined Steuben's preeminence in that area.

The following March, "Emile Gallé: Dreams into Glass" was mounted in the New York shop. It previewed the first major United

States exhibition of works by French glass artist Emile Gallé—a show organized for The Corning Museum of Glass by Buechner and associate curator William Warmus. Focusing on Gallé's late period, which celebrated his fantasies of the natural world, "Dreams into Glass" was immensely popular. Following an opening reception for the New York Blood Center, more than 35,000 guests streamed through the shop during the show's three-week run.[17]

Steuben's Fifty-year Retrospective

But the high point of Chiodo's tenure was the retrospective exhibition "50 Years on 5th," organized to celebrate the 1934 opening of the first New York shop. The show was launched on October 3, 1984, with a glittering benefit reception for the Municipal Art Society, followed by a VIP dinner at nearby Lever House. Jacqueline Kennedy Onassis, resplendent in silver chain metal, was honorary chair of the event, along with Mr. and Mrs. Amory Houghton, Jr.[18]

Organized by Paul Schulze with installation design by Bernard X. Wolff, the widely publicized exhibition attracted 36,000 visitors in three weeks. It centered on forty representative Steuben designs from the previous five decades, selected by an advisory committee of decorative arts curators from major American museums. Steuben's design staff chose additional pieces, including "New York, New York," Paul Schulze's seventeen-inch abstract "city of glass" sculpture designed especially for the exhibition and featured on its catalogue cover.[19] In a *New York Times* review, Douglas C. McGill described the curated portion of "50 years on 5th" as "a timeline of taste in American decorative arts since the 1930s," in contrast to the "commercially popular" pieces chosen by Steuben, which represented "the personal artistic tastes of individual designers."[20] The review quoted Paul Schulze's assertion that the exhibition's contemporary slant demonstrated "the increasing influence at Steuben of designers who consider themselves primarily artists," a view that Schulze expressed in other media interviews as well.[21]

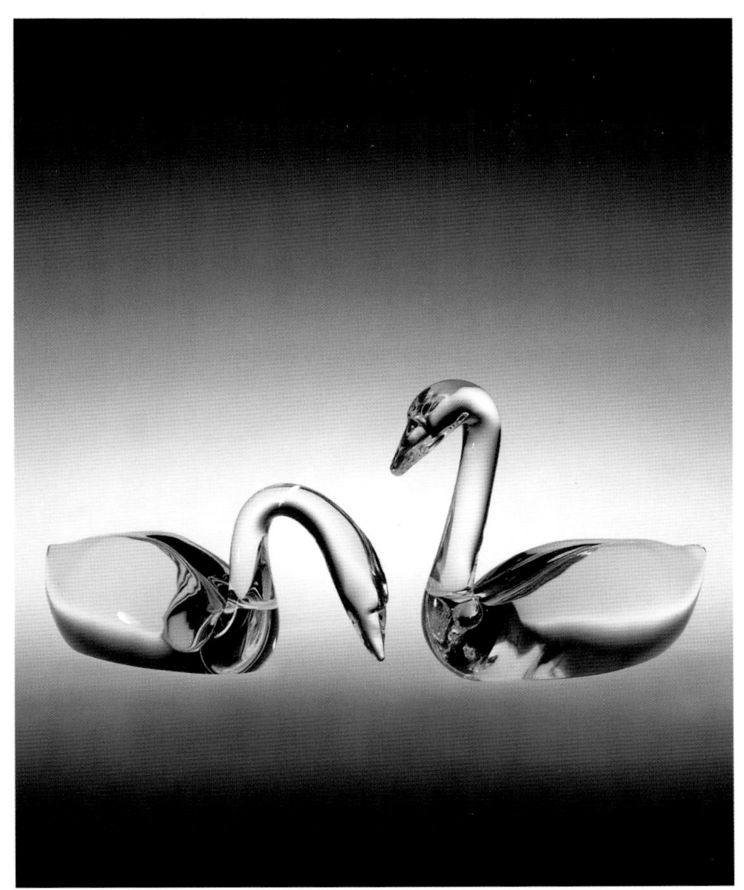

Lloyd Atkins. Pair of Swans. 1984.

Arthur Houghton was probably not pleased with such publicity. The matter of Steuben's design direction was a sore point with the retired but still influential chairman, who criticized the design department's growing autonomy and considered its focus on abstract sculpture a risky abandonment of tradition. Soon after "50 Years on 5th" closed, Houghton squared off in a note to Chiodo. "I am deeply concerned about our Design Department. It should be the strongest of all our departments. It is the weakest," he wrote, laying out a blunt five-point remedy: "Let me present my opinions. 1) The policy of design must be set by the President of Steuben Glass. 2) It is the responsibility of the Director of Design to implement the policy set by the president. 3) The personnel of the Design Department must realize

Bernard X. Wolff. Balloon Rally. 1985. Height 10¼".

they are employed as designers and not as artists . . . to design in the determined style of Steuben. 4) The Design Department should strive to design objects that will appeal to the customers . . . not attempt to educate the customers nor to change their tastes. 5) The Sales Department is the customer of the Design Department. It, not the Design Department, should determine which objects will be made and offered for sale. Please give this your consideration. I shall welcome your views."[22] To this last in a series of increasingly critical letters from Houghton, Chiodo stiffly replied, "While the design department can always do better, I would not call it the weakest department in Steuben. Your opinions on how the department should be run do not differ greatly from mine. There are, however, some points worthy of further discussion."[23] No discussion is recorded, but a few weeks after this exchange, in January 1985, Davis Chiodo stepped down.

Kirt Gardner: Setting Business Goals

Kirtland C. Gardner, III, had been at Corning Glass Works for nearly thirty years when Jamie Houghton appointed him president of Steuben on February 1, 1985. A seasoned executive, Gardner rose through the ranks of production management, serving as president of Corning Glass Works of Canada Ltd. and as Corning's general manager for Latin America. Though he lacked the design background of his predecessors, Gardner's management credentials and familiarity with the Corning culture were considered positive factors in helping Steuben meet corporate goals.[24]

Though the presidential succession at Steuben drew little public notice, considerably more publicity attended the presentation of two Steuben bowls to President of the United States Ronald Reagan and his vice president George Bush at their January 25 inaugural luncheon.[25] The engraved bowls, designed by Paul Schulze after classic pieces of Paul Revere silver, were presented on network television by Arthur Houghton's senator, Charles Mathias, Jr., of Maryland. Thirty Steuben Tetrahedrons were also given to the Inaugural Committee at this VIP event, which was attended by top Corning Glass executives. Clearly, Sally Walker's re-energized Gifts of State program was now in high gear, helping Steuben carry out its mandate to "add luster" to the Corning Glass Works image.

In Steuben's New York shop that April, the traditional spring flower show took on an Elizabethan air with "A Shakespeare Garden." Joseph Papp of New York's Public Theater gave a reading at the preview reception, where fruits and flowers mentioned by the bard were arranged in Steuben vases and bowls, including the new limited-edition Twist Collection—a vase, bowl, and candlesticks by David Dowler. Later that year, the commemorative show "Steuben Crystal in Private Collections: An Exhibition Dedicated to the Work of the Institute of International Education" opened at the Glass Center in Corning. Putting the Gifts of State program in the limelight, the show included duplicates of thirty-one pieces of crystal presented to royals and other heads of state. Concurrently, the second edition of *Steuben Crystal in Private Collections*, picturing one-of-a-kind gifts of state presented to Queen Elizabeth, the Pope, Nikita Khrushchev, and Emperor Hirohito, among others, was published.[26]

A Repositioning Plan

Though Kirt Gardner resided in Corning (where he also administered the Corning Glass Center and attached Steuben factory), he was nonetheless deeply immersed in affairs at the New York office. Within months, he formulated a comprehensive three-year repositioning proposal—a broad set of strategies intended to transform Steuben from a break-even business to a consistently profitable one.[27] The plan had five

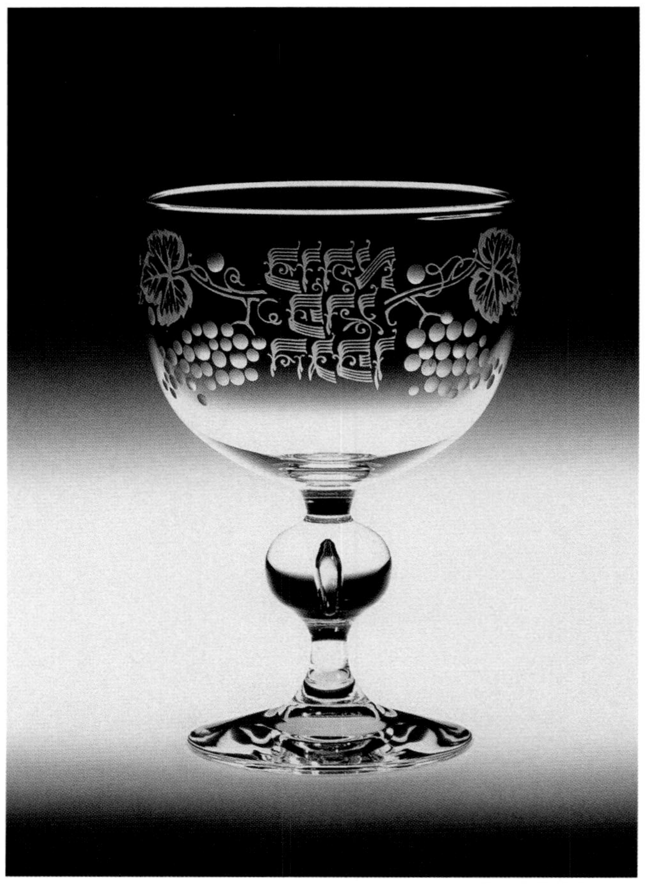

Bernard X. Wolff. Kiddush Cup. 1984. Height 7½".

objectives: achieving sales growth, improving profitability, "strengthening Steuben's position as one of the world's premiere crystals through product and image," developing new buyers by means of "special—but not exclusive—attention to contemporary designs," and finally, using production capabilities in a more efficient and profitable way. Integral elements included a revised ad campaign to attract younger customers (while continuing to keep old ones through direct mail and catalogue offerings), and the realignment of regional shops for greater profitability.

By mid-1986, some of these changes were in the works. Gardner brought in former Ogilvy and Mather public relations executive Sandra Jenkins Carr as vice president for advertising and public relations. "We began with a series of market surveys and found we needed to change the attitude that Steuben is such an institution it isn't relevant to people's lifestyles," Carr recalled.[28] To help "educate a new generation to the value of Steuben" she commissioned a series of ads showing a "warmer, more accessible" Steuben being used by teachers, stockbrokers, and other "real people" in anecdotal situations.

On the design front, Gardner made no radical changes. He approved plans for a major exhibition of contemporary sculptural pieces by Steuben designers David Dowler, Eric Hilton, and Peter Aldridge at the Heller Gallery, a New York City showcase well known to collectors of contemporary craft. Originally scheduled for the autumn of 1986, the show was rescheduled to May of 1988 "when Steuben discovered that its factory couldn't handle the load."[29]

Improvements at the Plant

From the start, cutting production costs and speeding up factory output were priorities for Gardner. In April 1985, a "standard operating procedure" for new products was adopted, and a coordinator of new products was named to act as liaison between the glass designers and the working gaffers.[30] Before a design could be approved for production, the cost of blowing, finishing, accessories, and packaging for the piece would be closely figured to ensure profitability.

Over the next several years, under the direction of plant manager Ed Vatcher and new plant engineer Thomas C. Messmer, many changes took place at the factory. The most extensive revisions were in the finishing room, where automated cutting, grinding, and polishing machines—some proprietary—were introduced "not just to decrease costs but to increase the quality of the finished glass," and to reduce worker exposure to particulate matter, recalled Messmer.[31]

By special agreement with the New York State Labor Department, Steuben's six incomparably skilled but aging engravers, including the masters Peter Schelling and Ladislav Havlik, were allowed to work from their homes, spending only six weeks a year in rotation at the factory.

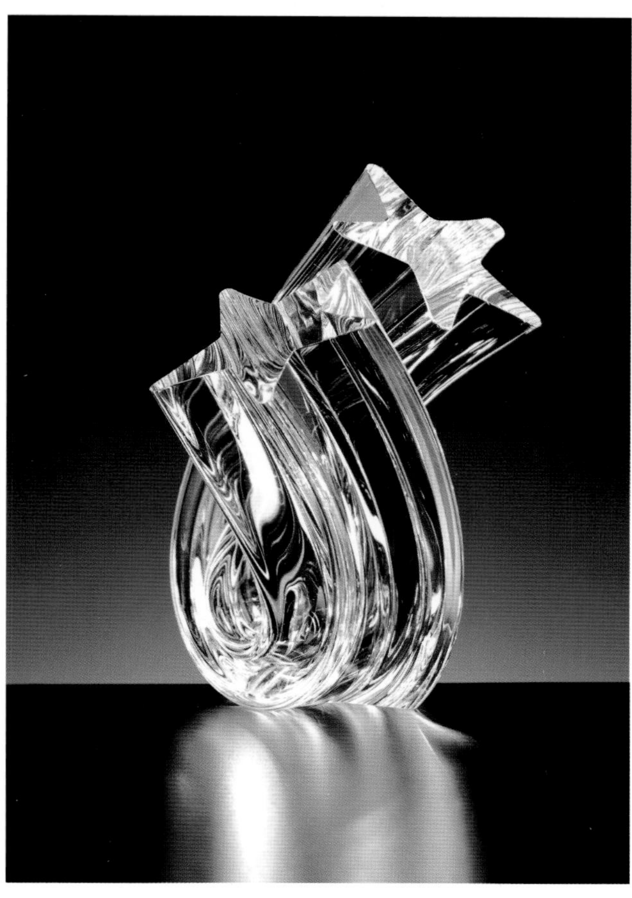

Neil Cohen. Star Stream. 1988. Height 5¼".

Steuben subsidized the renovation of home studios so the engravers could enjoy north light and the best possible working conditions, increasing their output and extending their working years.

In the factory blowing room, a robotic feed for the melting tank was introduced in the summer of 1988, reducing the risk of lead exposure for batch mixers; the automation also helped ensure more uniform crystal. Many pieces were now made by pressing or by sagging into molds. Veteran gaffers like Harry Phillips embraced the effort, helping to find pieces that could be pressed and hardcut rather than created off-hand by blowing. Under plant manager Ed Vatcher, the factory became a model for Total Quality Management, involving the gaffers and finishers in inspecting the completed pieces and striving for "zero defects."[32] In June 1986, the Steuben Shop at Corning Glass Center, adjacent to the factory, was expanded to 1,000 square feet, with floor-to-ceiling cases that could hold many more pieces of crystal.[33]

Steuben in the News

During Gardner's tenure, the Gifts of State program continued to get wide press coverage. In July 1986, President and Mrs. Reagan presented Britain's Prince Andrew and Sarah Ferguson, the Duchess of York, with a pair of Marriage Goblets designed by Donald Pollard, engraved in the classic seventeenth-century diamond-point style after a design by Bernard X. Wolff, with special calligraphy by Patricia Weisberg.[34] The goblets had been introduced at the "Marriage à la Mode" exhibition in New York two months earlier, where designer dresses were arranged in a wedding-reception setting along with ten new pieces of Steuben, including Eric Hilton's Sunflower Bowl and Bernard X. Wolff's Peacock.

The Designer Advisory Board

By late 1986, Steuben had about 185 pieces in active production, ranging from pressed hand coolers to popular animals to major ornamental designs and sculptural pieces in a wide mix of styles from traditionally narrative to abstract. The question of what would best appeal to younger customers, however, remained unanswered. That October, on the advice of Steuben's recently appointed public relations firm, Keeble Cavaco & Duka, Gardner invited an elite group of architects and interior designers (among them Robert A.M. Stern, Michael Graves, Albert Hadley, and Mark Hampton) to have lunch at Steuben and critique the line.[35]

Critique they did. The designers pronounced Steuben "aggressively anti-classical" and thus lacking appeal for their own younger clients, who "preferred simple classic forms." They suggested reissuing some "simple and timeless" pieces from the late 1930s and early 1940s including those by Walter Dorwin Teague, and recommended that Steuben consider a new, "simple and functional" line of bowls, ashtrays, decanters, and "thin" stemware. For Steuben to be credible as "real art," the Board said, big-name artists, architects, and interior designers (like themselves, presumably) would have to be commissioned to create special works; Steuben's in-house designers were, after all, "glass craftsmen" and not artists. The Board's recommendations catalyzed some immediate design initiatives at Steuben (its members were invited to participate in an exhibition the following autumn) and continued to influence design decisions for years afterward.

Susan B. King: Focus on Operations

Though Gardner accomplished much in two years, having a resident executive in New York would help speed implementation of the five-point 1986 repositioning plan. On January 1, 1987, Gardner was named chairman, senior vice president, and manager of international affairs for Steuben, ceding the presidential title—and responsibility for the New York operation—to Susan Bennett King, who moved to Manhattan from Corning soon afterward.[36] While King ran the New York operation, reporting to Corning Glass Works CFO Van Campbell (and for a time, to Gardner as well), Gardner continued to hold responsibility for the factory and for "outside" affairs. (In April 1988, for example, he traveled to Danilov Monastery in Moscow, to join Congressman Amory Houghton in presenting a gold-mounted Steuben cross designed by Bernard Wolff to Patriarch Pimen of the Russian Orthodox church. The gift, sponsored by churchgoers of New York's Southern Tier counties, commemorated one thousand years of Christianity in Russia.)[37]

As vice president and director for corporate communications and consumer affairs at Corning Glass Works, Susan King had been a key player in Jamie Houghton's Total Quality Management program, a business philosophy she implemented at Steuben. With a strong background in government service (she had chaired the United States Consumer Product Safety Commission under Jimmy Carter), King was also a politically astute strategist and manager. Initially, she was given a generous budget to make operational improvements at Steuben.[38] "The mandate was to bring Steuben into the 21st century, but first we had to bring it into the 20th," King recalled. "For example, there were no cash registers in the shop. Someone took the money to the bank twice a day in a little box. We had a huge transition, modernizing the business operation with computers and new systems. We devoted a lot of time to staff recruitment and training and to upgrading customer service."

There were marketing challenges, too, she recalled, "an entire generation that didn't have and didn't want Steuben" because they had "more options for luxury spending, from cars to travel; while for collectors, studio glass and art pottery were increasingly available." On another level, there was the pricing issue. "Some Steuben designs were being knocked off by retailers who had similar pieces made inexpensively abroad and sold them for less," King noted. "We needed to become more competitive, updating not only the look of the shop, but Steuben's image and its product line as well."

To lead this effort, King hired Nancy Neumann, "a top-flight marketer who understood the luxury business" as vice president of marketing and design. For a younger slant, the old snowflake logo was scrapped and the word "Glass" was dropped from the company's official title. "Steuben: The Clearest Form of Expression" became its new slogan, accompanying the new "poster" series of ads showing Steuben juxtaposed to everyday objects. One memorable image—a dalmation nosing a blue ball on a table next to the Equinox Bowl—won *Ad Week*'s Ad of the Year award in 1989.[39] King also brought in direct mail expert Bill Gibson to expand catalogue sales.

Julie Shearer. Iris Vase. 1986. Height 13½".

Malcolm Baldridge National Quality Award, designed by Chris Hacker.

Houghton Lobbies for Pictorial Glass

Though he disagreed with many of King's changes, Arthur Houghton welcomed her graciously and urged her to uphold Steuben's commitment to pictorial glass. "It is engraved glass that has made the reputation of Steuben Glass. Our customers love it and are eager to purchase it regardless of price. The market lies in pictorial, not abstract, themes," he wrote.[40] Soon after King's arrival, Houghton's favorite designer (and good friend) James Houston was honored with a retrospective exhibition celebrating his twenty-five years with Steuben. In April 1987, "James Houston: A Retrospective" opened in New York, with forty characteristic pieces plus the newly introduced Elephants of Kilimanjaro, a major engraved work Houston designed specifically for the event. Arthur Houghton himself wrote the introduction to the exhibition catalogue, describing his first meeting with Houston in the Canadian Arctic, where Houston was then a civilian administrator charged with developing indigenous Eskimo arts. The Houston retrospective drew 44,000 visitors to Steuben in less than a month, while forty-two orders were received for the $12,000 Elephants of Kilimanjaro.

This success fueled Houghton's lobbying efforts on behalf of both pictorial design and his friend Jim Houston. He urged King to start work on a 1989 African theme exhibition with twenty-five engraved pieces and a masterwork of "crystal panels engraved with wild game, mounted in African gold or platinum, and ornamented with African gem stones such as Kimberly diamonds and Red River rubies," all to be designed by Houston.[41] Houghton also proposed a show of eight pieces based on drawings by his first cousin, actress Katharine Houghton Hepburn, with a catalogue foreword by Houston (who would be engaged to assist Hepburn in carrying out the project).[42] King—who had her own agenda—gracefully sidestepped these potentially costly requests, though Houston was the focus of several other Steuben exhibitions over the next few years.

Changes on the Design Front

In March 1987, soon after King's arrival, Paul Schulze announced his impending retirement as design director after a quarter-century with Steuben ("My management style was aesthetic, not corporate," he reflected).[43] Associate design director Bernard Wolff also retired, and was replaced by a new designer, Rob Cassetti, while Mark Tamayo was hired to do visual merchandising. In late July, King recruited Christopher Hacker, creative director at Dansk, to be vice president and design director. "I wanted somebody who was a coordinator and decision maker, not necessarily a glass designer," she explained. Trained in industrial design, Hacker saw himself "not as product designer but as design manager, one who could manage the creative process."[44] The collegial Hacker was attuned to the realities of commerce and well able to put King's business strategies into play. He accompanied her to Washington in 1989 in a successful bid to secure a commission for the Malcolm Baldridge Quality Award—one of the few pieces that Hacker himself designed for Steuben.

Several exhibitions initiated under Schulze's direction were already in the pipeline when Hacker arrived, including "Separate Tables: A Presentation of Innovative Ways to Use Steuben," which opened at the shop in the autumn of 1987.[45] The show was inspired by comments of the 1986 Designer Advisory Board, whose members were invited to create vignettes using existing pieces of Steuben crystal "as the adjunct to a sophisticated lifestyle." Forty thousand visitors came to see such imaginative arrangements as Michael Graves' life-size, three-dimensional reproduction of a Juan Gris still life replete with painted-over pieces of Steuben, and Suzie Frankfurt's Christmas tree bedecked with Steuben jewelry.[46]

In a nod to Steuben's more traditional customers, a major loan exhibition of historic glass animals curated by French specialty glass manufacturer Albane Dolez and cosponsored by The Corning Museum of Glass opened in September 1988 with a benefit for The New York Zoological Society. "3,500 Years of Glass Artistry" included twenty Steuben animals along with masterpieces of earlier eras, documented by Dolez's book of the same title.[47] The following month, Crown Corning of Australia sponsored an exhibition of Steuben at David Jones, a prominent Sydney store; it was Steuben's first foray abroad since the postwar exhibitions in London and Paris.[48]

The Steuben Project: Sculptures in Crystal

Hacker also brought to completion "The Steuben Project: Sculptures in Crystal," which had been two years in the making, and supervised its installation at the Heller Gallery in May 1988. The show then moved to the Steuben shop from June 15 through July 16. For this landmark exhibition—the first collection of crystal introduced outside Steuben's own showrooms—Peter Aldridge, David Dowler, and Eric Hilton had each been provided with a stipend and given carte blanche to produce eight one-of-a-kind sculptural objects. Working from their own studios, they also had unlimited use of the Steuben factory—an extraordinary commitment of production resources. Freed from normal commercial constraints, the three designers "pushed the possibilities of glass to their very limits" in pieces ranging in size up to six feet.[49]

For the exhibition, David Dowler used his signature combination of matte and polished glass in several wall pieces in an ongoing "exploration of what glass is, what glass does, and its capacity for expression." Eric Hilton produced minutely detailed and engraved works inspired by remote areas of northwest Scotland, capturing "the visual rhythms of our planet" and the "complex universe of inner and outer space." Peter Aldridge, "developing the language of visual harmonics," used precisely cut prismatic forms to explore "the pure geometry of light."[50] According to Paul Hollister, writing in *The New York Times*, "What all the work in this show does with light is simply uncanny. If the prices, which range from $4,000 to $75,000, seem stiff, they nevertheless represent a net loss to Steuben against what they cost to produce. 'Sculpture in Crystal' was a big gamble, but it represents an even bigger step up from the fancy engraved presentation pieces of the past."[51]

The gamble paid off. The show generated enormous publicity, and like Jim Houston's retrospective of the previous year, it found a ready market. Only seven pieces remained unsold, and these went immediately to the Steuben shop at Neiman Marcus in Dallas, where all but one were purchased by a local collector before the opening reception.[52]

A New Image for the New York Shop

While building its reputation among art collectors, Steuben needed to put on a friendlier, more accessible face for its wider market. That meant updating the rather formal New York shop, which after thirty years was also showing wear. Hacker brought in New York City architects Bentley LaRosa Salasky, who eliminated the museum-like red velvet showroom where major ornamental designs had been displayed, opening up the spaces to make them warmer and more inviting to a younger clientele. A new 500-square-foot customer service room equipped with four rosewood desks with recessed computers was installed to help streamline the purchasing process. In the adjacent showroom, quartz halogen pin spots illuminated the open shelves of crystal from above, giving the pieces a far more

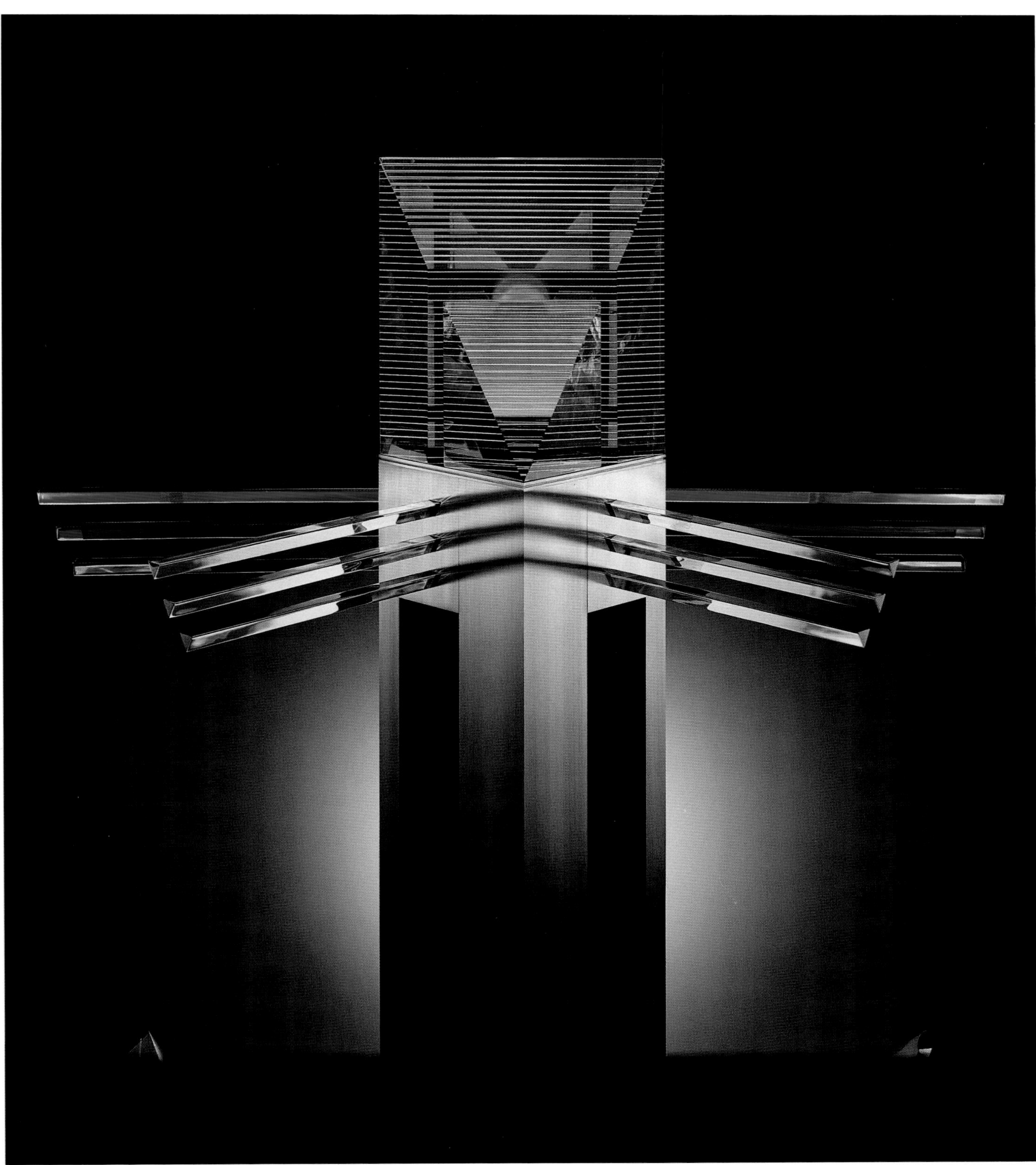

Peter Aldridge. Sentinel. 1988. Created for "The Steuben Project" exhibition at the Heller Gallery, New York City. Height 65¾".

Opposite: Eric Hilton. Light Bird Alignment. 1988. Height 68". Created for "The Steuben Project."

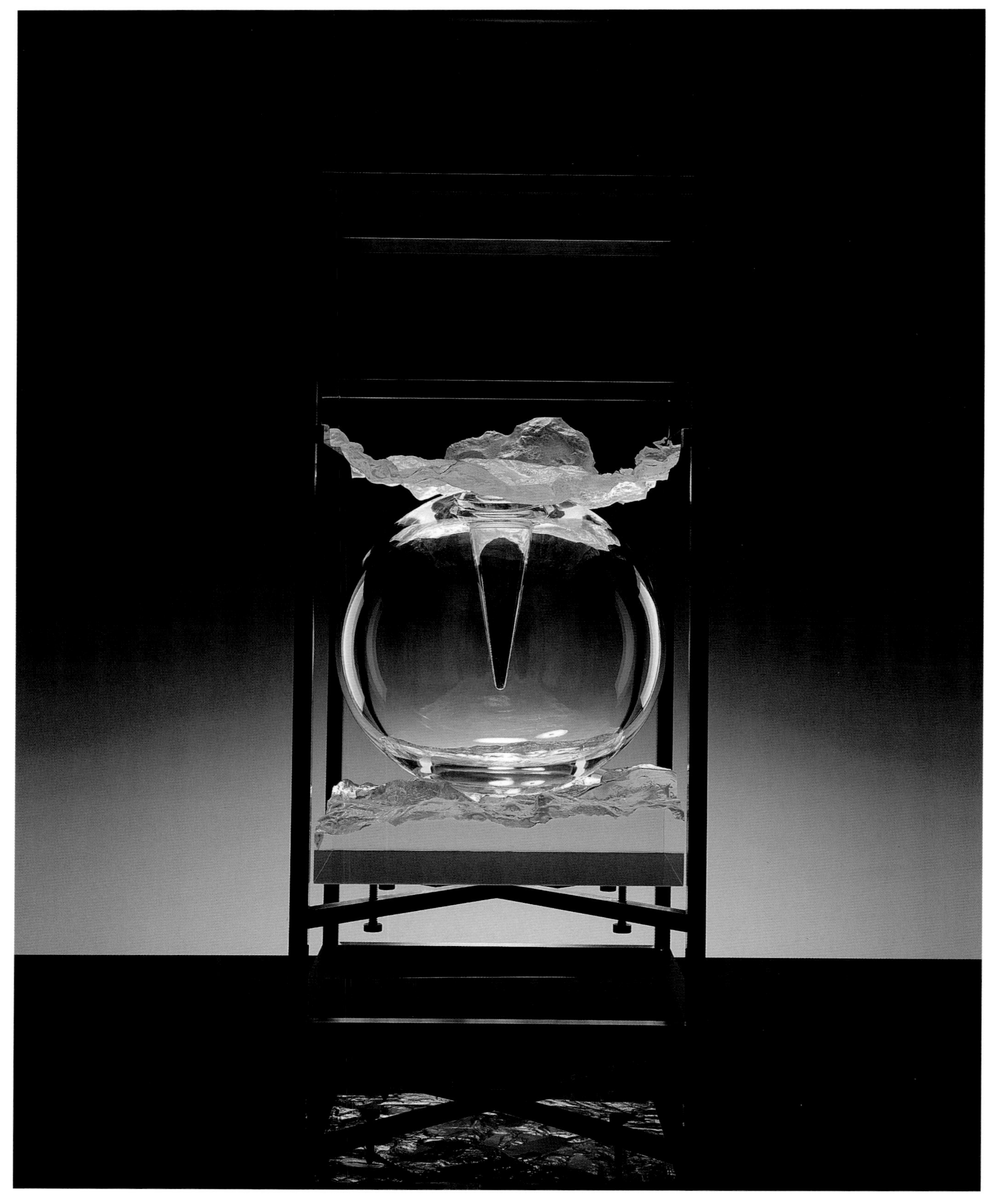

David Dowler. Poetry, Precision, and Fate. 1988.
Height 24". Created for "The Steuben Project."

Opposite: David Dowler. Poetic License. 1989.
Height 34½".

The Michael Graves Collection, 1988.

approachable look than was possible with the old fluorescent underlighting. The refurbished shop opened in June 1989 with an exhibition celebrating "The History of Steuben Design: 1903–1989," organized by Susanne Frantz of The Corning Museum of Glass, with sixty classic works on loan from various museums and collectors. The exhibition traced Steuben's design evolution decade by decade, beginning with examples of Frederick Carder's iridescent Aurene, on display at Steuben for the first time since Arthur Houghton banished Carder's colored glass from the line.[53]

In the year and a half following its renovation, the shop hosted an ambitious series of high profile events and exhibitions designed to attract younger customers, beginning with the debut of architect Michael Graves' Archaic Vessel Collection on September 13, 1988. A prominent member of the Steuben Designer Advisory Board, Graves spent the winter of 1987–88 commuting from Princeton to the factory in Corning, where he worked with senior gaffer Harry Phillips to produce three pieces inspired by a small Etruscan vase he'd purchased when a student in Rome. Graves' Archaic Vessels—two vases and a bowl—were introduced to the Steuben line as "models of latter-day classicism," with pointy, amphora-like bottoms supported in armatures of cast bronze.[54]

Driven by the Designer Advisory Board's suggestion to bring back some earlier classic pieces, "Steuben at the '39 World's Fair" opened in late September 1989 with a benefit for the Municipal Art Society. The exhibition highlighted seven major pieces designed for the original fair, among them Sidney Waugh's 300-pound Atlantica (a cast glass mermaid sculpture on loan from The Corning Museum of Glass), and also included a number of simple line items from the period, including the John Dreves Olive Dish, which was first introduced at the fair. Two other original fair pieces—John Gates' Heritage Cut Vase and Sidney Waugh's Gazelle Bowl—were

Richard Meier. Framed Vessels. 1992.

reintroduced for sale.[55] The embrace of simpler, more classic designs continued. "To welcome the new year and the new decade," a January 1990 reception introduced works by four new Steuben artists—Robert Cassetti (then serving as Hacker's associate director of design); Joel Smith; and the Swiss-based team of Monica Guggisberg and Philip Baldwin. Cassetti's first design for Steuben was the New Hellenic Urn, "a crystal vase with a heavy base incorporating both the dignity of ancient Greek vessels and a classic Steuben design signature, the curled bit," but otherwise unadorned. Joel Smith's minimalist Nimassi bowl, inspired by southwestern Native American pottery, also expressed classic simplicity, as did the pristine Small Pocket Vase by Baldwin and Guggisberg.[56]

From late January through February 1990 the shop exhibited "American Glassmaking: The First Russian Tour." Director of The Corning Museum of Glass Dwight Lanmon organized the show, which previewed an exhibition of historic American glass from the eighteenth through twentieth centuries destined for The Corning Museum of Glass, the Hermitage in St. Petersburg, and two other museums in Russia. Among the exhibition's 173 pieces were eight examples of Steuben, including John Gates' 1941 Valor Cup and Paul Schulze's 1986 New York, New York.[57]

(Meanwhile, in Corning, a massive work by Eric Hilton called Creation, was briefly displayed at the Glass Center prior to its shipment to the International Garden and Greenery Exposition in Osaka, Japan. The 1,100-pound centerpiece, six and a half feet high, was commissioned by Suntory for its pavilion at the Expo, where thirty million people were expected to view it over a seven-month period. Designed to "show respect for science and reverence for life," in Susan King's words, the Suntory sculpture engaged the efforts of fifty Steuben workers for four months—stretching the company's resources but proving once again the virtuosity of its craftspeople.)[58]

Designer Eric Hilton with Creation.

In New York later that spring, "Form & Content: Vessels in Crystal" introduced works by consulting designer Thomas Tisch, an Austrian-born glass designer who left his Oakland, California, art glass studio to join Steuben's atelier for a time. A dozen one-of-a-kind Tisch pieces—pared-down forms inspired by southwestern landscapes—were shown together with "Image and Framework: Sculpture in Crystal," a collection of eight new David Dowler pieces that arrived from the Heller Gallery, where they had been on display for the previous month.[59]

The highlight of the shop's 1990 fall season was "A Toast to Shakespeare's Globe," mounted to raise funds for reconstruction of the historic sixteenth-century Globe theater in London. At a gala benefit reception the night of October 3, guests wandered through a display of forty drinking vessels and other period artifacts lent by The Corning Museum of Glass, including a "rare goblet" by Giacomo Verzelini (who brought Venetian glassmaking techniques to England in the late sixteenth century). The goblet was later found to be a fake. Ivor Noel Hume, former director of Archeology at Colonial Williamsburg, curated the historical portion of the exhibition, which was augmented by a collection of major ornamental designs created especially for the event. Among them were A Wide and Universal Stage—an eight-sided interpretation of the Globe, designed by Joel Smith with engraving by artist Barry Moser; Jane Osborn-Smith's playful Shakespeare's Animals bowl; and Eric Hilton's memorable Macbeth, engraved with dark images from the Scottish play. These were accompanied by a series of four plates and four goblets engraved with Shakespearean themes and characters.[60]

A Legend Passes

The only thing missing at the "Shakespeare's Globe" preview was Steuben's staunch Anglophile and defender of engraved pictorial glass—Arthur Amory Houghton, Jr., himself. After a brief illness, Houghton passed away on April 3, 1990, at a hospital in Venice, Florida, near his winter home in Boca Grande where he had been awaiting "a visit from our young" to go tarpon fishing. Despite his increasing frailty, Houghton had remained a feisty steward of Steuben tradition, carrying on a crisp correspondence with Susan King until nearly the end. His final letter, written on February 28, chided her gently for limiting the edition of Jim Houston's recently introduced "Dolphins," and it contained a familiar appeal: Would she consider commissioning a new masterwork by Houston—an Eskimo Igloo, perhaps?[61] Houghton's obituaries listed his long history of cultural beneficence: the founding of The Corning Museum of Glass; the donation of land on Spencer Hill in Corning for a community college; the endowment of the Houghton Library at Harvard to house his Keats collection, for which he remained the honorary curator; and his bequest of Wye Plantation itself to Aspen Institute for use as a conference center. But Arthur Amory Houghton, Jr.'s best and most enduring gift to Steuben was his insistence on excellence without compromise.

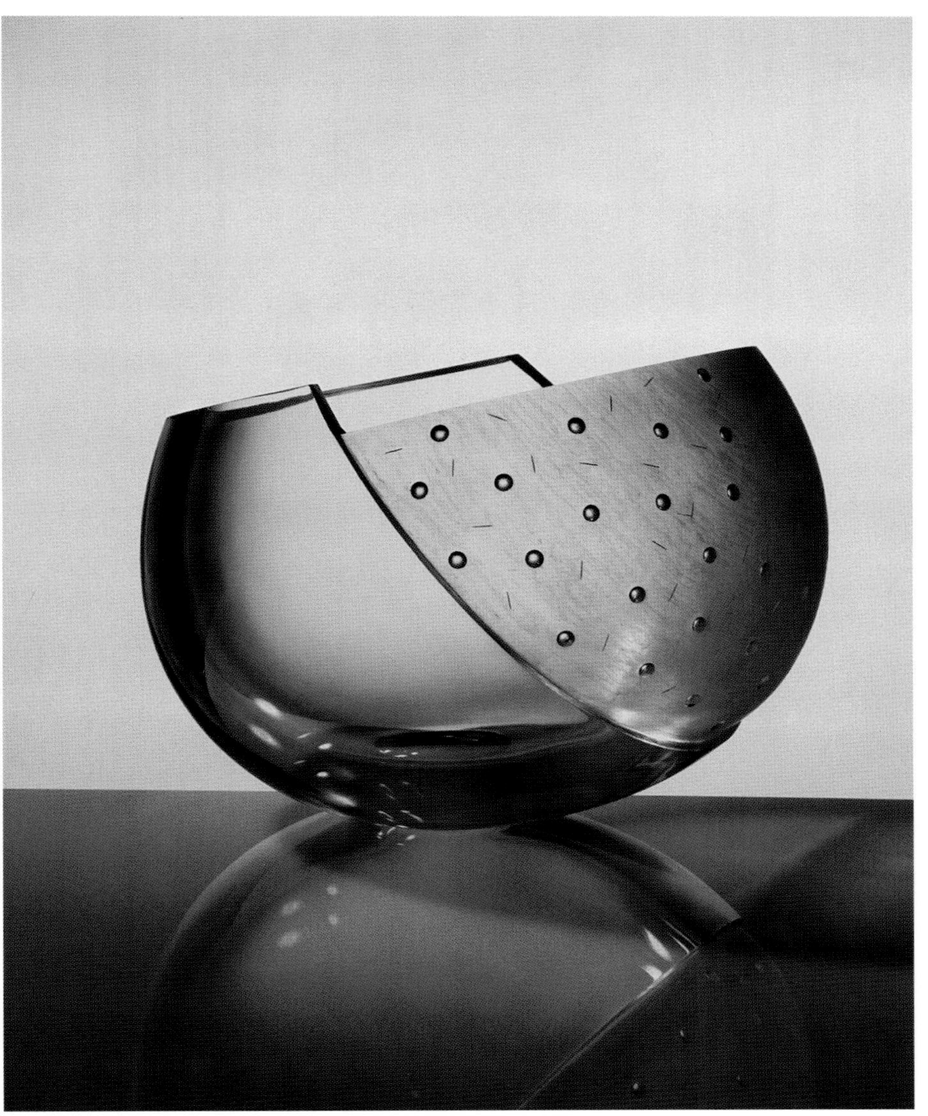

Thomas Tisch. Simple Arithmetic II. 1990.

Though Susan King began her tenure in 1987 with the mandate (and the budget) to upgrade Steuben's operations, buff its image, and broaden its market to younger buyers, the economic downturn later that year stalled many of her initiatives just as they were getting underway.[62] Soon after her arrival, a first-quarter order from Dow Corning for 7,300 Eagle hand coolers (one for each employee) assured a profitable 1987 performance—but this pig-in-the-python commission stretched factory resources painfully and raised corporate revenue expectations unreasonably for 1988 and beyond. The stock market plunge of October 1987 didn't help matters. In King's words, the young Wall Street brokers Steuben saw as its emerging market were "fleeing their Park Avenue apartments in the middle of the night without their furniture."

Despite this, King forged ahead optimistically in her efforts to upgrade and re-image Steuben. But "investments for the future in staff training, new equipment, and new product design" dug deeply into the expected operating margin in 1988.[63] In early 1989, while renovation of the shop was under way, Steuben was also busy consolidating its Fifth Avenue operations into half the space to make room for the Corning Glass Works executive offices, which were being moved down from a higher floor in the building. During the shift, Steuben's entire accounting, design, and customer service departments were transferred to Corning, and the staff was cut as well. Concurrently, advertising budgets were reduced so that the new award-winning ads could not be placed as planned.[64] Capping a difficult year, the factory had a bad run of "seeds" in the glass toward the end of 1989, hampering production during the normally profitable holiday season.[65] (King had already stopped making decanters, following reports that alcoholic beverages fostered the leaching of lead out of the crystal.) During this period, King and Nancy Neumann attempted to pare back marginal Steuben Rooms in retail stores nationwide, retaining only those in the most affluent areas, but they met with resistance. In Milwaukee, George Watts & Son, a specialty tableware store, took Steuben to court to defend its right to continue selling the crystal (and prevailed).[66]

Sam Wanamaker, Alice Tully, and Susan King.

Opposite: Eric Hilton. Macbeth. 1990. Width 16".

Although Steuben maintained its ambitious schedule of public events and exhibitions in 1989 and 1990, King was obliged to cut back on future shows, including plans for a retrospective of the 1940 "Twenty-seven Artists in Crystal" exhibition—an idea first proposed by the Designer Advisory Board in 1986.[67] A search was already

The Angela Cummings Oak Collection. 1991.

Opposite: Jane Osborn-Smith. Shakespeare's Flowers. 1991. This piece was presented by President Bush to HRH Queen Elizabeth on the occasion of her state visit to the United States in 1991.

underway for the original drawings Steuben had commissioned from Georgia O'Keeffe, Raoul Dufy, Henri Matisse, Fernand Léger, and other great artists in 1940. These were found "scattered around . . . in both New York City and Corning, most hanging in offices and some in flat files. Most were in terrible shape."[68] Though the "Twenty-seven Artists" retrospective would not come to pass for another decade, the drawings were sent to the Williamstown (Massachusetts) Regional Art Conservation Laboratories in May 1991, where they were restored and reframed. That November, they were hung in Corning Incorporated's New York City boardroom.

Angela Cummings Jewelry

The last major exhibition during King's tenure was "Glass Jewelry: Twenty-five Centuries of Style," which chronicled the history of glass jewelry from ancient times with artifacts borrowed from major museums. The show, curated by art consultant Alastair Duncan, went on view in September 1991—setting the stage for the "Angela Cummings for Steuben" line of crystal and 18-karat gold jewelry introduced at the same time. The Cummings collection included three sets of choker necklaces and matching earrings, with motifs of seafoam, latticework, and finely grained wood. To understand "what crystal could and could not do and how to highlight its extraordinary beauty," the noted jewelry designer spent days in the Steuben factory while her pieces were being produced.[69]

Other high points of 1991 were the opening of the new company-owned Steuben store in Stamford, Connecticut, as a convenience to suburbanites in the New York area; and Steuben's expansion in Asia, where in-store galleries were opened at Lane Crawford in both Hong Kong and Singapore and at Takashimaya in Japan. Steuben once again made news as a gift of state when President Bush presented Queen Elizabeth II with a Shakesepeare's Animals Bowl on the occasion of her 1991 visit to the United States.

King Returns to Corning

To reflect its global reach and evolution from glass to high technology products, Corning Glass Works had changed its name to Corning Incorporated in 1989. When its new corporate headquarters in downtown Corning, designed by Kevin Roche, opened in 1991, it became an architectural metaphor for the company's transformation as well as a symbol of its ongoing commitment to good design. King's talents—honed by her experience at Steuben—were needed in this broader arena; in early 1992 she returned to Corning to take charge of corporate communications once again.[70]

I know a bank where the
with lilies boast

XI.
DRIVEN BY DESIGN: 1992–1998

As the expansive 1980s gave way to the conservative 1990s, Steuben, like many other American companies, strove to ensure a steady return on its earlier investments. Under Kirt Gardner and Susan King, operations had been modernized, sales expanded, and the factory and shop updated, setting the stage for further progress under its next two presidents, Donald M. Rorke and Marie McKee.

Don Rorke was named president of Steuben in March 1992. He had recently retired as executive vice president of design worldwide at The Knoll Group, a design-driven company renowned for its impeccable furniture, office systems, textiles, and accessories. Trained in industrial design, Rorke was a modernist, influenced by the International School. He was well known in the field, with the confidence and credentials to carry out the Corning Incorporated mandate for respectable financial performance while imposing his own high aesthetic standard on every aspect of Steuben's operation—an approach not unlike Arthur Houghton's own. He arrived at Steuben "committed to cost/process controls and to learning what needed to be done to sustain a robust identity and secure the long term interest of both existing and new customers."[1]

Animal Kingdom: The Robert W. Nelson Collection

Planning for the only major Steuben exhibition scheduled for 1992 was already well under way by the time of Rorke's arrival. "Animal Legends and Lore: Sixty-five Years of Steuben Animals" was borrowed almost entirely from Robert E. Nelson, a Chicago businessman whose collection of Steuben animals was the largest in the world.[2]

David Dowler and Robert Cassetti. City Lights: Manhattan. 1995. Width 10".

The show opened in early October with seventy-five of Nelson's animals, spanning more than six decades of Steuben design. Early pieces included Frederick Carder's one-of-a-kind Eagle, made by the *cire perdu* process in the 1930s, as well as three colored-glass elephants designed as a hood ornament for Mrs. Amory Houghton's Bentley to signal her staunch support of the Republican Party. Nelson's collection was augmented by a group of new Steuben animal figures introduced in 1992. Among these were Lloyd Atkins' Monkey, David Dowler's Good Dog, Harold Gross' Elusive Buck, and Jane Osborn-Smith's Endangered Species Bowl. Like all Steuben animal exhibitions, this one was predictably popular, though it probably did not reflect the purist design vision Rorke had for Steuben.

Staff Changes and Design Challenges

In the turbulence that accompanied ongoing corporate change in the early 1990s, there was significant turnover at Steuben. Several key managers including Nancy Neumann and Christopher Hacker left in what Rorke described as a "flattening out" of staff.[3] With a strong design background and ideology of his own, Rorke functioned ex officio as Steuben's design director after Hacker's 1993 departure, while day-to-day design operations were carried out initially by associate design director Rob Cassetti, and, after Cassetti left to work at The Corning Museum of Glass, by designer David Dowler.[4] Eric Hilton also left Steuben during the Rorke years, while Peter Aldridge had returned to London in 1990 to head the glass department at the Royal College of Art. (In 1997, Rorke persuaded Aldridge to come back to Steuben as vice president and creative director of product design and development.)[5] At the plant, manager Ed Vatcher was succeeded by Dick Jack and later, by Craig Dunham.[6]

Rorke saw as his greatest challenges "the limited scope of the product line" (clear crystal only); the "decorative/ornamental nature of most Steuben designs" (which he considered equally limiting); and the need to expand customer awareness of Steuben both nationally and worldwide. He believed this would require a new brand identity program with consistent graphic standards for all print materials, packaging, and advertising.[7]

Big Names, Small Prices

High on Rorke's list of priorities was the introduction of "products that were more relevant to contemporary life, that would attract a broader range of collectors and offer a value proposition to younger customers." That meant a new emphasis on functional glass for the tabletop and home priced in the lower range of Steuben's traditional structure. For Rorke, it also meant bringing in prominent outside designers and architects including Massimo Vignelli, Marco Zanini, and Paul Haigh—all of them contacts from his days at The Knoll Group—to design collections or individual pieces of glass for the line.

Modernist architect Richard Meier, who had served as a member of the 1986 Designer Advisory Board, was first to complete a collection for Steuben during Rorke's tenure, although the project had been initiated by Susan King. Meier's Framed Vessels group of 1992 consisted of a bowl and two vases, each seated in an architectural, angular metal base. Unlike other more moderately priced designer collections that followed, these ranged from $11,000 to $13,000 with bases of solid handmade sterling silver. (The collection was shortly thereafter offered with bases of nickel plate for about a quarter of that amount.)[8] In 1994, Italian designer Marco Zanini—protégé of Memphis Group founder Ettore Sottsass—was commissioned to create two large-scale vases and a bowl with fluid, undulating lines. All were priced at less than a thousand dollars. Introduced as the Calypso Collection,

David Dowler. Mountain. 1994. Width 12".

Paul Haigh. Drape Bowl. 1995. Diameter 9¾".

Zanini's vessels received the Chicago Athenaeum's Good Design award the following year.

The Sequence Collections

In 1993, designer Massimo Vignelli's Whirlwind group of tablewares made its debut as the first phase of Steuben's Sequence Collections of accessories for the home. Inspired by the classic forms of Venetian glass that influenced Vignelli as a youth, the Whirlwind group was a daring departure from Steuben tradition. Thin and light, it was made entirely without lead to conform with strict product safety codes in states like California. A second small melting tank made it possible to manufacture the Whirlwind pieces without interrupting the production of fully leaded crystal. The collection included two carafes, a serving platter, an aperitif glass, and a tumbler costing between $45 and $275 each—at the bottom of the Steuben pricing structure.[9] Whirlwind was followed in 1994 by two other groups of items in the Sequence Collections: the Aurora line of pewter and glass dressing-table accessories (a trinket box, perfume bottle, bud vase, hand mirror, and tray) designed by Philip Baldwin and Monica Guggisberg; and the Interplay group of desktop objects—a clock, box, and picture frame by "the Steuben Design Group."[10] All were priced under $300.

Marking Steuben's 90th Anniversary

To elevate Steuben's design image, Rorke looked to prominent designers of the past as well as the present. In honor of the company's ninetieth anniversary year in 1993, he had Walter Dorwin Teague's polka-dotted Compote from 1932 reintroduced as part of the Heritage Collection; and he organized and promoted the Anniversary Collection of all-time favorites from past decades, among them George Thompson's 1959 Rose Vase, Sidney Waugh's 1937 Horse Head Paperweight, and Angus McDougall's 1940 Apple, with a "whimsically applied bit" as its stem. A "host of new designs that will reinforce our relevance to sophisticated modern lives" was also created during Steuben's ninetieth anniversary year, ranging from the Little Handkerchief Vase (at $225, it was promoted as "an ideal receptacle for an intimate bouquet") to Peter Drobny's $8,900 Mobius Prism, inspired by the mathematical symbol of infinity.[11] Later in 1993, President Bill Clinton presented the Mobius Prism to Crown Prince Naruhito and Crown Princess Masako of Japan as a wedding gift.

Some Special Commissions

In its tradition of accepting special commissions to commemorate important events, Steuben undertook two especially notable assignments during the Rorke years. The first was for Joel

Massimo Vignelli. Whirlwind Collection. 1993.

Smith's monumental sculpture Remembrance, completed in 1992 to memorialize victims of the Holocaust. Thirty inches high and weighing 150 pounds, Remembrance was commissioned by Deborah and David Schultz to stand as the centerpiece of the Harry Wilf Holocaust Memorial at the Alex Aidekman Family Jewish Community Complex in Whippany, New Jersey. The piece consists of six central flamelike elements symbolizing the six million who perished, rising from a field of fragmented pieces, each engraved with hundreds of tiny refractive points of light.[12]

The second commission was notable for its sheer production volume. In 1994 Hershey Foods placed an order for 17,000 Lyre Vases, each with an engraved image of the original 1897 Hershey logo, for distribution to all Hershey employees in commemoration of the company's centennial. This enormous order took many months to produce, challenging the Steuben factory's capacity during a time when it was also heavily involved in working with new glass concepts and outside designers.[13]

New Stores and a New Image

Along with introducing new collections and design concepts to Steuben, Rorke boosted its image and distribution network through several tastefully conceived shops in upscale resorts. In 1992, Walter Dorwin Teague's grandson, collaborating with Chris Hacker, was engaged to design a shop in Aspen, Colorado (owned by designer Jim Houston's son); and New York designer Lee Stout later created interiors for shops at The Greenbrier in West Virginia (1994) and The Breakers in Palm Beach, Florida (1995). Both of Stout's concepts subsequently received design awards from the Institute of Store Planners. In 1996, new Steuben galleries were opened at Asprey in London and Meister Juwelier in Zurich; while stateside, the network of galleries was extended to Marshall Field's, as well as to additional Neiman Marcus stores across the country. In all, there were more than forty retail Steuben outlets by 1998, including a shop at the Americana in Manhasset, New York.

Along with the new shops, Rorke commissioned a "new, cleaner, and more up-to-date" logo and packaging for Steuben products and "established a new commercial message: 'Timeless—Elegant—American,' intended for all Steuben stakeholders to identify with and rally around."[14] Along with the new logo, this message accompanied print ads in a new campaign designed by Takaaki Matsumoto. Matsumoto, a New York–based graphic designer whose aesthetic sensibilities reflected Rorke's own, was also commissioned to design Steuben's annual catalogues, its shopping bags, and other print materials "with a unified and consistent look that worked well with the new stores . . . designed by Lee Stout." (The shopping bag collection was subsequently made part of the permanent collection at the Montreal Museum of Decorative Arts, and in 1998 it received awards from the prestigious Art Directors Club and from the Industrial Design Society of America.)

Reaching Out to the Design World

A familiar figure in industrial and interior design circles, Rorke helped Steuben achieve wider recognition in the national and international design communities. He established several highly visible awards, including the Steuben Award for glass design, a component of the Alliance for Artists and Writers National Scholastic Awards program, which exhibits each year's winning entries at the Corcoran Gallery of Art in Washington, D.C., and at Scholastic Inc. in New York City. He personally initiated and funded the Steuben award for drawing at the Silvermine Guild Arts Center in Connecticut, and expanded Steuben's participation in such design organizations as the American Association of Interior Designers, the Industrial Design Society of America, and the Worldesign Foundation.

Another Strategy Study for Steuben

In 1996, Corning Incorporated engaged the Boston Consulting Group to examine Steuben's policies and operations. As a result of the study, Rorke developed an "Image & Design Strategy" for Steuben built around the word IMAGE as the basis for a one-word mission statement and the focus of its positioning strategy. According to Rorke, the letters of the word symbolized key points of the mission—"to be Innovative, to sustain Museum-quality design, to advance the Art form, to Grow profitably, and to strive for Excellence."[15] The Boston Consulting Group made a number of specific recommendations, including a cutback of marginally profitable Steuben retail outlets, while "building on the past instead of discarding it" by re-emphasizing traditional design to retain the loyalty of Steuben's old-line customers. The Group also recommended introducing more products with higher price points.[16] Though Rorke did not close any Steuben galleries or stores, he was attentive to balancing the kinds and styles of glass produced by Steuben, including many animals and decorative pieces of proven appeal to various market segments. Annual catalogues for 1997 and 1998 reflect this balance.[17]

Exhibitions: Sag-molded Glass and "Structure Revealed"

To heighten appreciation for Steuben's handcrafted methods—especially that of sag molding—"Breaking the Mold: The Art of Sculptural Glass at Steuben" went on view in the New York shop in January 1997 (the same month Peter Aldridge returned from the Royal College of Art as Steuben's new design director). At the opening reception, Steuben designers Peter Drobny and Bill Sullivan were on hand to personally explain the intricacies of sag molding. Their new piece, Regal Lion (1996), was used to illustrate the step-by-step transformation of an unformed 45-pound block of glass into a polished sculpture, through various stages of the sag-molding process. Preliminary sketches, wooden models, and master molds for this and other sagged pieces, including architect Paul Haigh's Colonnade (1996) and David Dowler's Star-Spangled Banner (1991) and Castle of Dreams (1986), were included in the educational display.[18]

With its focus on Steuben's peerless craftsmanship, "Breaking the Mold" set the stage for a technically stunning and artistically groundbreaking exhibition, "Structure Revealed: Glass Designs by David Dowler," that opened the following November. Always in the vanguard of experimental design at Steuben, Dowler had been given the freedom to concentrate exclusively on the development of designs for the show, resulting in five monumental one-of-a-kind sculptures offset by five intimately scaled and exquisitely crafted jewel boxes.

"My goal with this group of works was to expand the expressive palette of what has been done with the Steuben material over the years," Dowler explained. "The challenge was to coax the crystal into doing something new."[19] Typical of Dowler's approach, the pieces exploited the contrast of brilliantly polished and textured opaque surfaces, utilizing the most advanced techniques of molding and cutting. The most daring piece, Grotto, incorporated two subtly colored pieces of salmon-colored and pale-green glass—Steuben's first use of color since 1932. Thomas Hoving, who wrote the show's catalogue, called Grotto (priced at $50,000) "a landmark move" and praised another piece, Chasm ($32,500), as "one of the top works of contemporary glassmaking."[20] The catalogue described "Structure Revealed" as "a reaffirmation of (Steuben's) commitment to contemporary sculpture in glass. . . . the first in a series of current significant annual exhibitions aimed at advancing glass as an artistic medium." But the series did not materialize, leaving "Structure Revealed" as the artistic zenith of the Rorke years.

Some Milestones

In January 1997, Jim Houston's thirty-five years as a Steuben designer were marked by the unveiling of three new works—Polar Bear Cub, Polar Bear Mother, and Green Heron—at a gala cocktail event at the New York store, co-hosted by the Canadian consul general. (Houston continues to design for Steuben.) In March 1997, veteran Steuben designer Lloyd Atkins—beloved for his animal figures and the ever-popular line of hand coolers he initiated in 1974—celebrated his fiftieth year with the company. To honor Atkins' many contributions in his half-century of service, Steuben reintroduced some early Atkins pieces, including the Giraffe and Ram hand coolers, into the Heritage line.

On June 1, after six years at Steuben's helm, Don Rorke retired to pursue other design-related interests. Like Susan King before him, Rorke moved to North Carolina where he now teaches at Duke University. Among the achievements of his tenure, the elevation of Steuben's image in the worlds of interior, graphic, and product design stands out. His high visual standard helped set an aesthetic benchmark for Steuben in the new millennium. One of Rorke's final initiatives, carried out in concert with Peter Aldridge, was to open discussions with the Venetian glass master Lino Tagliapietra, "resulting in Lino working in the Steuben plant" the following year as an artist-in-residence.

STEUBEN

XII.
APPROACHING THE MILLENNIUM: 1998–2002

Upon Rorke's retirement on June 1, 1998, Marie McKee was named president and chief executive officer of Steuben. McKee, at the time a senior vice president of human resources at Corning Incorporated, had joined the company in 1979, rising quickly through the ranks and earning a reputation as a trailblazer. Among her first achievements was establishing one of the country's first corporate-community child care centers, which was soon recognized nationwide as a model for such collaborative services. As part of a high-level team, she also helped to define Corning's innovation process, tracing the evolution of new products from research and development through manufacturing and marketing. The project yielded an innovation-management process that required dialogue and collaboration among disparate units and resulted in much higher rates of success in selecting, developing, and commercializing new products.[1]

Respected for her insight, honesty, compassion, and ability to balance multiple high-level priorities, as well as her leadership skills, McKee was appointed president of the Board of Trustees of The Corning Museum of Glass, chairman of the Corning Foundation, and senior vice president of Corning Incorporated at the same time that she assumed responsibility for Steuben. The rationale for the multiple appointments was a new, closer relationship among these organizations; their new leader was to advance the potential of these entities individually and collectively.

In joining Steuben, McKee's mandate was to turn it into a successful business, a challenge that she thought would require "a substantial change in the culture inside Steuben, as well as in the vitality of the brand outside. Historically, we

The main floor of the New York flagship store on Madison Avenue.

have focused so intently on our artistic side that we have sometimes gazed right past critical business issues. When I joined Steuben and assessed the situation, I felt my first order of business was to bring the organization into better balance. While we must always focus on the art and design—these are, after all, the very heart and soul of Steuben—we must also realistically address important matters like production, people, and profitability."[2]

Improvements at the Plant

In December 1998, McKee tapped Peter Aagaard, then operations manager at another Corning Incorporated facility, to take charge of the Steuben factory. Aagaard knew the territory well; he had been an engineer at Steuben in the mid-1980s, reporting to Tom Messmer. Taking up the challenge of "making improvements dictated by ergonomics, health, and operational efficiency," Aagaard directed a fast-track renovation of the plant.[3] Throughout the factory redesign, Aagaard formed teams, inviting many employees into the process. Working together, they achieved not only a vast number of efficiency gains, but a real sense of ownership, which was also reflected in dramatic improvements to employee morale.

Aagaard moved operations previously carried out at the Fulton Street finishing and shipping facility into the Steuben factory, and completed a physical overhaul of the finishing room during the factory's regular two-week summer shutdown in 1999. A year later, he generated enough inventory to stop production for four weeks, during which more extensive improvements were made. The major goals this time were to improve product and environmental quality by reducing particulate matter in the air, and to create a more comfortable work environment by reducing the temperature. To achieve these ends,

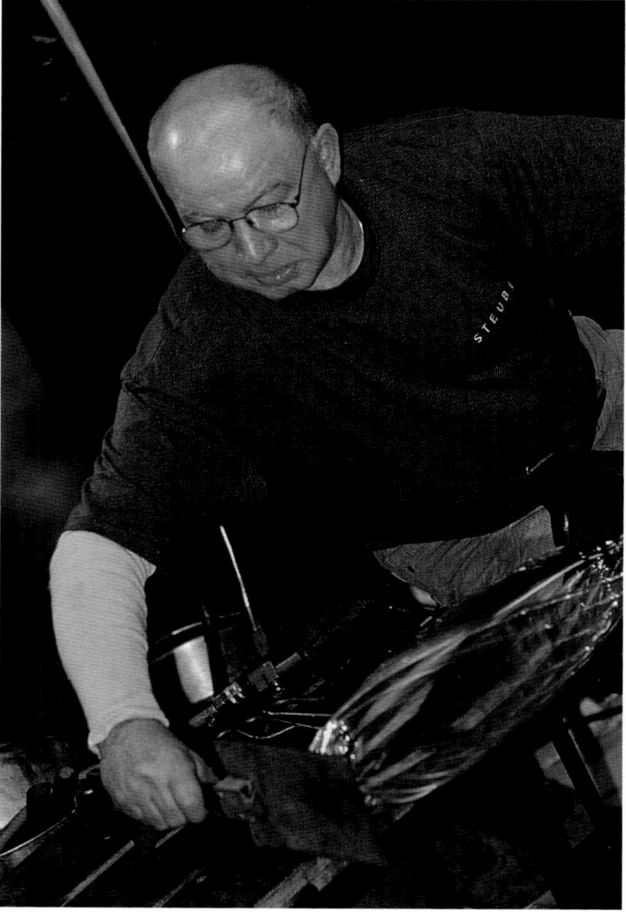

Lino Tagliapietra at work in the Steuben factory, 1998.

Aagaard directed the renovation of the blowing room and the installation of a new air-conditioning system. He enclosed the great north window wall to eliminate a seasonal problem with dust and partitioned off the big glass-melting tank from the main blowing room to reduce heat and particulates. Six old monolithic reheating furnaces, each with four glory holes opening into the same roaring central flame, were replaced by four quieter and more fuel-efficient units, each housing three individually fired glory holes. About the size of a barrel, these are lined in brick. Unlike their old monolithic counterparts, the new glory holes can be shut down one at a time for repair.

These and other improvements at the factory have increased efficiency, partially through increased automation, but equally important, through better ergonomics and working conditions for employees. As Aagaard points out, "We were able to eliminate completely the risk of certain types of injuries, and we also made the factory more comfortable for our workers by creating a more ergonomic environment overall. Both of these were high priorities." A new onsite "bag house" collects particulate matter removed from the air, so the air quality inside the factory is safer for workers and meets or exceeds all OSHA regulations. While increasing the use of automated polishing, cutting, and grinding machines in the renovated finishing room has improved efficiency in these routine processes, Aagaard emphasizes that "the important individualized work of engraving, design cutting, and repair is all still done by hand."

Next on the list of factory improvements is replacement of the factory's two large lehrs (annealing ovens), where finished pieces of glass are slowly cooled to prevent stress cracks. The current lehrs have been in service since 1951, and Aagaard anticipates they will need to be replaced sometime before 2006.

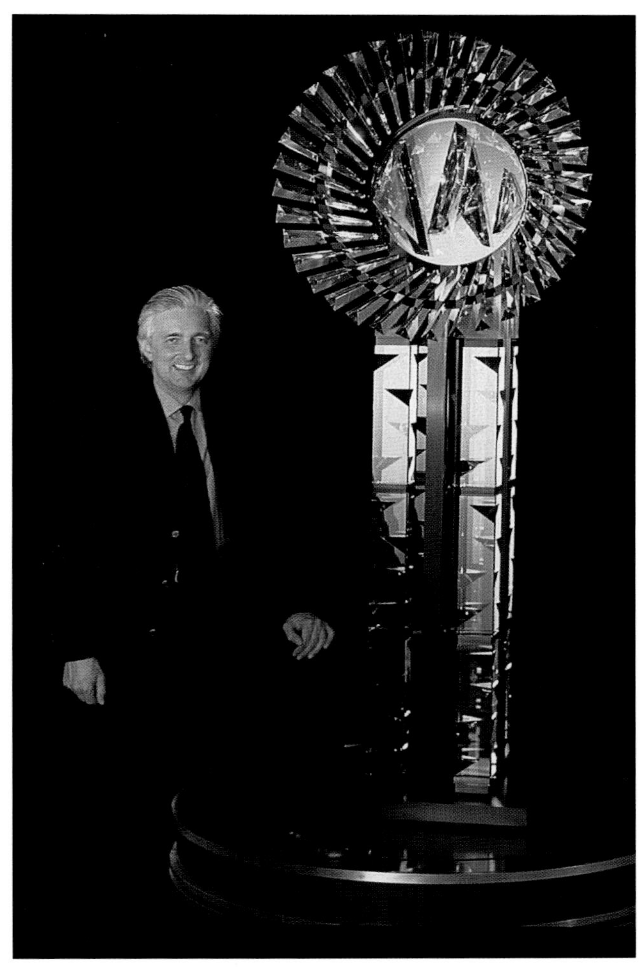

Disney Fantasia 2000 Masterwork, with its designer, Peter Aldridge.

Steuben and The Hot Glass Show

Since The Corning Museum of Glass opened in 1951, one of its visitors' most memorable experiences has been watching gaffers at work in the adjacent Steuben factory. Typically, visitors sat in bleachers, staring in fascination as gaffers gathered glass, blew it into specified shapes, added bits, measured with calipers, and finally carried the unfinished piece away for annealing. As they exited, visitors walked along the side of the factory floor, where they could see inspectors and engravers at work. Although they could observe work being done on actual Steuben items through windows into the factory, they were never able to see a piece of glass worked from start to finish. As popular as the experience was, The Corning Museum of Glass team felt this peek into glassmaking

Lino Tagliapietra. Canework Vessels. 1998.

Opposite: Joel Smith. Starlight Runner Table. 2000.

could be a much more compelling and educational visitor event. So they set out to create The Hot Glass Show.

The show takes place at the visitor entrance to the Steuben factory, with the blowing room floor as a backdrop. Visitors sit in a tiered bank of seats, facing a concrete demonstration platform equipped with a small melting tank, glory hole, annealing oven, and all the tools used to produce a piece of glass. Just beyond the platform, they can glimpse the activity on the "real" blowing room floor. But their attention is invariably riveted on The Hot Glass Show gaffer and his assistant, who explains each step of blowing, forming, decorating, and annealing as they create an entire vase or bowl. Unlike the colorless Steuben, these demonstration pieces are usually made of colored glass, so that the gaffer can demonstrate color processes, the results of which visitors see in many pieces at the museum. Strategically positioned cameras, including one positioned to reveal what is happening *inside* the fiery glory hole, and three sets of ceiling-mounted monitors, ensure that each visitor has a detailed view of the entire process, except for annealing, which takes an additional eight hours. The whole show takes fewer than twenty minutes. The Late Show—the last show of the afternoon—is a little longer. Then, the gaffer makes a larger piece of glass, spending about an hour in front of the crowd. If an earlier piece has cooled sufficiently, it is given away to a lucky Late Show visitor.

The Hot Glass Show became so popular that in the summer of 2001, The Corning Museum of Glass added a second outdoor stage and open-air amphitheater adjacent to the Steuben factory, to accommodate more visitors. This demonstration platform, complete with melting tank, glory hole, and annealing oven, is mounted on a large truck parked at the edge of the visitor parking lot. Once the weather grows too cool for outdoor seating, the entire demonstration unit is transported to schools and educational events around the country.[4] Its inaugural season was marked by an important first—a stint at the Winter 2002 Olympic Games in Salt Lake City, where visitors from around the world stood fascinated, watching the age-old "sport" of glassmaking.

Lino Tagliapietra: A Collaboration

When McKee arrived at Steuben, Peter Aldridge had already set in motion a plan to bring Venetian glass master Lino Tagliapietra to Corning, where he would collaborate with Steuben craftsmen on a collection of colorless crystal. An icon in the studio glass community, Tagliapietra spent two weeks in March 1998 at the Steuben factory, completing sixty pieces of crystal in an artist-in-residence program of unprecedented scope. "It was a challenge, because I was using crystal instead of glass to make my designs," Tagliapietra remarked. "The quality of crystal is high, but it is more difficult to work with. It has broadened my appreciation for this medium."[5] Twenty-five pieces from the collection were exhibited in "Clearly Lino Tagliapietra: Masterworks in Steuben Crystal" at the Fifth Avenue shop from October 5 through November 7, 1998, and another group of fifteen pieces was shown at the annual SOFA (Sculptural Objects and Functional Art) exhibition in Chicago, from October 8 through 11—the first time Steuben took part in this studio glass showcase.

Joel Smith. Orbit Bowl. 2000. Diameter 8¾".

Commissions and Awards

During McKee's first two years, Steuben earned several notable commissions and awards. ABC News selected Steuben to custom-design an icon for their award-winning six-part historical program, *The Century*. The following year, Steuben was commissioned to create one of seven unique masterworks to accompany the world premiere of the Walt Disney company's film *Fantasia 2000*. Peter Aldridge designed the eight-and-a-half-foot, 870-pound Fantasia sculpture. The largest and most complex piece ever produced by Steuben, it did not survive storage in Disney's unheated London warehouse. During the same time period, however, two of Aldridge's other Steuben designs were recognized with impressive honors. His Runway Vase, mounted on a runway-like base, received a Good Design award from the Chicago Athenaeum and was accepted into the permanent collection of its Museum of Architecture and Design. His more sculptural Passage: An Interval of Time was made part of the permanent collection of the Metropolitan Museum of Art.[6]

A Venture into E-Commerce: Steuben.com

Having commissioned extensive research, McKee decided to open an e-commerce channel for Steuben. "We understood that the Web presented a new way for us to reach people outside the realm we have traditionally served, as well as to provide additional services to our past and present customers," she says. "It was a fast-track project, first conceived in April 1999. In June we did the research; in July Corning agreed to fund the project; and at the end of August we did a quiet launch. We soaked up information over the first few months, perfected the site, and by the end of October, we were really in business."

The site offers Steuben customers round-the-clock access to Steuben products for purchase, as well as educational information, interviews with individual Steuben designers, and a list of store locations and events. According to McKee, Steuben.com has been well received, particularly by younger customers and those in geographic areas far from Steuben's retail outlets. "More than half of those who buy through this channel are new customers," she reports.[7]

A New Flagship Store on Madison Avenue

While a new "space" on the internet was under development, McKee was also masterminding plans for a new physical space—a Steuben flagship store at 667 Madison Avenue. The move to Madison, first proposed by Arthur Houghton following the sale of the Corning Building at Fifth Avenue and 56th Street, had been contemplated for years. Soon after McKee's arrival, it became a priority, since Steuben's lease for the Fifth Avenue store would soon expire. In pondering where to position a brand new primary site, she considered a Rockefeller Center location, but opted instead for a larger space in a neighborhood of luxury retailers on Madison Avenue south of 61st Street. "It offered us the chance to display Steuben as never before in a neighborhood that supported our image. The parcel actually included more space than we needed, but we saw in that an opportunity to use part of the space as a gallery, creating an additional draw for art lovers. Corning Incorporated agreed to underwrite it," she recalls. Ten million dollars were allocated for the project. Several architects proposed cold, minimalist interiors. But, emphasizes McKee, "although Steuben is certainly elegant and deserves to be the center of attention, it also has a very human appeal. So we wanted to create an environment that would put our products in a warmer, more friendly setting. For that, we turned to Ralph Applebaum, who had successfully redesigned the interior of The Corning Museum of Glass."

Based in New York City, Ralph Applebaum Associates is renowned for its visitor-centered museum installations. For the 6,100-square-foot Steuben store, Applebaum conceived an open, two-level sales floor with a 23-foot ceiling. A circular mezzanine surmounting a tall column symbolizes a bubble of glass at the end of a blowpipe. A graceful suspended staircase descends to the lower level gallery for rotating art exhibitions.[8] Flooded with light from the double-height front window and a sophisticated computer-controlled lighting system, the store's main 2,700-square-foot sales floor and mezzanine are planned for flexibility and frequent changes in merchandise display. A long, brightly lit display cabinet spans one wall, showcasing a wide variety of crystal. Versatile round tables with plasma screens are illuminated from within and can be rearranged to accommodate changing displays of Steuben. At the front of the store, a rotating, floor-to-ceiling column is partially enclosed by a scrim curtain. This forms a backdrop for imaginative window displays conceived by Steuben's director of visual presentation, Mark Tamayo. A second scrim can be drawn around the perimeter of the 900-square-foot circular mezzanine, where specially designed cases hold important pieces of ornamental and sculptural Steuben.

In May 2000, the new flagship store opened with a series of gala receptions for customers, the press, and the New York cultural community. In the spirit of the spring season—a time of weddings, graduations, and other celebratory events—inaugural displays highlighted the reintroduction of Steuben's classic Air-Twist Champagne Flutes, first introduced in 1949 and reintroduced in boxed pairs, along with other items of classic Steuben stemware. A harbinger of things to come, Joel Smith's Starlight Runner Table, made in a limited edition of ten, integrat-

Opposite: Joel Smith. Star Flight. 1999. Height 8½".

ed crystal with finely figured sapele pomele wood. It was the first time Steuben had been used in a piece of furniture.

An Inaugural Exhibition: "Celebrating by Design"

In the same gala mood, the lower-level gallery was launched on May 17, 2000, with a benefit champagne preview of its inaugural exhibition, "Celebrating by Design." Organized by Steuben and DIFFA (Design Industries Foundation Fighting AIDS), the exhibition featured ten vignettes using Steuben crystal—especially the champagne flutes—in celebratory or whimsical ways. Each vignette was created by a prominent designer from the worlds of fashion, architecture, and interior design: Avi Adler, Richard Meier, David Rockwell, Courtney Sloane, Kate Spade, Ali Tayar, Adam Tihany, Isabel and Ruben Toledo, and Eric Warner all participated.[9] The inaugural show remained on view until July 8 and was followed by three other exhibitions that year.

"Twenty-seven Artists in Crystal"

One of these was the long-planned revival of Steuben's 1940 exhibition, "Twenty-seven Artists in Crystal."[10] The show opened on October 2, 2000, with a gallery talk by Peter Aldridge. Although it was not possible to assemble all twenty-seven of the actual Steuben pieces from the original exhibition, its artistic spirit was realized through the display of signed original drawings made by participating artists, including Jean Cocteau, Salvador Dalí, Paul Manship, Thomas Hart Benton, Henri Matisse, Isamu Noguchi, Georgia O'Keeffe, and Grant Wood. Steuben had found and restored these drawings a decade earlier in anticipation of just such a retrospective. At the opening reception, Marie McKee officially presented these artistic treasures to David Whitehouse, executive director of The Corning Museum of Glass. He accepted them for the collection of the Juliette K. and Leonard S. Rakow Research Library in Corning, an adjunct of the museum. They are now available to scholars there.

The Golden Bowl

The world premiere party for the Merchant Ivory film inspired by the Henry James novel, *The Golden Bowl,* was held at the Madison Avenue store and gallery in April 2001, with film stars Uma Thurman, Angelica Huston, Nick Nolte, and others in attendance. Steuben was commissioned to create a Golden Bowl masterwork in crystal and gold as the centerpiece for the film. The new Golden Bowl was designed by Eric Hilton and Michele Beckman, and produced in a limited edition of fifty. The first bowl in the series, signed and numbered by Hilton, was auctioned at the opening party for charity.[11]

New Design Directions

In line with her mandate to "make Steuben a successful business," soon after her arrival McKee made it a priority to review each piece of crystal in production to see whether it should become a regular item in the Steuben product line, or whether it fell into the category of a short-term promotional piece, designed primarily to enhance the image of Steuben. Through this exercise, McKee became convinced that Steuben must become more purposeful in developing new pieces. "We had to consider the return on investment, whether we were creating an important sculpture or adding a new piece of crystal to the line," she said.

To implement this strategy, McKee established a Commercial Viability Team, comprised of representatives from marketing, design, and manufacturing. The team reviews every new product proposal from multiple perspectives,

Eric Hilton. Dragonfly. 2001. Height 10¼".

including cost of production and projected revenues it will generate. Senior product designer Joel Smith was named new product design manager to expedite this process. Before a piece can be approved for production, Smith says, it must meet a defined market need and go through a series of steps "to determine its viability as a commercial product."[12] Information and opinions from the marketing department are given equal weight to those of the design department, with manufacturing providing critical information on costs and scheduling impact.

McKee emphasizes that this commercial strategy is intended to ensure the success of the business, but it does not mean that fewer new pieces are being introduced, or that design excellence is compromised in any way. Although some pieces have been taken out of production, the number of new products has doubled under McKee's direction. More than forty new items per year have been added to the line since her arrival, ranging from utilitarian stemware and vases to new animals and major ornamental designs.

Beginning in 2000, McKee's team implemented a new design strategy. Individual members of the Steuben design staff were given responsibility for specific categories reflecting their particular skills and talents. Eric Hilton, who returned to Steuben as a designer in the late 1990s, is charged with designing virtually all of the corporate special-commission work—an important part of Steuben's business today. Peter Aldridge, the consummate artisan of angled glass, creates finely calibrated prismatic sculptures (though he has also contributed such elegant offhand pieces as the Antherium Vase, introduced in 2000). Joel Smith turns out many line items in response to specific marketing needs. Animal figures, especially the hand coolers, are now the specialty of consulting designer Taf Lebel Schaefer. (Lloyd Atkins, whose animals remain Steuben classics, officially retired from Steuben in 2000, marking the event with the production of a Rhinoceros for the hand cooler line. Atkins died in February 2002.) David Dowler, now retired, designs occasional ornamental and functional pieces for Steuben. Apart from these assignments, all members of the design team use their creativity by designing special pieces of exhibition glass from time to time. For example, David Dowler elected to make a unique Pastoral Epergne of crystal and bronze, introduced in 2001. At $19,000, it is limited to an edition of five. It is McKee herself, however, who makes the final decisions on which items will be produced.[13]

Late in 2001, Peter Aldridge stepped down as Steuben's director of design, and McKee asked Rob Cassetti to fill the joint role of design director and marketing director. Concurrently, he is also director of marketing, creative services, and guest services for The Corning Museum of Glass. Having served as Steuben's associate design director before leaving to focus on the museum in 1995, Cassetti has remained close to Steuben. "The more I worked with the vast world of glass at the museum, the more I pondered Steuben's role in it," Cassetti recalls. "I came back to Steuben with the philosophy that design-wise, we need to create things that are inherently about Steuben—the most perfect glass the world has ever known. There's a quality about certain Steuben pieces like the John Dreves Olive Dish that our customers recognize intuitively as being classic Steuben. It's all about maintaining the integrity of the glass. One function of the Steuben object is to hold meaning—each piece so touches the receiver that somehow, memories stick to it. It's one of the few times in life that you can touch perfection."[14]

Looking to Steuben's Centennial—and Beyond

During 2001, Steuben explored the potential of untraditional product categories like furniture and lighting. At the threshold of its 2003 centennial, however, the company is returning to its roots with the kind of glass that resonates with its customers as quintessentially Steuben. "We're going back to the future, in a sense, to the ideals first propounded by Arthur Houghton," Rob Cassetti says. "His Steuben trilogy—perfection of material, design, and workmanship—is still the essence of Steuben, as it was in his day." There will be a renewed emphasis on the pictorial, engraved glass that was the mainstay of the Houghton years, and that has remained enduringly popular with Steuben customers. Houghton himself would have looked with approval on plans for an exhibition commemorating Jim Houston's fortieth year with Steuben, scheduled for the fall of 2002. Along with the centennial, there are plans to reissue a number of all-time Steuben favorites as part of an expanded Heritage series. And, of course, there will be an ongoing succession of new pieces, which, without slavishly imitating the past, will still reflect the very heart of Steuben.[15]

To underscore Steuben's image of quality, the elegant grey linen boxes and soft grey flannel bags familiar to Steuben collectors a half-century ago are being reintroduced in all Steuben shops worldwide. And the famous snowflake logo, adopted in 1950 and retired in 1987, will be brought back into use.

Moving into the future, Steuben's importance as a symbol of quality for Corning Incorporated, and as a touchstone to the company's past, continues to grow. "One of our goals was to reintegrate Steuben with Corning Incorporated, and we've accomplished that," McKee states. "New generations of Corning management are now involved with Steuben, and they are as proud of what it stands for as Steuben employees have always been."

As Steuben's centennial approaches, McKee sums up the company's ongoing challenge: "to serve a new generation of customers, while upholding the standard of uncompromising excellence that has prevailed at Steuben since its founding. As the world's leading brand of crystal, unsurpassed in purity and brilliance, we will continue to offer our customers the artistry and craftsmanship they desire, along with the attentive personal service that has been a cherished, century-long Steuben tradition."[16]

EPILOGUE

Steuben: The Next Hundred Years

One hundred years—a milestone for any enterprise. But for an American firm to engrave its distinctive signature on the world of decorative arts for an entire century is remarkable. To do so in a single material is indeed rare. Steuben has earned a stature that accrues only through time and a heritage of perfection. When Arthur Houghton became President of Steuben Glass Works in 1933 and revolutionized the company, he proclaimed a mission to create "the most perfect crystal the world has ever known." And so it is—a material refined to its peak of optical brilliance and clarity through science, and formed into works of arresting beauty by some of the world's most extraordinary artists, designers, and glassworkers.

Centenary anniversaries are pivotal: we reflect on our past and anticipate our future. As I consider our hundred-year history at Steuben, I return time and again to three constants of our endeavor. Each is simple, yet profound in its effect.

First, we work solely in a single, ancient medium, elevated to perfection through science. Here at Steuben, we have privileged access to the largest, most technologically advanced and highly innovative group of glass scientists and engineers in the world. Our parent company, Corning Incorporated, has unparalleled strengths in glass and ceramics. No other glassmaker in the world has such a distinguished pool of scientific talent available to it. Thus our crystal earns its reputation for brilliance and clarity through continuing advances in science.

Second, the techniques we use to make glass are centuries old. As with the medium itself, we have refined our models of ancient tools and furnaces to improve reliability. Yet we still literally breathe life into glass—a practice that has

Peter Aldridge. Gazing Crystal. 1981.
Black slate base. Crystal, diameter 4½".

changed very little since Roman times. It is these very acts of forming and blowing glass that allow the human spirit to enter Steuben—to shape each crystal treasure individually. No matter how skilled our society becomes at mass production, the most cherished objects will always be made this way—one at a time, directly by human hands.

Third, we have consistently sought out such hands as can work magic with glass. Time and again, we have brought together some of the world's finest artists and designers with their uniquely skilled counterparts in glassmaking, and charged them with imagining possibilities in glass and light. And time and again, the result has been a symphony, a work of virtuosity greater than either composer or performer—artist or artisan—could have achieved alone.

Beauty wrought from high technology, ancient tradition, and the combined talents of artist and artisan: what other commercial enterprise has sustained such an elegant formula? Steuben creates classics, refining each creative new idea until its essence gleams. Is it any wonder that works of Steuben have been commissioned by or for every U.S. President since 1947, for countless international heads of state, opera stars, scientists, business magnates, astronauts and for others who have reached for the stars?

Now, having achieved the milestone of one hundred years, what does our rich history mean for us today and for the next one hundred years? Where do we go from here?

As we planned our future, we spent many months in searching, listening, looking, and reflecting on a myriad of ideas through the unique lens of Steuben. The course we have set resonates deeply with all of us. It is this: we will build gracefully on the strong and elegant pedestal that is our past. Our quest for the twenty-first century is to design new classics, to perpetuate perfection in execution, to be the worthy vessel and purveyor of dreams.

How will we achieve this? How better than to tune to the perfect pitch of our muses. We will seek sonority through our artists, designers, glassworkers, and scientists—the sources of Steuben's matchless beauty—in order to perpetuate their incomparable legacy. We will also aim to resonate with the life stories and moments of special meaning, and we will honor these with containers that cradle their innermost melodies. Finally, we will match our tone to that of our collectors, honoring and upholding the significance of their collections. For them, we will create new works of crystal art that beautifully augment and harmonize with their existing collections and inspire new ones.

It makes me smile to recall that the metaphor for divining the future is a crystal ball. Here at Steuben, I foresee future products of astonishing clarity and brilliance, working their alchemy with light. We will continue to create "the most perfect crystal the world has ever known," using the world's most exquisite material, individually crafted by master glassworkers who execute the visions of the world's most creative minds. As we have for the past century, we will fuse skill and imagination in the hot flames of our furnaces. The shapes, of course, will change over time, but we will align each with the perfect center of Steuben.

Our first hundred years established this firm as the maker of the world's most perfect crystal. As we enter our second century, we rededicate ourselves to creating new generations of classics. Steuben will remain exquisitely, timelessly Steuben.

E. Marie McKee
July 2002

CATALOGUE

ARTISTS' BIOGRAPHIES

PETER ALDRIDGE, vice president and creative director for Steuben from 1997 through 2001, is known internationally as a designer and sculptor in glass whose works embody complex prismatic geometries. Born in England, he was educated at the Royal College of Art, London, where he later served as a teacher, visiting professor, external examiner, and from 1993 to 1996, as head of the Glass Department. Aldridge began his long association with Steuben as an artist in residence in 1977. He has received many awards and honors, including Fellowships from the National Endowment for the Arts and the New York Foundation for the Arts, as well as two Good Design awards from the Chicago Athenaeum. Aldridge's works are represented in many museum collections including those of the National Museum of Modern Art in Tokyo, The Metropolitan Museum of Art in New York, the Musée des Arts Décoratifs in Paris, the Frankfurt Museum für Kunsthandwerk, and the Victoria and Albert Museum in London. His architectural glass commissions include an atrium installation in the Corning Incorporated Headquarters and a dichroic glass tower sculpture for Pembroke College, Cambridge. Aldridge is also a trustee of The Corning Museum of Glass.

TIMOTHY C. ANGELL, a botanical artist and sculptor, has worked with Steuben's designers to create numerous engraved pieces and vessels that reflect the beauty and complexity of the natural world. Educated at the Cleveland Institute of Art and the Cranbrook Art Academy, his sculpture and illustrations have appeared in many exhibitions, including those at The Missouri Botanical Garden, the New York State Museum, and Longwood Gardens. He received the American Society of Botanical Artists Award for Excellence in Botanical Art in the year 2000.

LLOYD ATKINS joined Steuben in 1948 as a staff designer. Over the next fifty years, he became one of Steuben's most versatile and prolific designers, renowned for his delightful animal sculptures as well as scores of other representational and decorative figures, forms for engraving, and geometric sculptures. Born in Brooklyn, Atkins studied at the Pratt Institute before serving in the Army Air Corps during World War II. After the war he received a Bachelor of Industrial Design degree at Pratt while working at Steuben. Atkins' crystal has been shown in innumerable Steuben exhibitions, including those at the Palais du Louvre, Paris; Park Lane House, London; the National Gallery of Art, Washington, D.C.; and The Metropolitan Museum of Art, New York. His work is represented in the permanent collections of the Art Institute of Chicago, the University of Kyoto, the National Museum of the Philippines, and the Dwight David Eisenhower Library, as well as in many private collections. Atkins marked his retirement from Steuben in the year 2000 with a Rhinoceros hand cooler, his last in the series of small pressed animal sculptures he initiated in 1974. Lloyd Atkins died in February 2002.

CARY AUSTIN, an illustrator, was born in Salt Lake City and educated at Utah State University and the Columbus College of Art and Design. He received the Society of Illustrators Gold Medal in 1994, and subsequently joined The Greenwich Workshop. He collaborated with Steuben designer Joel Smith on Our Love and with Peter Drobny on Eagle's Flight.

SAMUEL AYRES was born in Dedham, Massachusetts, and graduated from the Vesper George School of Art, Boston, in 1934. A Steuben glass designer from 1935 until 1939, he was responsible for designing many outstanding pieces of glass during the early Houghton years, including Whirlpool Vase, a very successful piece.

IRENE BENTON, a Steuben Glass designer from 1942 until 1944, was born in Poland. She studied in Warsaw and Brussels before obtaining a Bachelor of Arts degree from Smith College in 1942.

STEVE BERTRON, a master gaffer at Steuben since 1973, was born in Corning and educated at the Art Students League in New York City. Equally adept at blown vessels and hand-formed animals, he has collaborated with Joel Smith on Powerful Bull and Great Bear and designed the piece Free Spirit.

ZEVI BLUM created several designs for Steuben, including the Crusaders Bowl—a fine example of difficult *Hochschnitt*, or high-relief engraving—that was presented by President Reagan to Prince Charles and Princess Diana on the occasion of their marriage. A draftsman, etcher, and watercolor painter, Blum received a degree in architecture from Cornell University, and later served as head of the art department in the School of Architecture. His illustrations have appeared in *The New York Times*, and his work has been exhibited in group and one-person shows in the United States and in France.

THOMAS C. BUECHNER, president of Steuben Glass from 1972 to 1981, has enjoyed a distinguished career as a painter, museum director, and arts administrator. He designed the Ariadne necklace for Steuben in 1981.

LETTERIO CALAPAI—engraver, painter, teacher, and leader of the avant-garde school of etching and engraving in the United States—conceived the engraved design for a single Steuben piece, Canto V, in 1959. Calapai was head of graphics at the Albright Art School in Buffalo, and has taught at the New School in New York City. Calapai's works are represented in many private and museum collections, including those of The Metropolitan Museum of Art and the Boston Museum of Fine Arts.

JAMES CARPENTER born in 1949, contributed many innovative designs to Steuben over the years. A graduate of the Rhode Island School of Design, Carpenter is also a naturalist and botanical illustrator. He has taught at the Rhode Island School of Design, Ohio University, and other institutions of higher learning, and has received an award from the National Endowment for the Arts. Carpenter's work is represented in collections of The Corning Museum of Glass; the Musée du Verre in Liège, Belgium; the Museum Bellerive in Zurich; the Museum für Kunst und Gewerbe in Hamburg; and the Seattle Art Museum. His works travelled with the exhibition "New Glass" in 1979 and 1980.

STEVE CARVER, a graphic designer and illustrator, has worked for a wide variety of clients for more than 25 years. Born and raised in Oklahoma, Carver currently is based in Ithaca, New York. In addition to contributing images for engraving on Steuben crystal, Carver has received commissions from *The New York Times, The Atlantic Monthly, Time, Newsweek, Fortune,* CBS Records, Citicorp, and other clients.

ROBERT CASSETTI, who became a designer for Steuben in 1987, was born in Pittsburgh and graduated from the Carnegie-Mellon College of Fine Arts with honors. Known for his designs that exploit crystal's ability to magnify and reflect an image, Cassetti also served for a time as Steuben's associate director of design. Currently he is director of marketing and guest services for The Corning Museum of Glass, and serves as design and marketing director for Steuben. Among many other works created for Steuben, he designed several one-of-a-kind special commissions. His work has been published in such magazines as *Elle Décor, Print, Graphis, International Design, HG,* and *New York,* and exhibited at the American Institute of Graphic Arts and at the Art Directors Clubs in New York and Los Angeles.

NEIL COHEN, a Steuben staff designer from 1984 through 1988, conceived the popular Equinox Bowl in 1985, as well as Star Stream—a 1988 design that remains a Steuben best seller. A member of the Industrial Design Society of America, he graduated from the Industrial Design program at the Rhode Island School of Design. Currently he works as a freelance glass designer, based in New York City.

DONALD CROWLEY, an illustrator, designed the engraving for Steuben's Dandelions in 1973. Crowley received his training at the Art Center School, Los Angeles. His illustrations and cover renderings have appeared in many books and magazines. He is represented in a variety of public and private collections including that of the United States Air Force. Crowley created the Explorer mural for the Explorer's Club of New York City.

ANGELA CUMMINGS, renowned for her jewelry designs, collaborated with Steuben in 1991 to produce the Angela Cummings for Steuben collection—three sets of choker necklaces and matching earrings of crystal and 18-karat gold. Trained as a goldsmith as well as a gemologist, Cummings began her career in 1968 as an assistant designer at Tiffany & Co. By 1971, Tiffany had begun to sign her work and by 1977 her designs were featured in their own display on the main floor. Cummings left Tiffany's in 1984 to form her own company for the manufacture and sale of fine jewelry, porcelains, and accessories. The first Angela Cummings Boutique opened at Bergdorf Goodman that same year.

PATRICIA F. DAVIDSON, a goldsmith, collaborated with Steuben's Paul Schulze on the design of Quintessence (1971). Davidson was educated at Mount Holyoke College, Columbia University, and the New York Craft Students' League. However, she achieved her goldsmithing expertise primarily through self-instruction. Her work has been exhibited at the Museum of Contemporary Crafts in New York and in other institutions. Co-author of *Greek Gold Jewelry from the Age of Alexander,* published by the Brooklyn Museum in 1965, Davidson has also been a research associate in the Brooklyn Museum's Department of Ancient Art, where she studied ancient goldsmithing techniques.

GARY DAVIS, a freelance illustrator, was co-designer with Joel Smith of Steuben's The Pitch in 1996. Trained at the Massachusetts College of Art, Davis focuses on sports-related subjects and continues to work on a series that deals with the game of baseball and its early players.

MARSHALL DAVIS, an illustrator with a deep interest in French life, designed the engraving for Steuben's Balloons in 1968. A graduate of the Cleveland Institute of Art, Davis also studied with Harvey Dunn in New York City. His illustrations have appeared in various books and periodicals both in the United States and abroad.

DONALD DEMERS, renowned for his illustrations of ocean life, was trained at the Worcester Art Museum and at the Massachusetts College of Art in Boston. A member of the American Society of Marine Artists, Demers has received commissions from such prestigious clients as the

National Park Service, Reader's Digest, and American Airlines. His work has been published in many magazines including *Sail, Yankee,* and *Down East,* and has been honored by the Society of Illustrators. Demers is based in Kittery, Maine.

KATHERINE DE SOUSA was a member of the Steuben Glass design team from 1969 until 1972. Born in Fort Wayne, Indiana, she graduated from the Rhode Island School of Design and worked for Walter Gropius at The Architects Collaborative in Cambridge, Massachusetts. There, she designed a tea set that won the Gold Medal of the Senate at the 1970 International Exhibit in Faenza, Italy. Since 1978 she has worked as an independent designer for companies in the tableware, giftware, and housewares industries, specializing in fine crystal, ceramics, and other products.

RUSH DOUGHERTY joined Steuben's design staff in 1971. Before graduating from New York's Parsons School of Design, he also studied at the American College, Paris, and at the University of Strasbourg, France. In his years with Steuben, Dougherty concentrated on a series of geometric forms and variations in crystal. He also assisted with the design and installation of such Steuben exhibits as "Studies in Crystal," which appeared at the Corning Glass Center during the summer of 1971.

ARTHUR DOUGLASS graduated from the Massachusetts Institute of Technology and became a member of the Steuben Glass design department in June 1939. During his brief tenure at Steuben, which ended in May 1940, Douglass was responsible for the design of stock as well as exhibition glass.

DAVID DOWLER, a Steuben Glass designer since 1972, was born in Pittsburgh. An honors graduate of the Syracuse University School of Art, he was trained as an industrial designer and silversmith. At Steuben, he was the first to explore the unique aesthetic effects of combining textural, unpolished glass with highly polished transparent crystal. Dowler participated in a number of important exhibitions at Steuben culminating in his 1995 one-person show, "Structure Revealed," a group of glass sculptures both massive and intimate, inspired "by the natural world." These pieces, like much of his past work, combine contrasting brilliant polished and textured opaque glass, creating strong juxtapositions and dialogues between the two. Dowler's works have been exhibited in and are part of the permanent collections of many museums including the National Design Museum, the American Craft Museum, and the Renwick Gallery in the United States. Abroad, his pieces have been shown at the Musée des Arts Décoratifs in Paris and Lausanne, and at the National Museum of Modern Art in Tokyo and Kyoto.

JOHN DREVES worked for many years during the 1940s and 1950s as a Steuben designer. He was the second design staff member assigned to work in residence at Corning. During the World War II period, Dreves held weekly staff meetings for the factory production staff, working with them on problems relating to the implementation of designs. He is perhaps best remembered for his classic stock piece, the Olive Dish.

PETER DROBNY joined Steuben as a staff designer in 1989. Educated at the Rhode Island School of Design, where he focused on sculpture with a specialization in glass, Drobny has created many designs for Steuben, including special commissions and a range of functional works. His pieces exemplify his strong interest in geometry and spatial relationships and are strongly influenced by natural forms. Drobny's glass has been exhibited at the New York Experimental Glass Workshop, the Foster White Gallery in Seattle, and the Woods Gerry Gallery in Providence, Rhode Island.

STEPHEN DALE EDWARDS, a glass designer, received his training at the University of Iowa. He later taught glassblowing there and at the Pilchuck Glass Center and at the Miasa Bunka Center in Japan. His work appears in many public and private collections, including those of The Corning Museum of Glass and the Seattle Arts Commission.

FRANK ELISCU, a sculptor, collaborated with Steuben's staff designers on a half-dozen pieces between 1962 and 1972. A fellow of the National Sculpture Society and an Associate of the National Academy of Design, Eliscu studied at the Pratt Institute, Brooklyn; and the Beaux Arts Institute of Design and the Clay Club, both in New York City. He has received several awards for sculpture. His works in bronze and slate have been shown at the Pennsylvania Academy of the Fine Arts, Philadelphia; the Cleveland Museum; and other institutions. Eliscu's commissions include a fountain at Brook Green Garden, South Carolina, and heroic slate horses for the Banker's Trust Building in New York City. He is the author of *Sculpture: Techniques in Clay, Wax, and Slate.*

SHELDON FINK, a painter and illustrator who often depicted nature's creatures, designed the engravings for Steuben's Dragonfly Bowl (1978) and Butterfly Bowl (1979). Fink studied art in his native city, New York. He is represented in various museum collections including those of New York's Metropolitan Museum of Art, the Brooklyn Museum, and the Yale University Art Gallery. Fink's work has frequently appeared in various one-man and group exhibitions on the East Coast.

GOLDA FISHBEIN, an illustrator and graphic designer, graduated from the Cooper Union School of Art, New York

City. She was on the design staff of Steuben Glass for many years. She also designed numerous book jackets for Alfred A. Knopf and Random House.

JOHN MONTEITH GATES, a former vice president of Steuben Glass and director of design for Corning Glass Works, held overall responsibility for Steuben Glass design from the time of the company's reorganization in 1933 until his retirement in 1969. Born in Elyria, Ohio, in 1905, he was educated at Harvard, received his architectural degree from the Columbia University School of Architecture, and studied at the École des Beaux Arts in Paris. In 1930, he joined the architectural firm of Charles A. Platt. In 1933, he was awarded first prize in an international competition to replan central areas of Stockholm, Sweden. As Steuben's chief of design, he was also the architect for the former Corning Glass building and Steuben Glass shop at 718 Fifth Avenue, as well as the Steuben Glass shop that occupied the corner of Fifth Avenue and 56th Street until it was relocated to Madison Avenue in 2000. During World War II, he was a much-decorated member of the United States Navy. In 1952, he was made a life fellow of the Royal Society of Arts, London, and in 1963 was appointed Benjamin Franklin Fellow of that Society.

MICHAEL GRAVES, an internationally renowned architect, developed the Archaic Vessel Collection of two vases and a bowl for Steuben during the winter of 1988-1989 when he commuted regularly from his office in Princeton to the Steuben factory in Corning. Born in Indianapolis, Graves received his architectural training at the University of Cincinnati and at Harvard. In 1960 he was awarded the Rome Prize for Study at the American Academy in Rome. Currently Graves is the Schirmer Professor of Architecture at Princeton University, where he has taught since 1962. A Fellow of the American Institute of Architects, he has designed many important projects around the globe, including office buildings, hotels, museums, and education facilities. His work has been documented in a number of museum exhibitions, including eight at the Museum of Modern Art in New York City.

HAROLD R. GROSS, a fine arts engraver, has been with Steuben since 1973. He served a six-year apprenticeship program at Steuben, which included attending Corning Community College and the Elmira College for Art. As a designer, he has contributed several designs for private collectors, and is the creator of a popular ornamental piece, the Elusive Buck.

MONICA GUGGISBERG and PHILLIP BALDWIN, who design as a team, contributed their first pieces to Steuben in 1989. Guggisberg was born in 1955 in Bern, Switzerland, and was trained as a glass flame worker. Baldwin, born in 1947 in New York City, received his bachelor's degree from American University in Washington, D.C. After meeting at the glass school at Orrefors in 1979, they worked as assistants to Wilke Adilfsson and Ann Wolff at their glass studio in Sweden. The pair opened their own studio in 1982 near Lausanne, Switzerland, producing designs for major glass manufacturers. Their work has been widely exhibited in Europe and is represented in many collections, including those of the Musée Ariana in Geneva, the Musées des Arts Décoratifs in Paris and Lausanne, The Corning Museum of Glass, the Denver Art Museum, and the Kunsthandwerk Museums in Berlin and Hamburg, among others.

TERRY HAASS, an American painter and graphic artist, contributed the engraving designs for two Steuben pieces, Genesis (1959) and Cosmos (1978). Czechoslovakian-born Haass fled to France at the start of World War II and came to New York in 1941. There she studied at the Art Students League and with printmaker Stanley William Hayter, whose influence may be discerned in her designs for Steuben. Haass' prints are found in the New York Public Library; the Museum of Modern Art, New York; the Carnegie Institute, Pittsburgh; and the Bibliothèque Nationale, Paris. A former co-director of Hayter's Atelier 17, Haass also taught graphics at Brooklyn College and the City College of New York. She holds a degree in Mesopotamian archeology and has done archeological research for the École des Hautes Études, the Sorbonne.

CHRISTOPHER HACKER, Steuben's design director from 1987 to 1994, was trained in industrial design at the University of Cincinnati's College of Design Architecture and Art. After working as a product designer for Henry Dreyfuss Associates and J.C. Penney, among other firms, he embarked on a corporate career as design director for such prominent companies as Estee Lauder and Dansk International. At Steuben, he supervised the design team and was in charge of the redesign of the Fifth Avenue shop, among other responsibilities. Hacker himself designed Steuben's commission for the Malcolm Baldridge Quality Award, presented annually. After leaving Steuben he worked as a creative director for Warner Brothers' stores division, and since 2000 has been vice president and creative director for the Aveda Corporation, a division of Estée Lauder.

THOMAS HACKER, a brother of Christopher Hacker, is a founding principal of Thomas Hacker and Associates Architects of Portland, Oregon, and has taught architectural design at the Universities of Pennsylvania and Oregon. For Steuben, he designed the Dervish Vase in 1991.

PAUL HAIGH, a British-born architect and designer, is a graduate of the Leeds Polytechnic Academy and the London

Royal College of Art. After working for Knoll International in Milan, Haigh emigrated to the United States in 1978. With his wife and partner Barbara H. Haigh, he established an architecture and design studio, Haigh Space, in New York City in 1981. The studio expanded to Greenwich, Connecticut, in 1989 where it still operates as Haigh Architects + Designers. Beginning in 1995, Haigh designed a number of contemporary vessels and ornamental sculptures for Steuben, including the Drape Bowl, which received an honorable mention in the 1997 Chicago Athenaeum Good Design Awards.

CHARLOTTE-LINNEA HALLETT contributed the engraving designs for several Steuben pieces in the 1970s. She is an artist and designer, trained at the Silvermine Guild of Artists, New Canaan, Connecticut, and at the University of Bridgeport in Connecticut. Hallett's drawings and paintings have been exhibited in a number of group shows in the Northeast. She and her husband have a product design studio in Connecticut.

MEREDITH HAMILTON, a freelance illustrator, has contributed whimsical line drawings to a number of adult and children's books, and magazines. She was educated at Brown University and received her MFA in Illustration from the School of Visual Arts in New York City, going on to work as an art director of graphics for Time, Inc. and *Newsweek*.

JIRI HARCUBA, an internationally renowned glass artist and engraver, was born in Czechoslovakia, where he learned engraving between 1942 and 1945, studying at the Glasfachschule in Novy Bor and the Art Academy in Prague. He taught at the Kunstgewerbeschule in Prague from 1961 until he was dismissed for political reasons. Harcuba then worked as an individual artist and teacher in Austria, Germany, England, and the United States, where he was an instructor at the Pilchuck Glass School. In 1990 he was called back to the academy in Prague and became director in 1991. His work is exhibited widely and held in many private and public collections in the United States and abroad.

LADISLAV HAVLIK, a master copper-wheel engraver, was born in 1925 in Bila, Czechoslovakia, and trained at the School for Gem and Glass Engraving in Turnov and at the School for Applied Arts in Prague. In 1960 he joined Steuben, where he engraved many important pieces and masterworks including Carrousel of the Sea, Dreams of Alice, and Crown of Oberon. He has taught glass engraving at Corning Community College.

MILTON HEBALD, a sculptor born in New York City on May 24, 1917, studied at the National Academy of Design and the Beaux Arts Institute. He soon had his first sculpture shows, winning a number of awards. After a brief period of teaching, he applied for and received the Rome Prize granted by the American Academy in Rome. He remained in Italy, settling permanently in Bracciano, and fulfilling many major commissions for public buildings, as well as for smaller pieces.

WALTER HEINTZE was one of the early members of Steuben's in-house design staff. He worked primarily on stock pieces of glass.

DAVID HILLS, a Steuben Glass staff designer from 1948 to 1952, is perhaps best remembered for his popular stock piece, Bud Vase, but he also was responsible for a number of pieces of exhibition glass. Hills attended Amherst College, Columbia University, and Pratt Institute.

ERIC HILTON, a Steuben designer since 1974, was born in northern Scotland and educated at the Edinburgh College of Art, where he later taught. He has been responsible for many of Steuben's finest pieces of jewelry, and has created many other sculptural pieces expressing his concerns with cosmic order, the unity of life, and the oneness of time and space. Hilton has also drawn inspiration from the lochs and moors of his native land. His glass has been exhibited at many museums and galleries including The Metropolitan Museum of Art, the Museum of Contemporary Art in Chicago, and the Musée des Arts Décoratifs in Paris, among others. His works are in the permanent collections of the Hokkaido Museum of Modern Art in Sapporo, Japan; the Pilkington Glass Museum in Liverpool, England; the Musée des Arts Décoratifs in Lausanne, Switzerland; the Renwick Gallery of the Smithsonian Institution; and The Corning Museum of Glass. His sculptural architectural glass has been installed at the World Golf Hall of Fame, ships of the Royal Caribbean and Celebrity cruise lines, and the International Conference Center in Racine, Wisconsin, among other sites.

JAMES HOUSTON, a prolific Steuben designer best known for his works inspired by wildlife and the Arctic, was born in 1921 in Canada. He studied at the Art Gallery of Toronto and the Ontario College of Art. After wartime service with the Toronto Scottish Regiment, he studied at the École Grande Chaumière in Paris and learned engraving at William Hayter's Atelier 17. As a civil administrator for the Canadian government in the Eastern Arctic, he lived on Baffin Island and promoted exhibitions of Eskimo art throughout the world. At Cape Dorset, he introduced printmaking to the Eskimos. There he met Arthur Houghton, who had come to the Arctic on a hunting expedition. In 1962, he accepted Houghton's invitation to become associated with Steuben Glass. Among his many writings are a number of award-winning children's books. His work is represented in the collections of the British Museum, the Philadelphia Museum of Art, the Winnipeg Art Museum, the Montreal Museum of Fine Arts, the National Museum of Canada, and the Glenbow Museum in Calgary, as well as in the private collections of the Queen Mother of England and King Carlos of Spain, among others. Today, Houston spends winters in Stonington, Connecticut, and summers in a cottage on the Queen Charlotte Islands off the coast of Alaska, where he continues to draw, write, and design glass.

GARY HUGHES, a gaffer, was first employed by Steuben in 1973 as an apprentice gatherer. Born and raised in Corning, he trained with master gaffer Harry Phillips. Hughes has contributed his expertise to the development of a range of Steuben stemware. He also created the glass design for the limited edition series of engraved Wild Game Flasks—Quail, Mallard, Turkey, and Pheasant—in collaboration with James Houston and others.

ZORAH HURD, a freelance illustrator and painter, studied at the Parsons School of Design, New York City. For several years she was staff illustrator for two fashion companies.

LUIS JIMINEZ, a sculptor, received his degree in art and architecture from the University of Texas. Formerly an assistant to Seymour Lipton, examples of his sculpture have been shown at the Whitney Museum of American Art in New York; the Fogg Art Museum, Cambridge, Massachusetts; and the John F. Kennedy Center for the Performing Arts, Washington, D.C.; and are in other private and public collections. His design for Steuben, Sea Girl, is limited to a single example.

DAVID JOHNSTON, an illustrator, was born in South Bend, Indiana. He is a graduate of the Art Center School, Los Angeles, and has been the recipient of both a silver and a gold medal from the Art Directors Club, Detroit. Johnston's work has frequently been shown in the annual Society of Illustrators Exhibition, New York City. Formerly a partner in the Detroit firm Designers and Partners, he has designed many book covers for such publishing houses as Bantam, Signet, and Harper and Row (now HarperCollins).

LEON KELLY is an American painter of Spanish-Irish descent, known for his vivid paintings in the surrealist and semiabstract style and for his themes taken from Irish fairy tales, fables, and folklore. His work is represented in most of the leading museums of the United States and he has also exhibited widely outside this country.

ALICE KOETH, a freelance artist specializing in decorative lettering, attended New York City schools and the Brooklyn Museum of Art School where she studied calligraphy and graphic design. In addition to routine inscription work, her special projects for Steuben include designing the inscriptions for a glass cross presented to the citizens of Kiev, Russia, to commemorate the thousand-year anniversary of Christianity there. She also fashioned the calligraphy for Shakespearean texts on Jane Osborn-Smith's Shakespeare's Flowers Bowl, presented to Queen Elizabeth II.

JACOB LANDAU, painter, lithographer, and engraver, is a graduate of the Philadelphia Museum School of Art. He also studied at the Académie de la Grande Chaumière in Paris and at the New School in New York City. Landau has taught at both the Philadelphia Museum School and at the Pratt Institute, Brooklyn. His work has been widely exhibited in France and in the United States at the Corcoran Gallery and the Museum of Modern Art, among other venues.

MICHAEL LANTZ, a sculptor, was born in New Rochelle, New York, and educated at the Beaux Arts Institute of Design and the National Academy of Design, New York City. He received his professional training as assistant to Lee Lawrie. A member of the National Sculpture Society, Lantz won the competition to design two equestrian groups for a terrace of the Federal Trade Commission building in Washington, D.C., in 1938. His work has been shown at the Philadelphia Association of Fine Arts and at the Philadelphia Art Alliance.

TOM LEA, a native of Texas, has written and illustrated many books. His murals decorate the Court House and Public Library in El Paso and United States Post Office buildings in a number of cities, including Washington, D.C.

CLARE LEIGHTON, printmaker and designer, was educated in her native London at the Slade School of Art and the County Council Central School of Art. After arriving in the United States in 1939, she became an American citizen. She wrote and illustrated twelve books of her own and provided the illustrations for many books by other authors. She designed the stained glass windows for St. Paul's Cathedral, Worcester, Massachusetts, and her prints are included in the permanent collections of The Metropolitan Museum of Art, New York City; the Victoria and Albert Museum, London; and other museums in Europe and the United States.

LINCHIA LI, a painter and teacher, was born in Fujian (Fukien) province, China, in 1920. Li taught painting at the China Institute, St. John's University, and the University of Pennsylvania; he lectured at many noted museums. In addition to flowers and animals, Li painted portraits of such notables as presidents Eisenhower, Kennedy, and Johnson. Li's work is represented in the collection of the

National Museum of History, Republic of China, in Taipei, and has been exhibited in many parts of the Far East and the United States.

EMIL LIE, a noted Norwegian sculptor, was born in 1897. He studied in Oslo and Rome and at the École des Beaux Arts, Paris, and exhibited his work at such prestigious Paris exhibitions as the Salon des Indépendents and the Salon d'Automne. Lie won the competition for sculptural decoration in the City Hall Plaza of Oslo and in 1930 was awarded the Prix Viking in Paris. His work is held in many private collections, and three of his best-known sculptures are in the Nasjonalgalleriet of Oslo, Norway.

MARY LOU LITTRELL was born in Kansas City, Missouri, and studied at the Kansas City Art Institute. She graduated from the Cooper Union Art School in New York City in 1960 and joined the Steuben design staff the same year. Littrell designed numerous calligraphic inscriptions for Steuben before concentrating on the design and production of Steuben's catalogues, promotional material, and other publications. She has won several awards for graphic design, including a silver medal from the Art Directors Club in 1981.

BRUNO LUCCHESI, sculptor, was born in Lucca, Italy, and studied at the art institute there. He taught at the University of Florence before coming to the United States in 1958. In 1960, Lucchesi began to teach at the New School in New York City. His sculpture is in the Whitney Museum of American Art, the Brooklyn Museum, and the Hirshhorn Museum and Sculpture Garden, Washington, D.C. Among Lucchesi's best-known works is Icarus, a bas-relief at Cornell University.

LYLE LUCE began his career with Steuben glass in 1979. A design cutter and finishing specialist, his proficiency in hand grinding and machine cutting techniques enabled him to co-design the Steuben Cross with Peter Drobny in 1997. Luce's works are in the collections of the U.S. Navy and in private collections in the United States. He is a veteran of the Vietnam War and the Gulf War.

GWEN LUX, a sculptor, was born in Chicago. She studied at the Maryland Institute of Art and the Boston Museum of Fine Arts, and with Ivan Mastrovi in Yugoslavia. Lux was awarded a Guggenheim Fellowship in 1933. Her work has been widely exhibited in the United States and abroad; her best-known commissions include Eve in the Radio City Music Hall of Rockefeller Center in New York City and Adolescence at the Detroit Institute of Arts.

ORONZIO MALDARELLI—a sculptor and educator—was born in Naples, Italy, and became a United States citizen in 1920. He taught sculpture at Columbia University. Maldarelli's work has been widely exhibited throughout the United States and is represented in the collections of such museums as the Art Institute of Chicago; the Pennsylvania Academy of the Fine Arts, Philadelphia; and New York's Metropolitan Museum of Art.

STANLEY MALTZMAN, a New York City painter and printmaker, studied at the New York–Phoenix Schools of Design. His works have been shown at the National Academy of Design, New York City; the Smithsonian Institution, Washington, D.C.; and the Albany Institute of History and Art. Maltzman received a Gold Medal Award in graphics from the American Artists Professional League.

BOLISLAV MANIKOWSKI was hired in 1917 by Frederick Carder and served as an etching worker. He was foreman of the etching department during the twenties. After 1933, he served for a time as Steuben's resident designer.

BRUNO MANKOWSKI came to the United States in 1933 from his native Germany. He received his early training under the supervision of his father, Tadeusz Mankowski, and later studied at the Beaux Arts Institute in New York City. A Fellow of the American Sculpture Society, Mankowski received many awards for his works, which have been shown at The Metropolitan Museum of Art, the Corcoran Gallery of Art, the National Sculpture Society and the National Academy of Design, and the Philbrook Art Center.

EZIO MARTINELLI, a painter, sculptor, and graphic artist, studied at the National Academy of Design in New York City; at the Barnes Foundation; and at the Accademia delle Belle Arti in Bologna, Italy. He taught at Sarah Lawrence College and at the Parsons School of Design. Martinelli received many awards for his work, including two Guggenheim Fellowships. Examples of his work are in the collections of the Whitney Museum of American Art, the Solomon R. Guggenheim Museum, and the Philadelphia Museum of Art, among other public institutions.

ANGUS MCDOUGALL, a sculptor, was a member of the Steuben design staff for a brief period during 1940. A native of Oxford, England, he was educated at the Royal College of Art, London.

JAMES MCNAUGHTON was a member of the Steuben Glass design department from October 1938 until January 1939.

DAN MEHLMAN, a freelance designer, artist, sculptor, and ceramist, has worked with Steuben for more than fifteen years in the hands-on development of many pieces of crystal. Trained at the Rhode Island School of Design with a Master of Arts from California State University at Fullerton, he has also taught product design and model making at a number of art schools and universities.

RICHARD MEIER, an eminent architect, designed a collection of two vases and a bowl for Steuben in 1994. After receiving his architectural training at Cornell University, Meier went on to an illustrious career as a designer of private residences, museums, high-tech and medical facilities, commercial buildings, and major civic commissions in the United States and Europe. In 1984, he received the Pritzker Architecture Prize and was selected as architect for the Getty Center, which opened in Los Angeles in 1997. Meier received the Royal Gold Medal from the Royal Institute of British Architects in 1989. He is a fellow of the American Institute of Architects and of the American Academy of Arts and Sciences.

RICHARD MILLER, a sculptor, was born in Ohio. He studied at the Cleveland Institute of Art and won a scholarship to study Pre-Columbian sculpture in Mexico. His work is held by many private collectors in the United States and Europe, and is represented in the Butler Institute of American Art, Youngstown, Ohio, and in the Hirshhorn Museum and Sculpture Garden, Washington, D.C.

GREGORY MIROW, a graphic artist and textile designer, was a supervisor of engraving at Steuben. He has been a stylist and colorist for New York textile firms and a designer of consumer products at the Corning Glass Works, Corning, New York. He published *A Treasury of Design for Artists and Craftsmen* in 1969.

BENI MONTRESOR, best known for his Caldecott Award–winning children's book illustrations and for his design of operatic sets and costumes, contributed the engraving design for Donald Pollard's masterwork, the Crown of Oberon. Born in Bussolengo, Italy, in 1929, Montresor was educated at the Arts Academy of Verona, later working as a designer for such film directors as Federico Fellini and Roberto Rossellini. He came to New York in 1960, and thereafter focused on operatic set design, dividing his time between Italy and Manhattan. Montresor died on October 11, 2001, in Verona, Italy.

BRUCE MOORE, a sculptor, designed many works for Steuben Glass. A native of Kansas, he studied at the Pennsylvania Academy of the Fine Arts in Philadelphia, and worked as a studio assistant to James Earle Fraser. Best known for his animal figures in stone, bronze, clay, and terra-cotta, Moore received many important commissions. His work is represented in the collections of the Whitney Museum of American Art in New York City, the Wichita Art Museum, the Pennsylvania Academy of the Fine Arts, and elsewhere. Moore was an academician of the National Academy of Design, New York City, and was director of the Rhinehart School of Sculpture, Baltimore, during the early years of World War II.

BARRY MOSER, a preeminent wood engraver, studied art at Auburn University and at the University of Tennessee. His illustrated versions of classics such as *Moby Dick*, Dante's *Divine Comedy*, and *Alice's Adventures in Wonderland* won numerous awards, including a National Book Award for Design in 1983. A member of the National Academy of Design, Moser has taught at The Rhode Island School of Design, Princeton University, and Vassar College, among other institutions of higher learning. In 1991, the Massachusetts native collaborated with Joel Smith on a collection of pieces celebrating the Globe theater, including the masterwork The Wide and Universal Stage.

FRANK NICHOLS, a graphic and product designer, graduated from the Art Center College of Design in Pasadena and has spent most of his career in New York City, working with a variety of design studios. He has earned awards from the New York Art Director's Club and the Industrial Designers Society of America.

JAMES NOLL, freelance designer, is a graduate of the University of Cincinnati. He has designed a wide range of products as well as graphics and interiors. In 1987 he was first commissioned by Steuben to design a number of pieces including Saturn, Scallop Sea Shell, and Starfish.

BRUCE NORTH, a painter, scenic designer, and cloisonné enamelist, studied at the School of Visual Arts, New York City, and at the Brooklyn Museum Art School. His work has appeared in exhibits throughout the eastern United States.

JANE OSBORN-SMITH, an independent artist best known for her remarkably detailed illustrations of animals, flowers, and plant life, has designed many engraved pieces of Steuben crystal since 1985. Born in England, she is a graduate of the Hornsey College of Art and the Royal College of Art in London. Her work has been widely exhibited in England, including at the Queen's Silver Jubilee Exhibition of 1978, the Edinburgh Festival of 1979, and at the Victoria and Albert Museum in London. Her one-of-a-kind Steuben bowl, Shakespeare's Flowers, was presented by President George Bush to Queen Elizabeth of England on the occasion of her state visit to the United States.

PETER PARNALL, a designer and illustrator, worked in commercial design for many years before becoming a teacher of design at Lafayette College. *Alfalfa Hill*, written and illustrated by Parnall, was published by Doubleday in 1974.

JERRY PFOHL, a painter, studied art in Paris and London, where he received gold and silver medals from the Regent Street Polytechnic. His paintings have been exhibited by museums throughout the United States, including the Pennsylvania Academy of the Fine Arts, Philadelphia; the Nebraska Art Association (courtesy the Sheldon Memorial Art Gallery), Lincoln; the National Academy of Design, New York City; and the Philbrook Art Center, Tulsa, Oklahoma.

WILLIAM PHILIPS, a sculptor, studied at the Massachusetts Institute of Technology's School of Architecture and at the Rhinehart School of Sculpture in Baltimore. He received the National Sculpture Society's John Gregory Award in 1959. Philips' work has appeared at the National Sculpture Society and the National Academy of Design, both in New York City, and is represented in many private collections.

DONALD POLLARD joined the Steuben design staff in 1950. A designer and painter, he was born in Bronxville, New York, in 1924. At the Rhode Island School of Design, he worked in silver under the trainee program of the Institute of Contemporary Art, Boston. Later, he worked for a time in architectural theater design, and served in the United States Navy during World War II. Over a long career with Steuben, he designed many decorative and functional pieces, including the Great Ring of Canada, which was presented by the president and people of the United States to the prime minister and people of Canada on the Centenary of Canada's nationhood. His masterwork, the Crown of Oberon, was introduced in 1981 as the centerpiece of a retrospective exhibition of Pollard's works organized to mark his retirement after thirty years at Steuben. Examples of Pollard's work in crystal are held in private and public collections throughout the world.

LUBOMER RICHTER, a master of copper-wheel engraving, was born in 1936 in Dobruska, Czechoslovakia. He studied engraving at the Glass Trade School in Novy Bor, receiving the school's highest accolades. In 1979 he came to the United States to join Steuben as an engraver.

LUCIANA G. ROSELLI studied art history at the universities of Pisa and Pavia, Italy. She has designed jewelry, textiles, and tableware. As an illustrator, her work has appeared in many magazines and children's books. She has also designed jewelry, textiles, and tableware.

DONALD RUSSELL was one of the first staff designers hired for Steuben by John Gates after the company's reorganization. Among his early exhibition pieces was a heavy-walled bowl in the Art Deco manner that was shown in the Paris Exhibition of 1937.

TAF LEBEL SCHAEFER, a sculptor in wood, stone, and cast bronze, earned a BFA from the Rhode Island School of Design. She later taught sculpture at the Maryland Hall for the Creative Arts in Annapolis and at the Corcoran Gallery's School of Art in Washington, D.C., as well as in her private studio in Maryland. Schaefer joined Steuben in 1998 as a designer of animals, but soon expanded her range to include a number of engraved designs, corporate pieces, and special commissions.

PETER SCHELLING, a master of copper-wheel engraving, was born in 1933 in Neustadt, Germany. He studied at the Glass Manufacturing School in Zweisel and the School of Fine Arts in Berlin before coming to the United States in 1953 and joining Steuben as an engraver. A member of the New York State Craftsmen, Schelling has taught engraving at Corning Community College.

PAUL SCHULZE, born in New York City in 1934, is a graduate of New York University and the Parsons School of Design, where he later taught for many years. After working in industrial design, Schulze joined the Steuben Glass design department in 1961 and became director of design in 1970, a position he held until his resignation in 1987. Schulze designed a wide range of pieces for Steuben, ranging from line items to major engraved decorative pieces to abstract sculptures such as New York, New York. His work has been exhibited in many museums including The Corning Museum of Glass and the American Craft Museum. Schulze's designs are also represented in the permanent collections of the National Air and Space Museum and of North Carolina State University, as well as in many private collections. In addition to his work with glass, Schulze is an accomplished watercolorist.

ALEXANDER SEIDEL, who designed the engraving for several of Steuben's masterworks, was born in Germany. A painter, he first studied art in Munich and then in Rome. Seidel came to the United States in 1939. For many years, he was staff artist for the American Museum of Natural History, New York City, where he illustrated many ornithological books and scientific papers and painted murals of extinct birds, saurians, and primates. His illustrations have appeared in several encyclopedias, and he published two books for young people on wild birds and water mammals.

PAUL SEIZ, a designer, is also a filmmaker, sculptor, and painter. A graduate of the Architectural Program at the Pratt Institute, Brooklyn, Seiz has been supervisor of the Corning Glass Works' architectural design department and chief of the Museum of the Performing Arts at Lincoln Center, in New York City. His exhibition installations include Corning Glass Center's "Hall of Science and Industry" and Burlington Industries' "The Mill."

ROGER SELANDER, a copper-wheel engraver, was born in 1945 to a glassmaking family in Corning. His grandfather, a gaffer, came to the United States from Finland, and his father was also a glassworker. Before joining Steuben as an apprentice engraver in 1966, Selander attended Corning Community College.

JULIE SHEARER, a painter and illustrator, was born in Charleston, South Carolina. For Steuben she designed the limited edition Iris Vase. Her artworks have been exhibited at shows organized by Audubon Artists, the Salmagundi Club, the Society of Illusrators, and The National Arts Club.

OREN SHERMAN, a graphic artist, is best known for his award-winning poster designs for such clients as the Kentucky Derby, Ringling Brothers Barnum & Bailey, and the Disney Resort and Cruise Line. He has also designed eight U.S. postage stamps, as well as covers for L.L. Bean catalogues, and he illustrated the Random House *Book of Greek Mythology*. Sherman graduated from the Rhode Island School of Design, where he currently serves on the faculty.

EMILY BROWN SHIELDS, a calligrapher, designed inscriptions and logos at Steuben for eleven years, including the lettering for David Dowler's 1986 Composers Bowl and Bernard X. Wolff's Liberty Crystal. A fine arts graduate of Wilson College, she studied with master calligrapher Donald Jackson, scribe to the House of Lords. She is a founding member of the New York Society of Scribes, and her work has appeared in several editions of the *Calligrapher's Engagement Calendar*, among other publications.

JUDYTHE SIECK, a calligrapher and specialist in children's book design, has won numerous awards for her book designs. Her work has been exhibited at Brown University and the Athenaeum Library of Art and Music in La Jolla, California, among other venues. For Steuben, she created the calligraphy for Joel Smith and Barry Moser's 1995 Infinite Love and for Joel Smith's 1997 Sundial.

ELIZABETH SILVAGNI, painter, studied in Boston at the School of the Museum of Fine Arts with Karl Zerbe and at the Boston Museum Summer School with Oskar Kokoschka. She received a B.S. degree in art education from Tufts University and an M.F.A. degree from Boston University. In 1952, a Ruth Sturdevant Scholarship sent her to Italy and France for thirteen months of study. Among her works are paintings in public and private collections; the Stations of the Cross for St. Jerome's Nuns' Chapel, South Weymouth, Massachusetts; and for the Librairie St. Michel, Boston. She has taught art at Cardinal Cushing College in Brookline, Massachusetts.

JUDY SMILOW, a product designer and graphic artist, graduated from Parsons School of Design and in 1985 founded her own company, Judy Smilow Design, in New York City, focusing on the design of dinnerware, giftware, jewelry, and tabletop items. She has worked for the Museum of Modern Art and many private clients. Her glass designs are held in the collections of the Cooper-Hewitt Design Museum, the Brooklyn Museum, and Yale University.

JOEL SMITH joined the Steuben design staff in 1988, later served as head of new product design, and is currently Steuben's design manager. Smith, who attended the Sorbonne, holds B.F.A. and Bachelor of Industrial Design degrees from the Rhode Island School of Design, as well as a bachelor's degree in history from George Washington University. In addition to numerous works in crystal created for the Steuben line, Smith designed a limited edition of glass-inlaid console tables, Steuben's first pieces of furniture. His special commissions include Remembrance, a sculpture produced in 1992 as the centerpiece of the Wilf Holocaust memorial in Whippany, New Jersey; and he created the masterwork The Wide and Universal Stage in 1990.

SUSAN VANDERBILT SMYLY, sculptor and designer, was born in Detroit, Michigan, and studied at Memphis Academy of Arts, Tennessee, and the Cranbrook Academy of Art, Bloomfield Hills, Michigan. She received a Fulbright Fellowship to Rome, twice won the Rome Prize given by the American Academy in Rome, and was given the Art Award of the American Academy and Institute of Arts and Letters, New York City. She has taught at Boston University, Temple University, and Queens College, and has been a visiting artist at the Rhode Island School of Design, the Cleveland Institute of Art, and Syracuse University. Her works have been exhibited by the Smithsonian Institution Traveling Exhibition Service, as well as in the Memorial Art Gallery of the University of Rochester, the Boston Athenaeum Gallery, and the Museum of Fine Arts in Springfield, Massachusetts.

BILL SULLIVAN, a self-taught sculptor best known for his woodcarvings, also works in clay, bronze, and glass. His works have been commissioned by such design notables as Parish-Hadley, Peter Marino, and Ralph Lauren. Sullivan's sculptures have been documented in many interior design books and periodicals, including *Architectural Digest* and *House and Garden* magazines.

LINO TAGLIAPIETRA, a celebrated Venetian glassmaker, was born in 1934 on the island of Murano, Italy. From the age of twelve, he apprenticed with other Muranese masters including Archimede Seguso, and became a master himself by the age of twenty-one. Later he worked at Galliano Ferro and Venini Glass, and was named head designer and glassblower at Effetre International in the mid-1970s. Since 1979 he has taught at leading international glass schools including the Pilchuck School, the Rhode Island School of Design, and the Studio of The Corning Museum of Glass, among others. Renowned among studio glass artists as both traditionalist and innovator, Tagliapietra came to Steuben in March 1998 to collaborate on a series of sixty masterworks. His glass has been exhibited by or is in the permanent collections of innumerable museums worldwide, including Palazzo Grassi, Italy; the Hokkaido Museum of Modern Art, Japan; the Danish Royal Museum; the Victoria and Albert Museum, London; the Musée des Arts Décoratifs in Paris; the Seattle Art Museum; and The Corning Museum of Glass.

TAKEO TAKEMASA, a copper-wheel engraver, was born in 1950 in Kubokawa Kochi, Japan. He received his bachelor's degree in art history from Cambridge University and his master's degree from the University of Tokyo. Before joining Steuben as an engraver in 1982, Takemasa completed the copper-wheel engraving program at the Tirol School in Austria.

GEORGE THOMPSON, for many years a senior staff designer, joined the Steuben design department upon its formation in 1936. Born in Nebraska, he received degrees in architecture from the University of Minnesota and the Massachusetts Institute of Technology. In 1936, he won the M.I.T. Class Medal and the Boston Institute of Architects Prize. Thompson's designs were included in every Steuben Glass exhibition held from 1937 until his retirement in 1974. His works are in the collections of The Metropolitan Museum of Art, New York City; the William Rockhill Nelson Gallery, Kansas City; Palais du Louvre, Paris; and the National Gallery of Modern Art, New Delhi.

CHRIS TOWNSEND, a servitor at Steuben for ten years, joined Corning Glass Works in 1973. Born into a family of glassworkers in Corning, he worked for a time with his father, a gaffer who was with the company for forty years. Townsend developed two of Steuben's holiday ornaments, the 1997 Acorn and the 2000 Pineapple.

ROBERT VICKREY, a painter, graduated from Yale University. He also studied at the Art Students League and with Kenneth Hayes Miller and Reginald Marsh. Vickrey's paintings are in many private and public collections in this country and abroad, including the Whitney Museum of American Art in New York City, the Atlanta Art Association, and the Dallas Museum of Fine Arts.

MASSIMO VIGNELLI, renowned as a designer of graphics, exhibitions, interiors, furniture, and consumer products, created the Whirlwind collection of six bar and serving pieces for Steuben in 1993. Born in Milan, Vignelli studied architecture in Milan and Venice. In 1971 he founded his firm, Vignelli Associates, with his wife and partner Lella; and in 1978 he initiated a second business, Vignelli Designs, in New York City. He has been widely recognized for a wide range of design contributions, and the recipient of numerous honorary doctorates of art and architecture from prominent institutions of higher learning, as well as prestigious international design prizes. Examples of his work have been exhibited widely in museums in the United States and abroad, and are represented in the permanent collections of the Museum of Modern Art, the Brooklyn Museum, and the Cooper-Hewitt Museum, among others.

TOM VINCENT, a painter, was a scholarship student at the University of Missouri at Kansas City and the Kansas City Art Institute, where he received his M.F.A. degree. At various times in his career, he was a professional ballet dancer, a semiprofessional football player, and a designer of stage settings in New York City. Among his awards for painting have been first and second prizes at New Jersey state shows and the Speiser Memorial Prize from the Pennsylvania Academy of the Fine Arts (1962).

SIDNEY WAUGH, together with Arthur Houghton and John Gates, was responsible for Steuben's reorganization in 1933, and was chief associate designer for the firm until his death in 1963. As a sculptor, Waugh received many awards, including the Rome Prize and the Herbert Adams Memorial Award for outstanding contribution to American sculpture. He was born in Amherst, Massachusetts, and was educated at Amherst College, the Massachusetts Institute of Technology School of Architecture, and the École des Beaux Arts in Paris. For a time, he was a pupil of and assistant to Henri Bouchard. Among his sculptural commissions were works for the United States Federal Courts Building, Washington, D.C.; Johns Hopkins University; and the United States Battle Monument in Florence, Italy. He was director of the Rhinehart School of Sculpture in Baltimore, Maryland, from 1942 to 1957, and the author of *The Art of Glassmaking* (1938) and *The Making of Fine Glass* (1947). Over the years, he designed both the form and the engraved decoration for many important pieces of Steuben glass, including the timeless Gazelle Bowl. His works in crystal are held in many collections, both public and private, in the United States and abroad.

ALBERT WEIN, a sculptor, was born in New York City. He studied at the National Academy of Design and the Grand Central School of Art there, and at the Beaux Arts Institute of Design, where his work won many competitions. He studied abroad as a recipient of the Rome Prize and of a Tiffany Foundation grant for sculpture. During his lifetime, Wein was accorded many honors for his work, including the Architectural League's Henry O. Avery Prize. His sculpture is represented in many collections, including those of New York City's Metropolitan Museum of Art and Whitney Museum of American Art.

PATRICIA WEISBERG, a calligrapher, collaborated with Donald Pollard on the engraving design for Steuben's Bicentennial Goblet, introduced in 1975 to commemorate the Bicentennial of the United States of America. For many years she designed most of Steuben's calligraphic inscriptions.

DON WIER, a designer, painter, and graphic artist, joined Steuben's design staff in 1945. He was educated at the University of Michigan and studied art at the Chicago Academy of Fine Arts and at the Grand Central School of Art, New York City. Wier was a faculty member of the latter institution for eight years. During his early career, Wier painted portraits of children, made flower paintings, and illustrated books. His designs for Steuben include many pieces now represented in such public collections as the Detroit Institute of Art; the Musée Royaux d'Art et d'Histoire in Brussels, Belgium; and Lincoln Center for the Performing Arts, New York City.

LAURENCE WHISTLER, an English poet, began to engrave glass in 1936. He became the foremost exponent of the diamond-stipple engraving technique, which he incorporated into his designs for Steuben. Educated at Stowe and at Balliol College, Oxford, Whistler won the King's Medal for Poetry and published several volumes of poems, in addition to a biography of Sir John Vanbrugh, the architect of Blenheim Palace.

ROBERT WINTHROP WHITE, a sculptor, is also known for his drawings. He studied at the Rhode Island School of Design in Providence and later received a fellowship at the American Academy in Rome. White's work has been exhibited in New York, Boston, Pennsylvania, Washington, D.C., and in Rome.

BERNARD X. WOLFF joined Steuben in 1973 as assistant director of design, a position he held until 1987. Born in California, he studied at the Chouinard Art School, Los Angeles, before joining Walt Disney Productions as assistant director of publications. Afterward, he moved to Rome to study at the Academy of Fine Arts and to work as art director for *Rome Daily American* and the music magazine *Discotecca*. He returned to the United States as chief designer for the Brooklyn Museum. At Steuben, Wolff was responsible for the design of major exhibitions in the New York shop, and he personally designed many pieces of crystal as well, including the popular engraved ornamental, Balloon Rally.

PETER YENAWINE, who was a member of the Steuben design department from 1969 to 1976, was born in Athens, Georgia, in 1944. He graduated from the Syracuse University School of Art, where his special interests were sculpture, silversmithing, and aesthetics. While a student, he received an Alcoa Aluminum award for package design, and he was selected for a General Motors internship. His work in silver has been shown at the Museum of Contemporary Crafts, New York City. During his tenure at Steuben, Yenawine designed a wide range of pieces. He later opened a studio for metal and glass art in Swarthmore, Pennsylvania.

MARCO ZANINI, a designer and architect, was born in Trento, Italy, in 1954. After graduating from the University of Florence, he spent three years traveling in the United States before returning to Milan in 1977 as an assistant to Ettore Sottsass. Later, as a partner and managing director of Sottsass Associates, he was design manager for a wide range of interiors, exhibits, and products, including furniture. A founding member of the Memphis movement in 1980, Zanini created pieces for all of its collections. Apart from his work with Sottsass Associates, Zanini works privately on the design of ceramics, jewelry, furniture, and objects in blown glass. For Steuben he designed the Calypso group, two vases and a bowl, in 1994.

ROBERT ZIERING, a painter, illustrator, and graphic designer, studied at New York University and at the School of Visual Arts, also in New York City. Examples of his work may be found in the John Fitzgerald Kennedy Library in Dorchester, Massachusetts, New York's Metropolitan Opera Association, and numerous private collections.

CATALOGUE INTRODUCTION

The catalogue is as nearly definitive as we could make it. Although Steuben continues to introduce a number of new designs each year, we had to decide on a termination date; thus the listing for stock and exhibition pieces is through the year 2001. At Steuben's request, we have omitted a large category of crystal specially commissioned by private individuals or business firms. In another category called Form and Function, we have listed by name but not provided photos or line drawings for a group of 127 one-off or few-of-a-kind pieces that never went into full production but were sold to collectors at a number of special sales at the New York shop. Finally, for some very early pieces of crystal, we were unable to find visual documentation, and these pieces have consequently not been illustrated. In the main, however, the catalogue documents the preponderance of Steuben's output between 1933 and 2002—some 1,499 pieces of stock glass and 1,384 decorative or exhibition pieces.

In arranging and describing pieces listed in the catalogue, we have followed Steuben's market categories (Stock Glass, Major Ornamental Designs, etc.) and we have retained their descriptive terminology. Exhibition Pieces in Series are presented first, arranged in roughly chronological order ("Twenty-seven Contemporary Artists in Crystal" was an exhibition in 1940, "British Artists in Crystal" in 1954, and so on). Exhibition pieces that are not part of any series are listed by designer in an alphabetical arrangement. The name of the designer of the glass form always precedes the name of the engraving designer, and the key to the artist abbreviations is given separately on page 248. There are instances where two or more designers have collaborated on a single piece of glass. Such a piece is listed under the designer's name whose contribution, whether to form or engraved decoration, was deemed most important to the final character of the piece. Stock glass comprises the largest section of the catalogue, and we have illustrated stock items with line drawings, keyed to captions giving the essential information where available—number, designer, introduction date, introduction price, and dimension. For space reasons, only the largest dimension is given (h.=height, w.=weight, l.=length, dia.=diameter). Although the major ornamental designs are stock pieces in the true sense of the word, we have listed these in a separate section and illustrated them with photographs; this documents more clearly than a drawing the special details of many pieces embellished with gems, precious metals, or engraved decorations. Jewelry, too, has been given its own section, owing to its detailed nature.

A word about Steuben's numbering system is perhaps in order. Steuben assigns a special stock number to each of its designs. These numbers remain the best means of identifying specific articles of Steuben glass since many pieces from the early Houghton years are so similar physically as to defy identification by title. (We have noted verbal titles in all instances where they are known.)

In Carder's day, pieces of Steuben were numbered in simple progressive sequence corresponding to the order of their introduction. Under Houghton in the early 1930s, a new system was initiated: When the design department accepted a tentative design for trial, it was numbered with an X followed by three digits. Stock pieces that successfully made it into the line were given a new SP (stock piece) number followed by three digits. If the stock piece was commercially successful, it was reassigned a four-digit number without an alphabetical prefix. Because exhibition pieces were made in relatively small quantities, they usually retained their trial X number even in production. However, if an exhibition piece was made as part of a special series or show, it was assigned a number beginning with a special letter prefix. ("Twenty-seven Contemporary Artists in Crystal" pieces begin with the letter A, followed by three digits, for example.) Designs reserved for sale to the State Department were given an OX prefix, blanks intended for special engraving carried an E prefix, and major ornamental designs were assigned the letters MOD before their three-digit number.

This system prevailed until 1967, when electronic data processing was introduced. Then all designs in production—regardless of date of introduction—were assigned four-digit code numbers, with the first digit defining the category to which the piece belongs. Pieces of exhibition glass, for example, are now assigned four-digit numbers beginning with a zero. Major ornamental designs (pieces in this category are distinguished from "exhibition glass" by price at introduction—currently under $4,000) carry the number 1 as their first identifying digit; engraving blanks and custom designs for private customers carry a 4; hand coolers a 5; and stock pieces are numbered beginning with an 8. Pieces that don't fit any of those categories are assigned a 6 as the first identifying digit—some exceptional exhibition pieces and furniture, for example. A series of 64 special works created by Lino Tagliapietra in 1998 is also numbered beginning with the number 6. (Not all the Tagliapietra pieces were photographed and thus are listed in this catalogue by name and number only.)

A final category of glass that does not precisely follow the numbering system described above is called Form and Function. About 127 pieces of ornamental or functional glass designed, created, and signed Steuben (but not put into full production for one reason or another) fall into this group. Usually only one to three examples of such pieces were made, and unlike full production pieces, they were not photographed. Form and Function items were offered in a number of special sales at the New York shop beginning in 1990. A list of such pieces is included in this catalogue, identified only by title and number. Form and Function pieces offered for sale in 1992 carry a four-digit number beginning with 8; those sold in 1993 and 1994 carry a four-digit number beginning with 6.

Hundreds of new pieces of Steuben glass have been produced in the twenty years since this book first appeared, and they have all been incorporated into the appropriate categories of the catalogue in this revised edition in chronological order wherever possible. Two of the numbering systems described above (the simple four-digit system and the SP-plus-digits system for stock pieces) were used simultaneously over a period of decades, though no pieces produced after 1981 carry the SP designation. To make it easier to find specific pieces in this much-enlarged catalogue (though it deviates from straight chronology) all the pieces with SP prefixes are presented first within specific categories, followed by those having the sequential run of four-digit numbers without prefix.

Readers should note that many of the prices given for pieces made in or after 1981 are not introductory prices, but the last price at which the piece was sold by Steuben before being discontinued. However, the group of pieces produced for the 1980 "Sculpture by David Dowler" exhibition are accompanied by accurate introductory prices, obtained from an insert in the exhibition catalogue.

KEY TO ARTISTS AND DESIGNERS

A.A.H.	Arthur A. Houghton, Jr.
A.C.	Angela Cummings
A.D.	André Derain
A.Do.	Arthur Douglass
A.K.	Alice Koeth
A.M.	Aristide Maillol
A.Mc.D.	Angus McDougall
A.S.	Alexander Seidel
A.Sch.	Albert Schaller
A.W.	Albert Wein
B.L.	Bruno Lucchesi
B.M.	Bolislav Manikowski
B.Ma.	Bruno Mankowski
B.Mo.	Bruce Moore
B.Mon.	Beni Montresor
Ba.M.	Barry Moser
B.N.	Bruce North
B.S.	Bill Sullivan
B.X.W.	Bernard X. Wolff
C.A.	Cary Austin
C.B.	Cecil Beaton
C.H.	Chris Hacker
C.J.	Clain Johnson
C.L.	Clare Leighton
C.L.H.	Charlotte-Linnea Hallett
Ch.B.	Christian Bérard
Ch.L.	Charles Liedl
C.T.	Chris Townsend
D.C.	Donald Crowley
Des.	Design Department
D.D.	David Dowler
D.Da.	Dan Dailey
D.De.	Donald Demers
D.G.	Duncan Grant
D.H.	David Hills
D.J.	David Johnston
D.Joe.	Dale Joe
D.M.	Dan Mehlman
D.P.	Donald Pollard
D.R.	Donald Russell
D.W.	Don Wier
E.B.S.	Emily Brown Shields
E.G.	Eric Gill
E.H.	Eric Hilton
E.L.	Emil Lie
E.M.	Ezio Martinelli
E.O.	Elliot Offner
E.Si.	Elizabeth Silvagni
E.St.	Earl Stampp
F.C.	Frederick Carder
F.D.	Frank Dobson
F.E.	Frank Eliscu
F.L.	Fernand Léger
F.N.	Frank Nichols
G.	Giampietro
G.D.	Gary Davis
G.D.C.	Giorgio de Chirico
G.F.	Golda Fishbein
G.L.	Gwen Lux
G.M.	Gregory Mirow
G.O.K.	Georgia O'Keeffe
G.S.	Graham Sutherland
G.T.	George Thompson
G.W.	Grant Wood
H.D.S.	Herike Dolwer-Steinauer
H.G.	Harold Gross
H.M.	Henri Matisse
H.R.	Howard Rogers
I.B.	Irene Benton
I.N.	Isamu Noguchi
I.S.	Irene Schelling
J.B.	J. Battersby
J.C.	James Carpenter
J.Co.	Jean Cocteau
J.D.	John Dreves
J.E.	Jacob Epstein
J.G.	John Gregorey
J.Ha.	Jiri Harcuba
J.H.	James Houston
J. Hu.	Jean Hugo
J.L.	Jacob Landau
J.Le.	Jeanne Leach
J.M.	John Minton
J.Mc.N.	James McNaughton
J.M.G.	John M. Gates
J.M.S.	José Maria Sert
J.N.	John Nash
J.No.	James Noll
J.O.S.	Jane Osborn-Smith
J.P.	Jerry Pfohl
J. Pi.	John Piper
J.S.	Joel Smith
J.S.C.	John Stuart Curry
J.Sh.	Julie Shearer
J.Si.	Judythe Sieck
K.D.S.	Katherine De Sousa
K.J.	Karin Jonzen
K.V.E.	Kenneth Van Etten
L.A.	Lloyd Atkins
L.C.	Letterio Calapai
L.D.	Leslie Durbin
L. F.	Louis Feron
L.Fr.	Lucian Freud
L.H.	Ladislav Havlik
L.J.	Luis Jiminez
L.Ke.	Leon Kelly
L.Kr.	Leon Kroll
L.L.	Linchia Li
L.Lu.	Lyle Luce
L.P.	Leonard Parker
L.R.	Lubomer Richter
L.Ro.	Luciana G. Roselli
L.T.	Lino Tagliapietra
L.W.	Laurence Whistler
M.B.	Muirhead Bone
M.D.	Marshall Davis
M.G.	Michael Graves
M.H.	Meredith Hamilton
M.He.	Milton Hebald
M.Ho.	Michael Horen
M.K.	Moise Kisling
M.L.	Michael Lantz
M.Lau.	Marie Laurencin
M.S.	Matthew Smith
M.V.	Massimo Vignelli
M.Z.	Marco Zanini
N.C.	Neil Cohen
N.H.	Nien-tsu Hu
O.Ma.	Oronzio Maldarelli
O.Me.	Omer Menard
O.Mes.	Oliver Messel
O.S.	Oren Sherman
P.A.	Peter Aldridge
P.B./M.G.	Phillip Baldwin & Monica Guggisberg
P.D.	Patricia Davidson
P.Dro.	Peter Drobny
P.G.	Philip Grushkin
P.Ga.	Paul Gardner
P.Gr.	Paul Greiff
P.H.	Peter Hurd
P.Ha.	Paul Haigh
P.M.	Paul Manship
P.P.	Peter Parnall
P.S.	Paul Seiz
P.Sche.	Peter Schelling
P.Schu.	Paul Schulze
P.T.	Pavel Tchelitchew
P.W.	Patricia Weisberg
P.Y.	Peter Yenawine
R.C.	Robert Cassetti
R.D.	Rush Dougherty
R.Da.	Robin Darwin
R.Du.	Raoul Duft
R.E.	Roland Erlacher
R.M.	Richard Meier
R.Mi.	Richard Miller
R.Mo.	Rodrigo Moynihan
R.R.	Ruth Ray
R.S.	Reynolds Stone
R.V.	Robert Vickrey
R.W.	Robert White
R.Y.G.	R.Y. Godden
R.Z.	Robert Ziering
S.A.	Samuel Ayres
S.B.	Steve Bertron
S.C.	Steve Carver
S.D.	Salvador Dali
S.D.E.	Stephen Dale Edwards
S.D.T.	Steuben Design Team
S.F.	Sheldon Fink
S.M.	Stanley Maltzman
S.S.	Susan Smyly
S.W.	Sidney Waugh
T.A.	Timothy Angell
T.B.	Thomas Buechner
T.H.	Terry Haass
T.Ha.	Thomas Hacker
T.H.B.	Thomas Hart Benton
T.L.	Tom Lea
T.L.S.	Taf Lebel Schaefer
T.T.	Thomas Tisch
Ta.T.	Takeo Takemasa
T.V.	Tom Vincent
W.D.T.	Walter Dorwin Teague
W.H.	Walter Heintze
W.P.	William Philips
Z.B.	Zevi Blum
Z.H.	Zorah Hurd

CONTENTS

PIECES 1933–2001

Exhibition Pieces in Series

TWENTY-SEVEN ARTISTS IN CRYSTAL

A300 *The Cat*
I.N. (1940) 10" dia.

A301 *Engraved Vase*
G.D.C. (1940) 11¾" h.

A302 *Acrobats*
P.T. (1940) 13½" h.

A303 *Engraved Plate*
G.O.K. (1940) 14" dia.

A304 *Engraved Plate*
T.H.B. (1940) 13⅛" dia.

A305 *Engraved Vase*
D.R. and H.M. (1940) 14¾" h.

A306 *Adam and Eve*
G.T. and E.G. (1940) 14" h.

A307 *Engraved Plate*
Ch.B. (1940) 13" dia.

A308 *Engraved Vase*
J.Co. (1940) 11¼" h.

A309 *Engraved Vase*
J.G. (1940) 15⅛" h.

A310 *Engraved Urn*
M.Lau. (1940) 11" h.

A311 *Engraved Plate*
J.S.C. (1940) 14" dia.

A312 *Engraved Bowl*
F.L. (1940) 11" h.

A313 *Engraved Bowl*
S.D. (1940) 8¾" h.

A314 *Engraved Bowl*
J.Hu. (1940) 8¾" h.

A315 *Engraved Bowl*
R.Du. (1940) 11⅝" h.

A316 *Archipelago*
S.W. (1940) 15½" h.

A317 *Engraved Vase*
P.H. (1940) 12⅜" h.

A318 *Engraved Vase*
G.T. and G.W. (1940) 13¾" h.

A319 *Engraved Vase*
P.M. (1940) 13¾" h.

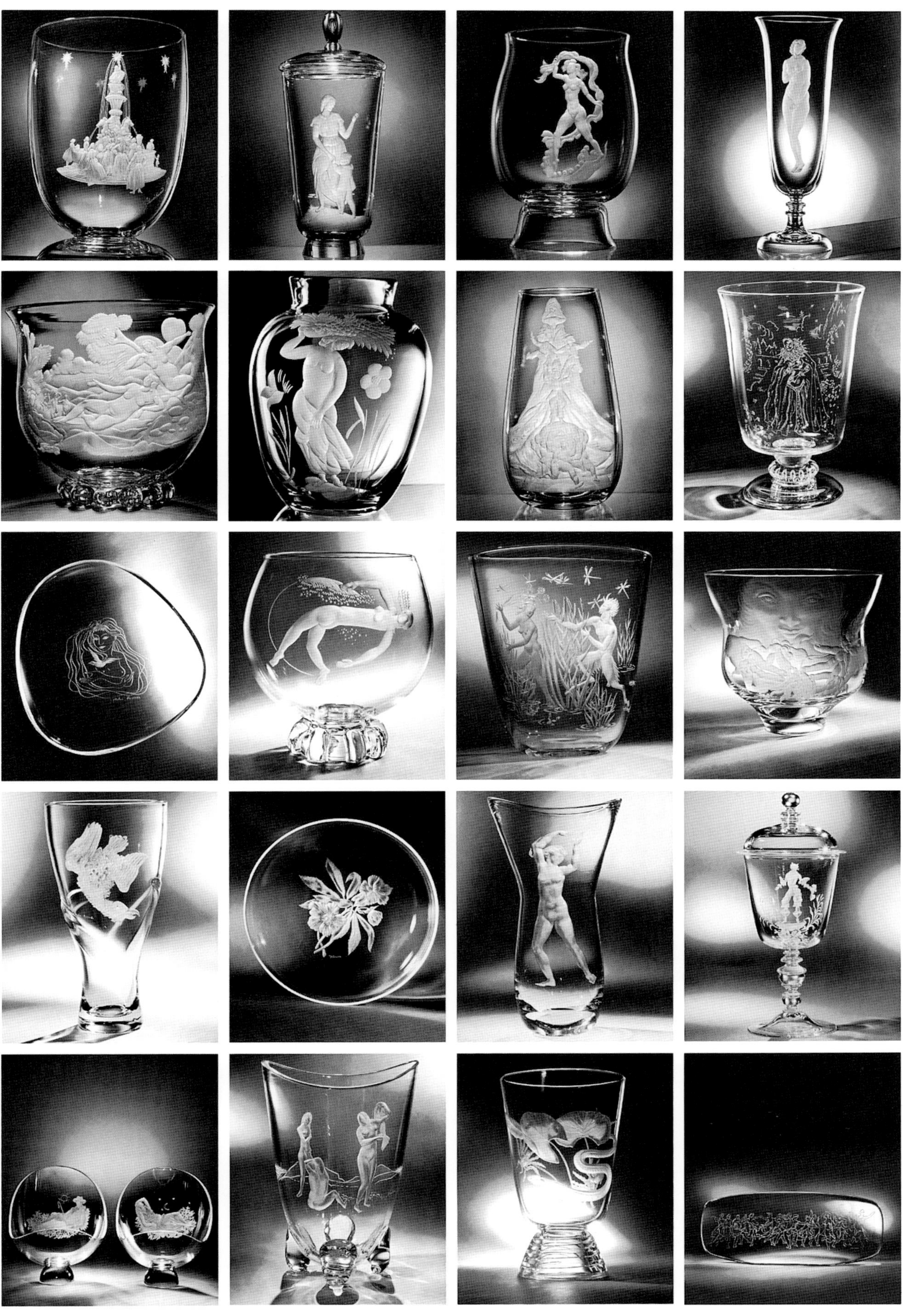

A320 *Fountain in Spain*
M.B. (1940) 11½" h.

A321 *Engraved Vase*
L.Kr. (1940) 18½" h.

A322 *Engraved Vase*
A.M. (1940) 12" h.

A323 *Engraved Vase*
J.M.G. and M.K. (1940) 19⅝" h.

A325 *Engraved Bowl*
A.D. (1940) 11¼" h.

A326 *Summer*
D.G. (1940) 11½" h.

A327 *Engraved Vase*
J.M.S. (1940) 13" h.

BRITISH ARTISTS IN CRYSTAL

B500 *Lady-in-Waiting*
C.B. (1954) $850, 14" h.

B501 *The Dove*
R.Da. (1954) 13" dia.

B502 *The Wave*
F.D. (1954) $1200, 11" h.

B503 *Pan and Nymph*
L.D. (1954) $850, 10" h.

B504 *Orchids*
D.P. and J.E. (1954) $2,000, 11" dia.

B505 *Bird of Prey*
G.T. and L.Fr. (1954) 12¾" h.

B506 *Christmas Rose*
R.Y.G. (1954) 14" dia.

B507 *Dancing Nude*
G.T. and K.J. (1954) 12½" h.

B508 *Puss in Boots*
O.Mes. (1954) $950, 15¾" h.

B509 *Day and Night*
L.A. and J.M. (1954), $1,000, 9½" h.

B510 *The Bathers*
R.Mo. (1954) $750, 11¼" h.

B511 *Snake and Frogs*
J.D. and J.N. (1954) 12" h.

B512 *Frieze*
G.T. and J.Pi. (1954) $1,150, 19" l.

B513 *Reverie*
D.P. and M.S. (1954) 10½" h.

B514 *Wood Anemone*
R.S. (1954) 13½" dia.

B515 *Mantis*
G.T. and G.S. (1954) 14¾" h.

B516 *Civilization*
L.W. (1954) $1,000, 12¾" h.

ASIAN ARTISTS IN CRYSTAL

Y2909 *Momoyama*
L.A. and Suekichi Akaba, Japan (1956) 14" h.

Y2910 *The Lone Bamboo in All Its Gracefulness*
L.A. and Ma Shou-hua, China, 15½" h.

Y2911 *Korean Sword Dance*
G.T. and Kim Ki-chang, Korea, 12¾" h.

Y2925 *New Year in Formosa*
G.T. and Ran In-ting, China, 13¾" h.

Y2926 *The Floating Village*
L.A. and Nguyen-van-Long, Vietnam, 13½" h.

Y2929 *The Village of Malinao*
L.A. and Manuel R. Rodriguez, The Philippines, 10" h.

0144 *Saying of Confucius*
D.P. and Cho Chung-yung, China, 7¼" h.

Y2931 *Bhima and the Snake*
G.T. and Raden Basoeki Abdullah, Indonesia, 15½" h.

Y2932 *Ananda, Disciple of Buddha*
D.P. and Shiko Munakata, Japan, 17½" h.

0145 *Bodhisattva*
D.P. and Kiyoshi Saito, Japan, 9½" h.

Y2935 *The Temple Dance*
G.T. and Agus Djaya, Indonesia, 11½" h.

Y2936 *Balinese Funeral*
L.A. and Made Djate, Indonesia, 19" h.

Y2937 *Nang Fa—Siamese Angel*
D.P. and Narumol Sarobhassa, Thailand, 13¼" dia.

Y2938 *Burmese Royalty*
G.T. and U Ohn Lwin, Burma, 16" h.

Y2939 *Gopis in the Grove of Vrindavana*
G.T. and Jamini Roy, India, 10¾" dia.

Y2940 *The Unicorn*
G.T. and Sheikh Ahmed, Pakistan, 8¾" h.

Y2942 *Spring Festival of Krishna and Radha*
D.P. and Rama Maharana, India, 13¼" h.

Y2944 *The Turkish Tray*
L.A. and Bedri Rahmi Eyuboglu, Turkey, 18¾" h.

Y2946 *Blind Minstrel*
G.T. and Pat Roy, Iraq, 12½" h.

Y2947 *Cypress of Shiraz*
G.T. and Ja'far Shoja, Iran, 19" h.

Y2948 *The Crane*
D.P. and Hossein Khatai, Iran, 12" h.

Y2954 *The Goddess Tara*
D.P. and L.T.P. Manjusri, Ceylon, 12½" h.

Y2956 *Returning Home*
G.T. and Phani Bhusan, India, 9 ¼" h.

Y2957 *Kinnaras*
L.A. and Virojna Nutapundu, Thailand, 13¼" h.

Y2958 *Khajuraho Temple*
D.P. and K.S. Kulkarni, India, 16¾" h.

Y2959 *The Poppy*
L.A. and Kenan Ozbel, Turkey, 15¼" h.

Y2960 *The Bodhisattva Vishvantara Gives Away His Wife*
D.P. and George Keyt, Ceylon, 17¼" h.

Y2961 *Tonaya*
L.A. and U Mya, Burma, 12¼" h.

Y2962 *Harana in Manila*
D.P. and Arturo Rogerio Luz, The Philippines, 11" h.

Y2963 *Monkeys*
G.T. and Gopal Ghose, India, 16" h.

Y2965 *Lions Rampant*
L.A. and Parviz Mofidi, Iran, 11½" h.

Y2966 *Bread*
G.T. and Hussein Amin Bikar, Egypt, 14¾" h.

Y2967 *Gazelles*
D.P. and Alfred Baccache, Syria, 9¾" dia.

Y2969 *Dawn*
L.A. and Gamal Sagini, Egypt, 10½" h.

Y2970 *Lovers on Shemm-en-Neseem*
D.P. and Hamed Abdalla, Egypt, 9¼" h.

Y2971 *Eve*
G.T. and Al Hussein Fawzi, Egypt, 10¾" h.

UNITED STATES IN CRYSTAL

W200 *The United States of America*
S.W. (1959) $3,250, 18" h.

W201 *Alabama*
S.W. (1959) $1,650, 15" h.

W202 *Arizona*
S.W. (1959) $1,650, 15" h.

W203 *Arkansas*
S.W. (1959) $1,650, 15" h.

W204 *California*
S.W. (1959) $1,650, 15" h.

W205 *Colorado*
S.W. (1959) $1,650, 15" h.

W206 *Connecticut*
S.W. (1959) $1,650, 15" h.

W207 *Delaware*
S.W. (1959) $1,650, 15" h.

W208 *Florida*
S.W. (1959), $1,650, 15" h.

W209 *Georgia*
S.W. (1959) $1,650, 15" h.

W210 *Idaho*
S.W. (1959) $1,650, 15" h.

W211 *Illinois*
S.W. (1959), $1,650, 15" h.

W212 *Indiana*
S.W. (1959) $1,650, 15" h.

W213 *Iowa*
S.W. (1959) $1,650, 15" h.

W214 *Kansas*
S.W. (1959) $1,650, 15" h.

0157 *Kentucky*
S.W. (1959) $1,650, 15" h.

W216 *Louisiana*
S.W. (1959) $1,650, 15" h.

W217 *Maine*
S.W. (1959) $1,650, 15" h.

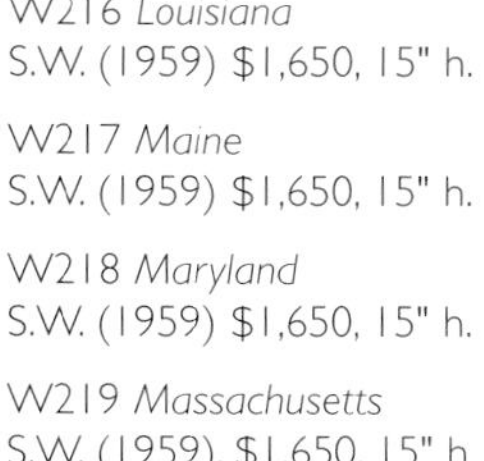

W218 *Maryland*
S.W. (1959) $1,650, 15" h.

W219 *Massachusetts*
S.W. (1959), $1,650, 15" h.

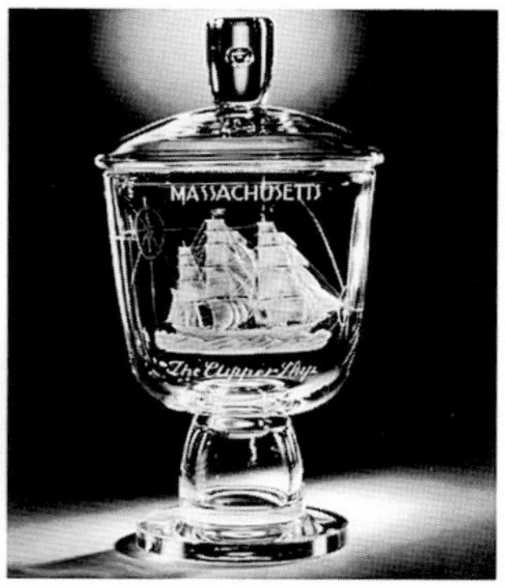

W220 *Michigan*
S.W. (1959) $1,650, 15" h.

W221 *Minnesota*
S.W. (1959) $1,650, 15" h.

W222 *Mississippi*
S.W. (1959) $1,650, 15" h.

W223 *Missouri*
S.W. (1959) $1,650, 15" h.

W224 *Montana*
S.W. (1959) $1,650, 15" h.

W225 *Nebraska*
S.W. (1959) $1,650, 15" h.

W226 *Nevada*
S.W. (1959) $1,650, 15" h.

W227 *New Hampshire*
S.W. (1959) $1,650, 15" h.

W228 *New Jersey*
S.W. (1959) $1,650, 15" h.

W229 *New Mexico*
S.W. (1959) $1,650, 15" h.

W230 *New York*
S.W. (1959) $1,650, 15" h.

W231 *North Carolina*
S.W. (1959) $1,650, 15" h.

W232 *North Dakota*
S.W. (1959) $1,650, 15" h.

W233 *Ohio*
S.W. (1959) $1,650, 15" h.

W234 *Oklahoma*
S.W. (1959) $1,650, 15" h.

W235 *Oregon*
S.W. (1959) $1,650, 15" h.

W236 *Pennsylvania*
S.W. (1959) $1,650, 15" h.

W237 *Rhode Island*
S.W. (1959) $1,650, 15" h.

W238 *South Carolina*
S.W. (1959) $1,650, 15" h.

W239 *South Dakota*
S.W. (1959) $1,650, 15" h.

W240 *Tennessee*
S.W. (1959) $1,650, 15" h.

W241 *Texas*
S.W. (1959) $1,650, 15" h.

W242 *Utah*
S.W. (1959) $1,650, 15" h.

W243 *Vermont*
S.W. (1959) $1,650, 15" h

W244 *Virginia*
S.W. (1959) $1,650, 15" h.

W245 *Washington*
S.W. (1959) $1,650, 15" h.

W246 *West Virginia*
S.W. (1959) $1,650, 15" h.

W247 *Wisconsin*
S.W. (1959) $1,650, 15" h.

W248 *Wyoming*
S.W. (1959) $1,650, 15" h.

W249 *Hawaii*
S.W. (1959) $1,650, 15" h.

W250 *Alaska*
S.W. (1959) $1,650, 15" h.

W251 *Puerto Rico*
S.W. (1959) $1,650, 15" h.

POETRY IN CRYSTAL

C700 *The Aim*
G.T. (1963) $3,250, 10¼" h.

C701 *April Burial*
L.A. and L.Kr. (1963) $4,500, 16½" h.

C702 *Aria*
L.A. and L.Kr. (1963) $2,250, 10½" h.

C703 *Bird Song*
G.T. and A.S. (1963) $2,500, 12" h.

0002 *Birds and Fishes*
D.P. and R.V. (1963) $8,500, 13" h. (w/base)

C705 *The Breathing*
D.W. (1963) $2,250, 6½" h.

0190 *The Certainty*
D.P. and D.Joe. (1963) $3,250, 8" w.

C707 *The Dragon Fly*
G.T. and B.Mo. (1963) $2,500, 9½" h.

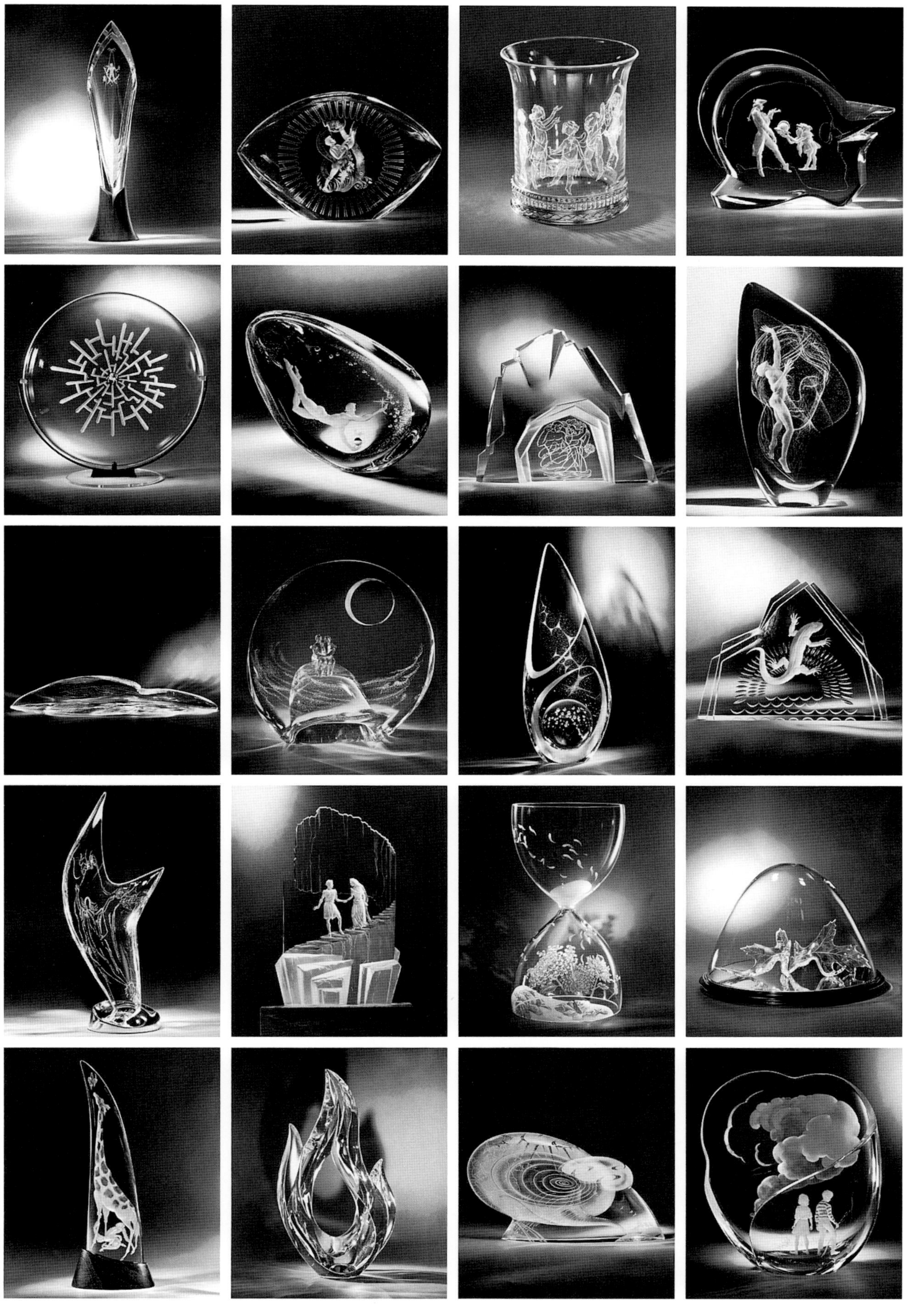

0003 *Harvest Morning*
L.A. and B.Mo. (1963) $2,500, 18" h. (w/base)

C709 *Horn of Flowers*
L.A. and C.L. (1963) $2,750, 12¼" l.

C710 *Leaving*
D.P. and F.E. (1963) $2,750, 5½" h.

C711 *The Maker*
D.P. and S.W. (1963) $4,250, 10¾" w.

C712 *A Maze*
L.A. (1963) $2,250, 15¾" h. (w/base)

0004 *Models of the Universe*
D.P. and W.P. (1963) $2,750, 8" w.

C714 *Off Capri*
G.T. and S.W. (1963) $4,250, 10½" w.

C715 *Orpheus*
G.T. and T.V. (1963) $3,000, 11¼" h.

C716 *Pacific Beach*
D.P. and J.La. (1963) $5,000, 20¾" l.

C717 *Partial Eclipse*
J.H. (1963) $3,300, 8¼" h.

C718 *Standstill*
G.T. (1963) $3,000, 15" h.

C719 *Stories*
G.T. and S.W. (1963) $3,000, 10" w.

C720 *Strong As Death*
D.P. and E.Si. (1963) $3,850, 18" h.

C721 *Telos*
D.W. (1963) $5,250, 13" h.

C722 *This Season*
D.P. and A.S. (1963) $4,250, 13½" h.

C723 *Threnos*
D.P. (1963) $6,500, 17" w.

0005 *To a Giraffe*
L.A. and F.E. (1963) $3,000, 18" h. (w/base)

C725 *To Build a Fire*
L.A. (1963) $2,500, 12" h.

C726 *Tornado Warning*
L.A. and B.Mo. (1963) $4,250, 13" l.

C727 *Trip*
G.T. and R.V. (1963) $3,000, 10¾" h.

C728 *The Victorians*
G.T. and D.W. (1963) $3,750, 8" h.

C729 *Voyage to the Island*
G.T. (1963) $3,000, 15¾" h.

0006 *Who Hath Seen the Wind?*
D.P. (1963) $6,600, 15" l.

STUDIES IN CRYSTAL

R101, R102 *Arctica*
G.T. (1955) $300, 9½" h.

R103 *Flight*
D.P. (1955) $550, 12½" h.

R104 *Sea Bird*
D.P. (1955) $650, 17" h.

0022 *Illusion*
G.T. (1955) $250, 9" h.

R106 *Mirage*
G.T. (1955) $250, 12" h.

R107 *Enigma*
D.P. (1955) $1,350, 12" h.

R108 *Largo*
L.A. (1955) $700, 10" l.

0023 *Cathedral*
G.T. (1955) $1,200, 15¾" h.

R110 *Firebird*
D.P. (1955) $450, 17½" h.

R111 *Ascent*
G.T. (1955) $350, 13¾" h.

0024 *Sea Breeze*
G.T. (1955) $1,250, 14½" h.

0025 *Counterpoise*
D.P. (1955) $900, 21¼" h.

0026 *Illusion*
G.T. (1955) $250, 9" h.

R115 *Polyhedra*
G.T. (1965) $2,000, 11" h.

R116 *Spiral*
G.T. (1965) $1,400, 18" h. (w/base)

R117 *Oval Inclusion*
G.T. (1965) $750, 6½" h. (w/stand)

R118 *Double Leaf*
P.Schu. (1965) $1,000, 19¼" h.
(w/base)

R119 *Free Inclusion*
G.T. (1965) $600, 8¼" h.

R120 *Totem*
P.Schu. (1965) $1,250, 15½" h. (w/base)

R121 *Cut Inclusion I*
G.T. (1965) $750, 6½" h. (w/base)

R122 *Expanding Inclusion*
G.T. (1965) $850, 4½" h.

R123 *Root-Two Solid*
P.Schu. (1965) $500, 4½" h.

R124 *Extended Totem*
P.Schu. (1965) $1,350, 29½" h. (w/base)

R125 *Ball Interior*
P.Schu. (1965) $250, 13½" h.

R126 *Spiral Column*
P.Schu. (1965) $1,600, 20" h. (w/base)

R127 *Cut Totem*
P.Schu. (1965) $1,250, 20" h. (w/base)

R128 *Cut Inclusion II*
J.H. (1965) $750, 5½" h.

0027 *Prismatic Column*
P.Schu. (1965) $1,500, 16" h.

R130 *Prism I*
G.T. (1965) $1,400, 5¾" h.

R131 *Prism II*
G.T. (1965) $1,400, 8½" h.

R132 *Incised Cone*
G.T. (1965) $300, 8¾" h.

R133 *Open Inclusion I*
G.T. (1965) $600, 6¼" h.

R134 *Pyramid*
G.T. (1965) $300, 4½" h.

R135 *Open Inclusion II*
G.T. (1965) $600, 5¼" h.

R136 *Rounded Inclusion*
G.T. (1965) $350, 6" h.

R137 *Floating Forms I*
G.T. (1965) $300, 4½" h.

R138 *Floating Forms II*
G.T. (1965) $300, 4½" h.

R139 *Square Spiral*
P.Schu. (1965) $1,750, 8¾" h.

R140 *Supported Crystal*
J.H. (1965) $900, 8" h.

R141 *Blade*
G.T. (1966) $1,850, 21" h. (w/base)

R142 *Spiral II*
G.T. (1966) $1,750, 11½" h.

R143 *Prism III*
G.T. (1966) $1,850, 13½" h. (w/base)

R144 *Construction*
P.Schu. (1966) $2,750, 11½" w.

R145 *Oval Inclusion II*
G.T. (1966) $800, 6½" h. (w/base)

R146 *Floating Forms III*
G.T. (1966) $400, 5½" h. (w/base)

R147 *Tensions*
G.T. (1966) $800, 9¼" h.

R148 *Torque*
P.Schu. (1966) $1,950, 7" dia.

R149 *Subtraction*
P.Schu. (1966) $1,750, 4" h.

R150 *Intersection I*
P.Schu. (1966) $1,750, 10¼" h. (w/base)

R151 *Intersection II*
P.Schu. (1966) $1,650, 5" h.

R152 *Open Sphere I*
G.T. (1966) $1,250, 7" w.

R153 *Open Sphere II*
G.T. (1966) $1,500, 7" w.

R154 *Tangents*
L.A. (1966) $1,800, 17" h. (w/base)

R155 *Trihedron*
P.Schu. (1966) $1,250, 8" w.

R156 *Interplay*
G.T. (1966) $800, 8½" h.

R157 *Tetra*
P.Schu. (1966) $500, 5" w.

R158 *Open Ball*
P.Schu. (1966) $1,600, 10" h. (w/base)

R159 *Loop*
L.A. (1966) $2,000, 14" h. (w/base)

R160 *Totem II*
P.Schu. (1966) $2,250, 14¼" h. (w/base)

R161 *Fish*
L.A. (1966) $1,650, 13½" l.

R162 *Alation*
L.A. (1966) $1,250, 15½" h. (w/base)

R163 *Volute*
L.A. (1966) $2,000, 10" h.

R164 *Spheres*
P.Schu. (1966) $850, 5½" h. (w/base)

R165 *Cubisphere*
P.Schu. (1966) $400, 7¼" h. (w/base)

R166 *Convolution*
P.Schu. (1966) $2,250, 8" h. (w/base)

0028 *Cut Ball*
P.Schu. (1968) $2,500, 9" h. (w/base)

0029 *Cut Prism*
G.T. (1969) $1,400, 8" h.

0030 *Rotating Sphere*
P.Schu. (1969) $2,750, 9¾" h. (w/stand)

0031 *Cubed Sphere*
P.Schu. (1969) $400, 6" h. (w/base)

R171 *Cut Cones*
G.T. (1969) $2,500, 9½" h., 13 ¾" h., 16" h.

4312 *Composition*
P.Schu. (1969) $3,750, 8½" h. (w/base)

R173 *Oval Inclusion III*
G.T. (1969) $1,650, 9½" h.

0032 *Hyperbolas*
G.T. (1969) $3,500, 12" h.

0033 *Cut Prism II*
G.T. (1969) $1,100, 6" h.

0034 *Pyramidon*
G.T. (1969) $1,100, 8¼" h. (w/stand)

0035 *Convolution II*
P.Schu. (1969) $3,000, 6¾" h. (w/base)

R178 *Totem III*
P.Schu. (1969) $3,000, 15½" h. (w/base)

R179 *Squares and Circle*
G.T. (1969) $1,250, 7¼" h.
(w/stand)

0036 *Ellipses and Circles*
G.T. (1969) $1,475, 8" h.

0037 *Cut Prism III*
G.T. (1969) $1,250, 6¼" h.

R182 *Concurrence*
D.P. (1970) $5,000, 19" h.
(w/stand)

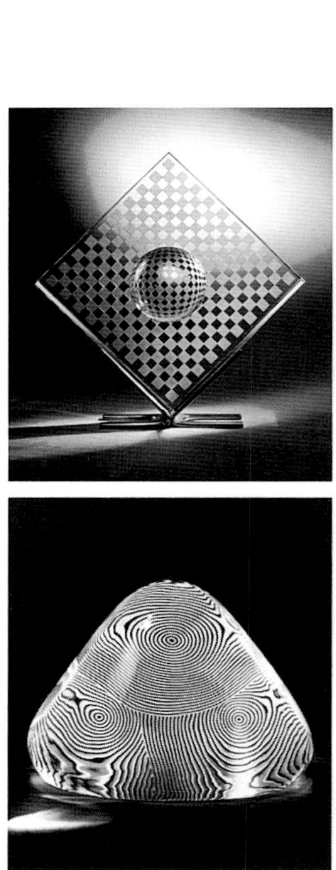

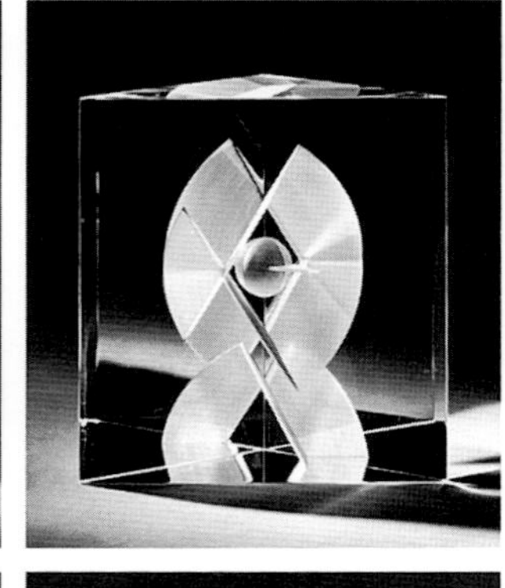

0038 *Concentric Circles*
G.T. (1970) $750, 6¾" w.

0039 *Diagonals*
L.A. (1970) $3,000, 9" h.
(w/stand)

R185 *Trihedrons*
G.T. (1970) $3,750, 11½" h.

R186 *Interplay I*
P.Schu. (1970) $1,750, 7¼" h.

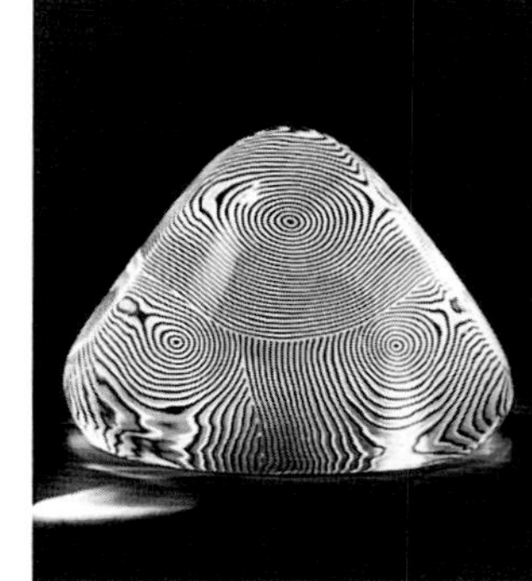

0040 *One Plus One Equals Three*
G.T. (1970) $2,000, 5" h.

0041 *Galaxy I*
G.T. (1971) $3,750, 36" h.
(w/base)

0042 *Triangles*
R.D. (1971) $1,550, 6" h.
(w/base)

R190 *Cylindra I*
G.T. (1971) $1,250, 10½" h.

0043 *Cylindra II*
G.T. (1971) $1,500, 10" h.

R192 *Cylindra V*
G.T. (1971) $1,600, 11½" h.
(w/base)

0149 *Cylindra III*
G.T. (1971) $1,500, 8" h.

R194 *Cylindra IV*
G.T. (1971) $1,500, 8¼" h.

0044 *Tetrahedra*
L.A. (1971) $1,850, 12½" h.
(w/base)

0045 *Offright*
R.D. (1972) $3,300, 11¼" h.
(w/base)

0046 *Triangles II*
R.D. (1972) $425, 4¾" w.

0047 *Circles*
P.Y. (1972) $985, 6½" h. (w/base)

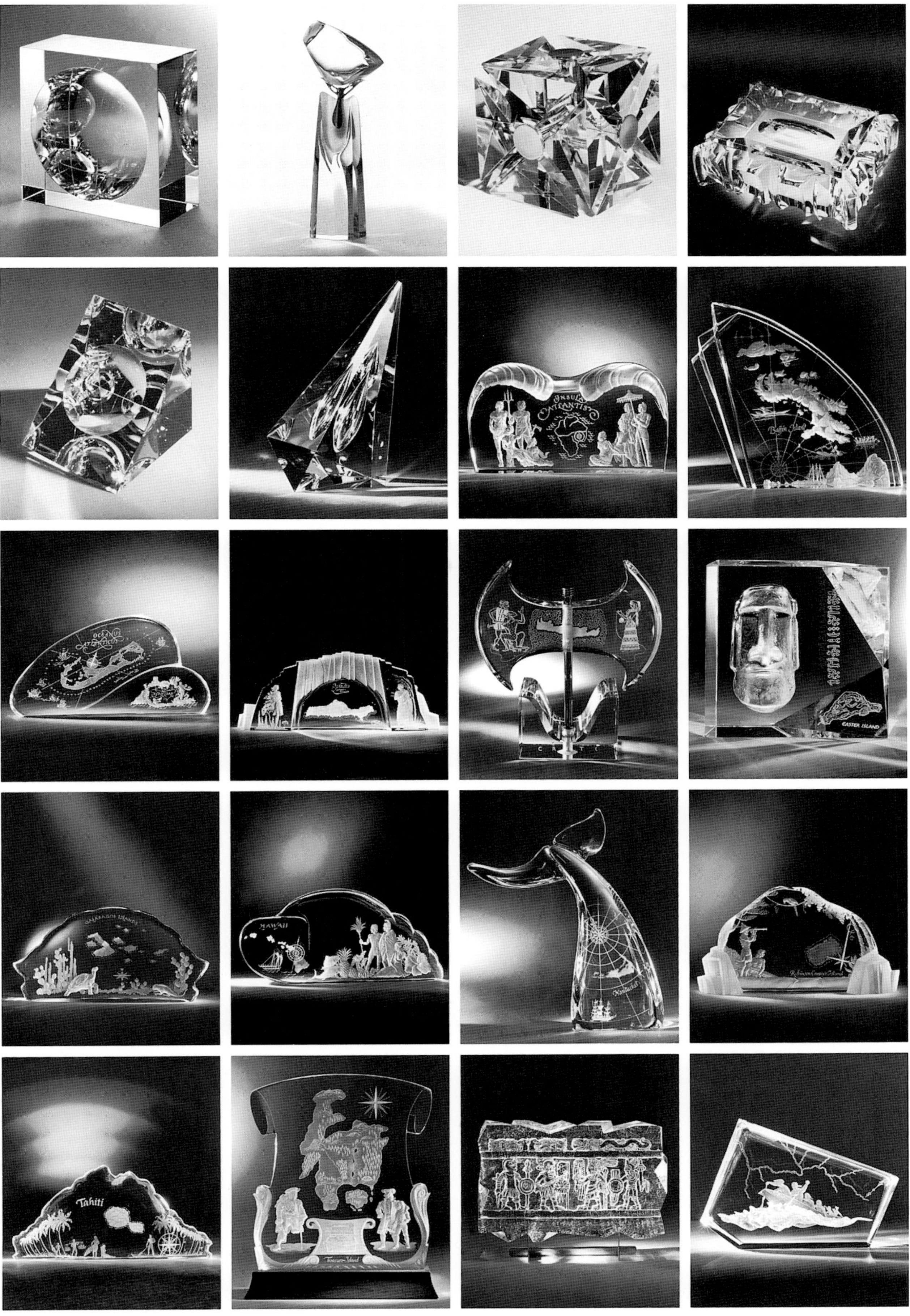

0048 *Circle in a Square*
P.Schu. (1973) $1,000, 6" h.

0049 *Duolith*
P.Y. (1974) $4,250, 14¾" h.

0050 *Spaced Cube*
R.D. (1973) $5,750, 4¾" h.

0051 *Prismatic Box*
E.H. (1974) $3,750, 7¼" l.

0052 *Circle in a Prism*
L.A. (1974) $750, 4½" h.

R204 *Pointed Prism with Teardrop*
G.T. (1974) $1,650, 8" h.

ISLANDS IN CRYSTAL

F900 *Atlantis*
D.W. (1966) $8,500, 11" l.

0016 *Baffin Island*
G.T. and J.H. (1966) $6,750, 9¼" l.

0017 *Bermuda*
D.W. (1966) $6,000, 15" l.

0018 *Capri*
D.W. (1966) $8,000, 14½" l.

F904 *Crete*
D.P. and A.S. (1966) $5,500, 10½" h.

0019 *Easter Island*
P.Schu. (1966) $6,500, 8" h.

0020 *Galapagos*
D.W. (1966) $5,000, 11½" l.

0021 *Hawaii*
D.W. (1966) $6,000, 13½" l.

F908 *Nantucket*
J.H. (1966) $3,500, 10" h.

F909 *Robinson Crusoe's Island*
D.W. (1966) $5,250, 10½" l.

F910 *Tahiti*
D.W. (1966) $4,750, 11¼" l.

F911 *Treasure Island*
L.A. and M.Ho. (1966) $7,800, 12½" h. (w/base)

GREAT EXPLORERS

0007 *Hernando Cortes*
P.Schu. (1970) $9,500, 9" h. (w/stand)

0008 *Lewis and Clark*
P.Schu. and J.H. (1970) $6,500, 9¾" l.

0009 *Leif Erikson*
J.H. (1970) $5,500, 8" h.

0010 *Ferdinand Magellan*
L.A. (1970) $6,750, 7" h.

0011 *David Livingstone*
D.P. (1971) $7,200, 13¼" h. (w/base)

0012 *Henry Hudson*
J.H. (1971) $5,750, 10½" h.

0013 *James Cook*
G.T. (1971) $7,000, 10½" w.

0014 *Christopher Columbus*
D.P. and R.Z. (1971) $8,350, 15½" h.

0015 *Robert Falcon Scott*
J.H. (1972) $7,000, 14½" l.

FLOWER DOMES

0169 *Dogwood I (Virginia)*
B.X.W. and A.S. (1975) $2,950, 5½" dia.

0170 *Violet I (Rhode Island)*
B.X.W. and A.S. (1975) $2,950, 5½" dia.

0171 *Mountain Laurel I (Connecticut)*
B.X.W. and A.S. (1975) $2,950, 5½" dia.

0172 *Wild Rose (New York)*
B.X.W. and A.S. (1975) $2,950, 5½" dia.

0173 *Dogwood II (North Carolina)*
B.X.W. and A.S. (1975) $2,950, 5½" dia.

0174 *Black-Eyed Susan (Maryland)*
B.X.W. and A.S. (1975) $2,950, 5½" dia.

0175 *Violet II (New Jersey)*
B.X.W. and A.S. (1975) $2,950, 5½" dia.

0176 *Trailing Arbutus (Massachusetts)*
B.X.W. and A.S. (1975) $2,950, 5½" dia.

0177 *Mountain Laurel II (Pennsylvania)*
B.X.W. and A.S. (1975) $2,950, 5½" dia.

0178 *Yellow Jessamine (South Carolina)*
B.X.W. and A.S. (1975) $2,950, 5½" dia.

0179 *Peach Blossom (Delaware)*
B.X.W. and A.S. (1975) $2,950, 5½" dia.

0180 *Cherokee Rose (Georgia)*
B.X.W. and A.S. (1975) $2,950, 5½" dia.

0181 *Purple Lilac (New Hampshire)*
B.X.W. and A.S. (1975) $2,950, 5½" dia.

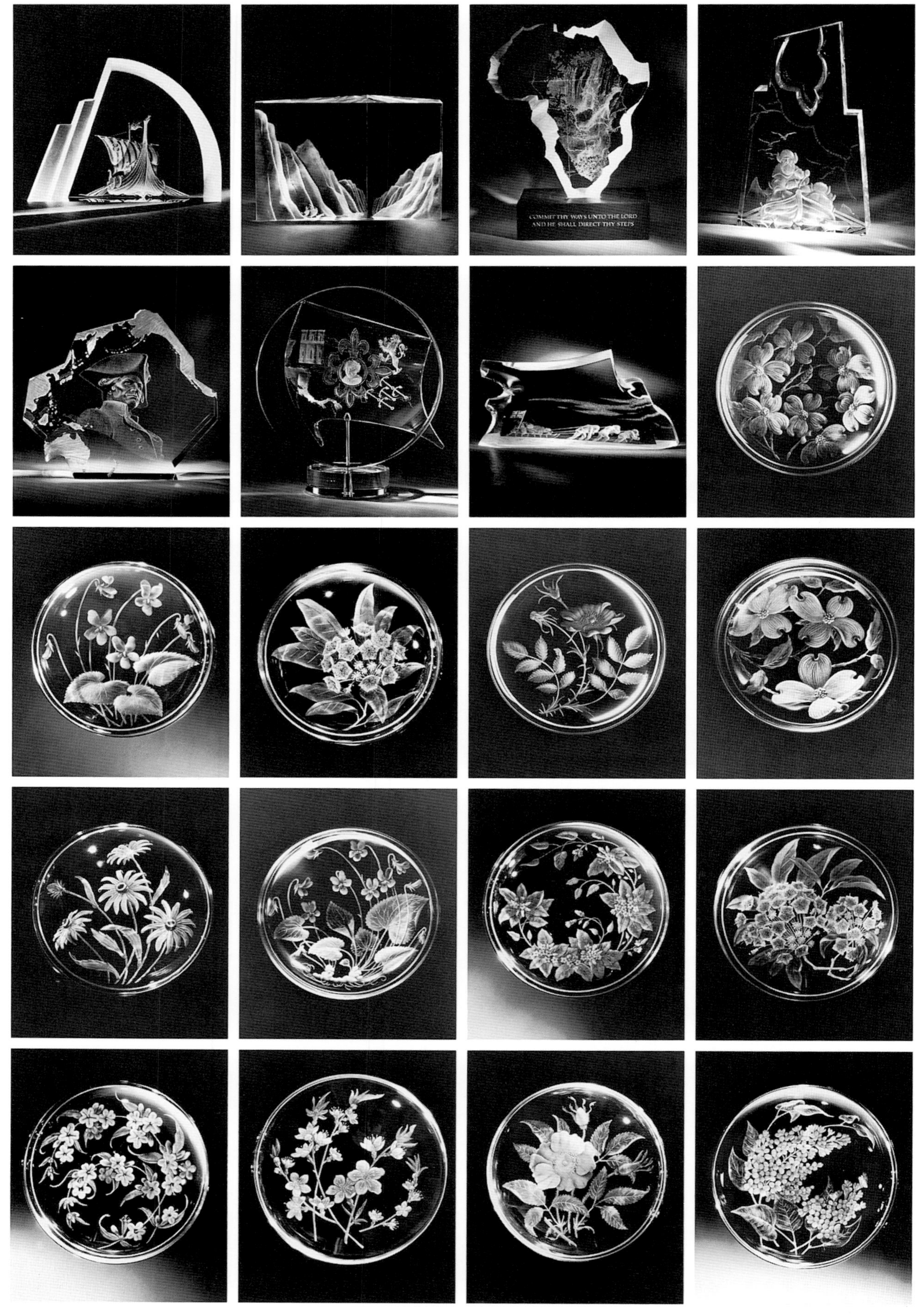

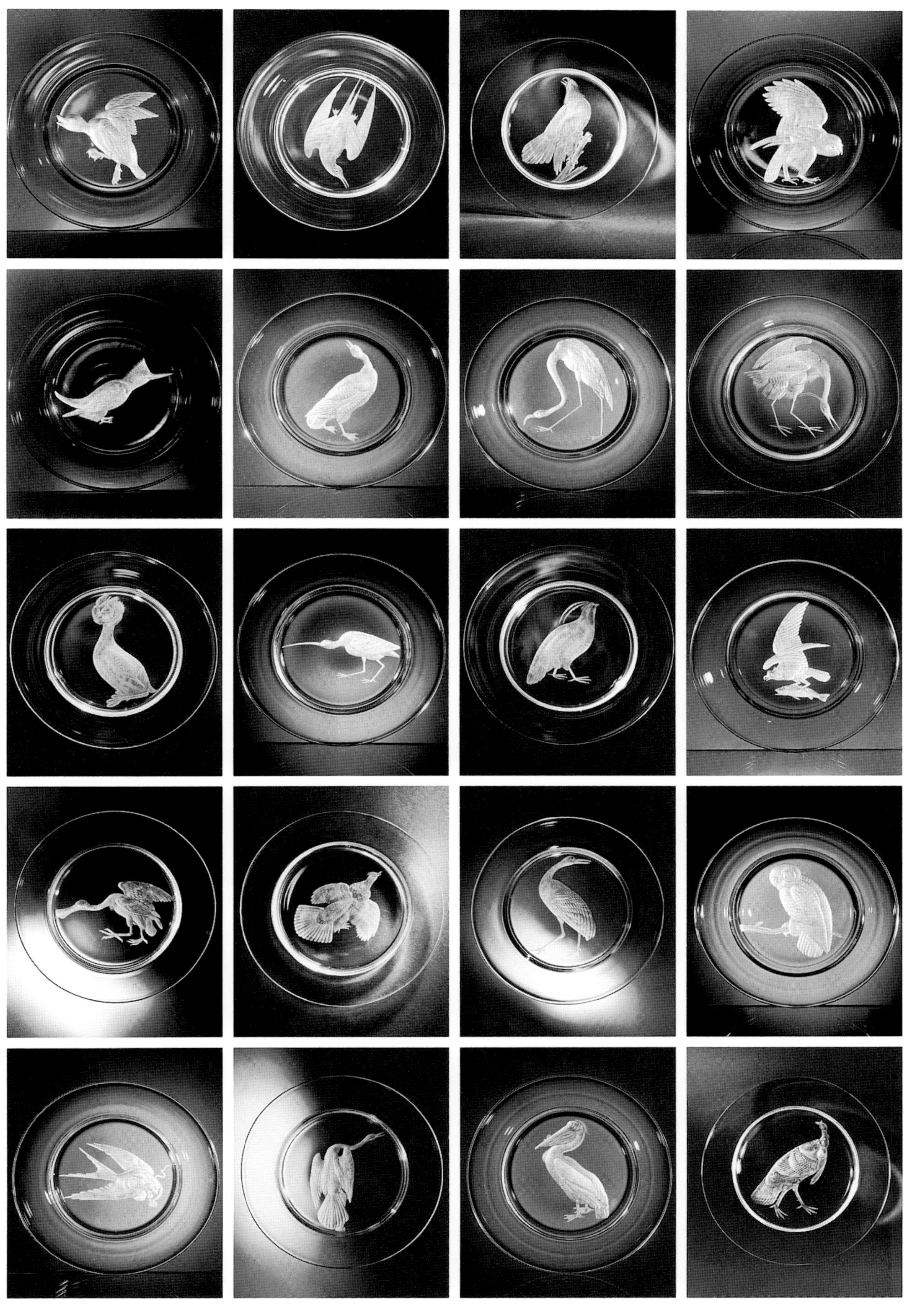

AUDUBON PLATES

2028 *American Golden-eye*
S.W. (1943–50) $300, 10" dia.

2028 *Arctic Tern*
S.W. (1940) $300, 10" dia.

2028 *Bald Eagle*
S.W. (1940) $300, 10" dia.

2028 *Barred Owl*
S.W. (1940) $300, 10" dia.

2028 *Belted Kingfisher*
S.W. (1943–50) $300, 10" dia.

2028 *Canada Goose*
S.W. (1943–50) $300, 10" dia.

2028 *Flamingo*
S.W. (1940) $300, 10" dia.

2028 *Great Blue Heron*
S.W. (1940) $300, 10" dia.

2028 *Horned Grebe*
S.W. (1940) $300, 10" dia.

2028 *Long-billed Curlew*
S.W. (1943–50) $300, 10" dia.

2028 *Mountain Quail*
S.W. (1940) $300, 10" dia.

2028 *Osprey*
S.W. (1943–50) $300, 10" dia.

2028 *Roseate Spoonbill*
S.W. (1940) $300, 10" dia.

2028 *Ruffed Grouse*
S.W. (1940) $300, 10" dia.

2028 *Sandhill Crane*
S.W. (n.d.) $300, 10" dia.

2028 *Snowy Owl*
S.W. (1943–50) $300, 10" dia.

2028 *Swallow-tailed Kite*
S.W. (1940) $300, 10" dia.

2028 *Water-turkey*
S.W. (n.d.) $300, 10" dia.

2028 *White Pelican*
S.W. (1940) $300, 10" dia.

2028 *Wild Turkey*
S.W. (1940) $300, 10" dia.

STAR PLATES

2028 *Pisces*
D.W. (1960) $450, 10" dia.

2028 *Aries*
D.W. (1960) $450, 10" dia.

2028 *Taurus*
D.W. (1960) $450, 10" dia.

2028 *Gemini*
D.W. (1960) $450, 10" dia.

2028 *Cancer*
D.W. (1960) $450, 10" dia.

2028 *Leo*
D.W. (1960) $450, 10" dia.

2028 *Virgo*
D.W. (1960) $450, 10" dia.

2028 *Libra*
D.W. (1960) $450, 10" dia.

2028 *Scorpio*
D.W. (1960) $450, 10" dia.

2028 *Sagittarius*
D.W. (1960) $450, 10" dia.

2028 *Capricorn*
D.W. (1960) $450, 10" dia.

2028 *Aquarius*
D.W. (1960) $450, 10" dia.

SHELL PLATES

X3347 *Bear's Paw*
D.W. 10" dia.

X3347 *Bonnet*
D.W. 10" dia.

X3347 *Caranaria*
D.W. 10" dia.

X3347 *Chambered Nautilus*
D.W. 10" dia.

X3347 *Crusaders' Scallop*
D.W. 10" dia.

X3347 *Harp Shell*
D.W. 10" dia.

X3347 *Slit Shell*
D.W. 10" dia.

X3347 *Tabled Neptune*
D.W. 10" dia.

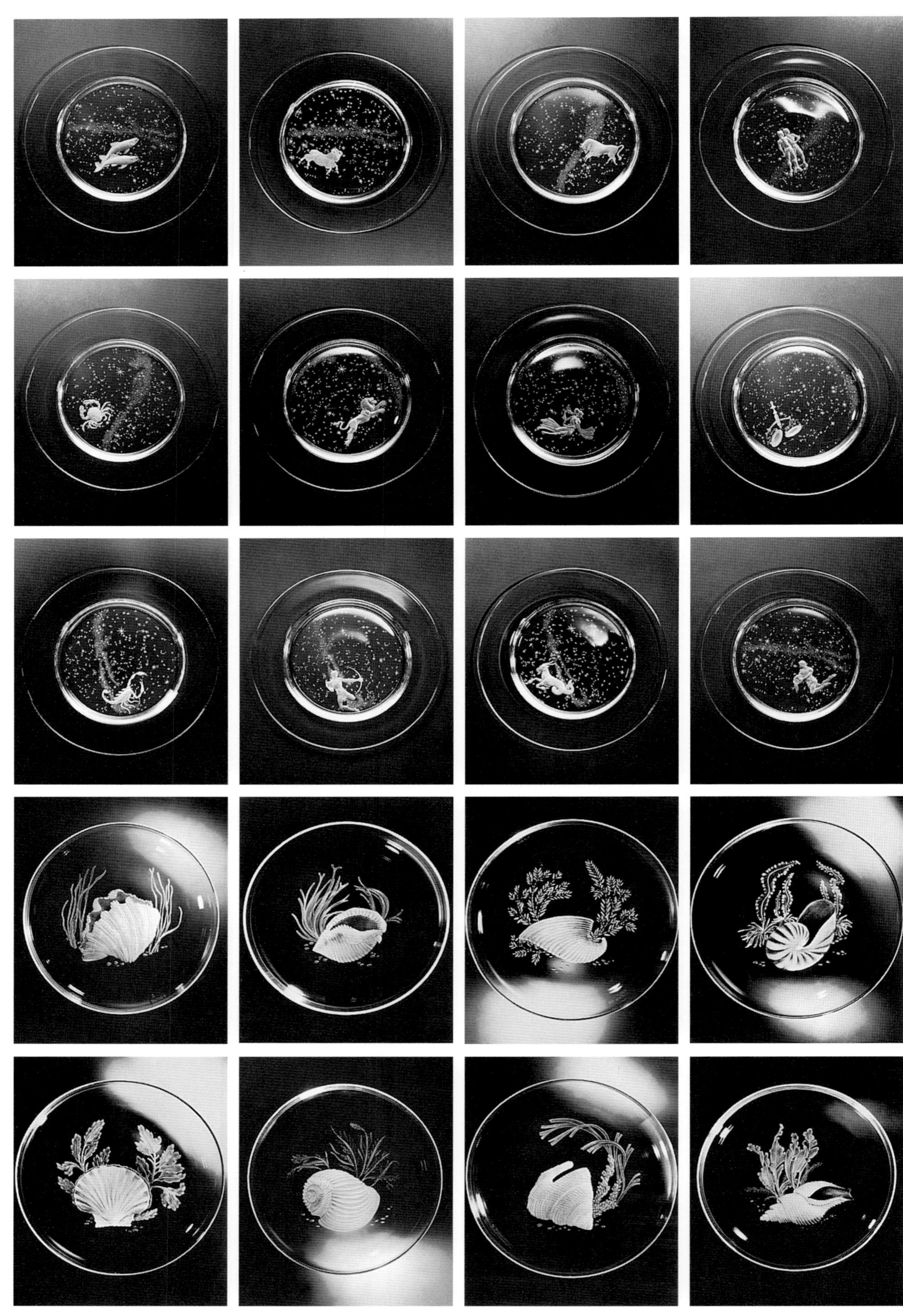

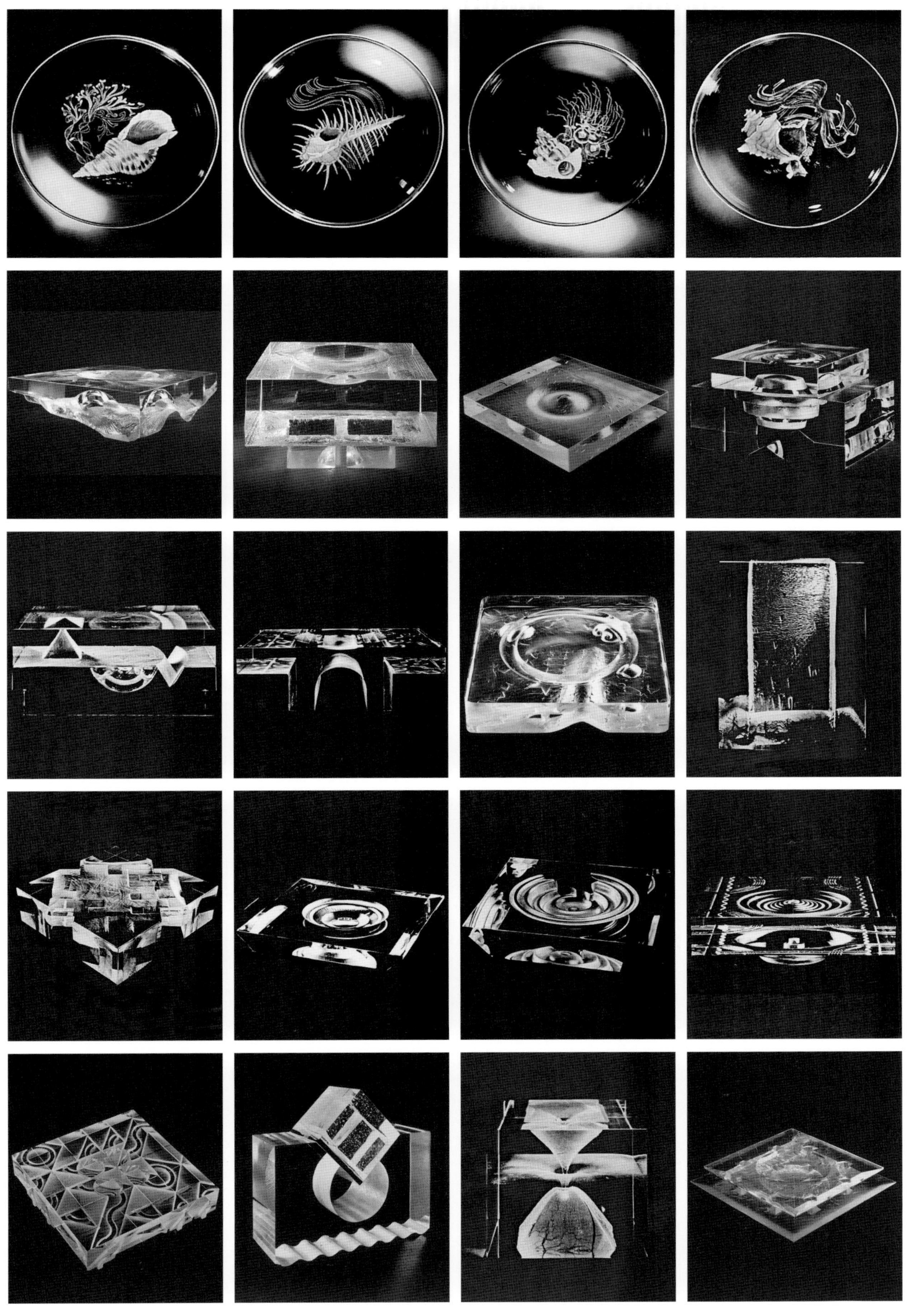

X3347 *Trumpet Triton*
D.W. 10" dia.

X3347 *Venus's Comb*
D.W. 10" dia.

X3347 *Wentletrap*
D.W. 10" dia.

X3347 *Banded Murex*
D.W. $800, 10" dia.

GLASS SCULPTURE

0274 *Interception*
D.D. (1980) $9,100, 11¼" l.

0275 *Oracle*
D.D. (1980) $4,850, 7" l.

0276 *Earth Rising*
D.D. (1980) $6,000, 11¾" w.

0277 *Magus Coffer*
D.D. (1980) $2,750, 5¾" l.

0278 *Pyramid Box*
D.D. (1980) $3,150, 7" l.

0279 *Archive*
D.D. (1980) $4,000, 10½" l.

0280 *The Other Earth*
D.D. (1980) $4,850, 10⅞" l.

0281 *Charismatic Offering*
D.D. (1980) $4,000, 5½" w.

0282 *Four Bright Corners*
D.D. (1980) $7,000, 10" w.

0283 *Meteorite*
D.D. (1980) $4,250, 11¼" w.

0284 *Canyons and Rivers*
D.D. (1980) $4,750, 10¾" w.

0285 *Temple in the Sand*
D.D. (1980) $6,500, 10" w.

0286 *Shrine*
D.D. (1980) $5,750, 9¾" square.

0287 *Monument*
D.D. (1980) $5,250, 7¾" l.

0288 *Model for the Creation of the Universe*
D.D. (1980) $3,000, 4" w.

0289 *Inland Lakes* (not illustrated)
D.D. (1980) $4,100.

0290 *Tableau*
D.D. (1980) $8,000, 11¾" square.

0291 *Relic*
D.D. (1980) $6,500, 7½" l.

PASSAGES

0294 Passage: *Function of Eleven*
P.A. (1981), $62,500, 20" h.

0296 *Wedged Vase*
P.A. (1981) $4,000, 15" h.

0297 *Triadic Vessel*
P.A. (1981) $4,575, 14½" h.

0298 *Dyadic Vessel*
P.A. (1981) $4,575, 14½" h.

0300 *Passage: State of Consciousness*
P.A. (1981) $36,050, 15¼" w.

0301 *Moment of Illumination*
P.A. (1981) $45,000, 30" l.

0302 *Passage: Interval of Time*
P.A. (1981) $27,500, 10¾" h.

0303 *Passage: Unity of Opposites*
P.A. (1981) $14,075, 12" w.

0304 *Space and Time Are Nothing but Names*
P.A. (1981) $30,250, 25" w.

0305 *Harmonic Trail 3.3.3*
P.A. (1981) $15,500, 19½" w.

0306 *Spanned Vessel*
P.A. (1981) $10,475, 17¼" w.

0307 *Triple-Wedged Vessel*
P.A. (1981) $9,350, 9½" w.

0308 *Cryptic Container*
P.A. (1981) $8,550, 9⅞" w.

0310 *Bridged Vessel*
P.A. (1981) $9,125, 19¼" l.

0312 *Passage: Alternative Realities*
P.A. (1981) $21,400, 26" l.

0313 *Encounter*
P.A. (1981) $29,500

0317 *Channeled Vessel*
P.A. (1981) $4,950, 14½" h.

1092 *Passage II*
P.A. (1981) $1,400, 4" h.

1093 *Passage I*
P.A. (1981) $2,700, 4" h.

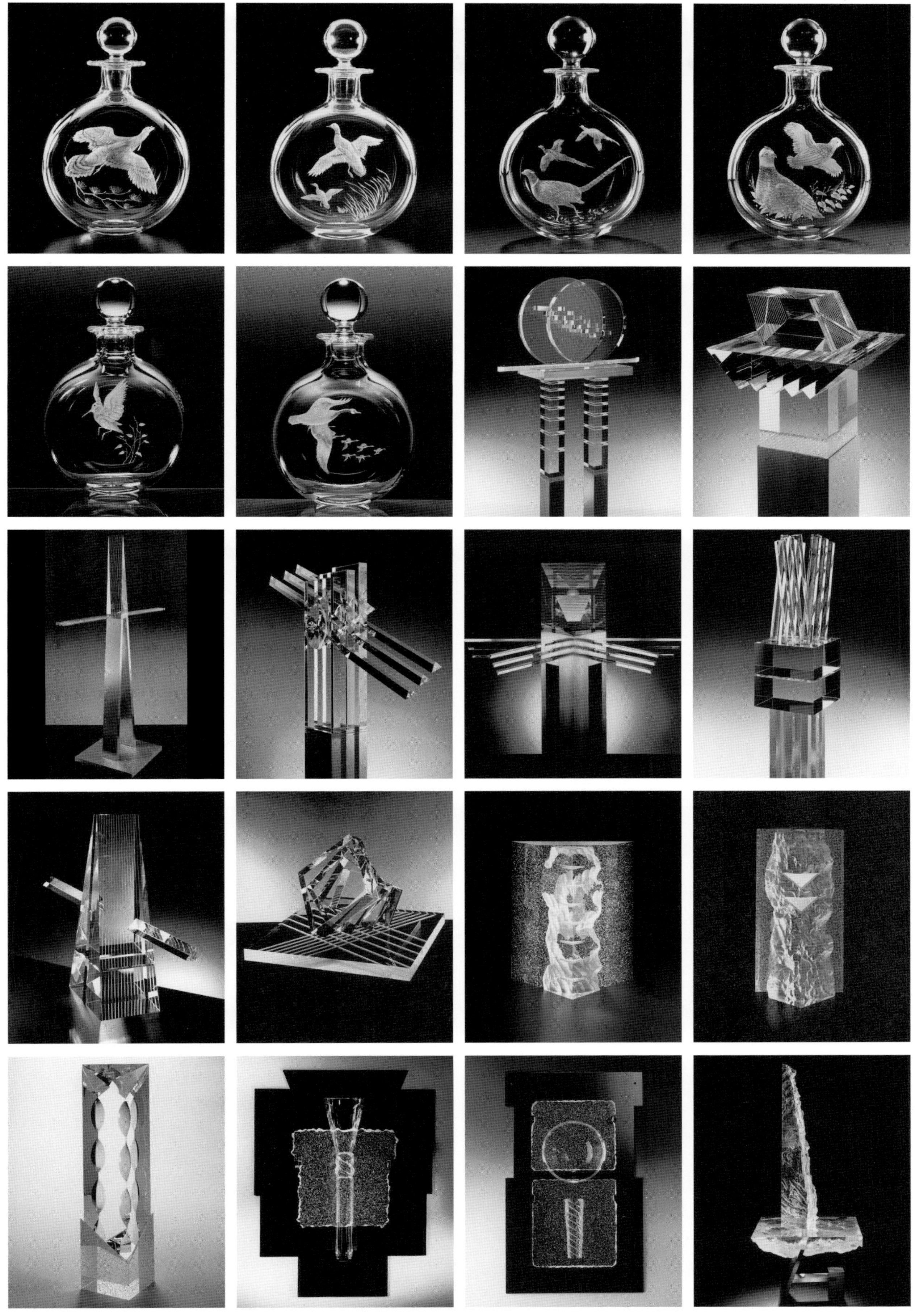

WILD GAME FLASKS

0367 *Wild Turkey Flask*
J.H. and G.H. (1985) $3,250, 8¼" h.

0368 *Wild Mallard Flask*
J.H. and G.H. (1985) $3,250, 8¼" h.

0377 *Wild Pheasant Flask*
J.H. and G.H. (1986) $3,250, 8¼" h.

0378 *Wild Quail Flask*
J.H. and G.H. (1986) $3,250, 8¼" h.

0448 *Wild American Woodcock Flask*
J.H. and G.H. (1988) $3,250, 8¼" h.

0449 *Wild Canada Goose Flask*
J.H. and G.H. (1988) $3,250, 8¼" h.

THE STEUBEN PROJECT: SCULPTURES IN CRYSTAL

0421 *Figures: Silent Sister*
P.A. (1988) $75,000, 75½" h.

0422 *Figures: Gnomon*
P.A. (1988) $25,000, 62¼" h.

0423 *Figures: Alto*
P.A. (1988) $32,500, 77¼" h.

0424 *Figures: Echo*
P.A. (1988) $50,000, 77" h.

0425 *Figures: Sentinel*
P.A. (1988) $55,000, 65¾" h.

0426 *Figures: Midi*
P.A. (1988) $30,000, 65¾" h.

0427 *Metronome*
P.A. (1988) $31,000, 25" h.

0428 *Harmonic Sequence* 3.3.3
P.A. (1988) $21,000, 15" w.

0432 *Totems* (3)
D.D. (1988) $20,000 for all.
Totem I: 13½" h.
Totem II: 12¾" h.
Totem III: 17¾" h.

0433 *Cartouche*
D.D. (1988) $3,500, 26½" h.

0434 *Phrases*
D.D. (1988) $4,500, 30" h.

0435 *Encouragement and Order*
D.D. (1988) $10,500, 31½" h.

0436 *Lens Object*
D.D. (1988) $11,500, 16¼" w.

0437 *Directional Response*
D.D. (1988) $40,000, 35" h.

0438 *Poetry, Precision and Fate*
D.D. (1988) $19,500, 24" h.

0439 *Precision and Impact*
D.D. (1988) $18,500, 36½" h.

0440 *Time's Arrow*
E.H. (1988) $35,000, 46" h.

0441 *Singularity*
E.H. (1988) $35,000, 39" h.

0442 *Silver Darling*
E.H. (1988) $57,500, 50" l.

0443 *A Way Through Time*
E.H. (1988) $30,000, 36" l.

0444 *No End No Ending*
E.H. (1988) $22,500, 28¼" l.

0445 *Light Bird Alignment*
E.H. (1988) $53,750, 68" h.

0446 *Beginning of the Beginning*
E.H. (1988) $17,500, 9½" h.

0447 *Threshold*
E.H. (1988) $72,500, 48" l.

IMAGE AND FRAMEWORK: SCULPTURES IN CRYSTAL

0457 *Reason, Integrity, Doubt*
D.D. (1990) $13,000

0458 *The Advocate*
D.D. (1990) $8,500

0459 *In the Zone*
D.D. (1990) $10,000

0460 *Light Is Speech*
D.D. (1990) $14,500

0461 *Intuition Is Fact*
D.D. (1990) $16,500

0462 *Night Speeds Quickly into Day*
D.D. (1990) $18,500, 20" h.

0463 *Surrender the Best*
D.D. (1990) $12,000

0464 *Bound Variable*
D.D. (1990) $16,000, 17" h.

0465 *Expanded Explanation*
D.D. (1990) $15,000

FORM AND CONTENT

0466 *Shield Bowl*
T.T. (1990) $3,500

0467 *Calypso*
T.T. (1990) $3,700

0468 *Jazz Composition*
T.T. (1990) $5,700

0469 *Water in the Desert*
T.T. (1990) $3,400

0470 *Roman Vessel II*
T.T. (1990) $2,700

0471 *Classical Composition*
T.T. (1990) $3,800

0472 *Simple Arithmetic*
T.T. (1990) $4,500

0473 *Roman Vessel III*
T.T. (1990) $6,000

0474 *Roman Vessel V*
T.T. (1990) $4,000

0475 *Roman Vessel I*
T.T. (1990) $3,400

0476 *Roman Vessel IV*
T.T. (1990) $5,800

0477 *Yosemite Falls*
T.T. (1990) $3,500, 15" w.

0478 *Simple Arithmetic II*
T.T. (1990) $4,500

0482 *Stars in the Desert*
T.T. (1990) $4,500

STRUCTURE REVEALED

0521 *Chasm*
D.D. (1997) $32,500, 10¼" h.

0522 *Grotto*
D.D. (1997) $50,000, 22½" h.

0523 *Cascade*
D.D. (1997) $45,000, 20½" h.

0524 *Promontory*
D.D. (1997) $50,000, 26" h.

0525 *Ozone*
D.D. (1997) $35,000, 15" h.

0527 *Natural Bridge*
D.D. (1997) $35,000, 10½" h.

1182 *Queen Anne's Lace*
D.D. (1997) $5,500

1183 *Impatiens*
D.D. (1997) $5,500, 4¾" w.

1184 *Mountain Laurel*
D.D. (1997) $5,500, 6" w.

1185 *Forget-Me-Not*
D.D. (1997) $5,500, 5¾" w.

CLEARLY LINO TAGLIAPIETRA

6176 *Batman II*
L.T. (1998) $23,000

6186 *Butterfly III*
L.T. (1998) $26,000

6188 *Anemone II*
L.T. (1998) $25,000

6191 *Eve III*
L.T. (1998) $24,000

6195 *Tampere II*
L.T. (1998) $20,000

6216 *Pompeii*
L.T. (1998) $24,000

6233 *Akira VII*
L.T. (1998) $22,000

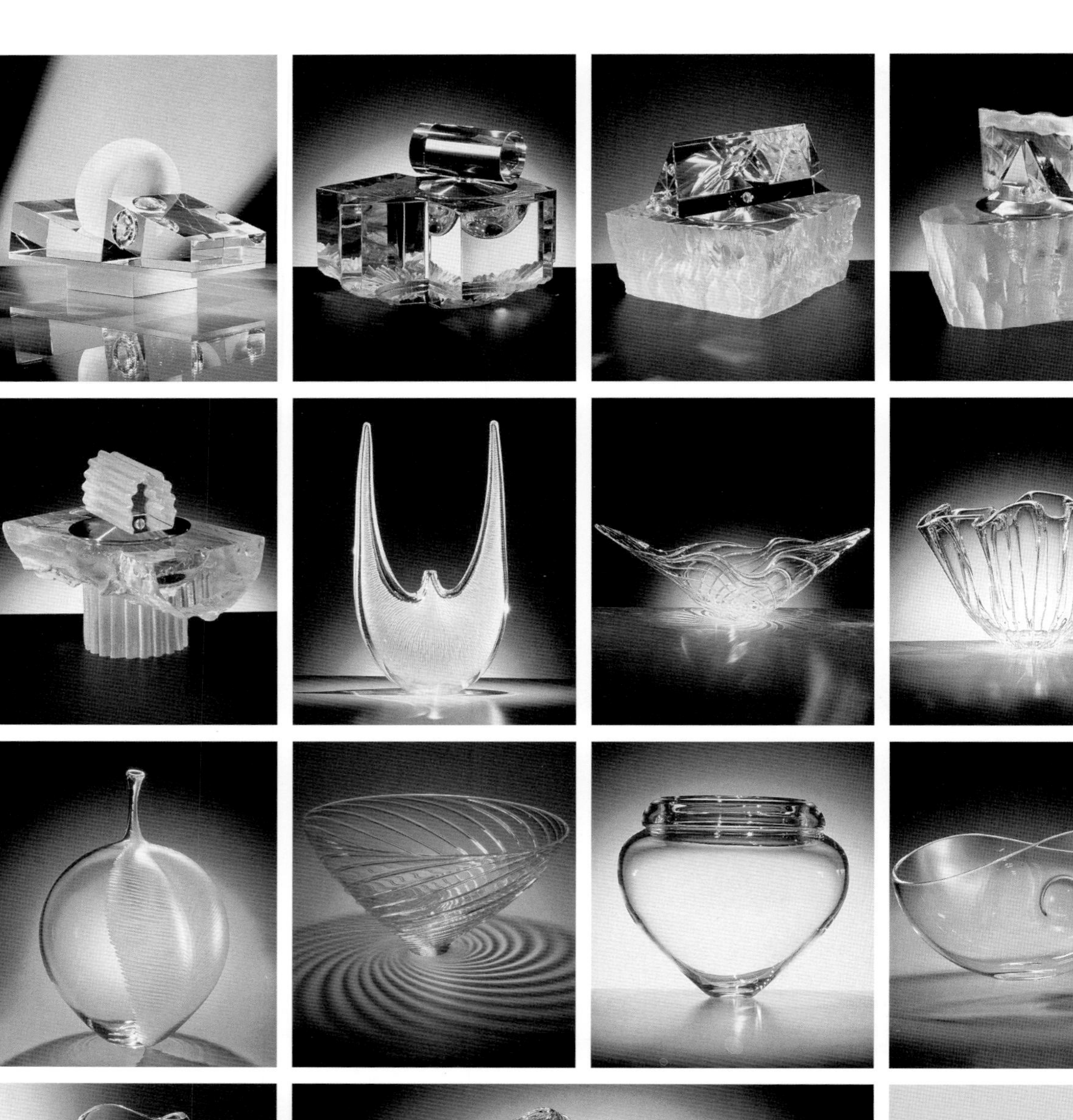

6235 *Foiba*
L.T. (1998) $30,000

From left: 6198 *Trullo I* ($15,000); 6212 *Riflessi II* ($22,000); 6199 *Riflessi I* ($21,000); 6211 *Trullo II* ($15,000), L.T. (1998)

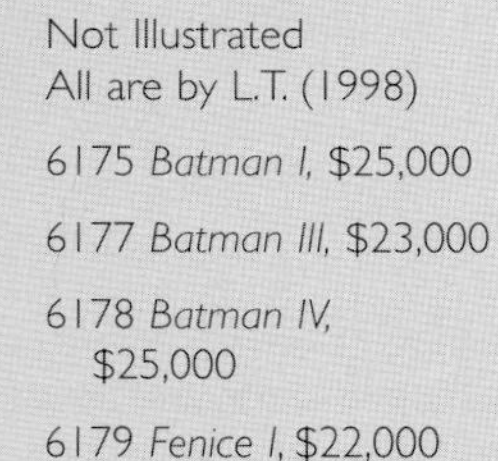

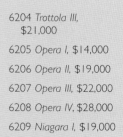

Not Illustrated
All are by L.T. (1998)

6175 *Batman I*, $25,000

6177 *Batman III*, $23,000

6178 *Batman IV*, $25,000

6179 *Fenice I*, $22,000

6180 *Fenice II*, $22,000

6181 *Pago Pago*, $23,000

6182 *Butterfly I*, $24,000

6183 *Butterfly II*, $19,000

6187 *Anemone I*, $20,000

6189 *Eve I*, $15,000

6190 *Eve II*, $19,000

6191 *Eve III*, $24,000

6192 *Trionfo I*, $18,000

6193 *Trionfo II*, $14,000

6194 *Tampere I*, $16,000

6196 *Uovo Alchemico I*, $15,000

6197 *Uovo Alchemico II*, $18,000

6200 *Oval Con Linea I*, $16,000

6201 *Oval Con Linea II*, $24,000

6202 *Trottola I*, $15,000

6203 *Trottola II*, $19,000

6204 *Trottola III*, $21,000

6205 *Opera I*, $14,000

6206 *Opera II*, $19,000

6207 *Opera III*, $22,000

6208 *Opera IV*, $28,000

6209 *Niagara I*, $19,000

6210 *Niagara II*, $18,000
6213 *Riflessi III*, $22,000
6214 *Riflessi IV*, $19,000
6215 *Dogale*, $24,000
6217 *Aureo*, $20,000
6218 *Ascentis*, $26,000
6219 *Columba*, $30,000

6220 *Vela*, $32,000
6221 *Saturno I*, $30,000
6222 *Saturno II*, $30,000
6223 *Saturno III*, $32,000
6224 *Edison*, $15,000
6225 *Detro I*, $24,000
6226 *Detro II*, $22,000

6227 *Akira I*, $23,000
6228 *Akira II*, $21,000
6229 *Akira III*, $24,000
6230 *Akira IV*, $24,000
6231 *Akira V*, $26,000
6232 *Akira VI*, $26,000
6233 *Akira VII*, $22,000

6234 *Genesis*, $18,000
6236 *Omega I*, $18,000
6237 *Omega II*, $22,000

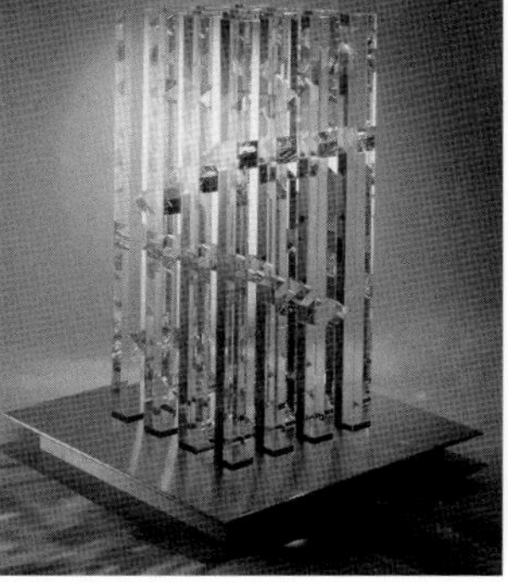

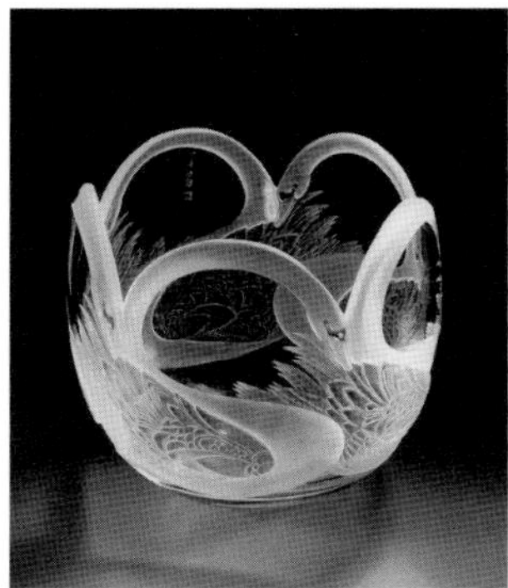

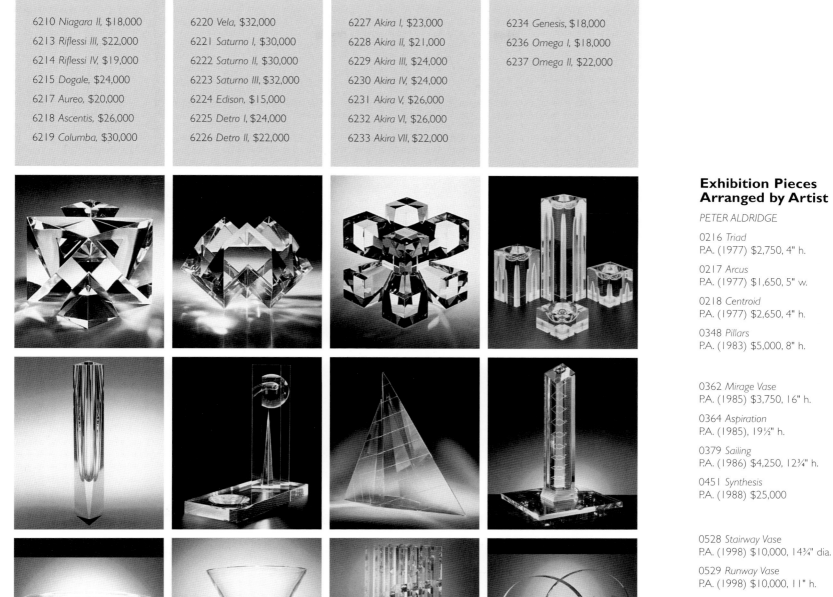

Exhibition Pieces Arranged by Artist

PETER ALDRIDGE

0216 *Triad*
P.A. (1977) $2,750, 4" h.

0217 *Arcus*
P.A. (1977) $1,650, 5" w.

0218 *Centroid*
P.A. (1977) $2,650, 4" h.

0348 *Pillars*
P.A. (1983) $5,000, 8" h.

0362 *Mirage Vase*
P.A. (1985) $3,750, 16" h.

0364 *Aspiration*
P.A. (1985), 19½" h.

0379 *Sailing*
P.A. (1986) $4,250, 12¾" h.

0451 *Synthesis*
P.A. (1988) $25,000

0528 *Stairway Vase*
P.A. (1998) $10,000, 14¾" dia.

0529 *Runway Vase*
P.A. (1998) $10,000, 11" h.

0530 *Interval Vase* (not illustrated)
P.A. (1998) $7,500.

6249 *Construct II* (not illustrated)
P.A. (2000) $35,000.

6276 *Highrise*
P.A. (2000) $46,000, 20" w.

6278 *Construct I*
P.A. (2000) $35,000

PETER ALDRIDGE AND JANE OSBORN-SMITH

0369 *Swan Bowl*
P.A. and J.O.S. (1985) $35,000, 9" dia.

0535 *Birdsong*
P.A. and J.O.S. (1998) $14,000, 9" h.

LLOYD ATKINS

X2083 *Flared Bowl*
L.A. 15" dia.

X2143 *Bowl*
L.A.

X2253 *Six-Branched Candelabra*
L.A. 15" h.

X2345 *Covered Urn*
L.A.

X2716 *Crystal Vase*
L.A. (1953) 12½" h.

X2769 *Bowl*
L.A. (1953)

E4100 *Crystal Bowl*
L.A. 11" dia.

X2801 *Vase with Cut Base*
L.A. 12¾" h.

X2832 *Bowl with Cut Base*
L.A.

X2869 *Bowl*
L.A.

X2875 *Covered Urn*
L.A. 14" h.

X3058 *Punch Bowl*
L.A. (1956) 9" dia.

X3066 *Crystal Cup*
L.A. 15¾" h.

X3067 *Covered Urn*
L.A. 16½" h.

E3077 *Crystal Vase*
L.A. 13¼" h.

X3097 *Covered Urn*
L.A.

X3098 *Covered Urn*
L.A. 16¾" h.

X3099 *Covered Centerpiece*
L.A.

X3104 *Covered Urn*
L.A.

E3149 *Crystal Bowl*
L.A.

4105 *Crystal Bowl*
L.A. 10¾" dia.

X3201 *Crystal Bowl*
L.A. (1957) 9½" dia.

E4108 *Covered Urn*
L.A. (1958) $350, 14" h.

X3463 *Crystal Bowl*
L.A. (1960) $125, 8¼" h.

0073 *Game Fish*
L.A. (1966) $750, 10½" h.

X3769 *Shakespeare Chalice*
L.A. (1964) $1,000, 11" h.

X3820 *Dolphin Bookends*
L.A. (1966) $1,500 pr., 7" h.

X3841 *Obelisk I*
L.A. (1966) $1,750, 18" h. (w/base)

X3914 *Obelisk II*
L.A. (1966) $1,750, 16½" h. (w/base)

0082 *Star Obelisk*
L.A. (1967) $1,750, 12½" h.

X3976 *Flame*
L.A. (1967) $4,500, 10¼" h.

0097 *Madonna with the Angels*
L.A. (1968) $12,500, 13½" h.

X4184 *Sea Chase*
L.A. (1969) $9,000, 10¾" h. (w/base)

X4197 *Partridge in a Pear Tree*
L.A. 5¾" h.

0102 *Partridge in a Pear Tree*
L.A. (1969) 5¾" h.

X4199 *Partridge in a Pear Tree*
L.A. 5¾" h.

X4232 *Partridge in a Pear Tree*
L.A. (1969) $10,550, 7½" h.

0104 *Partridge in a Pear Tree*
L.A. (1969) $3,800, 5¾" h.

0109 *Scarab*
L.A. (1971) $850, 6" l.

0120 *Paneled Obelisks*
L.A. (1973) $7,000, 14¾" h.

X4474 *Tiered Prism*
L.A. (1972) $2,750, 14⅞" h.

0146 *Tetrasphere*
L.A. (1974) $8,800, 7½" h. (w/base)

0186 *Cityscape*
L.A. (1976) $7,250, 16" h.

0239 *Bird Song*
L.A. and K.V.E. (1978)
$40,000, 9¾" dia.

0319 *Conversation*
L.A. (1981) $24,500, 17" h.

SAMUEL AYRES

X564 *Whirlpool Vase*
S.A. (1939) 14½" h.

IRENE BENTON

X1405 *Vase*
I.B.

ZEVI BLUM

0126 *The Thousand and One Nights*
G.T. and Z.B. (1974) $31,500, 11" h.

0141 *The Crusaders Bowl*
Z.B. and R.E. (1975) $65,000, 10⅜" w.

0200 *Shepherd's Cup*
P.Y. and Z.B. (1976) $1,975, 8¼" h.

LETTERIO CALAPAI

X3240 *Canto V*
D.P. and L.C. (1959) $2,250, 16" h.

ROBERT CASSETTI

0506 *Night Voyage*
R.C. (1992) $6,800

DONALD CROWLEY

0124 *Dandelions*
P.Schu. and D.C. (1973) $5,100, 7¾" w.

NEIL COHEN

0393 *Racing Bowl*
N.C. (1986) $2,500

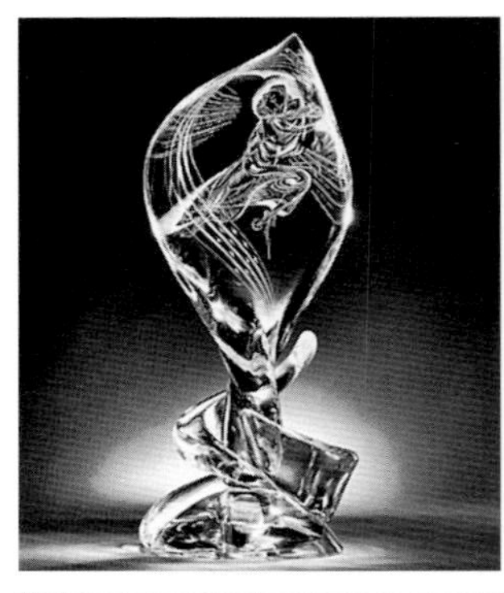

0394 *Puzzle Piece*
N.C. (1986) $4,000, 4½" h.

SALVADOR DALÍ

X1040 *The Sleep of Nautilus*
S.D. (1938) 16" h.

PATRICIA DAVIDSON

0091 *Quintessence*
P.Schu. and P.D. (1971) $15,000, 8" dia.

MARSHALL DAVIS

0094 *Balloons*
P.Schu. and M.D. (1968) $5,500, 11¼" h.

KATHERINE DE SOUSA

0115 *Hatshepsut*
K.D.S. (1972) $5,500, 9½" h.
(w/base)

0116 *Atlantic*
K.D.S. (1972) $5,250, 9" w.

0119 *Enchanted Jungle*
K.D.S. (1972) $11,250, 14" h.

DAN DAILEY

0344 *Ice Dancers*
D.Da. (1984) $9,500, 9½" h.

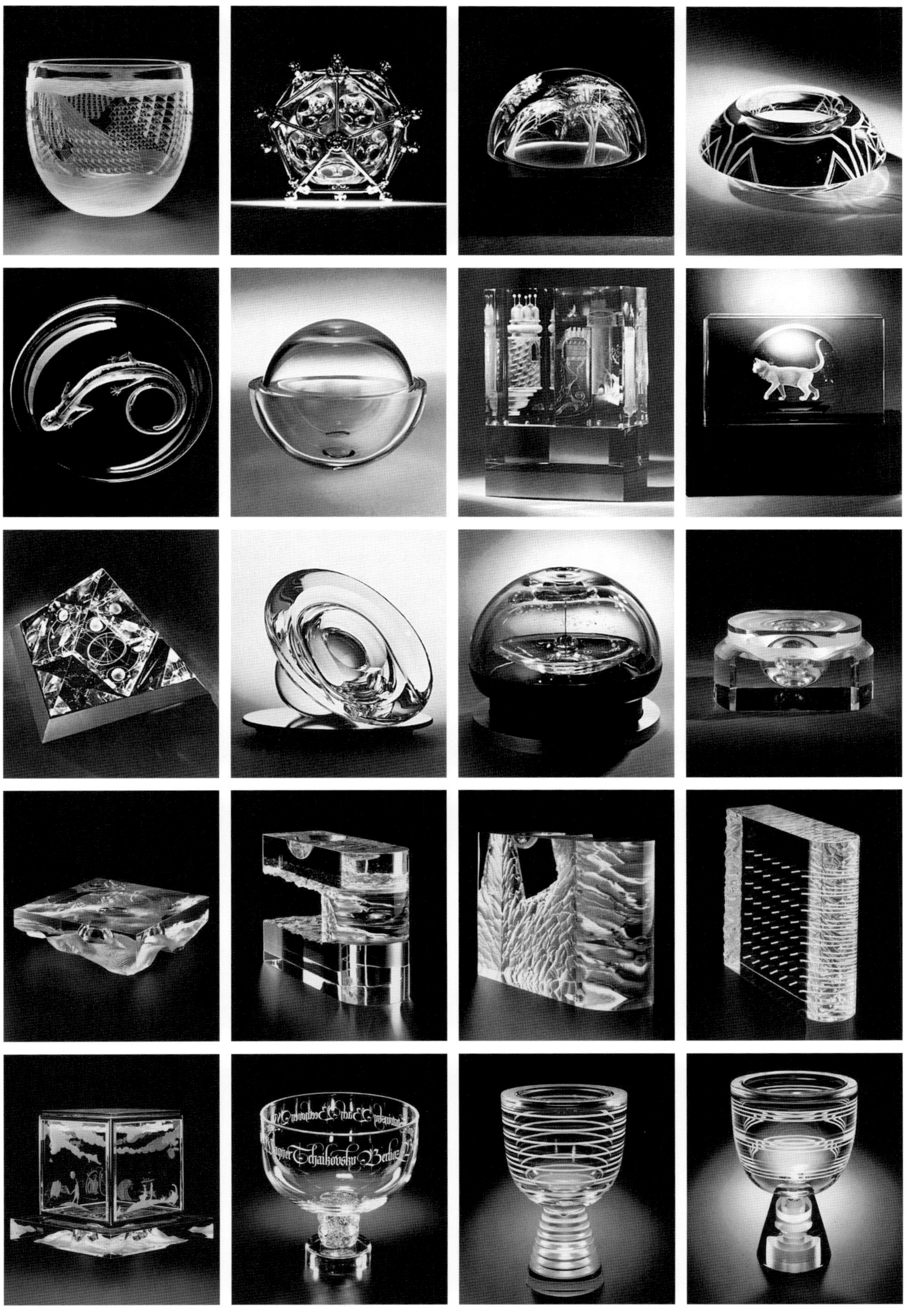

HERIKE DOLWER-STEINAUER

0330 *The Landscape Bowl*
H.D.S. (1982) $5,000, 5¾" h.

DAVID DOWLER

X4057 *Encased Sphere*
D.D. (1973) $2,500, 6" dia.

0130 *Grove of Trees*
D.D. (1973) $7,850, 8" dia.

0137 *Geometrics*
D.D. (1974) $3,100, 8½" dia.

0139 *Salamander Pond*
D.D. (1974) $2,500, 5¾" dia.

0163 *Spherical Bowl*
D.D. (1975) $950, 6" dia.

0165 *Enchanted Castle*
D.D. (1975) $5,800, 6¾" h.
(w/base)

0203 *Moonlight Cat*
D.D. (1976) $4,500, 9" l.

0212 *Pyramid*
D.D. (1977) $11,500, 12¼" w.

0226 *Solar Wind*
D.D. (1977) $5,950, 9½" dia.

0240 *Pendulum Universe*
D.D., L.H., P.Schu., and
P.Gr. (1978) $22,500, 13⅛" dia.

0273 *Box of Illusion*
D.D. (1980) $2,750, 6" w.

0333 *Interception II*
D.D. (1982) $9,100, 11¼" l.

0335 *River Lens*
D.D. (1982) $7,575, 9" w.

0336 *Land Ship*
D.D. (1982) $6,800, 9½" w.

0341 *River Cascade*
D.D. (1983) $6,500, 8" h.

0357 *Odyssey*
D.D. (1984) $90,000, 10¾" w.

0366 *Composer's Bowl*
D.D. (1985) $4,200, 10½" dia.

0391 *The Henry James Bowl*
D.D. (1986) $4,500, 11½" h.

0392 *The Ring Bowl*
D.D. (1986) $4,500, 11¾" h.

0395 *Day & Night*
D.D. (1986) $2,850, 2¼" h.

0396 *Starfield*
D.D. (1986) $2,850

0419 *In Central Park*
D.D. (1988) $12,000, 12½" h.

0450 *Poetic License*
D.D. (1989) $4,500, 34½" h.

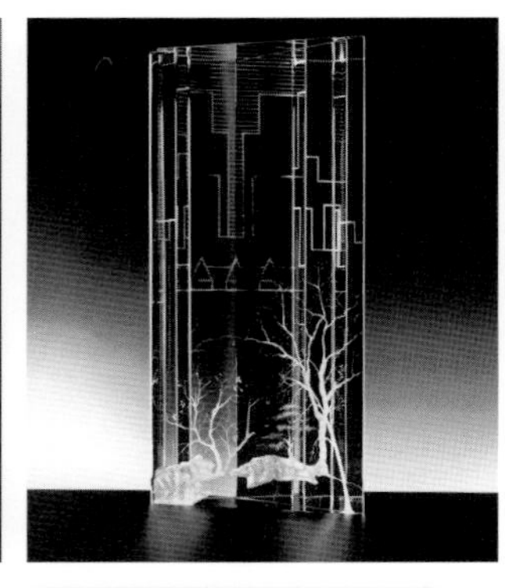

0499 *Mountain*
D.D. (1991) $7,500

0501 *Universe Bowl* (not illustrated)
D.D. (1991) $2,500.

0508 *Safe Harbor* (not illustrated)
D.D. (no date) $8,400.

0510 *Silent Flight*
D.D. (1994) $4,500, 15¾" h.

0511 *Mountain*
D.D. (1994) $9,800, 12" w.

0512 *Achievement*
D.D. (1995) $8,500, 18" h.

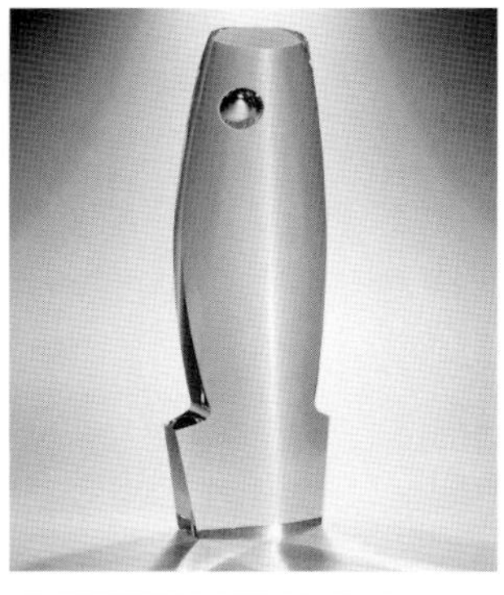

0540 *Gateway to the Millennium*
D.D. (1999) $15,000, 17" h.

6248 *Spiral to the Millennium*
(not illustrated) D.D. (1999) $7,450.

6238 *Crest*
D.D. (1999) $25,000

6239 *Thunder & Lightning*
D.D. (1999) $18,000

6240 *Violin*
D.D. (1999) $15,000

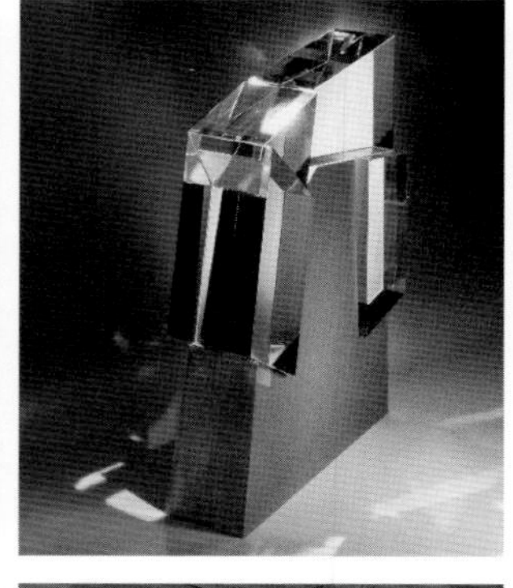

6246 Eye of the Storm
D.D. (1999) $12,000

6275 *Innerlight*
D.D. (2000) $260,000, 9' h., 7' w.

6279 *Pastoral Epergne*
D.D. (2000) $19,000, 22" h.

DAVID DOWLER AND TIM ANGELL

0543 *First Blooms*
D.D. & T.A. (2000) $10,000, 8" h.

JOHN DREVES

X2254 *Airtrap Vase*
J.D. (1950) 8½" h.

PETER DROBNY

0507 *Mobius Prism*
P.Dro. (1993) $8,900, 11¾" h.

PETER DROBNY AND CARY AUSTIN

0534 *Eagle's Flight*
P.Dro. and C.A. (1998) $14,500, 9¼" h.

STEVEN DALE EDWARDS

0375 *The Swimmers*
S.D.E. (1986) $27,500, 17½" w.

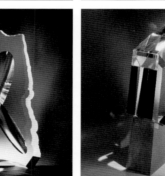

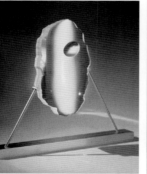

FRANK ELISCU

X3536 *Daniel*
L.A. and F.E. (1962) $4,000, 13½" h. (w/base)

X3539 *Saint Francis*
L.A. and F.E. (1962) $2,500, 14⅝" h.

0080 *Carrousel of the Seasons*
P.Schu. and F.E. (1966) $8,500, 12" h.

X3967 *Noah's Ark*
G.T. and F.E. (1966) $6,800, 11¾" h.

X4320 *Noah*
P.Schu. and F.E. (1970) $7,500, 14" h.

X4442 *Thumbelina*
G.T. and F.E. (1972) $8,200, 11½" h.

SHELDON FINK

0228 *Dragonfly Bowl*
P.Y. and S.F. (1978) $2,650, 17½" h.

0266 *Butterfly Bowl*
P.Y. and S.F. (1979) $3,650, 17½" h.

GOLDA FISHBEIN

X4612 *Forest Spires*
G.F. (1973) $6,000, 13¾" h.

0128 *Winter Trees*
G.F. (1973) $5,350, 16" h. (w/base)

JOHN M. GATES

X566 *World's Fair Cup*
J.M.G. (1939) 28" h.

X623 *Crystal Ciborium*
J.M.G. 12½" h.

X1516 *Five-Branched Candelabra*
J.M.G. 16½" h.

X1740 *The Valor Cup*
J.M.G. (1941) 15" h.

X2314 *The Centenary Cup*
J.M.G. and D.W. (1951) 14" h.

HAROLD GROSS

0503 *Elusive Buck*
H.G. (1992) $7,500, 7¼" h.

TERRY HAASS

X3311 *Genesis*
D.P. and T.H. (1959) $2,000, 9" h.

0238 *Cosmos*
D.P., T.H., and L.H. (1978) $27,500, 17" dia.

PAUL HAIGH

0519 *Colonnade*
P.Ha. (1996) $7,500, 15" h.

CHARLOTTE-LINNEA HALLETT

0195 *Angel Window*
D.P. and C.-L.H. (1976) $13,500, 9½" w.

0198 *Mare and Foal*
P.Y. and C.-L.H. (1976) $17,500, 8½" h.

0204 *Western Horses*
B.X.W. and C.-L.H. (1977)
$9,850, 10¼" w.

0268 *St. George and the Dragon*
D.P. and C.-L.H. (1979) $22,500, 8¾" h.

JIRI HARCUBA
0359 *Icarus*
J.Ha. (1985) $10,000, 11½" h.

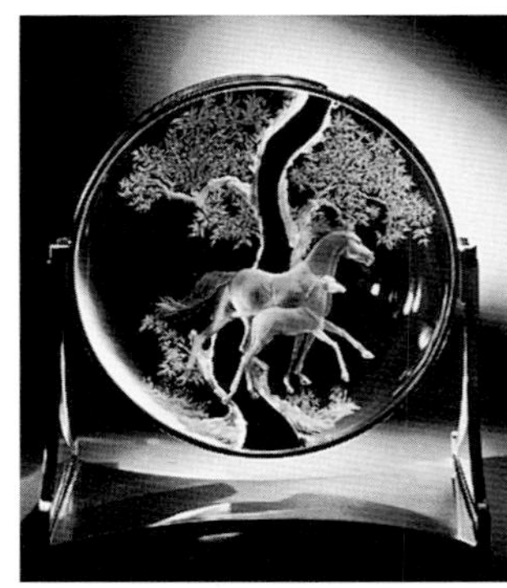
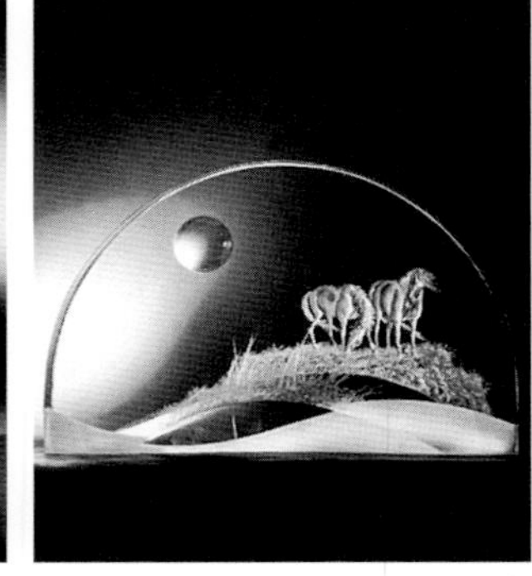

MILTON HEBALD
X1543 *The Railroad Cup*
G.T. and M.He. (1954) 13¾" h.

WALTER HEINTZE
X486 *Dolphin Urn*
W.H.

X512 *Covered Jar*
W.H.

DAVID HILLS
X2108 *Covered Urn*
D.H. 14" h.

E2109 *Covered Urn*
D.H. 14" h.

X2113 *Centerpiece*
D.H.

X2226 *Vase*
D.H.

X2342 *Tall Vase*
D.H. $150, 15" h.

ERIC HILTON
0135 *The Wave*
E.H. (1975) $9,500, 15½" h.

0136 *Prismatic Flight*
E.H. and L.H. (1975) $11,500,
14½" l.

0160 *The Tower*
E.H. (1975) $2,900, 4¼" h.

0161 *Matrix I*
E.H. (1975) $1,150, 6½" h.

0162 *Matrix II*
E.H. 5¾" w.

0194 *Land Beneath the Waves*
E.H. (1976) $7,500, 7" h.

0205 *Supported Sphere*
E.H. (1976) $5,500, 6¾" h.

0293 *Innerland*
E.H. (1980) $275,000, 19⅜" l.

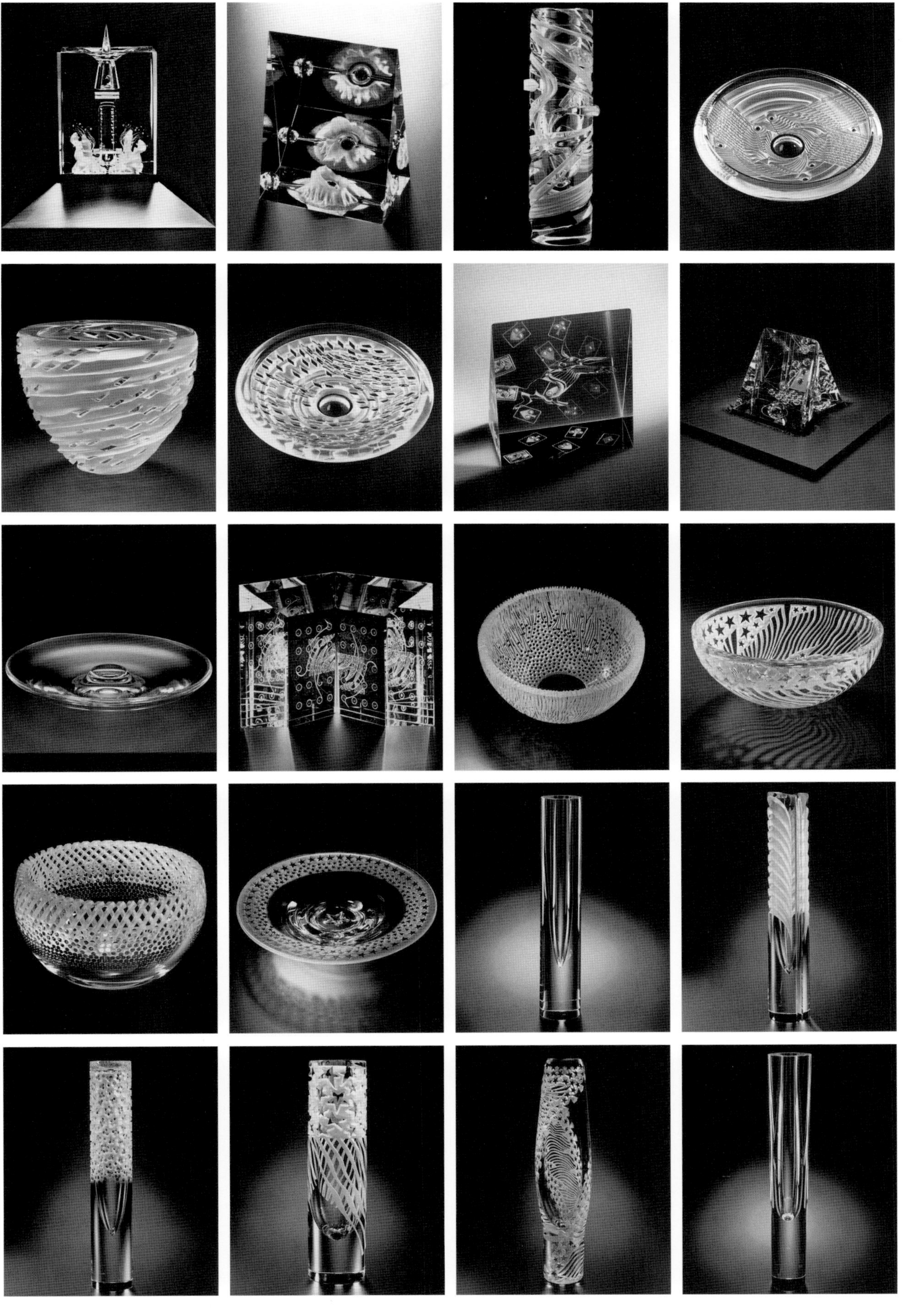

0321 *Point of Departure*
E.H. (1981) $41,725, 9" h.

0322 *Mountains of the Inner Eye*
E.H. (1982) $3,950, 7" h.

0337 *Will-o'-the-Wisp*
E.H. (1982) $9,175, 15" h.

0338 *Cosmic Wind*
E.H. (1982) $8,750

0339 *Dark Vortex*
E.H. (1982) $7,200, 7" h.

0340 *Cosmic Influence*
E.H. (1982) $8,000

0342 *Alice in Wonderland*
E.H. (1983) $6,350, 6¾" h.

0347 *Cosmic Journey*
E.H. (1984) $15,500, 19" w.

0349 *Triumph Bowl*
E.H. (1983) $3,950, 15½" dia.

0356 *Prism Pages*
E.H. (1984) $8,100

0365 *Pool of Asrai*
E.H. (1985) $7,500, 9¾" dia.

0371 *Stars & Stripes Bowl*
E.H. (1985) $5,500, 11½" dia.

0374 *Lattice Bowl*
E.H. (1986) $6,250, 7⅝" dia.

0380 *Star Bowl*
E.H. (1986) $3,500, 16" dia.

0381 *Ellipse Vase*
E.H. (1986) $2,000, 13¾" h.

0382 *Deco Vase*
E.H. (1986) $3,500, 14" h.

0383 *Lace Flower Vase*
E.H. (1986) $2,500, 13⅞" h.

0384 *Stars & Stripes Vase*
E.H. (1986) $2,500, 10½" h.

0385 *Tall Stars & Stripes Vase*
E.H. (1986) $3,500, 16" h.

0386 *Reverse Ellipse Vase*
E.H. (1986) $4,000, 18⅜" h.

0387 *Tall Ellipse Vase*
E.H. (1986) $4,000, 18⅜" h.

0388 *Crosshatch Vase*
E.H. (1986) $2,500, 12⅜" h.

0389 *Lace Flower Bowl*
E.H. (1986) $3,500

0390 *Middlearth Bowl*
E.H. (1986) $4,000, 6½" dia.

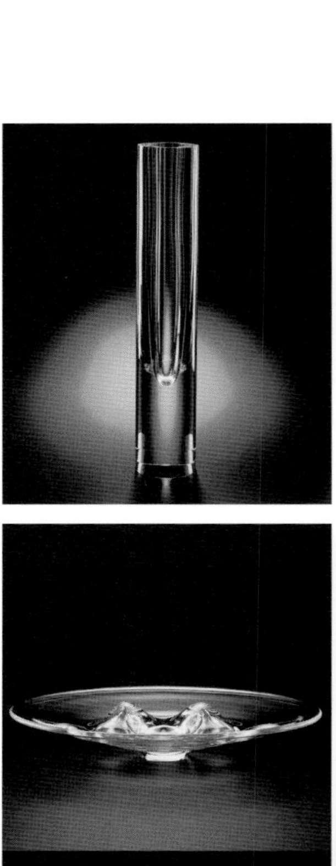

0397 *Double Glory Bowl*
E.H. (1986) $5,000

0402 *Flight of Eagles*
E.H. (1987) $22,500, 9½" h.

0403 *Dreams of Alice*
E.H. (1987) $45,000, 16¼" h.

0417 *Waterfall Vase*
E.H. (1988) $10,500, 11" h.

0455 *Sanctuary (not illustrated)*
E.H. (1990) $12,500, 16" dia.

0456 *Bird Disk*
E.H. (1990) $12,500, 16" dia.

0481 *Macbeth*
E.H. (1990) $42,000, 16" w.

0484 *Lions*
E.H. (1990) $12,000, 12" h.

6242 *Threshold to the Universe*
E.H. (1999) $32,000

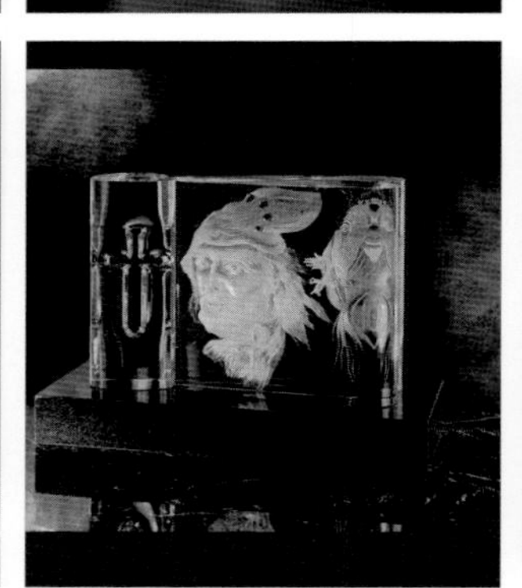

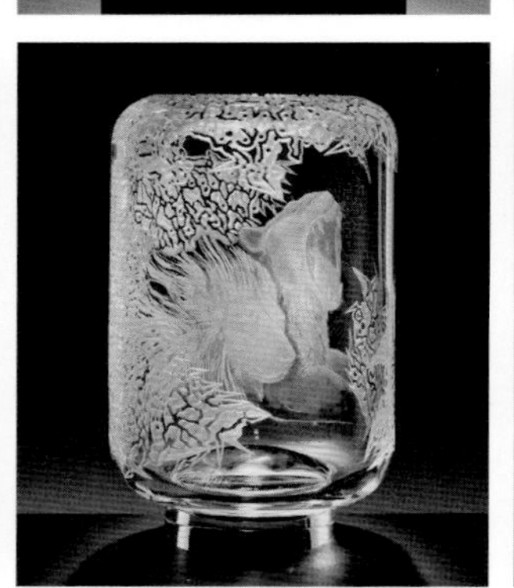

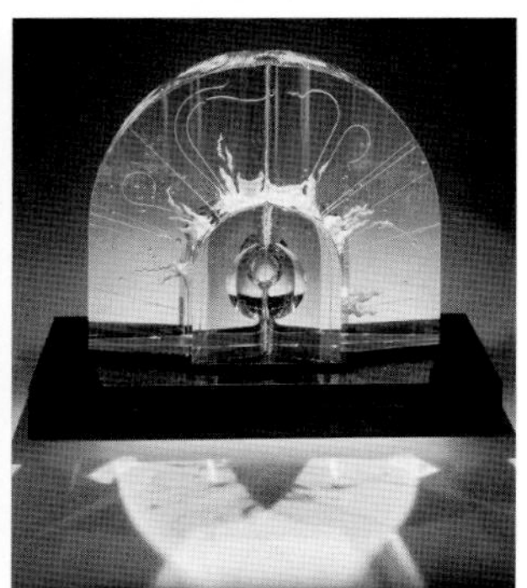

6280 *Earth's Pages*
E.H. (2000) $54,000, 36" h.

6281 *The Far Flight*
E.H. (2000) $19,000

6282 *Candelabra*
E.H. (2000) $16,000

6284 *The Imperial Way*/Candlestick
E.H. (2000) $8,500, 12" h.

Not Illustrated—All are by E.H.

0483 *Wheat Vase* (1990) $4,000

0485 *Architectural Bowl* (1990) $8,900

0489 *Ascending Twilight* (1990) $3,500 (list continues in grid)

0544 *Ruby-Throated Hummingbird*
E.H. (2000) $12,000, 8½" h.

0548 *Dragonfly*
E.H. (2001) $19,900, 10¼" h.

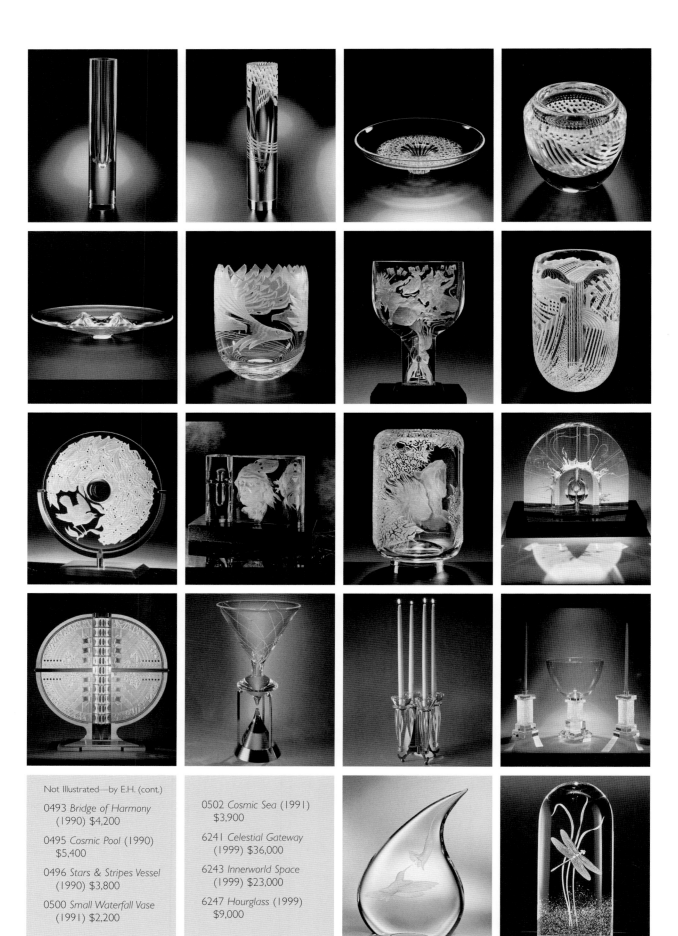

Not Illustrated—by E.H. (cont.)

0493 *Bridge of Harmony* (1990) $4,200

0495 *Cosmic Pool* (1990) $5,400

0496 *Stars & Stripes Vessel* (1990) $3,800

0500 *Small Waterfall Vase* (1991) $2,200

0502 *Cosmic Sea* (1991) $3,900

6241 *Celestial Gateway* (1999) $36,000

6243 *Innerworld Space* (1999) $23,000

6247 *Hourglass* (1999) $9,000

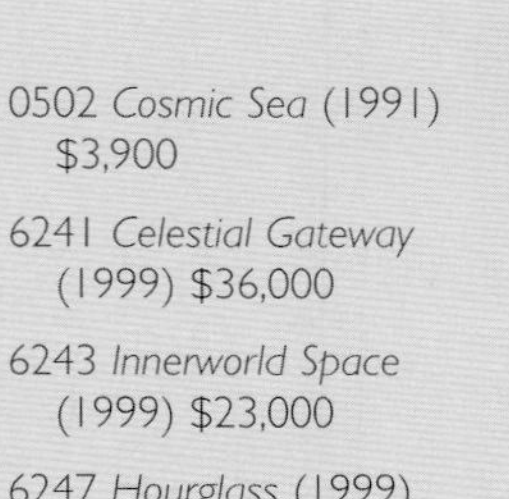

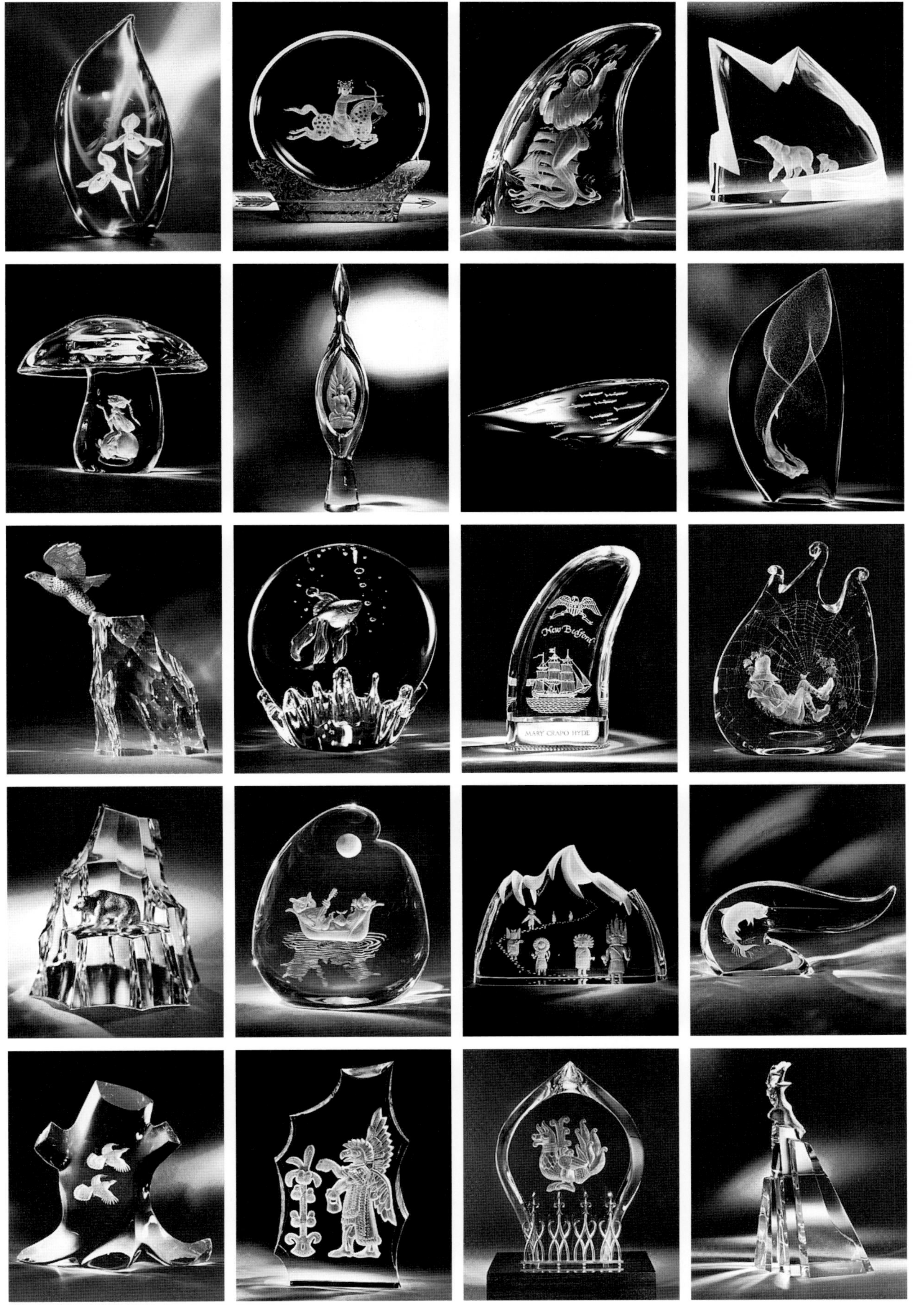

ERIC HILTON AND TIM ANGELL

0542 *Island Orchid*
E.H. and T.A. (1999) $10,000, 10¼" h.

JAMES HOUSTON

X3691 *Medieval Horseman*
J.H. (1964) $3,000, 12" dia.

0070 *Saint Elmo*
G.T. and J.H. (1964) $2,800, 9" h.

0071 *Polar Bears*
G.T. and J.H. (1964) $1,650, 5¼" h.

0072 *Elf and Mushroom*
J.H. (1964) $1,500, 6" h.

X3704 *Siva*
G.T. and J.H. (1965) $2,800, 16½" h.

X3723 *Salmon Run*
G.T. and J.H. (1965) $3,600, 17½" l.

X3802 *Mermaid*
G.T. and J.H. (1965) $2,000, 12" h.

X3957 *Eagle Rock*
J.H. (1967) $2,500, 8¼" h.

0086 *Veiltail*
J.H. (1968) $2,250, 7½" h.

X4108 *Whale's Tooth*
J.H. (1968) $1,750, 8¼" h.

0092 *Rip Van Winkle*
J.H. (1969) $5,000, 12" h.

X4113 *Guardian Rock*
J.H. (1968) $2,250, 5½" h.

X4151 *The Owl and the Pussycat*
J.H. (1969) $4,250, 8¾" h.

X4157 *San Francisco Peaks*
J.H. (1969) $6,000, 11" w.

0100 *Silver King*
J.H. (1970) $2,350, 10¼" l.

0101 *Grouse Grove*
J.H. (1971) $2,300, 8½" w.

0106 *Nisroch*
J.H. (1970) $5,500, 14½" h.

X4287 *Fire Dragon*
J.H. (1971) $2,500, 9½" h. (w/base)

0110 *Moses Breaking the Tablets*
J.H. (1970) $2,500, 11" h.

0111 *Blue Marlin*
J.H. (1971) $2,750, 11" h.

0121 *Diving Seals*
J.H. (1972) $5,500, 12" w.

0122 *Shark's Fin*
J.H. (1972) $3,900, 7½" h.

0125 *Salmon Pool*
J.H. (1973) $2,300, 6½" w.

X4537 *Northern Lights*
J.H., A.Sch., and L.H. (1973)
$48,500, 12⅝" h.

0131 *Woodcock*
J.H. (1974) $3,750, 10¾" h.

0150 *Autumn Moon*
J.H. (1972) $4,300, 8" w.

0153 *Snipe Bowl*
J.H. (1975) $7,500, 10" l.

0168 *Colonies Bowl*
P.Schu. and J.H. (1975) $1,950,
6¾" dia.

0182 *Night Owl*
J.H. (1975) $5,350, 7¾" w.

0196 *Water Disk—Muskellunge*
P.Schu. and J.H. (1977) $6,000,
12" dia.

0213/215 *Water Disk—Trout*
P.Schu. and J.H. (1977) $6,000,
12" dia.

0222 *Night Hawks*
J.H. (1977) $5,350, 7¾" w.

0224 *Water Disk—Bonefish*
P.Schu. and J.H. (1977) $6,000,
12" dia.

0241 *Raccoon*
B.X.W. and J.H. (1978) $4,950,
8½" w.

0262 *Beaver*
B.X.W. and J.H. (1979) $5,750,
8½" w.

0272 *Blue Whale*
J.H. (1980) $5,500, 7½" h.

0292 *Arctic Exploration*
J.H. $8,350, 7¾" h.

0325 *Salmon Leap*
J.H. (1982) $4,650, 7½" l.

0328 *Kingfisher*
J.H. (1982) $6,950, 7¼" h.

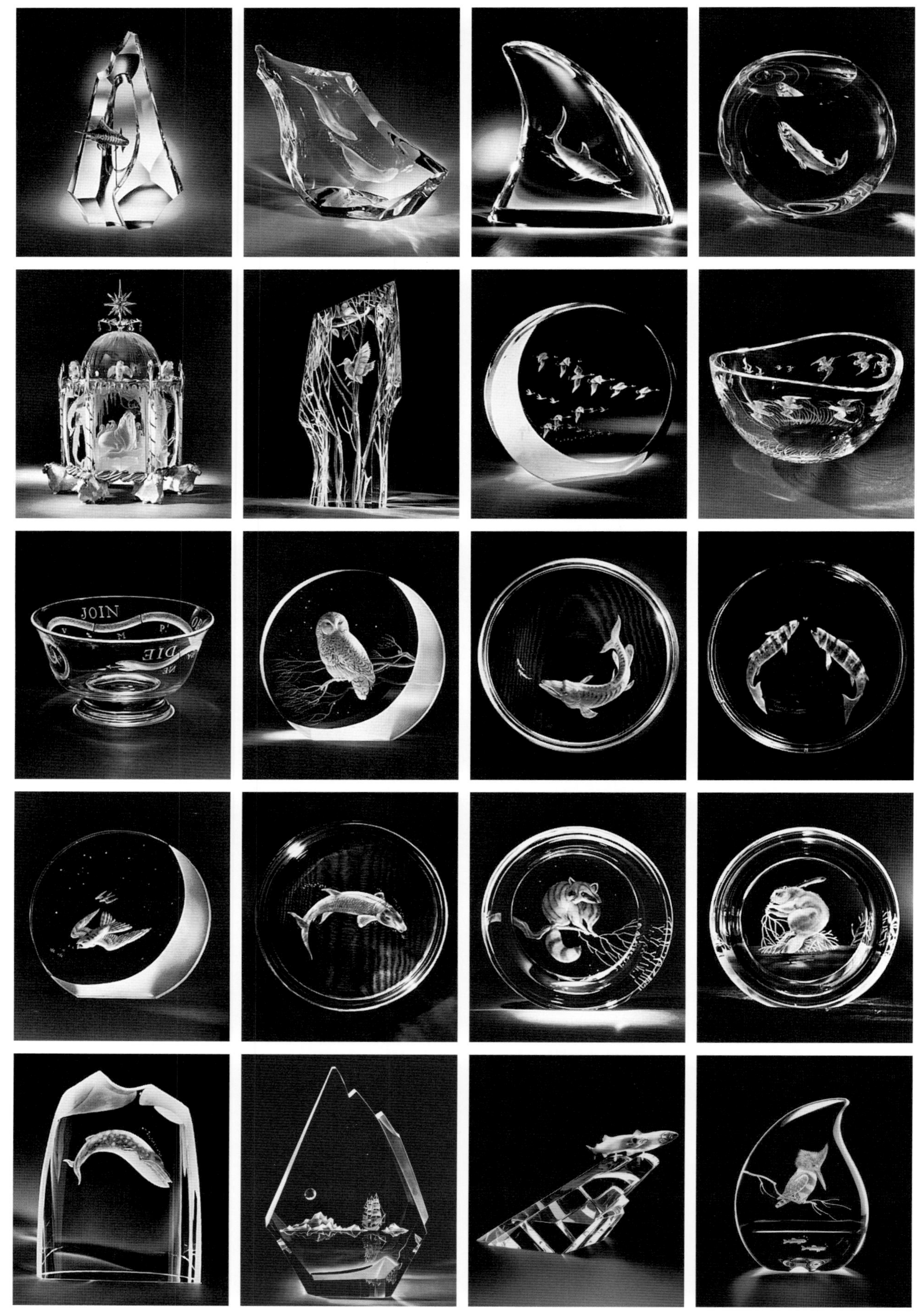

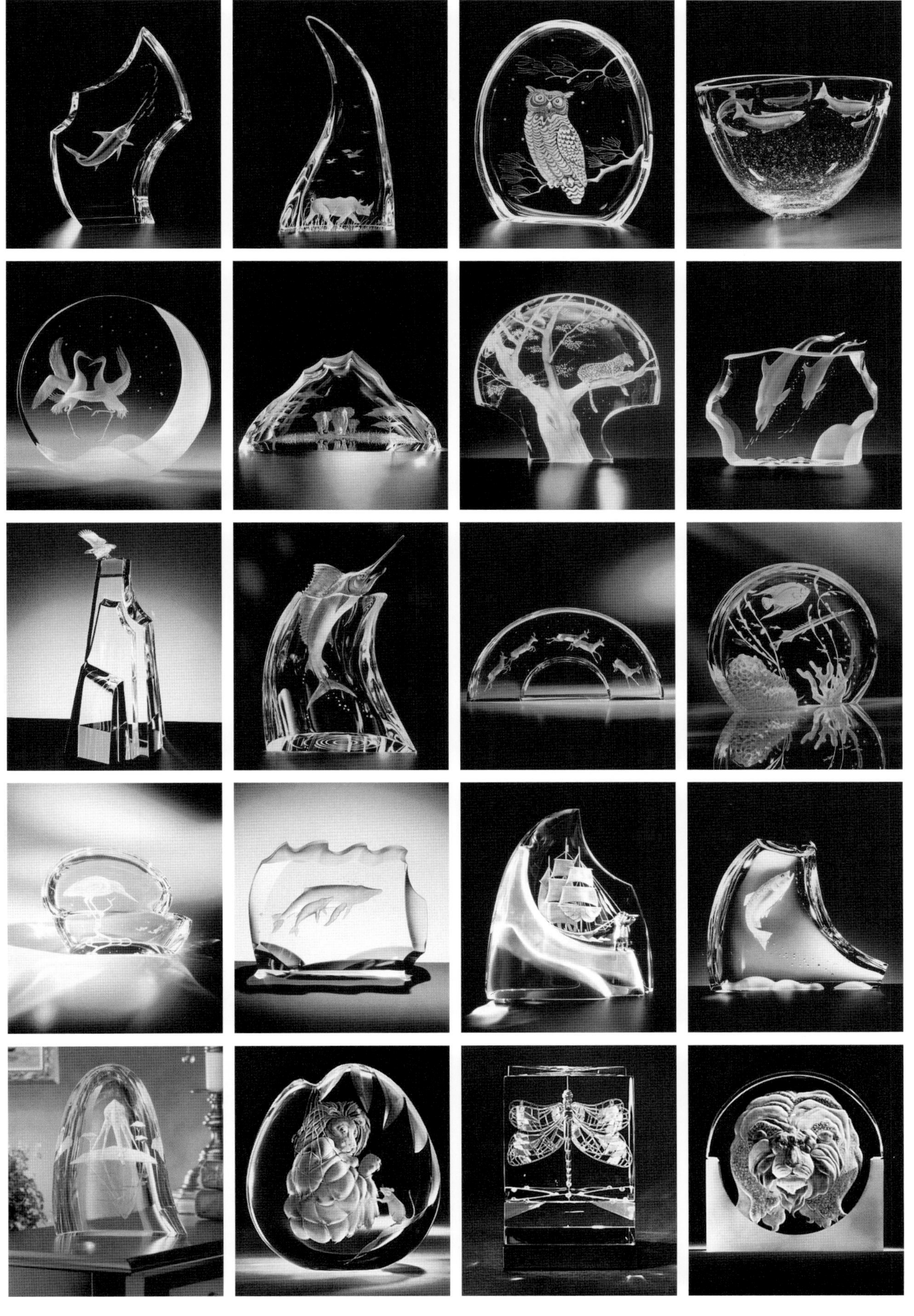

0343 *Sea Sword*
J.H. (1983) $5,950, 8¾" h.

0355 *Rhino Horn*
J.H. (1984) $6,750, 10¼" h.

0363 *Great Horned Owl*
J.H. (1985) $13,925, 8" h.

0372 *Salmon Bowl*
J.H. (1985) $16,000, 10¼" w.

0376 *Dancing Cranes*
J.H. (1986) $9,000, 8" dia.

0400 *Elephants of Kilimanjaro*
J.H. (1987) $12,000, 8½" h.

0401 *Leopard in the Moonlight*
J.H. (1988) $12,500, 7½" w.

0453 *Dolphins*
J.H. (1989) $5,750, 6½" h.

0497 *Eagle's Crag*
J.H. (1991) $13,000, 10¾" h.

0498 *Sailfish Rising*
J.H. (1991) $11,000, 7½" h.

0505 *American Pronghorn*
J.H. (1992) $22,000, 14" w.

0516 *Diver's Paradise*
J.H. (1995) $8,950, 8½" w.

0520 *Green Heron: Nature's Fly Fisher*
J.H. (1997) $9,850, 8¼" w.

0536 *Ocean's Majesty*
J.H. (1998) $9,750, 6½" w.

0538 *Exploration*
J.H. (1999) $13,400, 7" h.

0539 *Rainbow River*
J.H. (1999) $11,000, 7½" w.

0546 *Giraffe at Sunset*
J.H. (2000) $17,500, 9½" h.

0547 *Arctic Seal: Mother & Pup*
(not illustrated)
J.H. (2001) $8,000, 5¼" h.

ZORAH HURD

0093 *The Lion and the Mouse*
P.Schu. and Z.H. (1968) $5,250, 8"

0142 *Dragonfly*
P.Schu. and Z.H. (1975) $4,850,
7" h. (w/base)

0185 *Lion's Head*
D.D. and Z.H. (1976) $3,400, 5¼" h.

LUIS JIMINEZ

0117 *Sea Girl*
L.J. (1973) $5,000, 12½" w.

DAVID JOHNSTON

0123 *Butterfly Girl*
P.Y. and D.J. (1973) $8,600, 11" h.

0140 *Childhood*
P.Y. and D.J. (1974) $2,850, 4¾" h.

0152 *Disk of Angels*
P.Y. and D.J. (1975) $10,500, 14¼" h. (w/stand)

LEON KELLY

X2534 *Aurora Vase*
G.T. and L.Ke. (1952) 11¾" h.

JACOB LANDAU

X3295 *Tree of Life*
D.P. and J.La. (1959) 14" h.

X3343 *A Child's World*
D.P. and J.La. (1959) $2,250, 13¼" h.

X3354 *Four Seasons*
D.P. and J.La. (1960) $6,000, 11¼" w.

X3483 *Jazz*
D.P. and J.La. (1962) $5,500, 11" w.

MICHAEL LANTZ

X1858 *The Christmas Font*
G.T. and M.L. (1949) 15¼" h.

TOM LEA

X3325 *Trail Driver*
L.A. and T.L. (1959) $2,750, 10" dia.

CLARE LEIGHTON

X3091 *The Catch*
G.T. and C.L. (1957) 11¾" h.

X3092 *Tobacco Harvest*
L.A. and C.L. (1956) 15¾" h.

LINCHIA LI

0229 *Peony Jar*
D.P. and L.L. (1978) $2,150, 6½" w.

0237 *Bamboo Vase*
D.P. and L.L. (1978) $2,150, 7" h.

0263 *Lotus Flower Vase*
D.P. and L.L. (1979) $3,600, 8½" h.

0264 *Carp Bowl*
D.P. and L.L. (1979) $2,750, 7¾" dia.

0265 *Plum Blossom Bowl*
D.P. and L.L. (1979) $2,850, 7¼" dia.

0270 *Chinese Sun*
D.P. and L.L. (1980) $13,500, 8½" h.

0271 *Chinese Moon*
D.P. and L.L. (1980) $13,500, 9" h.

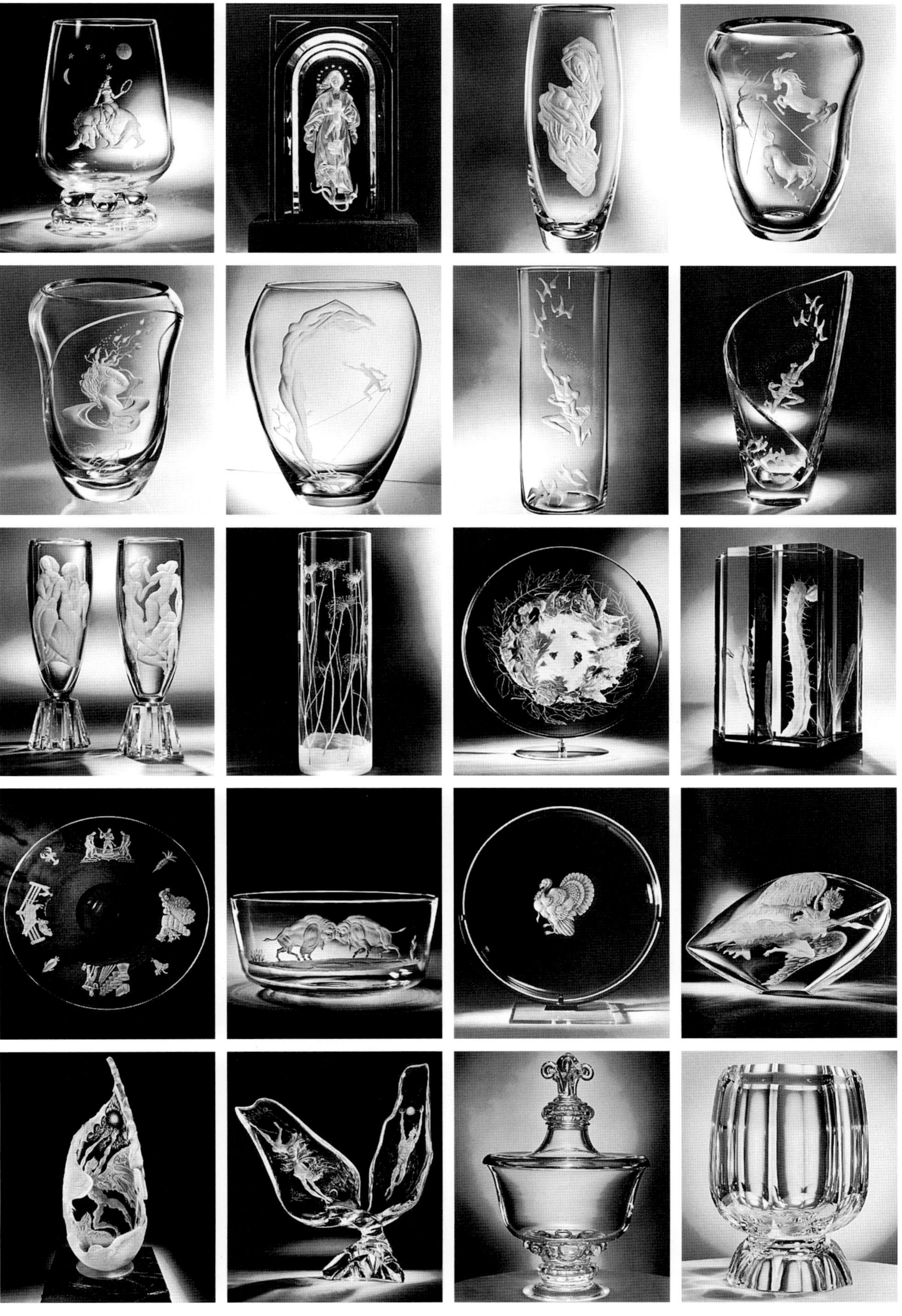

EMIL LIE

X2802 *East of the Sun and West of the Moon*
G.T. and E.L. (1942) 12½" h.

BRUNO LUCCHESI

0167 *Madonna and Child*
B.X.W. and L.R. (1975) $18,500, 15¾" h. (w/base)

GWEN LUX

X1639 *The Madonna*
G.T. and G.L. (1947) 14" h.

X1650H *Turbulent Horses*
G.T. and G.L. (1948) 8" h.

X1650P *Primavera*
G.T. and G.L. (1948) 8" h.

X1698 *The Daphne Vase*
G.T. and G.L. (1947) 11½" h.

X1699 *The Capistrano Vase*
G.T. and G.L. (1947) 15" h.

X3079 *The Swallows*
G.T. and G.L. (1959) $1,250, 13½" h.

ORONZIO MALDARELLI

X2384RE/RH *Repose and Rhythm*
G.T. and O.Ma. (1952) 12¾" h.

STANLEY MALTZMAN

0184 *Queen Anne's Lace—Winter*
B.X.W. and S.M. (1976) $6,300, 19¾" h.

0193 *Winter Leaves*
P.Y. and S.M. (1976) $12,500, 17½" h. (w/stand)

0206 *Cacti*
P.Schu. and S.M. (1976) $15,750, 11½" h.

BRUNO MANKOWSKI

X2841 *The Bowl of Plenty*
G.T. and B.Ma. (1954) 14¾" h.

X3070 *Buffalo Bowl*
L.A. and B.Ma. (1954) 13" dia.

X3100 *Turkey Plate*
Des. and B.Ma. 14" dia.

EZIO MARTINELLI

0067 *Angel*
G.T. and E.M. (1959) $2,250, 13" l.

X3353 *Icarus*
D.P. and E.M. (1960) $15,000, 14¾" h.

X3388 *Light*
D.P. and E.M. (1960) $4,000, 11½" h.

JAMES MCNAUGHTON

X477 *La Panache*
J.McN. (1939) 19" h.

X511 *Lotus Vase*
J.McN. (1939) $500, 15½" h.

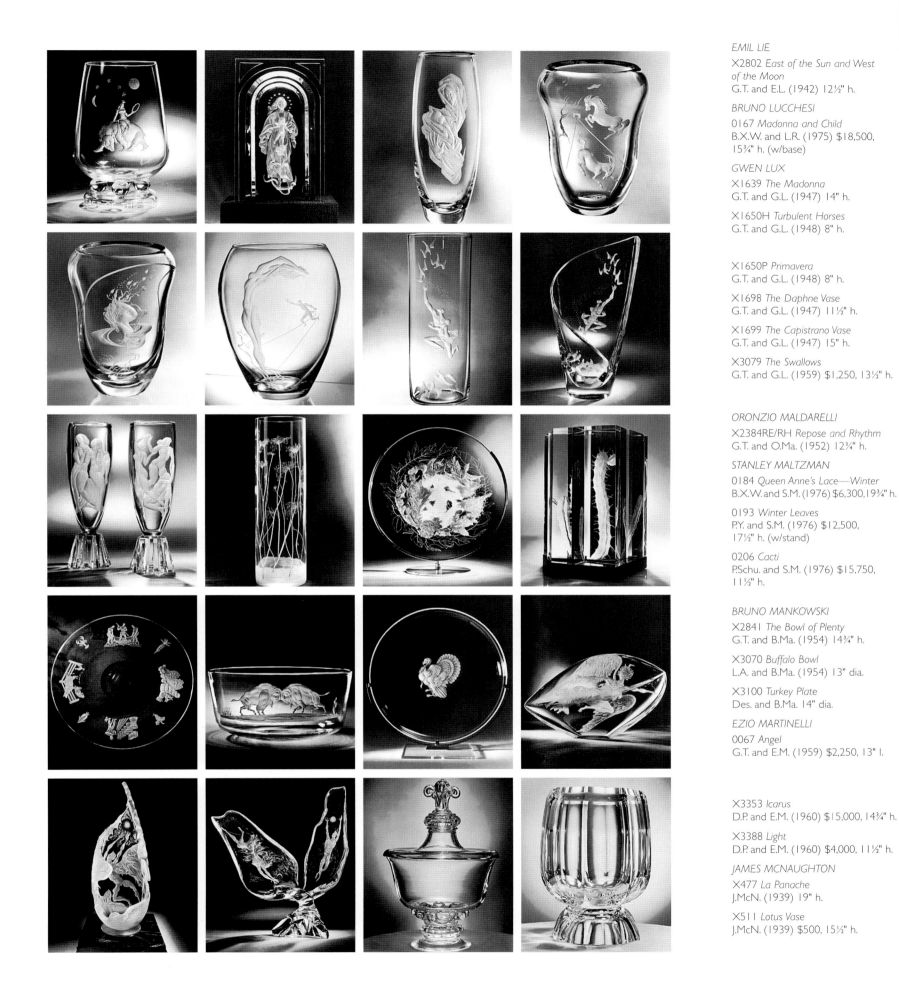

RICHARD MILLER

0112 *Nude*
R.M. and P.Schu. (1970) $5,600, 8¼" h.

X4405 *Nude II*
R.M. and P.Schu. (1973) $7,500, 8" w.

GREGORY MIROW

0133 *Spreading Pines*
G.M. (1973) $4,800, 8" h.

0159 *Floral Egg*
L.A. and G.M. (1975) $5,500, 10¼" h. (w/base)

BRUCE MOORE

0147 *Tiger Bowl*
B.Mo. (1950) 14" dia.

X2349N *Northern Lights*
G.T. and B.Mo. (1951) 14" dia.

X2349S *Southern Cross*
G.T. and B.Mo. (1951) 14" dia.

0060 *The Explorers*
G.T. and B.Mo. (1952) 10" h.

X2352 *The Plains*
L.A. and B.Mo. (1952) 13" h.

X2353W *The Woodland*
L.A. and B.Mo. (1952) 7" h.

X2353P *The Prairie*
L.A. and B.Mo. (1952) 7" h.

X2623 *Aerialists*
G.T. and B.Mo. (1953) 10½" h.

X2657 *Susanna*
B.Mo. (1953) 13" h.

0227 *Bombus*
B.Mo. (1953) 10" h.

0061 *Holiday Bowl*
G.T. and B.Mo. (1954) 12½" dia.

X2949 *The Village Blacksmith*
B.Mo. 12" h.

X2950F *Huckleberry Finn*
B.Mo. (1956) $800, 13" h.

X2950S *Tom Sawyer*
B.Mo. (1956) $800, 13" h.

X2997 *Hawkeye*
L.A. and B.Mo. (1956) 13½" h.

X3018 *The Raven*
G.T. and B.Mo. (1956) 13" dia.

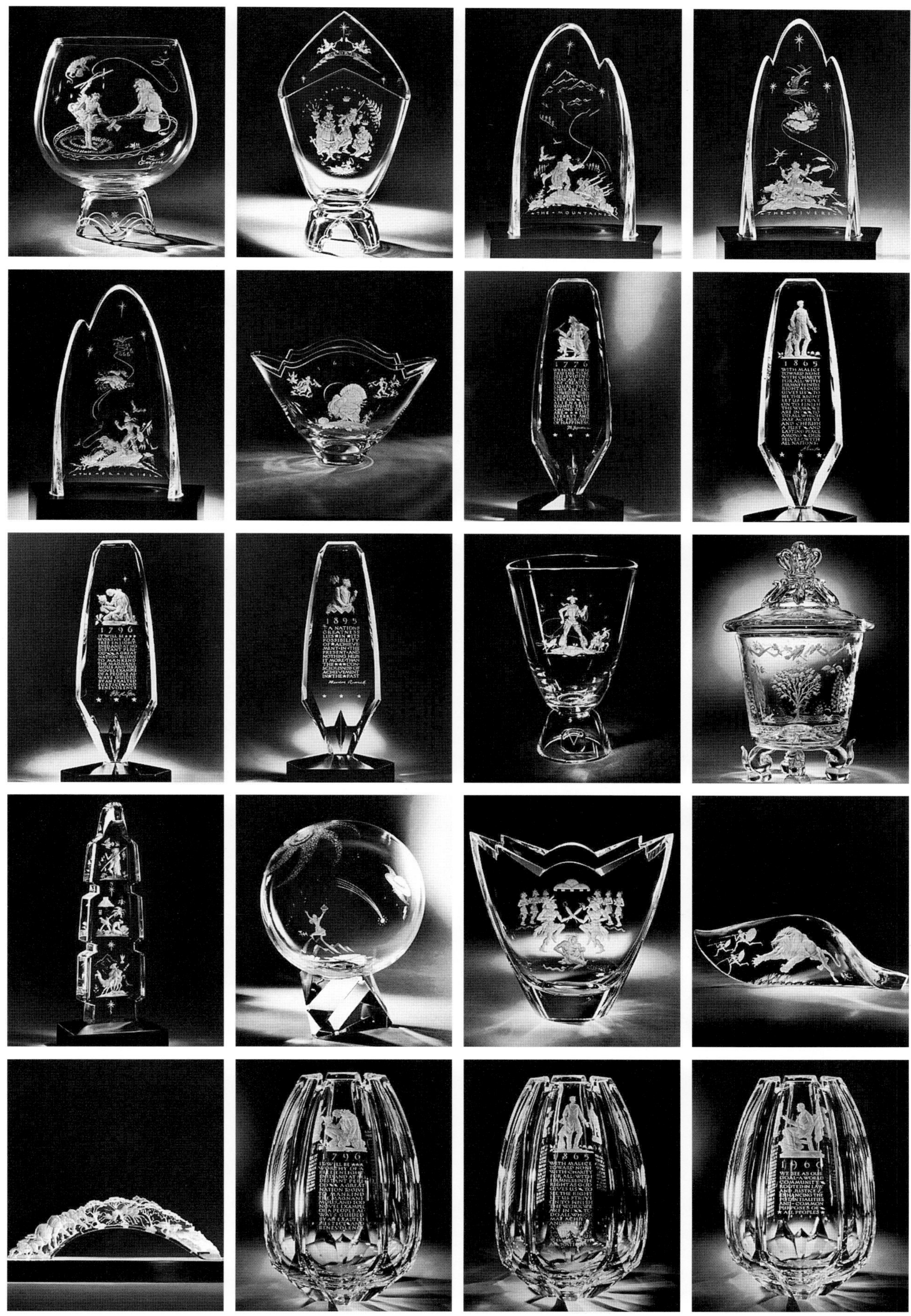

X3019 *The Circus*
G.T. and B.Mo. 10¼" h.

X3123 *The Magi*
B.Mo. (1957) $2,500, 15" h.

X3124 *The Mountains*
G.T. and B.Mo. (1957) $1,750, 11" h.

X3125 *The Rivers*
G.T. and B.Mo. (1957) $2,000, 14" h.

X3126 *The Prairies*
G.T. and B.Mo. (1957) $1,750, 11" h.

X3183 *Thanksgiving Bowl*
G.T. and B.Mo. (1957) $1,800, 13" l.

0062 *Thomas Jefferson*
D.P. and B.Mo. (1959) $2,000, 15½" h.

0063 *Abraham Lincoln*
D.P. and B.Mo. (1959) $2,000, 15½" h.

0065 *George Washington*
D.P. and B.Mo. (1959) $2,000, 15½" h.

0064 *Theodore Roosevelt*
D.P. and B.Mo. (1962) $2,250, 15½" h.

X3253 *The Rodeo*
G.T. and B.Mo. (1957) $900, 10" h.

X3255 *The Queen's Cup*
G.T. and B.Mo. (1957) 14½" h.

X3267 *Totem of the Americas*
L.A. and B.Mo. (1959) $2,500, 13¾" h.

X3323 *Cosmos*
L.A. and B.Mo. (1959) $2,500, 12" h.

X3327 *Rain Dance*
G.T. and B.Mo. (1959) $2,500,
10" dia.

X3363 *Ngatuny*
G.T. and B.Mo. (1960) $3,000, 15¼" l.

X3389 *Kisima*
D.P. and B.Mo. (1960) $5,000, 15½" l.

X3497 *Vase of the Three Presidents*
(three views) D.P. and B.Mo. (1961)
$3,750, 12¼" h.

X3535 *Moth and Flame*
D.P. and B.Mo. (1962) $900, 10½" h.

X3688 *Fireflies*
P.Schu. and B.Mo. (1964) $800, 8¼" h.

0074 *African Elephant*
L.A. and B.Mo. (1966) $5,500, 7¾" h. (w/base)

0076 *Chui*
L.A. and B.Mo. (1965) $3,500, 9½" l.

0077 *Tembo*
L.A. and B.Mo. (1965) $4,000, 7½" l.

X4324 *American Bison*
L.A. and B.Mo. (1970) $5,850, 16¼" l.

X4356 *Gibbons*
G.T. and B.Mo. (1970) $6,500, 10" h.

BRUCE NORTH

0151 *City Scene*
G.T. and B.N. (1973) $4,350, 6½" w.

JANE OSBORN-SMITH

0345 *Bird Song*
J.O.S. (1983) $10,000, 6" w.

0431 *Moth to Flame*
J.O.S. (1988) $19,500, 10" h.

0480 *Shakespeare's Animals*
J.O.S. (1990) $28,000, 12¼" dia.

0488 *Climbing Rose Vase*
(not illustrated) J.O.S. (1990) $8,700

0504 *Endangered Species Bowl*
J.O.S. (1992) $23,500, 8¼" h.

0552S *Enchanted Unicorn* (not illustrated) J.O.S. (2001) $9,000, 7¾" w.

PETER PARNALL

0129 *Apple Tree*
D.D. and P.P. (1974) $7,250, 8½" w.

JERRY PFOHL

X3842 *The Myth of Adonis*
D.P. and J.P. (1966) $28,500, 6⅞" h.

WILLIAM PHILIPS

X3531 *Pied Piper*
G.T. and W.P. (1962) $2,500, 11½" h.

X3770 *Crescendo*
P.Schu. and W.P. (1965) $1,500, 8¼" h.

DONALD POLLARD

X2682 *Covered Centerpiece*
D.P. 12½" h.

X2705 *Vase*
D.P. (1953)

X2805 *Bowl*
D.P.

X2872 *Vase on Cut Base*
D.P. 10" dia.

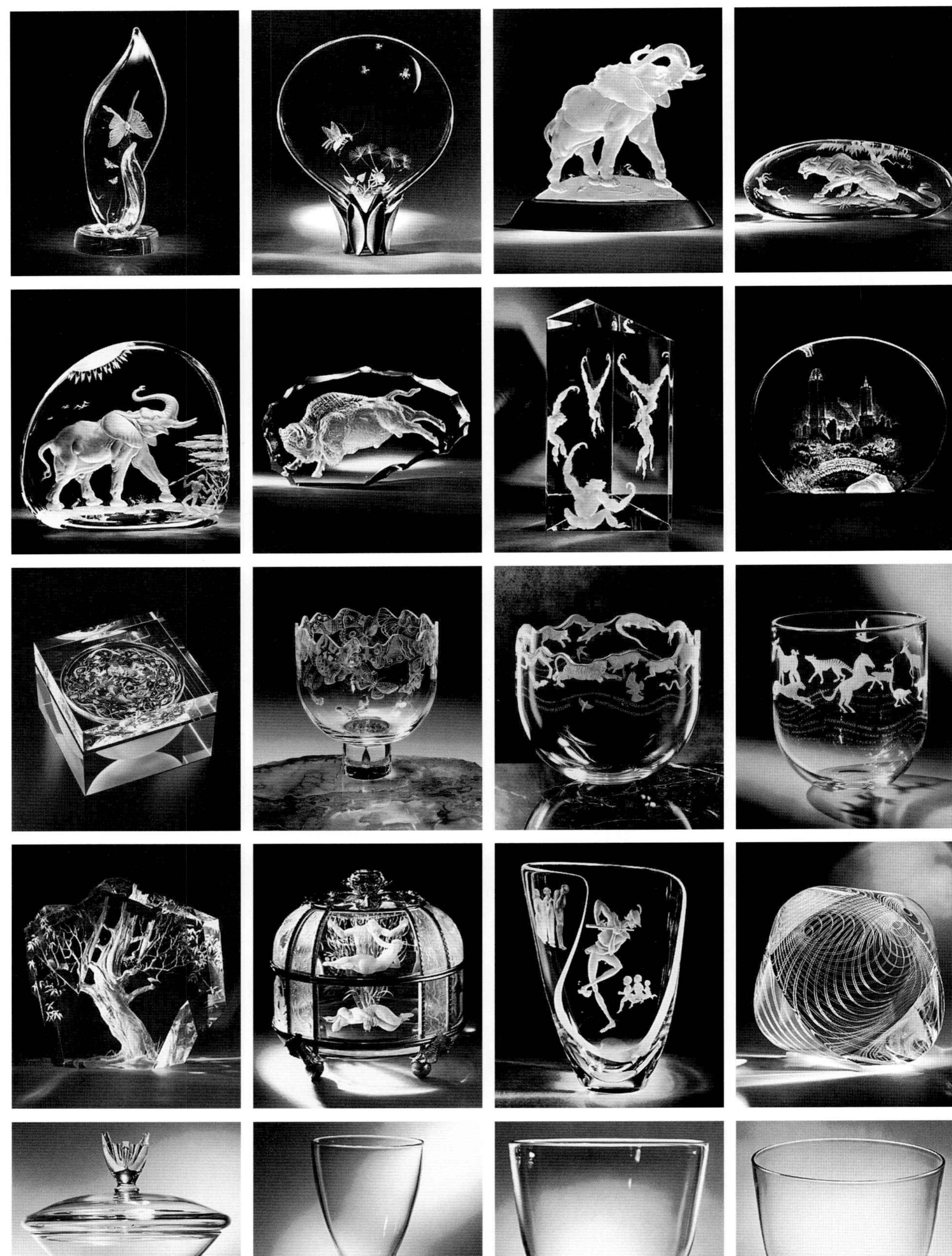

E3061 *Crystal Bowl*
D.P. 9" dia.

E3062 *Covered Urn*
D.P. 14½" h.

4106 *Crystal Bowl*
D.P. 10½" dia.

X3230 *Eisenhower Globe*
D.P. (1959) 6½" h.

X3250 *Covered Urn*
D.P. (1958) $1,250, 19" h.

X3251 *Covered Urn*
D.P. 15½" h.

X3434 *Decanters*
D.P. (1969) $800 ea., 12" h.

X3467 *Renascence*
D.P. (1963) $2,500, 18¼" h.

X3500 *The Eisenhower Crystal*
D.P. (1961) $5,000, 10½" h.

X3529 *Voyage*
D.P. (1961) $3,300, 10" l.

0075 *Manhattan*
D.P. (1965) $2,250, 18¼" l.

X3834 *Pine Seed*
D.P. (1966) $4,000, 17" h.
(w/base)

X4254 *The Moon and Man*
D.P. (1971) $4,800, 10¾" h.

0113 *American Eagle*
D.P. (1970) $3,750, 10" w.

0134 *Cross*
D.P. (1974) $5,600, 13" h. (w/base)

4128 *Chalice*
D.P. (1978) $395, 8¾" h.

0166 *The Bicentennial Goblet*
D.P. and P.W. (1975) $1,600, 8" h.

0199 *Square-Cut Vase*
D.P. (1976) $1,500, 7¾" h.

X4180 *The Four Seasons*
D.P. and A.S. (1969) $48,500, 6⅛" w.

X4181 *The Carrousel of the Sea*
G.T. and A.S. (1970) $47,500, 9¾" h.

X4346 *The Unicorn and the Maiden*
D.P. and A.S. (1971) $73,500, 14½" h.

0210 *Chinese Pavilion*
D.P., A.S., and R.E. (1975) $142,750, 11¼" h.

0143 *Nosegay*
D.P. and A.S. (1975) $7,450, 6¾" h.

0188 *Sphere of the Zodiac*
D.P., A.S., and R.E. (1976) $78,500, 19¼" h.

0324 *Chinese Waterfall*
D.P. (1982) $9,250, 9½" h.

0327 *Box of Dreams*
D.P. (1982) $4,250, 5½" l.

DONALD POLLARD AND BENI MONTRESOR

0332 *Crown of Oberon*
D.P. and B.Mon. (1983) $175,000, 9½" h.

RUTH RAY

7913 *Vase*
R.R. (1947) 8½" h.

HOWARD ROGERS

0225 *The Romance of the Rose*
D.P., H.R., and R.E. (1977) $95,000, 9½" w.

LUCIANA G. ROSELLI

0311 *Tulip Bowl*
L.Ro. (1981) $35,000, 12½" d.

0326 *Carnation Vase*
L.Ro. (1982) $8,000, 11½" h.

0360 *Bird of Paradise*
L.Ro. (1985) $29,500, 13½" h.

TAF LEBEL SCHAEFER AND TIM ANGELL

0545 *Manatee: Siren of the Sea*
T.L.S. and T.A. (2000) $13,500, 6¾" h.

PAUL SCHULZE

4115 *Crystal Plaque*
P.Schu. (1962) $95, 5" h.

X3720 *Space*
P.Schu. (1965) $1,200, 15½" h. (w/base)

4120 *Crystal Plaque*
P.Schu. (1964) $175, 6½" h.

X4055 *Crystal and Gold Egg*
P.Schu. (1969) $2,800, 6" h.

0098 *Cut Vase*
P.Schu. (1969) $750, 6½" h.

0099 *Puma Rock*
P.Schu. (1969) $2,750, 8" h.

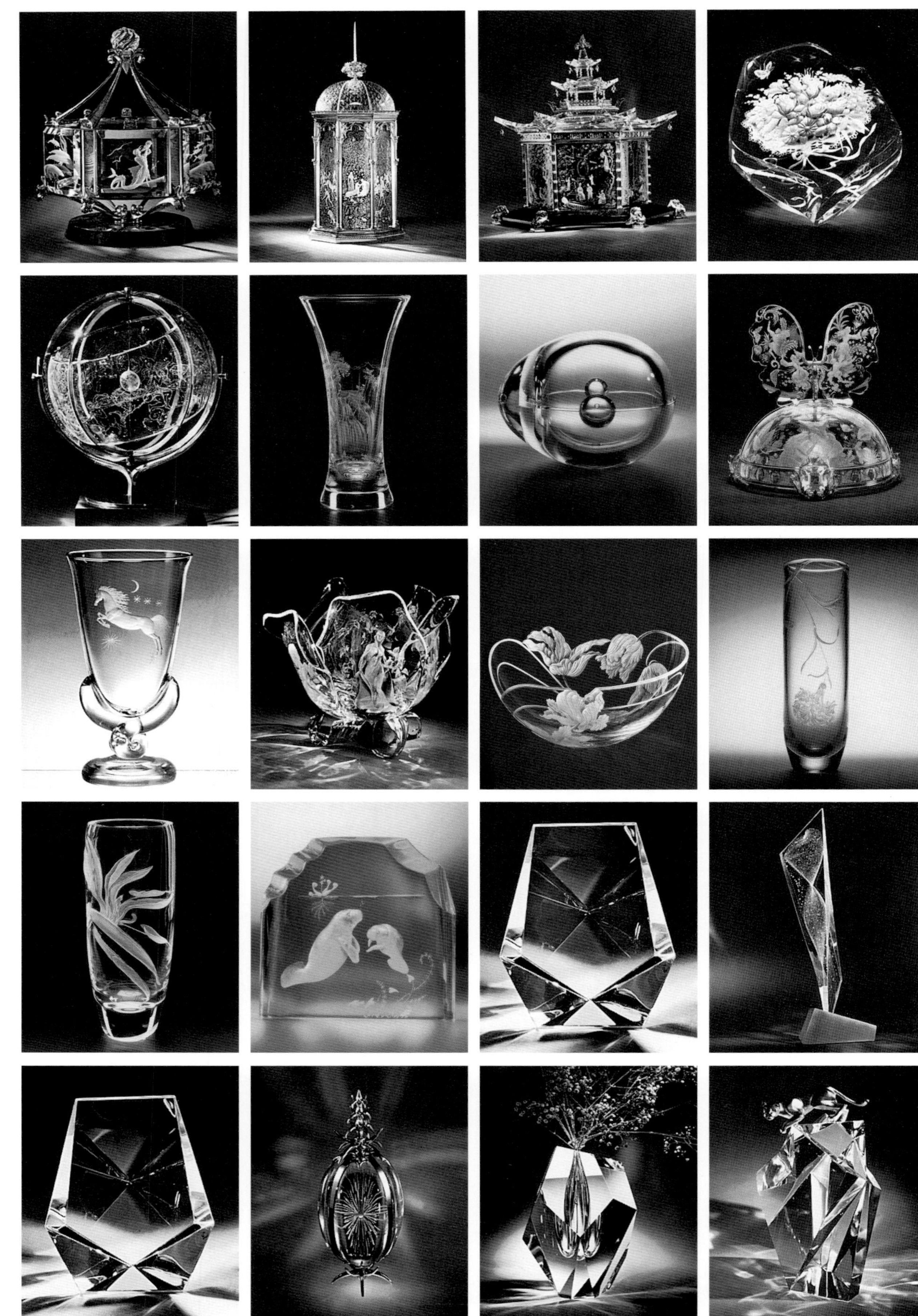

0155 *Flying Eagle*
P.Schu. (1975) $1,950, 14½" l.

0267 *Earth Zone*
P.Schu. (1979) $3,750, 8" h.

0346 *Soaring*
P.Schu. (1982) $10,500, 9⅞" dia.

0353 *New York, New York*
P.Schu. (1984) $27,500, 17" h.

ALEXANDER SEIDEL
X3721 *Partridge in a Pear Tree*
D.P. and A.S. (1964) $1,000, 5¾" h.

X3839 *The Enchanted Birds*
G.T. and A.S. (1966) $15,000, 13" h.

X3860 *Spring Trilogy*
D.P. and A.S. (1966) $7,800, 15½" h. (w/base)

0081 *Phoenix Nest*
D.P. and A.S. (1967) $7,000, 8½" w.

0085 *The Butterfly*
G.T. and A.S. (1967) $3,300, 8" h.

PAUL SEIZ
0208 *Lioness*
P.S. (1976) $9,500, 10" w.

JULIE SHEARER
0373 *Iris Vase*
J.Sh. (1986) $37,500, 13½" h.

JOEL SMITH
0541 *Winds of the Future*
J.S. (1999) $15,000, 8½" h.

6286 *Autumn Table*
J.S. (2000) $14,500 42" w.

6287 *Runner Table*
J.S. (2000) $12,500, 46" w.

6288 *Bubble Lamp* (not illustrated)
J.S. (2000) $3,800

JOEL SMITH AND GARY DAVIS
0517 *The Pitch*
J.S. and G.D. (1996) $10,000, 8" h.

JOEL SMITH AND DONALD DEMERS
0518 *Windward Passage*
J.S. and D.De. (1996) $10,500, 10" w.

JOEL SMITH AND BARRY MOSER
0479 *Wide and Universal Stage*
J.S. and Ba.M. (1990) $56,000, 13¼" h.

0514 *Infinite Love*
J.S. and Ba.M. (1995) $8,400, 10¾" h.

GEORGE THOMPSON
X509 *Primavera*
G.T.

X519 *Galapagos Bowl*
G.T.

X1428 *Vase*
G.T.

X1543 *Covered Centerpiece on Domed Foot*
G.T. (1946)

X1562 *Fountain*
G.T. 30" h.

X1575 *Covered Crystal Jar with Cane Twist Finial*
G.T. 11½" h.

X1576 *Vase*
G.T.

X1577 *Crystal Vase*
G.T. 8½" h.

E1586 *Crystal Vase*
G.T. 8¾" h.

E4123 *Crystal Bowl*
G.T. 9" dia.

X1626 *Bowl on Pedestal Base*
G.T. (1947) 15" dia.

X1632 *Zodiac Vase*
G.T.

X1653 *Crystal Decanter*
G.T. 12½" h.

X1684 *Crystal Cross*
G.T. (1950) 17¼" h.

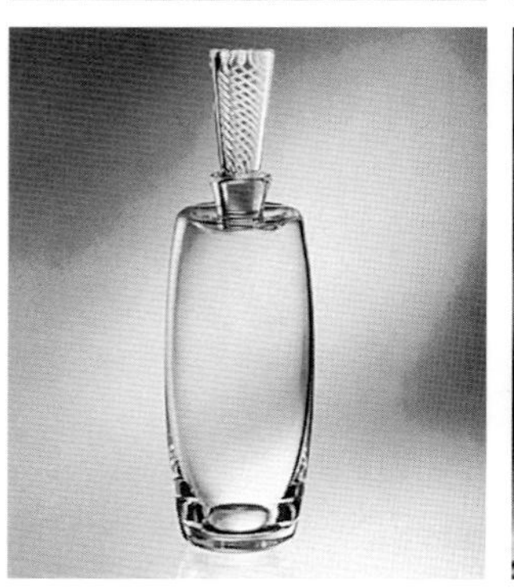

X1896 *Ornamental Champagne Glass*
G.T. 18½" h.

X1897 *Cut Punch Bowl*
G.T. 13" dia.

X1898 *Plate*
G.T.

X1991 *Vase*
G.T.

X2007 *The Wave*
G.T. (1949) 8¼" h.

X2009 *Sea Fight*
G.T. 7¼" h.

X2098 *Crystal Fountain*
G.T. 27" h.

X2206 *Covered Vase*
G.T. (1950)

X2232 *Bowl with Crenelated Base*
G.T. 9½" dia.

X2240 *Three-Tiered Fountain*
G.T. 26" h.

X2244 *Bowl*
G.T.

X2348 *Crystal Bowl with Cut Base*
G.T. 15½" dia.

E2354 *Trophy Cup*
G.T. 10½" h.

E2359 *Crystal Bowl*
G.T. 9" dia.

X2535 *Obelisks*
G.T. (1953)

X2539 *Pedestal Bowl*
G.T. 11½" dia.

E2547 *Covered Urn*
G.T. 14¾" h.

X2555 *The Crown Cup*
G.T. (1954) 19½" h.

X2678 *Crystal Centerpiece*
G.T. 15" dia.

X2680 *Bowl*
G.T.

X2696 *Crystal Bowl*
G.T. 9⅜" h.

X2715 *Vase*
G.T. (1953)

X2787 *Crystal Fountain*
G.T. (1954) 28" h.

X2788 *Crystal Bowl*
G.T. (1954) 9" dia.

X2795 *Covered Urn*
G.T. 21" h.

X2796 *Bowl*
G.T.

X2826 *Covered Urn*
G.T. 18¼" h.

E2827 *Bowl*
G.T. 11¼" dia.

X2847 *Crystal Vase*
G.T. 13" h.

X2857 *Crystal Vase*
G.T. 13¼" h.

E2878 *Crystal Vase*
G.T. 9½" h.

E2880 *Crystal Bowl*
G.T. 5¼" dia.

E2881 *Crystal Bowl*
G.T. 5½" dia.

4101 *Crystal Bowl*
G.T. 6" dia.

E2883 *Oval Bowl*
G.T. 6¼" l.

E2884 *Crystal Vase*
G.T. 12¼" h.

X3002 *Vase with Cut Base*
G.T. 16½" h.

X3013 *Fountain*
G.T. (1959) $3,000, 22" h.

4102 *Covered Urn*
G.T. (1961) $65, 8½" h.

E3056 *Covered Urn*
G.T. 18" h.

X3096 *Covered Urn*
G.T.

X3101 *Centerpiece*
G.T. (1957) $200, 12¼" h.

4107 *Ornamental Plaque*
G.T. (1957) $60, 8" l.

X3314 *Allegro*
G.T. (1958) 12" h.

X3348 *Rainbow*
G.T. (1960) $5,000, 12" w.

0068 *Nautilus*
G.T. (1959) $1,750, 9¾" h.

0069 *Mountains of the Moon*
G.T. (1960) $2,000, 9" w.

4111 *Crystal Plaque*
G.T. (1962) $750, 9¼" h.

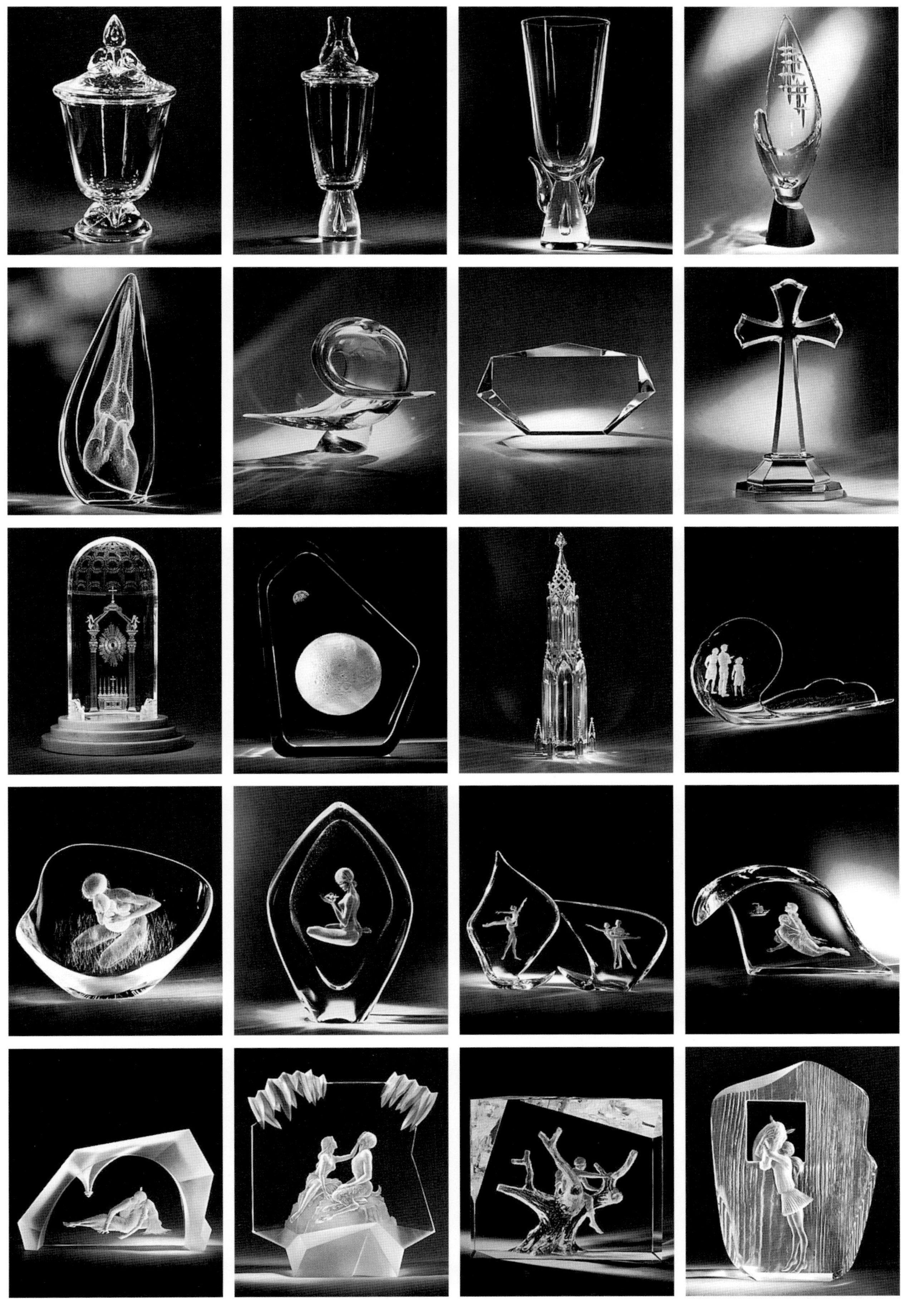

E3459 *Covered Urn*
G.T. (1960) $110, 10" h.

4112 *Covered Urn*
G.T. (1960) $100, 10¾" h.

E3464 *Crystal Vase*
G.T. (1960) $65, 10¼" h.

X3494 *Crystal Trophy*
G.T. 19¼" h. (w/base)

X3495 *Jet*
G.T. (1964) $2,000, 16" h.

X3667 *Crystal Ornament*
G.T. (1963) $325, 9¾" l.

4119 *Crystal Plaque*
G.T. 7" w.

X3779 *Crystal Cross*
G.T. (1964) $2,800, 13½" h. (w/base)

0078 *Altar*
G.T. (1965) $4,000, 12½" h. (w/base)

X4247 *The Moon*
G.T. (1969) $8,500, 12½" h.

X4374 *Cathedral Spire*
G.T. (1972) $20,500, 18¼" h.

ROBERT VICKREY

X3904 *Morning*
G.T. and R.V. (1966) $3,500, 14¾" l.

TOM VINCENT

X3549 *Mother and Child*
G.T. and T.V. (1962) $3,300, 12" w.

0079 *Girl and Bird*
G.T. and T.V. (1965) $3,000, 10¼" h.

0083 *Adagio I and II*
G.T. and T.V. (1966) $6,000, 11" h.

0087 *Tristan and Isolde*
G.T. and T.V. (1968) $4,200, 12¾" l.

0088 *Romeo and Juliet*
G.T. and T.V. (1968) $6,250, 11¾" l.

0090 *Afternoon of a Faun*
G.T. and T.V. (1968) $7,250, 10½" h.

0158 *The Tree*
P.Schu. and T.V. (1967) $6,500, 9½" w.

0107 *Girl with Horse*
G.T. and T.V. (1970) $5,350, 10¼" h.

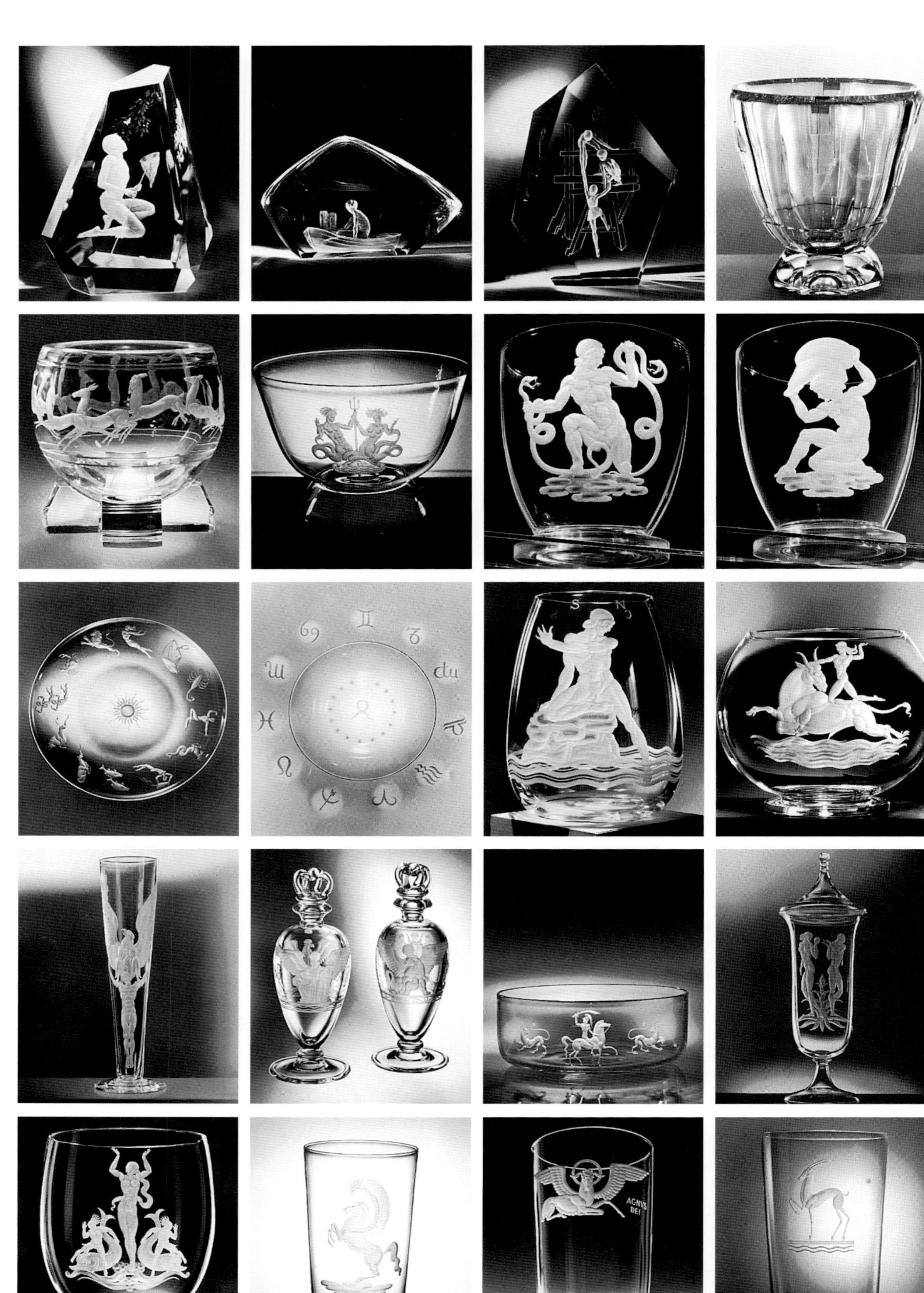

0108 *Boy and Butterfly*
G.T. and T.V. (1970) $6,000, 8¼" h.

0114 *Boy in Boat*
G.T. and T.V. (1971) $5,100, 13" w.

0118 *Ladder of Dreams*
G.T. and T.V. (1971) $4,500, 11¾" h.

SIDNEY WAUGH

X2928 *Massive Cut Vase*
S.W. (1935) 11" h.

0053 *Gazelle Bowl*
S.W. (1935) 6½" dia.

W102 *Trident Punch Bowl*
S.W. (1935)

W103 *Hercules and Snake*
S.W. (1938)

W104 *Hercules*
S.W. (1938)

W105 *Zodiac Bowl*
S.W. (1935) 16" dia.

W106 *Zodiac Plates*
S.W. (1946) 8¼" w.

W107 *Narcissus Bowl*
S.W. (1938)

W108 *Europa Bowl*
S.W. (1935) 8" dia.

W109 *Ganymede*
S.W. $700

W110 *Ecclesiastical Cruets*
S.W. 6¾" h.

W112 *The Lion Hunter Bowl*
S.W. 12" dia.

W113 *Adam and Eve Vase*
S.W. (1938)

W114 *The Venus Vase*
S.W. (1935) 11¾" h.

8206 *Pegasus Vase*
S.W. 7¼" h.

8207 *Agnus Dei Vase*
S.W. 7¼" h.

8208 *Gazelle Vase*
S.W. 7½" h.

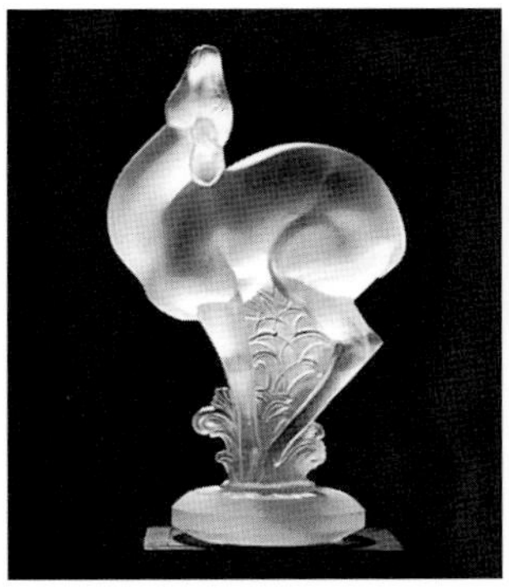

W118 *Fawn*
S.W.

8209 *Diana Vase*
S.W. 4¾" h.

8210 *Peasant Vase*
S.W. 5¼" h.

8211 *Woman with Trumpet Vase*
S.W. 5½" h.

W129 *Atlantica*
S.W. (1939)

0054 *Mariner's Bowl*
S.W. 15¾" dia.

W131 *Wine, Women and Song*
S.W. (1939) 10" dia.

W136 *Atalanta Cup*
S.W. (1939)

W138 *Paul Revere Vase*
S.W. (1942) 12½" h.

W139 *Bowl of American Legends*
S.W. (1942) 10" dia.

W140 *American Ballad Bowl*
G.T. and S.W. (1942) 9½" dia.

W141 *Transportation*
G.T. and S.W. (1943) 7½" dia.

W142 *Trade and Commerce*
G.T. and S.W. (1943) 7½" dia.

W143 *The Arts*
G.T. and S.W. (1943) 11¾" h.

W144 *The Sciences*
G.T. and S.W. (1943) 11¾" h.

W145 *Agriculture*
G.T. and S.W. (1943) 11¾" h.

W146 *Industry*
G.T. and S.W. (1943) 11¾" h.

W147 *The Indian*
S.W. (1943) 5¾" h.

W148 *The Trapper*
S.W. (1943) 5¾" h.

W149 *The Pioneer*
S.W. (1943) 5¾" h.

W151 *Prairie Smoke*
S.W. (1946) 12" dia.

W152 *The Sea*
S.W. (1946) 14" dia.
(top and side views)

W153 *The Forest*
S.W. (1946) 18" h.

W154 *The Desert*
S.W. (1946) 18" h.

W155 *The Merry-Go-Round Bowl*
S.W. (1947) 10" h.

W156 *Stephen Foster Bowl*
S.W. (1947) 11" dia.

W157 *Christopher Columbus*
L.A. and S.W. (1957) 14½" h.

W158 *The Puritan Vase*
S.W. (1957) 14" h.

W159 *The Eisenhower Cup*
G.T. and S.W. (1954) 12" h.

W160 *The Papal Cup*
G.T. and S.W. (1956) 22" h.

W161 *The LaFayette Medallion*
S.W. (1957) 11½" h. (w/stand)

8212 *Lust*
S.W. 7½" h.

8213 *Envy*
S.W. 7½" h.

8214 *Avarice*
S.W. 7½" h.

8215 *Sloth*
S.W. 7½" h.

8216 *Gluttony*
S.W. 7½" h.

8217 *Pride*
S.W. 7½" h.

8218 *Anger*
S.W. 7½" h.

W169 *The Norway Cup*
S.W. (1955) 13½" h.

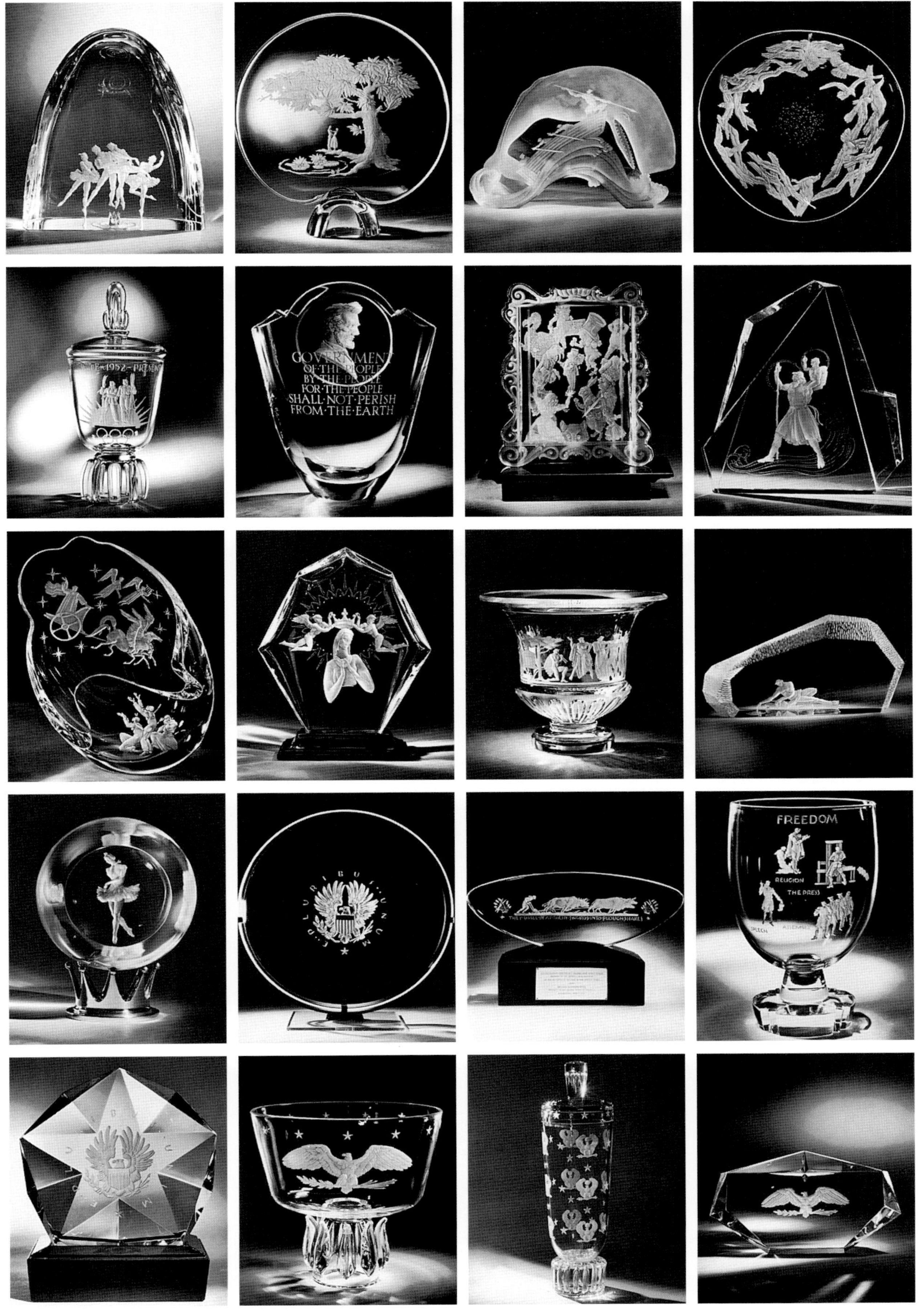

W170 *Swan Lake*
G.T. and S.W. (1959) $2,250, 6¾" h.

W171 *The Green Idyll*
G.T. and S.W. (1959) $1,500, 11¼" h.

0055 *Moby Dick*
D.P. and S.W. (1959) $3,500, 11¼" l.

W173 *Sea Gulls*
D.P. and S.W. (1960) $3,000, 16¼" dia.

W174 *The Winter Games Cup*
S.W. (1962) 15⅛" h.

W175 *Lincoln Vase*
G.T. and S.W. (1962) $2,000, 10" h.

W176 *The Adventures of Alice*
G.T. and S.W. (1962) $12,500, 11¾" h. (w/base)

0056 *Saint Christopher*
G.T. and S.W. (1962) $3,000, 9" h.

W178 *Swing Low*
G.T. and S.W. (1962) $3,000, 10½" h.

0057 *Sancta Virgo*
D.P. and S.W. (1962) $2,500, 9" h. (w/base)

0058 *Grecian Urn*
D.P. and S.W. (1962) $4,500, 6½" h.

0059 *Narcissus*
G.T. and S.W. (1962) $2,250, 11" l.

W182 *Ballerina*
P.Schu. and S.W. (1964) $500, 4½" h.

W183 *American Eagle Plate*
S.W. 13" dia.

W184 *Ploughshares*
S.W. (1959) 16" l.

W185 *The Four Freedoms*
G.T. and S.W. (1957) 11" h.

W186 *The Eagle and the Star*
D.P. and S.W. (1964) $2,500, 10" h. (w/base)

W187 *Engraved Bowl, Eagle*
G.T. and S.W. (1964) 10" dia.

W188 *Covered Urn, Stars and Eagles*
D.P. and S.W. (1961) $2,500, 19" h.

0105 *Plaque Engraved with American Eagle*
G.T. and S.W. (1969) $1,100, 9¼" l.

0132 *Zodiac Crystals*
G.T. and S.W. (1974) $1,125, 4" w.

ALBERT WEIN

X2859 *Communication*
G.T. and A.W. (1955) 13" h.

X2873 *The Pony Express*
D.P. and A.W. (1955) 14¾" h.

X3069 *Prairie Schooner*
L.A. and A.W. (1956) 12½" h.

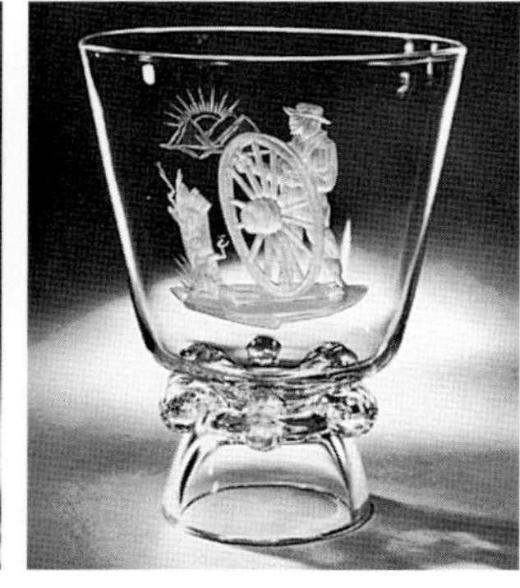

PATRICIA WEISBERG

0084 *Makara*
J.H. and P.W. (1967) $2,600, 13¼" h. (w/base)

LAURENCE WHISTLER

0214 *Freedom and the Spirit*
L.W. (1977) $25,000, 17¼" w.

0230 *Eye to Eye*
L.W. and P.Schu. (1978) $12,500, 10¾" h.

0231 *Sun Worship*
L.W. (1978) $12,500, 16" h.

0232 *Ode to Morning*
L.W. (1978) $12,500, 11⅞" h.

0242 *Winter*
P.Schu. and L.W. (1978) $2,500, 9¾" h.

0243 *Spring*
P.Schu. and L.W. (1978) $2,500, 9¾" h.

0244 *Summer*
P.Schu. and L.W. (1978) $2,500, 9¾" h.

0245 *Autumn*
P.Schu. and L.W. (1978) $2,500, 9¾" h.

0246 *Kissing Bough*
P.Schu. and L.W. (1978) $3,000, 10¼" h.

0247 *Moth and Flame*
P.Schu. and L.W. (1978) $2,650, 10¼" h.

0354 *Whistler Landscape*
L.W. (1984) $5,500

ROBERT WHITE

X3094 *Buffalo Hunt*
G.T. and R.W. (1958) 11" dia.

DON WIER

X1924A *Ariel*
G.T. and D.W. (1948) 9½" h.

X1924R *Rosalind*
G.T. and D.W. (1948) 9½" h.

X2096TH *The Thistle*
G.T. and D.W. (1950) 8" h.

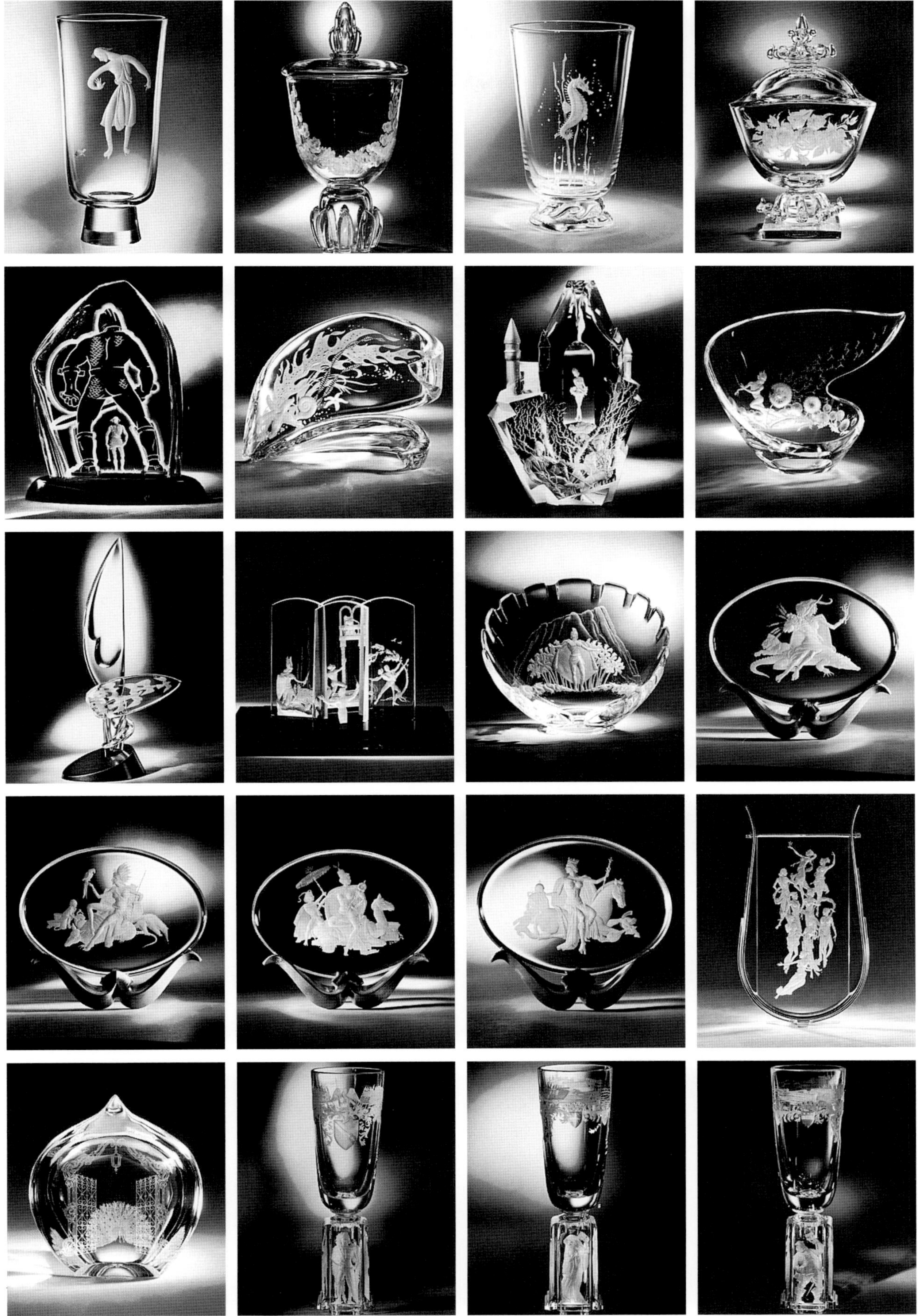

X2096TO *The Tortoise*
G.T. and D.W. (1951) 8" h.

X2536 *The Tulip Bowl*
D.W. (1952) 18" h.

X3115 *Sea Horse Vase*
L.A. and D.W. (1962) $200, 7½" h.

X3254 *The Rose Bowl*
D.P. and D.W. (1959) $2,500, 13¾" h.

0066 *David and Goliath*
D.W. (1959) $2,250, 9¾" h. (w/base)

X3303 *Sea Drift*
G.T. and D.W. (1959) $1,250, 8½" l.

X3324 *Sleeping Beauty*
D.P. and D.W. (1960) $7,500, 10¾" h.

X3351 *Zephyr*
G.T. and D.W. (1960) $2,500, 9" h.

X3387 *Alar*
D.P. and D.W. (1961) $2,250, 22" h. (w/base)

X3522 *The Performing Arts*
D.W. (1962) $12,500, 13" h. (w/base)

X3537 *Aloha*
L.A. and D.W. (1962) $4,000, 11½" w.

X3577AF *Africa*
L.A. and D.W. (1962) $3,750, 11½" w.

X3577AM *America*
L.A. and D.W. (1962) $3,750, 11½" w.

X3577AS *Asia*
L.A. and D.W. (1962) $3,750, 11½" w.

X3577E *Europe*
L.A. and D.W. (1962) $3,750, 11½" w.

0148 *The Muses*
D.W. (1964) $6,000, 10½" h.

X3706 *The Peacock*
G.T. and D.W. (1964) $400, 5¼" h.

X3810 *Shakespeare Memorial Cup* (three views)
D.W. (1964) $12,500, 16" h.

X4001 *Commedia Dell'Arte*
D.W. (1968) $8,500, 11¾" w.

X4005 *Fox and Grapes*
D.W. (1967) $4,000, 7¾" h.

0089 *Jonah*
D.W. (1967) $3,500, 8½" w.

0095 *Moses and the Burning Bush*
D.W. (1968) $4,200, 8¼" w.

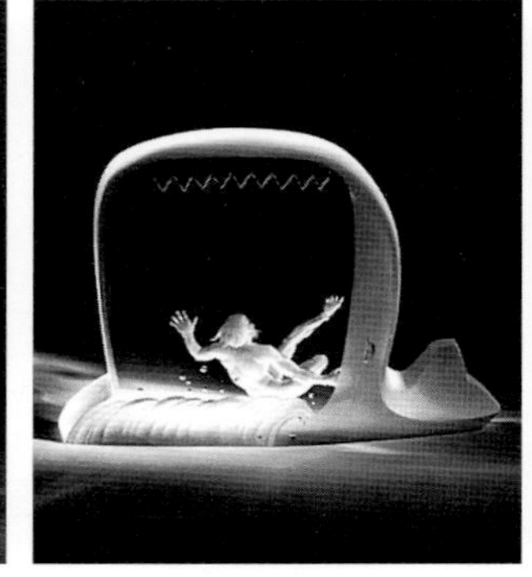

0096 *Canyon*
D.W. (1968) $8,000, 9½" h.

BERNARD X. WOLFF

0138 *Horses*
D.D. and B.X.W. (1974) $4,850, 11¼" w. (w/base)

0202 *Ballooning*
B.X.W. (1976) $5,750, 12" h. (w/base)

0219 *Odette, Odile*
B.X.W. (1977) $14,500, 15" h. (w/base)

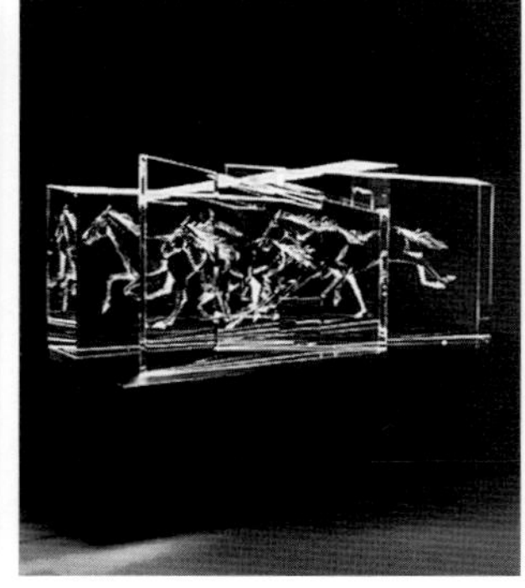

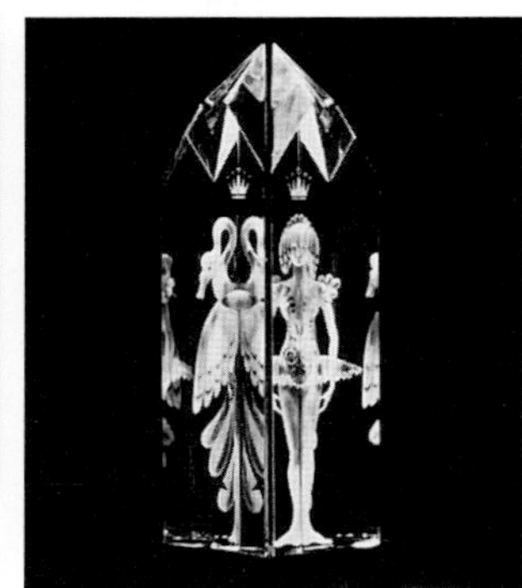

0223 *Music, Baroque*
B.X.W. (1977) $9,350, 10½" h.

0248 *Sirius*
B.X.W. (1978) $7,800, 10" h.

0269 *Water Windows*
B.X.W. (1980) $3,500, 4" h.

0318 *Dreaming Butterfly*
B.X.W. (1981) $5,450, 6" h.

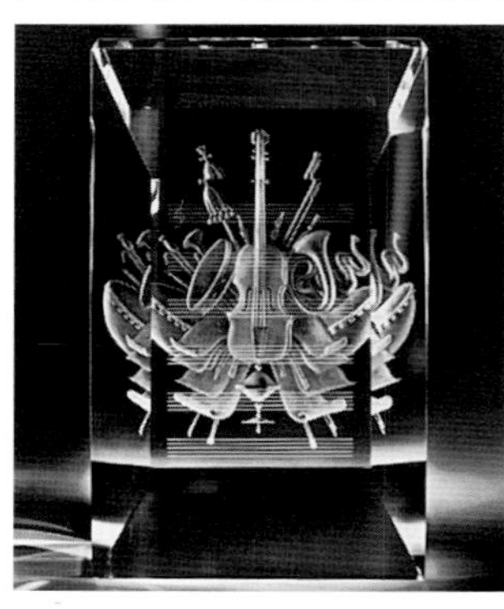

0320 *Dreaming Butterfly II*
B.X.W. (1981) $6,475, 6" h.

0323 *Floating Orchid*
B.X.W. (1982) $5,450, 6" h.

0329 *Hilltown*
B.X.W. (1982), $6,750, 8¾" h.

0331 *Floating Orchid II* (not illustrated)
B.X.W. (1982) $6,475

0350 *The First Trial of Hercules*
B.X.W. (1983) $6,950, 7⅜" h.

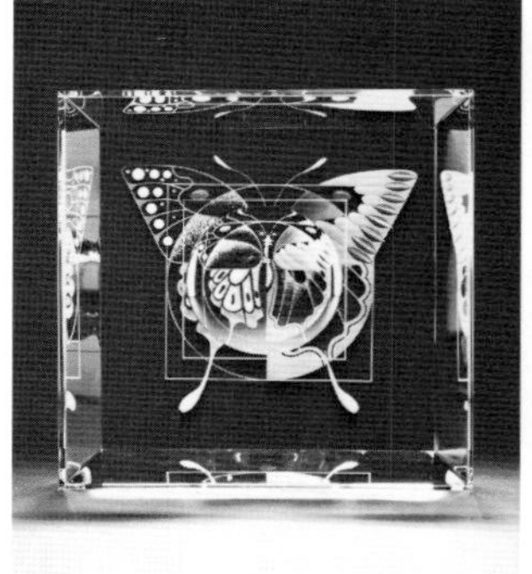

0351 *The Second Trial*
B.X.W. (1984) $6,950

0352 *The Third Trial*
B.X.W. (1984) $6,950, 7¾" h.

0358 *Monument Valley*
B.X.W. (1984) $3,500, 8¾" w.

0361 *Balloon Rally*
B.X.W. (1985) $11,000, 10¼" h.

0370 *Holly Bowl*
B.X.W. (1985) $15,000, 7½" dia.

0398 *America: 1851 Carafe*
B.X.W. (1987) $2,500, 10" h.

0399 *Baltimore Clipper Carafe*
B.X.W. (1987) $2,500, 10" h.

0416 *Osprey*
B.X.W. (1987) $8,750, 10¼" h.

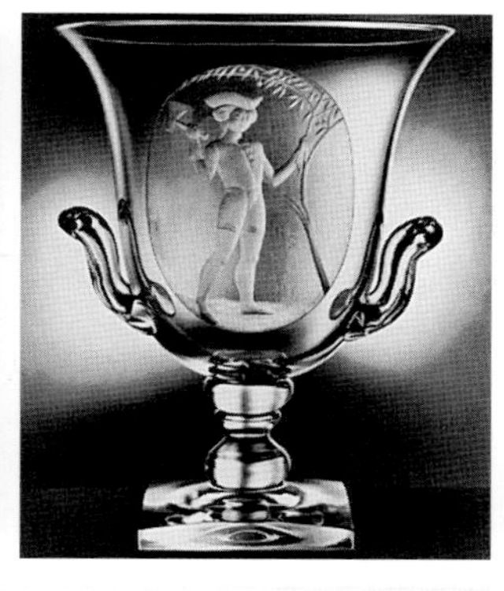

0420 *Saddlebred Horse*
B.X.W. (1988) $10,000

GRANT WOOD

X1039 *Washington Urn*
J.M.G. and G.W.

PETER YENAWINE

0127 *Optic Flower*
P.Y. (1974) $4,350, 7¾" h. (w/base)

0183 *Love Wreath*
P.Y. (1976) $2,550, 4¾" h.

0192 *Sea Serpent*
P.Y. (1976) $4,650, 9½" l.

0197 *Cup of Elijah*
P.Y. (1976) $11,500, 12" h.

0220 *Punty Cube*
P.Y. (1977) $2,150, 8" h. (w/base)

UNATTRIBUTED
(not illustrated)

0454 *The Woodland*
(1989) $20,250

0486 *Geometric Play Vase*
(1990) $3,600

0487 *Geometric Play Bowl*
(1990) $3,500

0490–0492 *Dialogue Studies I–III* (1990)
$2,000

ROBERT ZIERING

X4302 *Beethoven*
D.P. and R.Z. (1970) $7,600, 11¾" h.

UNATTRIBUTED (with photo)

0452 *French Bicentennial Bowl*
(1989) $950

0494 *Morning Lilies*
(1990) $12,000

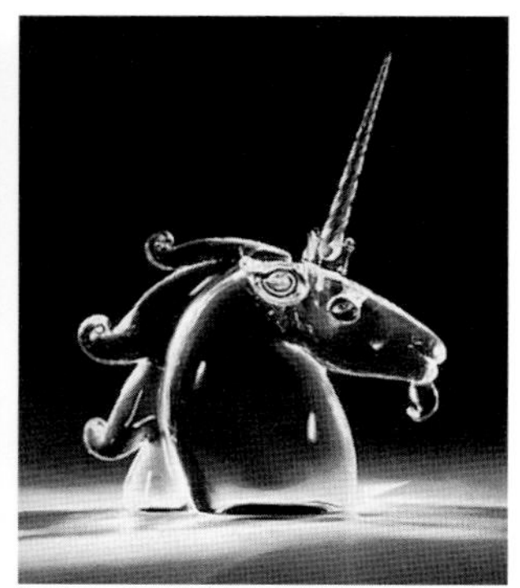

Major Ornamental Designs

1000 *Excalibur*
J.H. (1963) $650, crystal, 4½" w., sword 8" h.

1002 *Trout and Fly*
J.H. (1966) $625, 9½" h.

1003 *Beehive*
J.H. (1966) 5" w.

1004 *Unicorn*
J.H. (1966) 7" h.

1005 *Column of the Owl*
J.H. (8/6/74) 7¾" h.

1006 *Mouse and Cheese*
J.H. (4/10/75) 4" h.

1007 *Heart and Key*
J.H. 3¾" l.

1008 *Cupola with Golden Cock*
J.H. (7/24/67) 8" h.

1009 *Cupola with Golden Horse*
J.H. (10/26/73) 8" h.

1010 *Cupola with Golden Whale*
J.H. (7/24/67) 8" h.

1011 *Thistle Rock*
J.H. (9/1/67) 7" h.

1012 *Christmas Tree*
J.H. (2/12/70) 12" h.

1013 *Apple of Eden*
J.H. (9/3/71) 6" h.

1014 *Partridge in a Pear Tree*
L.A. (10/21/68) 5¾" h.

1016 *Crystal and Vermeil Turtle*
P.Schu. (4/7/69) 5½" l.

1017 *Bird Cage*
G.T. and A.S. (7/21/72) 8" h.

1019 *The Orb and the Eagle*
J.H. 6½" h.

1020 *Penguin Floe*
G.T. (2/16/70) 5" h.

1021 *Seal Rock*
J.H. (2/16/70) 6" h.

1022 *Ice Bear*
J.H. (2/20/74) 6" w.

1023 *Arctic Fisherman*
J.H. (6/1/70) 6½" h.

1024 *Orbiting Crystal*
P.Schu. (5/24/71) 5¾" h.

1025 *Mistletoe*
D.P. (9/8/70) 5¾" h.

1026 *Lilies*
D.P. (4/10/75) 5" h.

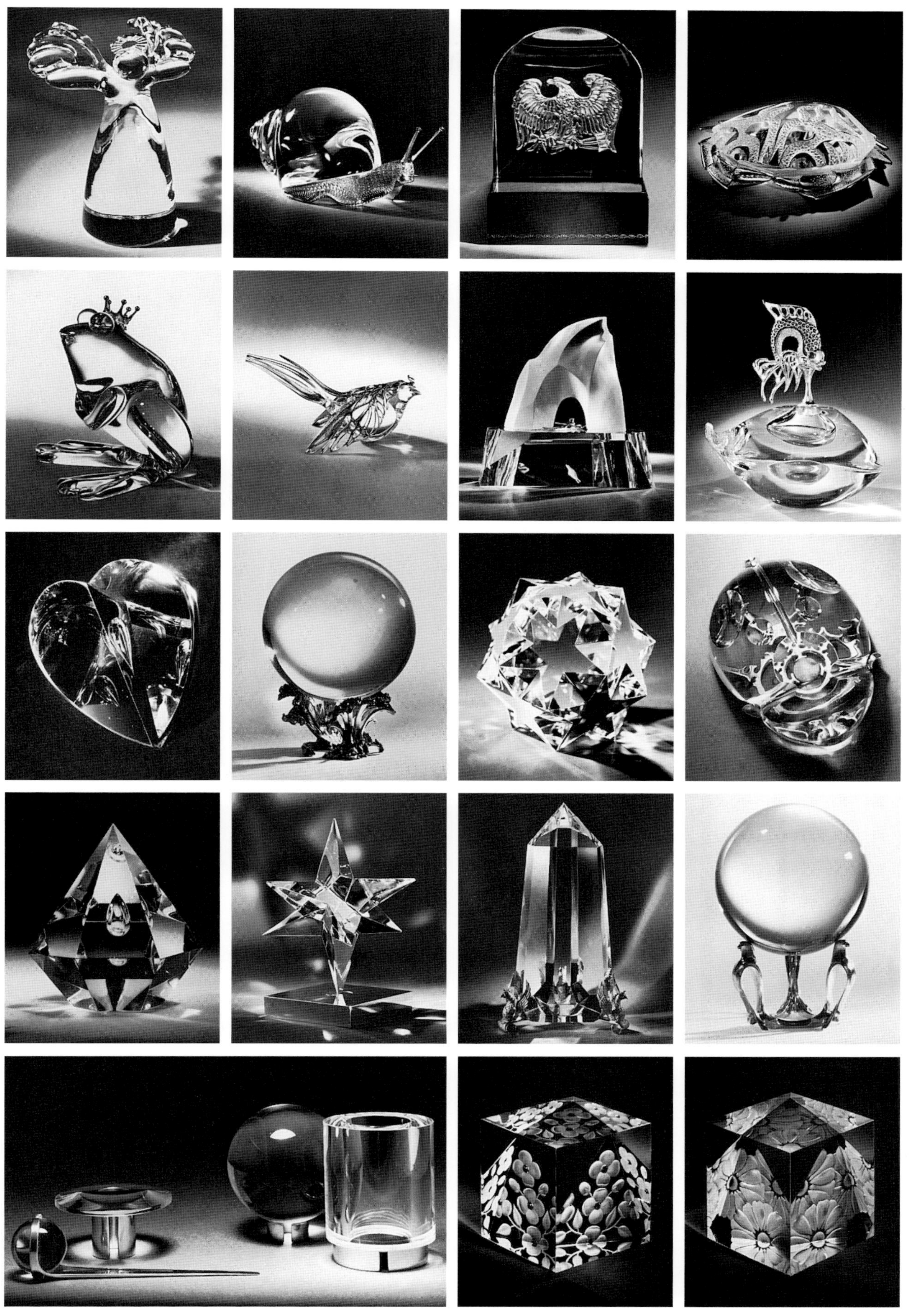

1027 *Guardian Angel*
K.D.S. (4/10/75) 6" h.

1028 *Crystal and Vermeil Snail*
P.Schu. (9/1/71) 7" h.

1029 *Prism of the Eagle*
J.H. (9/25/71) 6¼" h.

1030 *Crystal and Silver Crab*
L.A. (5/18/72) 7" w.

1031 *Frog Prince*
L.A. (6/25/73) 6" h.

1032 *Bird with Golden Wings*
P.Y. 6¼" h.

1033 *Ice Hunter*
J.H. (6/9/72) 6¼" h.

1034 *Dolphin Bottle*
K.D.S. 7" h.

1035 *Heart*
E.H. (9/3/74) 2¼" l.

1036 *Crystal Ball on Wave Base*
D.P. (7/1/74) 5½" h.

1037 *Star Sphere*
G.T. (5/1/75) 4¼" d.

1038 *Goldbug*
D.D. (10/15/74) 4¼" l.

1039 *Cut Paperweight with Teardrop*
G.T. (11/1/74) 3¼" h.

1040 *Eight-Pointed Star*
R.D. (6/2/75) 7½" h.

1041 *Pillar of the Griffins*
G.T. 7½" h.

1042 *Crystal Ball on Falcon Base*
P.Y. (3/5/75) 6¼" h.

1043 *Desk Set*
P.Y. (9/10/75)

1044 *Spring Crystal*
P.Schu. and B.X.W. (9/10/75) 3" h.

1045 *Summer Crystal*
P.Schu. and B.X.W. (9/10/75) 3" h.

1046 *Autumn Crystal*
P.Schu. and B.X.W. (9/10/75) 3" h.

1047 *Winter Crystal*
P.Schu. and B.X.W. (9/10/75) 3" h.

1048 *Punty Cube*
P.Y. (9/10/75) 6¼" h.

1049 *Starburst Crystal*
P.Y. (4/21/76) 5" h.

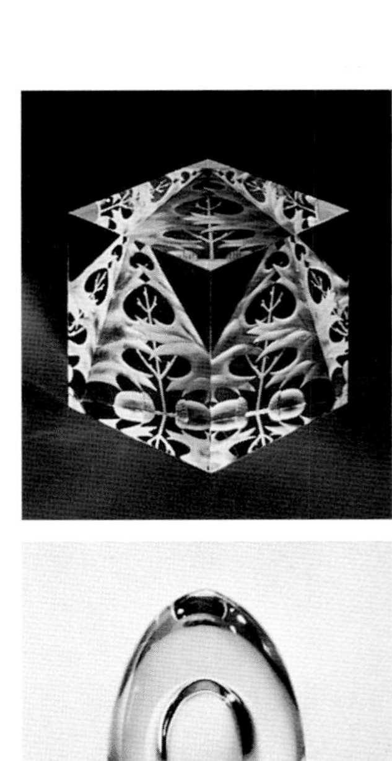

1050 *Egg with Ovoid Bubble*
E.H. (9/15/76) 4" h.

1051 *Butterfly*
P.Y. (9/15/76) 3" l.

1052 *Encased Void*
E.H. (6/15/76) 3¾" h.

1053 *Magnifying Glass*
B.X.W. (4/2/77) 9" l.

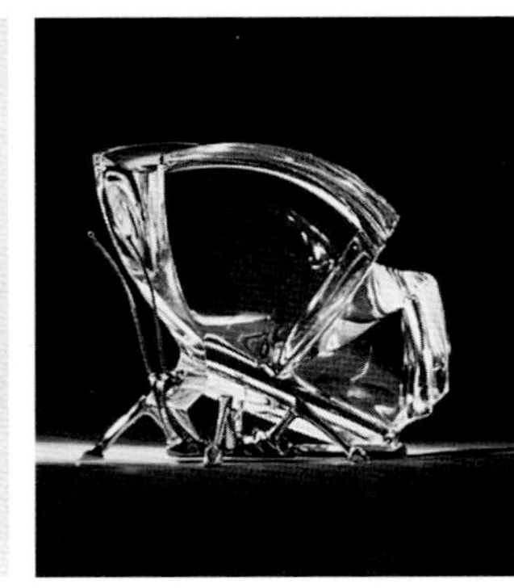
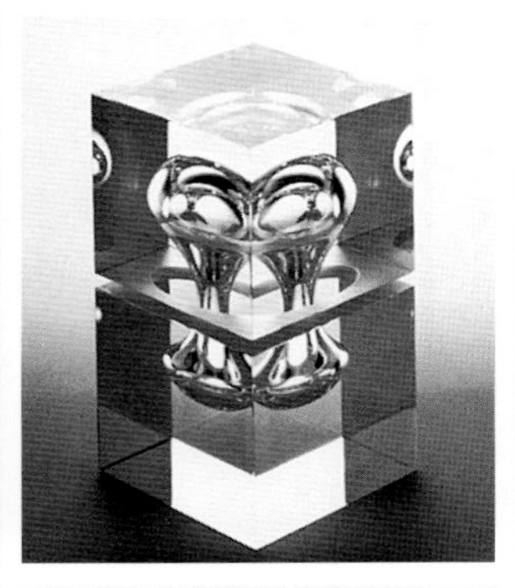

1054 *Cross*
L.A. (11/1/76) 6¾" h.

1058 *Shell Coffret*
D.D. (4/27/77) 4" h.

1059 *Flying Owl*
P.Schu. (5/2/77) 7¼" w.

1060 *Letter Opener*
B.X.W. (9/21/77) 10¾" l.

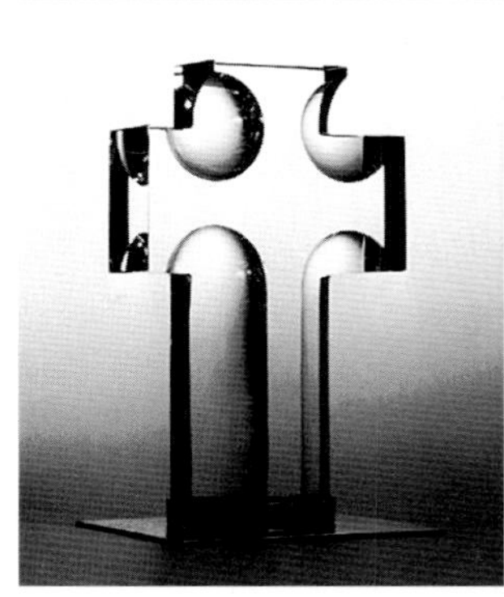

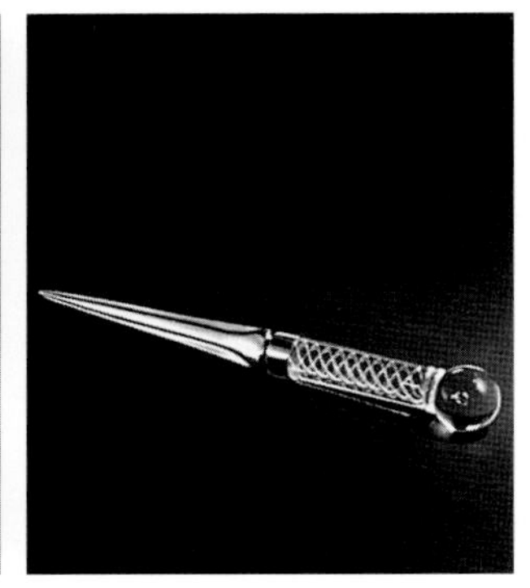

1061 *Moon and Earth*
D.D. (9/21/77) 4¼" dia.

1063 *Apple with Jade Seeds*
B.X.W. (5/15/78) 4½" h.

1064 *Pear with Jade Seeds*
B.X.W. (5/15/78) 5½" h.

1068 *Close to the Wind*
L.A. (4/28/80) 8" h.

1096 *Star of David*
D.D. (1981) $3,150, 6¼" l.

1097 *Cross*
D.D. (1981) $2,950

1098 *Fire Ball*
D.P. (1981) $1,375, 5½" h.

1106 *Sphere of Power*
E.H. (1982) $925

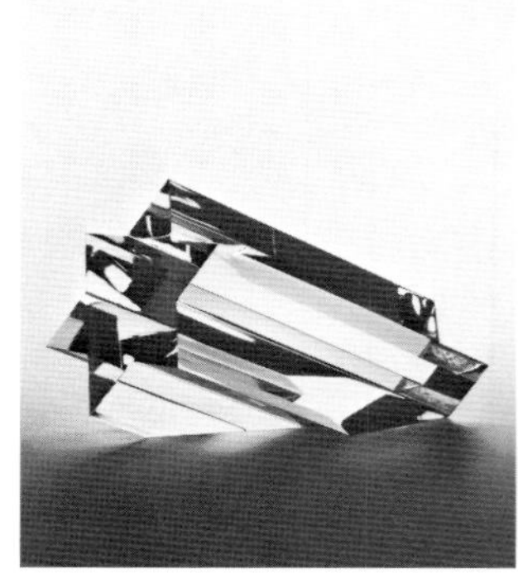

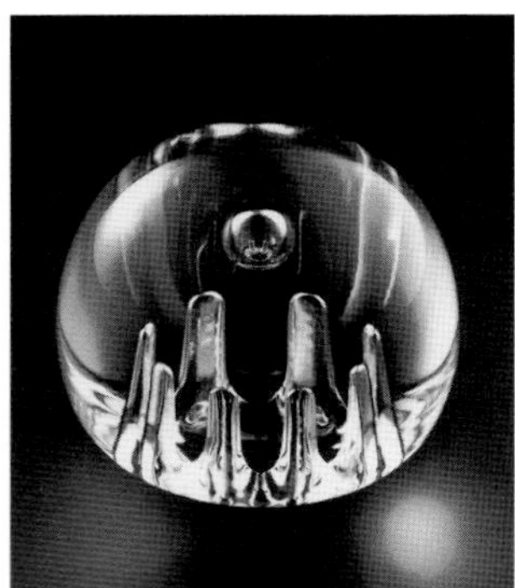

1107 *Sphere of Realization*
E.H. (1982) $925

1108 *Sphere of Energy*
E.H. (1982) $925

1109 *Sphere of Creativity*
E.H. (1982) $925

1112 *Ice Penguin*
J.H. (1982) $2,950, 5" h.

1113 *Stars and Stripes*
P.A. (1983) $2,950, 4" h.

1114 *Garden Butterfly*
B.X.W. (1983) $1,950, 6" h.

1115 *Phantom Skyline*
P.A. (1983) $1,950, 5¾" h.

1117 *Gull Rock*
J.H. (1983) $1,750, 8½" w.

1118 *Garden of Eden*
B.X.W. (1984) $1,950, 6" h.

1119 *Garden of Delight*
B.X.W. (1984) $1,950, 6" h.

1120 *Kiddush Cup*
B.X.W. (1984) $3,000, 7½" h.

1121 *Young at Heart*
E.H. (1984) $1,950, 3½" h.

1122 *Carrousel*
P.A. and J.O.S. (1985) $2,950, 7½" h.

1124 *Pyramid of Ascendance*
P.A. (1985) $1,950, 6" w.

1125 *Crescent of Glory*
P.A. (1985) $1,750

1126 *Lion*
L.A. (1986) $1,950, 9" w.
(Originally 8481 Lion w/o base)

1127 *Marriage Goblet*
D.P. and B.X.W. (1986) $2,250, 6¾" h.

1128 *Liberty Crystal*
B.X.W. & E.B.S. (1986) $1,975, 9" h.

1129 *Soaring Eagle*
P.Schu. (1986) $2,100, 9½" l.

1130 *Shooting Star*
D.D. (1986) $1,250, 5" h.

1131 *Castle of Dreams*
D.D. (1986) $1,950, 6" h.

1132 *Constitution Bicentennial Prism*
B.X.W. and P.W. (1987) $1,975, 9" h.

1133 *Prism Crystal*
D.D. (1988) $1,675, 7" h.

1134 *Day & Night*
D.D. (1989) $1,700, 9¾" dia.

1135 *Arrowheads*
D.D. (1990) $3,200, 13¾" h.

1136 *Fossils* (not illustrated)
D.D. (1990) $5,200, 14¼" h.

1137 *Globe* (not illustrated)
J.H. (1990) $4,200, 4" dia.

1138 *Music*
J.S. and Ba.M. (1990) $1,800, 12⅜" dia.

1139 *Tragedy*
J.S. and Ba.M. (1990) $1,800, 12⅜" dia.

1140 *Mirth*
J.S. and Ba.M. (1990) $1,800, 12⅜" dia.

1141 *Sovereignty*
J.S. and Ba.M. (1990) $1,800, 12⅜" dia.

1142 *Hamlet*
J.S. and Ba.M. (1990) $2,300, 11" h.

1143 *Lady Macbeth*
J.S. and Ba.M. (1990) $2,300, 11" h.

1144 *King Lear*
J.S. and Ba.M. (1990) $2,300, 11" h.

1145 *Cleopatra*
J.S. and Ba.M. (1990) $2,300, 11" h.

1156 *Planet Earth*
J.S. (1992) $5,500, 8½" h.

1159 *Lighthouse*
D.D. (1993) $2,150, 8½" w.

1160 *Prelude and Fugue*
R.C. (1993) $2,950, 6" h.

1161 *Exploration and Discovery*
R.C. (1993) $4,600, 8½" h.

1162 *Hypothesis*
R.C. (1994) $2,950, 6" h.

1163 *Adobe Landmark*
D.D. (1994) $2,450, 5½" h.

1164 *Rose Bouquet*
D.D. (1995) $5,300, 8½" h.

1165 *Wall Street*
R.C. (1995) $3,150, 6" h.

1166 *Wilderness Serenade*
J.H. (1995) $4,750, 7" h.

1167 *City Lights: Manhattan*
D.D. and R.C. (1995) $6,450, 10" w.

1168 *Harborside*
R.C. and D.de. (1995) $7,500, 8¼" h.

1169 *Top of the World*
D.D. (1996) $4,800, 7¾" w.

1170 *Swift Current*
J.S. (1997) $4,650, 18½" l.

1171 *Summit*
D.D. (1996) $2,450, 19¼" w.

1172 *Eagle*
D.D. (1996) $3,450, 7½" w.

1173 *Our Love*
J.S. and C.A. (1997) $6,850, 7¼" w.

1174 *Cross*
P.D. and L.Lu (1997) $3,450, 10" h.

1177 *Sundial*
J.S. and J.Si. (1997) $6,450, 9½" dia.

1178 *Regal Lion*
P.Dro. and B.S. (1996) $3,450, 8¼" h.

1180 *The Balance of Power*
D.D. (1997) $2,150, 6¾" h.

1187 *The Challenge*
P.H. (1998) $2,650, 5¼" h.

1191 *The Jungle*
J.S. and C.A. (1998) $6,750, 12" w.

1192 *Star Flight*
J.S. (1999) $4,500, 8½" h.

1193 *Loves Me?*
D.D. and T.A. (1999) $7,350, 7¼" h.

1194 *Evening in the Park*
J.S. and M.H. (2000) $2,500, 9½" h.

1195 *Butterfly Garden*
J.S. and T.A. (2000) $1,350, 7½" h.

1196 *Noble Tiger*
T.L.S. (2000) $2,250, 9" w.

1197 *Majestic Eagle*
T.L.S. (2001) $3,700, 8½" h.

OX Collection

OX200 *Covered Centerpiece*
13" h.

OX210 *Covered Urn*
17¼" h.

OX211 *Oveta Culp Hobby*
11¾" h.

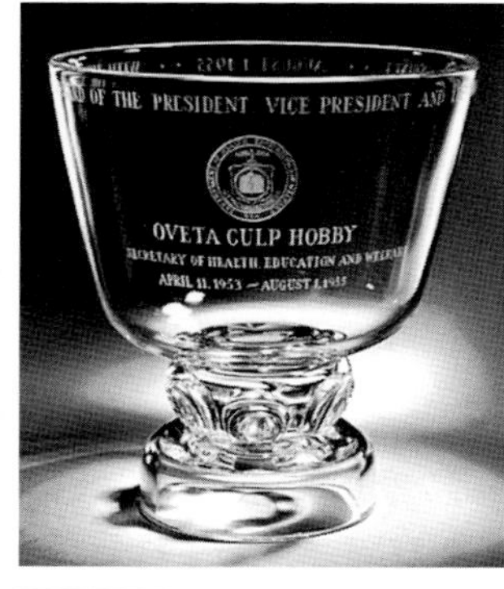

OX214 *Calumet*
A.W. 13¼" h.

OX218 *Covered Urn*
19½" h.

OX221 *Covered Urn*
15¾" h.

OX222 *The Costello Cup*
L.A. 15½" h.

OX2343 *Covered Urn*
D.H. 14" h.

OX2346 *Covered Urn*
L.A. 15½" h.

OX2389 *Bowl with Presidential Seal*
D.P. 12" dia.

OX2685 *Covered Centerpiece*
G.T. 10½" h.

OX2798 *Covered Bowl*
D.P. 18" h.

OX2804 *Covered Urn*
L.A. 15" h.

OX2870 *Vase with Presidential Seal*
L.A. 13¾" h.

OX3001 *American Eagle Vase*
L.A. 14" h.

OX3020 *Vase with Presidential Seal*
G.T. 13½" h.

OX3022 *Vase with Presidential Seal*
L.A. 11¾" h.

OX3023 *Cup with Presidential Seal*
L.A. 10½" h.

OX3025 *Bowl with United States Seal*
D.P. 8½" dia.

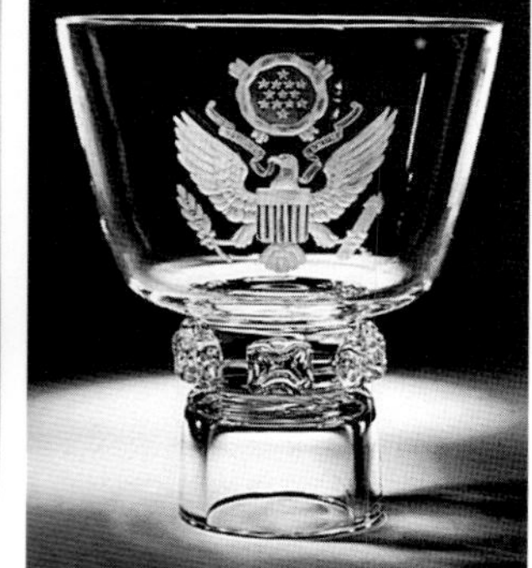

OX3027 *Vase with United States Seal*
D.P. 13¾" h.

OX3068(1) *Covered Urn with United States Seal*
L.A. 18" h.

OX3068(2) *Covered Urn with Presidential Seal*
L.A. 18" h.

OX3084 *Bowl with Presidential Seal*
D.P. 8" dia.

OX3086 *Cup with Presidential Seal*
D.P. 9½" h.

OX3103 *Engraved Covered Urn*
L.A. 20" h.

OX3106 *Bowl with Presidential Seal*
G.T. 8¼" dia.

OX3152 *Bowl with United States Seal*
D.P. 9½" dia.

OX3195 *Vase with Presidential Seal*
D.P. 13" h.

OX3246 *Vase with Presidential Seal*
L.A. 12¼" h.

OX3247 *Vase with Presidential Seal*
L.A. 13¼" h.

OX3248 *Bowl with Presidential Seal*
G.T. 8" dia.

OX3249 *Bowl with Presidential Seal*
G.T. 10" w.

OX3256 *Bowl with United States Seal*
L.A. 12" dia.

OX3404 *Bowl with Presidential Cipher*
G.T. 11" h.

OX3405 *Bowl, Eagle and Globe*
D.P. and S.W. 9" dia.

OX3474 *Plaque, Franklin Inscription*
D.P. 7¼" h.

OX3486 *Vase with Presidential Seal*
D.P. 11½" h.

OX3488 *Vase with Presidential Seal*
D.P. 11" h.

OX3490 *Bowl with Presidential Seal*
D.P. 9¾" h.

0103 *Presidential Plaque*
D.P. and S.W. 7¼" w.

Jewelry

0154 *Necklace with Crystal Pendant/ Leaf Engraving,* E.H. (3/5/75) 2" w.

0164 *Necklace with Crystal Pendant/ Seed Engraving,* E.H. (7/28/75), 2" w.

0187 *Necklace with Crystal Pendant/ Landscape Engraving*
E.H. and Z.H. (12/3/75) 2" w.

0189 *Necklace with Crystal Pendant/ Floral Engraving*
E.H. and Z.H. (2/2/76) 2" w.

0191 *Necklace with Crystal Pendant/ Butterflies Engraving*
E.H. and Z.H. (2/18/76) 2" w.

0201 *Necklace with Crystal Pendant/ Fire Engraving*
E.H. (5/12/76) 2" w.

0209 *Necklace with Crystal Pendant/ Geometric Engraving*
E.H. (9/15/76) 2" w.

0211 *Necklace with Crystal Pendant/ Sunlight Engraving*
E.H. 2" w.

0233 *Necklace with Crystal Pendant/ Element of Earth Engraving*
E.H. and L.H. (10/2/78) 2" w.

0234 *Necklace with Crystal Pendant/ Element of Air Engraving*
E.H. (10/2/78) 2" w.

0235 *Necklace with Crystal Pendant/ Element of Fire Engraving*
E.H. (10/2/78) 2" w.

0236 *Necklace with Crystal Pendant/ Element of Water Engraving*
E.H. (10/2/78) 2" w.

0250 *Brooch of the Four Winds*
E.H. (4/26/79) 2½" w.

0251 *Amuletic Ring*
E.H. (4/26/79) 1⅛" l.

0253 *Enigmatic Brooch*
E.H. (4/26/79) 2" w.

0257 *Pendant of the Four Winds*
E.H. (4/26/79) 2½" w.

0258 *Butterfly Pendant*
E.H. (4/26/79) 2½" l.

0259 *Amuletic Pin*
E.H. (4/26/79) 1⅛" l.

0260 *Touchstone Stickpin*
E.H. (4/26/79) 3¼" l.

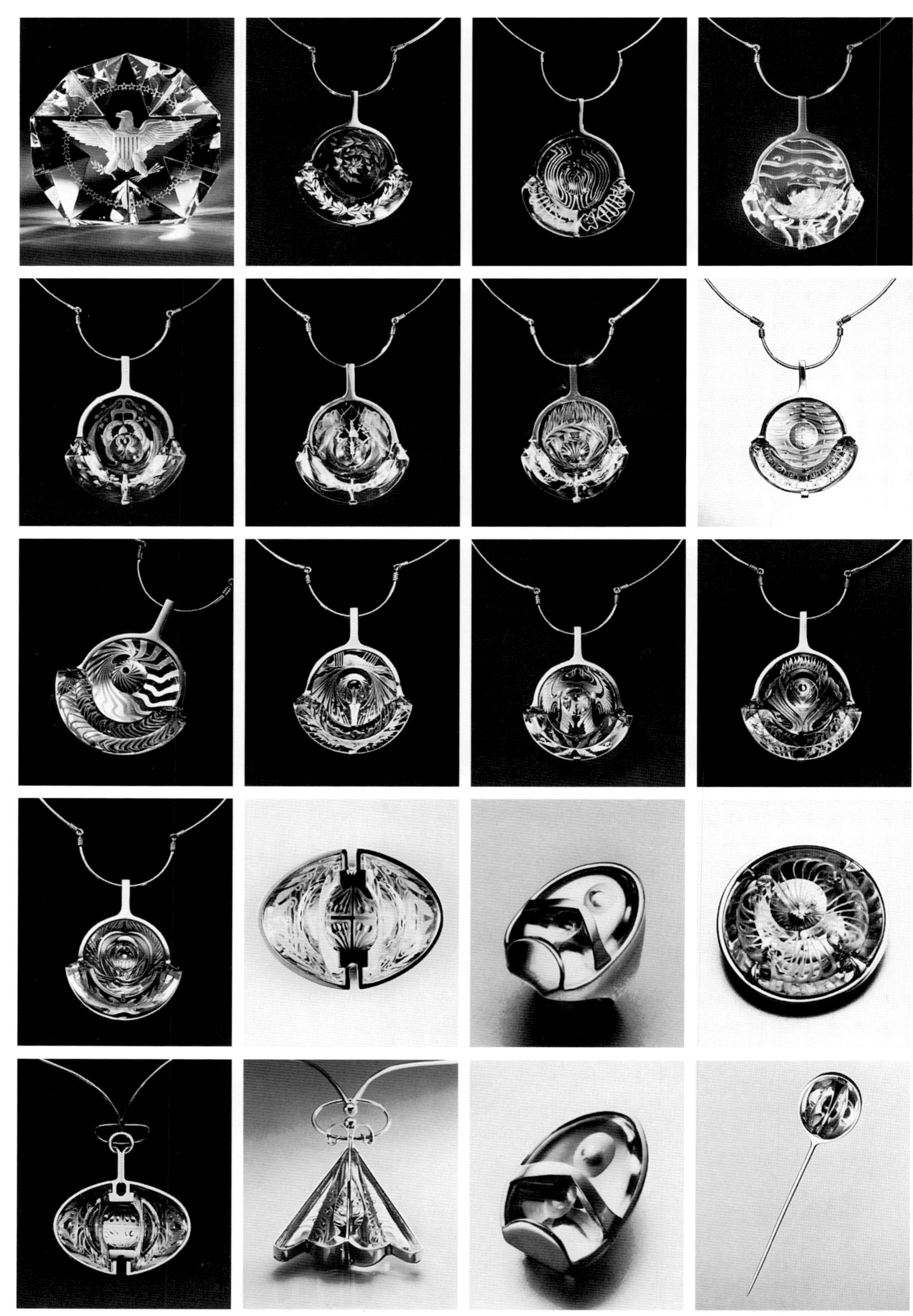

1055 *Strawberry Pendant*
D.P. and E.St. (1/21/77) 2" h.

1056 *Cross Pendant*
L.A. (4/27/77) 2¼" h.

1057 *Heart Pendant*
E.H. (4/27/77) 2" h.

1062 *Acorns Pendant*
P.Schu. 3" l.

1065 *Air-Twist Stickpin*
B.X.W. (10/23/78) 2½" l.

1066 *Air-Twist Cuff Links*
B.X.W. (10/23/78) ¾" h.

1067 *Cicada Pendant*
L.A. (12/11/78) 2¾" l.

1069–1072 *Air-Twist Necklace*
B.X.W. (10/29/79) 1" l.

1074 *Moondream Pendant*
P.A. (1/18/80) 1½" l.

1075 *Moondream Pin*
P.A. (1/18/80) 1½" l.

1076 *Moondream Bracelet*
P.A. (1/18/80) 1½" l.

1077 *Champagne Stickpin*
B.X.W. (4/17/80) 3⅜" l.

1078 *Champagne Button Earrings*
B.X.W. (4/17/80) ⅞" w.

1079 *Champagne Drop Earrings*
B.X.W. (4/17/80) 1⅞" l.

1080 *Champagne Brooch*
B.X.W. (4/17/80) 4½" l.

1081 *Champagne Cuff Links*
B.X.W. (4/17/80) 1³⁄₁₆" l.

1082 *Champagne Necklace*
B.X.W. (4/17/80) 16¼" cir.

1083–1087 *Champagne Ring*
B.X.W. (4/17/80) 5 sizes, $690

1088–1090 Air-Twist Ring Sizes 5–7
B.X.W. (1980) $675

1091 Jupiter Pendant
E.H. (1980) $1,000

1100 *Ariadne Pendant*
T.B. (1981) $650, 3⅛" l.

1102 *Horizon Pin* (not illustrated)
$1,575.

1103 *Crystal Cavern Pendant*
D.D. (1981) $2,350, 2½" h.

1110 /1111 *Nautilus Shell Pendant W/C*
J.C. (1982) $850. *Pendant only* $425

1116 *Rosebud Necklace*
D.D. (1983) $895, 1⅞" l.

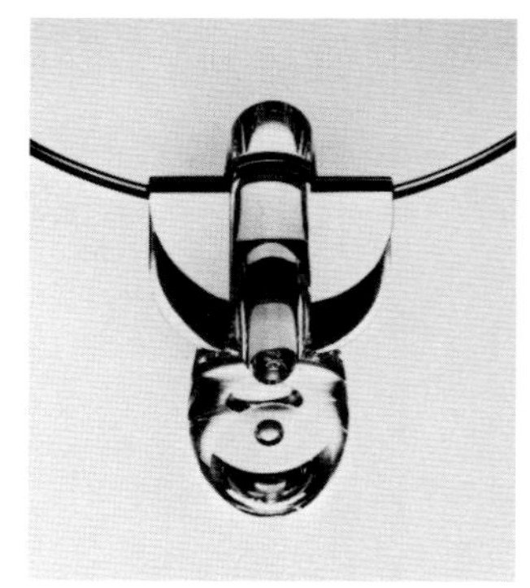

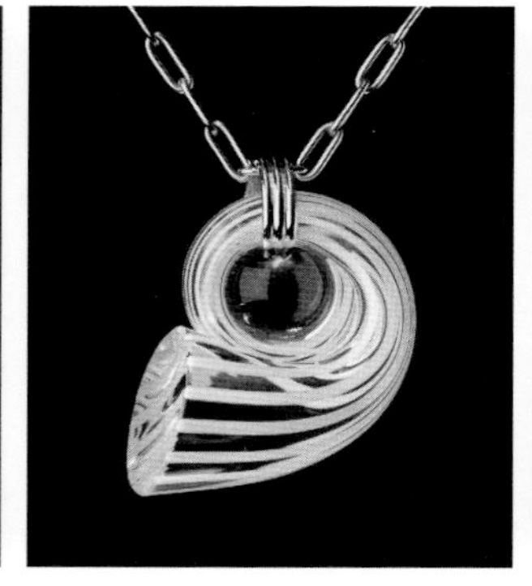

1147/1148 *Spiral Necklace and Earrings*
A.C. (1991) $2,300

1150 *Seafoam Necklace*
A.C. (1991) $15,000

1151/1152 *Seafoam Earrings Clip/Pierced*
A.C. (1991) $2,600

1153 *Oak Necklace*
A.C. (1991) $16,000

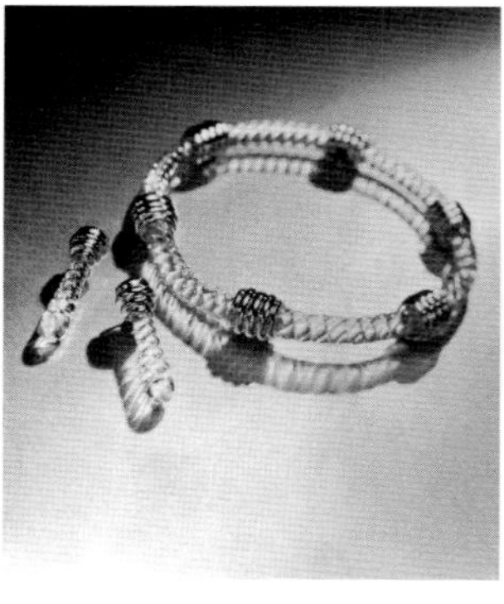

1154 *Oak Earrings Clip*
1155 (pierced)
A.C. (1991) $2,500

Stock Engraved Pieces

8076 *Star Crystal, Christmas*
5" w.

8159 *Covered Urn, Old Testament*
E.O. (1956)

8160 *Star Crystal, New Testament*
E.O. (1956) 5" w.

8161 *Plaque, Shakespeare*
E.O. (1957) $100, 8" w.

8162 *Bud Vase, R. Browning*
G.F. (1958) $47.50, 8" h.

8163 *Star Crystal, R. Browning*
(1960) $90, 5" w.

8164 *Plaque, Hippocratic Oath*
(1961) $150, 8" w.

8165 *Star Crystal, Tennyson*
(1961) $100

8170, 8183 *Ashtray and Cigarette Box, Mallard*
Ch.L. 4½" dia., 5" w.

8172 *Highball Glasses, Birds* (12)
Ch.L. $50 ea., 4⅜" h.

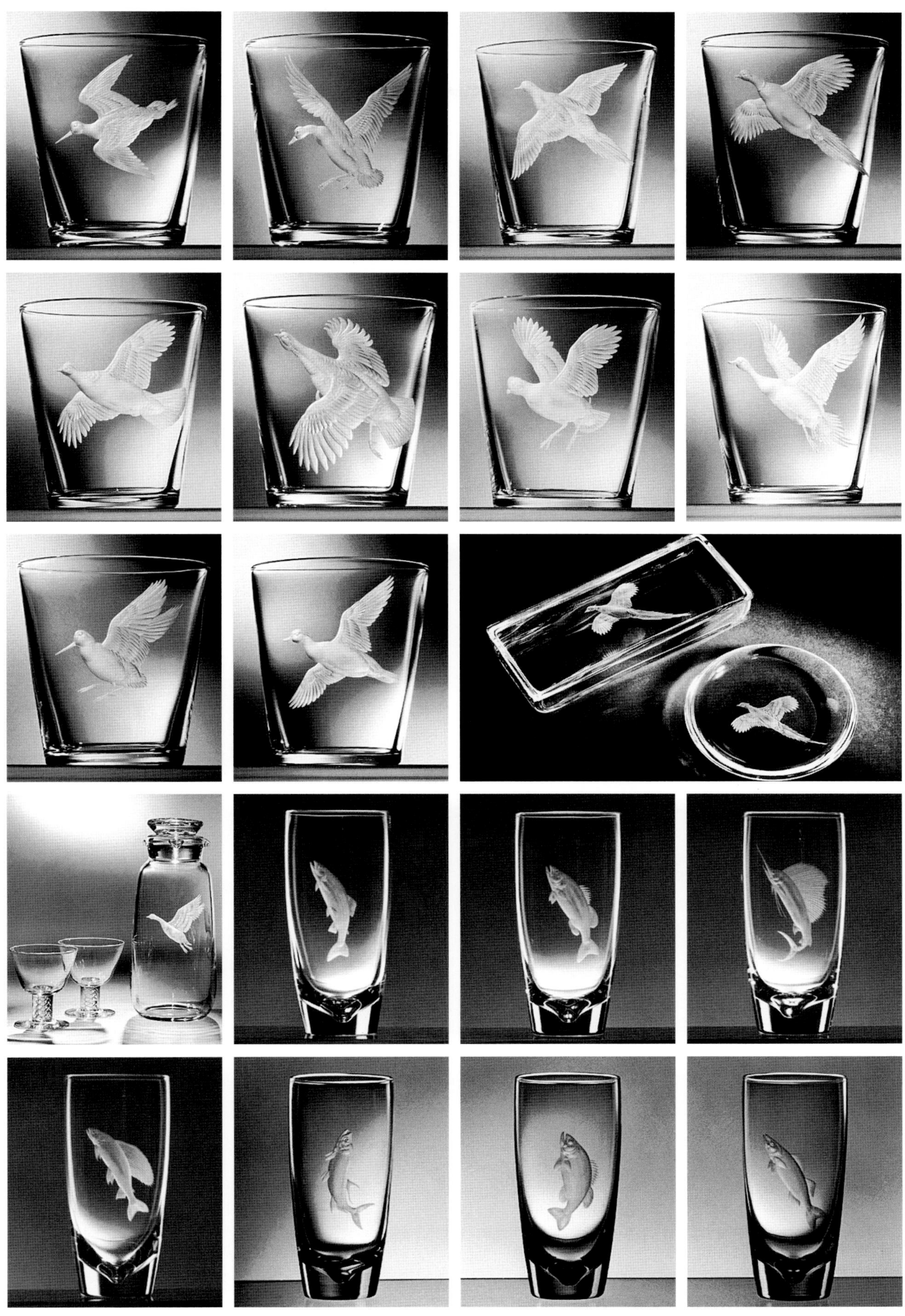

8185, 8187 *Ashtray and Cigarette Box, Pheasant*
Ch.L. 4½" dia., 5" w.

8189 *Cocktail Shaker, Canada Goose*
Ch.L. 8¾" h.

8190 *Highball Glasses, Fish* (12)
Ch.L. 6½" h.

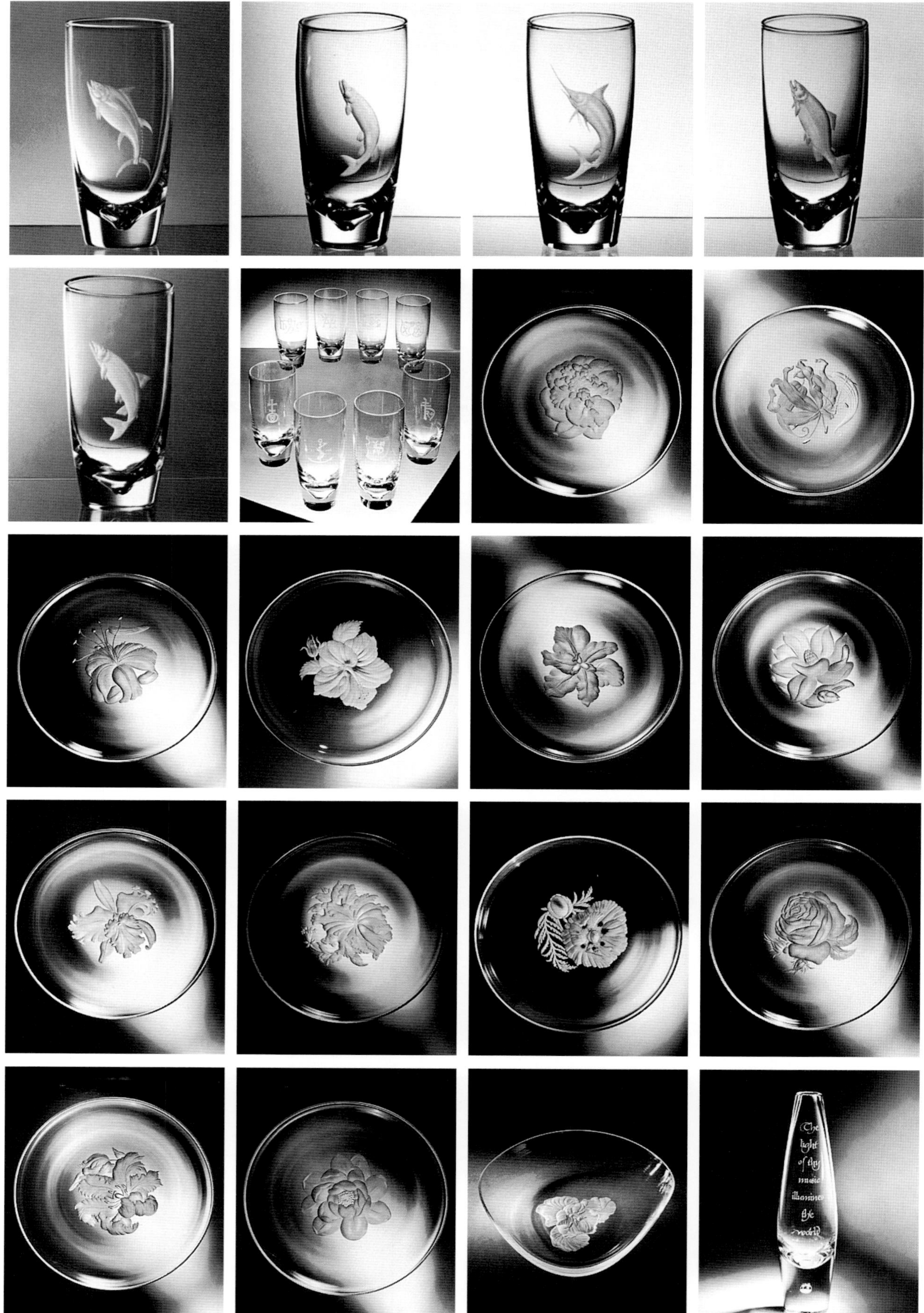

8191 *Highball Glasses, Printers' Marks*
6½" h.

8194 *Flower Plates* (12)
D.W. (1948) 8½" dia.

8195 *Tulip Bowl*
D.W. (1945) $100, 11¼" w.

8196 *Bud Vase, Tagore*
E.O. $45, 8" h.

8197 *Candle Shade, Old Testament*
E.O.

8198 *Bowl, Shakespeare*
E.O. (1956)

8199 *Toasting Goblet, Alexander Pope*
E.O. (1956) 12" h.

8200 *Plaque, Lewis Carroll*
E.O. (1957) $100, 8" w.

8202 *Toasting Goblet*
G.F. (1958) $100, 18" h.

8203 *Star Crystal, Crown of Thorns*
(1961) $80

8204 *Goblet, Shield of David*
(1961) $45

8248 *Plaque, Cicero*
(1970) $225, 8" w.

8249 *Star Crystal, James Montgomery*
D.P. (1970) $150, 5" w.

8250 *Plaque, Kahlil Gibran*
P.W. (1970) $215, 8" w.

8251 *Bud Vase, E. B. Browning*
G.F. (1970) $95, 8" h.

8278 *Tetron*
L.A. (1972) $225, 4¼" w.

8312 *Paperweight, White Birch*
P.Schu. and I.S. (1975) $850, 4¼" dia.

8313 *Paperweight, Silver Maple*
P.Schu. and I.S. (1975) $850, 4¼" dia.

8325 *Stars and Stripes*
P.Y. (1976) $160, 2¾" h.

8347 *Ashtray, Snowflake*
P.G. (1976) $55, 3", 4½", 6" dia.

8365 *Nova*
P.Y. and B.X.W. (1977) $165, 2¾" h.

8374 *Cube, Snowflake*
P.Schu. and P.G. (1978) $115, 2½" h.

8375 *Torch*
P.Y. and B.X.W. (1979) $375, 3" w.

Form and Function Pieces
(not illustrated)

Pieces numbered 8643–8701 were sold during 1992; those numbered 6100–6146 were sold during 1993; and those numbered 6147–6173 were sold during 1994.

8643 *Italian Urn*, $1,100

8644 *Signet Bowl*, $495

8645 *Fish Vase*, $1,200

8646 *Willow Bowl*, $450

8647 *Mica Vase*, $850

8648 *Mica Vase II*, $800

8649 *Mica Vase III*, $825

8650 *Caterpillar Vase*, $900

8651 *Snail Bowl*, $1,200

8652 *Tendril Vase*, $850

8653 *Medium Tendril Vase*, $950

8654 *Tall Tendril Vase*, $1,050

8655 *Jester Vase*, $850

8656 *Tall Mondo Vase*, $750

8657 *Wellspring Vase*, $550

8658 *Roulette Decanter*, $1,050

8659 *Pillow Bowl*, $850

8660 *Ribbon Bowl*, $1,750

8661 *Cordelia Bowl*, $475

8662 *Bubble-Base Bowl*, $550

8663 *Signorita Vase I*, $700

8664 *Signorita Vase II*, $750

8665 *Signorita Vase III*, $825

8666 *Tall Willow Bowl*, $550

8667 *Checkmate Decanter*, $1,100

8668 *Medium Checkmate Decanter*, $1,200

8669 *Tall Checkmate Decanter*, $1,300

8670 *Glissando Flask*, $450

8671 *Medium Glissando Flask*, $475

8672 *Tall Glissando Flask*, $550

8673 *Apostrophe Candlestick*, $500

8674 *Medium Apostrophe Candlestick*, $550

8675 *Tall Apostrophe Candlestick*, $600

8676 *Artesian Vase*, $850

8677 *Sanctuary Vase*, $1,950

8678 *Tall Pocket Vase*, $950

8679 *Parabolic Decanter*, $850

8680 *Turban Vase*, $675

8681 *Meditation Bowl*, $1,750

8688 *Worlds Without End*, $18,500

8689 *Tectonic Vase*, $4,900

8690 *Arioso Bowl*, $4,400

8691 *Autumn Leaves Bowl I*, $950

8692 *Autumn Leaves Bowl II*, $1,600

8693 *American Eagle Globe*, $18,000

8694 *Pronghorn Crossing*, $11,000

8695 *Vortex Vase*, $5,800

8696 *Inner Sanctum Glass I*, $3,350

8697 *Maasai Bowl I*, $700

8698 *Maasai Vase*, $1,200

8699 *Winter Trees Vase*, $4,900

8700 Inner Sanctum Glass II, $3,350

8701 *Maasai Bowl II*, $2,500

6100 *Cactus I*, $250

6101 *Cactus II*, $250

6102 *Cactus III*, $250

6103 *Seamless Vase*, $350

6104 *Large Seamless Vase*, $550

6105 *Large Seamless Bowl*, $475

6106 *Seamless Bowl*, $425

6107 *Airtrap Ring Bottle*, $275

6108 *Chapeau Bowl*, $450

6109 *Petite Chapeau Bowl*, $0

6110 *Airtrap Bud Vase*, $425

6111 *Airtrap Bud Vase II*, $425

6112 *Bubble Rim Bowl*, $500

6113 *Orbit Candy Dish*, $350

6114 *Airtrap Vase IV*, $250

6115 *Airtrap Vase III*, $900

6116 *Airtrap Vase I*, $950

6117 *Airtrap Vase II*, $850

6118 *Stepped Bowl*, $1,600

6119 *Low Pillar Bowl*, $2,650

6120 *Gear Bowl*, $1,500

6121 *Halo Bowl*, $1,350

6122 *Mollusk Vase*, $950

6123 *Mollusk Vase II*, $1,850

6124 *Mollusk Vase III*, $1,850

6125 *Wrapped Bit Carafe*, $825

6126 *Slender Vase*, $850

6127 *Balance Bowl III*, $1,200

6128 *Balance Bowl I*, $975

6129 *Balance Bowl II*, $1,300

6130 *Lens Plate*, $495

6131 *Footed Vase*, $385

6132 *Inside Out Bowl*, $985

6133 *Experiment I*, $1,400

6134 *Experiment II*, $1,400

6135 *Cut-Foot Bowl I*, $475

6136 *Cut-Foot Bowl II*, $400

6137 *Cut-Foot Bowl III*, $450

6138 *Cut-Foot Bowl IV*, $500

6139 *Sword*, $12,500

6140 *Triangle Bowl*, $5,300

6141 *Waterfall Vase*, $5,800

6142 *Egg Vase*, $9,300

6143 *Fish Bowl I*, $0

6144 *Fish Bowl II*, $0

6145 *Torch*, $6,300

6146 *Mountain/Sun*, $10,600

6147 *Column Vase I*, $425

6148 *Column Vase II*, $425

6149 *Cactus I*, $350

6150 *Cactus II*, $375

6151 *Cactus III*, $350

6152 *Drape Bowl*, $500

6153 *Chalis Vessel*, $850

6154 *Curvaceous Vessel*, $1,000

6155 *Topsy Turvy Vase*, $1,400

6156 *Closed Symmetry Vase*, $925

6157 *Open Symmetry Vase*, $925

6158 *Tornado Vase*, $975

6159 *Solar Plate*, $1,275

6160 *Trumpet Vase I*, $825

6161 *Trumpet Vase II*, $800

6162 *Exclamation Vase*, $775

6163 *Airtrap Bowl*, $475

6164 *Medium Airtrap Bowl*, $600

6165 *Large Airtrap Bowl*, $775

6166 *Mannequin Vase*, $800

6167 *Hourglass Vase*, $1,200

6168 *Oblique Bowl*, $700

6169 *Oblique Vase I*, $700

6170 *Oblique Vase II*, $800

6171 *Tall Oblique Vase I*, $950

6172 *Tall Oblique Vase II*, $1,000

6173 *Elizabethan Goblet*, $1,350

STOCK PIECES

VASES

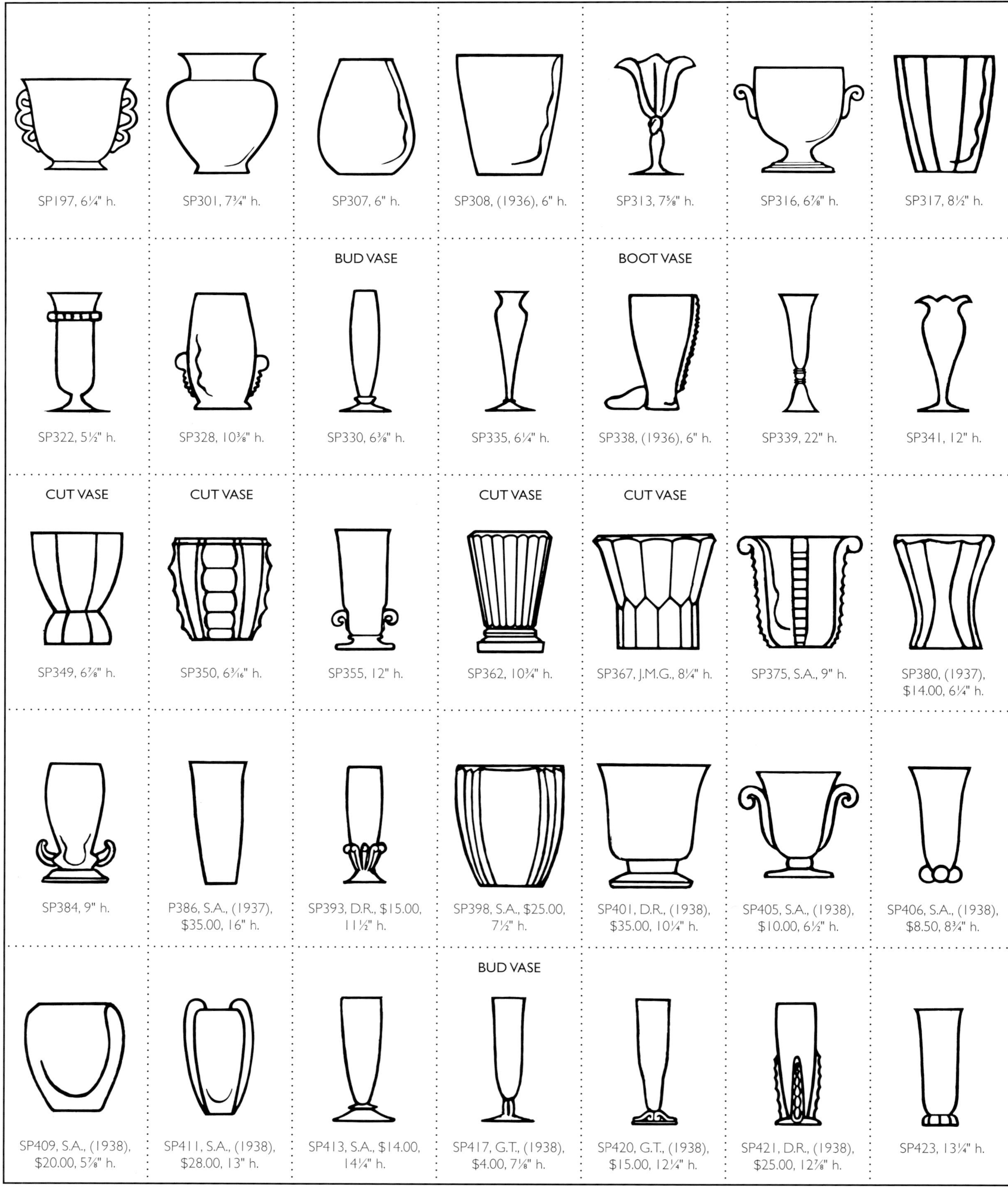
SP197, 6¼" h.
SP301, 7¾" h.
SP307, 6" h.
SP308, (1936), 6" h.
SP313, 7⅝" h.
SP316, 6⅞" h.
SP317, 8½" h.
SP322, 5½" h.
SP328, 10⅜" h.
BUD VASE
SP330, 6⅜" h.
SP335, 6¼" h.
BOOT VASE
SP338, (1936), 6" h.
SP339, 22" h.
SP341, 12" h.
CUT VASE
SP349, 6⅞" h.
CUT VASE
SP350, 6 3/16" h.
SP355, 12" h.
CUT VASE
SP362, 10¾" h.
CUT VASE
SP367, J.M.G., 8¼" h.
SP375, S.A., 9" h.
SP380, (1937), $14.00, 6¼" h.
SP384, 9" h.
P386, S.A., (1937), $35.00, 16" h.
SP393, D.R., $15.00, 11½" h.
SP398, S.A., $25.00, 7½" h.
SP401, D.R., (1938), $35.00, 10¼" h.
SP405, S.A., (1938), $10.00, 6½" h.
SP406, S.A., (1938), $8.50, 8¾" h.
SP409, S.A., (1938), $20.00, 5⅞" h.
SP411, S.A., (1938), $28.00, 13" h.
SP413, S.A., $14.00, 14¼" h.
BUD VASE
SP417, G.T., (1938), $4.00, 7⅛" h.
SP420, G.T., (1938), $15.00, 12¼" h.
SP421, D.R., (1938), $25.00, 12⅞" h.
SP423, 13¼" h.

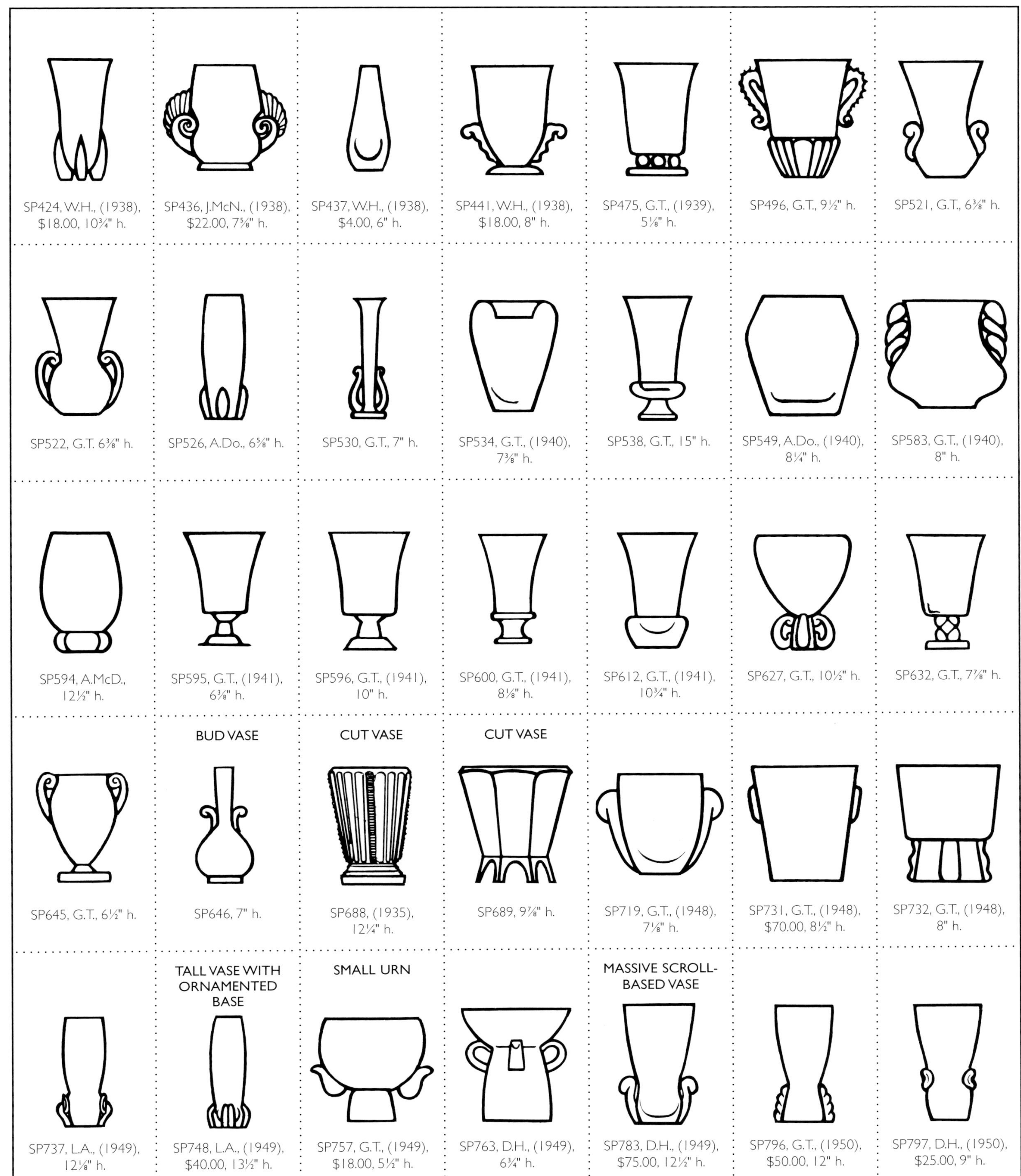
SP424, W.H., (1938), $18.00, 10¾" h.
SP436, J.McN., (1938), $22.00, 7⅝" h.
SP437, W.H., (1938), $4.00, 6" h.
SP441, W.H., (1938), $18.00, 8" h.
SP475, G.T., (1939), 5⅛" h.
SP496, G.T., 9½" h.
SP521, G.T., 6⅜" h.
SP522, G.T. 6⅜" h.
SP526, A.Do., 6⅝" h.
SP530, G.T., 7" h.
SP534, G.T., (1940), 7⅜" h.
SP538, G.T., 15" h.
SP549, A.Do., (1940), 8¼" h.
SP583, G.T., (1940), 8" h.
SP594, A.McD., 12½" h.
SP595, G.T., (1941), 6⅜" h.
SP596, G.T., (1941), 10" h.
SP600, G.T., (1941), 8⅛" h.
SP612, G.T., (1941), 10¾" h.
SP627, G.T., 10½" h.
SP632, G.T., 7⅞" h.
SP645, G.T., 6½" h.
BUD VASE
SP646, 7" h.
CUT VASE
SP688, (1935), 12¼" h.
CUT VASE
SP689, 9⅞" h.
SP719, G.T., (1948), 7⅛" h.
SP731, G.T., (1948), $70.00, 8½" h.
SP732, G.T., (1948), 8" h.
SP737, L.A., (1949), 12⅛" h.
TALL VASE WITH ORNAMENTED BASE
SP748, L.A., (1949), $40.00, 13½" h.
SMALL URN
SP757, G.T., (1949), $18.00, 5½" h.
SP763, D.H., (1949), 6¾" h.
MASSIVE SCROLL-BASED VASE
SP783, D.H., (1949), $75.00, 12½" h.
SP796, G.T., (1950), $50.00, 12" h.
SP797, D.H., (1950), $25.00, 9" h.

BUD VASE
WING VASE
WING VASE
DEEP FLOWER VASE
SP858, L.A., (1953), 8⅝" h.
SP873, L.A., (1954), 9" h.
SP884, L.A., (1955), $20.00, 8⅞" h.
SP886, G.T., (1955), $20.00, 6¾" h.
SP902, L.A., (1956), $50.00, 12¼" h.
SP919, L.A., (1957), $27.00, 7⅛" h.
SP945, D.P., (1959), $65.00, 11½" h.
TULIP VASE
FIVE-PRONG VASE
SP984, P.Schu., (1963), $37.50, 7" h.
2679, F.C., 10" h.
2683, F.C., 6", 10" h.
6053, F.C., 7", 8⅜", 12" h.
6876, B.M. and F.C., 6" h.
6968, B.M. and F.C., 10" h.
7035, F.C., 11¾" h.
CUT VASE
STRAWBERRY MANSION VASE
STRAWBERRY MANSION VASE
7090, B.M. and F.C., 9", 11" h.
7128, P.Ga. and F.C., 10" h.
7129, F.C., 14"h.
7305, F.C.
7311, B.M. and F.C., 6" h.
7389, F.C., (1934), 12½" h.
7389, F.C., (1934), 12½" h.
CUT VASE
7407, F.C.
7468, F.C., 6¾", 12" h.
7475, F.C., 8", 10" h.
7521, B.M. and F.C., (1933), 12" h.
7547, B.M., 5½" h.
7579, F.C., 6" h.
7580, F.C., 9" h.
BUD VASE
7581, F.C., 10" h.
7583, F.C., 12" h.
7646, S.W. and F.C., (1934), 11¾" h.
7674, 7⅛", 11⅞" h.
7690, B.M. and F.C., 8" h.
7697, B.M. and F.C., 7⅞" h.
7702

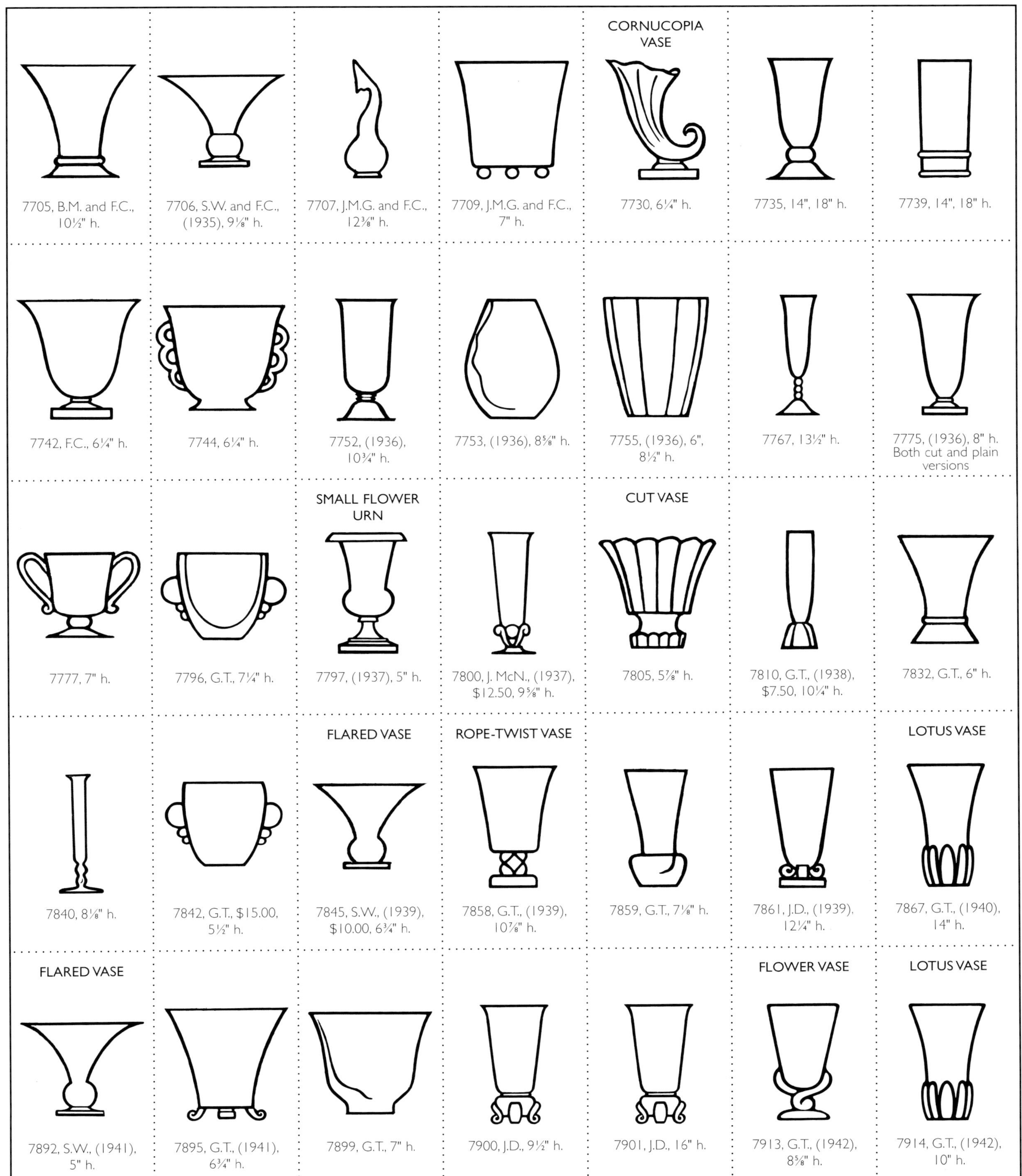

7705, B.M. and F.C., 10½" h.

7706, S.W. and F.C., (1935), 9⅛" h.

7707, J.M.G. and F.C., 12⅜" h.

7709, J.M.G. and F.C., 7" h.

CORNUCOPIA VASE
7730, 6¼" h.

7735, 14", 18" h.

7739, 14", 18" h.

7742, F.C., 6¼" h.

7744, 6¼" h.

7752, (1936), 10¾" h.

7753, (1936), 8⅝" h.

7755, (1936), 6", 8½" h.

7767, 13½" h.

7775, (1936), 8" h. Both cut and plain versions

7777, 7" h.

7796, G.T., 7¼" h.

SMALL FLOWER URN
7797, (1937), 5" h.

7800, J. McN., (1937), $12.50, 9⅝" h.

CUT VASE
7805, 5⅞" h.

7810, G.T., (1938), $7.50, 10¼" h.

7832, G.T., 6" h.

7840, 8⅛" h.

7842, G.T., $15.00, 5½" h.

FLARED VASE
7845, S.W., (1939), $10.00, 6¾" h.

ROPE-TWIST VASE
7858, G.T., (1939), 10⅞" h.

7859, G.T., 7⅛" h.

7861, J.D., (1939), 12¼" h.

LOTUS VASE
7867, G.T., (1940), 14" h.

FLARED VASE
7892, S.W., (1941), 5" h.

7895, G.T., (1941), 6¾" h.

7899, G.T., 7" h.

7900, J.D., 9½" h.

7901, J.D., 16" h.

FLOWER VASE
7913, G.T., (1942), 8⅝" h.

LOTUS VASE
7914, G.T., (1942), 10" h.

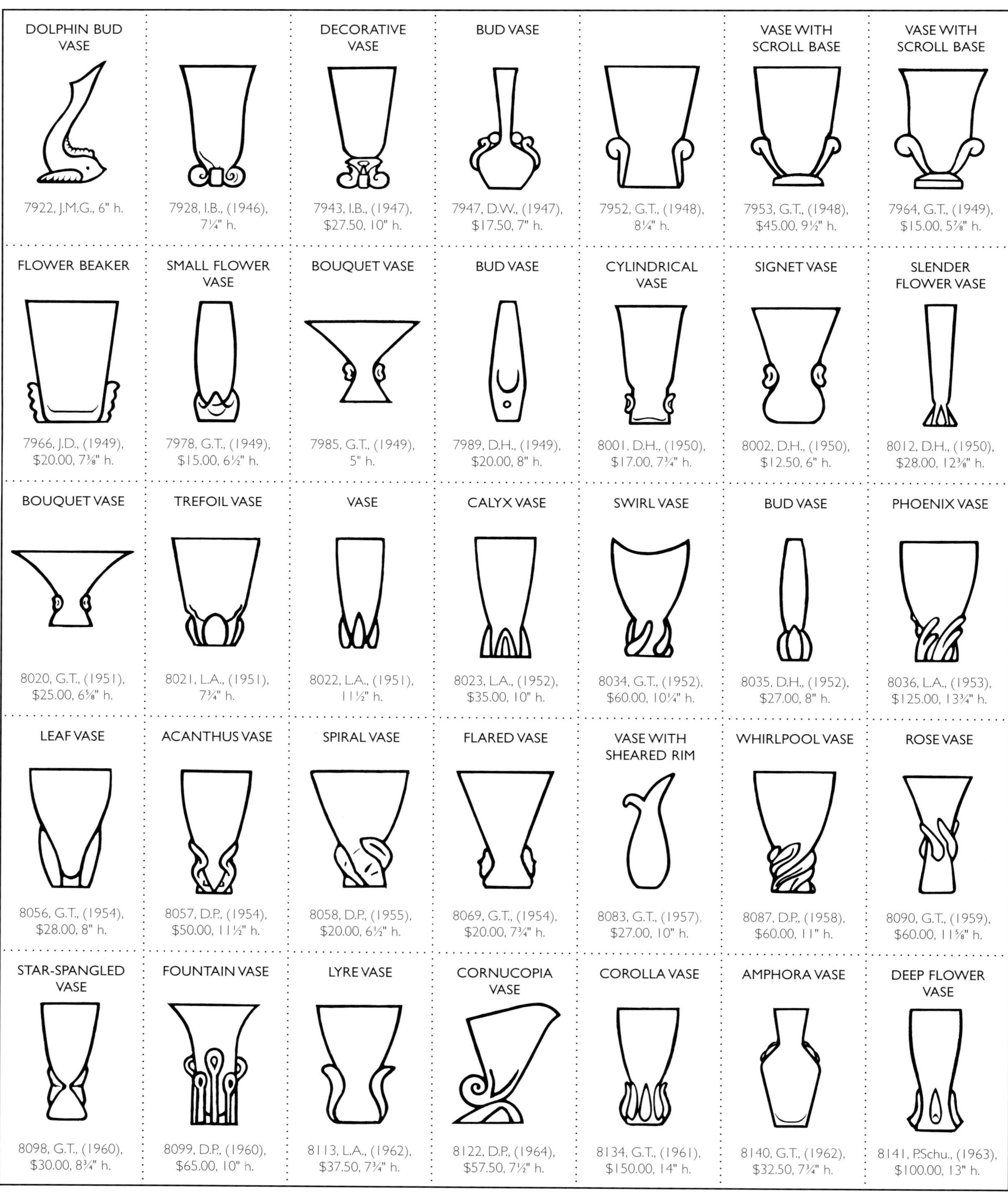
DOLPHIN BUD VASE
7922, J.M.G., 6" h.
7928, I.B., (1946), 7¼" h.
DECORATIVE VASE
7943, I.B., (1947), $27.50, 10" h.
BUD VASE
7947, D.W., (1947), $17.50, 7" h.
7952, G.T., (1948), 8¼" h.
VASE WITH SCROLL BASE
7953, G.T., (1948), $45.00, 9½" h.
VASE WITH SCROLL BASE
7964, G.T., (1949), $15.00, 5⅞" h.
FLOWER BEAKER
7966, J.D., (1949), $20.00, 7⅜" h.
SMALL FLOWER VASE
7978, G.T., (1949), $15.00, 6½" h.
BOUQUET VASE
7985, G.T., (1949), 5" h.
BUD VASE
7989, D.H., (1949), $20.00, 8" h.
CYLINDRICAL VASE
8001, D.H., (1950), $17.00, 7¾" h.
SIGNET VASE
8002, D.H., (1950), $12.50, 6" h.
SLENDER FLOWER VASE
8012, D.H., (1950), $28.00, 12⅜" h.
BOUQUET VASE
8020, G.T., (1951), $25.00, 6⅝" h.
TREFOIL VASE
8021, L.A., (1951), 7¾" h.
VASE
8022, L.A., (1951), 11½" h.
CALYX VASE
8023, L.A., (1952), $35.00, 10" h.
SWIRL VASE
8034, G.T., (1952), $60.00, 10¼" h.
BUD VASE
8035, D.H., (1952), $27.00, 8" h.
PHOENIX VASE
8036, L.A., (1953), $125.00, 13¾" h.
LEAF VASE
8056, G.T., (1954), $28.00, 8" h.
ACANTHUS VASE
8057, D.P., (1954), $50.00, 11½" h.
SPIRAL VASE
8058, D.P., (1955), $20.00, 6½" h.
FLARED VASE
8069, G.T., (1954), $20.00, 7¾" h.
VASE WITH SHEARED RIM
8083, G.T., (1957), $27.00, 10" h.
WHIRLPOOL VASE
8087, D.P., (1958), $60.00, 11" h.
ROSE VASE
8090, G.T., (1959), $60.00, 11⅝" h.
STAR-SPANGLED VASE
8098, G.T., (1960), $30.00, 8¾" h.
FOUNTAIN VASE
8099, D.P., (1960), $65.00, 10" h.
LYRE VASE
8113, L.A., (1962), $37.50, 7¾" h.
CORNUCOPIA VASE
8122, D.P., (1964), $57.50, 7½" h.
COROLLA VASE
8134, G.T., (1961), $150.00, 14" h.
AMPHORA VASE
8140, G.T., (1962), $32.50, 7¾" h.
DEEP FLOWER VASE
8141, P.Schu., (1963), $100.00, 13" h.

CARYATID VASE
8142, P.Schu., (1963), $75.00, 12⅞" h.
STEMMED VASE
8143, L.A., (1965), $65.00, 9¼" h.
LONG-NECKED VASE
8230, L.A., (1968), $80.00, 8¾" h.
CALYX VASE
8231, D.P., (1968), $100.00, 8⅞" h.
THREE-PRONG VASE
8232, P.Schu., (1968), $95.00, 8¾" h.
FLAME VASE
8235, G.T., (1968), $60.00, 10¼" h.
RING-HANDLED VASE
8239, L.A., (1968), $95.00, 9½" h.
UNDULATING VASE
8240, P.Schu., (1968), $150.00, 12¾" h.
CLOVER-FOOTED VASE
8245, P.Y., (1970), $110.00, 10" h.
DOLPHIN VASE
8275, L.A., (1972), $195.00, 10" h.
TRUMPET VASE
8308, D.P., (1975), $175.00, 7" h.
HEAVY CYLIN-DRICAL VASE
8309, G.T., (1975), $525.00, 5¾" h.
CYLINDRICAL BUD VASE
8319, G.T., (1975), $87.50, 9" h.
VASE
8320, D.D., (1975), $195.00, 7¾" h.
DOUBLE-FLARED VASE
8321, D.D., (1975), $150.00, 5½" h.
CRATER-BASE VASE
8328, P.Schu., (1976), $295.00, 13" h.
FLARE-NECK VASE
8329, L.A., (1976), $170.00, 8⅜" h.
PILLAR VASE
8341, D.D., (1976), $195.00, 8½" h.
LUNAR VASE
8350, D.D., (1977), $225.00, 10¾" h.
PRUNUS VASE
8353, D.P., (1977), $135.00, 7 1/16" h.
PALACE VASE
8354, D.P., (1977), $135.00, 8½" h.
TEMPLE JAR
8357, D.P., (1977), $167.50, 6 5/16" h.
DOLPHIN BUD VASE
8361, L.A., (1977), $135.00, 7⅜" h.
TALL WRAPPED VASE
8364, D.D., (1977), $650.00, 13¾" h.
VAULT OF HEAVEN VASE
8369, D.P., (1978), $140.00, 6½" h.
BEAKER VASE
8370, D.P.,(1978), $240.00, 9½" h.
DOUBLE GOURD VASE
8371, D.P., (1978), $235.00, 7⅞" h.
NIMBUS VASE
8390, P.Schu., (1980), $295.00, 6" h.
SOLAR VASE
8423, D.D., (1981), 6½" h.
CHRISTMAS VASE
8469, P.Schu., (1982), $320, 6¼" w.
SEAFOAM VASE
8473, D.D., (1983), $825, 8" h.
AURORA VASE
8492, P.Schu., (1984), $195, 4" h.
TALL AURORA VASE
8493, P.Schu., (1984), $310, 7¼" h.
TWIST BUD VASE
8499, D.D., (1985), $235, 8" h.
COILED VASE
8506, P.A., (1985), $250, 5¾" h.

TALL COILED VASE
8507, P.A., (1985), $395, 8¾" h.
TALL EMPYREAN VASE
8526, P.Schu., (1986), $350, 9½" h.
TALL MOMENTUM VASE
8540, P.A., (1986), $450, 7¼" h.
MOMENTUM VASE
8542, P.A. (1986), $410, 8½" dia.
TWIST VASE
8545, D.D., (1987), $375, 8½" h.
SEAWAVE VASE
8550, P.Schu., (1987), $310, 8" h.
TALL SEAWAVE VASE
8551, P.Schu., (1987), $510, 12" h.
COUNTERPOINT VASE
8562, D.D., (1988), $645, 13¾" h.
TALL ARCHAIC VASE
8584, M.G., (1989), $2,100, 10¾" h.
ARCHAIC VASE
8585, M.G., (1989), $1,500, 9¾" dia.
POCKET VASE
8591, P.B. and M.G., (1990), $265, 5" h.
HELLENIC URN
8592, R.C., (1990), $685, 9½" h.
DERVISH VASE
8598, T.Ha., (1990), $695, 6" h.
EMPIRE VASE
8601, J.S., (1990), $750, 11¼" h.
TOLIKAN VASE
8602, J.S., (1990), $550, 8" h.
DEEP POCKET VASE
8604, P.B./M.G., (1990), $375, 7½" h.
MONDO VASE
8616, P.B. and M.G., (1991), $725, 9½" h.
HANDKERCHIEF VASE
8618, S.D.T., (1991), $625, 9½" w.
JULIET VASE
8629, P.Dro., (1992), $195, 5¼" h.
TALL FRAMED VASE, STERLING
8630, Ref. in 8764 (1992), $13,000
FRAMED VASE, STERLING
8632, Ref. in 8766 (1992), $11,000
FEATHER VASE
8685, P.Dro., (1992), $600, 10" h.
LITTLE HANDKER-CHIEF VASE
8703, S.D.T., (1993), $225, 7" w.
SILHOUETTE VASE
8740, R.C., (1994), $350, 12½" h.
SCULPTURAL VASE
8744, D.D., (1994), $950, 17½" h.
AURORA INTIMATE VASE
8751, P.B./M.G., (1994), $175, 5¾" h.
LARGE CALYPSO VASE
8757, M.Z., (1994), $995, 13" h.
CALYPSO VASE
8758, M.Z., (1994), $795, 12½" h.
TALL FRAMED VASE, NICKEL SILVER
8764, R.Me., (1994), $4,420
FRAMED VASE, NICKEL SILVER
8766 R.Me., (1994), $4,195
ELEMENTS VASE
8773, D.D., (1995), $790, 11" h.
PIROUETTE VASE
8800, J.S., (1996), $275, 6¾" h.
GRAVITY VASE
8801, D.D., (1996), $895, 13" h.
TALL STARLIGHT VASE
8806, J.S., (1998), $1,175, 13" h.
LITTLE ELEMENTS VASE
8836, D.D., (1998), $380, 6½" h.

MARDI GRAS VASE
8844, D.D., (1999), $1,600, 15½" h.
WOODLAND VASE
8856, J.S. & T.A., (1999), $1,400, 10¾" h.
CLASSIC VASE
8857, P.A., (1999), $500, 6½" h.
TRANQUILITY VASE
8890, J.S., (2000), $1,100, 10¾" h.
MINOAN VASE
8896, J.S., (2000), $2,000, 12½" h.
ANTHERIUM VASE
8912, P.A., (2000), $300, 9½" h.
Not illustrated
SWING VASE
8772, P.Dro., (1995), $225
HERITAGE CUT VASE
8573, J.M.G., (reintroduced 1989), $10,500
BOWLS
SP277, 7" dia.
SP306, 13¾" dia.
SP309, 10½" dia.
SP335, A.Do., 15⅝" dia.
SP361, 9" dia.
CUT BOWL
SP363, J.M.G., 13¾" dia.
SP368, 10⅜" dia.
CUT BOWL
SP370, G.T., (1937), 10¼" dia.
CUT BOWL
SP371, D.R., (1937), 11⅝" dia.
CUT BOWL
SP372, J.McN., (1937), 13⅛" dia.
CUT BOWL
SP373, 9½" dia.
CUT BOWL
SP374, G.T., 12½" dia.
SP385, J.McN., (1937), $12.50, 9" dia.
SP395, D.R., (1937), $16.00, 9" dia.
SP403, D.R., (1938), $18.00, 8⅛" dia.
SP414, S.A., (1938), $15.00, 14" dia.
SP433, S.A., (1938), $25.00, 9" dia.
CUT BOWL
SP434, G.T., (1938), $28, 10¼" dia.
SP442, W.H., (1938), $20.00, 13½" dia.
CUT BOWL
SP447, G.T., (1938), $100.00, 14" dia.
SP451, G.T., (1938), $10.00, 6¾" dia.

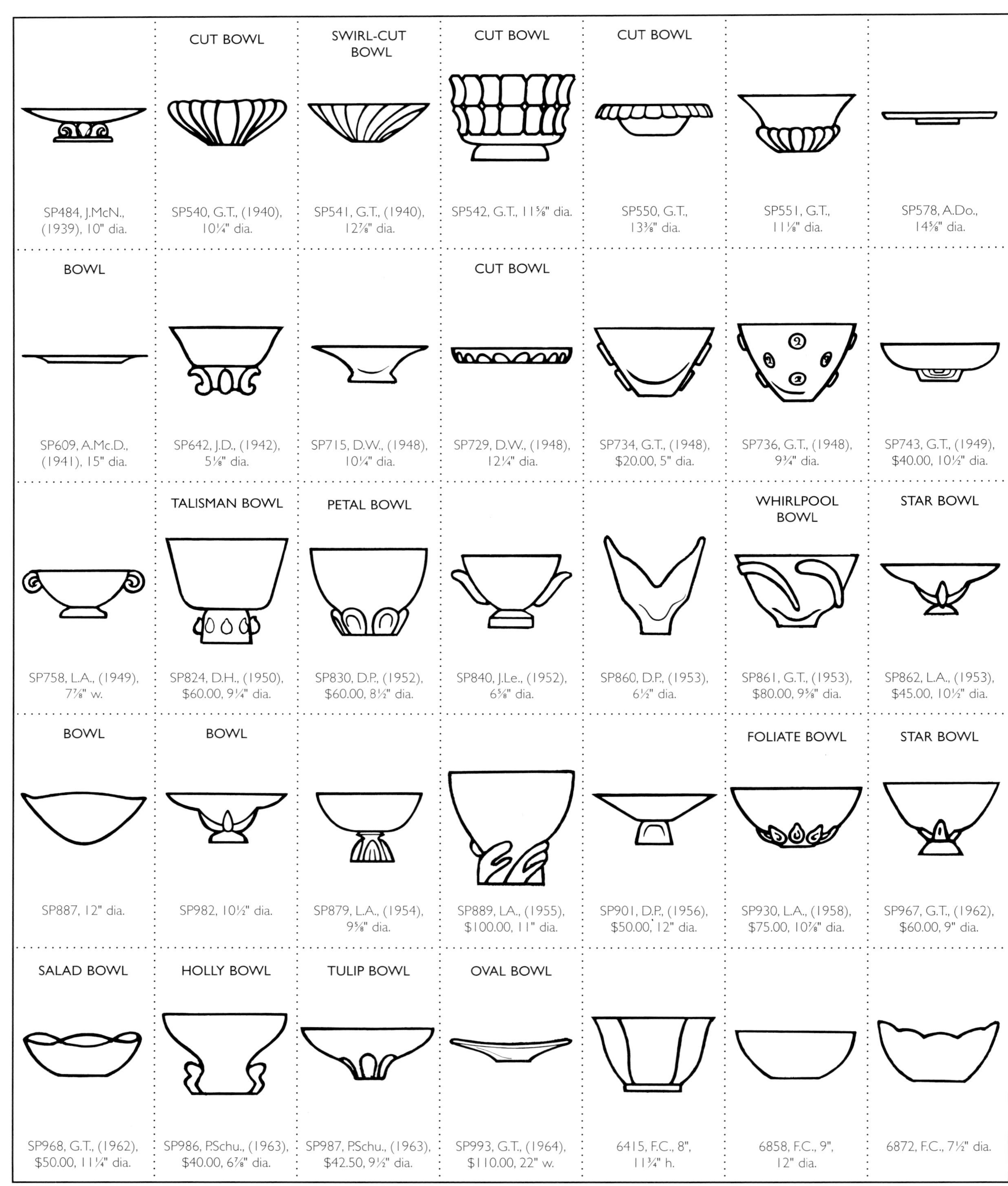
SP484, J.McN., (1939), 10" dia.
CUT BOWL
SP540, G.T., (1940), 10¼" dia.
SWIRL-CUT BOWL
SP541, G.T., (1940), 12⅞" dia.
CUT BOWL
SP542, G.T., 11⅝" dia.
CUT BOWL
SP550, G.T., 13⅜" dia.
SP551, G.T., 11⅛" dia.
SP578, A.Do., 14⅝" dia.
BOWL
SP609, A.Mc.D., (1941), 15" dia.
SP642, J.D., (1942), 5⅛" dia.
SP715, D.W., (1948), 10¼" dia.
CUT BOWL
SP729, D.W., (1948), 12¼" dia.
SP734, G.T., (1948), $20.00, 5" dia.
SP736, G.T., (1948), 9¾" dia.
SP743, G.T., (1949), $40.00, 10½" dia.
SP758, L.A., (1949), 7⅞" w.
TALISMAN BOWL
SP824, D.H., (1950), $60.00, 9¼" dia.
PETAL BOWL
SP830, D.P., (1952), $60.00, 8½" dia.
SP840, J.Le., (1952), 6⅝" dia.
SP860, D.P., (1953), 6½" dia.
WHIRLPOOL BOWL
SP861, G.T., (1953), $80.00, 9⅝" dia.
STAR BOWL
SP862, L.A., (1953), $45.00, 10½" dia.
BOWL
SP887, 12" dia.
BOWL
SP982, 10½" dia.
SP879, L.A., (1954), 9⅝" dia.
SP889, L.A., (1955), $100.00, 11" dia.
SP901, D.P., (1956), $50.00, 12" dia.
FOLIATE BOWL
SP930, L.A., (1958), $75.00, 10⅞" dia.
STAR BOWL
SP967, G.T., (1962), $60.00, 9" dia.
SALAD BOWL
SP968, G.T., (1962), $50.00, 11¼" dia.
HOLLY BOWL
SP986, P.Schu., (1963), $40.00, 6⅞" dia.
TULIP BOWL
SP987, P.Schu., (1963), $42.50, 9½" dia.
OVAL BOWL
SP993, G.T., (1964), $110.00, 22" w.
6415, F.C., 8", 11¾" h.
6858, F.C., 9", 12" dia.
6872, F.C., 7½" dia.

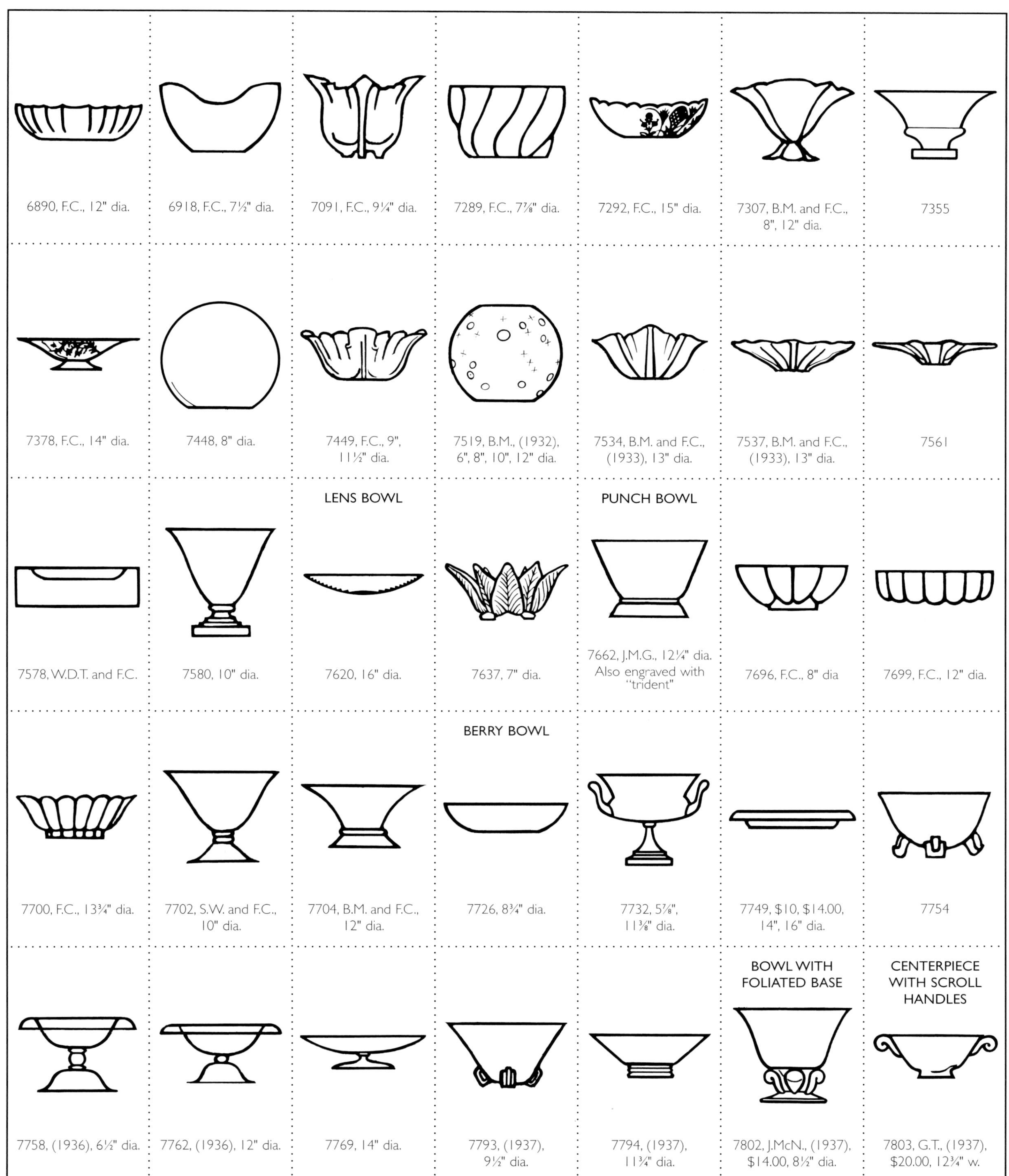

6890, F.C., 12" dia.
6918, F.C., 7½" dia.
7091, F.C., 9¼" dia.
7289, F.C., 7⅞" dia.
7292, F.C., 15" dia.
7307, B.M. and F.C., 8", 12" dia.
7355
7378, F.C., 14" dia.
7448, 8" dia.
7449, F.C., 9", 11½" dia.
7519, B.M., (1932), 6", 8", 10", 12" dia.
7534, B.M. and F.C., (1933), 13" dia.
7537, B.M. and F.C., (1933), 13" dia.
7561
7578, W.D.T. and F.C.
7580, 10" dia.
LENS BOWL
7620, 16" dia.
7637, 7" dia.
PUNCH BOWL
7662, J.M.G., 12¼" dia. Also engraved with "trident"
7696, F.C., 8" dia
7699, F.C., 12" dia.
7700, F.C., 13¾" dia.
7702, S.W. and F.C., 10" dia.
7704, B.M. and F.C., 12" dia.
BERRY BOWL
7726, 8¾" dia.
7732, 5⅞", 11⅜" dia.
7749, $10, $14.00, 14", 16" dia.
7754
7758, (1936), 6½" dia.
7762, (1936), 12" dia.
7769, 14" dia.
7793, (1937), 9½" dia.
7794, (1937), 11¾" dia.
BOWL WITH FOLIATED BASE
7802, J.McN., (1937), $14.00, 8½" dia.
CENTERPIECE WITH SCROLL HANDLES
7803, G.T., (1937), $20.00, 12¾" w.

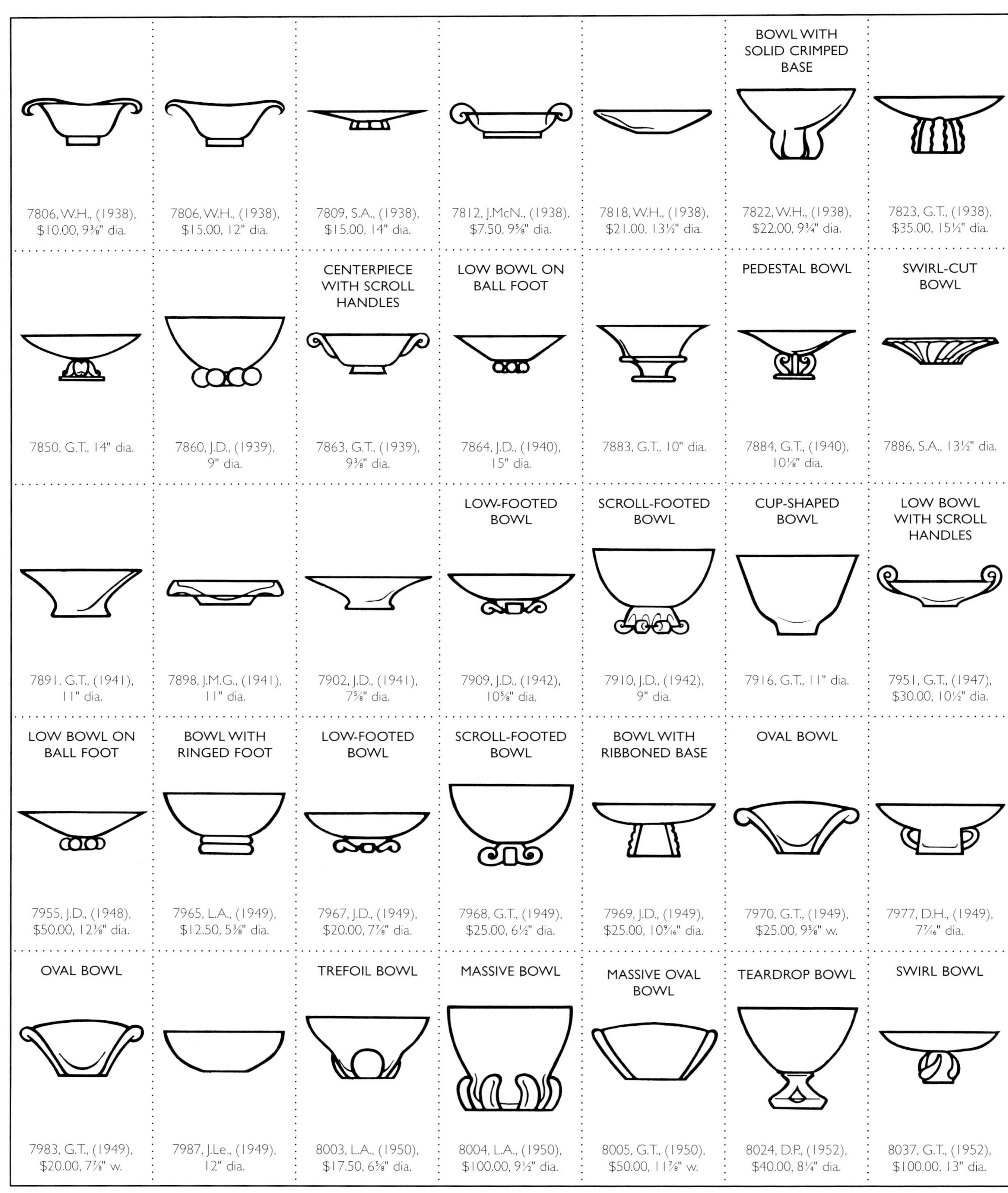

7806, W.H., (1938), $10.00, 9⅜" dia.
7806, W.H., (1938), $15.00, 12" dia.
7809, S.A., (1938), $15.00, 14" dia.
7812, J.McN., (1938), $7.50, 9⅝" dia.
7818, W.H., (1938), $21.00, 13½" dia.
BOWL WITH SOLID CRIMPED BASE
7822, W.H., (1938), $22.00, 9¾" dia.
7823, G.T., (1938), $35.00, 15½" dia.
7850, G.T., 14" dia.
7860, J.D., (1939), 9" dia.
CENTERPIECE WITH SCROLL HANDLES
7863, G.T., (1939), 9⅜" dia.
LOW BOWL ON BALL FOOT
7864, J.D., (1940), 15" dia.
7883, G.T., 10" dia.
PEDESTAL BOWL
7884, G.T., (1940), 10⅛" dia.
SWIRL-CUT BOWL
7886, S.A., 13½" dia.
7891, G.T., (1941), 11" dia.
7898, J.M.G., (1941), 11" dia.
7902, J.D., (1941), 7⅝" dia.
LOW-FOOTED BOWL
7909, J.D., (1942), 10⅝" dia.
SCROLL-FOOTED BOWL
7910, J.D., (1942), 9" dia.
CUP-SHAPED BOWL
7916, G.T., 11" dia.
LOW BOWL WITH SCROLL HANDLES
7951, G.T., (1947), $30.00, 10½" dia.
LOW BOWL ON BALL FOOT
7955, J.D., (1948), $50.00, 12⅜" dia.
BOWL WITH RINGED FOOT
7965, L.A., (1949), $12.50, 5⅜" dia.
LOW-FOOTED BOWL
7967, J.D., (1949), $20.00, 7⅞" dia.
SCROLL-FOOTED BOWL
7968, G.T., (1949), $25.00, 6½" dia.
BOWL WITH RIBBONED BASE
7969, J.D., (1949), $25.00, 10 9/16" dia.
OVAL BOWL
7970, G.T., (1949), $25.00, 9⅝" w.
7977, D.H., (1949), 7 7/16" dia.
OVAL BOWL
7983, G.T., (1949), $20.00, 7⅞" w.
7987, J.Le., (1949), 12" dia.
TREFOIL BOWL
8003, L.A., (1950), $17.50, 6⅝" dia.
MASSIVE BOWL
8004, L.A., (1950), $100.00, 9½" dia.
MASSIVE OVAL BOWL
8005, G.T., (1950), $50.00, 11⅞" w.
TEARDROP BOWL
8024, D.P., (1952), $40.00, 8¼" dia.
SWIRL BOWL
8037, G.T., (1952), $100.00, 13" dia.

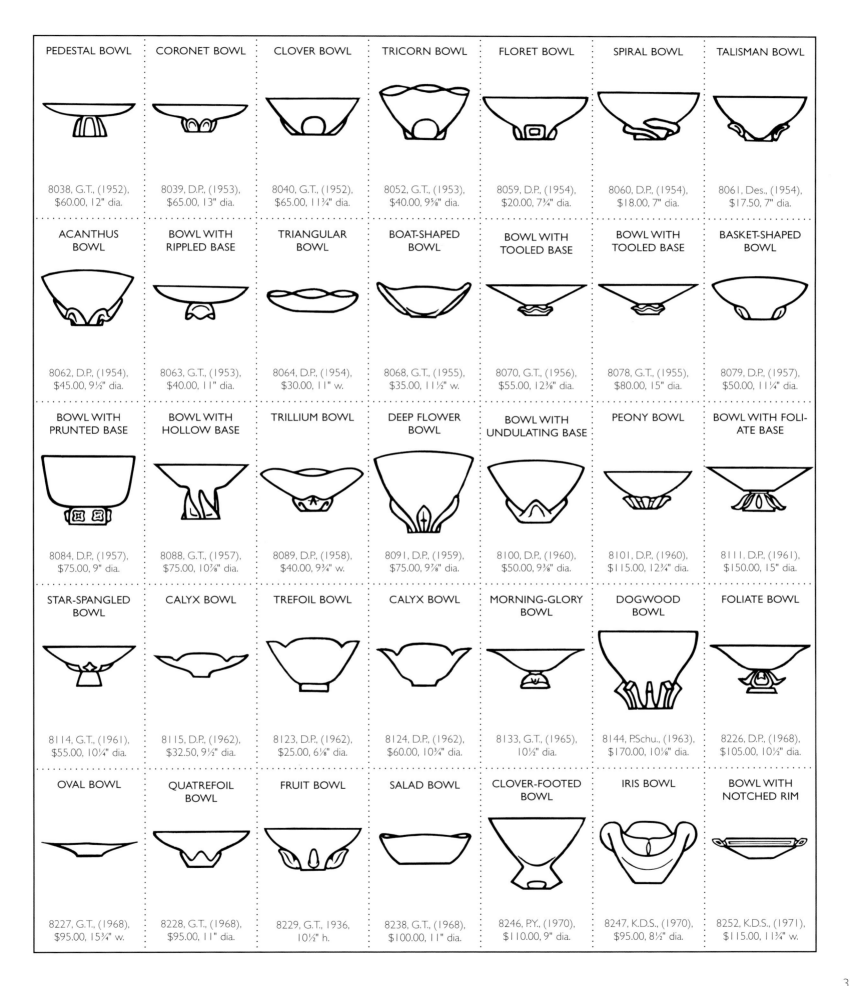

PEDESTAL BOWL	CORONET BOWL	CLOVER BOWL	TRICORN BOWL	FLORET BOWL	SPIRAL BOWL	TALISMAN BOWL
8038, G.T., (1952), $60.00, 12" dia.	8039, D.P., (1953), $65.00, 13" dia.	8040, G.T., (1952), $65.00, 11¾" dia.	8052, G.T., (1953), $40.00, 9⅝" dia.	8059, D.P., (1954), $20.00, 7¾" dia.	8060, D.P., (1954), $18.00, 7" dia.	8061, Des., (1954), $17.50, 7" dia.
ACANTHUS BOWL	BOWL WITH RIPPLED BASE	TRIANGULAR BOWL	BOAT-SHAPED BOWL	BOWL WITH TOOLED BASE	BOWL WITH TOOLED BASE	BASKET-SHAPED BOWL
8062, D.P., (1954), $45.00, 9½" dia.	8063, G.T., (1953), $40.00, 11" dia.	8064, D.P., (1954), $30.00, 11" w.	8068, G.T., (1955), $35.00, 11½" w.	8070, G.T., (1956), $55.00, 12⅜" dia.	8078, G.T., (1955), $80.00, 15" dia.	8079, D.P., (1957), $50.00, 11¼" dia.
BOWL WITH PRUNTED BASE	BOWL WITH HOLLOW BASE	TRILLIUM BOWL	DEEP FLOWER BOWL	BOWL WITH UNDULATING BASE	PEONY BOWL	BOWL WITH FOLIATE BASE
8084, D.P., (1957), $75.00, 9" dia.	8088, G.T., (1957), $75.00, 10⅞" dia.	8089, D.P., (1958), $40.00, 9¾" w.	8091, D.P., (1959), $75.00, 9⅞" dia.	8100, D.P., (1960), $50.00, 9⅜" dia.	8101, D.P., (1960), $115.00, 12¾" dia.	8111, D.P., (1961), $150.00, 15" dia.
STAR-SPANGLED BOWL	CALYX BOWL	TREFOIL BOWL	CALYX BOWL	MORNING-GLORY BOWL	DOGWOOD BOWL	FOLIATE BOWL
8114, G.T., (1961), $55.00, 10¼" dia.	8115, D.P., (1962), $32.50, 9½" dia.	8123, D.P., (1962), $25.00, 6⅛" dia.	8124, D.P., (1962), $60.00, 10¾" dia.	8133, G.T., (1965), 10½" dia.	8144, P.Schu., (1963), $170.00, 10⅛" dia.	8226, D.P., (1968), $105.00, 10½" dia.
OVAL BOWL	QUATREFOIL BOWL	FRUIT BOWL	SALAD BOWL	CLOVER-FOOTED BOWL	IRIS BOWL	BOWL WITH NOTCHED RIM
8227, G.T., (1968), $95.00, 15¾" w.	8228, G.T., (1968), $95.00, 11" dia.	8229, G.T., 1936, 10½" h.	8238, G.T., (1968), $100.00, 11" dia.	8246, P.Y., (1970), $110.00, 9" dia.	8247, K.D.S., (1970), $95.00, 8½" dia.	8252, K.D.S., (1971), $115.00, 11¾" w.

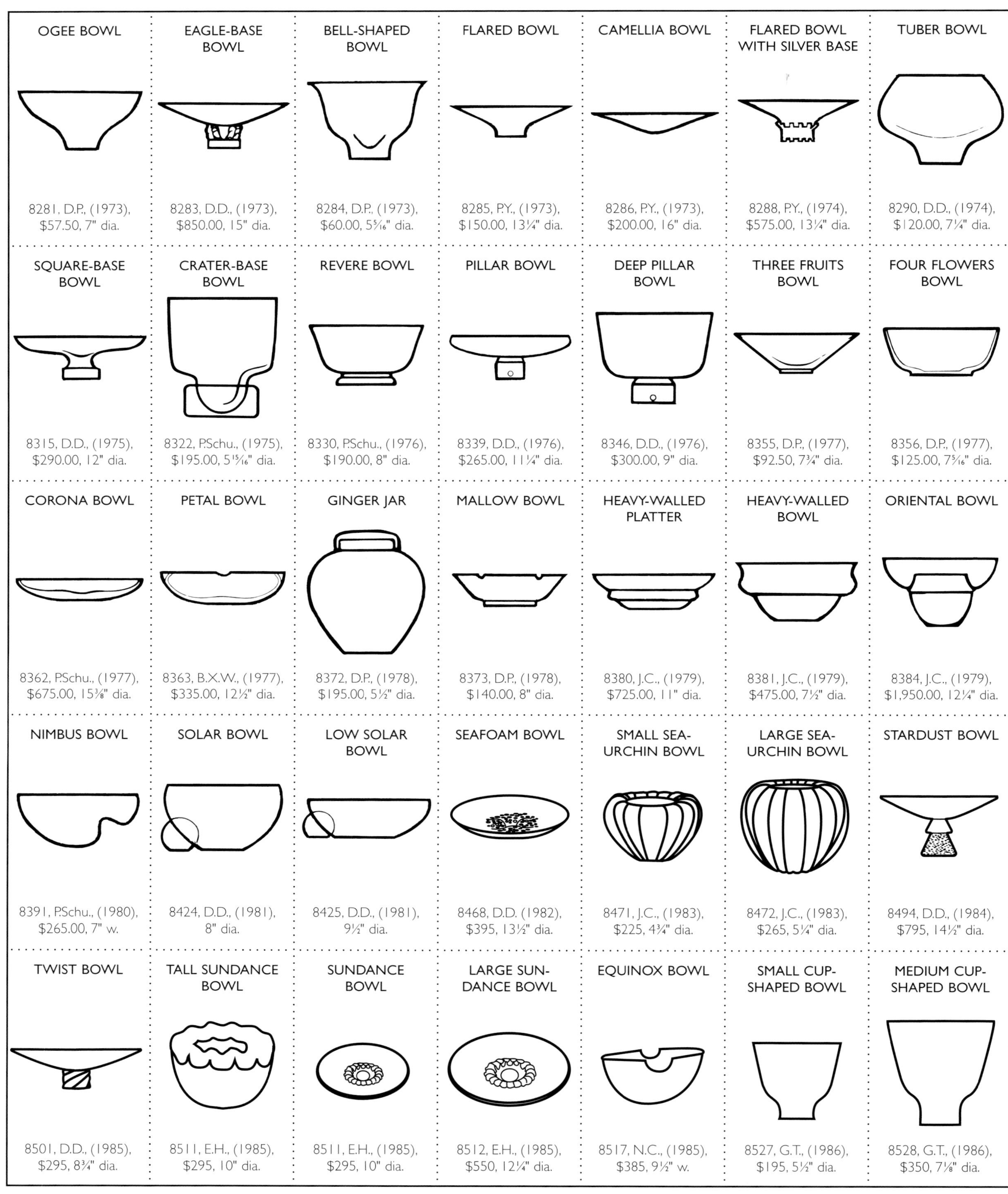
OGEE BOWL
8281, D.P., (1973), $57.50, 7" dia.
EAGLE-BASE BOWL
8283, D.D., (1973), $850.00, 15" dia.
BELL-SHAPED BOWL
8284, D.P., (1973), $60.00, 5 5/16" dia.
FLARED BOWL
8285, P.Y., (1973), $150.00, 13 1/4" dia.
CAMELLIA BOWL
8286, P.Y., (1973), $200.00, 16" dia.
FLARED BOWL WITH SILVER BASE
8288, P.Y., (1974), $575.00, 13 1/4" dia.
TUBER BOWL
8290, D.D., (1974), $120.00, 7 1/4" dia.
SQUARE-BASE BOWL
8315, D.D., (1975), $290.00, 12" dia.
CRATER-BASE BOWL
8322, P.Schu., (1975), $195.00, 5 15/16" dia.
REVERE BOWL
8330, P.Schu., (1976), $190.00, 8" dia.
PILLAR BOWL
8339, D.D., (1976), $265.00, 11 1/4" dia.
DEEP PILLAR BOWL
8346, D.D., (1976), $300.00, 9" dia.
THREE FRUITS BOWL
8355, D.P., (1977), $92.50, 7 3/4" dia.
FOUR FLOWERS BOWL
8356, D.P., (1977), $125.00, 7 5/16" dia.
CORONA BOWL
8362, P.Schu., (1977), $675.00, 15 3/8" dia.
PETAL BOWL
8363, B.X.W., (1977), $335.00, 12 1/2" dia.
GINGER JAR
8372, D.P., (1978), $195.00, 5 1/2" dia.
MALLOW BOWL
8373, D.P., (1978), $140.00, 8" dia.
HEAVY-WALLED PLATTER
8380, J.C., (1979), $725.00, 11" dia.
HEAVY-WALLED BOWL
8381, J.C., (1979), $475.00, 7 1/2" dia.
ORIENTAL BOWL
8384, J.C., (1979), $1,950.00, 12 1/4" dia.
NIMBUS BOWL
8391, P.Schu., (1980), $265.00, 7" w.
SOLAR BOWL
8424, D.D., (1981), 8" dia.
LOW SOLAR BOWL
8425, D.D., (1981), 9 1/2" dia.
SEAFOAM BOWL
8468, D.D. (1982), $395, 13 1/2" dia.
SMALL SEA-URCHIN BOWL
8471, J.C., (1983), $225, 4 3/4" dia.
LARGE SEA-URCHIN BOWL
8472, J.C., (1983), $265, 5 1/4" dia.
STARDUST BOWL
8494, D.D., (1984), $795, 14 1/2" dia.
TWIST BOWL
8501, D.D., (1985), $295, 8 3/4" dia.
TALL SUNDANCE BOWL
8511, E.H., (1985), $295, 10" dia.
SUNDANCE BOWL
8511, E.H., (1985), $295, 10" dia.
LARGE SUN-DANCE BOWL
8512, E.H., (1985), $550, 12 1/4" dia.
EQUINOX BOWL
8517, N.C., (1985), $385, 9 1/2" w.
SMALL CUP-SHAPED BOWL
8527, G.T., (1986), $195, 5 1/2" dia.
MEDIUM CUP-SHAPED BOWL
8528, G.T., (1986), $350, 7 1/8" dia.

CLOUD BOWL	SUNFLOWER BOWL	LARGE SUN-FLOWER BOWL	TRICORN BOWL	FLAIR BOWL	MOMENTUM BOWL	CASCADE BOWL
8529, D.D., (1986), $395, 10" dia.	8530, E.H., (1986), $275, 10" dia.	8531, E.H., (1986), $595, 15½" dia.	8535, D.D., (1986), $250, 7" dia.	8539, D.D., (1986), $395, 11¾" dia.	8541, P.A., (1986), $450, 12¾" dia.	8560, N.C., (1987), $545, 12½" w.
CELESTIAL BOWL	ILLUSION BOWL	LARGE ILLUSION BOWL	LARGE TWIST BOWL	ARCHAIC BOWL	NIMASSI BOWL	FERN BOWL
8563, D.D., (1988), $275, 8¼" dia.	8564, D.D., (1988), $325, 9¾" dia.	8565, D.D., (1988), $565, 15¼" dia.	8569, D.D., (1989), $525, 13½" dia.	8586, M.G., (1989), $1,400, 11½" dia.	8593, J.S., (1990), $550, 9¾" h.	8599, D.D., (1990), $2,950, 19¼" dia.
FEATHER BOWL	FRAMED BOWL, STERLING	CHRONOS BOWL	SMALL FOLDED BOWL	MEDIUM FOLDED BOWL	WHIRLWIND BOWL	MAGNOLIA BOWL
8612, P.Dr., (1990), $425, 7" dia.	8631, Ref. in 8765, (1992), $16,000	8706, D.D., (1993), $350, 7½" dia.	8707, J.S., (1993), $200, 7¼" w.	8708, J.S., (1993), $300, 9" w.	8721, M.V., (1993), $150, 5¾" dia.	8741, J.S., (1994), $485, 11¾" dia.
TALL CENTER-PIECE BOWL	CALYPSO BOWL	SKATING PARTY	FRAMED BOWL, NICKEL SILVER	DRAPE BOWL	OCEANA BOWL	HARMONY BOWL
8753, D.D., (1994), $775, 10" h.	8759, M.Z., (1994), $895, 11" dia.	8762, D.D., (1994), $550, 7½" dia.	8765, R.Me., (1994), $5,780	8797, P.H., (1995), $575, 9¾" dia.	8807, D.D., (1996), $750, 8¼" dia.	8814, P.A., (1997), $1,290, 15¼" dia.
STARLIGHT BOWL	HANDKERCHIEF BOWL	MARDI GRAS BOWL	ORBIT BOWL	MINT BOWL	TRANQUILITY BOWL	MINOAN BOWL
8835, J.S., (1998), $1,195, 10½" dia.	8841, P.Dro., (1998), $650, 12" dia.	8845, D.D., (1999), $1,750, 10" dia.	8849, J.S., (1999), $625, 8¾" dia.	8888, D.D., (2000), $350, 6" dia.	8889, J.S., (2000), $1,200, 13½" dia.	8899, J.S., (2000), $1,200, 12½" dia.

SMALL ORBIT BOWL

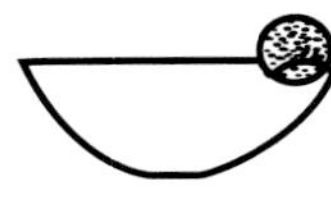

8908, J.S. (2000), $395, 6½" dia.

Not illustrated

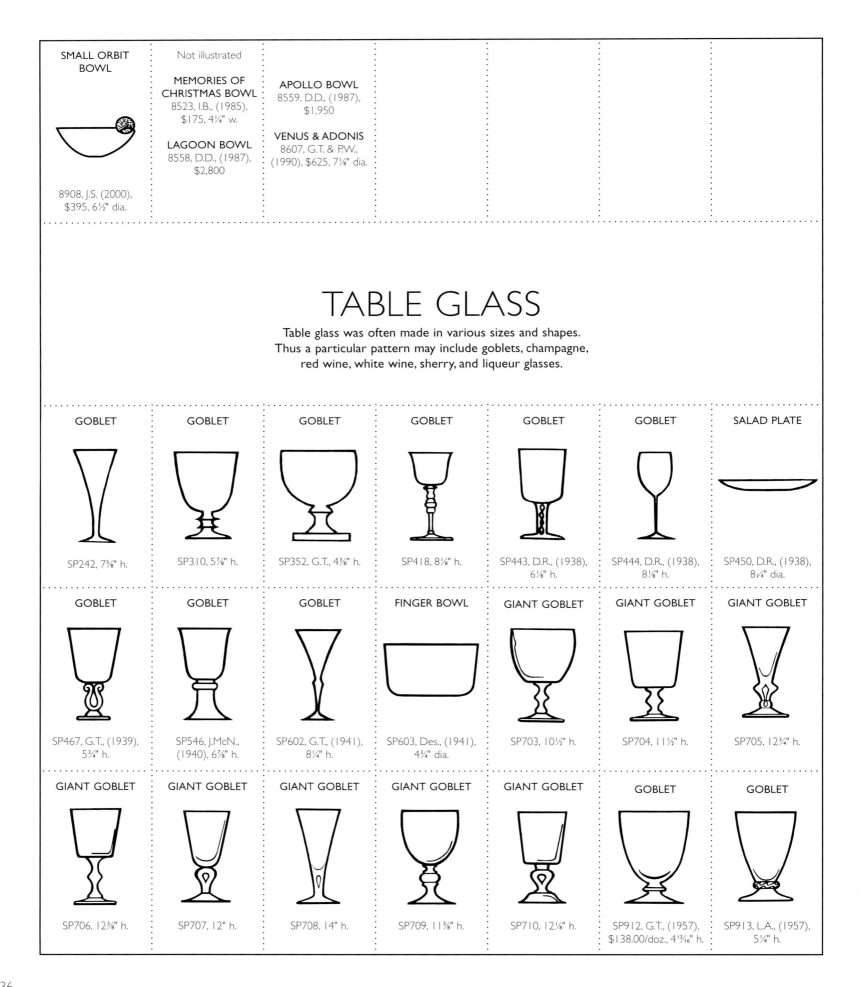

MEMORIES OF CHRISTMAS BOWL
8523, I.B., (1985), $175, 4¼" w.

LAGOON BOWL
8558, D.D., (1987), $2,800

APOLLO BOWL
8559, D.D., (1987), $1,950

VENUS & ADONIS
8607, G.T. & P.W., (1990), $625, 7⅛" dia.

TABLE GLASS

Table glass was often made in various sizes and shapes. Thus a particular pattern may include goblets, champagne, red wine, white wine, sherry, and liqueur glasses.

GOBLET 
SP242, 7⅝" h.

GOBLET 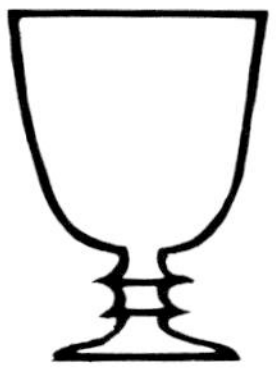
SP310, 5⅞" h.

GOBLET 
SP352, G.T., 4⅜" h.

GOBLET 
SP418, 8⅛" h.

GOBLET 
SP443, D.R., (1938), 6⅛" h.

GOBLET 
SP444, D.R., (1938), 8⅛" h.

SALAD PLATE
SP450, D.R., (1938), 8¼" dia.

GOBLET 
SP467, G.T., (1939), 5¾" h.

GOBLET 
SP546, J.McN., (1940), 6⅞" h.

GOBLET 
SP602, G.T., (1941), 8¼" h.

FINGER BOWL 
SP603, Des., (1941), 4¾" dia.

GIANT GOBLET 
SP703, 10½" h.

GIANT GOBLET 
SP704, 11½" h.

GIANT GOBLET 
SP705, 12¾" h.

GIANT GOBLET 
SP706, 12⅜" h.

GIANT GOBLET 
SP707, 12" h.

GIANT GOBLET 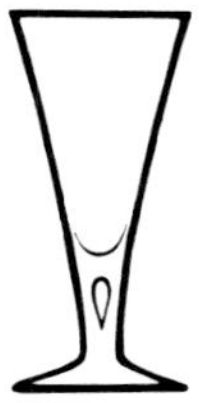
SP708, 14" h.

GIANT GOBLET 
SP709, 11⅜" h.

GIANT GOBLET 
SP710, 12⅛" h.

GOBLET 
SP912, G.T., (1957), $138.00/doz., 4$^{13}/_{16}$" h.

GOBLET 
SP913, L.A., (1957), 5¼" h.

GOBLET
SP914, L.A., (1957), 6⅛" h.
FINGER BOWL
SP915, D.P., (1957), 4¼" dia.
GIANT GOBLET
SP1016
PLAIN GOBLET
6268, F.C., 5¼" h.
CUT FINGER FLUTE GOBLET
6268, F.C., 5¼" h.
CUT QUEEN ANNE GOBLET
6268, F.C., 5¼" h.
CUT LEAVES GOBLET
6268, F.C., 5¼" h.
CUT WARWICK GOBLET
6268, F.C., 5¼" h.
GOBLET
6401, F.C., 8⅛" h.
FINGER BOWL
6401, 4⅞" dia.
STRAWBERRY MANSION GOBLET
7238, F.C., (1931), 6" h.
RIVIERA TABLE CRYSTAL GOBLET
7481, W.D.T. and F.C.
TABLE GLASS
7478, W.D.T., (1932)
TABLE GLASS
7478, W.D.T., (1932)
SPIRAL CRYSTAL WINE
7486, W.D.T. and F.C., (1932)
EMPIRE CRYSTAL GOBLET
7501, W.D.T. and F.C., (1932)
GOBLET
7602, F.C., 7½" h.
GOBLET
7611, F.C., 6⅞" h.
FINGER BOWL PLATE
7644, F.C., 7" dia.
PLATE
7644, F.C., 8½" dia.
FINGER BOWL
7644, F.C., 4⅜" dia.
PLAIN GOBLET
7644, B.M. and F.C., (1934), 5½" h.
CUT STAR AND PUNTY GOBLET
7644, B.M. and F.C., (1934), 5½" h.
PLAIN GOBLET
7666, F.C.
CUT GOBLET
7666, F.C.
PLAIN GOBLET
7667, F.C., (1936)
CUT STAR GOBLET
7667, F.C.
FINGER BOWL
7716, J.M.G. and F.C., 5½" w.
TABLE CRYSTAL WITH BUCKET BOWL
PLAIN GOBLET
7725, (1936), 5¾" h.
CUT GEORGIAN
7725, (1936), 5¾" h.
TRUMPET-SHAPED TABLE CRYSTAL
7737, S.W., 7¼" h.
SEAFOOD COCKTAIL
7766, G.T., (1937), 3⅛", 4⅛" dia.
BOUILLON CUP, PLATE
7770, (1936), 7" dia.

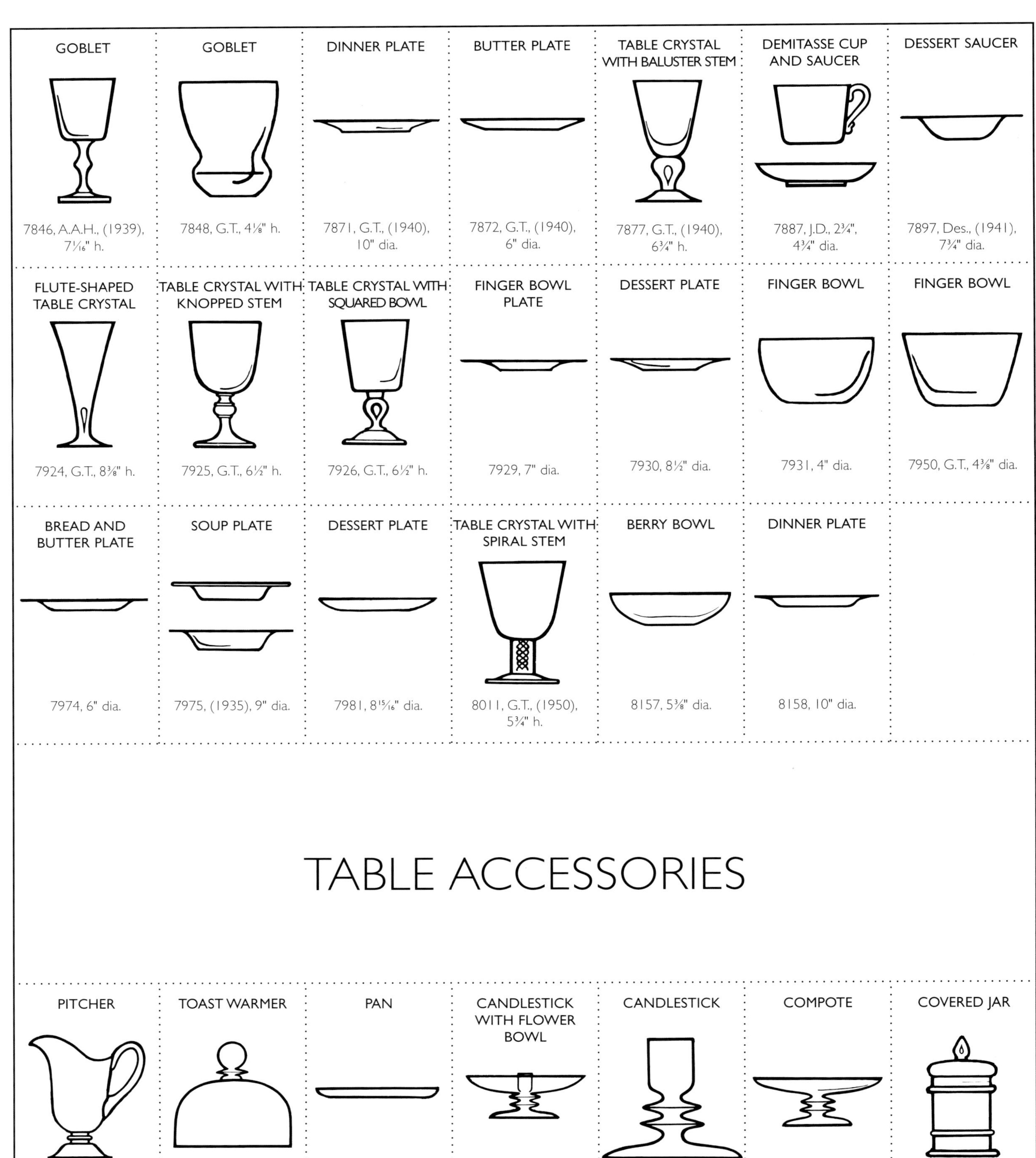

GOBLET
7846, A.A.H., (1939), 7 1/16" h.
GOBLET
7848, G.T., 4⅛" h.
DINNER PLATE
7871, G.T., (1940), 10" dia.
BUTTER PLATE
7872, G.T., (1940), 6" dia.
TABLE CRYSTAL WITH BALUSTER STEM
7877, G.T., (1940), 6¾" h.
DEMITASSE CUP AND SAUCER
7887, J.D., 2¾", 4¾" dia.
DESSERT SAUCER
7897, Des., (1941), 7¾" dia.
FLUTE-SHAPED TABLE CRYSTAL
7924, G.T., 8⅜" h.
TABLE CRYSTAL WITH KNOPPED STEM
7925, G.T., 6½" h.
TABLE CRYSTAL WITH SQUARED BOWL
7926, G.T., 6½" h.
FINGER BOWL PLATE
7929, 7" dia.
DESSERT PLATE
7930, 8½" dia.
FINGER BOWL
7931, 4" dia.
FINGER BOWL
7950, G.T., 4⅜" dia.
BREAD AND BUTTER PLATE
7974, 6" dia.
SOUP PLATE
7975, (1935), 9" dia.
DESSERT PLATE
7981, 8 15/16" dia.
TABLE CRYSTAL WITH SPIRAL STEM
8011, G.T., (1950), 5¾" h.
BERRY BOWL
8157, 5⅜" dia.
DINNER PLATE
8158, 10" dia.
TABLE ACCESSORIES
PITCHER
SP140, 10" h.
TOAST WARMER
SP290, (1936), 5⅛" dia.
PAN
SP292, 15" dia.
CANDLESTICK WITH FLOWER BOWL
SP295, 9" dia.
CANDLESTICK
SP311, 3½" dia.
COMPOTE
SP312, 6⅜" dia.
COVERED JAR
SP314, 12¼" h.

SALT DISH
SP318, 2" dia.
COVERED BOWL
SP319, 5" dia.
SQUARE-FOOTED CANDLESTICK
SP320, 3" w.
CANDLESTICK
SP326, 5" dia.
PITCHER
SP329, (1937), 8½" h.
JELLY DISH
SP342, (1936), 7⅛" w.
JAM POT
SP343, 5½" h.
MUSTARD POT
SP344, 3" h.
SAUCE BOAT
SP345, (1937), 8¼" w.
CANDELABRA
SP357, 11¾" w.
CUT COVERED JAR
SP365, 7⅞" h.
COVERED BOWL
SP366, 8¾" h.
COVERED VASE
SP369, G.T., (1937), 17½" h.
CANDLESTICK
SP382, S.A., (1937), $7.50, 3" dia.
CRUET
SP387, S.A., (1937), $10.00, 7⅝" h.
PITCHER
SP390, W.H., (1938), $12.50, 10¼" h.
CANDY JAR
SP400, G.T., $16.00, 7⅞" dia.
SYRUP DISH
SP404, D.R., (1938), $10.00, 7" l.
JAM POT
SP407, S.A., (1938), $7.50, 4½" h.
COVERED VASE
SP410, W.H., (1938), $25.00, 15¼" h.
CUT TRAY
SP416, W.H., (1938), $30.00, 14" dia.
CENTERPIECE
SP422, W.H., (1938), $35.00, 14" dia.
SMALL TRAY WITH HANDLES
SP428, G.T., (1938), $14.00, 10¾" w.
WATER PITCHER
SP435, D.R., (1938), $10.00, 6½" h.
LOW CANDY DISH
SP456, J.McN., (1938), $12.00, 6¾" dia.
WATER PITCHER
SP459, J.McN., (1938), $14.00, 11⅛" h.
SHALLOW PAN
SP464, S.A., (1939), 10" dia.
JAM JAR AND SAUCER
SP476, G.T., (1939)
FRUIT DISH
SP484, J.McN., (1939), 10" dia.
PEPPER SHAKER
SP485, J.M.G., (1939), 4¾" h.
SALT DISH
SP486, J.M.G., (1939), 3⁹⁄₁₆" w.
ICED TEA PITCHER
SP487, J.D., 11⅝" h.
SYRUP JUG
SP491, J.D., 8" h.
CANDY DISH
SP499, J.D., 6⅞" w.
SUGAR BOWL
SP503, J.D., 4⅝" dia.

SUGAR BOWL
SP505, J.D., 4 13/16" w.
CREAM PITCHER
SP506, J.D., 6 3/8" h.
COMPOTE
SP508, G.T., 9 5/8" dia.
COVERED CENTERPIECE
SP516, J.D., 9 1/8" h.
SHRIMP BOWL
SP527, A.Do., 7" dia.
TRAY
SP532, A.Do., (1939), 8 3/4" dia.
CENTERPIECE
SP535, A.Do., 15 5/8" dia.
COVERED JAR
SP543, J.McN., 17 1/2" h.
COVERED CANDY JAR
SP558, A.Do., (1940), 4 7/8" dia.
CANDLEHOLDER
SP559, J.D., 7 1/16" w.
PITCHER
SP569, J.D., 11 5/8" h.
COVERED CANDY DISH
SP573, G.T., 6" dia.
PITCHER
SP579, G.T., 8 1/4" h.
NUT DISH
SP581, A.Do., 3" dia.
PLATTER
SP609, A.McD., (1941), 14 7/8" dia.
CANDLESTICK
SP618, G.T., (1941), 5 5/16" w.
COMPOTE
SP622, J.D., 8 3/4" dia.
CANDLEHOLDER
SP641, J.D., 6 3/4" h.
MAYONNAISE BOWL
SP642, 5 3/16" dia.
PITCHER
SP696, I.B., (1947), $30.00, 9" h.
COVERED JAR
SP716, G.T., (1948), 9 3/8" h.
SALT AND PEPPER SHAKERS
SP722/3, G.T., (1948), 2 1/8" h.
CANDELABRA
SP726, I.B., (1948), 9 1/4" w.
COVERED CENTERPIECE
SP728, D.W., (1948), 8 1/2" dia.
CANDLESTICK
SP730, D.W., (1948), $120.00/pr, 13 1/4" h.
COMPOTE
SP735, G.T., (1948), $32.50, 10" dia.
PITCHER
SP738, G.T., (1949), $20.00, 6 3/8" h.
SUGAR BOWL
SP739, L.A., (1949), 4 7/8" w.
PITCHER
SP749, G.T., (1949), $18.00, 5 1/2" h.
SAUCE BOWL
SP764, J.Le., (1949), 6 1/8" dia.
TAPERSTICK
SP773, G.T., (1949, 5 3/8" h.
LOW CANDLESTICK
SP793, J.Le., (1950), $20.00/ea., 4 1/4" h.
CREAM PITCHER
SP798, L.A., (1950), $18.00, 6 9/16" h.
SUGAR BOWL
SP799, L.A., (1950), $10.00, 3 15/16" dia.
COMPOTE
SP801, D.H., (1950), 10" dia.

CREAM PITCHER
SP803, L.A., (1950), $12.50, 5 1/16" h.
SUGAR BOWL
SP804, L.A., (1950), $9.00, 3 1/16" dia.
COVERED JAR
SP817, D.H., (1950), 7" h.
CANDLESTICK
SP822, D.H., (1951), $80.00/pr, 10 1/8" h.
COVERED CENTERPIECE
SP846, G.T., (1952), 11 3/8" h.
CANDY DISH
SP857, L.A., (1953), $70.00, 7 1/4" h.
PITCHER
SP869, G.T., (1953), $22.00, 6 3/16" h.
CRUET
SP882, L.A., (1954), $45.00, 7 5/8" h.
COVERED URN
SP911, L.A., (1956), $65.00, 12" h.
CREAM PITCHER
SP925, G.T., (1957), $20.00, 5 1/4" h.
SUGAR BOWL
SP926, G.T., (1957), $18.00, 4 1/8" dia.
THREE-BRANCH CANDELABRA
SP927, L.A., (1957), $100.00, 8 7/8" w.
PITCHER
SP940, L.A., (1959), $40.00, 8 5/8" h.
CREAM PITCHER
SP941, L.A., (1959), $20.00, 4 7/8" w.
SUGAR BOWL
SP942, L.A., (1959), $20.00, 5 1/8" w.
PITCHER
SP961, D.P., (1961), $47.50, 8" h.
FOLIATE CANDLESTICK
SP974, D.P., (1962), $45.00, 5 3/4" h.
STAR COMPOTE
SP975, G.T., (1962), $35.00, 7 7/8" dia.
STAR CANDLESTICK
SP976, L.A., (1962), $37.50, 6 1/8" dia.
CREAM PITCHER
SP979, D.P., (1962), $37.50, 8 1/2" h.
COVERED URN
SP980, G.T., (1962), $125.00, 10 3/4" h.
AIR-TWIST CANDLESTICK
SP981, L.A., (1962), $65.00, 11 1/4" h.
CREAM PITCHER
SP991, L.A., (1963), $30.00, 4 3/8" h.
SCROLL PITCHER
SP992, L.A., (1963), $65.00, 12 1/4" h.
SHERBET OR FRUIT COCKTAIL
2680, 4" dia.
CANDELABRA
7242, P.G., 13 3/4" h.
FLATWARE
7478 F.C.
CANDLESTICK
7503, F.C., 4 1/2" h.
COMPOTE
7503, F.C., 7" dia.
COMPOTE
7503, F.C., 10" dia.
CANDLESTICK
7510, F.C., 3 5/8" h.
CANDLESTICK
7512, B.M. and F.C., (1932), 5 1/4" w.
CANDLESTICK
7516, B.M. and F.C., 5" w.
CANDLESTICK
7516, B.M. and F.C., 7" w.
CANDLESTICK
7554, F.C.

COMPOTE
7563, F.C., (1935), 7" w.
COMPOTE
7563, B.M., 14½" w.
CANDLESTICK
7564, F.C., 4⅝" w.
CANDELABRA
7616, W.D.T. and F.C., (1934), 13¾" h.
CANDLESTICK
7710, J.M.G. and F.C., 7½" h.
COMPOTE
7710, 7" dia.
BASKET
7717, F.C., 6⅜" w.
7717, F.C., 6⅜" w.
STRAWBERRY DISH
7726, 5", 8½", 11" dia.
COVERED CANDY DISH
7745, 6 3/16" h.
BALUSTER CANDLESTICK
7746, F.C., 10¼" h.
MAYONNAISE BOWL
7754, (1936), 5" dia.
CANDLESTICK
7756, S.W., (1936), 14½" h.
TURN-OVER BOWL
7758, J.M.G., (1936), 6¼" dia.
CREAM PITCHER
7765, (1936), 3¼" w.
SUGAR BOWL
7765, (1936), 3¼" w.
BELL
7768, (1936), 3¼" h.
COMPOTE
7772, (1936), 10" dia.
HURRICANE SHADE
7773, (1936), 18" h.
CREAM PITCHER
7778, (1936), 6¾" h.
SUGAR BOWL
7778, (1936), 6⅜" w.
NUT DISH
7783, (1937), 4" w.
CANDELABRA
7784, J.McN., 13" w.
SALT DISH
7785, 2" dia.
PEPPER SHAKER
7786, J.M.G., (1935), 3¼" h.
TEARDROP CANDLESTICK
7792, (1937), 8 13/16" h.
COVERED CANDY DISH
7799, (1937), 6½" w.
COMPOTE
7807, J.McN., (1938), $7.00, 6½" dia.
CANDLESTICK
7808, J.McN., (1938), $7.50, 5¼" w.
FLOWER HOLDER
7811, (1938), $4.00, 3⅞" w.
FLOWER HOLDER
7811, (1938), $5.00, 4⅛" w.
FLOWER HOLDER
7811, (1938), $5.50, 5⅜" w.
BELL
7813, S.A., (1938), $7.00, 3¼" h.
HURRICANE SHADE
7816, G.T., (1938), $15.00, 12½" h.
COMPOTE
7819, G.T., (1938), $8.00, 7½" dia.

CANDLESTICK
7820, G.T., (1938), $8.50, 5¼" w.
CREAM PITCHER
7829, J.M.G., (1939), 8⅛" h.
CANDELABRA
7830, G.T., (1939), 8" w.
JAM POT
7831, S.A., 4" h.
MUSTARD JAR
7833, S.A., (1939), 3" h.
CANDLESTICK
7834, G.T., 4¾" h.
WATER PITCHER
7837, J.D., (1939), 9¼" h.
TOAST COVER
7839, G.T., $7.50, 5½" dia.
CRUET
7841, $10.00, 6¾" h.
COVERED CENTERPIECE
7843, G.T., $35.00, 9⅝" h.
CANDLESTICK
7844, G.T., $10.00, 4⅛" w.
ROPE-TWIST CANDLESTICK
7849, G.T., (1939), 8" h.
CANDLE LAMP
7866, A.Do., 8" h.
PEPPER SHAKER
7868, A.Do., (1940), 4½" h.
SALT DISH
7869, A.Do., (1940), 2½" dia.
PITCHER
7881, G.T., 7½" h.
CANDLESTICK
7890, G.T., (1941), 3⅞" dia.
CANDELABRA
7893, G.T., (1941), 8¼" w.
SAUCE BOWL
7904, A.McD., (1941), 5⅝" dia.
LADLE
7905, Des., (1941), 5⅛" l.
CREAM PITCHER
7906, J.D., (1940), 3¾" w.
SUGAR BOWL
7907, J.D., (1941), 4 1/16" w.
CANDELABRA
7908, G.T., (1942), 8 5/16" h.
CANDY DISH WITH RAM'S-HEAD FINIAL
7936, I.B., (1943), 6" h.
CREAM PITCHER
7941, I.B., (1947), $12.50, 5" w.
SUGAR BOWL
7942, I.B., (1947), $12.50, 5" w.
JAM JAR
7944, Des., (1947), 3⅝" w.
CRUET WITH TEARDROP STOPPER
7945, G.T., (1947), $30.00, 4⅜" h.
NUT DISH
7946, G.T., (1947), 3" w.
MAYONNAISE BOWL
7949, D.W., (1947), 5⅜" dia.
CANDLESTICK
7957, D.W., (1948), $18.00, 5" w.
PITCHER
7959, G.T., (1948), 8" h.
SALT AND PEPPER SHAKERS
7971/2, G.T., (1948), 2⅛" h.
CANDELABRA
7979, G.T., (1949), $55.00, 8¼" w.
BELL WITH AIR-TWIST HANDLE
7986, J.Le., (1949), 5⅞" h.

LOW TEARDROP CANDLESTICK
7995, D.H., (1949), 4 3/8" h.
CANDLESTICK
7996, J.Le., (1949), 5 1/2" w.
PITCHER
8010, G.T., (1950), $35.00, 10 7/8" h.
SCROLL CANDELABRA
8017, L.A., (1950), $55.00, 9 5/8" h.
COVERED URN
8019, D.H., (1950), 10 7/16" h.
SALT DISH
8030, D.H., (1952), $8.50, 2 1/4" dia.
PEPPER SHAKER
8031, Des., (1952), $24.00, 2 7/8" h.
FLARED TEARDROP CANDLESTICK
8032, D.P., (1952), $25.00, 4 3/4" h.
COMPOTE
8033, D.P., (1952), $25.00, 7" dia.
CANDLEBOWL
8049, G.T., (1952), $60.00, 8 7/8" w.
CANDELABRA
8050, G.T., (1952), $80.00, 9 5/8" h.
PITCHER
8051, G.T., (1953), $30.00, 8 1/2" h.
LOW CANDLESTICK WITH RIPPLED BASE
8066, G.T., (1954), $25.00, 3 1/2" h.
SAUCE BOAT
8067, D.P., (1953), $22.00, 5 3/4" w.
MARTINI OR WATER PITCHER
8077, L.A., (1955), $40.00, 9 7/8" h.
LOW CANDLESTICK
8081, D.P., (1956), $25.00, 5 7/16" w.
SHALLOW COMPOTE
8082, L.A., (1957), $25.00, 8 1/8" dia.
COVERED CENTERPIECE
8085, D.P., (1956), $80.00, 9 7/8" h.
PEAR-SHAPED SAUCE BOAT
8086, L.A., (1957), $25.00, 7" w.
BALUSTER CANDLESTICK
8094, D.P., (1955), $90.00, 14 5/8" h.
SEA CENTERPIECE
8096, G.T., (1959), $160.00, 11 1/2" h.
PITCHER
8097, D.P., (1959), $27.50, 6 5/16" h.
STAR-FOOTED SERVING PLATE
8110, D.P., (1961), $37.50, 9 1/2" dia.
CANDLESTICK
8121, D.P., (1962), $62.50, 8 1/4" h.
BELL
8139, L.A., (1962), $32.50, 4 1/8" h.
BAR PITCHER
8224, G.T., (1968), $80.00, 7 1/2" h.
LOW-SCROLLED CANDLESTICK
8234, P.Schu., (1968), $50.00, 4 7/16" h.
BERRY BOWL
8241, 11" dia.
DOUBLE-DISK CANDLESTICK WITH SILVER CUP
8287, P.Y., (1974), $212.50/ea., 11 5/8" h.
COLONIAL CANDLESTICK
8305, D.D., (1975), $120.00/ea., 9 1/4" h.
COMPOTE
8311, B.X.W., 1975, $125.00, 7 3/8" dia.
SQUARE-CUT CANDLESTICK
8316, D.D., (1975), $450.00, 3 1/2" h.
CANDLESTICK CLUSTER
8326, P.Y., (1976), $750.00, 5 3/8" h.

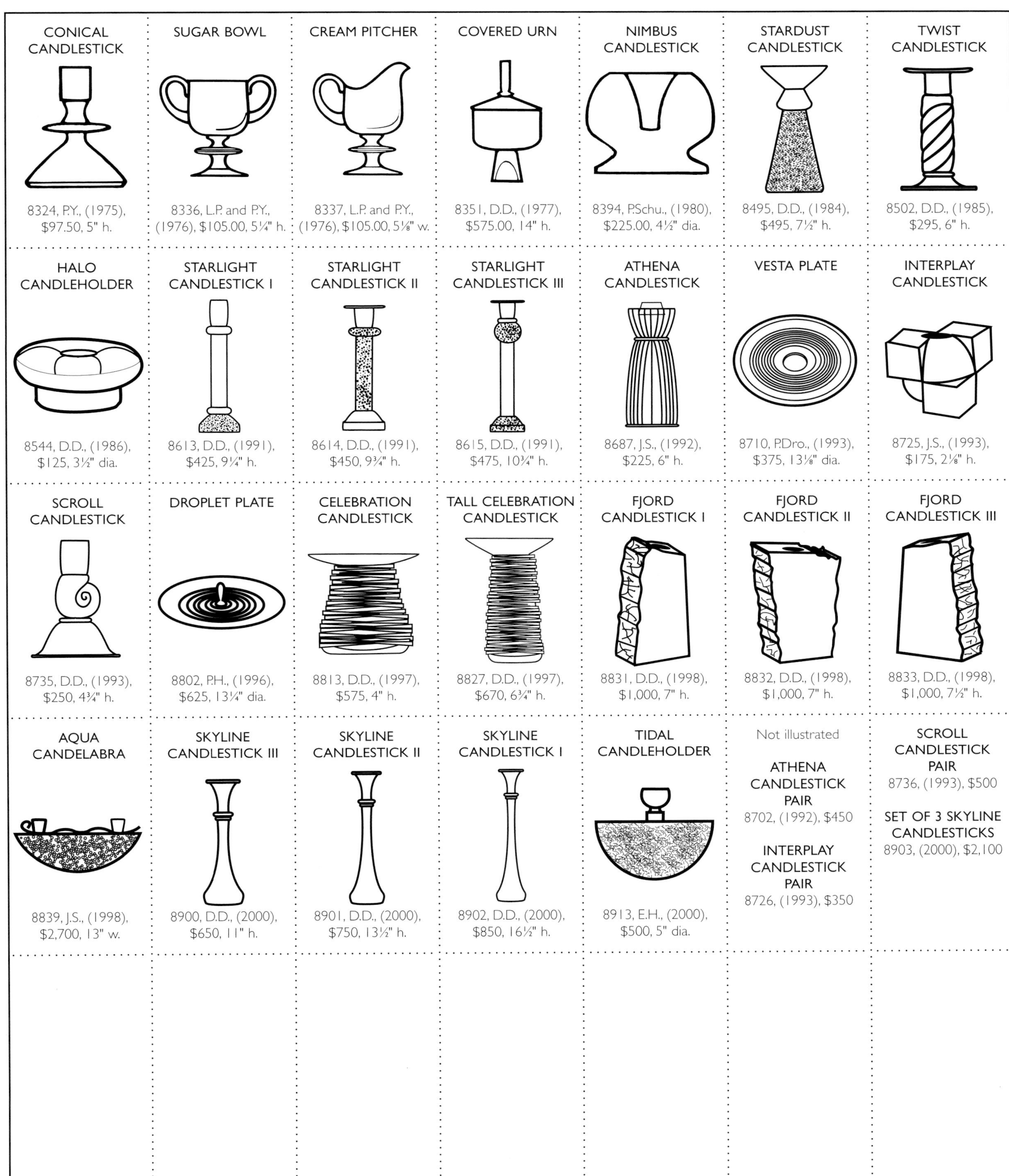

CONICAL CANDLESTICK 8324, P.Y., (1975), $97.50, 5" h.	SUGAR BOWL 8336, L.P. and P.Y., (1976), $105.00, 5¼" h.	CREAM PITCHER 8337, L.P. and P.Y., (1976), $105.00, 5⅛" w.	COVERED URN 8351, D.D., (1977), $575.00, 14" h.	NIMBUS CANDLESTICK 8394, P.Schu., (1980), $225.00, 4½" dia.	STARDUST CANDLESTICK 8495, D.D., (1984), $495, 7½" h.	TWIST CANDLESTICK 8502, D.D., (1985), $295, 6" h.
HALO CANDLEHOLDER 8544, D.D., (1986), $125, 3½" dia.	STARLIGHT CANDLESTICK I 8613, D.D., (1991), $425, 9¼" h.	STARLIGHT CANDLESTICK II 8614, D.D., (1991), $450, 9¾" h.	STARLIGHT CANDLESTICK III 8615, D.D., (1991), $475, 10¾" h.	ATHENA CANDLESTICK 8687, J.S., (1992), $225, 6" h.	VESTA PLATE 8710, P.Dro., (1993), $375, 13⅛" dia.	INTERPLAY CANDLESTICK 8725, J.S., (1993), $175, 2⅛" h.
SCROLL CANDLESTICK 8735, D.D., (1993), $250, 4¾" h.	DROPLET PLATE 8802, P.H., (1996), $625, 13¼" dia.	CELEBRATION CANDLESTICK 8813, D.D., (1997), $575, 4" h.	TALL CELEBRATION CANDLESTICK 8827, D.D., (1997), $670, 6¾" h.	FJORD CANDLESTICK I 8831, D.D., (1998), $1,000, 7" h.	FJORD CANDLESTICK II 8832, D.D., (1998), $1,000, 7" h.	FJORD CANDLESTICK III 8833, D.D., (1998), $1,000, 7½" h.
AQUA CANDELABRA 8839, J.S., (1998), $2,700, 13" w.	SKYLINE CANDLESTICK III 8900, D.D., (2000), $650, 11" h.	SKYLINE CANDLESTICK II 8901, D.D., (2000), $750, 13½" h.	SKYLINE CANDLESTICK I 8902, D.D., (2000), $850, 16½" h.	TIDAL CANDLEHOLDER 8913, E.H., (2000), $500, 5" dia.	Not illustrated ATHENA CANDLESTICK PAIR 8702, (1992), $450 INTERPLAY CANDLESTICK PAIR 8726, (1993), $350	SCROLL CANDLESTICK PAIR 8736, (1993), $500 SET OF 3 SKYLINE CANDLESTICKS 8903, (2000), $2,100

DRINKING GLASSES

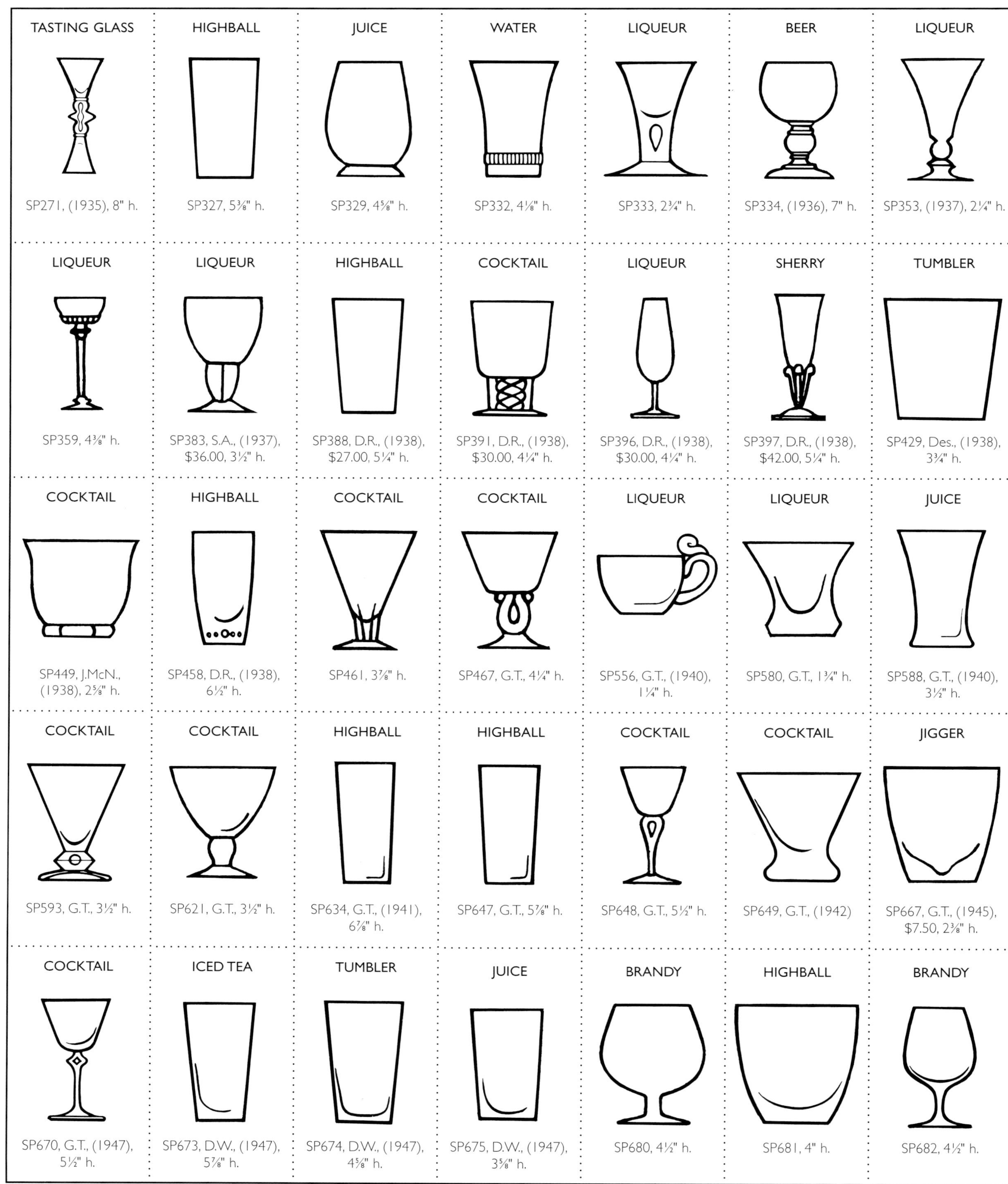

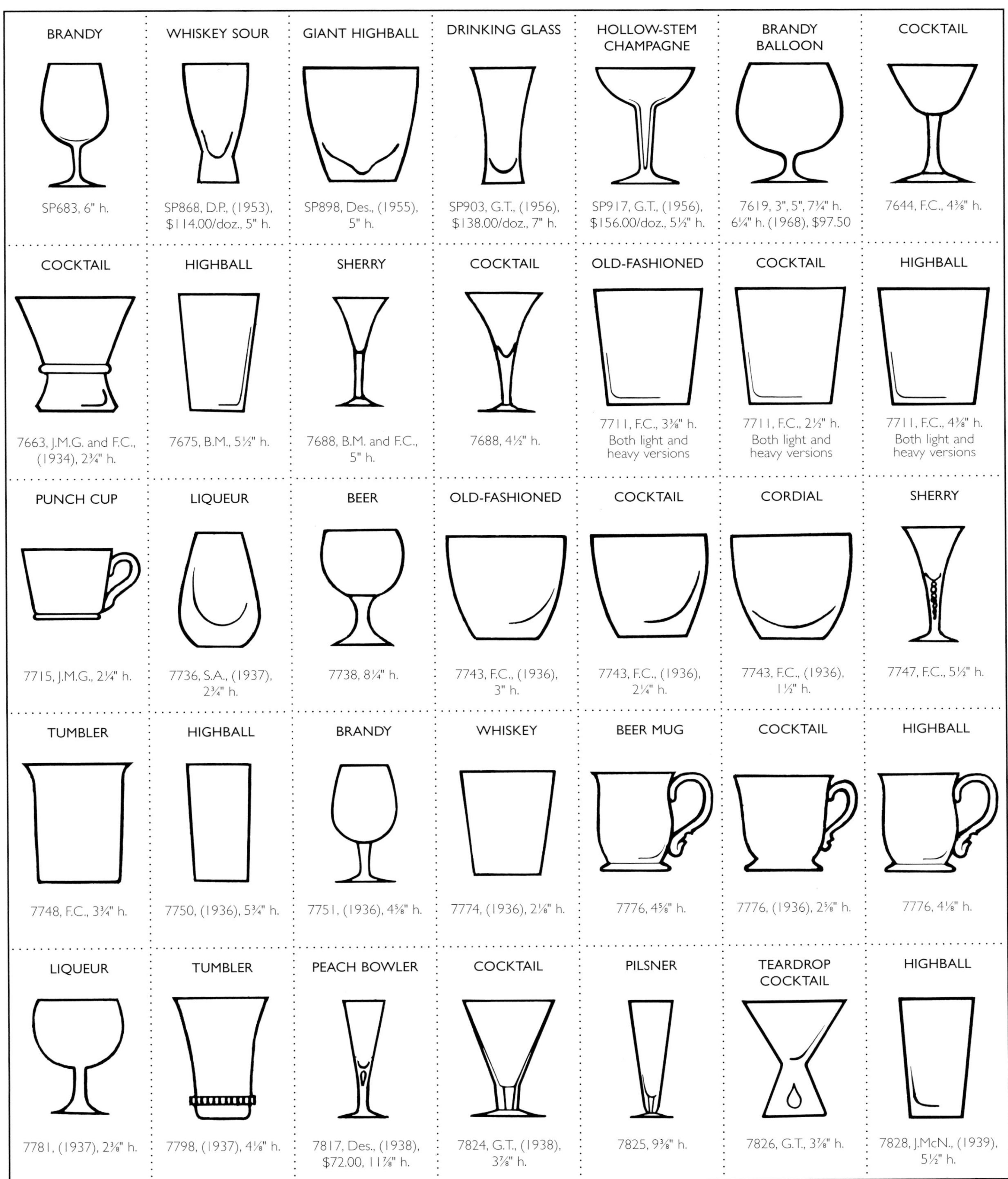
BRANDY
SP683, 6" h.
WHISKEY SOUR
SP868, D.P., (1953), $114.00/doz., 5" h.
GIANT HIGHBALL
SP898, Des., (1955), 5" h.
DRINKING GLASS
SP903, G.T., (1956), $138.00/doz., 7" h.
HOLLOW-STEM CHAMPAGNE
SP917, G.T., (1956), $156.00/doz., 5½" h.
BRANDY BALLOON
7619, 3", 5", 7¾" h. 6¼" h. (1968), $97.50
COCKTAIL
7644, F.C., 4⅜" h.
COCKTAIL
7663, J.M.G. and F.C., (1934), 2¾" h.
HIGHBALL
7675, B.M., 5½" h.
SHERRY
7688, B.M. and F.C., 5" h.
COCKTAIL
7688, 4½" h.
OLD-FASHIONED
7711, F.C., 3⅜" h. Both light and heavy versions
COCKTAIL
7711, F.C., 2½" h. Both light and heavy versions
HIGHBALL
7711, F.C., 4⅜" h. Both light and heavy versions
PUNCH CUP
7715, J.M.G., 2¼" h.
LIQUEUR
7736, S.A., (1937), 2¾" h.
BEER
7738, 8¼" h.
OLD-FASHIONED
7743, F.C., (1936), 3" h.
COCKTAIL
7743, F.C., (1936), 2¼" h.
CORDIAL
7743, F.C., (1936), 1½" h.
SHERRY
7747, F.C., 5½" h.
TUMBLER
7748, F.C., 3¾" h.
HIGHBALL
7750, (1936), 5¾" h.
BRANDY
7751, (1936), 4⅝" h.
WHISKEY
7774, (1936), 2⅛" h.
BEER MUG
7776, 4⅝" h.
COCKTAIL
7776, (1936), 2⅝" h.
HIGHBALL
7776, 4⅛" h.
LIQUEUR
7781, (1937), 2⅜" h.
TUMBLER
7798, (1937), 4⅛" h.
PEACH BOWLER
7817, Des., (1938), $72.00, 11⅞" h.
COCKTAIL
7824, G.T., (1938), 3⅞" h.
PILSNER
7825, 9⅜" h.
TEARDROP COCKTAIL
7826, G.T., 3⅞" h.
HIGHBALL
7828, J.McN., (1939), 5½" h.

JUICE
7854, J.D., 3⅝" h.
WATER
7855, J.D., 4½" h.
ICED TEA
7856, J.D., 5⅝" h.
OLD-FASHIONED
7889, G.T., (1941), 3¾" h.
AIR-TWIST COCKTAIL
7917, G.T., 3¾" h.
BEER MUG
7921, I.B., 5" h.
HIGHBALL
7923, G.T., (1943), 6½" h.
BEER MUG
7932, I.B., 5" h.
OLD-FASHIONED
7933, G.T., (1947), $84.00/doz., 3⅜" h.
COCKTAIL
7937, G.T., (1947), $72.00/doz., 2⅞" h.
PILSNER
7938, O.Me., (1947), $108.00, 9¼" h.
HIGHBALL
7940, G.T., (1947), $72.00/doz., 5½" h.
LIQUEUR
7954, G.T., (1947), $66.00/doz., 2½" h.
BEER MUG
7976, I.B., (1949), 5" h.
COCKTAIL
7980, D.H., (1949), 4 15/16" h.
PUNCH CUP
7994, L.A., (1949), $100.00, 2 3/16" h.
PILSNER
7997, D.H., (1949), 8 11/16" h.
NOGGIN
8013, D.H., (1950), $120.00/doz., 4⅞" h.
COCKTAIL
8014, G.T., (1950), $120.00/doz., 4⅞" h.
HIGHBALL
8041, D.P., (1952), $144.00/doz., 6½" h.
COCKTAIL
8042, D.P., (1953), $96.00/doz., 3¼" h.
OLD-FASHIONED
8054, D.P., (1953), $120.00/doz., 3 11/16" h.
LIQUEUR
8055, D.P., (1953), $96.00/doz., 4" h.
BRANDY
8152, 6¼" h.
PILSNER
8323, D.P., (1975), $70.00/ea., 7½" h.
JIGGER
8342, G.T., (1947), $66.00/doz., 2⅜" h.
STARDUST BAR GLASS
8579, D.D., (1989), $210, 4⅛" h.
WHIRLWIND VODKA GLASS
8714, M.V., (1993), $45, 3¾" h.
WHIRLWIND TUMBLER
8716, M.V., (1993), $65, 3¾" h.
AIR-TWIST CHAMPAGNE FLUTE
8859, S.D.T., (2000), $300, 7½" h.
TRUMPET MARTINI GLASS
8898, S.W., (2000), $300, 5" h.
Not illustrated
AIR-TWIST CHAMPAGNE FLUTE PAIR
8858, S.D.T., (2000), $600
TRUMPET MARTINI GLASS PAIR
8897, S.W., (2000), $600, 5" h.

DRINKING ACCESSORIES

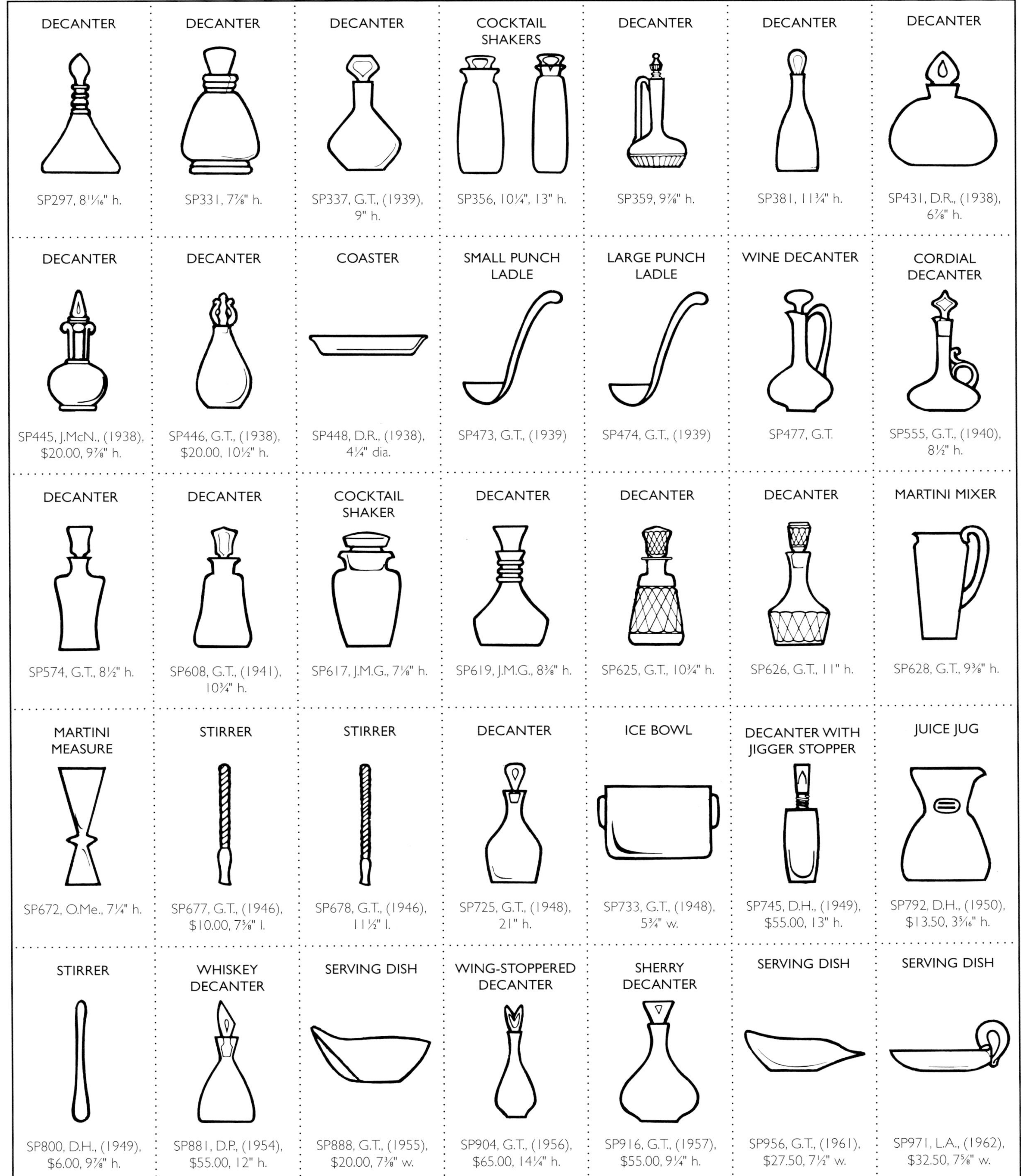

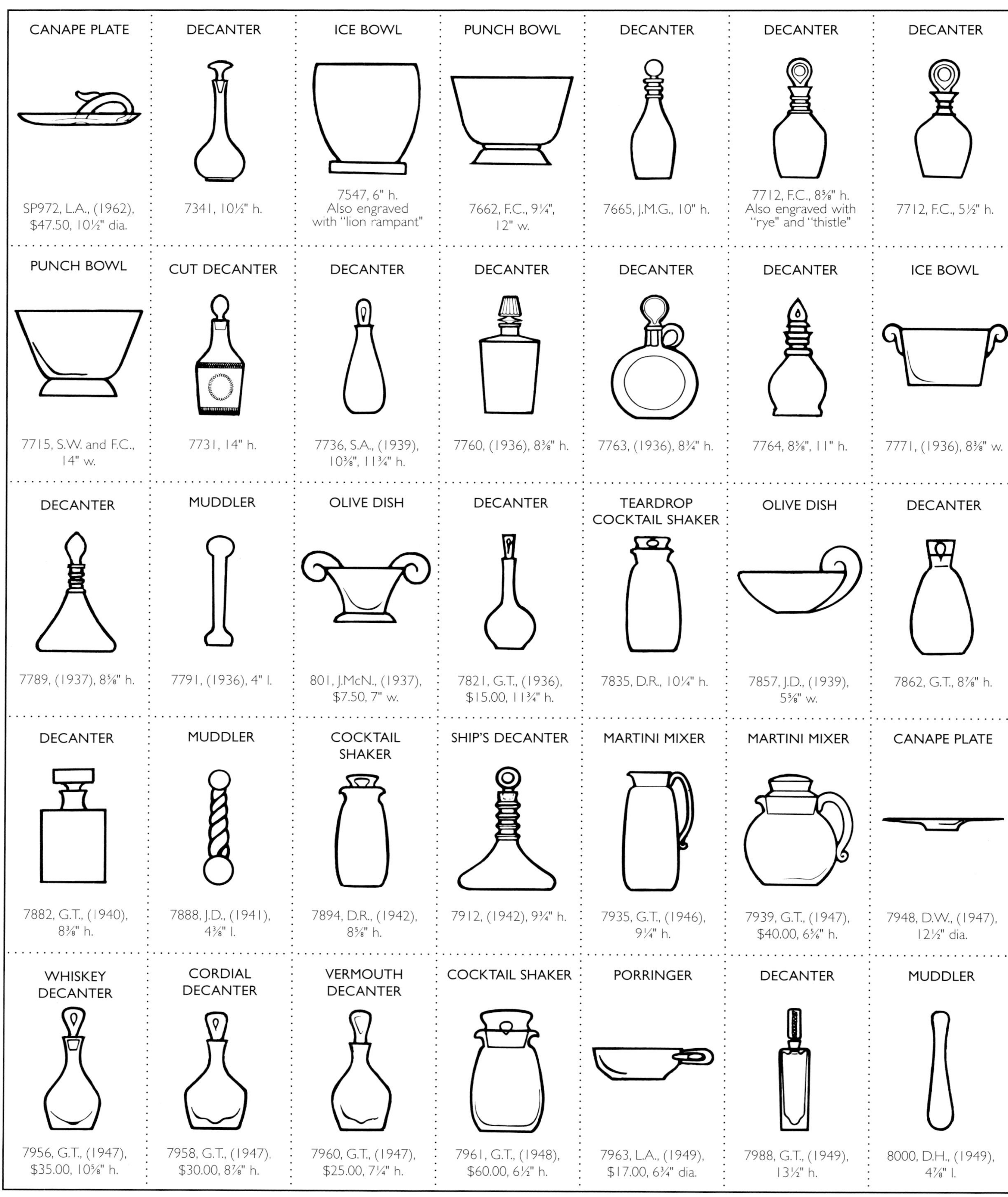
CANAPE PLATE
SP972, L.A., (1962), $47.50, 10½" dia.
DECANTER
7341, 10½" h.
ICE BOWL
7547, 6" h. Also engraved with "lion rampant"
PUNCH BOWL
7662, F.C., 9¼", 12" w.
DECANTER
7665, J.M.G., 10" h.
DECANTER
7712, F.C., 8⅝" h. Also engraved with "rye" and "thistle"
DECANTER
7712, F.C., 5½" h.
PUNCH BOWL
7715, S.W. and F.C., 14" w.
CUT DECANTER
7731, 14" h.
DECANTER
7736, S.A., (1939), 10⅜", 11¾" h.
DECANTER
7760, (1936), 8⅜" h.
DECANTER
7763, (1936), 8¾" h.
DECANTER
7764, 8⅝", 11" h.
ICE BOWL
7771, (1936), 8⅜" w.
DECANTER
7789, (1937), 8⅝" h.
MUDDLER
7791, (1936), 4" l.
OLIVE DISH
801, J.McN., (1937), $7.50, 7" w.
DECANTER
7821, G.T., (1936), $15.00, 11¾" h.
TEARDROP COCKTAIL SHAKER
7835, D.R., 10¼" h.
OLIVE DISH
7857, J.D., (1939), 5⅝" w.
DECANTER
7862, G.T., 8⅞" h.
DECANTER
7882, G.T., (1940), 8⅜" h.
MUDDLER
7888, J.D., (1941), 4⅜" l.
COCKTAIL SHAKER
7894, D.R., (1942), 8⅝" h.
SHIP'S DECANTER
7912, (1942), 9¾" h.
MARTINI MIXER
7935, G.T., (1946), 9¼" h.
MARTINI MIXER
7939, G.T., (1947), $40.00, 6⅝" h.
CANAPE PLATE
7948, D.W., (1947), 12½" dia.
WHISKEY DECANTER
7956, G.T., (1947), $35.00, 10⅝" h.
CORDIAL DECANTER
7958, G.T., (1947), $30.00, 8⅞" h.
VERMOUTH DECANTER
7960, G.T., (1947), $25.00, 7¼" h.
COCKTAIL SHAKER
7961, G.T., (1948), $60.00, 6½" h.
PORRINGER
7963, L.A., (1949), $17.00, 6¾" dia.
DECANTER
7988, G.T., (1949), 13½" h.
MUDDLER
8000, D.H., (1949), 4⅞" l.

COCKTAIL MIXER	LIQUEUR DECANTER	SCROLL PLATE	LIQUEUR DECANTER	SERVING DISH	CANAPE PLATE	SERVING DISH
8006, D.H., (1950), $25.00, 7⅜" h.	8015, G.T., (1950), $40.00, 9⅛" h.	8025, G.T., (1952), $25.00, 8⅝" dia.	8043, D.P., (1953), $45.00, 11¼" h.	8044, L.A., (1953), $25.00, 7¾" w.	8045, L.A., (1953), $35.00, 10½" dia.	8053, D.P., (1953), $30.00, 9⅛" w.
SERVING DISH	COCKTAIL MIXER	PUNCH BOWL	CANAPE PLATE	EAGLE DECANTER	SERVING DISH	NUT BOWL
8092, L.A., (1958), $25.00, 8¼" w.	8093, G.T., (1959), $30.00, 9" h.	8116, D.P., (1957), $150.00, 12" dia.	8233, P.Schu., (1968), $80.00, 14" dia.	8276, L.A., (1973), $350.00, 10½" h.	8343, B.X.W., (1976), $97.50, 8⅝" dia.	8345, B.X.W., (1976), $70.00, 6¹¹⁄₁₆" dia.
NIMBUS DISH	CANAPE PLATE	CARAFE	DECANTER	STARDUST DECANTER	WHIRLWIND PLATTER	WHIRLWIND CYLINDRICAL CARAFE
8392, P.Schu., (1980), $235.00, 7" w.	8398, L.A., (1980), $265.00, 10¾" dia.	8427, D.P., (1980), 8½" h.	8534, P.Schu., (1986), $950, 10" h.	8580, D.D., (1989), $725, 9½" h.	8718, M.V., (1993), $275, 11½" dia.	8719, M.V., (1993), $250, 7½" h.
WHIRLWIND ROUND CARAFE						
8720, M.V., (1993), $200, 7½" h.						

SMOKING ACCESSORIES

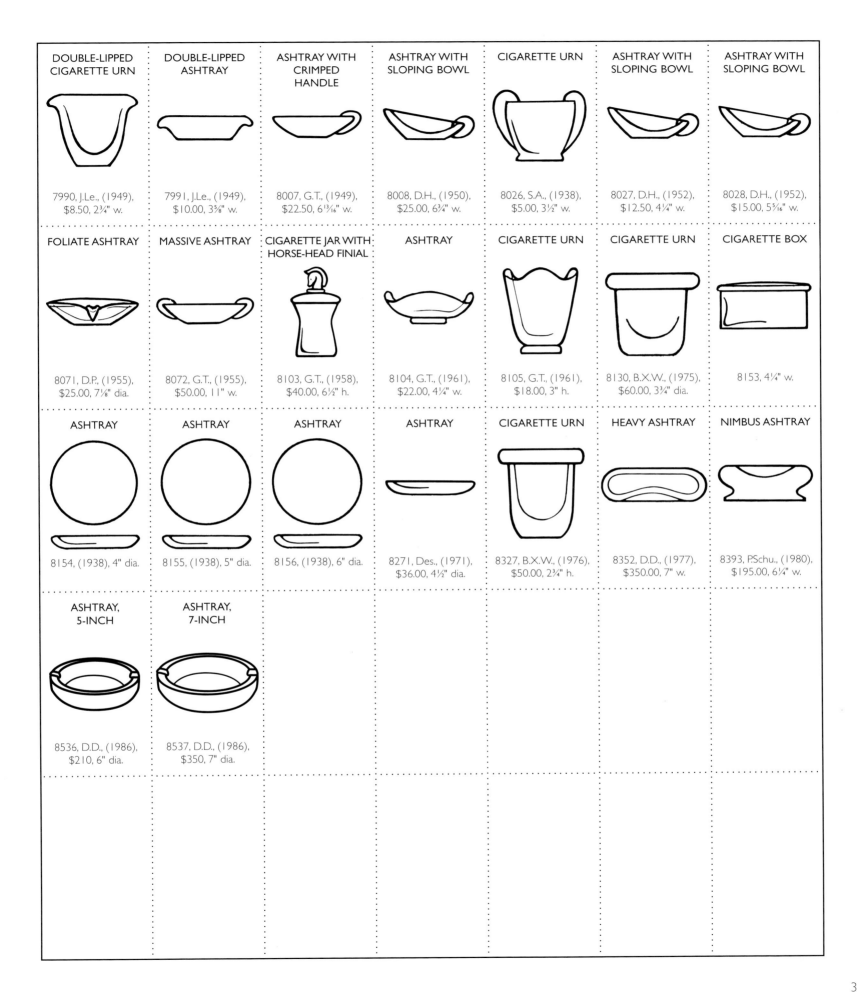

DOUBLE-LIPPED CIGARETTE URN	DOUBLE-LIPPED ASHTRAY	ASHTRAY WITH CRIMPED HANDLE	ASHTRAY WITH SLOPING BOWL	CIGARETTE URN	ASHTRAY WITH SLOPING BOWL	ASHTRAY WITH SLOPING BOWL
7990, J.Le., (1949), $8.50, 2¾" w.	7991, J.Le., (1949), $10.00, 3⅝" w.	8007, G.T., (1949), $22.50, 6$^{13}/_{16}$" w.	8008, D.H., (1950), $25.00, 6¾" w.	8026, S.A., (1938), $5.00, 3½" w.	8027, D.H., (1952), $12.50, 4¼" w.	8028, D.H., (1952), $15.00, 5$^{5}/_{16}$" w.
FOLIATE ASHTRAY	MASSIVE ASHTRAY	CIGARETTE JAR WITH HORSE-HEAD FINIAL	ASHTRAY	CIGARETTE URN	CIGARETTE URN	CIGARETTE BOX
8071, D.P., (1955), $25.00, 7⅛" dia.	8072, G.T., (1955), $50.00, 11" w.	8103, G.T., (1958), $40.00, 6½" h.	8104, G.T., (1961), $22.00, 4¼" w.	8105, G.T., (1961), $18.00, 3" h.	8130, B.X.W., (1975), $60.00, 3¾" dia.	8153, 4¼" w.
ASHTRAY	ASHTRAY	ASHTRAY	ASHTRAY	CIGARETTE URN	HEAVY ASHTRAY	NIMBUS ASHTRAY
8154, (1938), 4" dia.	8155, (1938), 5" dia.	8156, (1938), 6" dia.	8271, Des., (1971), $36.00, 4½" dia.	8327, B.X.W., (1976), $50.00, 2¾" h.	8352, D.D., (1977), $350.00, 7" w.	8393, P.Schu., (1980), $195.00, 6¼" w.
ASHTRAY, 5-INCH	ASHTRAY, 7-INCH					
8536, D.D., (1986), $210, 6" dia.	8537, D.D., (1986), $350, 7" dia.					

ORNAMENTALS

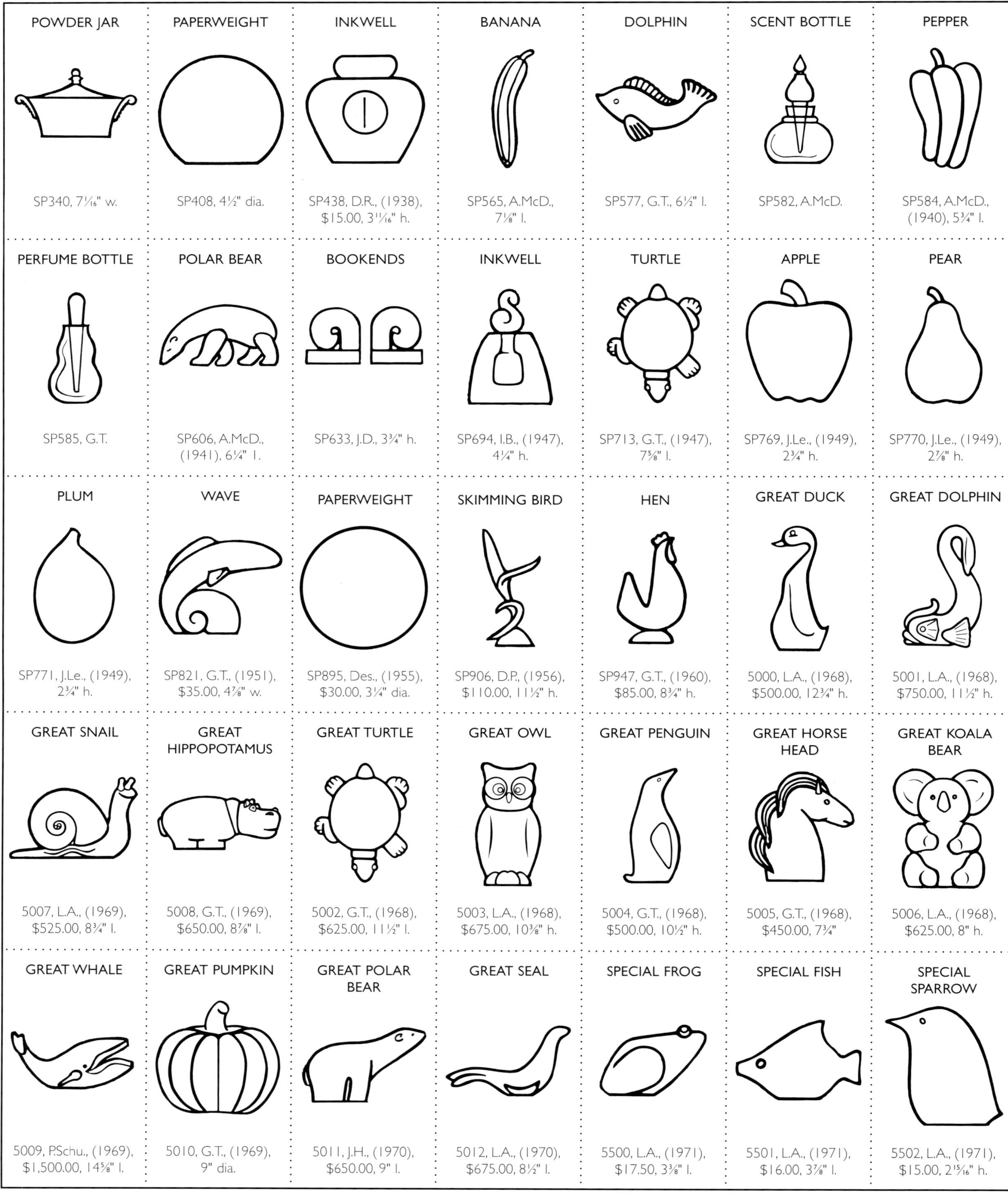

SPECIAL PIG	SPECIAL MOUSE	SPECIAL TURTLE	SPECIAL SNAIL	SPECIAL OWL	EAGLE	PHEASANT
5503, L.A., (1971), $18.50	5504, L.A., (1971), $16.00, 3⅛" l.	5505, L.A., (1971), $16.00	5507, L.A., (1972), $34.00, 3" l.	5508, L.A., (1972), $21.00, 2¾" h.	6502, F.C.	6504, B.M. and F.C., (1932), 11½" l.
MUSHROOM	PAPERWEIGHT	PIGEON	GAZELLE	BOOKEND	FISH	SAINT THERESA
6662, 4⅝" dia.	6821, F.C., 4½" h.	6824, F.C., 6⅝" l.	7399, S.W. and F.C., 7⅛" l.	7641, W.D.T. and F.C., (1934), 4½" h.	7698, S.W. and F.C., 10½" h.	7720, 5⅞", 8⅛" h.
HORSE	BEAR	POUTER PIGEON	HORSE HEAD	ELEPHANT	INKWELL	FISH
7727, S.W., 9¼" l.	7728, S.W., 8¾" l.	7729, S.W., 7¼" h.	7779, S.W., (1937), 5" h.	7780, (1937), 5⅛" l.	7782, 4¾" dia.	7790, (1937), 6" l.
INKWELL	DOLPHIN BOOKEND	PERFUME BOTTLE	ROOSTER	LOTION BOTTLE	BICARBONATE BOTTLE	POWDER BOX
7814, W.H., (1938), $15.00, 5¼" h.	7827, S.A., (1939), 7½" h.	7838, G.T., (1939), $18.00, 6¾" h.	7847, 8½" h.	7851, G.T.	7852, G.T., 5½" h.	7853, G.T.
PEAR	APPLE	GRAPES	FIG	SWIMMING DOLPHIN	LEAPING DOLPHIN	INKWELL
7873, A.McD., 4¾" h.	7874, A.McD., 4" h.	7875, A.McD., 6½" l.	7876, A.McD., 3¼" h.	7879, G.T., (1940), 6⅞" l.	7880, G.T., (1940), 5¾" h.	7885, A.McD., (1941), 4⅜" h.

ELEPHANT
7896, J.D., (1941), 6 3/8" l.
POWDER JAR
7903, G.T., (1941), 5 1/8" dia.
RABBIT
7911, J.D., (1942), 3 7/8" l.
PERFUME BOTTLE
7918, G.T. and J.B., 3 3/4" h.
POWDER JAR
7919, G.T. and J.B., 3 1/4" dia.
BOOKEND
7920, G.T., 5 7/8" h.
TOASTING GOBLET
7927, A.A.H., 17 3/4" h.
SNAIL
7984, G.T., (1949), $25.00, 3 5/8" dia.
PAPERWEIGHT
7984, G.T., (1949), $25.00, 3 5/8" dia.
GRAPES
7992, J.Le., (1949), 3 5/8" l.
BANANA
7993, J.Le., (1949), 6 1/8" l.
POWDER JAR
7998, J.Le., (1949), $40.00, 4 13/16" h.
PERFUME BOTTLE
7999, J.D., (1949), $36.00, 5 3/4" h.
DUCK
8009, L.A., (1950), $30.00, 4 1/2" l.
FISH
8016, G.T., (1950), $25.00, 4 1/2" l.
TOASTING GOBLET
8018, D.H., (1950), $35.00, 12" h.
PAPERWEIGHT
8029, G.T., (1952), $25.00, 3 1/8" h.
PERFUME BOTTLE
8046, G.T., (1952), $40.00, 6 7/8" h.
SEA SPRITE
8047, G.T., (1952), $90.00, 8 5/8" h.
READING GLASS
8048, G.T., (1952), 4 1/16" l.
OWL
8065, D.P., (1955), $45.00, 5 1/8" h.
KITTEN
8073, L.A., (1955), $35.00, 4 1/8" l.
ROOSTER
8074, D.P., (1955), $75.00, 10" h.
WHALE
8075, L.A., (1956), $37.50, 5" l.
STAR CRYSTAL
8076, D.P., (1956), $40.00, 5" w.
PENGUIN
8080, G.T., (1957), $40.00, 6 3/8" h.
WATERBIRD
8095, L.A., (1959), $120.00, 9 7/8" l.
CAT
8102, D.P., (1960), $90.00, 8 3/4" h.
ELEPHANT
8106, G.T., (1960), $80.00, 5" l.
FISH
8107, G.T., (1961), $65.00, 6 7/8" l.
SEA HORSE
8108, L.A., (1961), $100.00, 9 1/4" h.
FROG
8109, L.A., (1961), $50.00, 4 3/8" l.
SONGBIRD
8112, G.T., (1963), $45.00, 4 1/2" l.
PERFUME BOTTLE
8117, L.A., (1956), $50.00, 6 7/8" h.
SEAL
8118, G.T., (1962), $80.00, 8 3/4" l.

GIRAFFE	SQUIRREL	PORPOISE (SMALL)	PORPOISE (MEDIUM)	PORPOISE (LARGE)	ELEPHANT (TRUMPETING)	DUCKLING
8119, L.A., (1963), $135.00, 14½" h.	8120, L.A., (1963), $75.00, 5" l.	8125, L.A., (1964), $60.00, 6⅛" l.	8126, L.A., (1964), $95.00, 9¼" l.	8127, L.A., (1964), $160.00, 12⅛" l.	8128, J.H., (1964), $110.00, 7½" h.	8129, L.A., (1964), $75.00, 8" h.
EAGLE	EGG	HORSE HEAD	DINOSAUR	PHOENIX	DONKEY	CROWN
8130, J.H., (1964), $140.00, 12" w.	8131, L.A., (1964), $65.00, 4¼" h.	8132, G.T., (1964), $55.00, 4" h.	8135, J.H., (1964), $185.00, 12¾" l.	8136, L.A., (1965), $175.00, 12¾" h.	8137, L.A., (1965), $110.00, 10⅝" h.	8138, L.A., (1965), $60.00, 3⅞" h.
PIG	CHICK	PINEAPPLE	FLYING BIRD	SWAN	SEA LION	COTTONTAIL
8145, P.Schu., (1964), $55.00, 3⅝" l.	8146, P.Schu., (1964), $45.00, 3⅞" h.	8147, L.A., (1965), $70.00, 7⅛" h.	8148, L.A., (1965), $150.00, 11⅞" w.	8149, J.H., (1965), $115.00, 8" w.	8150, J.H., (1965), $110.00, 7¾" h.	8151, D.P., (1965), $75.00, 5⅜" l.
PELICAN	ALLIGATOR	TROPICAL FISH	STARFISH	MOUSE	PHEASANT	CATERPILLAR
8222, L.A., (1968), $125.00, 6⅞" l.	8225, J.H., (1968), $160.00, 10" l.	8236, L.A., (1968), $165.00, 8⅛" h.	8237, P.Schu., (1968), $130.00, 10¼" w.	8242, L.A., (1970), $70.00, 3⅓" l.	8243, L.A., (1970), $335.00, 15¼" l.	8244, P.Y., (1970), $225.00, 11" l.
LOVE	DOVE (SMALL)	DOVE (MEDIUM)	DOVE (LARGE)	CHICKADEE (SHORT)	CHICKADEE (MEDIUM)	CHICKADEE (TALL)
8253, K.D.S., (1971), $95.00, 4¼" h.	8254, P.Y., (1971), $130.00, 7⅛" l.	8255, P.Y., (1971), $150.00, 8" l.	8256, P.Y., (1971), $170.00, 8¾" l.	8257, P.Y., (1971), $150.00, 5¼" h.	8258, P.Y., (1971), $150.00	8259, P.Y., (1971), $150.00

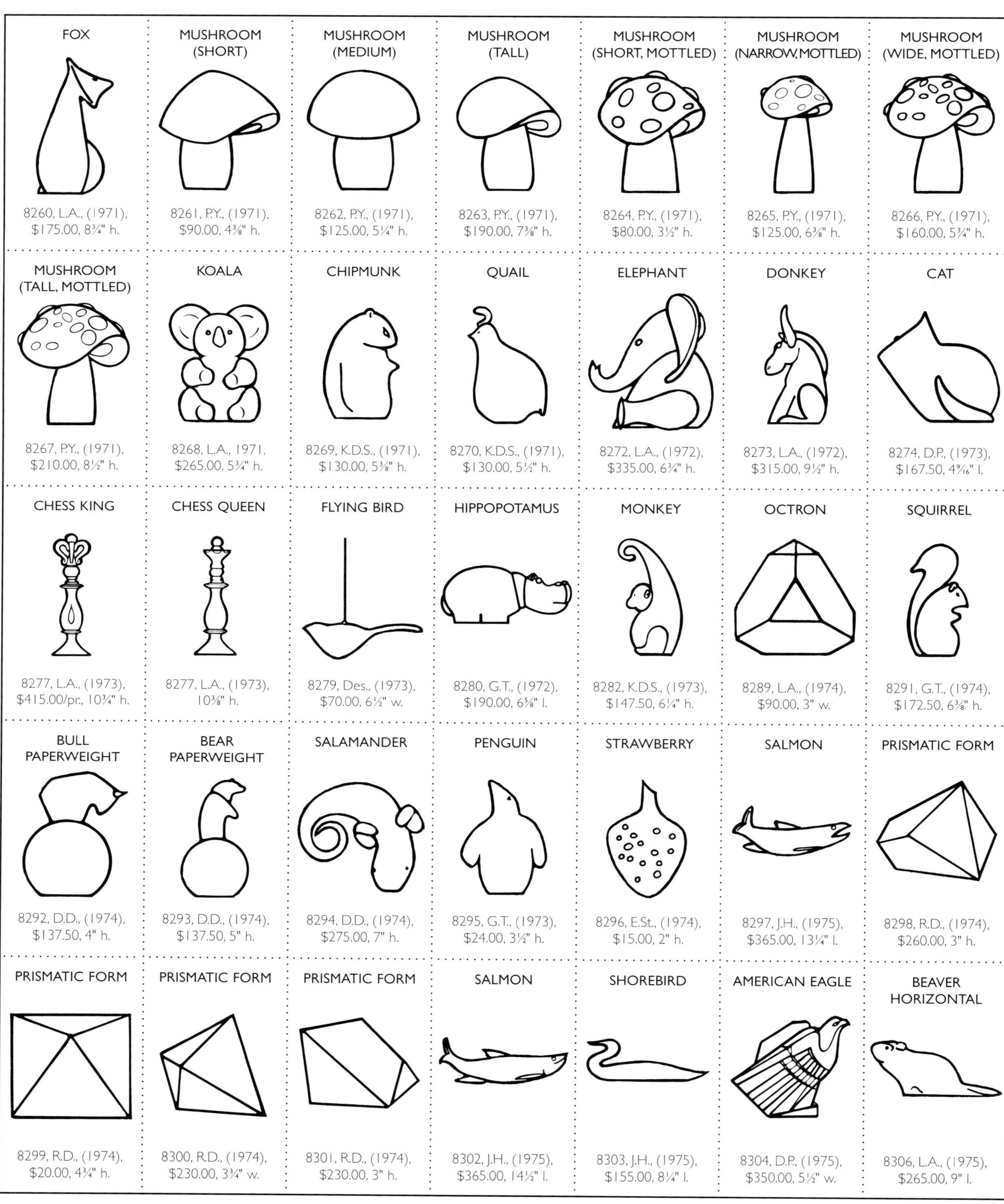
FOX
8260, L.A., (1971), $175.00, 8¾" h.
MUSHROOM (SHORT)
8261, P.Y., (1971), $90.00, 4⅜" h.
MUSHROOM (MEDIUM)
8262, P.Y., (1971), $125.00, 5¼" h.
MUSHROOM (TALL)
8263, P.Y., (1971), $190.00, 7⅜" h.
MUSHROOM (SHORT, MOTTLED)
8264, P.Y., (1971), $80.00, 3½" h.
MUSHROOM (NARROW, MOTTLED)
8265, P.Y., (1971), $125.00, 6⅜" h.
MUSHROOM (WIDE, MOTTLED)
8266, P.Y., (1971), $160.00, 5¾" h.
MUSHROOM (TALL, MOTTLED)
8267, P.Y., (1971), $210.00, 8½" h.
KOALA
8268, L.A., 1971, $265.00, 5¾" h.
CHIPMUNK
8269, K.D.S., (1971), $130.00, 5⅜" h.
QUAIL
8270, K.D.S., (1971), $130.00, 5½" h.
ELEPHANT
8272, L.A., (1972), $335.00, 6¾" h.
DONKEY
8273, L.A., (1972), $315.00, 9½" h.
CAT
8274, D.P., (1973), $167.50, 4 9/16" l.
CHESS KING
8277, L.A., (1973), $415.00/pr., 10¾" h.
CHESS QUEEN
8277, L.A., (1973), 10⅜" h.
FLYING BIRD
8279, Des., (1973), $70.00, 6½" w.
HIPPOPOTAMUS
8280, G.T., (1972), $190.00, 6⅝" l.
MONKEY
8282, K.D.S., (1973), $147.50, 6¼" h.
OCTRON
8289, L.A., (1974), $90.00, 3" w.
SQUIRREL
8291, G.T., (1974), $172.50, 6⅜" h.
BULL PAPERWEIGHT
8292, D.D., (1974), $137.50, 4" h.
BEAR PAPERWEIGHT
8293, D.D., (1974), $137.50, 5" h.
SALAMANDER
8294, D.D., (1974), $275.00, 7" h.
PENGUIN
8295, G.T., (1973), $24.00, 3½" h.
STRAWBERRY
8296, E.St., (1974), $15.00, 2" h.
SALMON
8297, J.H., (1975), $365.00, 13¼" l.
PRISMATIC FORM
8298, R.D., (1974), $260.00, 3" h.
PRISMATIC FORM
8299, R.D., (1974), $20.00, 4¾" h.
PRISMATIC FORM
8300, R.D., (1974), $230.00, 3¾" w.
PRISMATIC FORM
8301, R.D., (1974), $230.00, 3" h.
SALMON
8302, J.H., (1975), $365.00, 14½" l.
SHOREBIRD
8303, J.H., (1975), $155.00, 8¼" l.
AMERICAN EAGLE
8304, D.P., (1975), $350.00, 5½" w.
BEAVER HORIZONTAL
8306, L.A., (1975), $265.00, 9" l.

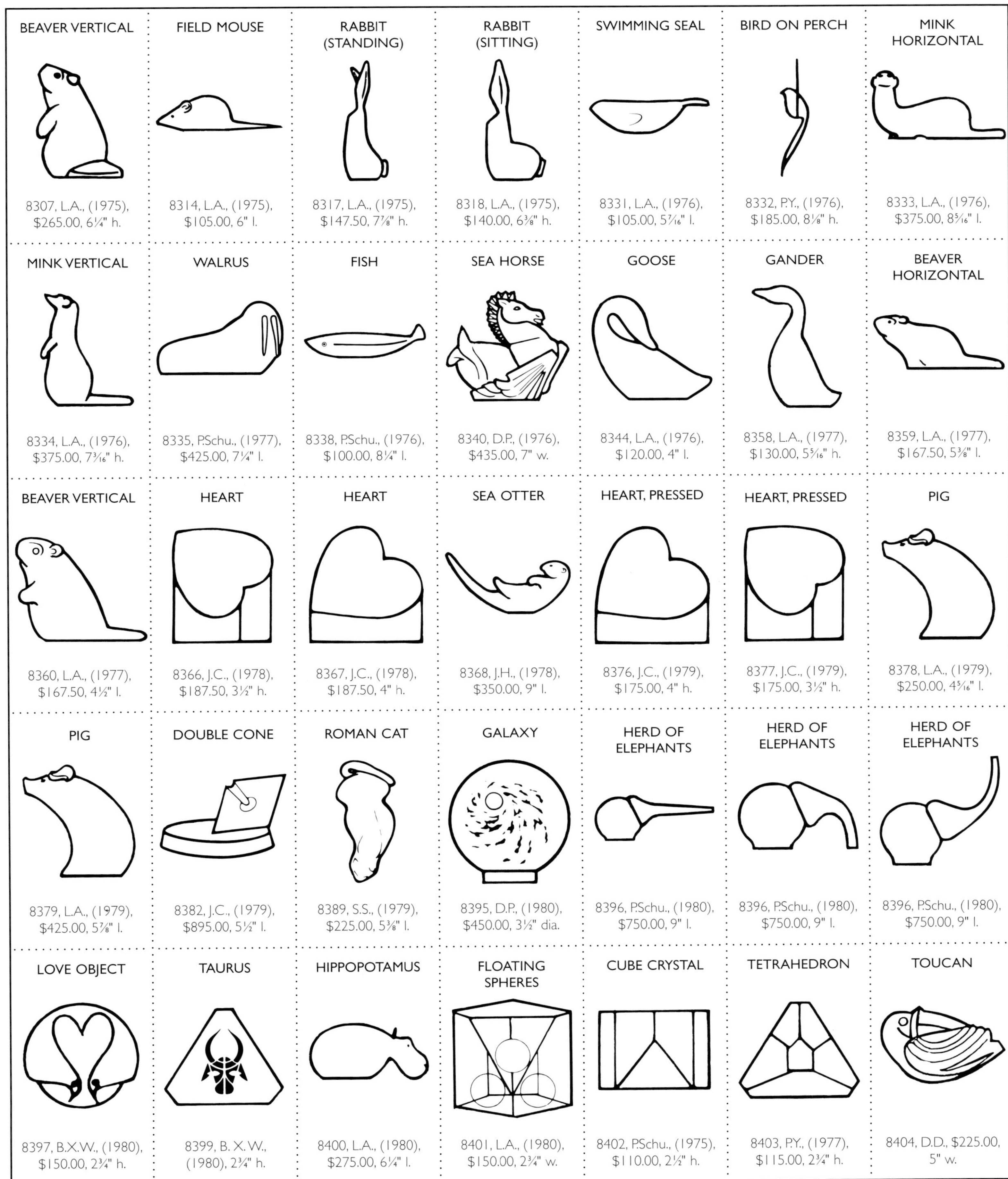
BEAVER VERTICAL
8307, L.A., (1975), $265.00, 6¼" h.
FIELD MOUSE
8314, L.A., (1975), $105.00, 6" l.
RABBIT (STANDING)
8317, L.A., (1975), $147.50, 7⅞" h.
RABBIT (SITTING)
8318, L.A., (1975), $140.00, 6⅜" h.
SWIMMING SEAL
8331, L.A., (1976), $105.00, 5 7/16" l.
BIRD ON PERCH
8332, P.Y., (1976), $185.00, 8⅛" h.
MINK HORIZONTAL
8333, L.A., (1976), $375.00, 8 5/16" l.
MINK VERTICAL
8334, L.A., (1976), $375.00, 7 3/16" h.
WALRUS
8335, P.Schu., (1977), $425.00, 7¼" l.
FISH
8338, P.Schu., (1976), $100.00, 8¼" l.
SEA HORSE
8340, D.P., (1976), $435.00, 7" w.
GOOSE
8344, L.A., (1976), $120.00, 4" l.
GANDER
8358, L.A., (1977), $130.00, 5 5/16" h.
BEAVER HORIZONTAL
8359, L.A., (1977), $167.50, 5⅜" l.
BEAVER VERTICAL
8360, L.A., (1977), $167.50, 4½" l.
HEART
8366, J.C., (1978), $187.50, 3½" h.
HEART
8367, J.C., (1978), $187.50, 4" h.
SEA OTTER
8368, J.H., (1978), $350.00, 9" l.
HEART, PRESSED
8376, J.C., (1979), $175.00, 4" h.
HEART, PRESSED
8377, J.C., (1979), $175.00, 3½" h.
PIG
8378, L.A., (1979), $250.00, 4 5/16" l.
PIG
8379, L.A., (1979), $425.00, 5⅞" l.
DOUBLE CONE
8382, J.C., (1979), $895.00, 5½" l.
ROMAN CAT
8389, S.S., (1979), $225.00, 5⅜" l.
GALAXY
8395, D.P., (1980), $450.00, 3½" dia.
HERD OF ELEPHANTS
8396, P.Schu., (1980), $750.00, 9" l.
HERD OF ELEPHANTS
8396, P.Schu., (1980), $750.00, 9" l.
HERD OF ELEPHANTS
8396, P.Schu., (1980), $750.00, 9" l.
LOVE OBJECT
8397, B.X.W., (1980), $150.00, 2¾" h.
TAURUS
8399, B. X. W., (1980), 2¾" h.
HIPPOPOTAMUS
8400, L.A., (1980), $275.00, 6¼" l.
FLOATING SPHERES
8401, L.A., (1980), $150.00, 2¾" w.
CUBE CRYSTAL
8402, P.Schu., (1975), $110.00, 2½" h.
TETRAHEDRON
8403, P.Y., (1977), $115.00, 2¾" h.
TOUCAN
8404, D.D., $225.00, 5" w.

ARMADILLO
8405, D.D., $225.00, 5⅛" w.
ABALONE
8406, D.D., $195.00, 3⅝" w.
ODALISQUE
8407, S.S., $235.00, 4¼" w.
ROSE
8408, S.S., $195.00, 4½" w.
STARFISH
8409, D.D., $225.00, 3¼" w.
GEMINI
8410, B.X.W., (1980), 2¾" w.
CANCER
8411, B.X.W., (1981), 2¾" w.
PYRAMID BLOCK
8413, L.A., $225.00, 3½" w.
LEO
8414, (1981), $195.00, 2¾" w.
VIRGO
8415, (1981), $195.00, 2¾" w.
LIBRA
8416, (1981), $195.00, 2¾" w.
SCORPIO
8417, (1981), $195.00, 2¾" w.
SAGITTARIUS
8418, (1981), $195.00, 2¾" w.
CAPRICORN
8419, (1981), $195.00, 2¾" w.
AQUARIUS
8420, (1981), $195.00, 2¾" w.
PISCES
8421, (1981), $195.00, 2¾" w.
ARIES
8422, (1981), $195.00, 2¾" w.
WILD DOVE
8426, B.X.W., (1981), 8⅝" w.
QUIDDITY
8428, C.J. and P.Y., (1981), 2¾" h.
DRAGON
8429, B.X.W., (1981), 7½" l.
GAZING CRYSTAL
8430, P.A., (1981), 4½" h.
ROTATION
8431, D.D., (1981), 3¼" l.
TUNNELS
8432, P.Schu., (1981), 2½" h.
ILLUSIONS
8433, L.A., (1981), 2½" h.
UNION JACK
8434, B.X.W., (1981), $250, 2¾" h.
SPRING CHICKEN
8435, D.P., (1982) $395, 6" w.
CROCUS
8436, P.Y. & P.W., (1982), $295, 2¾" h.
LILY
8437, P.Y. & P.W., (1982), $295, 2¾" h.
GENTIAN
8438, P.Y. & P.W., (1982), $295, 2¾" h.
DAFFODIL
8439, P.Y. & P.W., (1982), $295, 2¾" h.
A–Z ALPHABET CRYSTAL
8440–8465, P.Schu. & A.K., (1982), $275, 2½" h.
BROOK TROUT (STRAIGHT TAIL)
8466, J.H., (1982), $575
BROOK TROUT (CURVED TAIL)
8467, J.H., (1982), $575
FOX
8470, L.A., (1983), $495, 5½" h.
OLD GLORY
8474, P.Y. & B.W., (1983), $225, 2¾" h.

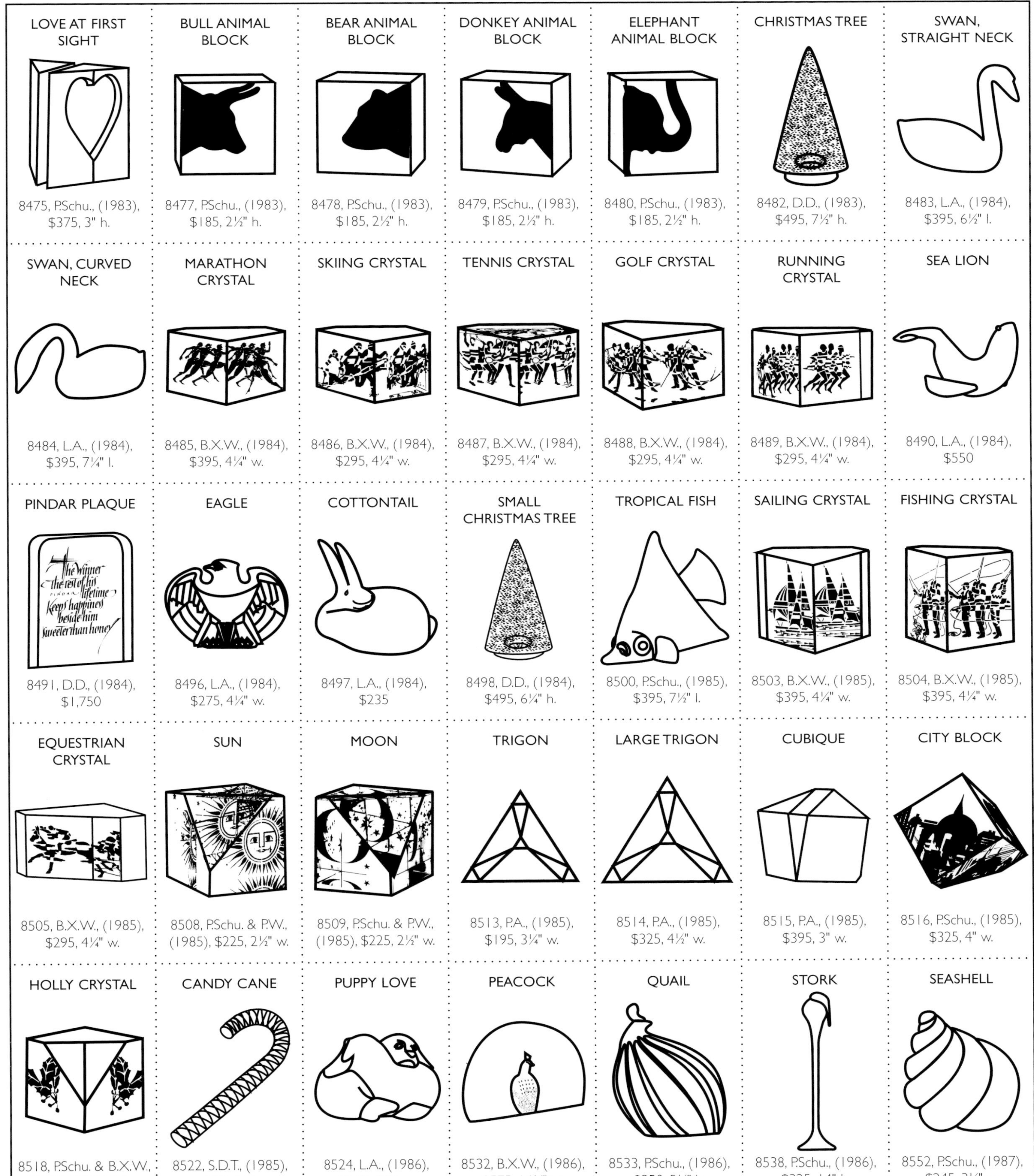
LOVE AT FIRST SIGHT
8475, P.Schu., (1983), $375, 3" h.
BULL ANIMAL BLOCK
8477, P.Schu., (1983), $185, 2½" h.
BEAR ANIMAL BLOCK
8478, P.Schu., (1983), $185, 2½" h.
DONKEY ANIMAL BLOCK
8479, P.Schu., (1983), $185, 2½" h.
ELEPHANT ANIMAL BLOCK
8480, P.Schu., (1983), $185, 2½" h.
CHRISTMAS TREE
8482, D.D., (1983), $495, 7½" h.
SWAN, STRAIGHT NECK
8483, L.A., (1984), $395, 6½" l.
SWAN, CURVED NECK
8484, L.A., (1984), $395, 7¼" l.
MARATHON CRYSTAL
8485, B.X.W., (1984), $395, 4¼" w.
SKIING CRYSTAL
8486, B.X.W., (1984), $295, 4¼" w.
TENNIS CRYSTAL
8487, B.X.W., (1984), $295, 4¼" w.
GOLF CRYSTAL
8488, B.X.W., (1984), $295, 4¼" w.
RUNNING CRYSTAL
8489, B.X.W., (1984), $295, 4¼" w.
SEA LION
8490, L.A., (1984), $550
PINDAR PLAQUE
The Winner the rest of his lifetime Keeps happiness beside him sweeter than honey
PINDAR
8491, D.D., (1984), $1,750
EAGLE
8496, L.A., (1984), $275, 4¼" w.
COTTONTAIL
8497, L.A., (1984), $235
SMALL CHRISTMAS TREE
8498, D.D., (1984), $495, 6¼" h.
TROPICAL FISH
8500, P.Schu., (1985), $395, 7½" l.
SAILING CRYSTAL
8503, B.X.W., (1985), $395, 4¼" w.
FISHING CRYSTAL
8504, B.X.W., (1985), $395, 4¼" w.
EQUESTRIAN CRYSTAL
8505, B.X.W., (1985), $295, 4¼" w.
SUN
8508, P.Schu. & P.W., (1985), $225, 2½" w.
MOON
8509, P.Schu. & P.W., (1985), $225, 2½" w.
TRIGON
8513, P.A., (1985), $195, 3¼" w.
LARGE TRIGON
8514, P.A., (1985), $325, 4½" w.
CUBIQUE
8515, P.A., (1985), $395, 3" w.
CITY BLOCK
8516, P.Schu., (1985), $325, 4" w.
HOLLY CRYSTAL
8518, P.Schu. & B.X.W., (1985), $250, 2½" w.
CANDY CANE
8522, S.D.T., (1985), $50, 6" l.
PUPPY LOVE
8524, L.A., (1986), $150, 2¾" w.
PEACOCK
8532, B.X.W., (1986), $575, 14½" w.
QUAIL
8533, P.Schu., (1986), $350, 5½" h.
STORK
8538, P.Schu., (1986), $325, 14" h.
SEASHELL
8552, P.Schu., (1987), $245, 3½" w.

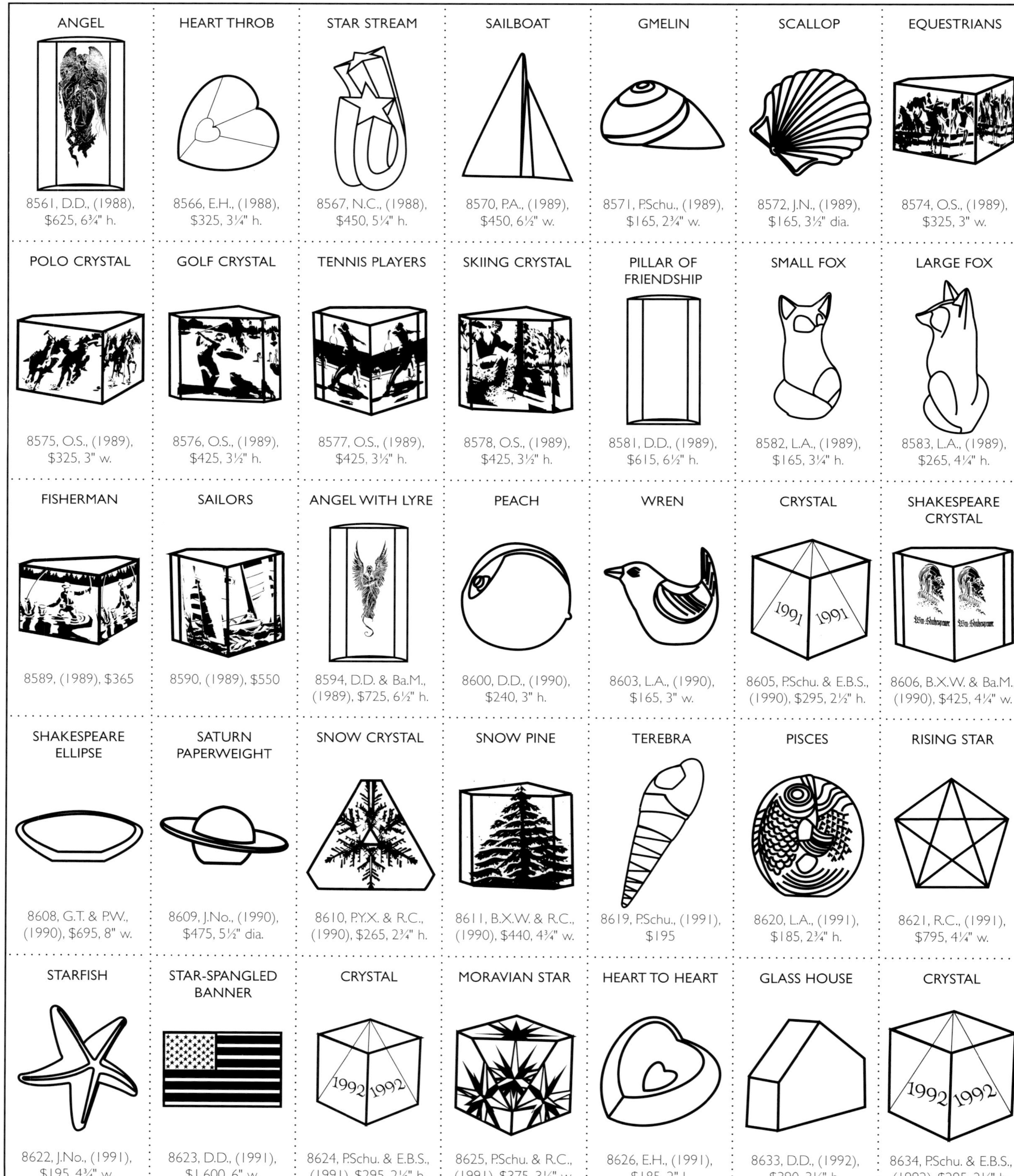
ANGEL
8561, D.D., (1988), $625, 6¾" h.
HEART THROB
8566, E.H., (1988), $325, 3¼" h.
STAR STREAM
8567, N.C., (1988), $450, 5¼" h.
SAILBOAT
8570, P.A., (1989), $450, 6½" w.
GMELIN
8571, P.Schu., (1989), $165, 2¾" w.
SCALLOP
8572, J.N., (1989), $165, 3½" dia.
EQUESTRIANS
8574, O.S., (1989), $325, 3" w.
POLO CRYSTAL
8575, O.S., (1989), $325, 3" w.
GOLF CRYSTAL
8576, O.S., (1989), $425, 3½" h.
TENNIS PLAYERS
8577, O.S., (1989), $425, 3½" h.
SKIING CRYSTAL
8578, O.S., (1989), $425, 3½" h.
PILLAR OF FRIENDSHIP
8581, D.D., (1989), $615, 6½" h.
SMALL FOX
8582, L.A., (1989), $165, 3¼" h.
LARGE FOX
8583, L.A., (1989), $265, 4¼" h.
FISHERMAN
8589, (1989), $365
SAILORS
8590, (1989), $550
ANGEL WITH LYRE
8594, D.D & Ba.M., (1989), $725, 6½" h.
PEACH
8600, D.D., (1990), $240, 3" h.
WREN
8603, L.A., (1990), $165, 3" w.
CRYSTAL
1991 1991
8605, P.Schu. & E.B.S., (1990), $295, 2½" h.
SHAKESPEARE CRYSTAL
8606, B.X.W. & Ba.M., (1990), $425, 4¼" w.
SHAKESPEARE ELLIPSE
8608, G.T. & P.W., (1990), $695, 8" w.
SATURN PAPERWEIGHT
8609, J.No., (1990), $475, 5½" dia.
SNOW CRYSTAL
8610, P.Y.X. & R.C., (1990), $265, 2¾" h.
SNOW PINE
8611, B.X.W. & R.C., (1990), $440, 4¾" w.
TEREBRA
8619, P.Schu., (1991), $195
PISCES
8620, L.A., (1991), $185, 2¾" h.
RISING STAR
8621, R.C., (1991), $795, 4¼" w.
STARFISH
8622, J.No., (1991), $195, 4¾" w.
STAR-SPANGLED BANNER
8623, D.D., (1991), $1,600, 6" w.
CRYSTAL
1992 1992
8624, P.Schu. & E.B.S., (1991), $295, 2½" h.
MORAVIAN STAR
8625, P.Schu. & R.C., (1991), $375, 3½" w.
HEART TO HEART
8626, E.H., (1991), $185, 2" l.
GLASS HOUSE
8633, D.D., (1992), $390, 3½" h.
CRYSTAL
1992 1992
8634, P.Schu. & E.B.S., (1992), $295, 2½" h.

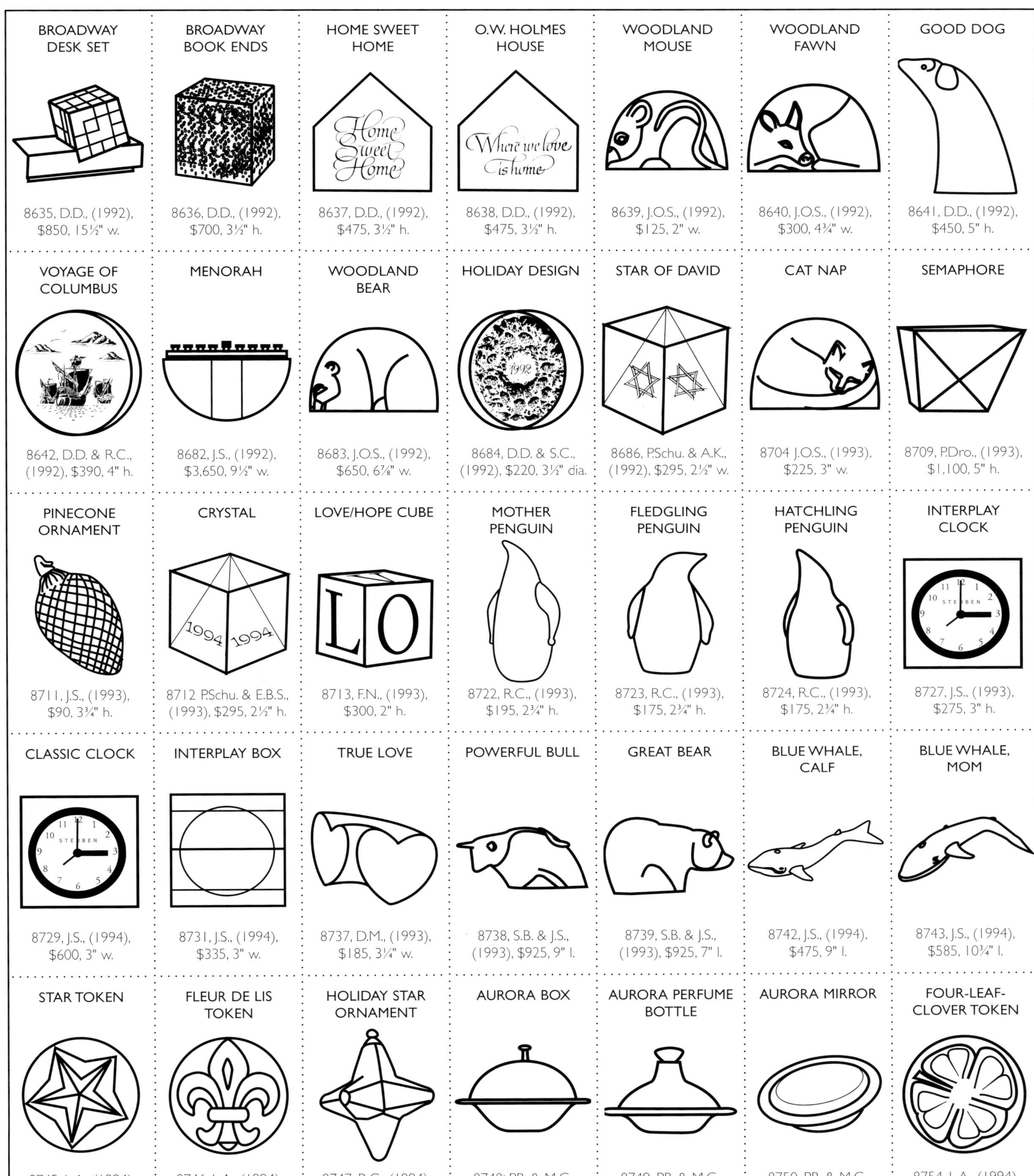
BROADWAY DESK SET
8635, D.D., (1992), $850, 15½" w.
BROADWAY BOOK ENDS
8636, D.D., (1992), $700, 3½" h.
HOME SWEET HOME
Home Sweet Home
8637, D.D., (1992), $475, 3½" h.
O.W. HOLMES HOUSE
Where we love is home
8638, D.D., (1992), $475, 3½" h.
WOODLAND MOUSE
8639, J.O.S., (1992), $125, 2" w.
WOODLAND FAWN
8640, J.O.S., (1992), $300, 4¾" w.
GOOD DOG
8641, D.D., (1992), $450, 5" h.
VOYAGE OF COLUMBUS
8642, D.D. & R.C., (1992), $390, 4" h.
MENORAH
8682, J.S., (1992), $3,650, 9½" w.
WOODLAND BEAR
8683, J.O.S., (1992), $650, 6⅞" w.
HOLIDAY DESIGN
1992
8684, D.D. & S.C., (1992), $220, 3½" dia.
STAR OF DAVID
8686, P.Schu. & A.K., (1992), $295, 2½" w.
CAT NAP
8704 J.O.S., (1993), $225, 3" w.
SEMAPHORE
8709, P.Dro., (1993), $1,100, 5" h.
PINECONE ORNAMENT
8711, J.S., (1993), $90, 3¾" h.
CRYSTAL
1994 1994
8712 P.Schu. & E.B.S., (1993), $295, 2½" h.
LOVE/HOPE CUBE
LO
8713, F.N., (1993), $300, 2" h.
MOTHER PENGUIN
8722, R.C., (1993), $195, 2¾" h.
FLEDGLING PENGUIN
8723, R.C., (1993), $175, 2¾" h.
HATCHLING PENGUIN
8724, R.C., (1993), $175, 2¾" h.
INTERPLAY CLOCK
STEUBEN
8727, J.S., (1993), $275, 3" h.
CLASSIC CLOCK
STEUBEN
8729, J.S., (1994), $600, 3" w.
INTERPLAY BOX
8731, J.S., (1994), $335, 3" w.
TRUE LOVE
8737, D.M., (1993), $185, 3¼" w.
POWERFUL BULL
8738, S.B. & J.S., (1993), $925, 9" l.
GREAT BEAR
8739, S.B. & J.S., (1993), $925, 7" l.
BLUE WHALE, CALF
8742, J.S., (1994), $475, 9" l.
BLUE WHALE, MOM
8743, J.S., (1994), $585, 10¾" l.
STAR TOKEN
8745, L.A., (1994), $80, 2¼" dia.
FLEUR DE LIS TOKEN
8746, L.A., (1994), $80, 2¼" dia.
HOLIDAY STAR ORNAMENT
8747, R.C., (1994), $90, 3¾" h.
AURORA BOX
8748; P.B. & M.G., (1994), $295, 5" dia.
AURORA PERFUME BOTTLE
8749, P.B. & M.G., (1994), $215, 2¼" h.
AURORA MIRROR
8750, P.B. & M.G., (1994), $285, 5" dia.
FOUR-LEAF-CLOVER TOKEN
8754, L.A., (1994), $80, 2¼" dia.

SOCCER PLAYERS	CRYSTAL	PARTNERSHIP	SHOU TOKEN	BASEBALL	SCALES OF JUSTICE	CADUCEUS
8755, O.S., (1994), $510, 4¼" w.	8756, P.Schu. & E.B.S., (1994), $350, 2½" h.	8760 R.C., (1994), $660, 12" w.	8761, L.A., (1994), $85, 2¼" dia.	8763, S.D.T., (1994), $295, 2¾" dia.	8767, P.Schu. & A.K., (1994), $360, 2½" w.	8768, P.Schu. & A.K., (1994), $360, 2½" w.
HOLIDAY LANTERN ORNAMENT	WESTERN WALL MENORAH	LOVING HEART	AMERICA	SAIL AWAY	HOME RUN	FREE SPIRIT
8769, P.Dro., (1995), $90, 2½" l.	8770, J.S., (1995), $725, 9¾" w.	8771, P.Dro., (1995), $190, 2½" h.	8789, D.D., (1995), $185, 2½" w.	8790, D.D., (1995), $185, 3¼" h.	8792, S.D.T., (1995), $675, 2¾" dia.	8793, S.B., (1995), $1,100, 11¾" l.
DOLPHIN, CHILD	DOLPHIN, MOTHER	GOLF PRISM	HOLIDAY PEAR ORNAMENT	HOLIDAY ACORN ORNAMENT	SWEETHEART	STRETCHING CAT
8794, J.S., (1995), $475, 7¼" l.	8795, J.S., (1995), $585, 9¼" l.	8798 P.Dro., (1996), $1,075, 7¼" h.	8799, D.D., (1996), $90, 3¾" h.	8804, C.T., (1997), $90, 3½" h.	8809, J.S., (1997), $200, 2½" w.	8811, T.L.S., (1999), $800, 11" l.
STAR PATH	FULL GALLOP	HOLIDAY APPLE ORNAMENT	BUNNY	POLAR BEAR, CUB	POLAR BEAR, MOTHER	BABY ELEPHANT
8812, D.D., (1997), $250, 4" h.	8817, P.Dro., (1999), $950, 9" l.	8818, D.D., (1998), $95, 3" h.	8822, R.C., (1997), $365, 3½" l.	8824, J.H., (1997), $485, 4" l.	8825, J.H., (1997), $685, 5¾" l.	8826, J.S., (1997), $595, 4¼" h.
HOLIDAY GIFT BOX ORNAMENT	PLAYFUL SEA LION	BUNDLE OF JOY	FOREVER YOURS	DOVE	BEST FRIEND	PERFECT BALANCE
8830, T.L.S., (1999), $95, 2¼" w.	8838, T.L.S., (1998), $795, 5¾" h.	8842, T.L.S., (1998), $220, 3" w.	8843, P.Dro., (1999), $480, 3¼" h.	8846, J.S., (1999), $500, 7¼" l.	8848, T.L.S., (1999), $985, 6¾" h.	8850, E.H., (1999), $750, 4¾" h.

KANGAROO
8851, T.L.S., (1999), $1,400, 10¼" h.

MENORAH OF LIGHT
8852, J.S., (1999), $1,350, 9¾" w.

GOLDEN ANGEL
8853, T.L.S., (1999), $800, 7¼" h.

SCULPTURAL CLOCK
8854, J.S., (1999), $650, 4¾" h.

CONCENTRICITY
8855, E.H., (1999), $750, 5" h.

CLEARLY LOVE
8861, D.D., (2000), $225, 2½" dia.

BABY'S BLOCKS A–Z
8862–8887, J.S., (2000), $225 ea., 2" w.

HOLIDAY PINEAPPLE ORNAMENT
8891, C.T., (2000), $95, 4" h.

HERITAGE SWINGING MONKEY
8892, K.D.S., (2000), $800, 6¼" h.

GRACEFUL HERON
8893, T.L.S., (2000), $1,200, 14½" h.

YOUNG HERON
8894, T.L.S., (2000), $900, 8¾" h.

ENCORE CLOCK
8904, J.S., (2000), $700, 5¾" h.

VISION
8905, E.H., (2000), $650, 3½" h.

BABY PUMPKIN
8906, D.D., (2000), $165, 2¼" dia.

PUMPKIN
8907, D.D., (2000), $225, 3½" dia.

BABY'S CUP
8909, T.L.S., (2000), $350, 3¼" h.

TURTLE
8910, T.L.S., (2000), $500, 5¾" l.

LOVING ANGEL
8911, T.L.S., (2000), $400, 6" w.

FOREVER MORE
8914, E.H., (2001), $375, 3½" l.

STARS & STRIPES
8915, P.A., (2001), $350, 3½" w.

SONATA
8916, P.A., (2001), $350, 3½" w.

TORCH OF STRENGTH
8918, T.L.S., (2001), $550, 8¼" h.

ACHIEVEMENT CRYSTAL
8919, J.S., (2001), $550, 8¼" h.

STARLIGHT
8920, D.M., (2001), $295, 3¼" w.

WELCOME HOME
8921, E.H., (2001), $795, 4¼" w.

HOLIDAY BELL ORNAMENT
8922, J.S., (2001), $95, 4" h.

Not illustrated

PATRIOTIC CRYSTAL
8476, (1983), $495

LION
8481, L.A., (1983), $975, 9½" w.

RED CANDY CANE
8543, S.D.T., (1986), $65, 6" l.

POLAR BEAR
8568, P.Schu., (1988), $575, 7½" l.

CRYSTAL
8595, P.Schu. & E.B.S., (1989), $265, 2½" h.

NOEL BELL
8596, L.A., (1989), $275, 4⅛" h.

CRYSTAL
8597, P.Schu. & E.B.S., (1990), $265, 2½" h.

SNOWCONE
8627, S.D.T., (1991), $95, 4⅛" h.

SNOWBALL
8628, S.D.T., (1991), $95, 3½" w.

PENGUIN FAMILY
8734, (1993), $735

RHINOCEROS
8840, J.S., (1999), $1,290, 9¼" l.

PAIR OF HERONS
8895, T.L.S., (2000), $2,000

HAND COOLERS

PRESSED FROG
5510, L.A., (1974), $28.50
PRESSED ELEPHANT
5511, L.A., (1974), $28.50, 2 5/16" h.
PRESSED RAT
5512, L.A., (1974), $28.50, 2 5/16" h.
PRESSED RABBIT
5513, L.A., (1974), $28.50, 2 7/16" l.
TURTLE
5514, L.A., (1978), $75.00, 2 5/8" l.
RAM
5515, L.A., (1980), 2 1/4" h.
OWL
5516, L.A., (1980), 2 1/4" h.
PRESSED HEN
5517, L.A., (1982), $100, 2 1/2" l.
PRESSED DRAGON
5518, L.A., (1982), $100, 2 3/4" h.
EAGLE
5519, L.A., (1983), $110, 2 3/4" w.
CAT
5520, L.A., (1983), $110, 2 1/2" w.
BEAR
5521, L.A., (1985), $125, 2 1/2" h.
PIG
5522, L.A., (1987), $125, 3" l.
RABBIT
5523, L.A., (1988), $125, 2 3/4" l.
BULL
5524, L.A., (1990), $135, 2 1/2" h.
MONKEY
5526, L.A., (1992), $150, 2 3/4" h.
ROOSTER
5527, L.A., (1993), $150, 3 1/4" h.
HORSE HEAD
5528, D.D., (1995), $155, 2" h
ELEPHANT
5529, L.A., (1995), $185, 3 1/4" h.
DOLPHIN
5530, L.A., (1996), $155, 2 1/2" h.
TEDDY BEAR
5531, D.D., (1995), $155, 2 1/2" h.
DOVE
5532, L.A., (1997), $155, 3" l.
PELICAN
5533, L.A., (1997), $185, 3 1/4" l.
DOG
5534, L.A., (1997), $185, 3 1/4" h.
HIPPOPOTAMUS
5535, L.A., (1998), $190, 3 1/2" w.
HERITAGE RAM
Same as 5515, L.A., 2 1/2" w. (reintroduced as 5536 in 1999)
SQUIRREL
5537, L.A., (1999), $190, 2 3/4" h.
LADYBUG
5538, T.L.S., (1999), $195, 2 1/2" l.
RHINOCEROS
5539, L.A., (2000), $195, 2 3/4" l.
LION
5540, T.L.S., (2000), $165, 2 3/4" h.
BISON
5541, T.L.S., (2001), $165, 3" l.
TURTLE
5542, T.L.S., (2001), $195, 3 1/2" l.
HARE
5543, T.L.S., (2001), $195, 3 1/2" l.
Not Illustrated
AMERICAN EAGLE
5545, T.L.S., (2001), $195, 3 1/4" h.

NOTES TO THE TEXT

Note: The Steuben Permanent File, a major source for the first edition and referenced in the notes below, was originally housed in Steuben's offices until the late eighties, when it was dispersed, presumably to the Corning Glass facilities in upstate New York. The Archive, Corning Glass Works, which existed at the time of publication of the first edition and is referenced in the notes for Chapters 1–8, is now known as the Corning Incorporated Department of Archives and Records Management (CIDARM).

I. HOW STEUBEN GLASS IS MADE

1. "Gaffer" is thought to be a corruption of the English word grandfather.
2. Cherrywood is still favored for forming molds and tools. It is heat resistant and not likely to become misshapen by cooling in troughs of water. Graphite is also a popular material for forming tools; unlike metal, it never loses its shape.
3. Sidney Waugh, *The Making of Fine Glass* (New York: Dodd Mead, 1947), p. 3.
4. Most current process information is from author's interviews with Steuben factory manager Peter Aagaard on May 10 and July 5, 2001.

II. FOUNDATIONS

1. Paul V. Gardner, *The Glass of Frederick Carder* (New York: Crown, 1971). Gardner's book is the single best source of information on Carder's years in England, and we are indebted to it for the facts recounted here, unless otherwise noted.
2. *Ibid.*, p. 25.
3. *Ibid.*, p. 28.
4. Estelle Sinclaire Farrar and Jan Shadel Spillman, *The Complete Cut and Engraved Glass of Corning* (New York: Crown, 1979), p. 196.
5. Gardner, *op. cit.*, p. 29.
6. Gardner, *op. cit.*, p. 31.
7. Photographs of the old Steuben plant in The Archives, Corning Glass Works, document this expansion (also cited by Gardner, and by Farrar and Spillman).
8. Taped conversation between Thomas S. Buechner, Paul V. Gardner, and others. The Archives, Corning Glass Works.
9. Clipping from the *Corning Leader*. The Archives, Corning Glass Works.
10. *Corning Leader*, January 7, 1918.
11. Untitled typescript history of the early years of the Houghton family's association with glassmaking and the founding of the Corning Glass Works. All information on Houghton family involvement with Corning and Steuben, unless otherwise noted, is taken from this account. The Archives, Corning Glass Works.
12. Farrar and Spillman, *op. cit.*, p. 2.
13. Memorandum, Arthur A. Houghton to Frederick Carder, December 28, 1921, incorporating memo of May 10, 1921. The Archives, Corning Glass Works.
14. For a complete description of Carder's various glasswares, together with many illustrations of the various kinds of glass he made to 1933, see Gardner, *The Glass of Frederick Carder*, and Thomas P. Dimitroff's *Frederick Carder and Steuben Glass* (Schiffer Publishing, 1998).
15. Biography of Robert Leavy, typescript. Steuben Permanent File, Steuben, New York City.
16. Gardner, *op. cit.*, p. 48.
17. Typescript manuscript of biography of Frederick Schroeder (incomplete), dated April 14, 1950. The Archives, Corning Glass Works.

III. THE TROUBLED YEARS

1. Report, M.J. Lacey to Dr. E.C. Sullivan, 1929. The Archives, Corning Glass Works.
2. Report, R.C. Vaughn to Amory Houghton, April 11, 1931. Houghton succeeded Sullivan as president in 1930. The Archives, Corning Glass Works.
3. Lacey, *op. cit.*
4. Vaughn, *op. cit.*
5. Various documents in The Archives, Corning Glass Works, document this move.
6. Vycor glass was made in the old Steuben plant during the 1940s. The buildings were torn down in 1962.
7. Paul V. Gardner, *The Glass of Frederick Carder* (New York: Crown, 1971), p. 51.
8. *Ibid.*
9. Toward the end of Carder's life, he was visited weekly by Thomas Buechner, who absorbed the old glassmaker's impressions of the industry in Corning as he had observed it for nearly sixty years. Apparently his initial bitterness toward Steuben never dissipated, for it was often a topic of conversation at these meetings between friends. The Archives, Corning Glass Works.
10. Letter, Walter Dorwin Teague to Amory Houghton, February 8, 1932. The Archives, Corning Glass Works.
11. General Bulletin #1 from John J. Mackay to Steuben staff, February 15, 1932. The Archives, Corning Glass Works.
12. General Bulletin #10 from John J. Mackay to Steuben staff, April 22, 1932. The Archives, Corning Glass Works.
13. General Bulletin #18 from John J. Mackay to Steuben staff, May 20, 1932. The Archives, Corning Glass Works.
14. Catalogue, 1932, The Steuben Division. The Archives, Corning Glass Works.

15. Letter, Walter Dorwin Teague to Amory Houghton, April 5, 1932. The Archives, Corning Glass Works.
16. Letter and memorandum, Walter Dorwin Teague to Amory Houghton, October 7, 1932; letter, Amory Houghton to Walter Dorwin Teague, October 12, 1932. The Archives, Corning Glass Works.
17. *Who Was Who in America*, Vol. 4 (Chicago: Marquis, 1951). Listing for Walter Dorwin Teague, industrial designer.
18. General Bulletin #37 from John J. Mackay to Amory Houghton and Steuben directors, October 11, 1932. The Archives, Corning Glass Works.

IV. A NEW BEGINNING

1. Recalling these days in an interview taped by the author on May 12, 1981, Arthur A. Houghton, Jr., noted that "Teague was a salesman plus—he was very smooth, very articulate and charming, superbly and quietly dressed, and it was months and months before I realized he couldn't design a goddamn thing."
2. Transcription of taped interview by Richard H. Andrews with John M. Gates and Arthur A. Houghton, Jr., May 14, 1969. Steuben Permanent File, Steuben, New York City.
3. Papers of Incorporation, Steuben Glass, Incorporated. The Archives, Corning Glass Works.
4. Transcription of taped interview, Gates and Houghton, *op. cit.*
5. *Ibid.*
6. Arthur A. Houghton, Jr., in a taped interview with the author, May 12, 1981.
7. *Ibid.*
8. Steuben staff list, 1933–34. The Archives, Corning Glass Works.
9. Unsigned memorandum listing "Steuben cutters and engravers, mid-30's." The Archives, Corning Glass Works.
10. Letters to Arthur A. Houghton, Jr., from Robert Leavy in the Steuben Permanent File attest to Leavy's strong support of Houghton's reorganization. As Houghton recalled in his May 12, 1981, interview: "We suggested things that violated what he believed, every tradition of glassmaking, but he'd go along with them."
11. Transcription of taped interview, Gates and Houghton, *op. cit.* Steuben Permanent File, Steuben, New York City. In a later interview with the author (May 1981), Houghton explained that some of the more "commercially minded people in Corning Glass Works felt the shop ought to be located in a busy district, around Grand Central, but Gates and I felt very strongly it should be uptown, just as swank as could be."
12. *Evening Leader*, Corning, February 8, 1934.
13. Fern Fenton, writing for *The New York Times*, February 8, 1934.
14. Transcription of taped interview, Gates and Houghton, *op. cit.*
15. Letter from Arthur A. Houghton, Jr., to Robert J. Leavy, December 27, 1965. Steuben Permanent File, Steuben, New York City.
16. Paul V. Gardner, *The Glass of Frederick Carder* (New York: Crown, 1971), p. 52.
17. John M. Gates, "The Design of Steuben Glass" (typescript, April 18, 1950). Steuben Permanent File, Steuben, New York City.
18. *Ibid.*
19. Houghton interview with the author, *op. cit.*
20. *Ibid.*
21. *The New York Times*, March 13, 1935.
22. *Ceramic Industry*, March 19, 1935.
23. Houghton interview with the author, *op. cit.*
24. London *News Chronicle*, March 30, 1935.
25. London *Times*, March 24, 1935.
26. London *Catholic Herald*, April 6, 1935.
27. Houghton interview with the author, *op. cit.*
28. *Christian Science Monitor*, November 9, 1935.
29. Houghton interview with the author, *op. cit.*; also *Bulletin*, Metropolitan Museum of Art, Vol. XX, No. 10 (October 1935).
30. Houghton interview with the author, *op. cit.*
31. *Ibid.*
32. *Ibid.*
33. *Ibid.*
34. Memorandum, John M. Gates to Isobel Lee Beers, May 22, 1965. Steuben Permanent File, Steuben, New York City.
35. Houghton interview with the author, *op. cit.*
36. Rough draft of biography of John (Jack) Hultzman, May 23, 1979. Steuben Permanent File, Steuben, New York City.
37. Typescript manuscript of biography of Frederick Schroeder (incomplete), dated April 14, 1950. The Archives, Corning Glass Works.

V. WORLD'S FAIR AND WORLD WAR

1. Examples of stationery with this gilt insignia are held in the Steuben Permanent File, Steuben, New York City.
2. Other members of the committee were Wescott Rathbone, Arthur A. Houghton, Jr., J.P. Cushman, and Howard Baker. All information on Steuben's booth at the fair is derived from a final report on the project now held in the Steuben Permanent File, Steuben, New York City.
3. *New York Sun*, February 3, 1940.
4. New York *Herald Tribune*, January 14, 1940.
5. Valor Cup file. Steuben Permanent File, Steuben, New York City.
6. Letters, Cecil Davis to John M. Gates, 1938–39. Steuben Permanent File, Steuben, New York City.
7. Arthur A. Houghton, Jr., in a taped interview with the author, May 12, 1981.

8. Steuben catalogue, 1941. New York Public Library.
9. *The Steuben Collection of Antique Glass,* n.d. but probably 1943, New York Public Library.
10. Houghton interview with the author, *op. cit.*
11. Among the regional shops carrying Steuben in 1941 were Neiman-Marcus, Dallas; Shreve, Crump & Low, Boston; Halle Brothers, Cleveland; M's Inc., Providence; Scruggs-Vandervoort-Barney, St. Louis; Austin Wyne, Detroit; and Marshall Field, Chicago.
12. Steuben's Christmas catalogue, 1943. New York Public Library.
13. Author's interview with Mrs. Elizabeth Pollard, June 23, 1980.
14. Houghton interview with the author, *op. cit.*
15. This date is the one recalled by Myles Madigan, a Corning Glass Works employee now deceased, who served as a representative of management in union negotiations for many years.

VI. GEARING FOR EXPANSION

1. Steuben sales catalogue, spring 1947.
2. Arthur A. Houghton, Jr., in a taped interview with the author, May 12, 1981.
3. Report, James S. Plaut to Arthur A. Houghton, Jr., September 15, 1947. Steuben Permanent File, Steuben, New York City.
4. Houghton interview with the author, *op. cit.*
5. Joseph Blumenthal, *The Spiral Press Through Four Decades* (New York: Pierpont Morgan Library, 1966).
6. Memorandum, Arthur A. Houghton, Jr., to Anthony Snow, March 9, 1979. Steuben Permanent File, Steuben, New York City.
7. James S. Plaut, *The Corning-Steuben Design Development Program* (Boston: Department of Design in Industry, Institute of Contemporary Arts, 1949).
8. John B. Ward, director of design for Corning Glass Works, "Product Design in the Corning Glass Works" (unpublished typescript). Steuben Permanent File, Steuben, New York City.
9. Plaut, *op. cit.*
10. Ward, *op. cit.*, p. 2.
11. Arthur A. Houghton, Jr., *Design Policy Within Industry as a Responsibility of High Level Management* (Steuben Glass, Inc., 1951).
12. Facts relating to the composition and melting of Steuben Glass are taken from various memoranda in The Archives, Corning Glass Works.
13. Memorandum, John M. Gates to Arthur A. Houghton, Jr., July 25, 1949. Steuben Permanent File, Steuben, New York City.
14. Houghton interview with the author, *op. cit.*
15. Letter, Arthur A. Houghton, Jr., to Julian Boyd, November 5, 1948. Steuben Permanent File, Steuben, New York City.
16. Houghton interview with the author, *op. cit.*
17. Letter, Carl Bridenbaugh to Arthur A. Houghton, Jr., February 8, 1949. Steuben Permanent File, Steuben, New York City.
18. Memorandum, J.B. Treddenick to Arthur A. Houghton, Jr., March 21, 1950. Steuben Permanent File, Steuben, New York City.
19. Memorandum, C. Lin Tissot to J.B. Treddenick, undated. Steuben Permanent File, Steuben, New York City.

VII. FROM AMERICA TO THE WORLD

1. Centenary Cup file. Steuben Permanent File, Steuben, New York City.
2. The author is indebted to Jack Hultzman, production director for Steuben, for a tour of the "cave" and a patient explanation of this process.
3. Notes on "Crystex." Steuben Permanent File, Steuben, New York City.
4. Memorandum, Robert J. Leavy to Arthur A. Houghton, Jr., October 24, 1951. Steuben Permanent File, Steuben, New York City.
5. Antique Glass Dispersal Reports. Steuben Permanent File, Steuben, New York City.
6. Sidney Waugh, *The Making of Fine Glass* (New York: Dodd, Mead, 1947), p. 10–11.
7. Memorandum, James M. Plaut to Arthur A. Houghton, Jr., September 15, 1947. Steuben Permanent File, Steuben, New York City.
8. Correspondence relating to this and other details of "L'Art du Verre" exhibition is in the Steuben Permanent File, Steuben, New York City.
9. Paris, *Le Matin*, July 8, 1951.
10. Paris, *Midi Libre*, July 10, 1951.
11. Letter, Mme. de Vandenay Tharand to Arthur A. Houghton, Jr., July 24, 1951. Steuben Permanent File, Steuben, New York City. In an interview with the author on May 12, 1981, Houghton asked: "Can you imagine what a warm feeling I got on receiving that letter?"
12. Dwight David Eisenhower was at that time living abroad as head of SHAPE.
13. Report, "British Artists in Crystal," Steuben Permanent File, Steuben, New York City, is the source of information for details of exhibition planning. Copies of the Houghton correspondence are included.
14. John Monteith Gates, Introduction, *British Artists in Crystal* (Steuben, 1954).
15. Report, "Park Lane House Exhibition," Steuben Permanent File, Steuben, New York City. Contains various memoranda and correspondence relating to the planning and implementation of the exhibition.
16. Isobel Lee Beers, in an interview with the author, September 15, 1980.
17. Memorandum, Harold Stassen to Arthur A. Houghton,

Jr., Steuben Permanent File, Steuben, New York City.
18. *Ibid.*
19. Kup actually traveled as a consultant of FAO, which paid his expenses and facilitated his entry into various countries en route; at Stassen's request, however, this agency's connection with the project was kept confidential. Only the participation of the USIS offices in Asia was publicized at the time the show opened. Steuben Permanent File, Steuben, New York City.
20. Correspondence and report, "Asian Artists in Crystal," Steuben Permanent File, Steuben, New York City.
21. *Ibid.*
22. Memorandum, Sally Walker to Steuben staff, January 17, 1955. Steuben Permanent File, Steuben, New York City.

VIII. EXPERIMENT AND CHANGE

1. Correspondence and memoranda relating to the Steuben Glass Incorporated–Corning Glass Works merger, July 1958. Steuben Permanent File, Steuben, New York City.
2. Elizabeth Pollard in a personal interview with the author, June 25, 1980.
3. Arthur A. Houghton, Jr., in a taped interview with the author, May 12, 1981.
4. Report, "Poetry in Crystal," Steuben Permanent File, Steuben, New York City.
5. John M. Gates, *Poetry in Crystal: Interpretations of Thirty-One New Poems* (Steuben Glass, 1963), Introduction.
6. Arthur A. Houghton, Jr., *Five Masterworks* (Steuben Glass, 1972), Introduction.
7. Houghton interview with the author, *op. cit.*
8. James M. Plaut, *Steuben: Seventy Years of American Glassmaking* (New York: Praeger, 1975), p. 69.
9. File on the Angels project. Steuben Permanent File, Steuben, New York City.
10. Houghton interview with the author, *op. cit.*
11. Islands file, correspondence with Alexander D. Vietor. Steuben Permanent File, Steuben, New York City.
12. Arthur A. Houghton, Jr., typescript of remarks made at Robert Leavy's retirement party. September 1, 1963. Steuben Permanent File, Steuben, New York City. Leavy was presented with Cathedral as a retirement gift.
13. Letter, Robert Leavy to Arthur A. Houghton, Jr., June 27, 1968. Steuben Permanent File, Steuben, New York City.
14. Baccarat file. Steuben Permanent File, Steuben, New York City. Baccarat was the second crystal manufactory, after Steuben, to institute tank melting. It requested Steuben's technical assistance in 1964 to make a tank furnace. When this was refused, Baccarat learned the secret of the "let-it-down-easy" process from an American who had helped build similar optical glass tanks for Corning Glass Works. Baccarat's tank was operational by 1967; and because the company used another system for making stemware, it was able to replenish its stock in a much shorter time than it took Steuben to turn out an equivalent number of pieces.
15. Letter, Arthur A. Houghton, Jr., to John M. Gates, July 1, 1969. Steuben Permanent File, Steuben, New York City.
16. Paul Schulze, in a personal interview with the author, October 17, 1980. Details of Perrot's brief tenure at Steuben are based on this interview.
17. All quotations in this paragraph are from Houghton interview with the author, *op. cit.*

IX: CELEBRATING THE ARTIST

Unless otherwise noted, Thomas S. Buechner quotes are taken from an interview taped by the author, April 30, 1981.
1. Letter, Arthur A. Houghton, Jr., to Robert Leavy, June 8, 1962. Steuben Permanent File, Steuben, New York City.
2. Steuben press release, May 15, 1971.
3. Steuben press release, January 3, 1973.
4. *Ibid.*
5. Steuben press release, March 15, 1976.
6. Steuben press release, April 15, 1977.
7. Steuben press release, September 2, 1980.
8. Steuben press release, April 27, 1977.
9. *Ibid.*
10. Steuben press release, March 6, 1979.
11. Steuben press release, September 2, 1980.
12. Steuben press release, April 5, 1981.
13. Steuben Public Relations File, Steuben, New York: Report on "Nine Florists" exhibition.
14. Steuben Public Relations File, Steuben, New York: Book of press clippings.
15. Thomas S. Buechner, in the epilogue to *Steuben Glass: An American Tradition in Crystal* by Mary Jean Madigan, New York: Harry N. Abrams, Inc., 1982.
16. *Ibid.*
17. Interview, Arthur A. Houghton, Jr., by Kathy Littleton, August 1988; author's interview with Marie McKee, July 9, 2001.
18. Corning Glass Works Bulletin 20–82, July 14, 1982, Corning Incorporated Department of Archives and Records (CIDARM).

X: STEUBEN IN TRANSITION

1. Davis Dyer and Daniel Gross, *The Generations of Corning*, (New York: Oxford University Press, 2001), p. 372–73.
2. Reprint of "Design at Corning," presentation by James Houghton to the Design Management Institute Conference, Halloran House, New York City, April 7, 1983; Steuben Public Relations file, Steuben, New York. Houghton remarked, "Good design is important to corporate success . . . a practice first developed and proven when Arthur A.

Houghton, Jr., established our Steuben Division . . ."

3. "Organization Changes," *Corning Glass Works Bulletin*, p. 20–82, July 14, 1982. Corning, Inc. Department of Archives and Records (CIDARM).

4. Letter, Arthur A. Houghton, Jr. (AAH), to Davis Chiodo (DC), November 17, 1982, Arthur Amory Houghton, Jr., File, CIDARM.

5. Memo, "A Plan for Gifts of State," Arthur Amory Houghton, Jr., File, CIDARM; letters, AH to DC, November 2, 1982, and DC to AAH, November 10, 1982, CIDARM.

6. Author's interview with Susan King, June 7, 2001.

7. Letter, AAH to DC, January 7, 1983, CIDARM.

8. Letter, AAH to DC, December 11, 1984, CIDARM.

9. Letter, AAH to DC, November 19, 1984, CIDARM.

10. Letter, AAH to DC, June 11, 1984, CIDARM.

11. Author's interview with Paul Schulze, June 10, 1988.

12. Jean Libman Block, "Steuben Glass," *American Craft*, February/March, 1985, p. 12–13.

13. Author's interview with Thomas C. Messmer, July 10, 1988.

14. *Ibid*; author's interview with Mary Minstrell, June 5, 2001.

15. Letter, DC to AAH, March 20, 1984, CIDARM.

16. Report, "One Dot at a Time," Chloe Zerwick to Steuben Staff, May 1983: Steuben Public Relations File, Steuben, New York.

17. Report, "Dreams Into Glass," Chloe Zerwick to Steuben Staff, April 1984: Steuben Public Relations File, Steuben, New York.

18. "At Lever House, a Benefit Party," *The New York Times*, October 5, 1984.

19. *50 Years on 5th* (New York: Steuben Glass, 1984).

20. Douglas C. McGill, "Exhibition of Steuben Glass to Open," *The New York Times*, October 3, 1984.

21. Barbara N. King, "Design Evolution at Steuben," *Pan Am Clipper*, October 1984.

22. Letter, AAH to DC, December 11, 1984, CIDARM.

23. Letter, DC to AAH, December 20, 1984, CIDARM.

24. Author's interview with Susan King, June 7, 2001.

25. *Steuben Glass Information Bulletin*, vol. xxviii, no.1, January 23, 1985.

26. *Steuben Crystal in Private Collections* (New York: Steuben Glass, 1985).

27. "1986 Expansion Report," Morey Houghton File, Box 2.7–1–2, CIDARM.

28. Author's interview with Sandra Carr, June 10, 1988.

29. Michelle Green, "The Ruling Glass," *Manhattan, Inc.*, October 1986, p. 159–70.

30. Memo, N.E. Naylor and P.J. Aagaard to Steuben Employees, April 22, 1985, Box 2.7–1–2, CIDARM.

31. Author's interview with Thomas C. Messmer, July 10, 1988 (all information on 1988 factory changes, except where otherwise noted, is from this source).

32. *The Corning Leader*, November 19, 1986. Vatcher was quoted as saying, "Steuben has become something of a symbol for the quality Corning Glass Works is trying to stress in its other facilities."

33. *Steuben Glass Information Bulletin*, vol. xxix, no.8, June 12, 1986.

34. *Steuben Glass Information Bulletin*, vol. xxix, no.9, July 22, 1986.

35. Memo from Keeble, Cavaco & Duka to Chloe Zerwick with attached transcript of Designer Advisory Board discussion of October 6, 1986. Steuben Public Relations File, Steuben, New York.

36. Author's interview with Susan King, June 7, 2001.

37. Press release, Office of Representative Houghton (Contact: Brian Fitzpatrick), March 25, 1988; *Elmira Star Gazette*, April 5, 1988, p. 1–4.

38. All King quotes, except where noted, are derived from the author's interview with Susan King, June 7, 2001.

39. Reprint, Philip H. Dougherty, "Steuben Has a New Form of Expression," *The New York Times*, April 20, 1988, Steuben Public Relations File, Steuben, New York.

40. Letter, Arthur Amory Houghton, Jr. (AAH), to Susan King (SK), February 26, 1987, Houghton File, CIDARM.

41. Letter, AAH to SK, June 4, 1987, CIDARM.

42. Letter, AAH to SK, June 9, 1987, CIDARM.

43. Author's interview with Paul Schulze, June 10, 1988.

44. Author's interview with Christopher Hacker, August 22, 1988; author's interview with Rob Cassetti, February 27, 2002.

45. Steuben press release, "Separate Tables: Seven Points of View," undated (Contact: Alexandra Smith—Keeble, Cavaco & Duka), Steuben Public Relations File, Steuben, New York.

46. Report, "Separate Tables," submitted by Public Relations and Advertising Department, Jane Kaufman to Sal Carulli et al., December 3, 1987, Steuben Public Relations File, Steuben, New York.

47. Albane Dolez, *3500 Years of Glass Artistry* (New York: Harry N. Abrams, 1988).

48. *The Sun Herald* (Sydney, Australia), November 6, 1988.

49. Betty Sargent, "Steuben Breaks the Mold," *Connoisseur*, June 1988, p. 80–85.

50. All quotes, *The Steuben Project: Sculptures in Crystal* (New York: Steuben, 1988).

51. Reprint of Paul Hollister, "Splendid Steuben, in a Dramatic Light," *The New York Times*, May 12, 1988, Steuben Public Relations File, Steuben, New York.

52. Report, "The Steuben Project," submitted by the Steuben Public Relations and Advertising Department, October 10, 1988. Steuben Public Relations File, Steuben, New York.

53. Steuben press release, "The History of Steuben Design," undated (Contacts: Harriet Blacker and Anita Hunter), Steuben Public Relations File, Steuben, New York.

54. Steuben press release, "Michael Graves: Archaic Vessels," undated (Contacts: Harriet Blacker and Anita Hunter),

Steuben Public Relations File, Steuben, New York.
55. Steuben press release, "Steuben at the World's Fair," undated (Contacts: Harriet Blacker and Anita Hunter), Steuben Public Relations File, Steuben, New York.
56. Steuben press release, "Meet the Artists," undated (Contacts: Harriet Blacker and Anita Hunter), Steuben Public Relations File, Steuben, New York.
57. Steuben press release, "American Glassmaking," undated (Contacts: Harriet Blacker and Anita Hunter), Steuben Public Relations File, Steuben, New York.
58. *The Corning Leader*, February 28, 1990, p. 3.
59. *Steuben Information Bulletin*, vol. xxx, no.5, May 1, 1990.
60. Steuben press release, "A Toast to Shakespeare's Globe," undated (Contacts: Harriet Blacker and Anita Hunter), Steuben Public Relations File, Steuben, New York.
61. Letter, AAH to SK, February 28, 1990, CIDARM.
62. Author's interview with Susan King, June 7, 2001.
63. Letter, SK to AAH, January 27, 1989, CIDARM.
64. Author's interview with Susan King, June 7, 2001.
65. Letter, SK to AAH, January 29, 1990, CIDARM.
66. Milwaukee *Sentinel*, October 24, 1989, p. 4, part 4.
67. Letter, SK to AAH, January 19, 1990, CIDARM; transcript of Designer Advisory Board notes, 1986, Steuben Public Relations File, Steuben, New York.
68. Memo, Anne Hanley to Susan King et al, January 7, 1992, Steuben Public Relations File, Steuben, New York.
69. Steuben press release, "Angela Cummings for Steuben," undated (Contacts: Harriet Blacker and Anita Hunt), Steuben Public Relations File, Steuben, New York.
70. Author's interview with Susan King, June 7, 2001.

XI: DRIVEN BY DESIGN

1. Memorandum, Donald M. Rorke to the author, May 10, 2001. All direct quotations that follow are taken verbatim from this memorandum.
2. Steuben Press Release, undated (Contacts: Harriet Blacker and Anita Hunter), Steuben Public Relations File, Steuben, New York.
3. Rorke memorandum to author, *op.cit.*
4. Author's interview with Joel Smith, July 20, 2001.
5. Memorandum, "Organizational Announcement," Donald M. Rorke to Steuben Staff, December 24, 1996. Steuben Public Relations File, Steuben, New York.
6. Rorke memorandum to the author, *op cit.*
7. *Ibid.*
8. *Steuben Annual Catalogue.* (New York: Steuben, 1993).
9. *Steuben Annual Catalogue.* (New York: Steuben, 1994).
10. *Steuben Annual Catalogue.* (New York: Steuben, 1995).
11. *Celebrating Ninety Years.* (New York: Steuben, 1993).
12. *MetroWest Jewish News*, November 21, 1995.
13. Author's interview with Mary Minstrell, June 21, 2001.
14. Memorandum, Don Rorke to author, *op. cit.*
15. *Ibid.*
16. Author's interviews with Mary Minstrell and Marie McKee.
17. *Steuben Annual Catalogue.* (New York: Steuben, 1997).
18. Memorandum, Cara Ferragamo to Mark Tamayo, December 24, 1996. Steuben Public Relations File, Steuben, New York.
19. David Dowler, quoted in the catalogue *Structure Revealed: Glass Designs by David Dowler.* (New York: Steuben, 1997.)
20. Thomas Hoving, *Structure Revealed: Glass Designs by David Dowler.* (New York: Steuben, 1997).

XII: APPROACHING THE MILLENNIUM

1. Steuben press release, "Zero Population Growth Honors Steuben's President and CEO," undated (Contact: Kathi E. Edelson).
2. Author's interview with Marie McKee, July 9, 2001. All McKee quotations, unless otherwise indicated, are from this source.
3. Author's interviews with Peter Aagaard, May 9 and July 5, 2001. All Aagaard quotations, unless otherwise indicated, are from this source.
4. For information on The Hot Glass Show, the author is indebted to John Cowden, who kindly escorted her through the show facilities in Corning following a presentation of the show on July 9, 2001.
5. William Warmus, *Lino Tagliapietra.* (New York: Steuben, 1998).
6. "A Timeline," updated March 25, 1999. Steuben Public Relations File, Steuben, New York.
7. Author's interview with Marie McKee, *op.cit.*
8. Steuben press release, "A New Manhattan Exhibition Space," undated (Contact: Kathi E. Edelson), Steuben Public Relations File, Steuben, New York.
9. Steuben press release, "Steuben Celebrates Its Move to Madison Avenue," undated (Contact: Kathi E. Edelson), Steuben Public Relations File, Steuben, New York.
10. Steuben press release, "Steuben to Present Retrospective of Celebrated 1940 Show," undated (Contact: Kathi E. Edelson), Steuben Public Relations File, Steuben, New York.
11. Steuben press release, "Steuben to Design a Limited Editon of The Golden Bowl for Merchant Ivory Productions' New Film to Be Released in April 2001," undated (Contact: Andrea J. Miles), Steuben Public Relations File, Steuben, New York.
12. Author's interview with Joel Smith, *op.cit.*
13. Author's interview with Marie McKee, *op.cit.*
14. Author's interview with Rob Cassetti, February 27, 2002. All Cassetti quotes are from this source.
15. Author's interview with Rob Cassetti, *op.cit.*
16. Author's interview with Marie McKee, *op.cit.*

SELECTED BIBLIOGRAPHY

Blaszczyk, Regina Lee. *Imagining Consumers: Design and Innovation from Wedgwood to Corning*. Baltimore, Maryland: Johns Hopkins University Press, 2000.

Block, Jean Libman. "Steuben Glass," *American Craft*, February/March, 1985.

Brooks, John A. *Glass*. New York: Golden Press, 1973.

Corning Glass Works. *Corning Glass Center*. Corning, N.Y.: Corning Glass Works, 1952.

Corning Incorporated. *Steuben: Celebrating Ninety Years*. New York: Corning Incorporated, 1993.

Dimitroff, Thomas P. *Frederick Carder and Steuben Glass*. Atglen, Pennsylvania: Schiffer Publishing, 1998.

Dolez, Albane. *3500 years of Glass Artistry*. New York: Harry N. Abrams, 1988.

Dyer, Davis. *Corning: A Story of Discovery and Reinvention*. Corning, New York: Corning Incorporated, 2001.

Dyer, Davis and Gross, Daniel. *The Generations of Corning: The Life and Times of a Global Corporation*. New York: Oxford University Press, 2001.

Farrar, Estelle Sinclaire and Spillman, Jane Shadel. *The Complete Cut and Engraved Glass of Corning*. New York: Syracuse University Press, 1997. First published, New York: Crown, 1979.

Gaines, Edith. "Seventy Years of Steuben Glass," *The Magazine Antiques*, August 1975.

Gardner, Paul V. *The Glass of Frederick Carder*. New York: Crown, 1971.

———*Glass*. New York: Cooper-Hewitt Museum of the Smithsonian Institution, 1979.

Graham, Margaret B.W., and Shuldinger, Alec T. *Corning and the Craft of Innovation*. New York: Oxford University Press, 2001

Green, Michelle. "The Ruling Glass," *Manhattan Inc.*, October 1986.

Gros-Galliner, Gabriella. *Glass : A Guide for Collectors*. New York: Stein and Day, 1970.

Houghton, Arthur A. Jr. *Design Policy within Industry as a Responsibility of High-Level Management*. New York: Steuben Glass, 1951.

Johnson, J. Stewart. *American Modern, 1925–1940: Design for a New Age*. New York: Harry N. Abrams in association with the American Federation of Arts, 2000.

King, Barbara N. "Design Evolution at Steuben," *Pan Am Clipper*, October, 1984.

Perrot, Paul N. with Gardner, Paul V. and Plaut, James S. *Steuben: Seventy Years of American Glassmaking*. New York: Praeger, 1974.

Plaut, James S. *Steuben Glass, a Monograph*. New York: H. Bittner, 1948.

———2nd revised and enlarged edition. New York: H. Bittner, 1951.

———3rd revised and enlarged edition. New York: Dover, 1972.

Redmond, Louis. *Enjoying Steuben Glass*. New York: Steuben Glass, 1960.

Revi, Albert Christian. *American Art Nouveau Glass*. Camden, N.J.: Nelson, 1968.

Sargent, Betty. "Steuben Breaks the Mold," *Connoisseur*, June 1988.

Skelley, Lelouise Davis. *Modern Fine Glass*. Garden City, N.Y.: Garden City Publishing Company, 1942.

Steuben Glass. *Modern Glass*. New York: Steuben Glass, 1939.

———*How to Care for Your Steuben Glass*. New York: Steuben Glass, n.d.

———*Your Steuben Glass and How to Care for It*. New York: Steuben Glass, n.d.

———*How to Take Care of Your Steuben Glass*. New York: Steuben Glass, n.d.

———*Designs in Glass by 27 Contemporary Artists*. New York: Steuben Glass, 1940.

———*Books on Glass: A Checklist of 183 Selected Titles*. New York: Steuben Glass, 1946.

———*A Primer of Glass Design*. New York: Steuben Glass, n.d.

———*A Primer of Glass History*. New York: Steuben Glass, n.d.

———*The Story of Steuben Glass*. New York: Steuben Glass, Inc. 1942; second edition, 1946.

———*Steuben Glass*, with an introduction by Sidney Waugh. New York: Steuben Glass, 1947.

———*Books on Glass: A Checklist of 256 Selected Titles*. New York: Steuben Glass, 1947.

———*British Artists in Crystal*. New York: Steuben Glass, 1954.

———*Steuben Crystal*. New York: Steuben Glass, 1956.

———*Asian Artists in Crystal*. New York: Steuben Glass, 1956.

———*Steuben Crystal in Private Collections*. New York: Steuben Glass, 1961.

———*The Story of Steuben Glass*. New York: Steuben Glass, 1962.

———*Poetry in Crystal*. New York: Steuben Glass, 1963.

———*Islands in Crystal*. New York: Steuben Glass, 1966.

———*The Myth of Adonis*. New York: Steuben Glass, 1966.

———*The Great Ring of Canada*. New York: Steuben Glass, 1967.

———*The Four Seasons*. New York: Steuben Glass, 1969.

———*The Carrousel of the Sea*. New York: Steuben Glass, 1970.

———*The Unicorn and the Maiden*. New York: Steuben Glass, 1971.

———*Five Masterworks*. New York: Steuben Glass, 1972.
———*Chinese Pavilion*. New York: Steuben Glass, 1975.
———*The Sphere of the Zodiac*. New York: Steuben Glass, 1976.
———*The Romance of the Rose*. New York: Steuben Glass, 1977.
———*The Art of Steuben*. Vol. I. New York: Steuben Glass, 1972. Vol. II. New York: Steuben Glass, 1974. Vol. III. New York: Steuben Glass, 1977. Vol. IV. New York: Steuben Glass, 1987.
———*Innerland*. New York: Steuben Glass, 1980.
———*About Steuben Glass*. New York: Steuben Glass, 1980.
———*50 years on 5th: A Retrospective Exhibition of Steuben Glass* with an essay by Brendan Gill. New York: Steuben Glass, 1984.
———*James Houston: A Retrospective* with a preface by James Houston. New York: Steuben Glass, 1987.
———*The Steuben Project: Sculptures in Crystal* with essays by Peter Aldrich, David Dowler, and Eric Hilton. New York: Steuben, 1988.
———*Structure Revealed: Glass Designs by David Dowler* with an essay by Thomas Hoving. New York: Steuben, 1997.
———*Lino Tagliapietra* with an essay by William Warmus. New York: Steuben, 1998.
Waugh, Sidney. *The Art of Glassmaking*. New York: Dodd, Mead, 1938.
———*The Making of Fine Glass*. New York: Dodd, Mead, 1947.
Zerwick, Chloe. *A Short History of Glass*. Corning, New York: The Corning Museum of Glass, 1980.

PHOTO CREDITS

All photographs were supplied by Steuben Glass with the following photographers indicated:

Anger International Photos, p. 124
Associated Press, p. 115
Bauer, p. 93
Brown Brothers, pp. 77 (bottom), 78 (bottom)
H. A. Bruno and Associates, pp. 84, 85 (top)
Michael Caputo, pp. 86 (both top), 89
Corning Glass Works, pp. 31, 33–34, 41, 49, 53 (both), 54 (both), 56, 57, 59, 63 (both)
Joyce Fay, p. 94
Gaffer News, p. 143
Samuel G. Gottscho, p. 87
Gottscho-Schleisner, pp. 78 (top), 92
Eugene Hutchinson, pp. 77 (top), 85 (bottom)
Constance Stuart Larrabee, pp. 35 (left), 36 (both), 38, 39 (bottom), 40 (right), 42, 45 (both)
J. Mastalir, pp. 35 (right), 40 (left), 83
Robert Moore, front cover, pp. 3, 5–8, 12–15, 18–19, 43, 137, 161, 169, 170, 171, 173, 178–182, 184, 185, 187–189, 190, 192, 193, 195, 196, 198–203, 205, 206, 208, 209, 227, 228, 230
National Foto Pressbureau, p. 142
Herbert Smit, pp. 2, 81, 132, 133, 135, 136, 149, 160, 177
St. Neill Studio, back cover
Underwood and Underwood, p. 86 (both bottom)
UPI Photo, p. 139
Wagner International Photos, p. 153

ACKNOWLEDGMENTS

While researching the original version of this book more than twenty years ago, it was my great good fortune to meet many of the people whose personal histories, taken together, are the story of Steuben. Although most of them have now passed on, their willingness to share their memories and insights about Steuben continues to invest this narrative with a personal flavor that no amount of archival research could ever produce. Among those who consented to be interviewed for the original book was Arthur A. Houghton, Jr., who died in 1990. Houghton and his gracious wife, Nina, welcomed me to Wye Plantation, where we taped his recollections of early Steuben. Otto Hilbert, an old-time resident of Corning who devoted himself to the history of Corning Glass, invited me into his home to share his personal recollections of Frederick Carder and other Steuben founders. Thomas Buechner, then Steuben's president, made time for conversations that reflected his vision for the company. Other employees, some retired at that time, cast light on other topics: Isobel Lee Beers described activities on the international scene; Betsy Pollard recalled Steuben during World War II; Jack Hultzman explained production processes and guided me through the factory at Corning.

Sally Walker, whose career spanned the Houghton and Buechner years, forthrightly responded to many difficult questions and arranged free access to the confidential Steuben "Permanent File" in the New York offices on Fifth Avenue (the file has since been dispersed). Paul Schulze, then director of design, shared recollections of Steuben in the sixties and seventies. Chloe Zerwick—now retired—and her assistant Marjorie McClung offered many kindnesses, as did Larry Szenyi, who assisted with the picture files.

James Thurston's near-photographic memory was an invaluable asset in compiling the master list of pieces from which the original catalogue entries were drawn; while Mary Lou Littrell and Loren Vincent reworked hundreds of shop drawings for the first version of the book. Anthony Snow, then marketing director, cheered me on. Joan Good, research assistant for the original book, worked tirelessly in both Corning and at Steuben's headquarters in New York City. In Corning, the Archives of the Corning Glass Works, then headed by Diane Vogt, provided valuable assistance, as did the staff of The Corning Museum of Glass Research library. Corning Museum of Glass curator Jane Shadel Spillman kindly read and criticized my manuscript. Myles and Rebekah Madigan, now deceased, offered limitless hospitality and encouragement during research trips to Corning and helped me understand the special pride longtime Corning residents feel for Steuben glass.

At Harry N. Abrams, Inc. Robert Morton initiated and oversaw work on the original book, and arranged for new printings in 1983 and 1987. (The 1987 edition contained some textual corrections and additional catalogue illustrations.) Nora Beeson edited the original manuscript, along with Emily Berns, while Darilyn Lowe Carnes designed the original layouts. Susan Meyer, to whom I reported in my "day job" as editor of *Art & Antiques* magazine, urged me to take on the project and remained a source of inspiration.

During the spring and summer of 1988, in preparation for a new edition intended to carry Steuben's history forward by another decade, I interviewed a number of Steuben executives including external affairs director Kirt Gardner, president Susan King, executive vice president Sally Walker, departing design director Paul Schulze, new design director Christopher Hacker, engineering manager Thomas Messmer, and vice president of marketing Sandra Jenkins Carr. As it happened, that ten-year revision of the Steuben book was not published as planned. But the detailed interview notes survived in my files, and they have provided an exceptionally clear window into Steuben's activities in the mid-to-late 1980s which adds immediacy to this new edition. I am especially grateful to Susan King, who agreed to a second interview for the present edition, recounting events that occurred later in her tenure.

Among those Steuben employees who provided first-person information for the present edition are: former Steuben president Donald M. Rorke; former director of wholesale accounts Mary V. Minstrell (who has worn many hats at Steuben over several decades of service); and former plant manager Peter Aagaard (now Steuben's general manager). Also, former director of design Peter Aldridge, product design manager Joel A. Smith, former director of commercial development Bill Gibson, director of visual presentation Mark A. Tamayo, director of design and marketing Rob Cassetti, and glass designers Eric Hilton and David Dowler. Thanks to all of them.

I am especially grateful to E. Marie McKee, Steuben's incumbent president, for her ongoing support of the project. She patiently answered a raft of questions and made the full range of Steuben's personnel and resources available for research. Her assistant, Shelley Pierri, was unstintingly helpful. Corning Incorporated's Meleny Peacock offered great encouragement at the start of the project, while Bill Gibson was my primary Steuben liaison throughout. In addition to other contributions, Gibson supervised the organization of materials for the massive post-1982 catalogue, supported by the dedicated efforts of Tamika Brown. In addition to proofreading catalogue entries, Jennifer Privette researched sources for more than 500 stock-piece line drawings, which were reviewed by Tom Heffernan and meticulously redrawn by Eric Townsend. Joel Smith was a font of valuable information for the updated artists' biographies section. Jeffrey F. Purtell, an Amherst, New Hampshire, dealer who specializes in the purchase and sale of Steuben glass, suggested ways to make the catalogue more useful to collectors.

In Corning, thanks are due to many people. Michelle Cotton, director of the Corning Incorporated Department of Archives and Records, assisted in locating important documents and other materials that had been part of the now-dispersed Steuben Permanent File; while at the Rakow Library, Patty Rogers and Gail Bardhan provided cheerful, ongoing assistance and ready access to Steuben-related materials. Tom Knott and David Whitehouse welcomed me to The Corning Museum of Glass, while Pete Aagaard guided me through the refurbished Steuben factory and explained improvements to the production process made over the last two decades. John Cowden provided a helpful, eye-opening tour of the new Hot Glass Show. Thomas Dimitroff—a longtime Corning public school teacher, local historian, Rockwell Museum curator, and author of the preeminent collector's guide to Carder-era Steuben—generously shared his scholarly insights and introduced me to the stunning new Carder Gallery, which he helped develop at The Corning Museum of Glass.

At Harry N. Abrams, Inc. sincere thanks are due to all who aided the project, most especially to editor Andrea Danese for her patient attention to detail; to Darilyn Lowe Carnes for the design of this new edition; to Mike Esposito and Arlene Lee for their work on the catalogue layouts; and to Margaret Chase, Kate Norment, and Eric Himmel for their ongoing guidance.

As always, I am grateful for the encouragement of my sons Richard, Dana, and Reese; and for the very special inspiration and perspective provided by Sarah Myles Madigan and Andrew Richard Kyle Madigan.

Mary Jean Madigan
December 2001

INDEX

All numbers refer to pages; those in *italic type* are illustrations; colorplates are so indicated.